Mastering Voice Interfaces

Creating Great Voice Apps for Real Users

Ann Thymé-Gobbel
Charles Jankowski

Apress®

Mastering Voice Interfaces

Ann Thymé-Gobbel
Brisbane, CA, USA

Charles Jankowski
Fremont, CA, USA

ISBN-13 (pbk): 978-1-4842-7004-2
https://doi.org/10.1007/978-1-4842-7005-9

ISBN-13 (electronic): 978-1-4842-7005-9

Managing Director, Apress Media LLC: Welmoed Spahr
Acquisitions Editor: Celestin Suresh John
Development Editor: Matthew Moodie
Coordinating Editor: Aditee Mirashi

Cover designed by eStudioCalamar

Cover image designed by Freepik (www.freepik.com)

Distributed to the book trade worldwide by Springer Science+Business Media New York, 1 New York Plaza, Suite 4600, New York, NY 10004-1562, USA. Phone 1-800-SPRINGER, fax (201) 348-4505, e-mail orders-ny@springer-sbm.com, or visit www.springeronline.com. Apress Media, LLC is a California LLC and the sole member (owner) is Springer Science + Business Media Finance Inc (SSBM Finance Inc). SSBM Finance Inc is a **Delaware** corporation.

For information on translations, please e-mail booktranslations@springernature.com; for reprint, paperback, or audio rights, please e-mail bookpermissions@springernature.com.

Apress titles may be purchased in bulk for academic, corporate, or promotional use. eBook versions and licenses are also available for most titles. For more information, reference our Print and eBook Bulk Sales web page at http://www.apress.com/bulk-sales.

Any source code or other supplementary material referenced by the author in this book is available to readers on GitHub via the book's product page, located at www.apress.com/978-1-4842-7004-2. For more detailed information, please visit http://www.apress.com/source-code.

Printed on acid-free paper

To all who strive to create better voice experiences—and all who want to use them.

Table of Contents

Part II: The Planning Phase: Requirements Discovery and High-Level Design Definition

Chapter 4: Define Through Discovery: Building What, How, and Why for Whom

About the Authors

Ann Thymé-Gobbel has focused her career on how people use speech and natural language to communicate with each other and with technology. She has held a broad set of voice-related UI/UX roles in large and small organizations, working within product development, client project engagements, and R&D. Her past work includes design, data analysis, and establishing best practices at Nuance; voice design for mobile and in-home devices at Amazon Lab126; and conversational multimodal healthcare app design at 22otters. Currently, she is Director of UX/UI Design at Loose Cannon Systems. Ann never stops doing research—she collects data at every opportunity and enjoys sharing her findings with others, having presented at conferences internationally. Her published work includes prosody-based automatic language detection and discourse structure. Ann holds a PhD in Cognitive Science and Linguistics from UC San Diego.

Charles Jankowski has over 30 years of experience in industry and academia developing applications and algorithms for real-world users incorporating advanced speech recognition, speaker verification, and natural language technologies. He has used state-of-the-art machine learning processes and techniques for data analysis, performance optimization, and algorithm development. Charles has in-depth technical experience with state-of-the-art technologies, effective management of cross-functional teams across all facets of application deployment, and outstanding relationships with clients. Currently, he is Director of NLP at Brain Technologies, creating the Natural iOS application with which you can "Say it and Get it." Previously, he was Director of NLP and Robotics at CloudMinds, Director of Speech and Natural Language at 22otters, Senior Speech Scientist at Performance Technology Partners, and Director of Professional Services at Nuance, and he has done independent consulting. Charles holds SB, SM, and PhD degrees from MIT, all in Electrical Engineering.

About the Technical Reviewers

David James is a speech industry veteran of three decades' standing who has practical experience of all stages of the application development and deployment lifecycle. Having joined Nuance as their third employee in Europe, his current role is as Principal Speech Consultant, bringing cutting-edge Artificial Intelligence to the customer contact center. David holds several patents in speaker verification, as well as master's and PhD degrees in Engineering from the University of Cambridge.

Cathy Pearl is Design Manager on Google Assistant at Google and a Women in Voice board member. Cathy has been creating conversational interfaces (voice, text, and multimodal) since 1999. She learned the ropes designing IVRs at Nuance and then moved on to building conversational mobile apps. She is the author of the O'Reilly book *Designing Voice User Interfaces* and was listed #1 in Voicebot.AI's 2020 Leaders in Voice for "Design and Product Pros." Cathy holds a BS in Cognitive Science and an MS in Computer Science.

Marius Wolf works at Bayer where he has held various digital leadership roles. He is also a trainer/author/community manager for voice assistants and voice user interface design. A digital leader with over 10 years of experience in establishing human-centric digital solutions and processes in an international business environment (B2B and B2C), Marius has the strong belief that technology can improve people's lives while also delivering clear business benefits. He has often been the one building crucial connections between different mindsets, skills, processes, and technologies. Marius holds a Master of Science degree in Computer Science and Human-Computer Interaction.

Acknowledgments

First and foremost, we'd like to thank everyone who has directly or indirectly contributed to this book: users and creators of voice solutions. We appreciate your hard work, your mistakes, and your solutions equally because we know how complex this is. When we point out suboptimal experiences, it's because of the learning opportunities they provide.

A huge thank you to our technical reviewers for their dedication to provide thoughtful comments. This book would be poorer without your meticulous work: David James, Cathy Pearl, and Marius Wolf. To everyone providing feedback along the way. And to the team at Apress who took us across the finishing line, always with encouragement, good humor, and helpful advice: Celestin Suresh John, Matt Moodie, and Aditee Mirashi.

To our friends, family, and study participants who provided data, anecdotes, and opinions, as well as the millions of users who have been exposed to our voice systems through the years. It's because of you that we are so passionate about providing great experiences.

To our colleagues and clients, past and present, for insightful discussions and data that continuously form our understanding of the field. In particular, our colleagues at Nuance Professional Services and R&D. Also, colleagues at Amazon Lab126, Brain Technologies, CloudMinds, Denon/Sound United, Gamgee/22otters, Loose Cannon Systems, MIT Lincoln Laboratory, MIT Spoken Language Systems Group, Natural Speech Technologies, Performance Technology Partners, and Voxware.

We're unable to call out everyone who's influenced our thinking through the years, so we limit ourselves to some in the field who have directly or indirectly influenced, supported, or contributed specifically to our completing this book, whether they know it or not: Aimee Percy, Bob Quinn, Carrie Armel, Claudia Pateras, Damien Dabrowski, Dave Noelle, Dave Rich, Diane Stephenson, Donald Burbano, Eric Tober, Erin Diehm, Hoi Young, Ian Menzies, Jan Houston Smith, Janice Mandel, Jared Strawderman, Jeff Shrager, Jennifer Balogh, Jenny DeGroot, Joseph Tyler, Karen Kaushansky, Laura Marino, Linda Thibault, Lisa Falkson, Malan Gandhi, Margaret Urban, Maria Astrinaki, Marikka Rypa, Martha Senturia, Neal Sikka, Peter Celinski, Philippe Charest, Rebecca Nowlin

ACKNOWLEDGMENTS

Green, Renee Schwall, Robby Kilgore, Ron Croen, Roxanne St Cyr, Sandy Hutchins, Shamitha Somashekar, Sondra Ahlen, Steve Springer, Sumedha Kshirsagar, Susan Hura, Teenie Matlock, Tony Sheeder, and Vitaly Yurchenko.

To all the fine teams who organize conferences that enable us to learn and share our experiences. A special shout-out to the ReWork AI Assistant Summit and Bruno Figueiredo's team at UXLx.

To the lovely town of Brisbane, California, its inhabitants and businesses, for providing great real-world examples, in particular, Na Na's Kitchen, Melissa's Taqueria, and Madhouse Coffee. "The City of Stars" most definitely.

And above all, to our families who finally can stop wondering, *When will you be done?!* Ann thanks Randy, whose never-ending support made all this possible, and her parents, Asta and Hans, who prove that love of learning and trying new things is not limited by age or native language. Charles expresses deep appreciation and thanks to his wife Jennifer and children Jarek, Alina, and Garin, who have endured him working on this project for way too long, and shouts out to a certain Swede who has dragged him into several worthwhile endeavors in the fascinating area of Voice UI Systems, such as this book!

Introduction

We live in a golden age of voice technology. Conversational voice-first interactions—human-computer interfaces that use automatic speech recognition (ASR) and natural language understanding (NLU)—suddenly seem to be everywhere, from dictation and questions answered by Siri; home interactions and assistants like Amazon Alexa, Google Assistant, Microsoft Cortana, and Samsung Bixby; and mobile voice requests and enterprise solutions with Nuance and others to in-car control, games, and more. Anywhere you turn, you see people talking to devices or talking about talking to them!

This explosion of voice comes out of a perfect storm of significant technology improvements and ease of access for anyone wanting to create something they and others can talk to. It's a glorious gold rush at its infant stages of untapped potential. It's exciting both for those new to talking to devices and to those of us who have been working in voice and natural language automation for many years. Voice interaction creation used to be the realm of a small handful of designers and developers (like us) in dark corners. Now it's out in the light, and everyone wants to do it. Many tools can help you build a functional voice interaction quickly. It seems like voice can do anything!

But with lofty promises comes the risk of letdown due to unfulfilled expectations, disappointed developers, and disenchanted users. It's already happening. Many voice solutions have low ratings, and it's not hard to see why. We both have several devices that we talk to: smart speakers on different platforms, lights, audio receivers, TVs, and, yes, even a fake fireplace. And we use these devices, but all too often, we run into unexpected and even undesired experiences, like this recent interaction one of us authors had when wanting to turn off a light. In Figure 1, we're letting our stick robot stand in for the actual intelligent voice assistant (IVA).

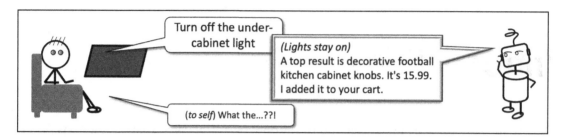

Figure 1. *An actual conversation between a user and a voice assistant controlling household lights*

We watch our friends ask voice devices for information and entertainment, try various approaches, and too often not get the result they hoped for. They settle on a few use cases that work while they also get frustrated. Yet other friends with voice development experience worry about a Voice Winter, where an emerging technology can't keep up with the hype once it's in users' hands. Large companies are betting big on voice, but only a few voice apps are delivering the ROI many hope for. Why? There's no lack of opportunity, but the streets aren't lined with gold either. Gartner's 2019 hype cycle analysis[1] concludes that voice assistants are at risk of falling into the dreaded "valley of despair" because of fundamental barriers and challenges.

Having been around voice for quite a while, we've seen what voice solutions can do, so we started wondering, *Why isn't it better?* And we started analyzing, *I see what happened there … It wasn't tuned enough …* or *There was an incorrect assumption about context …* or *That wording is too vague …* or *It's not taking meaning into account* and so on, which lead to *We want to use voice devices that work well!*

We looked at the available resources and found that even when the material is good, the typical focus is only on one portion of the full voice creation process, either design or development. Missing was something that brought it all together to explain the why and how of voice as an interface modality without the limitations of a specific platform. Something explaining why the needs of the users, system, and business all must be met and work together. Something incorporating voice-appropriate discovery and testing methods for complex real-world applications. Creating voice applications without understanding how people process and generate speech is a bit like judging

---

[1] www.gartner.com/smarterwithgartner/top-trends-on-the-gartner-hype-cycle-for-artificial-intelligence-2019/

the readiness of pasta by throwing it at the wall to see if it sticks. You can do it, but it's unnecessarily messy and probably doesn't have the result you hoped for.

This is where our motivation for this book began to take shape. *How can we share our experiences? Can **we** help others succeed and avoid unnecessary mistakes? What do we wish someone could teach us today based on what we now know about voice development?* Over the years, we've learned that success in this space starts with understanding what's special about spoken natural language. We've worked at big companies and small startups, in different organizations doing product development, client services engagements, R&D, design, development, testing, research, teaching, and even marketing research, strategy, and planning. All of it has convinced us that **the way to create successful voice interactions is to work with a team that understands real users' needs to apply the available technology and resources appropriately**.

Here's the good news: fully functional voice systems have been around for quite a while and analysis of spoken language much longer. Voice systems did not suddenly appear out of nowhere a few years ago, nor will they disappear anytime soon. If we thought voice had nothing to offer, we wouldn't stay in this field our whole careers! But we do think about how to avoid a Voice Frost. The core of Alexa and Google Assistant voice design is based on best practices built on years of well-tested observations. And there's a reason for that: **users are the same now as decades ago, because they're people using spoken language, which is the most human trait there is**. As the landscape matures and the technology evolves, the same constraints and issues still pop up because the interaction modality of spoken language remains the same. Any conversational system must understand regular speech from regular people and handle misunderstandings. Developers new to voice applications quickly realize that they're dealing with a large set of interconnected complex factors where deeper understanding is necessary. We give you concrete tips and guidelines so you can make smart choices, rather than blindly apply algorithms or be dependent on tools and platforms that suddenly change.

Our book draws on our practical experiences in services engagement and product development, using real-world examples to illustrate what can go wrong and why it often does and how you can avoid or solve issues when they occur. The result is a strategy of actionable steps and tips that can benefit any voice application of any size on any platform. To encourage everyone to have a grasp of the whole pie, not just their slice, we intentionally blend design, development, and product/project management concerns in every chapter.

Foundation: Chapters 1–3 provide a solid foundation for the technology used in most voice-first solutions today. You'll learn about how humans use language that leads you to understand the reasons behind the voice user interface (VUI) best practices that our code samples, design details, and discussions build on. You'll also get a first round of experiences with voice interaction code samples. These chapters assume no special background. When you understand what's special about spoken natural language, you're ready to take voice design and development to the next step.

Phase 1, Discovery: Chapters 4 and 5 focus on the first of three phases of voice-first development: planning. Voice-first success depends on a three-way balance of business/product needs, system/technology dependencies and limitations, and understanding user needs and goals. Voice-focused requirements discovery is not a topic covered in most voice development books, and we have seen how the final voice solution suffers when this phase is ignored. This part also dives into how to turn discovery findings into high-level architectural designs and detailed dialog specifications.

Phase 2, Design-informed development: This is the core of the book, covering the main phase of creating and implementing voice systems: we'll call it design-informed development. Each chapter introduces code and techniques addressing a specific characteristic of voice-first conversations, explaining what makes each a challenge and why some solutions are better than others. **Chapters 6–9** focus on the core characteristics. **Chapters 10 and 11** go into depth on recognition and interpretation. **Chapters 12 and 13** explore voice conversation when it fails and how to get it back on track. These topics are crucial for voice since users can't be limited in what they say. **Chapters 14 and 15** dive deeper into topics and methods that make voice-first solutions truly powerful.

Phase 3, Testing and tuning: Chapters 16 and 17 cover the third phase of voice-first development success: rollout and launch. You learn techniques for collecting and analyzing data, testing and tuning your voice solution, and how to interpret your findings to address issues quickly and appropriately before and after production deployment.

Because we focus on the how and why of good voice solutions, what you learn here applies to how people and machines communicate with voice, across device types and platforms, even when those platforms change. Our goal is to be agnostic, but that's tricky to do while also providing concrete examples from one human language and code samples that run with minimal setup. So, we use English examples. Though details differ across languages, the underlying concepts apply to all natural languages because it's about human cognition, perception and production. And, we decided to use the Google platform because of the broad availability of that platform and its convenient APIs (Application Programming Interfaces). However, this is not a cookbook for how to make skills or actions for a specific platform; it's an in-depth yet practical manual for creating successful voice applications for any platform or device, including smart speakers, call center routing, and mobile devices. When different device types need different voice interactions, we'll make that explicit. All code samples are available on GitHub (`www.apress.com/source-code`). There are many important topics that we barely touch, such as ethics, simply because they deserve a more in-depth treatment than we can provide in this book.

We illustrate the concepts via two fictitious assistants: one for finding a restaurant and another for health tasks. We pick these because they cover all aspects of design and implementation complexity you're likely to encounter and because some tasks, like health and finance, demand higher accuracy than others. Since we both have considerable first-hand voice design and development experience in the health domain, it lets us share real-life voice-first experiences with you, though we're in no way making medical claims of any sort when recommending design and implementation choice for this or any other medical voice application.

So welcome to the world of voice-first development! Please join us in our quest to create voice applications that users love with the voice technology available today. We're excited to share with you what we've learned from several decades of creating speech and natural language solutions. Some were great, and we're proud of those, and some, well not so much. You'll be hearing about both; the ones with issues are often more interesting! We avoid using names, and we change minor details in our stories and examples to obscure the source, but you can trust that they are real examples. We hope our book will help you overcome that "valley of despair" to enter the "slope of enlightenment." Come along and learn from our mistakes and our successes—and build great voice interactions for us all to use!

Tomorrow belongs to those who can hear it coming.

—David Bowie

PART I

Conversational Voice System Foundations

Welcome into the world of voice systems!

Whether you're a designer or developer from the world of mobile apps or online interfaces, a product manager, or just wondering what all this voice stuff is about, you'll have more knowledge and experience in some areas than in others. For that reason, we start by laying the groundwork that will let you take advantage of the rest of the book, no matter your background.

- Chapter 1 introduces voice-first systems, core concepts, and the three high-level voice development phases reflected in the book's layout. By addressing some common claims about today's voice technology and its users, we provide explanatory background for the current state and challenges of the voice industry.

- In Chapter 2, you learn how humans and computers "talk" and "listen," what's easy and difficult for the user and the technology in a conversational dialog, and why. The key to successful voice-first development lies in coordinating the human abilities with the technology to enable conversations between two very different dialog participants.

- In Chapter 3, you put your foundation into practice while getting your coding environment up and running with a simple voice application you can expand on in later chapters. Right away, we get you into the practice of testing, analyzing, and improving the voice experience with a few concrete examples.

At the end of this part, you'll be able to explain what's easy and difficult in today's voice user interface (VUI) system design and development, as well as why some things are more challenging than others. You'll understand the reasons behind the VUI design best practices. These are your basic tools, which means you're ready to learn how to apply them.

CHAPTER 1

Say Hello to Voice Systems

You've probably experienced it: you use an app and think, *I could've done this better.* Now here's your chance to create something with a promising cool new technology—an application that users can talk to and that responds with voice.

You've heard that practically everyone uses voice technology so you'd better hurry or you'll be left behind. Your newsfeed reports on the explosive growth: millions of voice devices in everyone's home and thousands of apps already available. It must be true: commercials on TV show the smiling faces of happy users who adopted conversational devices into their families, resulting in a perfect existence of clean, well-organized homes where machines handle the dreariness of everyday life. And, thanks to APIs and SDKs, it should be quick to put it all together. What's not to love? So you have an idea: maybe controlling everything in your own house with voice or something simpler, like a local restaurant finder. You pick a platform, maybe Amazon Alexa or Google Assistant or one of the others, and look at a few tutorials to learn the tools. You build your idea, you deploy it, you wait for the users...and they don't show up or give you a low rating.

What went wrong? Here're just a few likely reasons why people aren't using your voice app:

- It doesn't offer the functionality your users want.

- It covers the right features, but the design or implementation makes it difficult or slow to use—if other options are available to users, why would they bother using this solution?

- The functionality is there, but users can't find it.

- It doesn't respond appropriately or correctly to the phrases users say; the app doesn't understand its users.

© Ann Thymé-Gobbel, Charles Jankowski 2021
A. Thymé-Gobbel and C. Jankowski, *Mastering Voice Interfaces*, https://doi.org/10.1007/978-1-4842-7005-9_1

- Users are confused by the app's responses; users don't understand the app.

- Users don't like how the app talks: either the voice or the wording or both.

- Users are understood, but they don't get the content or action they requested.

- The app makes incorrect assumptions about the user or pushes its own agenda.

- The voice app doesn't integrate well with content or relevant external user accounts.

- For privacy reasons, users prefer silent interactions for what your app does.

- The app doesn't respond when it should or responds when it shouldn't!

These reasons fall into three categories:

- **Failing to understand the users**: How they talk and listen, what they need and want

- **Failing to understand the technology**: How it works, what's easy to do and what's not

- **Failing to understand that solutions need to work for both users and technology**

To create successful voice solutions, you need to address all three. Our book helps you do exactly that. This chapter first defines the voice tech space and then investigates some claims you'll hear about voice and the reality behind each. After an overview of the technology, architecture, and components of most voice-first systems, we discuss the phases of successful voice system development and what to watch out for in each phase. Understanding all aspects of voice-first development benefits everyone, designers, developers, and product owners—even users themselves. Everyone wants to build or use something that solves a problem. Let's make it happen!

Voice-First, Voice-Only, and Conversational Everything

First, what do we mean by voice-only, voice-first, and voice-forward, and why are those terms important?

We use voice-only to mean exactly what it sounds like: voice is the **only** mode of interaction, both for input and output. The user talks to the device, and it responds by voice or some other audio-only feedback. No screen, no buttons, no typing. There can be supporting lights that indicate if the device is listening, but those are optional in terms of meaning. We'll consider a "traditional" Amazon Echo or Google Home as voice-only since you don't need to look at the lights on the device to interact with it. Most phone-based call center enterprise systems are also voice-only systems, though many allow touch-tones for backup.

Voice-first, to us, has two related meanings: Voice is the primary mode of interaction, both for input and output. It should be the first modality you design and implement if your interaction is multimodal. That means you design and develop for voice-only with a plan for additional modalities, such as a screen or buttons, now or in the future. In later chapters, you'll see why your chances of success increase if voice takes the lead rather than being a later add-on. Different interaction elements and different levels of feedback are needed for voice user interfaces, or VUIs (pronounced *voo-ees*, to rhyme with GUIs, or graphic interfaces). Voice-forward is similar: voice is the primary interaction method, though other modalities are present to support input and/or output. Multimodal interfaces aren't the primary focus of this book—voice should always be able to stand on its own in the solutions you learn about—but we do highlight how modality affects your design and development choices. Look for the "Multimodal Corner" sections throughout the book.

Voice applications, or spoken dialog systems, come in many flavors on different devices: mobile phones, cars, in-home virtual assistants, customer service, and so on. Voice apps can be generalists that answer questions with Wikipedia snippets. They can be narrow and tied to a specific device, like a thermostat that changes the temperature in a single room. They can take the lead as a tutor, or they patiently wait for you to ask for something. Some can access your calendar, make an appointment, play your favorite song, find movies released in 2001, or even transfer money from your checking account to pay your credit card bill. Some will assume only one user, others will recognize who's talking or ask them to identify themselves, and yet others will give the same answer to everyone who asks. Some only use voice; others have a screen or physical buttons.

Some stay in one place; others move with the user. Most of what you'll learn in this book applies across devices, topics, and contexts. They all have one thing in common: spoken language is the primary mode of interaction.

In this book, we deal primarily with conversational spoken dialog systems. Outside the voice industry, conversational means an informal natural language chat between two people taking turns talking and listening, usually on a topic that needs no specialized technical expertise. What makes a voice system conversational? The important parts of the definition are natural and turn-taking.

"Natural" means no special training is needed. Natural means users are able to express themselves the same way as if talking to a person in the same context, be understood, and get responses similar to what a person would give. If the user says a command, like *Turn up the volume to 45 in the living room,* they should expect the audio currently coming out of a device with a 0–100 volume scale in that room to get louder. The VUI should not try to change lights in the room, nor should it try another audio device that's not on or has a 0–100 volume scale. The user should also expect to give the command in the many slightly different ways that would be understood by a person (*volume up..., living room volume..., increase the volume..., make the music louder...*) rather than be limited to a few prescribed words or phrases. Natural dialogs use words like *those* and *my* and expect them to be correctly interpreted. Natural also means the VUI responses are tailored to the context. Power users often prefer terse quick prompts over the detailed explanations novice users need. If a new user hears *How much would you like to transfer?*, an expert only needs *Amount?*

"Turn-taking" is part of any conversational dialog, a back-and-forth between two participants who take turns speaking and listening, building on previous information through short- and long-term memory, following established conversation patterns of when and how to comment, clarify, or correct something. Sometimes Participant A takes the lead, and sometimes Participant B does—this is the concept of mixed initiative you learn about in later chapters. Turn-taking follows learned and mostly subconscious patterns of when and how to ask a question, respond, or share new information.

Importantly, "conversational" doesn't mean chatty as in verbose. Nor is it conversational just because it's informal or uses slang. Conversational means a natural language dialog between two participants that meets expectations in behaving like a human-only dialog in the same context.[1]

---

[1] Read more about conversational dialogs in Clark, H. H. (1996). *Using Language.* Cambridge University Press.

Claims About Voice Technology

With those first definitions settled, let's now look at some common claims and beliefs about voice interactions today. After reading this book, you'll understand the reality behind these beliefs, which helps you create better voice solutions.

Claim: Everyone Has a Smart Voice Device and Uses It All the Time

It's true that millions of smart speakers have been sold and more are coming. Marketing reports aren't lying about those numbers, but does it matter if the device is just collecting dust in a corner? One of the biggest issues facing Alexa and Google and others is low return use, or retention. Finding accurate retention statistics can be challenging; understandably no business will share that data publicly. Studies by VoiceLabs[2] found only a 6% chance that a user is still active the second week. Voice is a mode of interaction. Sometimes people want to talk to a device because it's practical and quick; other times they don't. But if you solve a problem for them and do it well, they'll want to use your solution. One developer improved voice skill retention from 10% to 25% simply by caring about the users: analyzing what went wrong and fixing the issues. Ratings went up as well.[3]

Our own studies tell us that people love the idea of speaking to devices for specific tasks, but are held back by a combination of mistrust and poor experience. A categorization of over 200 online survey responses (Figure 1-1) show that voice tech users are held back by not getting what they want, with solutions lacking accuracy, integration, or result relevance.[4] Good news is that if you can offer people something that works for them, they'll want your solution.

---

[2]https://voicebot.ai/2017/09/20/voice-app-retention-doubled-9-months-according-voicelabs-data/

[3]www.dashbot.io/2018/06/06/how-this-alexa-skill-developer-increased-retention-of-voice-game-by-15/

[4]Results partly presented at UXLx Lisbon, 2018, "Designing and prototyping voice interfaces."

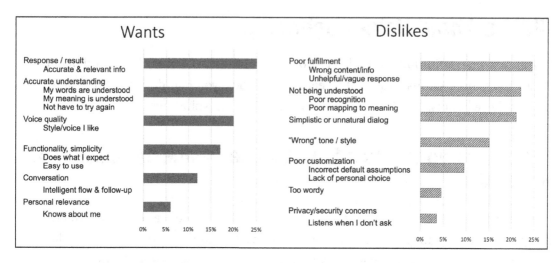

Figure 1-1. *What users want and what they feel like they're getting*

Claim: You Can Simply "Add Voice" to an Existing GUI or Touch Interface

You or someone you work for is bound to suggest, *We already built this device, and now everyone's doing voice—let's add voice to it!* Unfortunately, it's not that simple. We learned from phone-based voice-first IVR (interactive voice response) development that combining voice and touch-tone input is nontrivial. If you started with a physical device with a screen and buttons, you must be willing to revisit your original design. It's unlikely to work for voice without any changes. Even if you want to just add a few voice commands, you need to revisit earlier choices and be ready to redesign some or all of them. Drop-down menus, ubiquitous in GUIs, can be great for screens; but they're not the right choice for voice. Also, simply "adding speech" doesn't take advantage of the key strengths of voice: allowing people to use "normal" natural language to quickly find specific information or completing a complex task in a single step. Menus constrain choices, but voice users can't be constrained: they can and will say anything. We don't speak to each other using menus, unless we need to clarify an utterance or respond to a direct question, like *What salad dressing do you have?* Browsing a voice menu is difficult because of its fleeting nature—you will have menus in your VUIs to help users move forward when needed, but they must be designed carefully and include shortcuts using words that come naturally to users.

So if you're wanting to "add voice" to an existing UI, should you just put down this book and give up? No! Don't despair! You'll learn how VUIs and GUIs differ from each other and why—understanding those differences will make your whole development process smoother. Applying established best practices based on real user data is your tool for success. If you build a multimodal solution from scratch, lead with the modality that has the most implementation constraints. That's usually voice.

Claim: Voice or Chatbot, Both Are Conversational So Basically the Same

Chatbots are seldom voice-first. Bots can actually be less free-form than well-designed voice-only UIs. Some bots are like GUI versions of touch-tone systems with a few options presented as text-label buttons or canned responses and the bot side of the conversation presented as text on a screen. Even if the user can speak to a bot, few bots provide voice output, making the interaction very different from one where both sides use voice. You'll learn more how voice and text differ and why it matters.

Conversational is applied to both voice and text bots. Yes, there are similarities, but let's be clear: spoken and written conversations differ on many levels, including the words used, if sentences are complete, abbreviations, and so on. For simplicity, we'll assume that "chatbots" primarily use text and "voice assistants" use voice.

Claim: I Speak the Language; What More Is There to VUI Design?

As you'll learn, there is a whole lot to designing and implementing for voice. At the end of a voice design tutorial Ann gave recently, one participant exclaimed, *Even something as small as setting a timer has so many things that can go wrong. It's much more complex than I thought!* That participant got it. "Design by committee" is a related pitfall and time-sink in voice development. Learning how to think about what words imply and how to recognize ambiguity helps you make the right VUI choices for any situation as well as shorten unnecessary discussions.

Claim: Every Voice Solution Needs a Strong Personality

In most use cases outside pure entertainment, the goal of voice interactions is to get something done. You may be aware of the "form vs. function" spectrum. Voice interactions that have task goals are often closer to the function end of the spectrum, which is not to say style doesn't matter. Far from it: it all matters because it all interacts and influences the user. But without function, form becomes irrelevant. And not everyone likes the same form.

Don't worry; everything with a voice has a personality, whether you want it to or not. But not everyone will react with the same level of excitement to your choice of voice or the jokes it tells. And you can't control how people react. In an online survey, we asked voice assistant users about their likes and dislikes.[5] Some like a quirky sense of humor; others are very clear about not wanting jokes. Friendliness that's perceived as fake can be the kiss of death for a voice solution. Word choices and consistency are also aspects of personality that you need to be careful about, as you learn throughout this book.

Claim: Hire a Scriptwriter; They Can Write Conversations

Companies have difficulty keeping up with the demand to hire VUI designers and understandably aren't even sure what skill set or experience to look for, so they cast a broader net, often without understanding what types of thinking or knowledge matter most for this work. Just like a designer and a developer seldom have the same skill set, scriptwriting for theater or film is not the same as understanding how people naturally talk to each other or to machines. Many experienced scriptwriters are excellent VUI designers, and breathing life into a VUI is important, but not without having in-depth understanding of voice technology, human cognition, and speech perception and production. Whoever designs a VUI needs to be interested in how real people express themselves, how that changes with context and differs between individuals, and how a seemingly minor difference in prompt wording can result in a significant difference in users' responses. We've seen users roll their eyes when a banking VUI greeted them with *Hey!* and respond to *Got it!* with a *No, you didn't!* We've seen low system performance when VUIs use some common phrasing (*You wanna cancel the first or the second?*) instead of a clearer version (*Which should I cancel, the first or the second?*). Solid

---

[5]Results partly presented at the 2018 San Francisco AI Assistant Summit, "A Matter of Choice: Personalization vs. Personality in Interactive Voice Assistants."

voice responses can't be created in isolation or without understanding the full flow, the technology characteristics, and content access limitations. Spoken language has different characteristics from written language, and spontaneous speech is different from scripted acting in ways that matter in voice technology, as you'll see. You'll learn why more effort is spent on handling error conditions and edge cases than on the happy path (the perfect use case where everything goes as expected).

Claim: Recognition Is a Solved Problem; It's Basically Perfect Today

It should be obvious to anyone who uses any voice solution that they're far from perfect even with today's amazing recognition. As you saw in Figure 1-1, the top dislikes mentioned by voice assistant users in our survey were poor content (unhelpful responses or lack of information) and poor recognition (no understanding or incorrect understanding). Each was mentioned by a quarter of the survey participants. That's hardly a sign of perfection. These findings are supported by the 2020 Adobe Voice Survey.[6] While voice use is increasing, 57% of respondents say poor recognition performance and poor results keep them from using voice more. The survey estimates that accuracy is around 75%.[7] That means one in four requests fails in some fashion. That's terrible. Working with IVRs, we would not stop performance improvements until well over 90% because user frustration is death for voice implementations.

Because recognition isn't perfect, you can't just rely on the text result when evaluating performance. You need to listen to what users actually say, decide if the words were captured correctly, and then determine if the intended meaning was handled appropriately. If you only have access to the correct recognition and the successful interpretations and fulfillment, you don't know anything about the requests that were not mapped to something your VUI handles. There's also still a difference in recognition performance between non–regionally accented US English and strong regional accents or non-native accents. In later chapters, you learn how user characteristics affect design and development choices and how to improve performance based on real user data.

---

[6]https://xd.adobe.com/ideas/principles/emerging-technology/
voice-technologys-role-in-rapidly-changing-world/

[7]https://voices.soundhound.com/voice-assistant-adoption-surges-during-covid-while-
user-frustrations-remain/

Creating conversations with responses that are not misleading or vague or weird or simply wrong takes a lot of effort. Figure 1-2 shows just a few actual conversation examples between a user and an intelligent voice assistant (IVA); you'll see many more throughout the book. There are three take-home messages here:

- Designing for voice is complex. Even seasoned experts still get it wrong.

- Most odd IVA responses can be avoided or at least handled more smoothly.

- Responding well matters. You need to pay attention to the details and handle what you can handle, instead of hoping it'll be good enough.

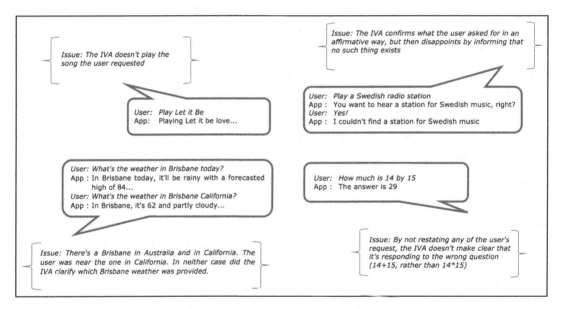

Figure 1-2. *Transcripts of four actual smart speaker voice interactions and the reasons why they're suboptimal. Each one is avoidable; each one lessens users' trust in voice and the app that's speaking*

You'll soon start learning about the close relationship between planning, designing, and building in voice-first development, more so than in many other disciplines. One reason for this is that the underlying voice technologies still are not perfect and all the parties involved need to account for the limitations each one has to deal with.

Voice technology is not yet accepted or standardized to a degree that you can just slap something together hoping users will figure it out or keep trying if they're not successful. They won't—unless they're voice experts who love to find out where something fails, but we're a strange bunch. Most people just won't bother using your voice application after trying a few times, and they'll happily share why on social media, often making valid points:

- *I'm annoyed that virtual assistants don't know the difference between a light system and a receiver both called living room. If I say, "Play Coldplay in living room," why can't it figure out that the lights don't output audio?*

- *I have a band called 'Megahit' in my library, so when I ask to hear it, [she] says "OK," playing mega hits and plays some pop garbage.*[8]

Worse yet, you might find yourself in a PR nightmare when your voice app doesn't understand something with serious consequences to the users, maybe privacy, financial, or health related. Examples go viral immediately. You may have heard about Alexa sending a private conversation to an unintended recipient, the vague responses to *Are you connected to the CIA?* or Samsung's S Voice responding to *My head hurts* with *It's on your shoulders.*[9] You can easily find these and others online. Better yet, start collecting your own examples and think about why something sounded weird and how you might solve it. We don't use these examples to point fingers—we know how complex this stuff is—we just want you to understand why it's important to get it right.

Claim: AI Takes Care of Understanding What People Say

Machine learning and neural networks make voice more powerful than ever, but AI does not yet "take care of everything." Today's VUIs are still very limited in scope and world knowledge compared to humans. One reason is that available development frameworks lack a complete model of world knowledge. As humans, even in narrow tasks, we bring with us knowledge of the world when we talk and listen.[10] One of the biggest issues for today's voice app creators is the lack of access to the data that could help address gaps in handling. You'll learn about what you can do with what's available to you without

---

[8]Anonymized chat between two acquaintances of us authors.

[9]www.washingtonpost.com/news/to-your-health/wp/2016/03/15/siri-i-was-raped-and-other-statements-that-will-probably-yield-unsatisfying-answers-from-your-phone/ and www.consumerreports.org/consumerist/why-amazons-alexa-cant-tell-you-if-its-connected-to-the-cia/

[10]Read more on this fascinating topic elsewhere by searching for "strong" vs. "weak" or "narrow" AI.

training models on large amounts of data and what you could do if you have more data. Any natural language understanding (NLU) in isolation also isn't enough, no matter how great it is at "understanding" the user. To communicate successfully with your users, you still need to convert that understanding into responses tailored to those specific users and their contexts. That complete start-to-end process is covered in this book.

AI has made huge strides in the last few years. This makes voice-first development a lot more accessible than it used to be. Voice automation has been broadly available for decades, just not with Amazon Alexa or Google Assistant, but typically in the form of telephone-based interactive voice response, or IVR, systems that you'll probably interact with still today if you call your bank or your airline. What's different today is the ease of access to voice platforms and tools and the expansion of voice to new devices. What's the same is how people talk and converse and the limitations and strengths of spoken language.

Claim: IVRs Are Irrelevant Today, Nothing to Be Learned from Them

IVRs have a bad rap, mainly thanks to the all-too-many examples where voice is treated like touch-tone and everything therefore is a tree of menus. But no competent VUI designer allowed to do their job has created a *Press or say 1* IVR in decades. Today's IVRs use a sophisticated combination of statistical natural language processing and rule-based pattern matching. While the same methods have been in place for well over a decade, they're constantly improving, giving the inaccurate impression that IVRs handling natural language requests are new on the scene.

Voice is a modality with specific strengths and limitations. Natural means users have leeway in how they say something, so not having to say *one* instead of *yes*, but saying anything from *yes* to *umm I think so* and *that's absolutely correct*.

Both of us have worked extensively with IVRs, as have the majority of those with extensive voice product experience today. We'd never claim that all IVRs are perfect, but we will tell you that you can learn a lot from them. IVRs are voice-first systems whose users, typically untrained, speak to technology using their own words to get some task done, often successfully when the IVR has been implemented well. The key difference between IVRs and in-home systems today relates to use cases: IVRs are for business relationships with companies, while in-home assistants have mainly focused on entertainment and household tasks. This is an important difference to understand when home assistants expand further into business applications because it affects how users talk and interact and what they expect in response, as you'll see. But the "rules" of spoken language still apply, making conversations more similar than not across devices and platforms. According to the Adobe Voice Survey, people are now asking for voice solutions for account balances, making payments, making reservations, and booking appointments—all common IVR tasks for decades.

Building something with voice input and/or output means building something that suits each user's needs and contributes to their success. Applied appropriately, voice makes some interactions easier for some people in some contexts. If not done well, the interaction becomes annoying, and the technology becomes a convenient scapegoat for corner-cutting, heavy-handed business logic, and poor choices. It's as true today as it was two decades ago. You'll learn how to apply it to your voice-first development in today's environment.

Claim: That Ship Has Sailed; Alexa Is the Winner

Maybe, maybe not. No shade on Alexa—she was first in the current field and tapped into a bigger market than even Amazon expected, giving Alexa a two-year lead time. The technology and the users were both ready; Siri had paved the way, but Amazon took the plunge, which we applaud. Thanks to the success of Alexa and the voice ecosystem as a whole, Google had the opportunity to architect their system from the ground up to incorporate lessons learned. Amazon's smart speaker market share is still largest, but their lead has shrunk, estimated from 72% in 2018 to 53% in 2020, while Google's share increased from 18% to 31%.[11] For user-centric voice assistants not focused on dictation or call center interactions, Amazon had what's called "first mover (dis)advantage"; being first to market with something that takes off means others can learn from your success and mistakes. We talk a lot about Amazon and Google; at the time of writing, they're the biggest players in the English voice assistant space today. But they're not the only ones. Apple has brought the HomePod to the party. And don't forget about Microsoft, Samsung, Facebook, and Nuance. The space changes constantly.

Even now, there's room for solutions that are fully native or built a la carte from the available technology or aimed at a particular user group or context. This creates opportunities for smaller and nimbler conversational platforms and speech engines,

---

[11]https://voicebot.ai/2020/04/28/amazon-smart-speaker-market-share-falls-to-53-in-2019-with-google-the-biggest-beneficiary-rising-to-31-sonos-also-moves-up/

including open source solutions. In addition, not all voice development is done for smart speakers. A significant amount of work is done today implementing voice in a wider set of devices and environments, including mobile devices. That's not likely to slow down; on the contrary, it's one reason for the agnostic goal of this book: we teach you how to apply voice-first thinking to any platform or solution while still being practical and concrete.

Claim: Everyone Needs a Voice Solution; Voice Is Great for Everything

We'd be lying if we tried to tell you that—and you should take any such claims with a large amount of salt. Everyone doesn't need a mobile app, so why should they need a voice solution? A hospital saw high contamination rates for urine sample collection. Thinking the issue was with patients handling instructions while holding the jar, they wanted a voice solution. While creating the design, we researched the environment and realized what was needed was a small table in the restroom. Sometimes voice isn't the necessary solution. If an app needs private or sensitive information from its users and those users use the app in a public location, voice isn't the right approach, or at least not for the whole interaction. Understand your users so you create what they want and need. In the 2020 Adobe Voice Survey, 62% feel awkward using voice technology in public. Only one in four uses voice for more sophisticated tasks than what's been available on virtual assistant devices for years. People set timers, ask for music, get weather updates, initiate calls, or dictate searches or text messages.

The good news is that people want voice solutions, simple and complex; they just want ones that work well. The strength of voice solutions is that it's like speaking to people: convenient, easy to use, and fast. Or should be. If recognition is poor and understanding leads to spotty results, it becomes frustrating. The field is wide open for your voice solutions, if you build ones that work for your users.

Introduction to Voice Technology Components

Before you dive into creating your first application, it's worth discussing the architecture of voice systems in light of what you learned so far. In Figure 1-3, you see the general core components of voice systems and how they interact, starting at the upper left and ending in the lower left. The figure is fairly abstract on purpose: the general approach holds true across most types of systems and platforms. Again, we stay agnostic and don't focus on any input or output component details outside this core box, like the location or type of the microphone or speaker. In Chapter 3, you'll see how it translates into the Google Dialogflow approach we use for most code examples in the book. In the Figure 1-3 example, imagine a user asking a voice system *What time does McDonald's close?* and the system finding the answer before responding, *McDonald's closes at 11 PM tonight.*

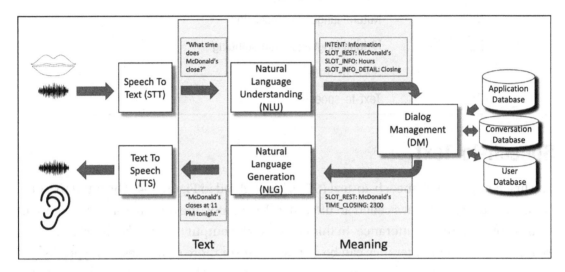

Figure 1-3. *Generic architecture of a voice-first system*

The components are laid out in this there-and-back way to highlight the two directions of a dialog: the top row represents the user saying something and the computer interpreting that utterance; the bottom row focuses on the computer's response. Simplistically, the user speaks, that audio signal is captured (automatic speech recognition) and converted to text (speech-to-text), and structure is assigned to the text (natural language processing) to help assign meaning (natural language understanding) and context (dialog manager). Having settled on a result, the system determines how to respond (natural language generation) and generates a voice response (text-to-speech). Acronyms for each component are captured in Table 1-1 for reference. Next, let's take a closer look at each of those components.

Table 1-1. *Acronyms for the components of a voice system*

Acronym	Component
ASR	Automatic speech recognition
DM	Dialog manager, or dialog management
NLG	Natural language generation
NLP	Natural language processing
NLU	Natural language understanding
STT	Speech-to-text
TTS	Text-to-speech

Speech-to-Text

The first component is speech-to-text (STT), highlighted in Figure 1-4. The input to STT is what the user says; that's called an utterance. Using ASR, the output is a representation of the captured spoken utterance. In this example, the output text is *What time does McDonald's close?* An utterance can be a word or one or more sentences, but typically in informational systems, it's no more than one sentence. The text result gets fed to the NLU, which is the next component of the voice system.

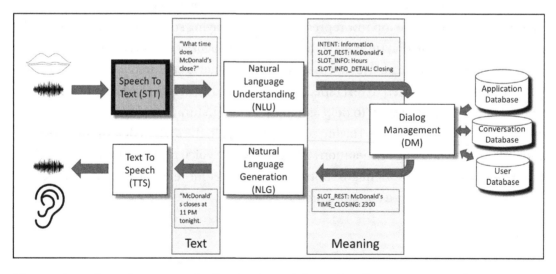

Figure 1-4. *Speech-to-text, the beginning of the voice-first system pipeline*

In-Depth: Is STT Better Than Human Recognition and Understanding?

Microsoft Research made a big splash a few years ago[12] when claiming they had achieved better-than-human performance on STT. Did that mean that all ASR engineers should go home? No. For starters, the Microsoft work was done in a lab setting. It's still difficult for production STT to be completely accurate and provide an answer quickly enough to be acceptable. Within some constrained scenarios, computers can understand some speech better than humans. But many common use cases don't fall within those constraints. Conversational human speech is messy, full of noisy accented incomplete words; and it builds on direct and indirect references to shared experiences, conversations from days ago, and general world knowledge. Most "smart AI" voice applications are still surprisingly brittle with much complex work to be done. Having said that, in the last few years, STT has improved remarkably. Why?

First, faster computation. By Moore's Law, the number of transistors per square inch doubles every two years. Your smartphone today has more compute power than the Apollo 11 guidance computer did. This dramatic increase in quantitative compute power has qualitatively changed possible interactions.

Second, new or improved algorithms. Neural networks have been around since the mid-1950s, but computers were too slow to realize the full power of the algorithms until recent years. With improved algorithms and new approaches that are now possible, ASR has made great strides using various large deep learning network architectures.

And third, data! Ask any experienced speech engineer if they'd rather have a slightly fancier algorithm or more data; they'll pick data because they know performance generally improves with more data. And bigger deep learning networks, running on faster servers, need to be fed the raw material that allows the networks to learn, and that is data—real data, from real users talking to deployed systems in the field. This is one reason Google deployed the free GOOG411 application years ago—to collect data for ASR models—and why Alexa and Siri are so much better now than when they first appeared. Once you get to a reasonable level of performance, you can deploy real applications and use that data to build better models, but you have to start with something that is at least usable, or you won't get good data for additional training and improvement.

---

[12]www.microsoft.com/en-us/research/blog/microsoft-researchers-achieve-new-conversational-speech-recognition-milestone/, Also www.wired.com/story/ai-beat-humans-at-reading-maybe-not/

Natural Language Understanding

Recognizing the words the user spoke is only the beginning. For the voice system to respond, it must determine what the user meant by those words. Determining meaning is the domain of the natural language understanding (NLU) component, highlighted in Figure 1-5. The input to NLU is the words from STT; the output is some representation of the meaning.

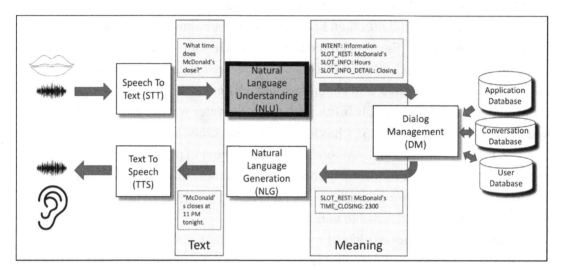

Figure 1-5. *Natural language understanding, or NLU, component in a voice-first system*

You may ask what's meant by meaning. That's actually an interesting and open question, but for our current discussion, let's focus on two parts of meaning:

- **Intent**: The overall result, assigning the likely goal of the captured utterance. What does the user want to do? In the example, the user is asking when McDonald's closes, so let's call the intent something like "information."

- **Slots (or entities)**: Along with the core intent, there's often another important content in the utterance. In this example, there are three such content pieces: what type of information we're looking for (hours), refining details on that information (**closing** hours), and which restaurant we're talking about (McDonald's).

Intents and slots are core concepts in voice-first development. There are various approaches to NLU, and you'll learn about the differences later. At the highest level, NLU can be either rule-based or statistical. Rule-based approaches use patterns, or grammars, where recognized key words or complete phrases need to match to a predefined pattern. These patterns need to be carefully defined and refined based on user data to maximize matching correctly with what the user says, as well as minimizing the chances of a mismatch. Their benefit is precise control, clarity in why something matched, and rapid creation. The other general NLU approach is statistical, where matches are based on similarity to training data. The drawback of that is a need for lots of training data, which slows down rollout in new domains and introduces some level of unpredictability to how specific phrases will be handled. The benefit is that exact matches aren't needed. You learn about creating grammars and assigning meaning in Chapters 10 and 11.

Does the NLU component apply to text chatbots as well? Yes and no. In its simplest form, a chatbot is what you get if you strip off the audio and just use text for input and output. If you have a text chatbot in place, you can start from what you've built for all components, but soon you'll find that you need to make modifications. The main reason is that spoken and written languages differ a lot at the levels that matter most. Your NLU models need to accommodate those differences. At first cut, simple string replacement could accomplish some of this, but it's far from that simple. Nonetheless, some of the fundamental issues in voice-first systems are shared by chatbots, and many of the tools that have sprung up in recent years to build bots are essentially designed to craft these components.

Dialog Management

Assuming you recognized what was said and interpreted what it meant, what's next? The reason for a voice system in the first place is to generate some sort of response to a request or question. This is where dialog management (DM) comes in, highlighted in Figure 1-6. DM is responsible for taking the intent of the utterance and applying various conditions and contexts to determine how to respond. Did you get what you needed from the user to respond, or do you need to ask a follow-up question? What's the answer? Do you even have the answer? In this example, the content is not very complicated: you want to tell the user McDonald's closing time.

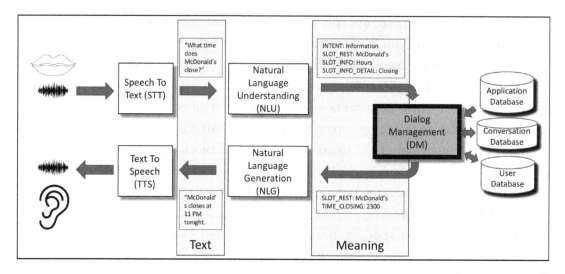

Figure 1-6. *Dialog management, or DM, component in a voice-first system*

Already you're spotting a complexity: how do you know which McDonald's? The answer might be the closest to the user's current location, but maybe not. Should you ask the user or offer some choices? Can you assume it's one they've asked about before? And if you need to ask all these questions, will any location still be open by the time you're sure of the answer? There's no one single correct choice because it depends on many contexts and choices. As voice interactions become more complex, DM quickly gets more complicated as well.

The output of DM is an abstract representation that the system will use to form its best response to the user, given various conditions and contexts applied to the meaning of what the user said. Context is the topic of Chapter 14.

You're already getting a taste of the complexity involved in that DM connects to no fewer than three important sources of information, highlighted in Figure 1-7. In most real-world cases, this is never one database or even three, but a tangled network of web services (such as accessing the McDonald's website or web service) and logic (extracting closing hours from what's returned) that hopefully provides the necessary information.

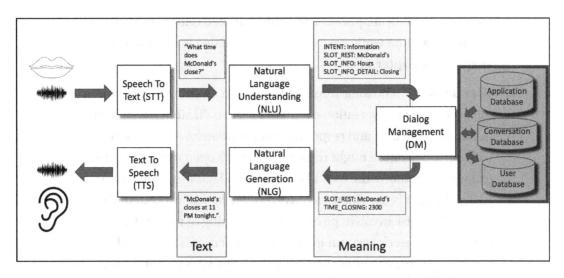

Figure 1-7. *Data access components in a voice-first system: application, conversation, and user databases*

Even with infrastructure being built to make information access easier, it's often a weak point of a system because it often involves external databases and content that you don't control.

- **Application database**: The source of information needed to answer the question. In our example, it's where you'd find the store hours. The raw data source may return additional information that's irrelevant to fulfill the request; DM needs to extract what's needed (closing hours) to craft the meaning of a sensible and informative response.

- **Conversation database**: A data store that keeps track of the dialog context, what's been going on in the current (or very recent) conversations with the voice system. It can be a formal database or something stored in memory. For example, if your user asks *Tell me a restaurant close to me that's open now* and McDonald's is one result, the user might follow up with the question, *What time does it close?* To answer naturally, the system must remember that McDonald's was the last restaurant in the dialog and provide a sensible answer accordingly. Humans do this all the time; interpreting "it" correctly in context to replace "McDonald's" and not having to keep saying the name is using anaphora. The conversation database is key to making anaphora work. No conversational dialog is natural without anaphora (**Chapter** 14).

- **User database**: The long-term context that keeps information about the user across conversations. It makes personalization possible, that is, knowing the user and responding appropriately. A voice system with personalization might respond to *What's open now?* with a list of restaurants it knows the user likes. The user database might also track where the user is to respond to ...*close to my house?* without having to ask. If the task involves payments or shopping or music streaming requests, the user's account information or access is needed. If something's missing, that also impacts the system's response. You learn about personalization in Chapter 15.

DM is often a weak point of today's more complex systems for one reason: it's tricky to get right. It often involves interacting with information in "the outside world," such as external account access or metadata limitations, and current user context, such as user location, preceding dialogs, and even the precise wording of the utterance. DM is also the controller of any results that depend on what devices are available for the requested action, like turning something up.

SUCCESS TIP 1.1 DIALOG MANAGEMENT IS YOUR SECRET SAUCE   A detailed and accurate DM with functional links to external data sources and relevant data is your key to voice-first success and impressed users. Without it, your solution won't be able to respond in a natural conversational manner but will sound clunky, like it doesn't quite understand. Without it, you can't give your users what they ask for. If you master DM and create responses that capitalize on it, you'll create an impressive conversational voice-first system.

Natural Language Generation

Natural language generation (NLG) takes the abstract meaning from DM and turns it into text that will be spoken in response to the user. In the pipeline, this is the fourth component shown in Figure 1-8. In the example, your DM databases gave McDonald's closing hours as "2300" so your NLG generates the text "McDonald's closes at 11 PM tonight." Note how you convert "2300" to "11 PM" in the text; one of the functions of NLG is to turn formal or code-centric concepts into ones that are expected and understandable by the users. It's crucial for your voice system to sound natural, both for reasons of user satisfaction and for success. Unexpected or unclear system responses lead to user confusion and possibly responses your system can't handle. If your user population is general US English speakers, you'd choose "11 PM"; if it's military, you might choose "2300 hours." Context matters for something as basic as how to say a number. Think about how you'd say a number like "1120" differently if it referred to time, a money amount, a street address, or a TV channel.

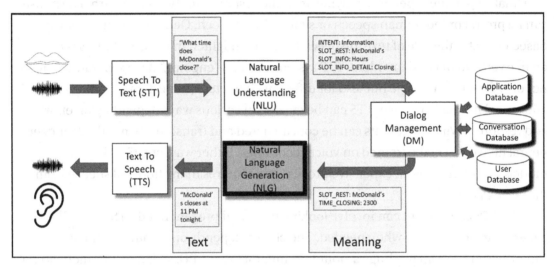

Figure 1-8. *Natural language generation, or NLG, in a voice-first system*

Your VUI needs to understand the different ways users say those as well as use context to produce the appropriate response. You learn about context and voice output in Chapters 14 and 15.

It's worth noting that NLG is not always a separate component of a voice system. In many systems, including those you'll build here, language generation is built into dialog management so that the DM essentially provides the text of the response. We separate those functions here because it's conceptually useful to think about systems as having text and meaning in, meaning and text out, and DM to bridge the two meanings. There are other systems, such as translation, that currently require separate NLG; the meanings are language-independent, and you can imagine NLG and NLU being based on different languages.

SUCCESS TIP 1.2 SEPARATE LAYERS OF ABSTRACTNESS   Treating the NLG as a separate component provides the flexibility to add other languages or even interaction modes without redoing your whole system from scratch. Even if you combine NLG and DM, get in the habit of separating abstract meaning from the resulting output and track both.

Text-to-Speech

The final step in the pipeline is playing an audio response to the user. A verbal response can be pre-recorded human speech or synthesized speech. Generating the response based on text is the role of text-to-speech (TTS), highlighted in Figure 1-9. TTS is of course very language-dependent. TTS systems, or TTS "engines," have separate models not only for each language but also for different characters (male/female, older/child, and so on) in each language. TTS can be created in various ways depending on effort and resources. Voice segments can be concatenated and transitions smoothed, or deep neural networks can be trained on voice recordings. Either way, creating these TTS models from scratch is an expensive process and requires many hours of speech from the voice talent.

The TTS component can involve looking up stored pregenerated TTS audio files or generating the response when needed. The choice depends on resources and needs. Cloud-based TTS can use huge amounts of memory and CPU, so larger TTS models can be used with higher-quality results but with a delay in response. On-device TTS uses smaller models because of limitations on memory and CPU on the device, so won't sound as good but will respond very quickly and not need a connection to a cloud server. This too is changing as compute power increases.

Today's TTS is almost indistinguishable from human speech (see the "In-depth" discussion). So why are many customer-facing voice systems still recording the phrases spoken by the system instead of using TTS? Recording is a lot of effort; but it also provides the most control for emphasizing certain words, pronouncing names, or conveying appropriate emotion—all areas of language that are challenging to automate well. For things like digits, dates, and times—and restaurant names—you'd need to record the pieces separately and string them together to provide the full output utterance. In the example, you might have separate audio snippets for *McDonald's*, *closes at, 11, PM*, and *tonight* or (more likely) some combinations of those. This is sometimes known as concatenative prompt recording, or CPR. You'll learn more in Chapter 15 about the pros and cons of using pre-recorded human speech or synthesized TTS.

This final step can also involve playing other content, like music or a movie, or performing some action, like turning on a light. You learn more about that in later chapters as well.

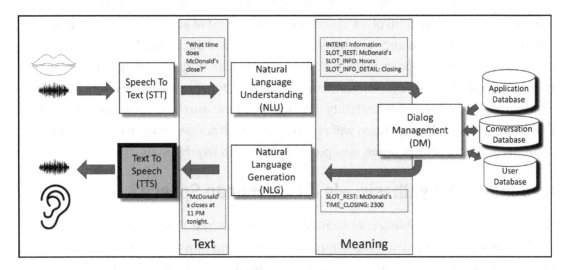

Figure 1-9. *Text-to-speech or TTS, the final step in the pipeline of a voice-first system*

Now you know the architecture and technology components of voice systems. Understanding the purpose and challenges of each component helps you anticipate limitations you encounter and choose the best implementation for your VUI. Existing voice development platforms are fairly complete for many uses, but as you build more complex systems, you'll find that you might not want to be shielded from some of the limitations each platform enforces. You could potentially modify any and all of the components and put together your own platform from separate modules.

So how difficult is each step and the end-to-end pipeline? In general, the further to the right in the voice pipeline diagram you are, the harder the problem is. Not that STT and TTS aren't incredibly hard problems, but those areas have reached closer-to-human-level performance than NLU and NLG so far. Fully understanding the meaning of any sentence from any speaker is a goal that's not yet been achieved. Part of the problem is that NLU/NLG bridges the gap between words and meaning, and there's still less understanding at a theoretical level of "meaning." The complexity of a complete model of human cognition and how people do it so well (or not) is hard to fathom and lacking in basically all voice systems, so any machines trying to emulate human behavior will be more of an approximation.

Then there's dialog. Correctly interpreting someone's intent and generating a reasonable response is clearly doable today. But the longer or more complex the dialog becomes, with back-and-forth between user and system, the less like a human conversation it becomes. That's because dialog reflects more than just the meaning of a sentence in isolation. It involves the meaning and intent of an entire conversation, whether it's to get the balance of a bank account or to find out where to eat dinner or to share feelings that a sports team lost! It involves shared understanding of the world in general and the user's environment and emotional state in particular. It involves responding with appropriate certainty or emotion. These are the current frontiers of the field, and breaking through them will require joint work across many fields including cognitive science, neuroscience, computer science, and psycholinguistics.

In-Depth: TTS Synthesis—Is It Like Human Speech?

As with all the other enabling core technologies, synthesized TTS has made great strides in the past few years. It has improved to the extent that a few years ago, the union representing voice actors recording audio books complained that the TTS on the Amazon Kindle was too good and might put them out of work! An exaggeration perhaps, but you know you're making serious improvements in technology when this happens. Not only has the quality improved but it's also easier and faster to create new voices.

The improvements of TTS synthesis have (re)ignited a firestorm of social commentary around whether systems should be built that are indistinguishable from humans—moving closer to passing the Turing test[13] and forcing us to ask "What's real?" in the audio world as in the past few years with images and video. The recent results are impressive, as judged by the Google Duplex demo at the 2018 Google I/O conference; you have to work to find where the virtual assistant's voice does not sound mechanical. It even adds human-sounding *mm hmms*, which isn't typically the domain of TTS but makes interactions sound more human. You learn more about the ramifications of this in Chapters 14 and 15.

---

[13]"Computing machinery and intelligence." Alan Turing. Mind 59 (October):433-60 (1950).

In particular, WaveNet from Google DeepMind[14] and Tacotron, also from Google, provide more natural-sounding TTS (as judged by human listeners) than other TTS engines. It still requires hours of very-high-quality studio recordings to get that result, but this is constantly improving. Today, anyone can affordably create a synthesized version of their own voice from a couple of hours of read text (descript.com), but the benefit of using TTS from one of the main platforms is that someone else has done the hard work for you already. We'll come back to the pros and cons of using TTS vs. recorded human speech in Chapter 15; we ourselves regularly use both.

The House That Voice Built: The Phases of Voice Development Success

You don't need to be on the cutting edge of voice research to quickly realize the complexity involved in creating a VUI—just look at the steps involved in a simple question about restaurant hours. What if, on top of that, you work with a team of people with different backgrounds and goals? How do you succeed? In this section, we'll introduce you to a strategy that works for creating high-quality voice systems of any size and type—it's the strategy that's mirrored in the overall layout of our book. We use building a house as an analogy that illustrates what's involved in building a voice solution. It's an analogy we've used successfully during project kickoffs to explain to clients and stakeholders new to voice what's involved. Feel free to use this analogy in your own meetings.

SUCCESS TIP 1.3 EDUCATE AND LEVEL-SET EVERYONE ON YOUR TEAM   If you work on a voice project or product with other people, assume nothing about shared knowledge. Because everyone shares a language and understanding seems easy to us as humans, assumptions need to be spelled out from Day 1. Include everyone who touches the project.

Voice-first development is a set of best practices and guidelines aimed specifically at maximizing success and minimizing risks of common pitfalls when creating conversational voice solutions.

---

[14]https://deepmind.com/blog/wavenet-generative-model-raw-audio/

Figure 1-10 shows a voice-first-focused version of a common lifecycle diagram. Some of you might notice that this looks a bit like a classic waterfall process, with defined steps leading to the next and where different people with different skill sets execute their part before handing it off, never to see it again. One valid criticism of waterfall is this "throw it over the wall" mentality, where the person doing step X need not worry about step X+1. This approach doesn't work well for voice. The same is true for building a house. Your planner/architect needs to understand design and architecture to not propose something that'll fall down. The designer should know about resources and regulations, as well as understanding what's feasible to build. The builder needs to understand the design specification and use the right materials. And so on. To facilitate communication with others and build a house people want to live in, each one needs to understand the others' tasks and challenges. At the same time, some tasks need to be further along than others before the latter start. That's the reason for the overlapping and connected blocks representing the Plan, Design, and Build phases. Think of it as a modified phased approach. Everything can't happen in parallel; some phasing is necessary. But the phases should overlap with a lot of communication across "borders."

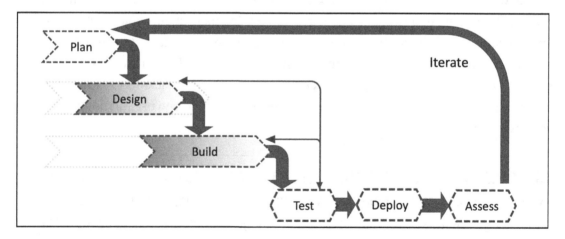

Figure 1-10. *Modified application lifecycle process appropriate for voice-first development*

So, if we agree waterfall-ish approaches can take a long time before actually seeing results in deployment, what about a more agile process, which is designed to see results and iterate faster? After all, we do have that whole cycle from Assess back to Plan; isn't that tailor-made for Agile? Maybe. We're very pragmatic: we're big believers in using any approach that works well to solve a problem. We only care that each step is well-informed by other steps and that assessment is done appropriately in iterative steps. And we know from experience that voice development isn't easily modularized. If you incorporate the small incremental approach of an agile process, do so with involvement from everyone on your voice team. In particular, account for tasks necessary in voice software development but not in other types of software development, such as voice-specific testing, and familiar tasks that may involve very different levels of effort. Take care not to ignore the interdependencies between steps, the need for detailed requirements discovery and design, and the benefits of extensive testing and gradually exposing the app to larger user populations. User stories, popular in agile approaches, are also one of the tools we use. You'll learn how to find the user data that's most valid so you can base your user stories on appropriate data. The "Assess" step in voice-first development relies on putting the VUI in the hands of actual users and observing behavior and results, which naturally takes time. You'll learn why rolling out limited features for voice is tricky and why defining a minimum viable product (MVP) by nature is different for speech than for other interface modalities. Hint: You can't limit what users say, so you need to handle it gracefully if you don't have full handling yet.

Plan

What's the first thing you do if you're building a house? Pick up a hammer? Buy lumber? Pour concrete? No, no, and no. First, you figure out what you're building—or if you should build at all! Voice technology is really cool, but let's be clear: it's not the only interface people will use from now on. It's perfectly natural to be excited about something new and promising, and "To the man with a hammer, everything looks like a nail." We've seen the most well-meaning salesperson convincing a customer that voice is the one solution for all users and use cases. Sadly, that's just not true for several reasons we'll explore in this book. If your users need to enter a credit card number while on a bus, guess what? Voice is not the right thing. Digit entry is fine with keypads, and of course there's the privacy issue. But if they're driving and need to enter a phone number, voice is a great option. The point is voice is an interaction modality, a means to an end. There are many modalities that allow your user to get something done; make sure you're implementing the right one in the right way and know when to suggest another solution. Think about the user and what their best way is to do a task in different environments. Voice is not the answer for all users at all times. If you want to create a voice solution that people want to use, don't ask "What can I build with voice?" but rather "What task can be solved better with voice?"

Any architect worth their salt asks these questions early, before going to the drafting table, let alone getting a crew of builders. So why wouldn't you plan your voice-first interaction before developing it? Start with the basics:

- Who'll live in the house? How many people? How old are they and what's their relationship? Young kids, roommates, extended families? Any special needs?

- What did they like about past residences? Do they plan to stay there long? Do they work from home? Have special collections? Like to cook, garden, throw parties?

- What can be built here? What's the budget? Timeline? Permit needs? Utility access?

The bullet list questions have clear parallels in voice development: understand the end user, the person who's going to be interacting with the voice solution, as well as what any product owner is hoping to get out of it. If you do this right, you'll actually learn quite a bit about the user that you and the product owner didn't know. The planning phase is so underrepresented today in voice development writing that we dedicate all of Chapter 4 to highlighting the core questions you should ask before you do any development. If you plan a one-story family home, you can't later build a ten-story apartment building on the same foundation. All voice platforms are also not the same—if some feature or data access is required for your VUI, this is the time to figure out if you can actually create what you want with what's available to you.

The planning stage needs the steady hand of a product/project manager who brings the designer(s) and engineer(s) into the room on Day 1. Make sure everyone knows not only the business goals of what's being built, but involve them directly in discussions with stakeholders and customers when refining requirements. This is the time to verify assumptions about feasibility from both a voice technology and user experience perspective. Early user experience research (UXR) is crucial to success. Chapter 5 covers UXR methods appropriate at this early stage.

SUCCESS TIP 1.4 BE CAREFUL WITH YOUR USER STORY ASSUMPTIONS   We have seen too many examples of "As a user..." stories turning into implemented features where there was no true research and understanding of what the user actually wanted or needed. If a consultant or customer tells you something about users, find out what that's based on beyond wishful thinking, self-as-user, or potentially misleading statistics.

Design

The needs and wants of the inhabitants will influence many design decisions: is there a need for a formal living room, a mudroom, a multicar garage? The same-size house could have different numbers of rooms and one or multiple stories. Those are fairly individual choices, within a common range. But building a house with ten stories and one room on each level or one with the garage between the kitchen and dining room is not recommended without a really good reason. And although the architect won't typically worry about what color the bathroom gets painted, it may be important to know that it will get painted so that the wall isn't the wrong surface. Architecture vs. interior design—they're different but related.

What about the voice-first design? How to convert the plan into design and implementation is of course a core focus of this book, but here's a sample:

- What functionality are you offering? (What can the user do?) What happens when users ask for something outside that functionality?

- How should you organize the functionality? Are there lists of options? If so, which option comes first, and why? How will users know what's possible? Do users make one request or several in a row? This is a little bit like the flow of the house; you could put the laundry room next to the front door, but you probably wouldn't. You want the most used functionality easily accessible and the less used not as prominent (but still easily available).

- Will you allow natural language, the ability to ask for a request very naturally, with a prompt like *What would you like to do?* as opposed to *Please say A, B, or C?*

- What does your system say to the user at each point in the dialog? Why are you choosing a particular formality style, voice or personality? What reaction do you hope for from your users?

- What do you expect the user to say at each point in the dialog? How do you know what they'll say so it's handled? How will they know what to say? How do they accomplish this task today?

- Are you using recorded system phrases (if so, recorded by whom?) or synthesis (if so, which one)? Are audio files stored or generated when needed? Can you edit pronunciations? Alter the speed? Make updates quickly? Is it expensive?

- What happens when the system doesn't understand the user? It will happen. How will users get back on track without getting frustrated?

- What happens when the user says nothing? This will also happen. Do you keep asking them to say something? Do they have to start over if the app times out?

- Are the design choices in line with what your chosen technology can do? Any plan can result in multiple designs, but if some part of your platform or pipeline can't provide some piece of metadata to work well, you need another design choice.

For a house, the output of the design phase is typically a set of blueprints and/or other documents that essentially allow the builders and tradesfolk to put the house together. For voice, detailed designs go into a VUI design specification; you'll learn more about options for creating these specs in Chapter 5. You don't necessarily need to be overly formal; it depends on your situation. If you're creating a solution for external clients or with a larger team, you'll all need something tangible to review. To be honest, even if you work with just one or two others or if there's any level of complexity to what you're building, you'll find out that it's still very useful to have something to drive the build process other than what's only in your head. There are also different aspects of design; voice user experience is more like architecture, while detailed VUI design is more like interior design, as you'll see in Chapter 5 and later. You learn things during design that don't match your assumptions. Sometimes the answers you got during planning were incorrect, and sometimes you didn't ask all the questions you should have. If that happens, you have to guess, use knowledge from other VUI designs, or dip back into planning. This phase is of course the realm of the voice UX and UI designer in close coordination with speech engineers and other engineers depending on what's being built. Visual designers will be involved if it's a multimodal solution.

SUCCESS TIP 1.5 NOT ALL DESIGN IS THE SAME   If you're building a device that uses voice and also has a physical shape, your device's industrial design needs to not just look great but also function well for voice input/output. Does the shape of the device encourage users to speak to where the microphone is located, or are they covering up the input with their hand or with stuff? Are lights not only pleasant to look at but also indicating meaningfully whether the device is listening or not? All aspects of design will matter; don't forget one to focus only on another.

Build

You've got your blueprints. Now pick up the hammer and the saw and build that house! One of the first choices to make for your voice-first development is what platform to use. This may not really be a choice at all; you or someone else may have said, "We need an Alexa skill to do X." The choice might be a smart speaker assistant, a mobile voice app, a phone-based IVR, a stand-alone device built from scratch, or something else. Again, much of what you learn in this book is agnostic enough to apply across platforms and devices. Along with each platform comes a set of tools. Later, you'll learn about when those tools are great and when they push against the limits of what you might need to do. A builder might have a favorite brand of hammer; you might have a favorite programming language. The builder can use another brand because they know how to hammer; once you learn to code, you can learn other languages while still applying your coding skills. With this book, you can apply voice best practices no matter what platform or device you're building for.

You'll find that the VUI specification has errors or things that are unclear, or it's missing use cases that need to be handled. Maybe design didn't get all the answers from planning. So now you either implement your best guess or revisit earlier decisions to make changes. What if you already built something that now has to be changed? Obviously not having the right plan can get expensive, whether it means tearing down the bathroom walls or redoing code. But it won't get easier to fix if you wait. While this phase is mainly the engineer and coder phase, there will always be a need for design changes. Those need to be done in coordination with both the designer and the speech scientist so that users get consistent responses throughout the voice system.

Test

The next big step is testing and verifying. Different types of testing and verifying obviously apply to house building and voice development, but the concept is the same. Does it work to spec? Is it safe? Voice has an extra level of complexity: users most likely didn't have direct say in the specification, and the solution has to work for many people, not just one household.

Most tools have simulation environments where you can test a phrase, either via text or voice, and see if it does what you expect. But that's only one aspect of testing. It's common to do some very early testing to validate whether users respond with the words and phrases you think they will (they often don't!). This can impact the flow of the dialog. You'll benefit greatly from letting some potential actual users try what you created, the earlier the better, and see if their requests are handled as both you and they expect.

Testing voice apps takes special training. The most successful testing involves every role on the team. The types of voice testing, how to perform them, and what they can tell you are other underrepresented aspects of voice-first development today, which is why we focus on several types of testing in Chapter 16.

Deploy and Assess

Great, you've tested what you created, and it performs well, so now you just "push the button" to deploy the app and consider it done, right? No, you don't want to do that. The main reason is the need to iterate, the assess/repeat notion that we've talked about. There's always something that can be improved, and when live users have never before interacted with your voice-first solution, there's likely a lot that can be improved. One possibility is to expose only a small portion of the user population at first and then do your assess/repeat cycle. Sometimes you just flip the proverbial coin to decide which users go first; sometimes you pick more deliberately.

Your voice-first solution is deployed, and you have users! That's a very exciting time. It's also (at least should be) one of the most unnerving times. You want the end product to be great and useful. But is it? How do you know?

This is where the assessment phase comes in. You want to monitor every available aspect of the application behavior. This could include analyzing the text interpretations of what people are saying (since speech recognition is imperfect, you're actually looking at hypotheses of what the system "thinks" people are saying). It could involve listening to the raw utterances to find out what users are **really** saying and how they're saying it. There's a difference between a cheery *Yes!* from an excited user who got what they needed and a rather annoyed *YES* when you've asked the user to confirm the same thing three times. There's listening to entire user conversations end-to-end to explore weird timings, latency, noise, and many other things. And that's from a qualitative perspective. There are also loads of statistics that tell a story if you know what to look for: what users are asking for, how long it takes to perform a transaction, how often the speech recognizer is returning the right answer, how often users have to rephrase and try again, and so on. This is the topic of Chapter 17.

Iterate

Once you've learned what can be improved, you make the changes. You find data that leads you to update the requirements, modify aspects of the design, add more phrases for training, and so on.

How often do you repeat? Forever? Well, no. For a decent-sized business-grade deployment, try to get one or two pilots before full 100% rollout, followed by another iteration after rollout. Finally, revisiting performance and doing another iteration on a quarterly basis (if things are changing rapidly) or a yearly basis is a very good idea, if only because your user population or business environment changes constantly in ways that may not be obvious. It's particularly important to check if things are still OK after any known big change in either user base (maybe you've just had a merger adding new customers who use different terminology or come from a different background) or business (maybe you've just added a new product or hiked your prices; see the "From the Trenches" section). Granted, these are guidelines for industrial-strength voice apps that could process tens of thousands of users a day; a smart home assistant app will likely not do that. This is also a topic of Chapter 17.

FROM THE VOICE TRENCHES: "CANCEL? WE DON'T WANT THAT!"

We worked on a voice solution for a prominent client where we started in a standard "by the book" manner—by figuring out what the functionality should be and how often users will want to do this or that.

We based the functionality on user interviews and meetings with the client's customer service and marketing folks. One of the things not in the original requirements was the functionality of canceling an account. We asked many times *Are you sure?* about leaving it out, explaining why we'd seen it needed in many other apps. But the client was adamant and of course they're paying the bills!

You can guess what happened when we deployed. A quarter of all user requests were for canceling accounts! We were actually prepared to quickly add account cancelation handling— we knew this would happen. We're not picking on those who insisted that we didn't need to cover canceling accounts. The point is that when you deploy voice, you stand to learn a great deal about what your customers and users want to do! Sometimes these discoveries are surprising and uncomfortable, as this one was. Usually they're not this dramatic.

Lesson learned: As you assess your system's performance and listen to what users actually say, you can learn a lot, and you must be open to revisiting previous decisions. The risk of having to start over is smaller the better prepared you are through planning and knowledge.

What Next?

You're probably thinking, *Wow, this all sounds like a lot of work and extra steps. Why should I do all this?* You certainly can build something without worrying about the details. You can find articles and videos online that explain how to use one of the great available tools. But will it be a great app? Will users want to use it? Will they return? All these phases—planning, testing, deploying, assessing, and repeating—are aimed at succeeding with any task on any platform, especially the complex tasks. It's not enough to pick up a hammer, drive some nails in, and hope that the resulting house will have happy inhabitants. You need to make sure it's a good house: not only a house that won't fall down but one that's functional and aesthetically pleasing—bottom line, a house that the residents want to live in!

We're covering a lot of ground in this book, but there's no need to get overwhelmed. You won't need to handle everything by yourself. In the next chapter, you learn what's special about spoken language, how speech is processed by humans and computers, and why some things are harder than others.[15]

Summary

- Many common claims about voice are based on misconceptions—you can avoid many pitfalls by understanding what's underneath those misconceptions. Address causes, not effects.

- Even though spoken and written communication have the same goals, they differ from each other in fundamental ways that are crucial to handle in voice-first development and conversational dialog.

- Incorporating the best aspects of agile and waterfall approaches and iterating at all phases of voice development leads to successful deployments, thanks to the interconnectivity of voice processing components.

- Understanding can fail at every step of a conversation with potential consequences at every other step.

- Creating a great voice application is more than just building and designing; you also need to plan, design, build, test, deploy, and assess.

---

[15]Read more about real-world implementation challenges: Falkson, L. (2018). *Ubiquitous Voice: Essays from the Field*. Seattle, WA: Amazon.com Services, LLC.

CHAPTER 2

Keeping Voice in Mind

Over the years, we've found that the people who create the most successful voice interactions understand both the underlying technology and how people use spoken language. A solid basis in these topics helps you choose between the many possible options you'll have at every step of designing and building a voice system. In the words of Bower and Cirilo,[1] "Modern civilization demands that a person acquire and use language. It is imperative that we learn how it operates."

This chapter begins with an overview of voice as a modality, a particular mode of interaction with its own particular characteristics. You learn how voice differs from other modalities and why that matters to the user experience and the ultimate success of what you create. You'll meet the two participants in voice-first dialogs, the "human" and the "computer," and learn how each talks and listens. From this, you'll understand what's easy and challenging for each and why they're different for each of them. Then you learn the core VUI principles that'll be your guiding light in every voice-first interaction you build from now on.

Why Voice Is Different

The secret to creating successful conversational voice dialogs is understanding voice. You might wonder what the big deal is or how it's even different from developing GUIs or text-based chatbots. Shouldn't Alexa handle the details for you? Does it really matter if someone has to ask Google Assistant twice to get their answer? If Cortana or Bixby gets a request almost right, isn't that good enough? Sure, these voice assistants take care of a lot for you, but certainly not everything. Even in simple voice interactions, it's easy to trip over something that results in a failed dialog from the user's perspective. How often do you dictate to Siri and end up with a word that sounds similar but makes

---

[1]Bower, G., and Cirilo, R. (1985). Cognitive Psychology and Text Processing. In T. van Dijk (Ed.), Handbook of Discourse Analysis, volume 1. London: Academic Press.

© Ann Thymé-Gobbel, Charles Jankowski 2021
A. Thymé-Gobbel and C. Jankowski, *Mastering Voice Interfaces*, https://doi.org/10.1007/978-1-4842-7005-9_2

absolutely no sense in the context? Don't get discouraged: experienced voice designers and developers themselves trip. This stuff is complex. When asked to *Play "Let It Be,"* one of our home voice assistants responded with *Playing "Let It Be Love,"* a nice tune but not the expected Beatles song. As a user, I didn't get what I wanted, from this request that's straightforward for a human listener.

Voice is about sound—making sounds, processing them, and interpreting them. The audio signal is fleeting and varied, created by different voices and practically unlimited within a shared language. A lot of information has to be conveyed through a very narrow stream of sound while relying on the listener's working memory. The risk of misinterpretation is constant. All this immediately differentiates it from other modalities, as you'll see later in this chapter.

Voice is a modality: a way in which information is encoded for human consumption that makes use of our senses. Written text, images, and signs are visual; voice, noises, and music are auditory. To us humans, there's a huge difference between how we process information in different modalities: how we understand something we read vs. how we understand information we hear. That difference is behind all the reasons why voice design and development is deeply different from that of visual or tangible interfaces. Multimodal interfaces combine modalities for a potentially richer experience.

If you're entering the voice world from a GUI or web-based background, you'll naturally apply what you know about visual interfaces to auditory interfaces. Many basic principles transfer, but how they're best implemented differs across modalities. As introduced in Chapter 1, voice-first implies developing a UI appropriate for the modality of voice without being constrained to fit into a framework that's better for other modalities. By the end of this chapter, you'll understand why and how this matters.

You'll hear the term conversational applied to text-based chatbot interactions as well as voice interactions. The two share being open-ended compared with other graphical interfaces, but they're not the same because of the differences in how they're processed. A conversational dialog implies a back-and-forth, or turn-taking, interaction between two participants. It implies an informal natural language broad-vocabulary interaction but can also be something more formal, following a pattern. It can be a short one- or two-turn interaction or a longer multi-turn one. More turns is more conversational. We don't consider dictation to be conversational because of its one-sided nature.

This book focuses on natural language conversational (by our definition) voice-first interactions **with a goal**: dialogs where users try to perform some task. Examples include making a flight reservation, requesting to hear a particular song, setting a timer, transferring money between accounts, turning on a light, changing TV channels, information lookup, and so on. It's the core use case for voice today. It's also the foundation for any back-and-forth turn-taking needed for more complex interactions.[2]

If a voice assistant doesn't understand its users, the users have to try again. Is that the end of the world? No, but it's an annoying waste of effort and leads to unhappiness and lack of trust. They'll receive inaccurate information and complain about not being understood. Eventually they'll stop using it, and even mock it in public, resulting in bad PR. Worse, users could lose money if a financial transaction is misunderstood, affecting everyone's financial bottom line. Obviously, you'd rather avoid all that in the first place than fix it later. As users become more familiar with voice, they expect more sophisticated "smart" behavior from their VUIs.

SUCCESS TIP 2.1 PRACTICE ANALYZING VOICE CONVERSATIONS   One of the best, quickest, and cheapest ways to get a sense of what makes a VUI good or bad is to experience it yourself—and do it consciously. Practice analyzing and thinking about voice. Find as many voice systems as you can, use them as intended, and take notes. Did you get the answer or result you expected? How was the level of detail, tone, speed, and accuracy? Do you trust the result? Why or why not? What happens if you rephrase a request? When does it fail? What if you try something nonsensical? Is it clear what you can do and say? Importantly, why did you think so? And what could be improved for your use and situation? Change your environment and think of other uses. Does that change things? Start the practice of analyzing your own reactions before expanding to observing other users—their reactions will be different.

---

[2]There are many forms and purposes of conversation: strengthening relationships, problem analysis, conflict resolution, and so on. Voice-based solutions may be able to support such conversations one day, but their complexity puts them outside the scope of our book for the foreseeable future.

Hands-On: A Precoding Thought Experiment

In Chapter 3, you'll set up and run your first functional conversational voice application: a simple version of a restaurant finder, maybe something like Figure 2-1.

Figure 2-1. *Sample restaurant finder dialog between a user and a voice assistant*

Think about the details involved as you read this chapter:

- **Geographical scope**: What geographical area will it cover? If there are limits, how do users know about them? What happens if users ask for a location you don't cover? Do you assume users want matches near their current location? Why or why not? How do you make your assumptions clear to the user, and what happens if you're wrong?

- **Search**: What search parameters are used for finding a restaurant? Name, location, cuisine, hours, price range, specific menu items…? How many results do you present to the user, and in what order? Closest, most popular? When and how do you clarify your assumptions? Can users override them? How do they know? Can they gradually narrow in on a result?

- **Information**: What information can a user get? Location, hours, and type of cuisine seem obvious. How do you keep the info up-to-date? How fuzzy is the match of a restaurant name, both in pronunciation and exact name? What happens when users aren't understood?

- **User information**: How tailored are the responses for each user? What do you know about the user, their preferences, their location, and their past restaurant visits? Can you build on past searches? Should you assume that they want something similar next time? Again, how do users know what's available, and what happens if they ask for something you can't provide?

Voice Dialog and Its Participants

Voice-first development requires taking advantage of the strengths and minimizing the weaknesses of both dialog participants, human and computer, and helping them reach their goal. Successful conversational voice interactions are built by designers and developers who understand the voice modality—people who understand the technology available to them and are interested in how people communicate by speaking and listening. That's it—that's the whole secret to voice. The rest is details... Of course, the devil is always in the details.

Our goal is to create interactions like the one in Figure 2-2, which represents a dialog between two participants who need to speak, listen, and understand each other.

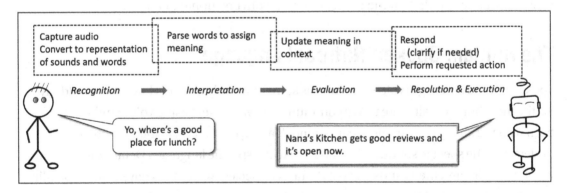

Figure 2-2. *The basic steps of one human-to-computer dialog turn*

The trick is that each of the two dialog participants has specific, and very different, strengths and weaknesses. The human side is based on human physiology and biology, out of which spoken language developed. The computer side depends on technology to process the spoken input and synthesized or recorded speech to respond. So the reality looks more like Figure 2-3.

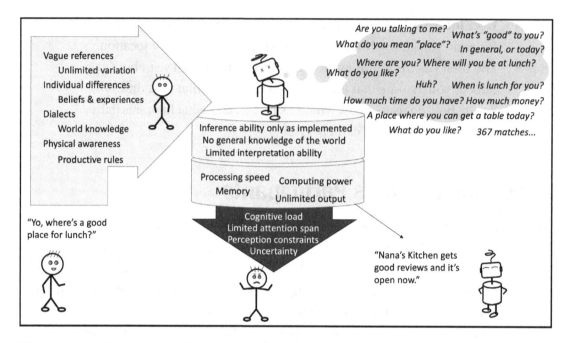

Figure 2-3. *The more realistic steps of one human-to-computer dialog turn*

To create successful voice interactions, you need to understand what's behind the dialog. So let's meet our two dialog participants—the human and the computer—first each separately and then in the context of their conversational dialog.

The Human: Spoken Natural Language

Spoken natural language (voice, for short) is something only humans have. You could say it's the most human trait there is. We communicate with others using voice, and we're born with the ability to hear and create sound, leading to our innate ability to create and understand the specific sounds and words used in a specific language. Details differ, like the words we know and the sounds we make, but as a species, all humans have voice capability.[3]

But what about AI bots or parrots or bees or apes, you ask? Don't they have language as well? Not by the complete definition of natural language. They can produce human language sounds or respond to some spoken words or communicate in other ways, but they don't share all traits of human (spoken) natural language, traits that make it uniquely both simple and complex:

---

[3]We deliberately don't discuss languages such as ASL here, which are fully functional languages but are less relevant to our focus on spoken language.

- **Discrete**: A small set of individual units (sounds) whose forms are mostly arbitrary (hence variation across languages).

- **Rule-based**: A system for combining smaller units into larger units that in turn combine to represent increasing levels of complexity.

- **Productive and limitless**: Ability to create infinite combinations of the units using the rules—and create new ones never before heard but easily understandable.

- **Displaced**: Ability to represent concepts in the past or future or in locations never visited, abstract ideas, lies, or fiction.

- **Learned and social**: The traits are general; but once a certain combination is established, it's rigid enough to be predictable and forming a specific language, one that kids easily learn but can also be learned by an adult.

Let's look at an example. Imagine how easily you can convert a feeling of hunger plus a knowledge of time of day into the concept [LUNCHTIME] and then turn that concept into sounds forming a string of words like *Wanna get some food?* Your friend, just as easily, hears your words, assigns a meaning, and responds with words based on their understanding and context, maybe *Sure* (Figure 2-4).

Figure 2-4. *Voice interaction: a dialog with a resolution between a speaker-listener pair*

You just created and participated in a voice dialog, a short conversation between two participants, in this case between you and your friend. You initiated the dialog and your friend responded, both taking turns and intuitively realizing when the goal had been reached, making the dialog complete. Pretty simple, right? As we start unpacking the many levels and steps involved in producing and understanding even this short dialog, you'll see it's anything but simple.

For now, we'll skip past how people form the concepts feeding into their speech and start by looking at the most fundamental piece: the speech audio signal.[4]

Speech sound is an acoustic waveform: vibrations in the air at specific frequencies determined by the movements we make (or articulate) with our mouths and vocal tracts. The "e" in "get" has different frequencies from the "oo" in "food." In reality, there's limitless variation in these sounds across speakers and words. The same word spoken by the same person is even acoustically different each time. What you hear (or perceive) as "oo" in "food"—designated as the sound [u]—is actually a group of sounds at slightly different frequencies.

Your human ability to categorize these auditory signals lets you group many instances of [u] across speakers and words and interpret them as instances of the same meaningful discrete unit of sound in your language, a phoneme, disregarding variation to a point of not even noticing it (Figure 2-5).

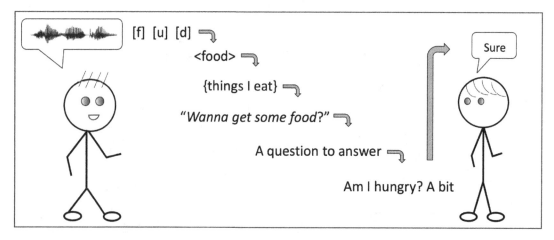

Figure 2-5. *Voice is an audio stream with enormous variation*

---

[4]For space considerations, we're greatly simplifying the details of how speech and language works.

Because voice is a waveform, it's created and heard as a linear sequence in time. It's fleeting: once something has been said, whether heard or not, it's gone. As a listener, you need to keep what you hear in working memory; you can't "rewind" or wait till the speech stops to look at the whole thing while you ponder a response. So you parse what you hear: you create and update hypotheses (working theories, or guesses) of sounds and words and meaning based on what you hear in real time while the stream continues. The vaguer or noisier the utterance, the longer you need to keep hypotheses active until you have enough information to settle on the most likely match. If you hear "Do you want some co-<NOISE>?" from the kitchen, your top hypothesis may be "coco" or "coffee," possibly "coke" or "corn." You'll automatically assign probabilities to each depending on other contexts. If you need to know which one is correct, you might just need to ask the speaker what they said. But if they immediately follow up with "I'll brew a fresh pot if you want some too," then you can pick "coffee" and drop the other hypotheses.

Using hypotheses to find the best match is a very important concept—it's what the computer side of the conversation uses, as you'll see, though a computer can easily track many hypotheses, while we humans are very limited. The more hypotheses, the greater the listener's cognitive load. This important concept comes out of cognitive psychology. It's the mental effort needed by someone to successfully complete some task, in particular, the effort needed to keep something in working memory. It isn't a voice-related concept per se; cognitive load applies to all types of human processing. But it's particularly relevant in voice processing because of the characteristics of voice as linear and fleeting. Limiting cognitive load is therefore at the core of VUI design. You'll hear much more about it throughout the book.

When you (subconsciously) decide you've heard enough to settle on a hypothesis, you end up with an interpretation of the utterance. Your friend gradually heard the sounds that formed *Wanna get some food? My turn to treat* and knew you were talking about eating before hearing the exciting last word and realizing that you're paying.

Meaning isn't just conveyed through words but also by how those words are spoken: pitch level, amount of pitch variation, duration, and loudness carry meaning about the speaker—where they're from, how they feel, and more. Changing an English sentence from falling to rising intonation can change its meaning from a statement or command (*Get food.*) to a question (*Get food?*). Imagine the pitch of your friend's *Sure!* compared with the pitch on the same word if you had asked, *Wanna get some food? My turn to treat, but I forgot my wallet* (Figure 2-6). We use this prosody and intonation to lessen the cognitive load for the listener by emphasizing new or important words in a phrase or by chunking longer information like numbers into groups with brief pauses. We also use it to convey our attitudes about what we're saying and our overall emotional state. It means there's a lot of information stacked in parallel in everything we say and hear!

Figure 2-6. *Voice interaction is sharing an understanding of the world*

Words are symbols that let us refer to things even when those things are not in front of us, things displaced in time and space. Displacement lets us refer to items and events and abstract concepts that are not here and now, like *Did you like that place we went to last week?*

There's limitless variation also in how we combine sounds into words and words into phrases and sentences to convey meaning. Much of that variation is relevant, like words with different meanings, while other variation is irrelevant to the core meaning of a phrase, like saying *yes* vs. *yeah* or the presence of disfluency, the hesitations and restarts, and little hitches in pronunciation, like *um* and *er*, that we as listeners usually are very good at ignoring. Disfluency is one area where spoken language differs from written language.

With all this limitless variation, how can anyone understand the meaning of anything? "Wanna get some food?" isn't even "proper English," you might point out, remembering school. If we talked like we write, we should say "Do you want to..." or at least "Want to...," but that would sound oddly formal.

The reason we can communicate at all is that we apply various strategies and "rules of engagement." We "know" these rules; we can't easily explain them, but we sure know when they're broken. We also expect other dialog participants to follow the same rules. The intended meaning of word combinations and acceptable interactions are things we learn and share with others in our specific culture and language.

Turn-taking is one such rule. Both participants can't talk and listen simultaneously without their communication suffering, so they need to take turns and sense when it's time to shift from talking to listening and vice versa. The details of turn-taking depend on the goal of the conversation, the participants' relationship, and their shared culture.

Another rule is Paul Grice's Cooperative Principle: dialog participants generally try to contribute to reach a common goal.[5] When I say, *Can you close the window?* I expect you to actually close the window, not respond *Yes, I can* and do nothing. On the surface, it's just a simple Yes/No question, so more than word and grammar knowledge is needed to respond appropriately. Breaking the rules of engagement can be an intentional source of humor—whether the other participant finds it funny or not is another question with its own set of rules of engagement. You'll learn more about this and related rules in later chapters.

Yet another relevant communication model is Friedemann Schulz von Thun's four-sides model.[6] This model highlights that all messages have four facets: fact, self-revealing, relationship, and appeal. The speaker filters every message through these facets, but at different degrees at different times. The listener hears it through the same filters, but likely at different levels of each.

People learn these "rules" more or less automatically by virtue of learning a language and interacting with other speakers. People also expect others to share the same abilities so that they can talk about a wide range of topics. That makes voice a rule-based productive and surprisingly robust system of a (to us) finite set of units that can be combined in infinite ways. The result is a very powerful system of communication—and a very human one (Figure 2-7).

---

[5]Grice, H. P. (1975). "Logic and conversation." In Cole, P., and J. L. Morgan (Eds.), Speech Acts (41–58). New York, NY: Academic Press. Different rules apply to different types of dialogs. The Cooperative Principle is a default that we assume applies to conversations unless we're faced with another more specific conversation type, like a political debate, an argument, a sales pitch, and so on. How to implement a well-functioning voice interaction for these and other conversations with their own rules is a fascinating topic outside the scope of this book, but any conversation will need to handle the underlying characteristics of spoken language.

[6]Friedemann Schulz von Thun. Miteinander reden: Störungen und Klärungen. Psychologie der zwischenmenschlichen Kommunikation. Rowohlt, Reinbek 1981.

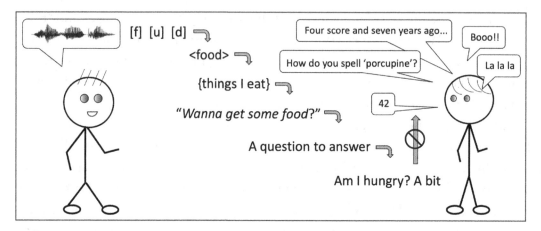

Figure 2-7. *Voice follows "rules" of natural language such as the Cooperative Principle*

Clarity is obviously important for being understood, but clarity entails precision. Legal documents are precise to avoid assumptions and are therefore very long. If we needed to talk like legal documents without making any assumptions, dialogs would never end. Problem is sometimes assumptions are wrong. Two people's concepts are never identical because mental models are based on past experiences and cognitive biases. They make assumptions about how much of their mental model is shared with their dialog partner. The vaguer the utterance, the more the listener has to either assume or clarify. When you proposed getting lunch, your friend heard the words correctly, but what if you had been unclear about the details? What if you wanted to have ramen and your friend was in a pizza mood? If your friend understood what you had in mind for lunch but didn't want ramen, was the dialog still a success? How do you know what needs clarification and to what level of detail? Some assumptions are more important than others to verify. The trick is knowing which are which (Figure 2-8).

Figure 2-8. *Voice is sharing assumptions and knowing something about your dialog partner*

As listeners, we often miss a portion of what was said. If the conversation topic is familiar, you might miss a word or two and still get the overall gist, so the process can be fairly robust. At other times, you misinterpret or hear something ambiguous or vague. If your friend responds with words you just don't understand, the dialog fails: you either need to try again, ask for clarification, or give up. You use disambiguation, clarification, verification, and confirmation strategies to repair errors and reach some confidence level that understanding is obtained, all strategies you'll learn more about starting in Chapter 7. If you'd asked your friend, *Wanna get some ramen?* the answer might have been different. And maybe your friend should have asked, *Where're we going?* or *Can we get pizza?* (Figure 2-9).

Figure 2-9. *Voice is clarifying ambiguity to minimize misunderstandings and convey shared understanding*

53

Having a conversation implies following these subconscious "rules": you assume and expect that anyone, or anything, that speaks will respond and interact in predictable ways and that they'll expect the same from you. You can even influence how others speak without them realizing it; if you talk louder or faster, so will your listener. Try it. People instinctively apply the same rules of conversation and social expectations when talking to technology—even when knowing the conversation is with a machine. That means the same strategies apply also when the dialog is between a human and a voice assistant. It's what makes VUI design possible.

To summarize the traits of the human dialog participant, the strength of human voice communication is that it's practically limitless yet rule-based and formed from a small number of established units. The challenges for a human listener are the cognitive load of keeping information in memory to interpret it and act on it. People rely on strategies for avoiding or repairing misunderstandings; we take a lot for granted expecting others to make sense of our vague and ambiguous expressions. Considering all the steps involved, it's amazing we can communicate with each other at all! How do computers do it? It sounds tricky, but don't worry! We're here to help with exactly that. Understanding how people talk and listen is half the battle. After we explain the basics of the computer side of the dialog, we're going to show you how to put it all together successfully in the remainder of the book. You'll see that you can achieve vast voice app improvements with the methods and tools already available today—no need to invent new things.

The Computer: Voice Recognition and Interpretation

In Chapter 1, you were introduced to the components of a voice system. Now let's dive further into those components to understand why some aspects are harder than others. How does a computer do what humans do? Just as people both talk and listen, so do computers. But a computer must be "taught" everything a human has learned, including how to handle vague or ambiguous utterances. In fact, most of your work will be aimed at minimizing and handling incorrect results. Computers, like humans, need strategies to minimize misrecognition and misinterpretations; to confirm, correct, and verify; and to resolve ambiguity. They don't need to use the same underlying strategies as humans—and they won't, since they're built differently—but the end result must be the same, or better, from the human's point of view. The trick for the computer, then, is to make use of its strengths when handling human input.

At the highest level, the computer has two tasks: first, capturing the user utterance and turning it into words and meaning and, second, responding to the user in a meaningful and appropriate way, either a spoken response or some action or both. Let's revisit the voice system introduced in Chapter 1 (Figure 2-10) and expand on some details; the reasons for the overlapping boxes will become clear soon. The two core tasks can be further divided into the following five steps, numbered 1–5 in the figure:

1. Recognition captures the voice utterance through automatic speech recognition (ASR) and converts the waveform signal frequencies into a format that can be used to map that signal into phonemes.

2. Interpretation maps the recognized phonemes into text (words and phrases) using methods for pattern matching and rules.

3. Intent evaluation maps the text result with a representation of its (hopefully) intended meaning using rule matching methods.

4. Intent resolution and execution attempts to fulfill the interpreted request with an appropriate action or response.

5. Computer vocal response has two core aspects: the content (the words chosen, level of detail, etc.) and its delivery (recorded vs. synthesized speech, emotional tone, gender of voice, etc.).

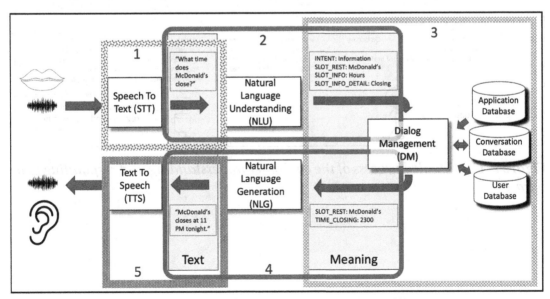

Figure 2-10. *Voice-first system expanded with additional details*

When your user asks, *Where's a good place for food?* the first part of recognition captures the analog waveform and converts it to a digital representation (A in Figure 2-11). This is done by measuring, or sampling, the waveform at very frequent regular intervals. The recognizer uses an **acoustic model** to map the digital representation to specific phonemes (B). The best acoustic models are trained on enormous amounts of speech data using various algorithms and approaches. The language model (LM) interprets the phoneme string by mapping it to the closest word and text string (C). Competing mappings will have an associated likelihood, or confidence score, that depends on context and other factors (D). The confidence score can be used to pick the most likely mapping out of many, as can parsing. Correct assignment of confidence is often what fails when you dictate a message on your phone and get the wrong text result. Confidence is used for some powerful techniques we'll show you later. The winning hypothesis is evaluated against grammars and/or statistical models mapping the text to an intent, a representation of its meaning (E). At that point, what's thought of as recognition and intent mapping is done, but the user hasn't gotten anything out of it yet. The last step is to generate an appropriate response based on context and provide the content or information that was requested (F).

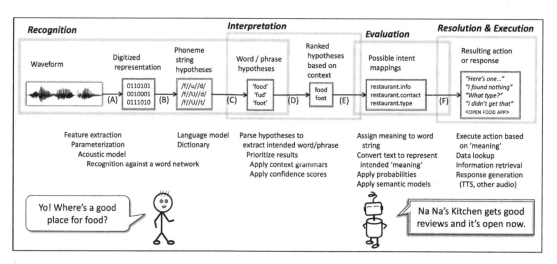

Figure 2-11. *Detailed process of the computer understanding and responding to a phrase*

At each step, something can go wrong. If the computer settled on the wrong hypothesis early in the process, one tiny error easily ignored by a human can snowball, so that by the end of the process, the result is nonsensical in a way that would never happen in human conversation. Background noise and other voices are especially problematic. As mentioned in Chapter 1, recognition performance has improved a lot in recent years, but it's not perfect, as you can easily see when dictating to your phone. Say any sentence out loud; you'll realize that you don't say words in isolation but as a continuous string, sounds mingling, one word flowing into the next and impacting how it's spoken. If you hesitate or start over or hiccup on some word, the resulting transcript will probably not be what you intended. If one sound is on the edge between two phoneme pattern matches and the unintended match wins, it can lead to a mistaken word boundary, and you end up with *engulfing them all* interpreted as *and golf in the mall*. Parsing into words is hard; assigning the intended meaning to those words can be even harder. Even with excellent recognition performance, the intent resolution step fails if the text-to-intent mapping isn't robust.

You'll probably work mostly on steps 3 and 4 (intent evaluation and resolution and execution). These are the steps where you specify what should happen for each user request. The main difference between working within platforms like Alexa or Google Assistant and in a native solution is that platforms provide the convenience of a black box that handles many details for you, particularly involving the transition from step 2 to step 3. For that convenience, you trade the benefits of accessing and affecting results at earlier steps, as you'll see later.

The first thing to understand about how the computer processes voice is that it's all about pattern matching and settling on the best hypothesis of many possible hypotheses at each step. The recognizer's goal is to find the best answer, the best match to what it knows about—think of it as a set of magnets that try to grab what's thrown at it. The recognizer creates many hypotheses that are updated with each additional slice of sound coming in. Each new sound slice provides additional information that affects the probability of all active hypotheses (the strength of each magnet). Lots of hypotheses need to be kept active at the start of an utterance, because later information may tip the scale of interpretation to another phoneme, another word, and so on. Context helps both humans and computers pare down potential hypotheses and occurs at all levels of an utterance: expectations about the other dialog participant, knowledge about the dialog topic and its relevant terminology, grammatical structure, preceding words and sounds, and so on. While context is used by both dialog participants, cognitive load is obviously not a concern for the computer. It can keep many hypotheses in parallel while additional voice input is captured and analyzed.

Tracking many hypotheses in parallel makes ASR possible. Contexts and constraints decrease the number of likely matches, gradually making one hypothesis bubble to the top. When the end of the user's utterance is reached, the highest-scoring utterance hypothesis wins. Often, there's a winner with one score clearly higher than others. Sometimes that highest score isn't very high or maybe just marginally higher than others. This means the computer isn't very confident in the accuracy of the top result. At this point, the computer makes a decision based on settings and predetermined criteria:

- If the confidence is below some chosen cutoff value, the pattern is rejected. If it would have been correct to pick that hypothesis, it's a false reject; if rejecting was the right thing to do, it's a correct reject.

- If the confidence is above the cutoff value, the pattern is accepted. If it was a "wrong answer," it's a false accept; if it matches the user's intended utterance, then it's good, a correct accept.

Obviously any of the "false" outcomes should be avoided and handled when they occur. You'll learn much more about how to do that in Chapters 10, 12, and 13.

SUCCESS TIP 2.2 SET APPROPRIATE EXPECTATIONS   Setting the appropriate expectations is crucial to VUI success. It means clarifying to your users what level of knowledge your implementation has on what topic. This isn't trivial. Within the VUI, you rely on the wording of what your VUI says. In IVRs, the VUI typically begins with either a menu or an open-ended question with illustrative examples. The more general the VUI, the harder this is, but a lot of information can be conveyed in the responses when some action can't be completed. You'll learn about this in Chapters 12 and 13. Outside the VUI interaction, it involves marketing and sales and resource materials. Broad information retrieval has been at Google's core from the start; Alexa's initial focus was more targeted in scope, such as playing music and a few information domains like weather. Users don't necessarily know that. They only know that one assistant can answer when another can't. You'll see blog posts and articles pitting assistants against each other, comparing which is "smarter." By all means, read these and anything else voice-related you come across. Learn from them, but you'd also be wise to take any conclusions with a grain of salt.

Not everything is difficult for the poor computer. Dialects are not necessarily as challenging as you might think.[7] Holding something in memory or producing a long list of hypotheses is obviously no challenge for a computer. Instead, the challenge is to present that information in a way that's digestible for the human.

To summarize the computer side of a voice conversation, its strength is massive parallel computing to help settle on a specific hypothesis mapping a sound to a word or phrase. It'll still fail catastrophically at times. Its weaknesses include having to be taught the intended meaning of "everything" in a signal full of variation, vagueness, and broader knowledge of the world that needs some level of reasoning or inference.

Human-Computer Voice Dialog

So here you are, ready to start creating conversations between two participants with very different strengths and weaknesses. Developing for voice means balancing those strengths and weaknesses: if you build to human expectations and limitations, your users will be successful and stick around. To do so, remember that a voice interaction is all about the sound, even when there's secondary visual backup. Table 2-1 summarizes the characteristics we just covered for humans and computers, comparing the strengths and weaknesses. We covered all these traits in the lunch examples earlier in this chapter, the first five being the traits of human language and the last two being traits of any audio stream.

---

[7]The more mature the acoustic models, the less problematic dialects are. That means American English models are less affected by dialectal differences today than languages trained on less data.

Table 2-1. *Comparison of human and computer perception of voice production traits*

Voice production trait	Perception challenge for humans	Perception implementation challenge for computers
Discrete	Minimal	Considerable
Rule-based	Minimal	Considerable
Productive and limitless	Minimal	Considerable
Displacement	Minimal	Considerable
Learned and social	Some	Considerable
Linear and sequential	Considerable	Minimal
Fleeting	Considerable	Minimal

You learned earlier that all human interactions with technology are basically social interactions, even more so with voice. People's expectations of anything voice-enabled directly impact how people converse with VUI devices. Every aspect of how the computer responds sets expectations about its abilities and affects how users will interact with it. You apply the same rules of conversation when you talk to technology, even when you know it's not a person. That's the beauty—and curse—of voice: everyone "knows how to have a conversation." If you want your voice interactions to be ubiquitous and perform well, you shouldn't need to explain to your users how to talk to your voice assistant. Anyone should be able to succeed without special training beyond the inherent knowledge of the intended user audience.

This makes voice different from other technologies and modalities and puts the burden on you as the developer to know enough about how people converse to help them succeed. Few things upset voice technology users more than systems that don't deliver on their promises. Our own experiences in the industry over the years have highlighted that the first few interactions with a voice device will determine how willing users are to continue using voice and to trust it. Early success is key. Sure, over time some users will tailor what they say to be understood, becoming more "computer-like"—the Cooperative Principle predicts this. But others will stop trying before that because they couldn't get what they asked for. If users need to change to succeed, the dialog will remain limited. Voice interactions can become truly ubiquitous only if people are allowed to talk like people. When users are faced with a new voice situation, they'll rely on what they expect from talking to people, following the human conversational rules of engagement exactly because voice is so "human." They'll make assumptions and respond to the voice assistant based on what it says and how it says it. As listeners, we even have similar emotional reactions and judgments about who the speaker is. It's as if we can't avoid it.

SUCCESS TIP 2.3 MAKE USERS SUCCEED EARLY   Successful early interaction increases likelihood of user satisfaction and continued use. Aim to make users' first voice interactions successful by including one or two very simple—and robust—interactions.

The good news is that the more you know about how people naturally talk and listen, the more you're able to avoid catastrophic failure by designing and implementing the right behavior for each context.

When you develop for voice, you need to realize that people can say anything at any time the VUI is listening. This is one of the biggest differences between a visual GUI and an auditory VUI: even if you explicitly tell users to *say yes or no*, they might say something else, like *maybe*, for good reason. Or they respond using words you didn't expect, like *yuppers* or *you betcha*. Or they cough or hesitate before responding. If the sounds are picked up as input by the VUI, you have to either respond or find a way to ignore it if it's unintentional noise. If it's a reasonable thing to say, you can't just tell them to use other words.

However, and this is important, while it's true that you technically can't limit what people say, it's also true by the Cooperative Principle that people want to communicate and succeed with their tasks. People vary greatly in **how** they say something, their voice quality, pronunciation, and words used—variation is part of human language, as you learned in this chapter. But **what** they say is usually more predictable than you might think. The vast majority of users stay within what's expected in some domain and task— that's also part of language. Some will try to trick your VUI and say something off-topic like *Who won the latest Formula 1 race?* in the middle of ordering pizza. Oh, well. If it's not your core use case, it shouldn't be your focus. Don't try to deal with every type of variation, certainly not at the start. Just focus on predicting the expected variation given the task or domain, maximizing recognition accuracy and correctly interpreting the meaning of what was said in-domain.

SUCCESS TIP 2.4 WORDING DIRECTLY AFFECTS HOW USERS RESPOND   When developing for voice, always start by asking yourself how two people in a similar dialog converse. Predict the responses, words used, next steps in the dialog, places of potential confusion, and so on. Base your VUI dialog on this. Make it clear and easy to understand. You influence users' responses with your VUI's prompt wording and delivery. The clearer your VUI dialog is, the more predictable your users' responses are—and the more successful everyone is.

The differences between GUI and VUI are summarized in Table 2-2. We're also including text bots in this comparison. Mobile app bots have similarities with both GUI and VUI: because they're visual, they're not fleeting like voice, and because the input is written language, they can use unconstrained language like voice.

Table 2-2. *Differences between visual and voice interfaces*

GUI/visual	Bot/visual language	VUI/audio language
User input is mostly **constrained** (tap, click, entry).	User input can be constrained (tap) or unconstrained (type).	User input **can't be constrained** (say anything).
Info **persists** until user moves on (text, images).	Info persists until user moves on (text).	Info is **fleeting**, user not in control of info stream (audio).
Info arrives in **parallel** (whole screen or page).	Info arrives linearly (one character at a time).	Info arrives **linearly** (one sound at a time).
Limited equivalence in human communication (expectations based on similarity with physical objects).	Familiar equivalence in human communication (expectations based on similarity with texting).	Strong parallel with ingrained **social** behavior (expectations based on similarity with human language).

MULTIMODAL CORNER

The fundamental differences in how humans process visual information vs. audio/voice information remind us that even when dealing with words, written and spoken languages are very different from each other. That's why it doesn't work well to retrofit a visual interface with voice: it doesn't take advantage of how people naturally speak or consider their listening and processing challenges—hence the need to think about voice first. It's also the reason why choosing from a spoken list is tricky. Tapping a screen is easy, but imagine the dialog in Figure 2-12: the poor human will have a great deal of difficulty remembering all the options in order to choose one. It's possible to present lists of choices in voice, but you need to know how to present the options and how to handle the responses. Choosing from results on a screen is clearly less cognitive load; it combines well with the lower cognitive load of speaking a complex request instead of typing it or navigating to it. Just remember that for most use cases, you need to voice prompts that apply both when users can see and touch the screen and when they can't. If user input was spoken, audio output can usually be assumed to be OK.

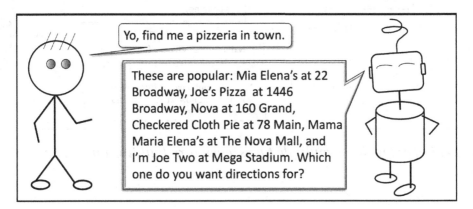

Figure 2-12. *Cognitive load is high for lists that are heard rather than seen*

SUCCESS TIP 2.5 VUI IS ABOUT SOUND, SO REVIEW IT AS SOUND   Seeing
information in writing is different from only hearing the same information. When
planning any voice interaction, always sanity-check it by reading it out loud to
someone else and observe where they hesitate and how they reply, especially if
they say things you didn't expect.

Now you understand the complexity involved when a VUI device is expected to
accurately handle one single user utterance. In a typical dialog, there's back-and-forth,
with each turn building on the context of what was said and understood in previous
turns (Figure 2-13). This means tracking more contexts to avoid misunderstanding at
each step. Pairs of dialog turns are sometimes referred to as **adjacency pairs**. They're
important because they limit the variation you need to handle in the second turn. You'll
see a lot more of turn-taking throughout this book.

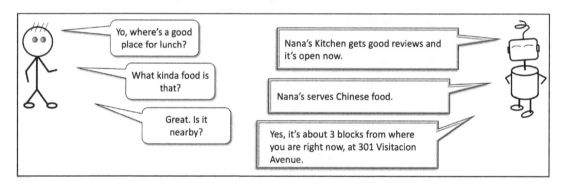

Figure 2-13. *Dialogs have multiple turns, each turn building on what came
before*

Great! Your voice UI has mapped the user utterance to some meaning. You're not
done yet—not until you've responded or fulfilled the user's request. If the user asked
to hear a particular version of a song but the music service provider doesn't have an
agreement with that artist, you might not be able to respond with anything more than a
Sorry, I can't help with that. Remember the example from the start of the chapter where
Play "Let It Be" resulted in hearing "Let It Be Love"? That happened because of the
search using fuzzy matching and favoring a music library that contained the latter but
nor the former. Nothing wrong with that approach, but again the devil is in the details.

You can have perfect recognition and assign the correct meaning to a user utterance and still fail because you couldn't execute the command. The user only notices that they didn't get what they asked for; they don't know what went wrong. This is one of the most overlooked aspects of voice assistants today and not easily addressed well. It's the **three-legged stool of voice** (Figure 2-14): the user only knows they fell off the stool; they don't know, or care, why or which leg was broken.

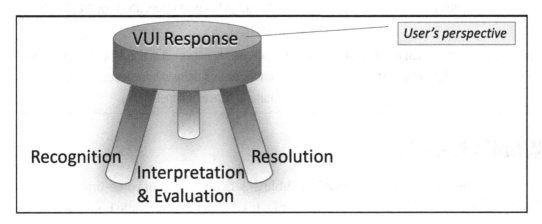

Figure 2-14. *The three-legged stool of voice*

SUCCESS TIP 2.6 DON'T PROMISE A VUI YOU CAN'T DELIVER   If users don't get what they want, they don't care what went wrong. Follow through to the "real" end of the interaction with real-life production constraints in real user environments. It's better to focus on doing fewer things well than adding new functionality that doesn't work well or isn't tested. Provide explanations as much as you can; users will be more forgiving of your inability to give them what they asked for if they feel understood, much like people.

Things that are inherently easy for humans are difficult for computers and vice versa. That's your challenge as a voice developer: balancing user expectations about human voice dialogs with technology limitations while also balancing human cognitive limitations with technological strengths, listed in Table 2-3. Conveniently, the third column is a concise summary of the core principles of voice design and implementation.

Table 2-3. *Challenges of voice and core design principles*

Voice is...	...which is a challenge for...	...so use core VUI design principles to...
Linear and fleeting	The user due to cognitive load	Balance clarity and efficiency
Limitless	Recognition and interpretation due to variation	Maximize accuracy and robustness through coverage to avoid errors and support graceful recovery
Social	Production and interpretation due to lack of cognitive models of the world	Incorporate expected dialog strategies, context, and user and domain knowledge to support natural conversational dialog

What's Next?

Before moving on, take one more look at Table 2-3. Every aspect of voice-first development is an effect of what's in this table. It's fair to say this whole book focuses on what's here, whether it's strategies for ambiguity resolution, handling anaphora, dealing with variation, understanding how wording impacts a response, choosing when and how to confirm, or even knowing when to stop trying to understand the user.

Of course, humans are also not limitless in their capacity to interpret voice. Your dentist probably can't help you debug your code or figure out why your oven won't turn on. They wouldn't ask the right questions to analyze the issue, but you wouldn't expect it. Think about possibilities to set the scene for a voice application so that users intuitively know what they can and cannot do.

If you're a developer, you don't need to become a VUI designer yourself, but you do need to understand the characteristics of voice so that you can focus on what's important. You're already well on your way! Whatever your role, we recommend reading *Wired for Speech* by Nass and Brave—it's full of information and it's very entertaining.[8] If you want to dig into the details of sound as used in speech and language, look for titles covering acoustic, articulatory, or auditory phonetics, perception, and production. For a great introduction to the cognitive principles underlying language processing, check

---

[8]Nass, C, & Brave, S. (2005). *Wired for Speech: How Voice Activates and Advances the Human-Computer Relationship*. Cambridge, MA: MIT Press.

out *Designing with the Mind in Mind* by Jeff Johnson.[9] If you're interested in the levels of meaning in human speech, look for books and articles on discourse, speech acts, turn-taking, and conversation analysis, including adjacency pairs.[10]

In Chapter 3, you'll start digging into implementation, starting with setting up your voice development environment. The devil is always in the details, and with voice you'll spend much of your effort dealing with those details. Voice users are demanding—precisely because it's voice. The good news is that by understanding what's easy and what's challenging to people using voice, you're already ahead of those who only build something because they have easy access to tools. You'll have what it takes to develop something your users will successfully interact with. A successful user is a happy user. So let's get you started on making users succeed!

Summary

- Voice has distinct characteristics from visual and touch-based modalities: it's fleeting, linear, and limitless. Designing and developing for voice must cater to those characteristics.

- A VUI is a dialog between two dissimilar participants with different strengths and weaknesses. A successful VUI builds on the strengths of both participants by applying core VUI principles.

- Users cannot be constrained; they can and will say anything. Your VUI needs to guide, anticipate, and respond in ways that meet your users' expectations.

- Human conversations build on information and assumptions that are not explicit in the words uttered. These references, world knowledge, contexts, and references to past and future interactions need to be handled by the computer as well.

- For a conversation to succeed, a VUI has to correctly recognize the users' spoken words, correctly interpret the meaning, and either give the result the users expect or provide some reason for why it can't do so.

---

[9]Johnson, J. (2014). *Designing with the Mind in Mind: Simple Guide to Understanding User Interface Design Guidelines*. Waltham, MA. Morgan Kaufmann.

[10]Sacks, H. (1992). Lectures on Conversation. Ed. Jefferson, G. Oxford: Blackwell.

CHAPTER 3

Running a Voice App— and Noticing Issues

In the first two chapters, we introduced you to voice interaction technology and the reasons why some things are harder to get right than others for humans and machines in conversational interactions. Now it's time to jump in and get your own simple voice-first interaction up and running. You'll stay in the familiar food domain; it's a convenient test bed for introducing the core concepts—finding a restaurant is probably something you're familiar with, and it covers many voice-first concepts. The task of finding a restaurant seems simple, but things get complicated fast. When you expand functionality to deal with real users, you'll stray from the happy path quickly, but let's not worry about real life yet.

Hands-On: Preparing the Restaurant Finder

Figure 3-1 (similar to Figure 2-1) illustrates a simple restaurant finder. A person asks for a recommendation; a voice assistant provides one. That's it. A word on notation: "AGENT" in panel 2 is shorthand indicating that you don't yet care about the name or platform of the voice assistant or how listening is initiated. It can be a **wake word**, like *Alexa* or *Hey, Google*, or a press of a button. For IVRs, it's calling a number. It merely suggests that this dialog is initiated by the user.

© Ann Thymé-Gobbel, Charles Jankowski 2021
A. Thymé-Gobbel and C. Jankowski, *Mastering Voice Interfaces*, https://doi.org/10.1007/978-1-4842-7005-9_3

Figure 3-1. *Plausible restaurant finder dialog between a user and a voice assistant*

Next, let's define this interaction so you can build it. In Chapter 2, you started thinking about the decisions you need to make for a restaurant finder. Many decisions are about scope: users ask for a restaurant recommendation for a specific city; the app responds with a few best-match suggestions based on parameters specified by the user, ordered by proximity. You learn about how and why to limit scope in Chapter 4; here's a first take:

- **Geographical scope**: Your initial restaurant finder is limited to a predefined area, one small town, because doing well at unconstrained name recognition is very complicated. So, we've picked a small city in the San Francisco area: Brisbane. There are only about 20 places in town that offer food.

- **Search scope**: Starting small, users can't refine their search or search for something based on food type or hours; they can only get a recommendation from a predefined set of responses.

- **Information scope**: Here too, you limit the initial functionality. You need a list of all restaurants in the city and a set of responses, such as business hours or street address, to play based on that list.

- **User scope**: No customized results based on user settings and no follow-on questions to refine searches. But make sure users don't hear the same suggestion every time, so something needs to be tracked. Assume there can be multiple users.

- **Interaction scope:** Start by creating a custom voice app, a skill (for Alexa) or action (for Google). Access will be primarily from a stationary device (as opposed to a mobile app or in-car), probably indoors, at home or work, and not requiring a screen.

SUCCESS TIP 3.1 VOICE SUCCESS IS BASED ON SCOPE AND LIMITATIONS   No matter what voice interaction you're creating, much of your time should be spent understanding the scope and limiting it where you can—and knowing you can't limit user behavior. That means you need to figure out how best to handle out-of-scope requests. "You" means you: designer, developer, and product owner.

Having settled on the scope, you define the basic dialog for when all goes well: the happy path. The recommended starting point is to write sample dialogs:

User   *AGENT, ask Brisbane Helper to recommend a restaurant.*

AGENT   *[Look up data and generate an appropriate response.]*

AGENT   *Na Na's Chinese gets good reviews.*

Sample dialogs show up throughout this book. They're high-level examples of the functionality a voice app offers, how it's offered, what's understood, and what responses the app will give. Sample dialogs are the conceptual draft drawings of voice, showing core functionality and representative conversations; they don't show every possible wording a user might say. Any "real" implementation will use more than one sample dialog, but this is all the first version of this restaurant finder will do, so one's enough. It's time to build it.

Choosing Voice Platforms

Today you have access to an ever-increasing number of voice platforms of ever-increasing abilities, so you don't need to start by building your own from individual modules. Build your simple restaurant finder using a platform you prefer and have access to. We assume many of you will use either the Amazon Alexa or the Google Assistant platform. If coding isn't your core strength, make use of one of the many no-code platforms that let you run your creations on either of those two platforms.[1] If you prefer the flexibility of open source, there are yet other options.[2] Any mature platform lets you get something functional running quickly, something concrete that's a sandbox for playing with and understanding the core concepts. And that's what we want right now. Remember: You're **not** reading a platform-specific cookbook—we cover concepts and provide concrete examples for you to run and play with to get a solid understanding of voice. We actually recommend you develop the simple dialog in this chapter using more than one platform, including any you're interested in that we don't cover. Seeing what's platform-specific vs. what appears across all platforms helps you become a stronger voice practitioner, and you'll be less dependent on any specific platform. Early on, you'll prefer platforms that handle as many details as possible for you. The more experience you gain, the more flexibility you want. And you'll be able to make use of that flexibility without getting in trouble. You want a stable robust platform with superior speech recognition. We have chosen to go the Google route in this book for several reasons that will get to a little later in this chapter. But first, let's jump into building something!

Hands-On: Implementing the Restaurant Finder

It's time to implement the basic restaurant finder in Figure 3-1. You'll be using Actions on Google, the developer platform for Google Assistant. So far, it's only one question, but that's enough to start. We'll walk you through the steps of getting set up, pointing out some things to watch out for without going into every detail. For more details, refer to one of the many available references for the most up-to-date information.[3]

---

[1]There are many; they come and go and change. Voiceflow, Botmock, and Botsociety are a few starting points.

[2]Rasa and Mycroft are good places to start.

[3]If you choose to work with the Google platform, you want to keep up-to-date on the great material available online. For a Dialogflow-specific start, look at `https://dialogflow.com/docs/getting-started` and for Amazon Alexa `https://developer.amazon.com/alexa`, Apple's Siri `https://developer.apple.com/siri/`, Samsung's Bixby `https://bixbydevelopers.com/`, and so on. Don't overlook the Raspberry Pi and Mycroft options.

Basic Setup

Here we go... *OK, Google, ask Brisbane Helper to recommend a restaurant.*

1.   Create a Google account, or log into an existing one.

2.   Open the Actions on Google Developers Console[4] and create a new project.

    a.   Click the New Project button, and then type BrisbaneHelper as the project name. Click Create Project.

    b.   Choose Custom for "What kind of Action do you want to build?" Click Next.

    c.   **Important**: On the screen asking "How do you want to build it?", scroll all the way to the bottom and click "Click here to build your Action using Dialogflow." Later in this chapter, we'll discuss why we're using Dialogflow.

    d.   Choose Build your Action and then Add Action(s).

    e.   Click Get Started and then Build.

3.   Dialogflow (Dialogflow Essentials) should open. Click Create.

On the referenced web page, it asks you to enable Fulfillment. Fulfillment is the ability for Dialogflow to connect with a web service that you build to do more detailed processing (analog to the AWS Lambda function used for Alexa). You don't need it here because Brisbane Helper is so simple. In Chapter 7, you'll add that flexibility.

Step 1: Respond to an Invocation

In Dialogflow, choose the "Default Welcome Intent" that's automatically created. This is the starting point of the interaction when the user invokes it—in other words, when saying, *OK, Google, talk to Brisbane Helper.*

1.   Click Responses. Click the trash icon to remove any existing responses.

---

[4]At the time of writing: https://console.actions.google.com/

2. Type something like "Welcome to Brisbane Helper. How can I help?" or "Hi, I'm Brisbane Helper. What's your question?" This adds a new response that plays when the user engages the action without specifying a question.

3. In the Intents window, click Save.

Step 2: Specify What the User Says

In Dialogflow (as with Alexa), an intent is the basic "unit" of the user "doing something," like requesting information (*Recommend a restaurant, When is it open?, Do they take reservations?*) or requesting some action (*Order a pizza for delivery, Make a reservation for 7 PM*).

1. Create a new intent. To the right of Intents, click the plus symbol (+).

2. Type RecommendRestaurant in the Intent name field. Save.

In a voice application, the way to "do something" is of course to say it. Specify what the user might say to make their request.

1. In the section Training Phrases, click Add Training Phrases.

2. In the box Add User Expression, type "Recommend a restaurant."

3. Press Enter, and then click Save. That's the phrase in the sample dialog.

Step 3: Specify What the VUI Says

Next, specify how the action should respond when the user says, *Recommend a restaurant*.

1. Find Enter a Text Response Variant. Type "Na Na's Chinese gets good reviews." Press return.

2. After the application has responded, this dialog is complete, and you're done. Click the slider to the left of Set this intent as end of conversation. If you don't do this, the action won't end, but will wait for the user to say more after it gives the recommendation. Click Save.

Step 4: Connect Dialogflow to Actions on Google

You've defined the conversation in Dialogflow, but you started with Actions on Google, which is the development environment to extend Google Assistant. You need to connect the two.

1. Click Integrations, then Google Assistant, and then Integration Settings. In Discovery, you see two sections—Explicit Invocation and Implicit Invocation:

    -   Explicit invocation is what you'll use here. It refers to the user starting their request by specifying the intent's name by itself or in combination with the intent, for example, *OK, Google, talk to Brisbane Helper* or *OK, Google, ask Brisbane Helper to recommend a restaurant.*

    -   Implicit invocation refers to specifying an intent that leads to invoking an action without invoking it by name, for example, *Hey, Google, I need a local recommendation for a restaurant.*

2. In Explicit Invocation, find Default Welcome Intent. Click the checkbox.

3. Where it says Auto-preview Changes, move the slider to the right.

4. Click Test, at the bottom of the box.

5. Leave the Auto-preview Changes checked.

6. Actions on Google should now appear, with the successful integration, in the Test section.

Step 5: Test Your VUI

You've built your simple app. Hooray! Time to test it. You can test in several ways: in Dialogflow, in the Actions console, or with a Google device.

Testing Using Dialogflow

In Dialogflow, you can test with either text or voice, as shown in Figure 3-2:

- **Text test**: Find Try It Now, and then type "recommend a restaurant."
  Press Enter. It should show the correct response, "Na Na's Chinese
  gets good reviews."

- **Voice test**: Find Try It Now, click the mic icon (just click; don't click
  and hold), and say *Recommend a restaurant.* Click the mic again to
  stop listening. You should get the same response as for text testing.

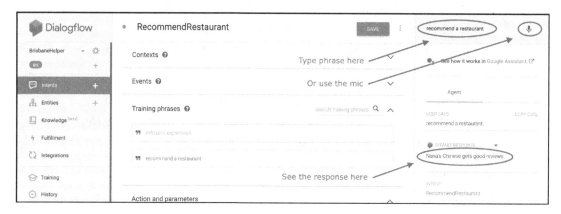

Figure 3-2. *Testing method #1: Dialogflow*

TROUBLESHOOTING

Before you test using Actions on Google, go to the Activity Controls page for your Google
account and turn on Web & App Activity, Device Information, and Voice & Audio Activity
permissions.

Testing Using the Actions console

In the Actions console, you can test with either text or voice:

1. In your Actions console window, click Test.

    - Make sure your volume isn't muted.

2. Invoke the action. Type "Talk to Brisbane Helper." Or click the mic and say it. This time, you don't need to click it the second time; it will stop listening on its own.

   - This invocation phrase wasn't necessary when you tested in Dialogflow. But now that you're in Actions on Google, you need to tell Google Assistant how to access your skill, so you set the invocation phrase to "Brisbane Helper."

3. You should hear the response *Sure, here's the test version of Brisbane Helper* and then maybe a different voice saying, *Welcome to Brisbane Helper. How can I help?* You added that prompt earlier.

4. Type, or click the mic and speak, the magic phrase: "recommend a restaurant."

5. You should get the expected response: *Na Na's Chinese gets good reviews.*

Testing with Assistant, Home, or Nest Devices

If you've read some of the resources we pointed to earlier, you've seen that there's a well-defined publishing process for making your creation available to other users. How cool is that? Refer to those resources for the current process—remember this stuff is in flux. For quick testing, as long as your device (Google Home, Nest Hub, or the Google Assistant app on iOS or Android) is logged into the same Google account as your development environment, you can test with that device, which is handy.

1. Set up your Google Home device with the same Google account you're using for Actions on Google and Dialogflow.

2. Now we need to define how you're going to access your app from Google Home or other devices. In the Actions console (where you just tested), click Develop on the top and then Invocation on the left. Under Display Name, type "Brisbane Helper." Click Save on the upper right.

3. When the device is ready, say, "OK, Google, talk to Brisbane Helper."

4. Here you need both the wake word and the invocation phrase.

5. You hear the same thing you heard in the simulator, but it's coming out of your device. Nice!

DO I NEED TO TEST WITH A GOOGLE HOME DEVICE?

You may wonder if you really need to test "on-device" with whatever platform will be the target platform of your application. Strictly speaking, no, not early in the process. But if you want to build a voice app that not only does something but also does it well, you'll need to put yourself in the mindset of your expected users. That's a recurring theme of this book. It means experiencing the app the way a user would. So whenever possible, we strongly recommend that you test what you build in the same environment, under the same contexts and conditions that your users will experience, and within the same platform and ecosystem they'll use.

Step 6: Save, Export, or Import Your Work

You have options for saving away your work to share with others and using work by others.

1. In Dialogflow, click the gear icon by your app's name.

2. Click Export and Import.

3. Click Export as ZIP. The file will be saved as APPNAME.zip in the Downloads directory. Rename it if you want to keep track of versions.

To load an app from a .zip file

1. In Dialogflow, click the gear icon by your app's name.

2. Click Export and Import.

3. Click Restore from ZIP. All current intents and entities will be cleared before loading.

You also have the option to Import from ZIP. If there are duplicates, existing intents and entities will be replaced. Note that you have to actually type the word "restore" to restore from a .zip file, since the process wipes out anything you currently have.

You've now built a voice app that does one very simple thing. You'll return to your restaurant app shortly to expand it. But first, let's take a closer look at the Google platform and why we chose to use it.

Why We're Using Actions on Google and Assistant

Short answer: We had to pick something. The main goal of this book is not to teach you how to create Google actions specifically, but to demonstrate the concepts and principles that apply to any voice development—no matter the framework. We happen to like many aspects of Google. And of Alexa and Nuance and Apple and Bixby and Mycroft and…and…and so on. We would've loved to compare half a dozen platforms throughout the book, but it's long enough as it is, so for brevity's sake, we had to pick one. Here are some of the reasons why we chose to use Google.

First, we wanted a widely available platform that was free to use, well supported, mature enough to be robust, flexible for a variety of use cases, and with top-of-the-line performance across all core voice system components. It should be familiar to end users as well as to designers and developers, with components and support in multiple languages. And it should "come with" all tools, hardware and software necessary to build something fully functional, while also not being completely tied to those components.

There are additional practical considerations. We'd like you to not worry about complexities unless it's necessary for some point we make. But we also don't want you to depend on what a specific platform provides. Nor do you want to be limited by it. That's not how you learn about voice. As your dialogs get more complex or you're working with a platform that doesn't offer some tool or feature, you'll want the ability to customize to provide the best experience for your users. That's our focus.

Meeting all those criteria basically narrowed the field to Amazon and Google. We simply have more experience creating voice interactions with Google (and Nuance and some open source platforms) than with Amazon, so we know that it will work well for our purpose, and it leads naturally into using Google for more hands-on development using the Google Cloud Speech-to-Text API. But don't worry: Alexa and Google share many concepts and approaches to conversational voice, so ideas you see in one will map to the other, as well as to other platforms.

For additional code, we personally favor Python over Node.js, again based on personal experience from product development; it's flexible and practically the standard in the voice and natural language community. Ultimately you should use what's appropriate for your particular use case and fits into your overall product development environment with the best speech and language performance available. There's no one single right answer for everyone.

Again, this isn't a cookbook or manual for Actions on Google or for a particular device or use case—we use the platform so you can take advantage of what's already available to you and build something quicker than if you have to put all the pieces together. Platforms and computing power change—the advanced features we discuss in later chapters may be available on the Actions platform by the time you read those chapters, which is great. But you still need to understand the reasons behind a tool to use it correctly. And that's what this book is about. Speech is speech; natural conversational interfaces rely on the same core principles this decade as they did last decade and the decade before that. The principles of spoken language apply across all platforms and devices, because it's about human language.

Google's Voice Development Ecosystem

Let's take a closer look at the Google voice development architecture to see how it maps to our voice discussion in Chapter 1. Figure 3-3 is a variant of Figures 1-3 and 2-10, showing how the same building blocks fit into the Google Assistant voice service and Actions on Google framework.

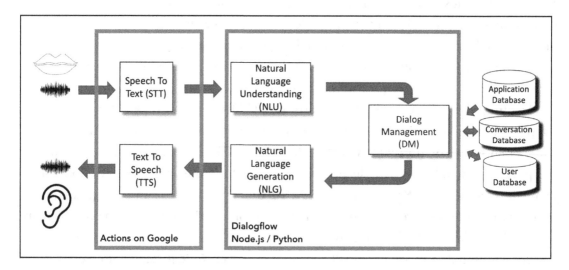

Figure 3-3. *Building blocks for a voice system using Actions on Google and Google Assistant*

The mapping here is approximate. Think of it as a big picture rather than as a definition of Google's voice architecture. Three main building blocks are involved in Google Assistant voice development:

- Actions on Google for STT and TTS

- Dialogflow for NLU, NLG, and DM

- Node.js or Python as the back end to handle anything but the simplest DM

Many of these components can be used separately, adding to the flexibility. Google has cloud APIs for speech-to-text,[5] text-to-speech,[6] natural language,[7] and translation,[8] among others. We use Actions on Google and Dialogflow since they package these components together nicely, letting you focus on application design, and they also interface with the hardware that we're going to test on such as Google Home.

Actions on Google

Actions on Google is the platform on which Google Assistant's "intelligent voice" functionality can be extended into actions. A great advantage of this framework is that the platform takes care of some of the thorniest components of voice development (STT, NLU, TTS) through its libraries and services. Your focus when starting out can therefore be on the core aspect of implementing the DM and NLG parts to build the app.

Dialogflow

There are at least three ways that you can design dialogs in Actions on Google:

- **Actions SDK**: A code-like API for specifying actions, intents, and so on

- **Dialogflow**: A more GUI-based application that provides a graphical wrapper around the Actions SDK, adds NLU functionality, and incorporates machine learning, allowing synonym expansion of phrases mapping to intents

---

[5]https://cloud.google.com/speech-to-text
[6]https://cloud.google.com/text-to-speech
[7]https://cloud.google.com/natural-language
[8]https://cloud.google.com/translate

- **Actions Builder**: A more recent GUI, more directly connected to Actions on Google.

You'll use Dialogflow for now so you can focus on application building rather than on code formats. Dialogflow is more or less responsible for handling the NLU, DM, and NLG components of the action. From the DM and NLG point of view, the main responsibility of the application is to decide what to say next, based on user input, contexts, and the progress of the dialog. There are two ways to specify the responses the system plays back to the user:

- Provide static responses in Dialogflow through the GUI.

- Use a webhook back end to provide responses. This can be very dynamic and depend on history, user data, or application data—all the data sources shown in Figure 3-3. We'll make extensive use of webhooks in later chapters.

Dialogflow provides a good balance of simplicity, extensibility, performance, and openness of various components. It's also mature and stable because it's been around for a while—for our goal of teaching you about design principles and best practices, that's more important than to include the latest platform features. So we use what's now called Dialogflow ES, rather than the more recent (and not free) Dialog CX, and we don't use the Actions Builder environment, which is less flexible than ES (currently only deployable to Assistant, not to third-party channels).[9]

The Pros and Cons of Relying on Tools

Until recently, it was next to impossible to create any kind of voice interaction unless you were in research or employed by one of the few enterprise companies directly working in voice. Today, there's easy access to tools and platforms that didn't exist a few years ago. Practically anyone with a standard laptop and a free account can quickly put together something that responds when spoken to. If you already have experience with Google Assistant or Amazon Alexa, you know that the platform provides a lot "for free" by handling many details for you.

---

[9]If you prefer using Actions Builder, you can use the migration tool available at developers.google. com. There are also tools for migrating from Dialogflow to third-party platforms, like the open source Rasa framework (`https://rasa.com/`). We don't mind if you do either with our sample code. The fact that there are so many tools migrating from Dialogflow to other tools is yet another cue that Dialogflow is commonly used.

But tools and platforms come and go, and they can change quickly, as we just mentioned in the previous section. Even while writing this chapter, at least one voice tool went from free to pay-for, another changed its name, and yet another was acquired. If you depend on tools to handle the details for you, you may be in trouble if those tools disappear or change. More importantly for our purpose, you won't learn how to improve your voice interactions if you don't understand why you got some result or can't access what you need to fix. As users become savvier and more familiar with voice, they become more demanding. Being too closely tied to a specific framework may limit your ability to create the right voice interaction or one that stands out from the crowd.

What if you need precise control over responses or secure access to data? What if you deal with large data sets, have branding needs, have integrations with other systems, or need access to your users' utterances for validation? Or what if you need precise control over accuracy and responses to specific requests? Well, then you'll need more than these platforms probably give you, and you need to take charge of a larger chunk of the development. Fortunately, none of these are new issues for voice. Techniques exist for addressing them, but they're either not yet available for developer modification, or their relevance is not fully understood. Most voice developers today are fairly new to the field and only have experience with one platform. One of our goals is to reintroduce some powerful techniques that have fallen by the wayside because of having been less accessible. As those features are added, you still need to know how to apply them. The choices you make affect every voice app you build, from the simplest question-answer to a full prescription refill system. Learning to "think in voice" will empower you to make the right choices.

If you choose to develop within the Google and Alexa platforms, you may trade ecosystem access, convenience, and development speed for various limitations. If you're willing and able to build up your own environment with your own parsing and designs, a new world opens up, offering choices at every step to create something different from what others do. But as is the case in life, with choices and flexibility come increased responsibility and careful planning. Only **you** know what's the right answer for you.

Each company also offers products for other voice use cases, such as the following:

- **The Internet of Things (IoT) use case**: *AGENT, dim the lights in the living room* or *AGENT, set the temperature to 70.* Controlling appliances via spoken commands addressed to and directed at an Alexa Echo device or Google Home device. The appliances themselves don't have microphones or speakers for voice responses. These are connected devices, usually referred to by the term smart home.

- **Third-party devices with built-in microphones and speakers that make use of the recognition and NL "smarts" of Alexa or Google**: *AGENT, play music by Queen.* The spoken commands are directed at a device that has its own microphones and speakers but is "inhabited" by one of the two voice assistants. These are built-in devices.

General voice UI best practices apply across all use cases, but details differ because users' needs differ, devices have different functionalities, and different overlapping architectures and ecosystems need to interact. Custom skills and actions need invocation, while smart home and built-ins don't. Because of the narrower focus and specific needs of smart home and built-in applications, we don't focus on those in this book.

You might not need an invocation or wake word at all. That's the case if the VUI is delimited in other ways, for example, a phone call to an IVR, a push-to-talk device, an always-on handsfree device, or a free-standing VUI outside the common smart home ecosystems. They're all valid and all current environments—and they're all equally able to produce both great and crummy voice interactions.

SUCCESS TIP 3.2 ARE YOU SURE THAT WORD MEANS WHAT YOU THINK IT MEANS?   Be aware that product names and features are in near-constant flux, as you might expect from quickly evolving high tech. What you see here is the landscape at the time of writing in 2020–2021. If you work with a team to build a custom skill or action, a smart appliance, or a speaker with its own audio input and output on the Amazon or Google platform, or anywhere else, make sure everyone on your team is clear on what's possible and what's not within that approach and that everyone matches the same name to the same product.

Hands-On: Making Changes

Back to the restaurant finder. You're up and running and talking to your voice assistant. Cool, it works. Better yet, you make your skill or action available and proudly tell your friends. They use it, and...they tell you it doesn't work well.

What happened? What did they say to make them complain when it worked for you? If you only built exactly what we covered earlier, very likely some of the following issues happened:

1. They made requests that were within your defined scope, but those requests

   a. Were rejected

   b. Resulted in a response that was wrong

   c. Resulted in a response that was misleading

   d. Resulted in a response that was uninformative

   e. Resulted in a response that sounded weird or off

2. They asked for things you knew were out of scope.

3. They heard only one response even though you had created several variants.

We recommend you don't ignore your friends or tell them they're stupid for not talking in just the right way! In reality, you didn't do your planning—understanding your users and designing for them—because we haven't told you how yet. This chapter is about getting a first taste of the process, so let's look at how you can address these issues.

SUCCESS TIP 3.3 IF USERS SAY IT, YOU HAVE TO DEAL WITH IT. PERIOD.   Your users are your users because they want to be, so treat them well, like friends, not like enemies or objects. This might seem obvious, but it's surprisingly easy to fall into thinking *Nobody will say that* or *What a stupid way to say that* or even *If they don't read my description of what's covered, it's their own fault*. Most of the time, users are not trying to trip the system, and they know when they are. Sure, you can create clever responses to out-of-scope requests, but don't do that at the expense of making the actual intended experience more robust.[10]

---

[10]Look at some of the great resources on UX and human-centered design, starting with the classic: Norman, D. *The Design of Everyday Things.* 1988. New York: Basic Books.

Adding More Phrases with the Same Meaning

In the case of issue 1a (rejection), your friends probably asked reasonably worded requests that were not covered by your training phrases or the auto-generated coverage based on those. Maybe they didn't say *restaurant* or *eat* but said *What's the best place?* or *Where to?* Or they included preambles you didn't cover: *I would absolutely love to hear about a new café I'm not familiar with.* Remember: A core strength of voice interactions is that people don't have to learn some set of commands—they can just speak normally. Your first solution is to add more variety; ask a few people how they would phrase the request if you think you covered all. Later, we'll show you more methodical exhaustive approaches.

Pushing the Limits

First, let's do a little testing. Recall that you added one training phrase, "recommend a restaurant." You might think that you'd have to say exactly that. Try some phrases:

- "Recommend a restaurant." (That had better work; it's the only one you added!)

- "Recommend restaurant." "Please recommend a restaurant."

- "Can you please recommend a restaurant for me?"

- "Would it be possible for you to recommend a restaurant for me to eat at?"

- "Can you tell me a good restaurant?"

- "What's a good restaurant?" "Can you suggest a good restaurant?"

- "Recommend a place to eat." "Got any restaurant suggestions?"

- "Where is a good place to eat?" "Where should I eat?"

- "Where can I get some food?"

Well, this is interesting. You should have found that, except for the last two sets of phrases,[11] it still responded with the right answer! Why is that?

---

[11]Interestingly, the first time we created this example, the third-to-the-last set of phrases also didn't work, but now they do—a great example of how Dialogflow and other systems constantly change and usually improve.

Look back to Chapter 1, specifically the section "Natural Language Understanding" (NLU). NLU is the module that takes a string of words and generates the meaning of the sentence. Here, the meaning is the Intent you created, RecommendRestaurant. If you have multiple Intents (you soon will), NLU will figure out which Intent, if any, matches the phrase that was spoken and produce an associated response for that Intent (we're capitalizing Intent here since that's a very specific Dialogflow concept that we saw).

How does it work? You may think, *Aha! If the sentence has both recommend and restaurant, that's it, right?* No: *What's a good restaurant?* and *Recommend a place to eat* both worked. Hmmm. Maybe it's either including "recommend" or "restaurant"? That would work for now, but you're about to add some more phrases that break this hypothesis. As you add enough phrases to make the app robust, rules like that would be too unwieldy, so you need some sort of automatic method.

What's happening is that Dialogflow is "learning" how to map your training phrases to intents automatically, using various technologies like natural language processing and machine learning. Or, rather, it's making use of rules and statistical mappings of words and phrases to meaning. When you add more phrases and click Save, it relearns using those new phrases. Automatically extracting meaning, especially training such a process from new data, is a problem that researchers have been working on hard for years, and the fruits of such work are what you see in Google, Alexa, and other systems. It's not the whole answer, but enjoy!

Rejection

Let's look at the last three phrases in the list. What happened when you said, *Where is a good place to eat?* It probably responded, *Sorry, could you say that again?*, *What was that?*, or something. This is a **rejection**, one of the most important concepts in building good voice apps and one you first learned about in Chapter 2. Basically, the app (specifically the NLU part) not only has to hypothesize which Intent is represented by a user's request but also *if it's none of them.* You hear *Sorry, could you say that again?* when the NLU doesn't think any of the Intents match. This response is a default response. Don't worry yet about if it's a good response (spoiler: it's not); only remember the importance of the concept of rejection. As you design and develop more complex voice interactions, you'll probably be shocked at how much of your effort is spent on handling rejections.

Fixing Rejection

As you might expect, if the app rejects too many reasonable user utterances and your users only hear *Sorry...*, that's no good. You address this by adding more phrases. Let's do that now in Dialogflow:

1. Make sure you're still in BrisbaneHelper in Dialogflow. If not, open it.

2. Select the RecommendRestaurant intent.

3. In Training Phrases, find Add User Expression. Type "Where is a good place to eat?" Press Enter.

4. Click Save.

5. When you see Agent Training Completed, retest *Where is a good place to eat?*

6. You should now get the correct answer.

You've added one of the rejected phrases. Keep testing. Try *Where should I eat?* It works too, even though you didn't add it as a phrase! Again, smart, machine learning NLU to the rescue; it figured out that *Where is a good place to eat?* and *Where should I eat?* have enough similar meaning. How about *Where can I get some food?* That's still rejected. Once we add that phrase as well, we should be good for the whole list.

TROUBLESHOOTING

After adding phrases, don't forget to not only click Save but also wait for Dialogflow to display the phrase Agent Training Completed. Only then will new phrases work. While you're waiting, the NLU is being retrained using machine learning, and that takes a little bit of time.

Expanding Information Coverage

Na Na's may get good reviews, but sometimes people need to eat something different. Now that you've added some variability on the input side, let's add some to the output, changing the response users might hear when asking for a restaurant recommendation. In Dialogflow

1. Make sure you're still in BrisbaneHelper. If not, open it.

2. Choose Intents, and then select the RecommendRestaurant intent.

3. Find the Responses section. At Enter a Text Response Variant, type "Don't forget to try a quiche at Star Box Food. And get there before the end of lunchtime." Press Enter. Then click Save.

4. When you see Agent Training Completed, test using the *Recommend a restaurant* phrase. You should get either of the two phrases for Na Na's or Star Box.

5. Add a few more phrases:

    -   "Did you know that Madhouse Coffee serves sandwiches and other bites?"

    -   "What about further outside, but still mostly Brisbane? 7 Mile House is on Bayshore, and WhiteCaps Drinks is out on Sierra Point."

How does a response get picked from the list? It's just random, with a slight tweak to avoid playing the same response twice in a row. Issue 3 (hearing the same response) would have been a logic oversight to not randomize responses. Watch out for those! Later, you'll learn about more detailed schemes where you might factor in what's open or what kind of food the user is looking for and so on.

Adding Granularity

Issues 1b–e (incorrect or odd responses) listed earlier have two related causes. One is simply knowing how to best word a clear unambiguous response. We'll cover that in great detail in later chapters. The other cause is one that's necessary even if the responses are worded well: intent granularity. Right now, there's only one single intent with no slots. If your friends asked *Recommend a restaurant for breakfast*, they may or may not have been understood. That is, *for breakfast* could have been dropped by the interpreter. Since there's no handling of [MEAL] yet, if the response happened to be for a dinner-only place, it would be wrong. Same for *…open now*, *…open late*, or *…open tomorrow* if it's not open and you don't yet track and compare time. And if they said *Recommend a Mexican restaurant*, they wouldn't want to hear about a great Chinese restaurant.

You want to support these sample phrases, starting with *Recommend a restaurant for breakfast*. In Dialogflow

1. Click the plus (+) to the right of Intents to create a new intent. Name it `RecommendRestaurantBreakfast`.

2. Add a training phrase "Recommend a restaurant for breakfast."

3. Add a response phrase "If you're hungry in the morning, you have several options. How about Madhouse Coffee or Melissa's Taqueria?"

4. In Responses, Set this intent as end of conversation.

5. Save and test.

Keep going to support more sample phrases for different search criteria:

1. "Recommend a restaurant open late":

    a. Create a new Intent `RecommendRestaurantLate` with the sample phrase "Recommend a restaurant open late."

    b. Add a response "Mama Mia Pizza is open late."

    c. Enable Set intent as end of conversation. Save and test.

2. "Recommend a Mexican restaurant":

    a. Create a new Intent `RecommendRestaurantMexican` with the sample phrase "Recommend a Mexican restaurant."

    b. Add the response "Hungry for Mexican food? Try Melissa's Taqueria."

3. Enable Set intent as end of conversation. Save and test.

Now you support breakfast, late, and Mexican food. You're thinking, *Wow, this could get really messy; there are all those other cuisines, types of meals, times of day, and intents for every one of those combinations?* Here you used static responses, and yes, with this approach it will be a crazy number of combinations. But you'll soon learn about a couple of enhancements, slots or entities, and dynamic or webhook responses, which will, believe it or not, allow you to support all those possibilities with one intent.

SUCCESS TIP 3.4 YOUR USERS ARE NOT YOUR UNPAID TESTERS   Of course you want to update your voice interactions based on data from real users, but don't expect your users to debug your voice apps for you. Get utterance examples from a varied group of alpha testers. Find beta testers who tell you if they felt understood **and** if responses were accurate. Without this, you'll never get rid of poor reviews.

Does this mean you have to answer every question? No. It means you can start by recognizing more of what's said to avoid problems and sound smarter until you add the actual functionality. You can add the most relevant information to every prompt. Maybe the user didn't ask for it, but they probably won't mind hearing it if it's brief. You could also handle some words, like *open now* and *dinner*, even if you can't provide an answer. Use sample dialogs to also show interactions that aren't on the happy path:

> **User**   *Hey, Google, ask Brisbane Helper to recommend a restaurant that's open now.*
>
> **VUI**   *Na Na's \gets good reviews. They're open for lunch and dinner every day except Saturday.*
>
> **User**   *Hey, Google, ask Brisbane Helper to recommend a restaurant that's open now.*
>
> **VUI**   *Na Na's gets good reviews. I'm not sure about their hours.*

SUCCESS TIP 3.5 EVERYONE WANTS TO BE HEARD AND UNDERSTOOD   The more unfulfilled requests you can shift from not handled to handled, the smarter your voice interaction sounds. When you acknowledge your user, they feel understood even if you can't do what they ask.

What about issue 2, real out-of-scope requests? You can't cover everything, and this is true for all VUIs on all platforms. So you need some appropriately vague response, like telling the user you can't help, but give them something general, maybe with a hint of what you can provide. Or you can ask the user to try again. Asking again, or reprompting, is more appropriate for some tasks and interaction types than others. It's a big topic you'll learn about in Chapter 13.

User	*Hey, Google, ask Brisbane Helper which place has the highest rating but isn't busy.*
VUI	[No matching handling.]
VUI	*I'm not sure how to help with that, but here's a general Brisbane recommendation. Na Na's gets good reviews.*

Preview: Static vs. Dynamic Responses

The way we've handled responses so far is by using static responses. You use these when you specify responses in the Responses section of the Intent. Other than the randomization we talked about, you can have no logic or decision making with static responses, which really limits you. The alternative is to use dynamic or webhook responses. These responses are generated by code (we'll use Python) that you write. Here you can imagine having unlimited logic to filter responses by cuisine, time of day, and so on. You use webhook responses when you enable Fulfillment for your Intent, which you'll do soon. Look at the documentation at `https://dialogflow.com/docs/intents/responses` for more details on using static vs. webhook responses.

What's Next?

Take a look at the last few sample dialogs and think about the context for when these responses work more or less well. What changes would you make in the wording to cast the net wider and have responses that sound "intelligent" but don't actually fulfill the requests?

With this quick and simple introduction to voice development, you're already starting to get a sense of what throws voice apps for a loop and what's no issue. This is what you need to master to succeed with voice: how to find big and small issues and fix them. The happy path is usually relatively straightforward; robustness is what's a bit tricky. By learning not just the "how" but also the "why," you minimize your dependency on specific tools and platforms while also learning how to choose the best implementation for a particular context and create conversational interactions where the platform doesn't limit you.

When you want to create a robust and well-functioning voice application, you start by asking the types of questions you've already started asking—just in greater detail. In the next chapter, we'll look at that "blueprints" part of the process.

Summary

- Because voice is fundamentally limitless, you need to define your VUI's scope carefully.

- It's possible to handle a request without fulfilling it. A well-worded voice prompt shows users they were understood even when they can't get what they asked for.

- Learn to anticipate what your users will ask for and how they'll say it. Available voice assistant ecosystem tools can get you far fast, but VUI performance will always involve iterations to improve coverage.

- A VUI can disappoint users in many ways: not recognize a reasonable request, not respond at all, respond incorrectly or in an uninformative manner, or respond in a way that the user doesn't understand. All must be addressed and all have different solutions.

PART II

The Planning Phase: Requirements Discovery and High-Level Design Definition

In this part of the book, we focus on the planning phase and how to find answers to the questions that are relevant for building any voice system. It's a phase that isn't covered in great detail in most voice resources, but one that we have seen over and over again makes a huge difference to the ultimate success—and level of pain—of voice system development. You quickly figure out that your own voice system's success depends on finding the right balance of (1) business and product needs, (2) system and technology dependencies and limitations, and (3) understanding user behavior, language, needs, and goals. In the two chapters in this part, you learn how to define the scope and functionality and how to determine your challenges and the options available for solving those challenges. You also learn how to capture your findings in ways that encourage voice UI design thinking while facilitating cross-functional team communication and development work.

- Chapter 4 covers voice-focused requirements discovery and definition. We haven't seen this covered in depth elsewhere, but we sure have seen how the final voice product suffers when this phase is ignored! No matter what your role is, you will be more successful if you understand the key points. Your future VUI system users will thank you for it!

- In Chapter 5, you're introduced to turning discovery findings into high-level architectural designs. Voice-first development is successful only when coordinated with solid design. You learn why flows, sample dialogs, and detailed dialog management specifications continue to be the most widely used tools and approaches for conversational voice system.

At the end of this part of the book, you understand how creating a voice system differs from designing and developing other interfaces and modalities. You have your plan; now you're ready for the "real" work: building your voice system.

Define Through Discovery: Building What, How, and Why for Whom

Because creating voice systems is such a hot topic, you can find lots of talks and online classes showing you how to build a VUI in a very short time. True, you can get something up and running very quickly, which is awesome. You already did exactly that in Chapter 3. And that's enough if your goal is something for your own use. But if you want to build something robust for others, what then? How do you build something that works well and meets their needs and expectations? And is it even possible to build that with the resources you have available?

You need a plan built on the answers from asking the questions that are relevant for voice—answers that will guide your design and development. That's what this chapter is about: asking the right questions and interpreting the answers. Even if you've written specifications before, you suspect VUIs are different. You're right.

So what are these questions? It's the ones usually grouped as functional requirements (What are you building? What does it do?) and nonfunctional requirements (Who will use it and why?). In this chapter, we step through discovery in a fair bit of detail to give you a sense of how we approach it. As you continue through the book, you'll understand the reasons behind the questions, why the answers matter, and why things go wrong when the right questions aren't asked or the answers are incorrect or ignored. Therefore, the focus is on requirements that matter most for voice. You might notice that we jump between categories of requirements questions. You're right. We do it on purpose to emphasize that you'll be more successful if you treat your discovery process as a whole, rather than separating it into functional vs. nonfunctional or business, user, and system requirements. Organizational separation is fine for

© Ann Thymé-Gobbel, Charles Jankowski 2021
A. Thymé-Gobbel and C. Jankowski, *Mastering Voice Interfaces*, https://doi.org/10.1007/978-1-4842-7005-9_4

documentation, not during the information gathering process. All answers are relevant to designers, developers, and product owners alike. Nobody gets to take a coffee break during a kickoff meeting because "their" portion isn't currently discussed.[1]

SUCCESS TIP 4.1 INVOLVE DESIGNERS AND DEVELOPERS FROM DAY 1   Avoid knowledge silos. If you work within and across teams, everyone needs to have a solid appreciation of the strengths and constraints of voice. Involve everyone from the start and listen to each other's concerns and advice. You cannot work well in a vacuum in this field: everything affects everything else, and no requirements are more important than others. Respect each other and include designers, speech scientists, and developers during discovery—they'll ask questions from different angles. VUI design, VUX research, NLU and grammar development, database programming, system architecture, marketing—they all involve different skills and it's rare to find all, or even most, in one person. You obviously need people with core expertise in their area for their role. If they have voice experience too, fantastic. If they don't, focus on finding those with a demonstrable interest in real user behavior and data, people who understand that interacting with voice versus interacting with text and images are fundamentally different, people who want to learn and who work well as a team.

Building for voice is always a balance. Even for the simplest VUI, it helps to have a plan before you start implementing. Experienced VUI designers and developers start all voice projects with a discovery process using their experience with voice to mentally check off nonissues while flagging potential complexities. Start practicing this habit— with the background from the first few chapters, you can already get far. There's a lot of text in this chapter. Use it as a resource when you need it. Just don't ignore doing discovery with voice in mind.

---

[1]Again, we're staying agnostic: we won't tell you to use any particular method for gathering requirements or tracking your progress. We also aim to highlight what's specific to voice, whether it's a startup's new multimodal product, your personal mobile app, an IVR for a Fortune 500 company, or anything in between. What we do say is if you don't plan and ask the right questions early on, you'll be sorry later.

General Functionality: What Are You Building?

Let's start with the most basic question: what is the goal of your voice app? You have some reason for the idea: you saw a need, or someone is paying you to implement their idea. Your answer affects every aspect of developing your voice solution—the need for and availability of specific content, security, accuracy, and so on—which in turn affects design choices and leads to trade-offs.

SUCCESS TIP 4.2 THERE'S NEVER ONLY "ONE CORRECT" WAY   No single VUI design guarantees success, but there are many ways to increase or decrease your success rate. Design choices always need to be made, and they'll depend directly on requirements, resources, timelines, and other constraints. The more you know at the start, the more likely you are to make the decisions that result in a VUI people want to use.

A good starting point is to put your idea into words: a few sentences that describe the purpose and goal of your VUI, the domain and main task, and the basic flow if you already have something in mind. This brief high-level summary, an elevator pitch, for the restaurant finder can be as follows:

- A restaurant finder for a specific city. Based on a search item, the app responds with a best-match suggestion. Users search for a local restaurant in city X by specifying a cuisine or hours of operation. The VUI responds with a match or asks for disambiguating restaurants if needed. Users can follow up with a request to make a reservation, specifying time, date, and number of guests.

Tell your pitch to a friend and ask them to describe to you in their own words what they heard and ask them what they'd expect to be able to accomplish, what they'd be able to say, and what responses it would provide. Did it match your view? Great. You're on your way.

Now, asking for restaurant information is something most of us have done, so we have a pretty good idea what it should look like. But part of the challenge of voice is to build something others want to use, even when they're different from you. What if you're building something you have less familiarity with? And what if your app's behavior could affect your users' health?

In this chapter, you'll plan a voice app that assists people preparing for an upcoming medical procedure. Assume this procedure is not life-threatening but unfamiliar to the user, a procedure with some level of instruction complexity, like a gastroenterology procedure or minor outpatient surgery. Here's why:

- The health and medical domain is complex while also incorporating the basics. It covers every key aspect of design and implementation complexity. It even involves food, so you didn't waste your time with restaurants!

- There's a lot of interest in using voice in the health and medical domain. Who doesn't want to do good? But this domain demands higher accuracy and confidence in the result than most simpler implementations can provide, making it a perfect topic for this real-life-focused book.

- Both of us authors have first-hand voice design and development experience in this domain, making it a realistic context for sharing real-life experiences and the reality of voice-first development with you.[2] We take you step-by-step through a process we've successfully used ourselves many times when creating voice interactions for mobile devices, smart home assistants, call center systems, and other devices.

So here's a new elevator pitch:

- A procedure preparation helper that guides a patient in the days leading up to a medical procedure to decrease chances of rescheduling due to lack of preparation. Users get timely notifications for necessary changes in diet or medication personalized for them based on the number of days before their procedure so they don't miss something that could affect their procedure. They can also ask questions about the procedure, such as if it's OK to eat a particular food or take some named medication, and hear a short informative response that they know is approved by their doctor. They can also contact their doctor.

---

[2]We are in no way making medical claims of any sort when recommending design and implementation choice for this or any other medical voice application.

Let's pause the functionality and take a closer look at your future users—understanding them will guide your next set of questions.

User Needs: Who'll Use It and What Do They Want?

The key to voice success is understanding your users' needs and expectations and speaking and understanding their language. Your assumptions affect everything from style, wording, and content to overall flow and what needs explanation for users to enjoy the interaction. How do you really know what users want? Get in the habit of starting every voice project with quick research. Start online. You quickly learn that people have questions about the procedure (what it is, how and why it's done) and the specific preparation tasks. Make note of the common questions and answers. In real life you'd base this on material provided by the health providers you build the app for, but the concept is the same. Also, you may need to scope the effort without much information to help create a sales quote. And if you do background research before meeting with the health provider, you can be much more effective in collecting the answers to your questions. Chapter 5 goes into some methods for finding user data. For now, let's assume you have access to a reliable source.

Keeping voice in mind, your main goal during the user needs discovery is to understand how people currently do the task your VUI will handle:

- Identify the user population (subject expertise, special terminology used, children's voices, heavy accents, one or several users on one device, etc.)

- Identify how the task is done today, in how many steps, and how does it "end."

- Identify any patterns in when and how often the task is done, including what triggers the start (prescription refill, wish to turn on a light or get directions, bill payment reminder, etc.)

- Identify users' environment, activity, and emotional state (type of background noise, stationary at home, walking outside, while driving, upset, etc.)

- Determine if there's a reason users can't talk or listen to a device doing the task.

FROM THE VOICE TRENCHES

A colleague designing a VUI for an international bank started by looking at the bank's website, making notes on types and names of accounts and services offered, style and formality of addressing readers, and so on. This information is critical for VUIs. It lays out the words and features people will expect and use. If there's a mismatch between that and the voice system, users won't be understood and get annoyed, and the VUI will look anything but "smart." Our colleague incorporated this information in the sample dialogs he presented during kickoff, which impressed the bank. It helped focus the discovery session: learning about the typical customer, how many accounts they typically have, how often they contact the bank, what the most common tasks are, how often they do one or several tasks in one session, when statements typically arrive, the format of account numbers and login access, and so on. It all informs design decisions, flow, prompt wording, confirmation needs, backend calls, recognition challenges, and where users are more likely to need contextual help.

Demographics and Characteristics

Who are your intended users? A broad population you know little about or a narrower user group, like kids, or a company's customers who have accounts and therefore available interaction history? You want to know if there are any significant characteristics different from a general population. You may need to tailor prompt wording, the speed and sound of the voice, how long to wait for a response, and various aspects of the flow and handling if a large chunk of users represents a particular generation or geographical location or has (a lack of) familiarity with the content or if they're non-native speakers unfamiliar with some words or pronounce words with a heavy accent. If you have several distinct user groups, such as novice and expert users, you can incorporate different handling for each group. More on this topic in Chapter 15.

FROM THE VOICE TRENCHES

In a multilingual app, the same name of a feature was used across all available languages. This was a trademarked name, so the company naturally wanted to use that name. The problem was that the name was an English word, not translated into the other languages. Recognition underperformed on the very phrase that was most important to the company because recognition is based on language models and non-native speakers don't pronounce a word the same as a native speaker does.

For general information, you don't need to know who the user is; the answers are the same for everyone in the same context. But the more you know about the user, the more interesting conversational voice dialogs you can design, from incorporating preferences to providing recommendations or handling secure data. More development work, but also greater potential payoff. Also, anything that narrows down options or potential matches can assist recognition and therefore contribute to success. And using context to predict something about the user behavior is key to success because it also narrows the search space for recognition and NL interpretation and speeds up the conversation.

SUCCESS TIP 4.3 USERS ARE STAKEHOLDERS TOO   You'll typically hear about gathering the business stakeholders during discovery, as well as involving technical representatives early. Make sure your end users are also accurately represented from the start. Business stakeholders, system implementers, and end users need to have equal representation at the table. Because voice is still typically less understood, plan for knowledge transfer and opportunities to involve everyone in learning about voice. The benefit is a better VUI.

Do you need to differentiate multiple users on the same account or access point? Mobile voice apps assume a one-user situation, but an in-home assistant device will either assume everyone accessing through an account is the same user or allow for multiple users in a household to be identified as separate users. For some medical apps, it makes sense to have different profiles for the patient and the caretaker, but for a simple outpatient procedure, it's not needed. Table 4-1 summarizes these concerns.

Table 4-1. *Demographics and user characteristics requirements for the procedure prep app*

Who are the users?	People who are scheduled for a specific procedure. Age skews older, but can be any adult.
User profile known?	Yes, to allow accurate and targeted responses.
Multiple users to differentiate?	No.
Access limitations?	Anyone can access general information. For personal information, some authentication is needed.

Engagement Patterns

FROM THE VOICE TRENCHES

In a financial stock voice system, we thought something was wrong when we saw calls as long as an hour or more. Turns out, multitasking traders continuously asked for real-time stock quotes by voice until they liked the price they heard. The dialog flow, quick pace, and information content worked well for the core power users.

Ignoring for now where to find the data, you need to know which functionality is most and least frequent. Remember: VUI differs from GUI in that the listener/user must keep everything in short-term memory. That's why you need to make use of things like task frequency: present options and information in the order that minimizes cognitive load for the user. Frequency of use also influences how users respond to multi-slot requests and ambiguous requests. In general, the less familiar a user is with the task, the more likely they'll let the VUI take the lead in requesting necessary information. You learn about this in depth in Part 3.

How often will your users engage with the VUI? If it's often, you want to aim for shorter prompts and use information from past user utterances to speed things up. If the task is complex and use is infrequent, you'll need more explanatory details, helpful hints, and error handling. And if you have both frequent and infrequent users, there are ways to personalize the experience on a "novice" vs. "expert" basis. Novice users can be presented with more detailed and explanatory prompts.

In some contexts, people have follow-on questions, even if their previous request was complete. Or they ask the same question again with different variables, like in the preceding stock quote example. You want to know if this is relevant for your voice app so you can make it easy for users in the flow. More on this in Chapter 14.

In the procedure prep app, you can expect mostly novice users and a mix of frequency depending on task. Expect lots of use for general questions, with more specific questions about foods increasing as the procedure gets close. Some tasks will happen only once, like specific procedure prep instructions. Within that task, the same step repeats multiple times, so assume you need to start with instructions for the task, but can taper off to short prompts quickly. You learn about tapering and other strategies in Chapter 13.

Mental Models and Domain Knowledge

FROM THE VOICE TRENCHES

A bank was concerned about the low completion rate for bill payment in their voice-first phone app. Turns out, users thought they were successful: they only wanted to know the due date and amount and happily hung up before completing any payment. It was a misunderstanding of users' mental models. Not everything that looks bad is bad.

Mental models, peoples' internal representations of how something works, are an important concept in voice. Mental models account for expectations for who says what when in a dialog, how to start and end a conversation, and even appropriate topics and words used. These expectations affect how users express themselves and what they expect to hear, which helps understanding what someone says when it's noisy. Therefore, your VUI should reflect these expectations and take advantage of them rather than ignore them or break them. If you're dealing with something that has a parallel method in real life or in an existing app, build on that. Users will be more successful if they can follow their expectations, express themselves naturally, and be understood.

If your restaurant finder expects users to search for the official name *Na Na's Kitchen* but all locals know it simply as *Na Na's*, you'd better handle both! Some people will give all information at once (*Make a reservation at Na Na's Kitchen for six people at 7 PM tomorrow*), while others will specify one piece of information and then hand over the conversational control to the person—or VUI—to step them through filling the rest. A stock trading voice app for expert traders needs a flow that mirrors how those trades are spoken to a person. How to build a specific dialog type is the core topic of Chapter 6. Chapter 15 goes into more detail about mental models.

FROM THE VOICE TRENCHES

It's natural for people to immediately follow a *no* in a confirmation with the corrected information—so responding *No, 1965* instead of just saying *No* and waiting for the other person, or VUI, to ask for the correct information. In a voice-first banking app, success increased by 8% just by adding this as a path based on understanding how people correct a misrecognition. Success comes from understanding how users naturally speak.

For some dialogs and devices, users expect some type of closure like the ability to say *goodbye* or hearing a confirmation number. If it's part of the mental model, be sure to allow for it without demanding an action from the user. Key points are summarized in Table 4-2.

Table 4-2. *Users' mental model requirements of the procedure prep voice app*

How do people do this today?	Look it up online, read instruction sheets, call the care team, and ask friends.
Terminology	People don't necessarily know the "right" terms for medical items. Users don't know how to pronounce names of many medications.
Expectations	High information accuracy, choices offered when relevant, confirmation before scheduling an appointment.

Environment and State of Mind

FROM THE VOICE TRENCHES

In a voice-first prescription refill app, users needed to provide their prescription number but often didn't have it nearby. We added the ability to pause the conversation until the user said *continue* to give them time to get the number without losing previous provided information and having to start over. Success comes from understanding users' environment.

In what environment will your voice app be used? Is it noisy? If so, what kind of noise? Loud white noise or mechanical noise is not as problematic for recognition as multiple voices (**side speech**) in the user's vicinity, including TV background noise. If you expect noise and have distracted or stressed users while also expecting high accuracy or difficult recognition, you'll need some methods to increase your success. Can you incorporate voice biometrics—recognition of the user based on their voice—to minimize responding to other voices? If you do, how do you handle multiple users, including guests and visitors? More about that in Chapter 15.

Why do users decide it's time to engage with the VUI: what's the triggering event? That one is obvious for the procedure prep app. Are they distracted? Are they stressed or relaxed? Are they multitasking, busy with hands or eyes or both? If you have a screen available for output, would that be useful in context or not? If the task is mentally or physically stressful, like most medical applications, your VUI should speak a bit slower and calmly, use simpler words, reiterate key information, or verify that the user understood by asking a simple comprehension question. The answers to all these questions will lead to different VUI solutions.

Do you need information from your users, like a product model number, credit card number, phone number, or prescription number? If so, do they know the information by heart and have it available, or will they need time to find it? If they're in the middle of completing the task, you'd want them to be able to pause rather than having to start over. People reciting information they know by heart, like their birth date, speak differently than those who are reading information, such as a credit card number. That will impact how your voice app listens, the pauses it allows, and the retries necessary. Table 4-3 shows environment and user state of mind information for the sample app.

Table 4-3. *Environment and user state of mind requirements of the procedure prep app*

What environment?	Home or in store; private or semiprivate; stationary or moving.
Noise or privacy impact?	For notifications, avoid potential embarrassment in wording.
User state of mind?	More nervous than normal, possibly distracted and tired.
User-provided information?	Needed for initial setup.
Modality benefit and challenge?	Screen is helpful but not required.
Special behaviors?	Just-in-time (JIT) hints; behavior tied to timing of procedure.

From General to Detailed Functionality

Now that we have a better sense of the user needs, let's return to defining the functionality. The goal is to define each task your VUI should handle and identify any red flags where voice will face challenges.

Step 1: Define the Core Features

List the core features you plan on including based on what you learned about user needs (Figure 4-1).

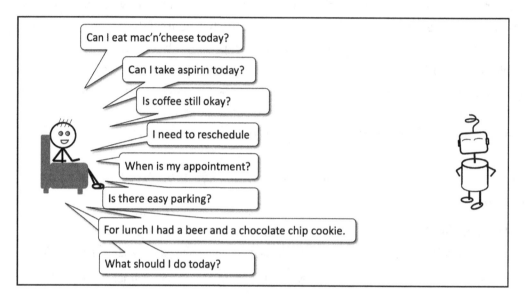

Figure 4-1. *Typical questions users have help you define the health assistant core features*

After your initial research helps you understand your users' pain points and needs, use that understanding to settle on the app's core features:

- People have questions about the procedure itself: *Will it hurt?, Is there parking by the lab?,* or *Is it covered by insurance?* A voice app is great for this: targeted answers instead of having to search through pages of material.

- People also have questions related to the low-fiber diet changes needed before the procedure. Some type of diet change is typical for many medical procedures. You want to allow users to ask about what foods are OK at any point before the procedure, both general (*What can I eat (today)?*) and specific (*Can I eat <food>? Can I drink coffee?*) Again, perfect for voice: quick information retrieval in a broad search space without stepping through menus.

- The same is true for medication questions related to medication change. Users should be able to ask both general questions (*What medications can I (not) take?*) and specific ones (*Can I take <medication>?*) No better way than voice: users don't need to spell weird names!

- It's important for people to do any prep task corrections, such as measuring blood pressure or consuming some liquid to prepare your body for the procedure. So you want to include step-by-step instructions for that. A spoken dialog allows for hands-free interactions, so again, great use of voice.

- The VUI can't answer all questions, so people need a way to contact their health team (*I'm running late for my appointment* or *I need to talk to my doctor*). Scheduling or rescheduling appointments is another important feature.

- Some people like to track what they ate each day. So let's include a food diary.

You've reached your high-level functionality goal when you can summarize what your VUI does, and you've settled on the features to address your users' most common and frequent needs. Include the core features (underlined in this section) into your functionality requirements (Table 4-4). Since this app deals with personal medical data, you'll need some form of login, but let's come back to that later.

Table 4-4. *General high-level initial description of sample procedure prep functionality*

Functionality	Description
Overall	A health assistant that helps a user prepare for their medical procedure. The voice assistant can answer questions relevant to preparing for a procedure, including general information, dietary and medication constraints, and day-of instructions. Users who are appropriately authenticated can get personalized answers, access their appointment calendar, and contact their care team.

SUCCESS TIP 4.4 LISTEN: DON'T LIMIT YOURSELF DURING DISCOVERY   Even if you know some functionality will be a bit tricky to get right with voice or you think only a few users want it, you don't know yet. We've seen project managers hurry the discovery discussion, not understanding the value of letting the technical team ask seemingly vague questions and allowing the stakeholder or customer to meander a bit. You'll learn about hidden expectations and even internal power struggles that become important later. Listening between the lines is not underhanded; it enables you to find the best solution.

Step 2: From Features to Intents and Slots

As you move from general toward detailed functionality, you need to "translate" your core features into intents. You were introduced to intents in Chapters 1–3. Think of an intent as the verb in a sentence: search, navigate, schedule, and so on. One discovery goal is to clarify enough details to define the intents for your design. Intents are at the core of all voice-first systems and architecture representing the users' goals. Separating intents makes design, coding, and future changes cleaner; combining them gains you nothing. A feature is a good candidate for being a separate intent if

- It's accessible from the VUI's top level.

- It covers a clearly different meaning and the outcome from other intents.

- It requires a dialog with distinct steps, different from others.

- It relies on a different data access from others.

Table 4-5 summarizes your eight core features for the procedure prep. Based on our guidelines, all eight features look like good candidates. How convenient. ☺

Table 4-5. *Features of the procedure prep voice app*

1. Get today's to-do list of tasks.	5. Navigate step-by-step instructions.
2. Ask for information about the procedure.	6. Contact the health care team.
3. Search for a food/beverage by name.	7. Schedule/change an appointment.
4. Search for a medication by name.	8. Update food diary.

Let's look at them in a little more detail before moving on. The first four are information requests, but they differ in topic, in how users make the request, and in the lookup logic the app needs to handle:

1. **Get to-do list**: Responses depend on time of query relative to the user's procedure: *What do I need to do today?* The VUI needs to calculate relative time based on the date and time of the procedure.

2. **Search for general info**: This info is not time sensitive and can be available to anyone with access to the voice app without privacy concerns: *How common is this procedure?, How long does the procedure take?*

3. **Search for foods (and beverages)**: Queries for specific items: *Can I eat pepperoni pizza today?, Can I still drink milk?* That means some database dip to find the answer.

4. **Search for meds**: Also queries for specific items (*Can I still take Aspirin?*) so another database dip to find these answers. Since food and meds need very different data sets, they should be handled separately while still allowing for very similarly worded requests.

The next four are different types of task completion requests:

5. **Prep**: A set of step-by-step interactions that allows some user navigation: *Repeat that, Continue.*

6. **Contact provider**: Contact details are user-specific and need information from the care team as well: *Send a message to my doctor, Call Dr. Smith's cell phone.* It's a task that starts with a data lookup.

7. **Schedule and change appointments**: Depends both on the user's and the care team's schedules: *I need to reschedule my follow-up appointment.*

8. **Update a food diary**: Updates involve the same database as the food search, plus handling multiple items in a single utterance.

There's one more feature that differs from the others in that the user doesn't initiate the dialog:

9. **Receive reminders**: Initiated by the app. Reminder content is tied to time relative until the scheduled procedure, so some background process will continuously check if it's time to play a reminder.

Give each intent a short descriptive name (Table 4-6).

Table 4-6. *Naming core intents*

1. ToDoInfo	5. PrepNav
2. GeneralInfo	6. Contact
3. FoodSearch	7. Schedule
4. MedSearch	8. FoodDiary

Add one or two archetype sentences, representative examples of well-formed user requests that lead to task completion. You already made a good start on those. You need a way to refer to the variable information in each intent. These are the slots (or entities) you were also introduced to in Chapters 1–3. If you think of intents as verbs, then slots are nouns: names of foods or medications. We often use all caps to indicate a placeholder for the variable information that fills a slot, and to make searches easier, we add curly brackets or a symbol, like $, so $FOOD and $MED. Add all that to your discovery documentation (Table 4-7).

Next, time to define successful task completion. Think about what information your voice app needs to fulfill each intent. Slots are the answer. A restaurant reservation request must fill three slots: TIME, DAY, and number of GUESTS. In the prep app, most intents need only one slot filled, but the food diary could take more than one slot, one for each FOOD and DRINK item. For contacting a care team member, it could be one slot (the person to call) or two (person plus which phone, if several). The information in Table 4-7 will be your input for high-level VUI dialog flows later in this chapter.

Table 4-7. *Detailed description of purpose and goal of each core user-initiated intent for the procedure prep voice app*

Intent	Functionality description	Archetype sentence	Task completion
ToDoInfo	User asks for upcoming prep tasks, based on procedure date. No TIME specified = "today".	<What should I do today?>	User hears a response of tasks.
GeneralInfo	User asks a question related to their procedure.	<How long will the procedure take?>	User hears a response to their question.
FoodSearch	User asks if they can eat or drink a named FOOD item. No TIME specified = "now".	<Can I eat $FOOD (today)?>	User hears a response to their food question.
MedSearch	User asks if they can take a named MEDication item. No TIME specified = "now".	<Can I (still) take $MED?>	User hears a response to their medication question.
PrepNav	VUI leads the user through multistep instructions to prepare and consume a prep solution.	<Continue>; <Pause>	Each step is completed, and end of task is reached.
Contact	User wants to contact their doctor or the procedure facility.	<Message my doctor>; <Call $NAME cell phone>	User hears the phone number for a care team member. Dialing is offered (if available).

(continued)

Table 4-7. *(continued)*

Intent	Functionality description	Archetype sentence	Task completion
Schedule	User wants to know when their appointment is or wants to change or cancel it.	<I need to reschedule>; <When is my appointment?>	User hears and confirms appointment. Appointment is made (if available).
FoodDiary	User lists >=1 FOOD and >=1 DRINK items they consumed for a specified meal. VUI confirms. Log result.	<(For $MEAL) I had $FOOD1, $FOOD2, and DRINK>	All necessary information is collected and added to their food diary.

Use this and other information you collect during discovery to draft dialog flows you can expand later in design. Figure 4-2 shows what the highest-level voice dialog flow looks like for this procedure prep VUI. Each intent is at this point only a box without details. You'll start expanding those details in the next chapter.

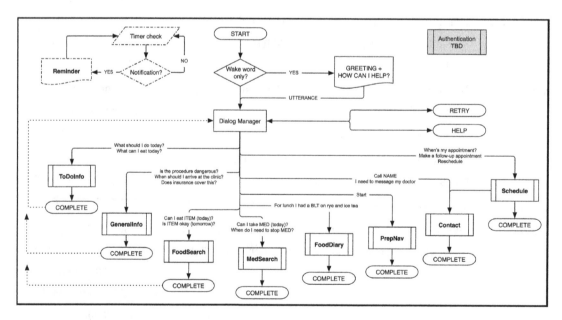

Figure 4-2. *High-level dialog flow of the sample procedure prep voice app*

Step 3: Identify Potential Complications

Once you've defined the features you'd like to include, determine what challenges a voice solution will face for each feature. Your conclusions directly affect how you structure the dialog flow, as you learn throughout this book. It also identifies which features are best left for later. Here's where understanding voice becomes important.

The rest of this chapter goes into detailed discovery exactly with this focus, asking, "With the available resources, platform choice, timeline, and so on, where are the complexities for voice and where can things go wrong?" Two core aspects of complexity are variation and cost.

Starting with variation, take another look at Figure 4-2. You can probably see some potential challenges right away: you learned in Chapter 2 that unconstrained variation in user utterances is a challenge for the VUI. Well, there's a lot of food people can ask about! And some of it is vague: If the user asks if rice is OK, the VUI needs to clarify, or disambiguate, the type of rice, since white and brown rice differ in fiber. So FoodSearch will be tricky. And because variation and complexity increase with more slots to fill, FoodDiary is even trickier: someone could list a whole meal in a single utterance. MedSearch will take some effort—not only do you need to understand the names of thousands of medications but you also need data access to provide the correct response. Contact means access to some contact list, as well as finding a way to actually connect. But the list of names is constrained, so it should be easier than all the foods. What about Schedule? Telling someone when their procedure is taking place isn't difficult assuming that info has been entered, but making or changing that appointment is a lot more work.

What about cost? Cost isn't about money here, but the consequences of misinterpreting something. If your VUI misrecognizes the name of a food, it's less costly if the question is about number of calories or to find a restaurant than if it concerns what's OK to eat the day before surgery. The costlier a potential mistake, the more effort you need to spend on minimizing that it happens. For this app, any response that results in inadequate prep has consequences of poor procedure results, rescheduling, time and money lost, and so on. Clearly not good. Again, FoodSearch and MedSearch are the red flags. For Contact the risk is that the wrong person gets contacted and for Schedule that the wrong appointment time is offered.

You end up with something like Table 4-8. Everyone needs this information. A salesperson needs this awareness to provide an accurate quote. The technical team, including designers, uses it for both settling on an approach and detailed development and testing. Product and project managers need this level of information and understanding to plan the detailed timeline and to evaluate what features to include in an MVP and a full project. You also refer to this to decide on success metrics.

Table 4-8. *Complications caused by variation in requests and cost of incorrect handling for each functionality of the procedure prep app*

Intent	Expected variation	Example	Cost of error
ToDoInfo	Some synonym variation.	*What can/should I do today?*	Low–Mid
GeneralInfo	Vague or ambiguous in wording. Broad topic; some answers won't be included.	*How common is this? How many people my age have this procedure?*	Low
FoodSearch	Ambiguity and large search space: many food and drink names. Pronunciation: Names borrowed from other languages.	*Can I eat cheese?* (different types) *Is* nasi goreng *still OK?*	Mid–High
MedSearch	Ambiguity (similar names, different versions): many drug names. Medication names are unfamiliar and can be hard to pronounce.	*Can I take Tylenol?* (different types) Is **idarucizumab OK?**	High
PrepNav	Different navigation commands. Some synonyms.	*Next, repeat/say again, go back.*	Low–Mid
Contact	Ambiguity (contacts with the same name, multiple phones). Contact list is user-dependent and limited in size.	*Call Joe. Message Dr. Brown.*	Low–Mid
Schedule	Ambiguity. Multistep dialog possible, filling time, day, appointment type, location. Dependent on user and health team calendar access.	*I'd like to move my appointment to Friday, February 12.*	Low–Mid
FoodDiary	Ambiguity: many food and drink names. Pronunciation: foods from other languages. Multiple items possible in one utterance.	*For breakfast, I had crumpets with bacon jam and Swiss cheese and some coffee.*	Low

Business Requirements: Why Are You Building It?

All voice implementations benefit from "doing it right." Even if it's just you building something for fun, you make choices (platform, domain, scope, task, flow, etc.) that affect your development effort and the VUI's performance. Make your choices consciously—it will help you later when you build more complex apps and products.

Keeping voice in mind, your business requirements need to focus on scope, timeline, budget, business rules, and legal constraints that affect VUI solutions:

- Settle on scope and features.

- Determine why voice is a preferred solution and what pain points can it improve most.

- Determine how to measure success—especially if that's tied to your payment!

- Determine if and how the VUI connects with other communication methods and if it supports backoff.

- Identify existing branding and style guides—or the need to create those.

- Identify any legal or compliance needs to affect design or development.

- Verify access to all necessary data sources and expert knowledge contributors, including resource needs if VUI is multilingual.

- Plan for performance improvement activities.

One fundamental decision is the type of device your VUI will exist on. Is it an Alexa/Google implementation, a hardware device, a multimodal app on a mobile phone, a telephone IVR, a stationary or moving robot, or an in-car solution? Can recognition happen in the cloud, or does it need to be local on-device because of the user's location? Does the device have a screen or not? To keep the discussion agnostic and maximally relevant to any voice solution, we assume it's a device that may or may not have a screen. In voice-first development, users should not need to rely on any visual feedback.

117

SUCCESS TIP 4.5 MVP FOR VOICE IS DIFFERENT   The answer lies in setting the right limits for voice. Yes, people can say anything, but they don't. That would break Grice's Cooperative Principle. Be clear about what your app can do, set expectations, and fulfill them. The biggest complaint by voice users is "It doesn't understand me," meaning "I asked for what I expect it to do in a reasonable way, and I didn't get what I wanted." The fastest way to get a one-star review is setting expectations you can't fulfill. Limit the **number** of features, **not** your **coverage**, what users must say to access those features. Pointing users to an FAQ with rules about how exactly to say something also breaks Grice's Cooperative Principle. Focus on fewer features and make those features robust by handling the expected variation in user utterances and fulfilling any requests. Some users will try to ask for things you haven't included yet, but if you're clear about your feature limits, that's OK. In the procedure prep app, if users are told they can ask about foods, you have to handle a large list of items (e.g., not just *cheese* but all common types of cheese) and the carrier phrases people use to ask the question (*Can I have...*, *Can I eat...*, *Is...OK to eat*, etc.). But you can let users know that you don't handle food brand names or restaurant specials. And if some user tries to order food in this dialog, that's not your problem. ☺

General Purpose and Goal

How will you measure success? That depends in part on your overall goals—and the goals of anyone paying for your work! This means this can be a bit of a sensitive topic. A solution focused on automation above all else may try to keep users in the system, hiding options to speak to a live agent; others offer automation for simple tasks to free up those agents when needed. IVR callers are usually happy to deal with a VUI for simple tasks if they know agents are available when needed, but they will not give your VUI good reviews if you put up hurdles when they ask to speak with a human. Whatever the purpose and goal, the more you understand voice, the better your chances of measuring success well.

Primary and Secondary Goals

Are you just creating something for your own use at home or making a demo, or are you building a product for others to use? When building a voice agent for an established company, you'll deal with a lot of constraints, including voice persona, data flow, and performance expectations. Every constraint will affect choices in your design and development.

Sometimes there are secondary goals that affect design. Are you pushing a particular product or brand? Are there reasons for engaging the user in a long conversation or giving them a response quickly, or are you trying to differentiate from other products? An answer might be "future monetization." Whatever it is, be honest and clear about it, because it will affect your dialogs and VUI responses. If your goal is to automate customer service, be aware of user backlash if you try to keep them from speaking to a person. There are better ways, as you'll learn.

Success Metrics

How will you even know if you succeed? That's the success metrics. It's not uncommon that VUI performance is tied to bonus payment amounts to the developer. If you have specific quantifiable metrics in mind, you should figure that out before you start building anything since your dialogs will impact things like time to completion. You may want a way to measure if the user reached a specific point in the dialog flow with a minimal number of steps or within some time frame. If accuracy is important, you'll need some way to track and measure that. Your choice of success metrics affects design decisions: higher accuracy means more explicit confirmation of what's recognized. If dialogs need to be short, you'll need to avoid superfluous conversational expressions. Track when specific changes are deployed for comparison with statistics on customer satisfaction, misrouted calls, or solved customer service tickets. If user engagement, repeat usage, or satisfaction is important, your dialogs need to maximize that. Chapters 16 and 17 go into further details.

FROM THE VOICE TRENCHES

In a healthcare voice-only system, each percentage point increase in containment was tied to payment by the customer to the voice service organization. By changing prompts and flows and tuning the recognition and grammars, containment increased by 10% and user satisfaction (CSAT) increased. Everyone was happy. In a banking voice-only system, increased customer satisfaction was key and was the result of design changes paired with speech tuning.

Domain, Device, and Other Modalities

VUIs can be built for any domain: medical, health, sports, entertainment, information, education, and so on. For procedure prep, the domains are "health and medical" and "food." Domain affects the dialog flow and terminology you'll use in responses, the need for confirmation and accuracy, and the utterances and behavior you can expect from users. It's more important to accurately interpret an utterance that deals with a user's money or health than to make sure you play the song they requested. Your flow will reflect that.

Table 4-9 summarizes this section for the procedure prep app. Accuracy is key since the domain is health. A valid success metric for the task is to increase user success in completing the prep. A secondary goal might be to encourage continued use for broader health. If you don't yet have some information that's needed, make a simple note, for example with TBD (to be decided/determined).

Table 4-9. *Business purpose and primary and secondary goals of the procedure prep app*

Purpose and main goal?	**Create a production-quality procedure prep helper that is easy to use, highly accurate, and secure.**
Secondary goals?	Building user data for future apps; creating stickiness through user engagement to encourage better eating habits.
Success metrics?	Significant increase of users completing procedure. Percentage TBD.
Domain?	Health and medical.

Underlying Service and Existing Automation

Think about the service your voice app is providing. If it were a live person performing the same task, what would their role be? Friend, DJ, teacher, entertainer, domain specialist? What's the relationship between the VUI and the user: equals, teacher-student, doctor-patient? This will affect the assistant's persona—the style of speaking, the words chosen, level of formality, emotional delivery, and so on. Any existing similar interactions will influence users' expectations of the order of the steps involved and how to respond. This is part of the users' mental model—you'll utilize existing dialog expectations and don't want to break them unnecessarily. If you do, you risk users behaving in ways you didn't account for, so you may need some just-in-time (JIT) hints or add additional paths to help more users succeed. For a restaurant finder, you'd want a local friend—not the same person you'd take medical advice from.

Is there live backup available, like a call center or doctor's office? If so, incorporate a handoff under some conditions. If a different backoff is available at different times of day, you need to know so that you can respond differently and appropriately. If you offer to connect the user to a person or business, make sure your system has access to the call center or business hours, so you don't send the user to a closed queue! Table 4-10 shows what's needed for the procedure prep voice app.

Table 4-10. *Metaphor and persona requirements of the procedure prep app*

Underlying service?	Always-available topic-specific hand-holding, information, timely reminders.
What would be the role if performed by a person?	A nurse or doctor, experienced and trustworthy health expert with specific knowledge about the user's situation. Doesn't provide medical diagnosis.
What exists today? Current pain points?	Some medical and health-related voice apps exist, but mostly with a different focus. Actual doctor or nurse not always available.
Available backoff?	Informational messaging. Contact information for the care team, possibly dialing.

Branding and Terminology

If your voice app needs strong product branding, you need to consider your system voice options. If your prompts use a lot of jargon, will users understand? If your users use a lot of specialized vocabulary, will your voice system understand?

The metaphor and persona question bleeds into the VUI branding. If you're building something for a company, this is a very important consideration. The brand needs to be reflected throughout the VUI, in the style, voice, and terminology. It needs to work well with other channels. If sound effects are appropriate for the task, branding affects those too. You need to be careful with branding requirements—they must never get in the way of the user's ability to succeed. Heavy-handed branding with sound effects and extraneous prompt verbiage can easily get in the way of success. Also think about how a company brand can coexist with a voice platform brand.

FROM THE VOICE TRENCHES

A bank wanted to appeal to a younger population, so they changed their voice app's greeting from "Welcome" to "Hey." Unfortunately, it didn't have the desired effect and instead resulted in scathing commentary during (fortunately) early testing.

A mobile phone company changed their voice talent to sound more "hip" thinking it would appeal to a younger population. This also resulted in negative reactions from users.

Prompt Format: Text-to-Speech or Recordings

The biggest question here is whether to use text-to-speech (TTS) synthesis or recorded prompts by a voice talent. There are benefits and drawbacks of both, and your choice affects your system architecture and level of effort. If the company has a famous spokesperson, can you use their voice? Should you? If you're using the Alexa or Google environment, TTS is a fine choice (assuming you don't need branding) because of the high quality for most situations.

Terminology and Pronunciation

If you go the TTS route, you may need to modify the pronunciation of some words, such as names of people or products. It's important to pronounce things correctly to instill trust in your VUI and be understood by the user. The pronunciation must also match what will be recognized since users will learn from what they hear. You need to get lists of any jargon and branded names from all channels, including websites and mailers, if applicable. You'll learn more about voice output in Chapter 18. You can see the summary of branding requirements for the health app in Table 4-11. Chapter 15 goes into further details.

Table 4-11. *Branding and terminology requirements of the procedure prep app*

Brand constraints on persona?	No branding constraints. Voice should be calm and mature.
TTS or recorded prompts?	TTS, with custom pronunciations as needed.
Terminology or pronunciation specifics?	Names of foods, names of medications, names in the contact list. Terminology needs to be accurate while also being easy to understand for all users.
Sound effects expected?	None planned—let's not imagine what those would be for a gastrointestinal app!

Data Needs

Your voice app will most likely need some data access. This includes data sets (e.g., names of medications or foods), information about user preferences or past use, payment information, ratings, and many other types. Think about what you'll need; later in this chapter, we'll look at how to find that data. When you start laying out the dialog, you'll work out where in the flow you'll need to fetch the data, what needs to be confirmed, and what needs to be saved for later access. Design and development need to work together on this. Table 4-12 shows the data needs for each intent in the procedure prep app.

Table 4-12. *Data type requirements of the procedure prep app*

	External data needed	User data needed
ToDoInfo	Procedure-relevant information; curated and mapped to procedure timing.	Date and time of procedure; procedure type details.
GeneralInfo	Procedure information and general health; curated.	Procedure location.
FoodSearch	Food names and ingredients; curated.	Date and time of procedure.
MedSearch	Drug names and category; curated.	Medications taken.
PrepNav	Food names and ingredients; curated.	Past food diary entries.
Contact	Access to latest updated instructions.	Prep type details.
Schedule	Care team contact info.	User contact list.
ToDoInfo	Care team schedule and availability.	User calendar.
FoodDiary	Food names and ingredients; curated.	Past food diary entries.

Access and Availability

There's more to privacy than pure data security. Imagine the potential embarrassment to the user if your VUI suddenly starts talking about procedure prep needs while other people are nearby. It happened with an early alpha version of our multimodal procedure app to the horror of one of our test users.

Your users must have easy access to their data while also believing their information is secure. Should your VUI respond differently to different people asking the same question? Should it respond differently to the same person in different contexts?

Privacy and Security Concerns

Will you need to handle any secure or private user data? Your answers affect backend integration and dialog design: you may need to authenticate the user—in the right way at the appropriate time in the flow—and you may need to be careful what information you read back. It's an area that's highly dependent on the platform and device your VUI runs on: you can make different assumptions about identity if something runs as an app on a mobile phone compared to as an IVR. Not all features within a voice app need the same level of security.

Access Limitations Based on Time or Place

Are there limitations on content and automation access based on time of day or geographical location? Automation should be available 24-7, but options and responses might depend on time of day or day of week. This has repercussions for flow and how to handle out-of-bounds requests. If your app limits geographical coverage, you need to respond to out-of-scope requests, even if you made the scope clear. If your app involves providing a closest location, can you assume it's closest to where the user is now? Locals and visitors have different needs for directions. If your app includes prescription refills, is there a cut-off time before the pharmacy closes? When and how do you make that clear? Do you even know where the user is, so you can respond correctly to *What's open **now?*** And is it worth risking being wrong by greeting someone with a *Good morning!* if there's any chance that time zone is unknown? Table 4-13 summarizes these expected needs for the health app.

Table 4-13. Access and availability requirements of the procedure prep app

Any privacy or security needs?	Yes, personal health information; check HIPAA regulations.
What's the geographical scope of usage?	United States. Assume any state, but expansion is gradual.
Any builder-side security or privacy demands?	User data must be kept secure and private.
Any limitation on availability: time of day, day of week, number of uses?	Information available 24-7. User requests referring to "now" or "today" need accurate time-sensitive responses. Calls should only be attempted when phones are staffed unless there's voice mail.

FROM THE VOICE TRENCHES

A medical company wanted to "not recognize" user questions on a specific topic so that they wouldn't have to respond. Problem: You can't <u>not</u> recognize something, but you can choose how to respond. And if it's a reasonable request for the app, why wouldn't they ask? Instead, tell users why you can't give them what they want.

Special Announcements

Some companies have announcements they want to communicate to users, such as holiday closures or special offers. There's nothing wrong with that per se, but it's important to consider the placement and frequency of such announcements. Users will welcome some of them, but once they've heard it, having to listen to the end of the same announcement again will only feel like a waste of time. An offer to upgrade the app for a special price is good; playing the same offer every time the user interacts with the VUI is bad. Notifying users about new updates or service outages is good; notifying them by voice at 3 AM on a device in their bedroom is bad. An IVR that has changed drastically, maybe from touch-tone to speech, can start with a very short concrete comment to that effect; saying *Please listen carefully as our options have changed* is pointless (if those options don't provide clarity on their own, you have a bigger issue). A pop-up on a screen is annoying but easy to close, and sometimes you can read "around" it. Because it's audio, voice announcements are more intrusive—you can't talk or listen to the VUI until the announcements are done. You learn more about this in Chapter 15. During the definition phase, settle on what announcements are necessary and the circumstances for playing them.

SUCCESS TIP 4.6 UNEXPECTED VOICE CAN AFFECT PERFORMANCE   If users have to listen to the VUI talking about things they don't care about, they'll tune out. This can result in them missing what the VUI says when they needed to pay attention.

Legal and Business Constraints

Legal disclaimers can be required, especially when dealing with sensitive information such as medical or financial advice and records. It's then important to follow best practices to lessen the impact on users. Can you ask only once or break it up in smaller chunks that are easier to process when heard? Can you get buy-in via email or text instead? Can you reword something to be less "legalese"? If you're offering a service that lets your users access external content, do they have to sign up for and link to other content providers? If so, can that be done with a link in email?

If you collect utterances for system tuning—and you'll want to, as you'll see in Chapter 17—you need to alert the user somehow. It's true over the phone (*Your call may be monitored or recorded...*), but it also applies to other devices. These types of constraints can be thorny; the wording of such alerts can negatively affect prompt wording. You can see in Table 4-14 how you might address these constraints in our sample app. Any medical application will have constraints on wording to off-load responsibility from automation: if collecting symptoms from the user, the VUI won't say *You have the flu* or *Nothing to worry about*, but rather *The described symptoms suggest the flu* and frequent *Contact your doctor* suggestions.

Compliance

Requesting, accessing, and storing personal data isn't just a question about finding the right database, finding space to store it, or following best practices. As time goes on and electronically collected and stored user data of any kind gets compromised, more regulation is put in place by necessity. If you collect any information about the user, as audio or text logs, that data must be kept secure, especially if it's financial or health data. A word of warning: For medical systems, regulations differ between countries—in the United States, for example, you need to use HIPAA-compliant servers for many tasks. You also need a Business Associate Addendum (BAA). These regulations change over time—it's your responsibility to comply. If your app is international, make sure you understand each country's regulations.

Table 4-14. Additional product constraints of the procedure prep app

Are you the decision maker?	No. Medical staff need to sign off on information provided to users. Need approval of product images on screen.
Are legal disclaimers needed?	Yes. Needed since medical. Needed when utterances are collected for tuning.
How many users are expected?	TBD. Unlikely to have many in parallel nor many per day.
Interaction with other channels or systems?	Yes. Food diary, procedure calendar, contact information, changes in procedure prep.

(*continued*)

Table 4-14. (*continued*)

Cost-control issues?	Assume free for end users. Unlikely to be high use that affects cost or service.
Usage constraints?	No limitations. User can keep asking questions and keep trying if not recognized. Normal response rate and latency expected. Some tracking of behavior for subsequent use. Expect tuning and updates needed to keep users happy and data reliable.
Logistics and timeline?	TBD. Urgent, but quality implementation is more important than schedule.

Identification and Authentication

FROM THE VOICE TRENCHES

A bank improved customer success significantly in a voice-only solution by changing how authentication was done. They offered different methods depending on the level of security needed for the task and different approaches depending on what the user knew.

Will you know the identity of each user? Do you need to? Think carefully about this because it affects the dialog flow, user experience, and system architecture. For most simple dialogs running on an in-home assistant, you probably don't need to worry about security. We differentiate between **identification**, recognizing who the speaker is, and **authentication**, verifying their identity to give them secure access. Identification is something you'll want to do if several people are likely to access the VUI on the same device and you want to incorporate past context and user preferences. Authentication is necessary when security and privacy is at stake, but only then.

For many tasks, user identity is not important: the answer to *Will it rain today?* is the same for me and you, assuming we're speaking to a device in the same location, and there's nothing private about the question or the answer. What's important in that case is user location, which is a trait of the user but not enough to identify them. Some tasks benefit from knowing who is talking: my request to *Play my workout music* is probably different from yours. When dealing with financial or medical information, it's obviously crucial to know who's talking. There are many ways to do either; you'll learn more in Chapter 15. For now, determine if you need to know who the user is. For the procedure prep voice app, you'd need to know something about the user: the date and time of their procedure, procedure type, procedure location, contact list, and maybe their calendar. You need to make sure to only give health information to the right user. You'd also need to track the user's food diary. How do you access the right diary if several people in the same household track their food intake using the same device? Again, you're only noting down your concerns, not potential solutions yet.

Error Handling and Navigation Behaviors

You know from Chapter 2 that misunderstandings will happen and users will need to try again. Or they missed what your VUI just said and want to hear it again. If the VUI plays content or covers a multistep task, users want to *skip*, *stop*, or *go back*. In the procedure prep VUI, you'll need to handle both retries and navigation behaviors. Best practices exist for different dialog types, as you learn in Chapters 9, 12, and 13. For now just realize that it's something you need to account for, at least to determine if it's all built-in or not in your platform (Table 4-15).

Table 4-15. *Supporting functionality needs of the procedure prep app*

Authentication needs?	Some needed. Could be one-time device based, up front before any response, or just-in-time as needed.
Identification needs?	Possibly. Multiple users in one household may have different preferences and usage history.
Error handling?	Standard for tasks and domain.
Navigation and control behavior?	Yes, for prep task (pause, next, repeat).

System Requirements: How Will You Build It?

If you're creating something small and simple, you can rely on the platform infrastructure. But if you go beyond those limits to where you need more control over the data—including collecting utterances—then system details become crucial.

SUCCESS TIP 4.7 BUILD FOR USERS AND COMPUTERS   It's popular to say you should design for humans and not for computers. We'd argue that's too simplistic. Your goal should be to design for success. To succeed, you need to consider both dialog participants and their different strengths and weaknesses. Designing for humans means designing for humans interacting with computers that sound and behave like humans. By creating a conversational VUI, you set user expectations. You succeed only if you fulfill those expectations.

Recognizer, Parser, and Interpreter

FROM THE VOICE TRENCHES

In a bank app, new account types were introduced in a marketing blitz. A disappointingly small number of users seemed interested in the number of users reaching that part of the conversation flow. The problem was that the voice app couldn't understand any questions about the new products because those names had not been added to the grammars.

What recognizer will you use? This is a big and basic question. If you're sticking with Alexa or Google or other full-feature platforms, you have your answer: you'll take advantage of the built-in intent handling. If not, you may need to write more of it yourself (Chapters 10 and 11). Within each platform, you'll find products aimed at specific voice use cases:

- **The Internet of Things (IoT) use case**: *AGENT, dim the lights in the living room* or *AGENT, set the temperature to 70*—controlling appliances via spoken commands addressed to and directed at an Alexa Echo device or Google Home device. The appliances themselves don't have microphones or speakers for voice responses. These are connected devices, usually referred to as **smart home**. The vocabulary is more limited to not conflict with other requests.

- **Third-party devices with built-in microphones and speakers that make use of the recognition and NL "smarts" of Alexa or Google**: *AGENT, play music by Queen.* The spoken commands are directed at a device that has its own microphones and speakers but is "inhabited" by one of the two voice assistants. These are built-in devices.

General VUI best practices apply across all, but details differ because the users' needs differ, devices have different functionalities, and different overlapping architectures and ecosystems need to interact. Custom skills and actions need invocation, smart home and built-ins don't, but need an explicit destination, like *in the kitchen*. Because of the platform-specific needs of smart home and built-in applications, we don't focus on those in this book.

Remember what you've learned already about voice in Chapters 2 and 3. What tasks are a challenge to the computer? Anything with large variation in user pronunciation or wording will take extra effort to handle well; the larger those sets are, the greater the challenge. Table 4-16 shows the situation for each intent for our medical app. To-do info is not a challenge since we expect simple requests like *What should I do today?* Prep instructions are only navigation commands like *Next*. Foods and medication names, on the other hand, are quite challenging, thanks to being very large sets of possible words with varied pronunciations.

Table 4-16. *Expected recognition, parsing, and interpretation challenges of each functionality in the procedure prep voice app*

	Recognition challenge	Parsing or interpretation challenge
ToDoInfo	Low.	Low.
GeneralInfo	Medium.	Medium. Broad open-ended set. Expect ambiguity.
FoodSearch	High. Huge list, varied pronunciation.	Low. Expect ambiguity.
MedSearch	High. Large list, hard to pronounce, varied pronunciation.	Medium. Users might include irrelevant info for the task (potency) or leave out relevant info (full drug name) or use generic names.
PrepNav	High. Huge list, varied pronunciation.	Medium. Users can say a whole meal at once including details of size and amounts.
Contact	Low. Hands-free use likely.	Low.
Schedule	Medium. Personal names from limited list.	Low.
ToDoInfo	Medium. Personal names, dates, times.	Medium. Users might request appointments with the wrong care team member.
FoodDiary	High. Huge list, varied pronunciation.	Medium. Users can say a whole meal at once including details of size and amounts.

As you move from smart home, via custom skills/actions, to fully custom solutions, you need more control over recognition performance, NL, and flow. If you're creating a voice app or IVR for medical or financial use, you'll be on the hook to get things right. You need to know exactly what went right and wrong.

There are other choices for recognition, parsing, and interpretation beyond what's made available by Amazon and Google, including the open source DeepSpeech, Kaldi, and Sphinx and paid-for solutions from Nuance and others.

Your choices depend on your need for recognition accuracy and functionality, including challenging tasks like address or name recognition, large data sets, or long alphanumeric strings. Your ability to combine modules is quite limited. Google and Alexa provide statistical language models that allow you to get far fast without a huge amount of your own parsing and interpreting. But eventually you'll run into limitations on what you can control because of decisions that have been made for you to enable simpler integrations. In Chapters 11 and 12, you learn some more hands-on techniques that allow you more flexibility and demand access to the speech data.

SUCCESS TIP 4.9 VOICE DATA IS HEARD AND VARIED   Content data for voice has a particular level of complexity and needs to be curated for voice. Even if you can find a database of food items or drug names, it's unlikely that the content has been curated for recognition or categorized for your intent handling needs. Working with large data sets is a key component for accurate recognition and intent resolution. Incorporating it correctly allows a restaurant finder to understand a request for "The Brisbane Inn" even when transcription gives you "the brisbane in." How do you handle names of artists that include symbols—and how do people pronounce those? You can get official lists of all current drug names, but they're categorized based on chemistry and usage, not on common mispronunciations of the names. Even if you find a comprehensive ontology or listing of all food terms, it won't include all regional names of some foods. That means someone needs to make sure that "grinder," "hero," "hoagie," "sandwich," "spuckie," "sub," "submarine," and "zeppelin" are all handled the same, especially if they're common on local menus. And that someone must verify that "faisselle," "organic small-curd cottage cheese," and "cottage cheese that's homemade" are recognized and mapped to the same food—assuming it should be for the VUI's context. And even if you create an in-house version with all the pronunciation and synonym details you need, you need to plan for updates. Who'll update your data and retest everything when a new drug list is published? It's very time-consuming and very important.

External Data Sources

Data is at the core of your recognition and intent resolution, as well as for output content and responses. Where do you find this data? Can you buy it or license it, or do you need to create it yourself? If you integrate with someone else's data, are there cost or access limits? If it's something like music or video content, do your users need to have their own direct account access to the content? Who keeps the data current? Will you need to handle updates to information that changes, or do you subscribe to updates? And what about secure info, like medical or financial records? What level of authentication is needed?

Is there some side benefit from building and maintaining the data? There can be. Even if you can get the data from somewhere, like names of foods or a drug name database, you need the right format for voice, for example, alternative pronunciations or content that's accessible when heard instead of read.

You need someone qualified to create and verify your voice responses. This is both content creation and QA testing; it's a crucial task when the information is in response to a health question. Responses need to convey content accurately as well as be designed for conversational voice dialogs. Very few people have the experience to do both well. Remember from Chapter 2 that you can never be sure that your VUI correctly understood the user. You'll learn more about how to minimize the risk of providing the wrong responses. For now, each intent in the procedure prep app relies on some level of data processing for lookup and updates, as well as careful content response curation.

Data Storage and Data Access

Storing and accessing data is not as tricky an issue if you rely on a platform like Amazon or Google, but very important if you're able to collect utterance data for tuning. Speech data takes a lot of space—plan for it.

If there's latency while a database is accessed, you'll need to mask it so users know their request is still being processed. After about 2 seconds of silence, users will start to wonder. Voice-only systems need audio, either a voice prompt or some sound; physical devices should also have sound but can also make use of lights, as you see on an Amazon Echo or Google Home unit. Ask Alexa or Google to play a song by name. The response feels instantaneous, but if you record the interaction and measure the time between your end of speech and the start of the song, it may be 7 seconds or more. Plenty of time to process the request, find a song even in a huge search space, and cue it up. Seven seconds of silence would feel like an eternity, but people are usually fine with about 2 seconds of silence, and that's what you get here, followed by a voice response with the name of the song. The key points are shown in Table 4-17.

Table 4-17. *Data storage requirements for the sample procedure prep voice app*

Collecting speech data?	Yes.
Collecting/updating user data?	Yes.
Security needs?	Yes.
Expected latency issues?	Investigate. Expect data lookup to be fast.

Other System Concerns

If you're building a business product, you'll need to interact and coordinate with other systems within the business, like websites, call centers, or mobile apps. Even if that's not what you're doing, you might interact with external systems to access ratings, send emails, or connect calls. Or you might want content output, like music. You'll need transitions of data coordination as well as wording.

MULTIMODAL CORNER

Some interactions are better suited for voice-only and others for multimodal solutions. Find out early if your VUI has a screen for input and/or output, the size and format of any screen, and what type of interaction is possible: touch/tap or remote control point-and-click. Is something already in place that you're voice-enabling? Previously implemented navigation controls can limit your implementation choices (or at least slow you down), as well as the effectiveness of voice interactions. If most users are expected to look at options and results on a screen, you rely less on longer explanatory prompts or the need to pause spoken information. If face detection or recognition will be available, you can use it both to know if the user is looking at the screen and for personalized responses. Any on-screen button labels need to be coordinated with prompts—they need to be short to fit on the screen and distinct enough to be recognized well. Establish a process early for keeping prompts and images in sync during all phases of development.

We focus on US English systems in this book; if you work with other languages, other concerns apply, as you can imagine. Table 4-18 is a quick summary of the concerns for our procedure voice app.

Table 4-18. *Additional system concerns of the sample procedure prep voice app*

Interactions?	Initiate calls.
Language?	US English.
Content output (music, video)?	None.
Multimodality (screen)?	Incorporate images for multimodal devices.

The default approach for multilingual VUIs is to first design the app in one language and start prototyping and implementation before adding other languages. At the planning stage, add time for translation and localization work and for every type of testing and tuning in each additional language. Plan the architecture: Will a VUI voice prompt have the same file name in all languages and be stored in separate directories, or will each name include a language tag? How will users pick a language? In an IVR it's likely a menu up front. A mobile app can rely on screen menu or the device settings.

What if it's a new hardware device? Clarify who will ultimately handle translations and localization—you can't just outsource it to someone with no voice experience, and you can't rely on online translation tools. More on this in Chapter 15.

What's Next?

That was a lot of information! What you learned here feeds directly into Chapter 5, where you learn about how to find real data to answer the questions raised here and how that data feeds into design.

Summary

- Learn to look at all aspects of discovery and resource needs from a voice perspective.

- You can't limit the limitless, but you can set your scope to do fewer things and handle those well and then add functionality over time.

- Technology choices made up front can limit your effort and success later in unexpected ways. Tradeoffs will be needed to handle the desired scope well.

- Different voice tasks have different risks and needs; calculating the cost of being wrong is crucial and affects design and development at every step. During planning, designers, developers, and product owners all need to be equally represented and heard during every planning phase.

- Databases and content need specialized curation for voice, both for information lookup and for result output.

- You need to know what your users expect, what words they use, and why they're talking to your app when they do.

- Keep design out of discovery—this is the time to understand what's behind the actual needs (user wants, business goals, resource limitations).

## CHAPTER 5

From Discovery to UX and UI: Tools of Voice Design

You've reached the final chapter of Part 2. After this, you move from the planning phase to the core building phase: detailed design and development. In this chapter, we look at how and where to find data that helps answer your discovery questions, data that can guide your design before you have users or when user access is limited. Fortunately, there's a lot you can do quickly and cheaply if you know what questions to ask and how to ask them. You'll be introduced to some common VUI design documentation approaches you can use for any platform. This isn't a how-to lesson on tools, but an overview of what some experienced VUI designers use and why. If you're in charge of VUI design in your organization, it gives you some options to choose from. If you enter an existing organization, of course you'll use what's standard. But who knows: maybe you can bring change! The chapter wraps up with an introduction to some powerful methods of testing your UI assumptions and what the results can tell you. You'll learn more about how to test in Chapter 16.

Where to Find Early User Data on Any Budget

Data is gold in the world of voice. The right data can tell you what people want, how they'll ask, what they expect to hear, if they're happy or not, and if you understood them or not. Data can point you to the right conversational design, help choose features, and help you improve existing voice apps. Your design is built on assumptions you make based on the data you have. You can find data in many places, some free, some cheap, some expensive. Good news: the expensive stuff isn't always the best. This chapter

© Ann Thymé-Gobbel, Charles Jankowski 2021
A. Thymé-Gobbel and C. Jankowski, *Mastering Voice Interfaces*, https://doi.org/10.1007/978-1-4842-7005-9_5

focuses on finding data that can inform your design before you have speech data from actual users. In the final part of the book, you'll discover what you can learn from voice recordings and text logs as people use your voice app. You'll understand why access to that data will be the future battlefield for voice.

Now, let's look at what you can learn and what to watch out for. We have grouped the methods loosely into three sets: first, data you can find online by searching or by actively engaging in crowdsourcing methods; second, direct observation data; and, third, data from actively engaging in observation and questioning. Keep in mind this is just an overview. Each method could be the topic of its own book. For each method, the devil is in the details, as always. It takes experience and practice to ask the right questions in the right way and analyze the answers. Our goal is to keep you from making big mistakes rather than teach you everything on the topic.

SUCCESS TIP 5.1 THE MORE DATA, THE BETTER   …as long as you know enough about its origin to evaluate the data and the claims. The relevance of the data depends on many aspects including how questions were presented, options given, context, participant characteristics, modality (text vs. voice), and exact wording of each question.

FROM THE VOICE TRENCHES

Remember that voice and text are not the same. Differences include types of errors (pronunciation vs. spelling) and emotion (prosody vs. emoticons). Utterances also differ in word choices, punctuation, hesitation, and overall structure. We collected data in our health app from voice and text user input that pointed to significant differences in use of complete sentences vs. only key words and phrases. For humans, this difference is trivial. For a voice system, it's huge.

Online Research and Crowdsourcing Options

In Chapter 4, we introduced the benefits of doing quick online research early on. You can learn loads by reading others' research and posing questions to end users.

Blogs and Articles

What is it?	Commentary based on one person's own experience or observation.
Pros	Easily available—someone else did the work for you. Free or inexpensive. Can provide interesting user-focused insights. Author usually independent.
Cons	Hit or miss, depending on author knowledge, insight, and agenda. Can be inaccurate or reflect an agenda. Results and conclusions are typically more anecdotal than significant.
Take-home	Read anything you have access to, but read it with a critical eye. Learn who and what to trust and why.

Industry Studies

What is it?	Surveys and studies performed by marketing or consulting companies, such as Gartner and others. Written reports with nice graphics, based on large sets of participants. Search online for "voice marketing industry studies" and similar.
Pros	Easy and fast access—someone else did the work for you. Provides general quantitative data of user behavior or preferences, with predictions about future directions of some technology. Can provide insights that can be further investigated and built on.
Cons	Very expensive. May not be targeted to your specific needs. Questions are often not formulated by voice experts, may be reused from other studies, or may not focus on voice input/output. Author pressured to provide insights and predictions; crucial details get overlooked, resulting in oversimplification or outright misleading conclusions. Participants are usually crowdsourced: the further participants are from their own concrete experiences, the higher the risk they're not truthful or engaged when responding.
Take-home	Read anything you have access to, but read it with a critical eye to evaluate all conclusions and the relevance of the questions.

Customer Reviews

What is it?	Reviews of existing or similar products or commentary on sites like reddit.
Pros	Quick and cheap. Reviewers want to be heard and can provide valuable information from a broad context with real-life conditions.
Cons	Passive info stream; you can't follow up with clarification questions. People usually don't know why something works or not. Negative reviews are more common than positive ones—some people just want to vent. Data is highly anecdotal. Complaints may be about unrelated aspects of the product.
Take-home	Don't use as your primary source of data for setting directions—try to understand what's behind each comment.

Supporting Materials

What is it?	Collect and read any material relevant to your tasks, particularly for anything with a specialized focus. For example, samples of instructions for a medical procedure, financial rules and terminology for stock trading, and options available for a hotel or cruise line reservation.
Pros	Easy to get far fast. Provides crucial information about words users will say and the pieces of information needed for completion. Layout of website and print material point to frequency of use that can be used in design flow and prompting.
Cons	The material you need might not be available to "outsiders." Most data will probably not be voice-specific.
Take-home	Build your own reference library for domains and tasks you're interested in.

Crowdsourced Data

What is it?	Data collection from Amazon Mechanical Turk, Figure Eight, and similar organizations. Each participant who provides feedback, responses, or behavior data on some task or topic gets paid a small amount. More on surveys in Chapters 16 and 17.
Pros	Inexpensive and quick. Questions and tasks can be targeted to address exactly the topic you're interested in. You can specify the size and type of your participants. Can provide a lot of valuable information from a very wide population.

(continued)

Cons   Passive info stream; you can't follow up with additional clarification questions. The further you get from asking participants about concrete experiences, the higher the risk they're not truthful or disengaged. Questions must be carefully worded to generate valid answers; get help with the details if not experienced with UX or survey creation.

Take-home   A great resource of general population data if you ask the right questions and recognize what data needs to get tossed out.

FROM THE VOICE TRENCHES

We, and others, have made great use of online crowdsourcing. For very little money, crowdsourcing platforms let you pose questions to readily available Internet users, resulting in quick turnaround data from a broad set of people. You can play audio prompts and ask comprehension and preference questions. Or play a set of names you're considering for a product and check which one is most memorable. Or ask participants what they had for breakfast. Or ask them to first think of a question they have about Procedure X, then say it out loud as if they were asking their doctor, and finally type in what they said out loud. What you can't do is capture audio from the participants or ask for clarification, so you have to think carefully about how you word questions and do a test run before starting a larger survey.

Dialog Participant Observation

The next set of methods focuses on observing potential users and their behavior. Observation is more passive than what's covered in the other sets, but no less important—and it plays a part of all other approaches. Whether you're creating a voice version of an existing human-human interaction or expanding a human-computer interaction to include voice or even working on a new version of an existing voice product, go forth and observe! The methods are the same, but your access to users differs. If you can do audio recordings, do so. But be careful about security and privacy.

FROM THE VOICE TRENCHES

Working on a voice project for a Fortune 500 company, we were shown detailed data on the reasons why customers contacted their large call center. The source of the data was the agents themselves, who after each call classified the call using a large set of predefined categories. It looked like most people called for just a few reasons. During a later agent observation session, we learned that because agents are in a hurry to get to the next call, they often just pick one of a few general categories. Finding the more precise category from a long set in a multilevel drop-down menu was just not going to happen. Had we relied only on the data reports instead of additional agent observations, we would have made the wrong decisions at several points in the flow that most likely would have had a negative impact on system performance.

SUCCESS TIP 5.2 LEARN TO WATCH—YOU'LL LIKE IT   Observing, analyzing, and making appropriate conclusions is something you should learn. Even if you work on a bigger team where you're not the one primarily in charge of data collection or design, the more you understand the implications, the better everyone can use their time and the more successful you'll be overall. Plus, it's really fun to understand what people want!

Actual or Potential Primary User Observation

What is it?	Watch and listen as people interact with existing tech or with other people to do what you're trying to do in your voice app. Can be formal or informal, with many or a few samples. Document each interaction in detail, what is said and done, what works, and what doesn't.
Pros	Can be quick and cheap and still teach you lots even after just a few observations. Should be part of anything you create.
Cons	Can be tricky to find the right interaction in the right environment if you're creating something new or something where you don't have access to representative users. Tricky to take notes or record without influencing the data.
Take-home	Find the most representative users and contexts without being intrusive.

Secondary Dialog Participant Observation

What is it?	Watch and listen as people interact with human agents, representatives, store personnel, nurses, or whoever now fulfills the task that your voice app will handle. Take note of their interaction style, words used, flow to fulfill the task, assumptions made, and so on.
Pros	Very informative. Can show what users are dealing with today and provide insights into what works well and what doesn't.
Cons	Not always available. If your voice app breaks from any aspect of what happens in the human-to-human interaction, know why (there can be good reasons) and plan for extra user guidance.
Take-home	A crucial source of information if you're automating any voice interaction that exists today.

Expert Reviews and Heuristic Evaluation

What is it?	Review designs of existing options to see what was done and understand why. Observe yourself interacting with existing options, human interactions, or apps; note what works or not and what your assumptions and needs are.
Pros	It doesn't get easier access than yourself—you'll probably cut yourself a deal too! If you're a representative target user, so much the better.
Cons	You are only one person. Experts have a different perspective from novice users.
Take-home	You can learn a lot from your own interaction and analysis; just don't rely exclusively on this approach.

SUCCESS TIP 5.3 YOU'RE NOT THE USER, AND...   You've probably heard the warning "You are not the user." Unless you are the only user, it's a valid and important warning. When you deal with voice, it's easy to fall into the trap of thinking everyone uses speech and language the same way you do. They don't. And you need to make sure they're all successfully understood. So, yes, "you're not the user." Never assume that you can put yourself into your users' place; know everything about their context or how they'll phrase requests. And, at the same time, don't assume you're completely different either. That's just the flip side of the same assumption coin. Only valid user voice data and utterances can show you users' behavior. Until you have that, make use of your own experiences and knowledge of how voice works, and try to cast your assumption net wide. Just be ready to change your assumptions.

FROM THE VOICE TRENCHES

Details matter—even who's asking the questions. When creating one of our health-related voice apps, we ran a focus group with all-female breast cancer survivors. Let's just say that the participants' willingness to share openly was considerably higher, thanks to the moderator being your female coauthor rather than your male one.

Focus Groups, Interviews, and Surveys

The final set of data source approaches differs from the others in that you're more actively involved—and so are your participants. Observation is also part of these approaches, but here we focus on your ability to interact with the data source, asking clarification or follow-up questions or knowing more about each participant. They're often performed in person and involve more preparation.

In-Depth Interviews and Focus Groups

What is it?	Formal or informal detailed conversations, typically one-time interaction, either one-on-one interviews or small groups of similar users who can answer your in-depth questions. For a medical procedure, separate patients and providers into two groups. If creating something for a business or organization, ask for a participant list through them to recruit from.
Pros	Participants with shared context can trigger ideas in other participants. One-on-one interviews can help when your topic is sensitive.
Cons	Focus groups should be handled by those with experience. Challenging to keep group on track and get everyone to participate. One participant can dominate others.
Take-home	Do your homework first to maximize everyone's time. A task for the trained.

Subject Expert Panel

What is it?	A particular type of focus group, this panel is a set of people who stay available for additional future questions and interactions. Create your own "VIP" group of people with experience or knowledge relevant to what you're creating. Find people who are honest and available to answer your questions on various topics. For a medical procedure app, you'd look for those who've had the procedure, those who will soon, and medical staff.
Pros	Great longitudinal resource later for testing and feedback of what you build. Can provide targeted valid information and a way to verify your assumptions quickly. Usually inexpensive; people like to be involved and provide feedback for the price of a gift certificate. Can often start with friends and family.
Cons	Need to find the right set of people for some tasks. Some will have strong opinions, and some will remember wrong or be poor at details—have a large enough set of participants to get a valid picture.
Take-home	A resource worth its weight in gold.

Targeted Surveys

What is it?	A survey with specific questions and distributed to targeted users with verified relevance. If creating something for a business or organization, ask for a participant list through them to recruit from. Usually only a one-time engagement with the participants, so not interactive, but you know something about each one, such as demographics and other relevant background.
Pros	Data quality and relevance is higher than online crowdsourced surveys or generic studies.
Cons	Can be difficult to find the right participants.
Take-home	Another resource worth its weight in gold.

In-App Data Collection

What is it?	If you already have a live app that doesn't use speech for the tasks you're building and if you have data access, add a step that seems to the user to understand voice. Or add a short survey or feedback question. Collect the data for analysis.
Pros	User data is highly relevant since spoken and worded naturally. Inexpensive and flexible, once infrastructure is in place. More on data in Chapters 16 and 17.
Cons	Prompts have to be carefully crafted to get relevant data. Need ability to collect user data.
Take-home	Lucky you if you're in this situation!

SUCCESS TIP 5.4 GET AS CLOSE TO REAL USERS AS YOU CAN   Possibly the most important tip of any related to finding data that informs your design. A target user is more informative than a general population user. Voice data is more relevant than written data. The behavior of someone performing the task in the expected environment tells you more than that person describing a past experience or future features. Collect it all but assign relevance accordingly.

FROM THE VOICE TRENCHES

A project manager offers up, "I'd like to share two learnings. First: Don't jump into development. Start with design, and even before that, be clear on what you have available. Know what you can and can't control, so you worry about the right stuff. It's not enough to pick a voice platform like Google or Alexa. There are several approaches and dependencies within each platform with direct consequences for your design and development choices. Second: Trust the voice-experienced people on your team. Work with them—they're usually geeks who love to get involved to solve problems. They know what works, and they can spec to any constraints. But only if they know the constraints."

A VUI designer discusses an expectation mismatch when starting a new job creating a voice product. "It was clear that nobody on the team understood what information mattered to the VUI architecture and design choices. I was hired to create the VUI design starting Day 1, so people were taken aback when instead of jumping right in, I started by asking questions about the available technology and data. Does the microphone close by itself after end-of-speech? What type of confirmation is available? What flexibility is there for error handling? What recognition engine is used? Can we track and make use of users' previous requests and account information? … It was a learning process all around."

How Discovery Informs VUI Design Decisions

Remember we said there's never only one way to design a VUI interaction? That's true for all approaches and platforms. However, your choices may be limited depending on what's available and feasible by the platform, tools, voice service, and development environment.

For example, if your chosen platform lets you differentiate between your own specified error conditions, you would be correct in thinking it would be helpful to your users if you can choose exactly how to word the responses to be clear about what went wrong. But now all platforms or environments will let you do that. If you have to map each of 20 error conditions to only three generic prompt responses, clearly this will impact your overall design and effectiveness. Mostly, you're dealing with platforms and technology that are far from mature and are ever changing. If you rely on a current feature or, worse, a promised one, that feature may not be there when you need it, or it's implemented in ways that don't match your expectations. Both have happened to both of us authors when relying on "packaged" solutions to speed things up. As always, choices are a tradeoff. No free lunch.

SUCCESS TIP 5.5 DON'T BURY YOUR REQUIREMENTS   Your discovery results should be documented and shared in some type of requirements specification, and it should be a living document. Keep it handy, refer to it, and update it when you modify the functionality or learn something about your users or data access. Add notes to remind yourself about your reasons. If you work with a team, get everyone onboard early to agree on a format and location that works for all, and refer to it frequently. Never lose your notes explaining the reasons.

One goal of discovery is to settle on the information needed to start defining your intents. Intents should have meaningful names that can be used in the same format by designers and coders. Importantly, they should capture the request from the user's perspective. That means with minimal interpretation from your side and not based on what you currently think you'll handle in your app. You'll learn more about the reasons behind this later.

Specifying intents at the appropriate level of granularity affects your design, code, and architecture. Intents are usually delineated by a combination of semantics and syntax on the user's part and various integration needs. You'll also have sublevels of intents within each core intent. Think of it as an intent family containing a set of more detailed intents. Like with other aspects of design and implementation, there's seldom one single answer for how to divide your intents, but give it some thought and planning.

We tend to be pretty detailed in our intent definitions, because we've found it makes things more flexible and precise. Naming choices and details actually influence how you and your team think of the whole voice interaction; they can impact the flow of the dialog and any module and prompt reuse. It's easier to talk to other team members and stakeholders about details when intent labels are clear. Little is gained by trying to ignore details and clump together behaviors under one label. You can easily handle two intents the same way, but you have to do extra work if you try splitting the handling of two user requests you grouped as one intent.

Discovery Informing Design: An Example

Let's look at an example. Figure 5-1 should look familiar from Chapter 4, except we've expanded it to add some responses. In Chapter 4, we settled on eight core intents for our procedure prep app. One core intent was food search. The first request in the figure (*Can I eat mac 'n' cheese today?*) clearly belongs in this intent. The user wants information about a specific food. So let's make the core intent label something like foodInfo or foodSearch. The second request (*Can I take Aspirin today?*) is similar from the user's perspective, but the details are different. Food and medication are not the same. So let's call this one something parallel like medInfo or medSearch. It captures both the difference and similarity, which seems appropriate also from a design and development perspective: they'll both involve open search of large databases. Could you just call them both Info or Search? You could, but knowing that these will be common requests and dip into different databases, we'd handle them as separate intents right away.

You're not done yet. Look at *Can I eat mac 'n' cheese today?* again. The user specified a food and a time frame. You don't want to ignore that information, so better capture those also. We'd probably start with something like foodSearch.specific.day. This tells us that we think the user is asking for information about a particular food item and that they specified the day. They could have left either or both unspecified (foodSearch.day, foodSearch.specific, *and* foodSearch.general *or* foodSearch), meaning we'd either have to ask a follow-up question or give a general response. More on this later. If a lot of users specify time of day, you might add *.time.* If it makes sense to keep "eat" and "drink" questions apart, then you'd add a drinkSearch intent family. You get the idea.

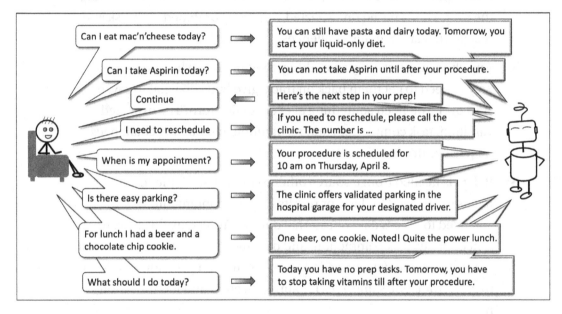

Figure 5-1. *Archetype user requests with representative voice app responses*

Your functional requirements feed directly into how you lay out the flow of your dialogs by pointing to where your VUI design needs to incorporate confirmations or disambiguation to fill multiple slots. Remember from earlier chapters that slots (or entities) are basically variables for capturing some specific bit of content, like a food item or time of day:

- Where several pieces of information fill slots, you need all required slots filled to reach your goal. That means every combination, including all or none of the slots or some slots, allowing users to speak naturally and continue without starting over or repeating. Your response ideally matches the user request in level of detail. You track this via archetype sentences—utterances that are representative for the most typical requests, like *What can I eat?* or *Can I eat $FOOD?* You also track task completion and expected variation.

- If the cost of being wrong is high, you need some type of confirmation. If it's also a tricky recognition task, you need more explicit confirmation. Determine your confirmation flow based on accuracy importance and on recognition and parsing challenges.

- If ambiguous user requests are possible, you need a way to narrow down the possibilities, either based on context and logic or by asking the user. This is based on expected variation combined with risk and recognition and parsing challenges.

- Anywhere users can say something, they can fail to be understood. So you need to get them back on track, give hints on what to say, or start over. You need something at every dialog turn. The expected variation, task completion, and recognition and parsing challenges help figure this out.

- If data is needed from a source other than the user, if the result needs to be saved for later or results in some content fulfillment, you need to access data or external devices. You know this by your functionality, task completion, and data needs. Capture at what point in the flow some data is needed, even if you don't yet know where to get it from. The same goes for authentication and identification needs.

Let's look at how this applies to one of the procedure prep intents: contacting one's care team. Table 5-1 provides a summary of some of the intent requirements from tables in Chapter 4. You can expect two slots (name and phone type). There's some trickiness in pronunciation and possible ambiguity that's constrained by knowing what's in the user's contact list. In terms of cost or risk, the worst that can happen is a call to the wrong person.

Table 5-1. *Summary of Contact intent requirements*

Functionality	User wants to call their doctor or the procedure facility.
Archetype sentence	<Call my doctor's office> <Call Dr. Smith's cell phone>
Task completion	User hears a phone number for a care team member. Dialing may be offered.
Expected variation	User's request can be ambiguous (same name, multiple phones). Data is user-dependent (contact list).
Cost/risk	Low–Medium
External data needed	Care team contact info.
User data needed	User contact list.
Recognition challenge	Medium. Personal names from limited list.
Parsing challenge	Low.

Assuming your care team has more than one contact, you have a core intent ("call") and two slots, one required (contact name or identity) and one optional (phone type; optional if we assume a default phone), resulting in four paths:

1. Core intent only (*Make a call*) needs follow-on dialog to get whom to call.

2. Core intent + contact (*Call my doctor, Call Doctor Jones*) could be a complete request or might need disambiguation if there are several Dr. Jones's or if Dr. Jones has multiple phone numbers.

3. Core intent + contact + phone type (*Call Doctor Jones' cell phone*) is a fully specified request, but it might not match any name or phone type in the user's contact list.

4. Core intent + phone type (*Call the cell phone*) is incomplete and unlikely, but could be the result of recognition failure so you need to deal with it, just in case.

If there's no match, tell the user and provide some guided advice. If Dr. Jones has no cell phone listing, you'd help the user by saying so rather than just responding *Sorry*. Depending on your integration, more helpful responses include offering another option or simply *There's no mobile listing for Doctor Jones. Calling the office instead*. What if your user asks: *What's Doctor Jones' phone number*? You could incorporate that in the flow and offer a choice of reading the number or connecting the user. You'll learn a lot more in later chapters about how to decide on these handling details. Figure 5-2 shows what an initial medium-level voice dialog flow might look like for paths 1–3.

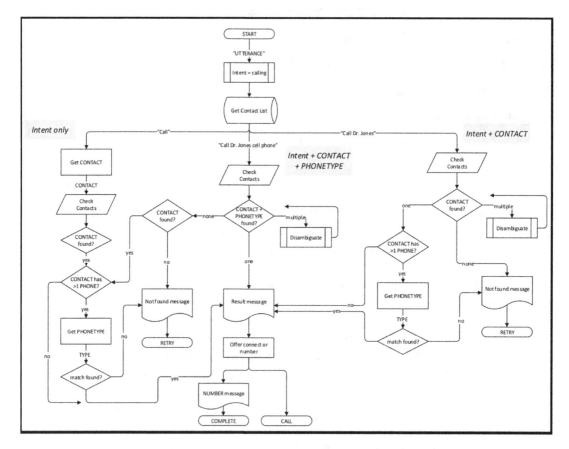

Figure 5-2. *A medium-level dialog flow for the partial Contact intent of the sample procedure prep IVA*

Do people create flows like this? Absolutely. Whether you use a simple drawing program or a tool that generates functional code, we highly recommend using some type of flow like this. It helps you track behaviors to avoid forgetting happy paths or error conditions. It helps establish where in the flow data dips are expected, which affects both design and coding.

Dialog Manager Graph, Yes; Hierarchical Decision Tree, No

Get in the habit of calling what's in Figure 5-2 a "flow" rather than a "tree." It's a common mistake to think that voice interactions follow only logical steps, that users won't start over or jump around to some degree, that they won't make mistakes or repeat a step, or that each end point should be reachable by only one path.

People have different mental models—there's no reason why they shouldn't be allowed to make a request in several different ways. There may be a logical best path to find one's account balance that doesn't involve asking for bill pay, but users have all kinds of reasons for doing things in various ways. Their reasons don't really matter to you—if they reach the result they want and they're happy taking five steps instead of one step, who are you to say your shorter way is better? If you block their way of doing it because it's extra work for you and you think *People don't/shouldn't do it that way*, guess what? Your users won't like what you created, and they'll think your smart voice app sounds and acts stupid. Instead, think about the interaction as a path from A to B, from initiation to fulfillment. B can be reached via one of many paths, including different conditions resulting in retries, different context for different users, and utterances with different wording and different levels of information or ambiguity. B is reached when your logic says it is: when you have the required and optional pieces of information to fulfill the user's request. You don't really care how the user got to B, only that you made sure the path they chose led them there.

One big reason that some voice interactions sound stupid to users comes from throwing every user request into the same NL interpretation without taking into account enough of the user's context. People build conversations on what was said previously and expect environmental awareness of their dialog partner. As a user, I keep context of what I just said and what happened as a result, what's happening with various things around me; this is my current foreground short-term context. I also know things about myself, like what relevant accounts I have, my geolocation, time of day, and so on; this is a longer-term context, a constant or predictable background. My conversation builds on these contexts. This means that a voice app needs to track and update the previous "state." That recent state, the short-term context, needs to be modified with each dialog turn based on outcome, like a narrow time slice of things that came before. You'll learn a lot about context in Chapter 14.

SUCCESS TIP 5.6 CHOOSE MEANINGFUL INTENT NAMES AND LABELS   Use intent names for flows and code and prompts—ideally, everyone on your team refers to them, so names should be logical and easy to write and remember and search on. Choose a naming convention where you can just look at the label and know a lot about what and how the user made their request. At a minimum, you have the same number as the number of slots that the intent takes. For example, the names foodSearch.item, foodSearch.day, and foodSearch.item.time tell you that the general intent is a food question and what else was specified. You'd add one for neither slot filled. This helps you being systematic about specifying necessary prompts and behavior for each context. Also take into consideration known future changes. So, if you already plan to split the Contact feature into email, text, and phone calls, you may as well split it right away even if you have no handling yet.

FROM THE VOICE TRENCHES

When asked what makes a VUI design spec, one developer said, "If you're a developer who's new to voice, you'll be surprised at the level of detail in quality VUI specs. Non-voice devs will naturally think 'How hard can this be?' to which my answer is often 'Harder than you think!' Dialog design has subtle complexities. A competent VUI designer takes the time and effort to spell out how it all ought to work, leaving nothing to interpretation. Using clearly specified logic is excellent. A good dialog designer has to understand basic programming logic, and a good developer needs to understand VUI designers have reasons for what they do. It's important to establish mutual common ground. Have regular meetings and ask each other questions."

A product manager points out, "Clearly separate intended behavior from implementation details. Let's say you're building some device. Instead of 'Feature X has the settings A, B, C, controlled with a toggle switch,' start with 'Feature X has the settings A, B, C.' Then link to and specify the UI for the different interfaces: 'X is controlled with a toggle on the top panel' for one and 'Typical requests for X are "Set X to A" or "Change X to B." If D or E is requested, respond that these are not supported' for the other. This helps you treat the different UIs equally while remembering they're not the same."

Capturing and Documenting VUI Design

VUI designs are typically captured and documented in three ways, each with its own strengths and purposes. You should make use of all three: dialog flows, sample dialogs (mocks), and detailed design specifications. Let's look briefly at each one.

Dialog Flows

Some dialog flows are high-level overviews of the core intents and experience; others are highly detailed. This is the best tool for everyone on the team to establish, for example, where data access takes place and the overall sequence of steps in multistep dialogs with multiple slots. You want to settle on the overall logic flow before getting into the detailed design. When you add prompt wording, use a notation that signifies draft status. We often use all caps or angle brackets. Once your detailed design is done, you might update your flows with the prompt wording. Figure 5-3 shows a few realistic examples.

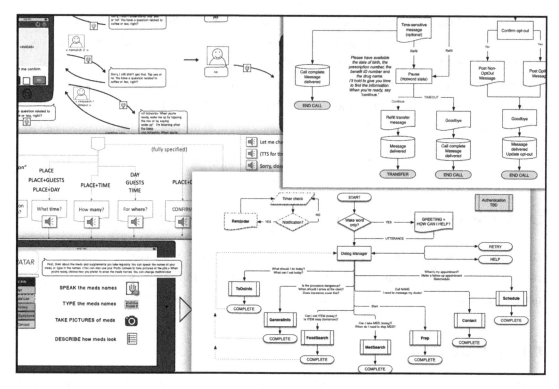

Figure 5-3. *VUI dialog flows take many shapes—literally*

SUCCESS TIP 5.7 STICK TO LOGIC AND DESCRIPTIONS IN EARLY FLOWS   To keep everyone focused on the flow and logic early on, rather than on the wording of prompts and other details, exclude fully phrased prompts in those flows but use descriptions. For example, all error messages might say "ERROR MESSAGE + OFFER OPTION" instead of a context-specific complete sentence like *Dr. Jones doesn't have an office phone. Want to call the lab instead*? Once you move into detailed design, you can easily change the descriptors to full prompts.

Sample Dialogs

Expanding each box in the flow involves creating the sample dialogs you first saw in Chapters 2 and 3. Also known as VUI mocks, they're a set of short dialogs, each illustrating a representative snapshot or path through the conversation between user and VUI. Each dialog should include clear descriptions of the context and condition for that dialog. You want to include successful happy paths of course. You also must show what unsuccessful interaction will be like for the user. You learn much more about error conditions in later chapters. Importantly, sample dialogs should exist as both written interactions (for convenience) and audio recordings (for relevance).

Sample dialogs are the basis for detailed design. They're the prototyping wireframes of VUI design. Together, sample dialogs and dialog flows are great tools for illustrating the intended style and features of any voice app and for making user stories concrete. You can think of a complete VUI design spec as a complete set of sample dialogs accompanied by logic or pseudocode and flows. It's fair to say that all experienced VUI practitioners make use of some combination of sample dialogs and flows when starting to create voice interactions. Figure 5-4 gives you a taste of what written sample dialogs might look like.

MULTIMODAL CORNER

Include examples of all expected multimodal interactions in every set of sample dialogs, starting from the very first ones, even if just simple descriptive notes at first. Include a simple visual version with the audiovisual mockups. Focus on showing how the modalities are coordinated and fit use cases with modality differences, such as hands-free vs. eyes-free. Show how listening is initiated (wake word, push-to-talk, etc.), different input modes (speech, buttons, keyboard), and how action states like listening, idling, or processing are indicated (icons, lights, etc.).

Direct match; 2 requests ("yes") – initial prompt v2

System:	Hi, I'm your Wine Steward. Always happy to pair a wine with your food. Tell me what dish or type of food you're having, like 'chicken' or 'fettuccini alfredo.'
User:	*chicken cacciatore*
System:	[All right.] With chicken dishes you can't go wrong with a Cha... Would you like help with another pairing?
User:	*yes please*
System:	Great. What food or dish?
User:	*blue cheese*
System:	[Excellent.] My personal choice for blues is a Merlot, but othe... even a Port. Would you like help with another pairing?
User:	*no thanks*
System:	Alright then. Enjoy. And remember: the best wine is the wine ...

Scenario: User has entered room, and tapped start button.

Speech	Screen
Hello. Your doctor has asked for a clean urine sample. To allow your doctor to get an accurate result, it's important that you follow all steps carefully. I'm here to help you with that. Don't worry: this is a recorded voice. No one is watching or recording you. Now, say '**repeat**' or say '**continue**'.	All screens: Complete text of VO. Arrows: 'go back'/ '**continue**'. Buttons: 'Repeat', 'Call Nurse'
Umm sure continue	
First, put the towelettes and the cup on the table near you so you can reach them later. Don't open the cup yet. Say '**continue**' when you're done with this step.	Picture of cup with lid on a table by toilet Arrows: 'go back'/ '**continue**'. Buttons: 'Repeat', 'Call Nurse'
Okay continue	
Wash your hands with soap and rinse thoroughly with warm water. Wipe your hands with paper towels and throw away the paper. Then say '**continue**'. You can also say '**repeat**' or '**go back**'.	Picture of hand washing and throwing towel without touching the garbage can

		Speech	Screen text	Screen graphics + REPEAT & BACK
	App	Let's verify that you have everything. You need two bottles of EasyLax, and a glass of cold or warm clear liquid to mix your first dose with. When you're ready, say START.	You should have • EasyLax; 2 bottles • Clear liquid; 8 oz	Buttons: START MORE INFO Graphics: Product pictures
	User	Start!		[START]
	App	In a glass, add one dose of EasyLax to approximately 8 ounces of liquid. Stir the mixture until the powder has dissolved completely. Now drink that first dose. Then say NEXT.	• 1 cap EasyLax+ 8 ounces of liquid • Stir until completely dissolved • Drink the whole glass	Buttons: NEXT MORE INFO Graphics: Stirring mix

Scenario: User is in the grocery store 2 days before procedure.

#	Speaker	Dialog
1	User	< MIC > can I have rice?
2	System	You can still have white rice today, but no brown rice. Tomorrow, you can only have clear liquids until after your procedure.
3	User	What about white bread?
4	System	Yes, white bread is still okay today, but not tomorrow.

Figure 5-4. *Sample dialog examples*

SUCCESS TIP 5.8 PRESENT SAMPLE DIALOGS AS AUDIO   Text versions of sample dialogs are useful for thinking through designs and discussing them with others, but never forget that spoken and written languages are quite different. In reviews, always start with an audio version, pre-recorded using the actual voice if possible; otherwise, read out loud, even role-play. Avoid showing the written text until later. In fact, review documentation sometimes includes "DO NOT TURN THIS PAGE" warnings. It's easy to see the issue, for example, with a list of options or long description of unfamiliar names or numbers. A written bullet list of ingredients is easy to scan visually to make sure you have everything, but with a voice-only version of the same recipe without pauses or navigation commands, you're likely to miss something. While working out the design, talk to yourself, and read samples to others around you. This is VUI: it's all about the sound.

Detailed Design Specifications

Your detailed VUI design should obviously strive for covering enough details to make the intended behavior clear in every context and condition during the development process. This is obviously true for any design in any modality, but it's probably less obvious how to do this for voice than for a visual interface where you include images of screens, exact measurements, and color codes. Detailed VUI design documentation should cover the following at a minimum:

- Every intent, name, and description

- For each intent

  - Archetype utterances and any expected words

  - Slot names and values, required and optional

  - Outcome and next step for every combination of context and conditions

- Context: user identity or category, user preferences, environment, previous user request and result (dialog path), current system activity, and so on

  - **Conditions**: Behavior for each expected user request status (recognized and handled, recognized and not handled, not recognized, etc.)

  - **Prompts**: Reference labels and exact wording for each context and condition, including error handling, retries, randomization, and so on

  - **Logic and pseudocode describing behavior clearly and consistently**

  - **Data needs**: Type, format, from where, and saved to where

Of course, the tool you use to document your design depends on where you work, whom you work with, and what platform and voice service you're using. Use a documentation style or tool that captures any system or platform limitations that affect the design. And use one that makes it easy to capture what can be done! You'll probably use different approaches for multistep dialog tasks vs. one-step "one and done" requests. And no matter what, of course you'll need to clarify and change your design as things change.

SUCCESS TIP 5.9 PICK A NOTATION   To convey the design (or interpret it as intended), you'll need a notation that is clear and easy to use, easy to type in flows and specs, and transfers well between design and development. We like to use all caps plus some symbol for easier search to indicate variable content, like $FOOD. Your choice is influenced by your developing environment, programming language, and your tools, but it should be usable for all involved. For archetype utterances, it's important to not lose track of them being illustrative rather than a promise of handling precise utterances. It's equally important to avoid detailed design too soon. Flag the "serving suggestion" or draft nature of a prompt. We often use angle brackets for this, but you can use anything that works well for your situation, for example, <OK. Calling $NAME, $PHONETYPE>. Pseudocode can be useful because it reduces the need for interpretation and is easy to search on. It can also help the design process when making sure all use cases are covered. We've made great use of simple pseudocode for contexts and conditions, such as "is_muted = TRUE" or "$AMOUNT >= maxAmount". Whatever you use, make sure everyone is onboard and clear on what things mean.

VUI Design Documentation Approaches

Let's take a look at your most common options for documenting VUI designs.

Self-Contained Design Tools

What is it?	Graphical software tools for VUI design. The goal is to minimize coding and worrying about details to quickly create a functional VUI dialog that can run on Alexa or Google or either. Examples: Voiceflow, Witlingo, Jovo, Voice Apps, and many others.
Pros	Fast. Can lay out a design and turn it into a functional dialog. Great for concepts and simple contexts. Don't need programming knowledge to get something up and running.
Cons	Typically limited in functionality and features. Many are not mature, still changing. All emphasize speed of creation over flexibility and quality design. Some favor one platform over another. Some ramp-up time needed.
Take-home	Great for smaller projects and sample dialogs. Find what works for you and doesn't limit you while staying true to the platform you'll develop and run on.

Open Platform-Specific Tools

What is it?	Examples: Google Dialogflow, Alexa Conversations.
Pros	Limited to what's available through the platform or voice service, which automatically keeps you from designing out-of-scope features and allows you to not deal with every detail. Can therefore be very powerful.
Cons	Limited to what's available through the platform or voice service. Always evolving; new versions can be unstable. Usually involves some coding, which can be a drawback for some designers. Some ramp-up time needed.
Take-home	If you know you'll design for one of the common platforms, these tools are well worth looking at.

Proprietary or Closed Platform-Specific Tools

What is it?	Highly flexible and powerful VUI design tools often created by a large effort over a long time. Examples: Nuance Application Studio (NAS), Nuance Mix, and others.
Pros	Powerful and often mature. Often tie together every kind of design documentation, automatically updating change in all relevant places to keep things synchronized. Can generate code and prompt lists, even a prototyping setup. Provide features corresponding to what's available in the platform and only those features.
Cons	Not accessible unless you're in a relationship with the company who controls the tool. Auto-generated code isn't optimized for production unless everything is streamlined, and it typically needs rework for larger realistic complex systems. Associated with a particular company's platform; it isn't generalized. Ramp-up time can be steep.
Take-home	Top of the top—use them if you have access.

Standard Documentation Tools

What is it?	Standard office software, sometimes with added tailored scripts. Examples: text (Word), spreadsheets (Excel, Google Docs), flow (Visio, Balsamiq). Can hook to databases and generate prompt lists.
Pros	Completely flexible, can tailor exactly to your needs. Not dependent on others changing feature availability. No training ramp-up time needed. Easily available.
Cons	You have to do all the work. Any auto-generation is limited to what you create. Make sure everyone referencing the documentation uses the same notation.
Take-home	Probably the most widespread VUI design tools today—don't underestimate the power of simplicity.

In Figure 5-5, you can see a couple of examples from different VUI design specifications. The spreadsheet approach is best for broad-but-shallow interactions, like initial open-ended interactions that are no more than one or two turns long. They provide an easy view of the big picture and patterns across contexts. For longer transactional dialogs, a combination of flow and a word processing format with clickable links is often the better choice. In bigger implementations, you'll probably combine both.

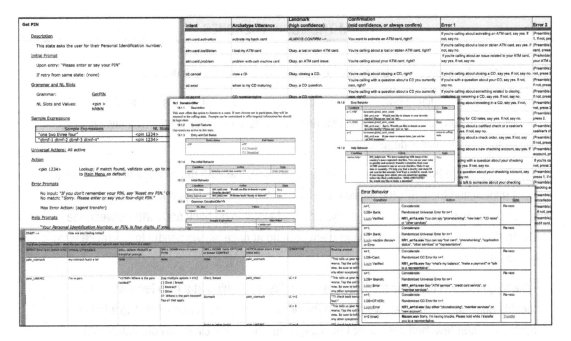

Figure 5-5. *VUI dialog specs can be a few tabs in a spreadsheet or hundreds of pages of documentation, but they all have more details than sample dialogs or flows*

As you can see, you have lots of choices. No "one way" to VUI documentation is used by all voice practitioners. You need to determine what works for you based on many factors: your work style, team structure, and familiarity with voice, company demands, voice platform, infrastructure, existing designs, tool availability, type of voice interaction, multimodality, or content. We used all approaches mentioned here in various combinations with varying results and levels of happiness. Investigate your options—options change constantly as tools come and go. Make use of anything already in place. It could be design patterns or existing designs for similar voice dialogs. Those may impact your documentation choice, or make it faster to get started. At times you'll have little or no choice because the approaches and formats have already been set.

FROM THE VOICE TRENCHES

A developer-turned-VUI-designer comments on how to review a VUI design:

"If there's a paired dialog flow, I always start with that. For me it makes the most sense. A lot of developers don't care about the dialog flow, and I have no #*@!! idea why. I always have. Big picture, then smaller details.

I can't emphasize the dialog flow's importance enough, like with mixed audiences. Business folks understand them. It's the easiest doc for the largest range of people to understand. It's great for orienting people in a bigger system. It's helpful to go back and forth between the dialog flow and VUI spec; even having them both up at once allows people to reference what you went over.

I like to go through the spec module by module, first explaining at a high level what the module does such that when we get into the details, people can connect that to what I said earlier. The first few modules might take longer, but then if it's clear and predictable (like similar conditions written the same way), even a non-techie person can learn the lingo and follow any detailed VUI design. Then I usually go node by node to a point. When there's a million conditions, it may become more 'In scenario A, we go down this path' and follow that through, then go back to scenario B. Specs must have clickable links which allow you to step through any scenario.

Explaining what to look out for and why helps folks who have less of a tech perspective, even with easy modules, like 'This is your transfer funds module… We have checks in place to ensure there's enough money, that this business rule is caught here, etc. etc.' Talking about business rules piques their interest because everyone knows what a transfer funds module does. Those small details up front help get them interested and also let them know you 'got it.'

I'm a developer who always cared about design. I like when developers say, 'If you do this part this way, the experience is the same, but it'll be much easier for me to code.' That's a good sign they understand, are paying attention, and can compromise."

Many tools today are aimed at letting developers jump in with little or no voice or design expertise. It's cool, and one reason for the explosion of voice development, but for enterprise-level voice systems, you'll probably need something else to coordinate and track details across teams. And you'll certainly start with design, not development.

MULTIMODAL CORNER

Include thumbnail images for screens in detailed specs. Show in parallel what's expected on screens (graphics/ images, static text, texts of users' recognized utterances, buttons/keyboard) with representative requests. Don't forget to show what happens when utterances are handled correctly and when errors occur (Chapter 13).

The detailed design references another important set of documented information: the VUI style guide. The core purpose of the style guide is to establish consistency. This means consistency on every level: prompt wording and delivery within and across conversations, VUI behavior, interpretation, and anything relative to any branding. Style guides are crucial when there's more than one designer working on portions of a VUI or on related VUIs for a company, but even a lone designer needs a style guide to keep dialogs consistent. Developers and speech scientists need it to ensure that user behavior is handled consistently and that words and phrases are consistently interpreted.

SUCCESS TIP 5.10 BEWARE OF DESIGN BY COMMITTEE   The biggest challenge during VUI design is funneling the (typically) good intentions of everyone involved in the project. Because the medium is voice, everyone has an opinion about what users will say and how best to respond. *I speak the language. How hard can this be?* is a natural thought. Your solution involves using recorded sample dialogs to settle on the overall conversational style. Capture decisions in your style guide to keep the style and behavior consistent. A useful approach can be to present multiple dialogs, where some are obviously bad experiences and others are great but also involve a lot of implementation work. Involve the team, asking them to find the good or bad in each. Early design is a good time to settle on the amount of variation you'll include in prompting because it'll likely impact the development effort. Keep detailed notes on decisions made and the reasons for each.

FROM THE VOICE TRENCHES

In-lab user testing can absolutely give you valid data. When running a study on using voice for texting while driving, we wondered how relevant the data would be since the whole study took place in a lab using a driving simulator. The task involved comparing driving performance while (1) using a mobile phone for text messaging and (2) using voice for dictation—asking participants to do the first task while actually driving would have been both dangerous and illegal. However, when one user held up his mobile phone to better see the screen while all other participants held their phones in their laps to "hide it from view," we knew the data was representative—and that people still text while driving (lab setup shown in Figure 5-6).

Figure 5-6. *In-lab participant driving simulator and moderator observation setup*

Prototyping and Testing Your Assumptions

As you create real-world VUIs of increasing complexity and breadth of functionality and for different user groups and domains, it becomes increasingly important to verify your assumptions. An Alexa skill or Google action running on your device at home is an example of a functional prototype before it's been optimized, or **tuned**. Such prototypes are easier than ever to put together for quick testing. But there are several reasons why you should also make use of nonfunctional and low-fi prototypes, such as paper prototypes and Wizard of Oz (WOZ) setups, where a person plays the role of the computer to elicit certain responses from a user.

Functional prototypes are limited for one crucial reason: no voice implementation has perfect performance, especially before it's been tuned based on real user data. A functional prototype, especially during early development, is likely to fail on some user requests, limiting your ability to do targeted testing on the functionality and users' behaviors. Another important limit of testing with functional systems, no matter how tuned they are, is that you can't force a specific behavior. So, for example, if you want to test how users respond to a particular error handling, your only option is to make a separate copy or other coding changes to force an error to take place where you want it to.

Lower-fi methods, including Wizard of Oz setups, provide that control. Low-fi nonfunctional prototypes also allow you quick testing of ideas that take some effort to implement before spending time and money to do so. You can even simulate data interaction.

SUCCESS TIP 5.11 IT'S NEVER TOO EARLY TO CHECK ASSUMPTIONS   Whether you're creating a restaurant finder, a companion for older users, or an investment tool, check your idea as soon as you can find a few representative users. Describe what you have in mind; ask what they'd find useful and what concerns they have. If you have prompts in mind, see how they respond. No tools needed, just role-play, and notice the responses. You're dealing with voice, so all interactions should be spoken, and responses should be heard. Make careful notes of your test users' responses and use them as archetype utterances in your use cases. Make equally careful notes on what prompt wording you're testing. Your users' responses may change drastically if you change prompt wording or delivery even a tiny bit.

Voice UX and Prototyping Approaches

While prototyping and user testing is a skill needing more depth and detail than we can cover in this book, you'll learn more about it and the data it provides in later chapters. For now, here's an introduction to the main methods used for testing voice apps. They are all valid and important techniques for collecting primary targeted voice data. Notice that they're all focusing on qualitative testing. It's what you want at this stage of development. Your best quantitative testing and analysis will take place once you have real user data from your tuned in-production voice app.

Hallway "Guerilla" Studies

What is it?	The name is descriptive: very quick manual testing in person, often without any props, such as describing a simple context, reading a prompt, and asking the participant to respond. Also used for asking about expected behavior in a context. Any prompts tested are read by the tester.
Pros	Very low overhead and inexpensive. Can test on friends, family, and coworkers who are "not in the know." Nimble: Can ask follow-up questions and modify the test instantly.
Cons	Extremely low-fi and informal; participant has an unrealistic experience. Consistent prompt delivery is difficult. If the task is unrealistic or inconsistent, results are misleading.
Take-home	Great for "sanity-checking" general assumptions and simple short voice interactions; less great for longer dialogs, specific user populations, or contexts.

Low-Fidelity Mockups (Voice Version of "Wireframes")

What is it?	One small step above hallway studies, voice mockups can be created in many of the tools we mentioned earlier in this chapter or by simply importing a set of audio files in an image of the flow you want to test. Simply click each in turn to respond to your test participant's utterance. It's a manual test of the sample dialogs. Any prompts tested should be pre-recorded or using TTS for consistency. Longer dialogs can be tested
Pros	Low overhead and inexpensive. Quick to modify. No need for coding or backend access. No need for tuned functional interaction, so easy to test alternative paths.
Cons	Unrealistic experience. Prompts are usually not using the production voice or final wording, so results can be misleading.
Take-home	Great for catching big issues as long as your prompts and participants are representative.

Wizard of Oz ("WOZ")

What is it?	The name comes from the concept of "the man behind the curtain" in *The Wizard of Oz* stories: what appears to be a machine is actually controlled by a person. The tester (the Wizard) uses a GUI to respond in predetermined ways to user voice requests. Often involves a Wizard and a moderator who sets context and asks follow-up questions. A few VUI development platforms include WOZ tools, but you can create your own. More on WOZ testing in Chapter 16.
Pros	Experience and "system behavior" can be controlled precisely. Participants don't know they're interacting with a nonfunctional system. When participants and context are representative, data is highly valid. Can be done in a lab or remotely.
Cons	Very difficult to be a consistent Wizard. Wizard needs to be very familiar with the design and voice technology to provide a realistic experience.
Take-home	The workhorse of VUI design. Find a setup that works best in your environment and learn how to use it to collect valuable data.

Functional Prototypes

What is it?	Several platforms and voice services allow you to test your designs with functional recognition and interpretation, allowing participants to speak and interact as if with a final product. More on functional prototypes in Chapter 16.
Pros	Realistic experience, especially when coming out of the intended hardware. Relatively quick and inexpensive to create a basic experience.
Cons	Limited accuracy when not tuned. Outcomes are not predictable and can't be easily controlled. If done using Google or Alexa voice service, you need to capture the results since you won't have direct access to the participant data.
Take-home	Realistic environment for the participant generates valuable data, especially the more effort you spend on making it robust.

FROM THE VOICE TRENCHES

Several years ago, we toured a local tech company where UX researchers lamented that some developers observing usability studies of features they had built would laugh and question the intelligence of any participant who behaved in ways their implementation hadn't accounted for. Don't be like one of those developers. We have observed similar reactions in the observation room during usability studies. Yes, sometimes user behavior really is entertaining—but don't ever laugh at a user who tried using something you created and failed because you didn't understand their mental model or needs. Don't kid yourself, and don't feel bad either: capturing the many ways people want to do things with your app takes effort, but it's not impossible and you don't have to get it "perfect" on Day 1. So do your best, and plan for future iterative refinements and updates as you collect more data.

What's Next?

If you want to learn more about voice design and related implementation topics on a foundation level, we recommend *Designing Voice User Interfaces* (Pearl, 2016),[1] *Voice User Interface Design* (Cohen, Giangola, and Balogh, 2004),[2] and *Voice Interaction Design* (Harris, 2004).[3] If you think some of those books are getting too old to be worth your while, remember that technology changes a whole lot faster than people do, especially when it comes to basic human senses and communication. So trust these sources and pair them with current platform-specific material.

This chapter ends Part 2. You now have a more solid foundation than most for creating awesome voice solutions. Chapter 6 dives into the first in-depth topic for voice design and development.

---

[1]Pearl, C. (2016). *Designing Voice User Interfaces*. Sebastopol, CA: O'Reilly Media, Inc.

[2]Cohen, M. H., Giangola, J. P., Balogh, J. (2004). *Voice User Interface Design*. Boston, MA: Addison-Wesley.

[3]Harris, R. (2004). *Voice Interaction Design: Crafting the New Conversational Speech Systems*. San Francisco, CA: Morgan Kaufmann.

Summary

- Sample dialogs should be presented as audio, not just in writing, because hearing a conversation gives insights written versions won't capture.

- Use data from multiple sources to best guide your design assumptions and high-level VUI design choices.

- Base design and implementation decisions on data that is representative of your users.

- Different users take different paths through a conversation. Your design and implementation must account for that variation.

- There are several options for VUI documentation. Your choices depend on what's available to you and the type of VUI project you work on, but you should get in the habit of always incorporating sample dialogs, flow diagrams, and detailed design specs as each one fills a particular purpose.

PART III

The Building Phase: Design-Informed Development

This part is the book's core. Each chapter introduces code and design techniques that introduce a particular characteristic of conversational voice systems.

The first four chapters focus on core spoken dialog characteristics:

- In Chapter 6, you learn that voice system users subconsciously apply turn-taking "rules" to reach dialog resolution. You learn about three common dialog types—question-answer, action requests, and task completion requests—as well as how to handle fully specified requests with multiple slots.

- In Chapter 7, you learn how to handle incomplete and ambiguous requests and how to apply common disambiguation methods.

- Chapter 8 teaches you the importance of conveying reassurance and how to apply different confirmation strategies. You're introduced to discourse markers and backchannels.

- In Chapter 9, you learn about the challenges of navigating an audio-first interaction and find out how to make use of global commands, landmarks, and non-verbal audio.

Time to delve into speech recognition, parsing, and interpretation:

- In Chapter 10, you learn about recognition and synonym coverage, including regular expressions, statistical models, dictionaries, normalizing, and bootstrapping.

- Chapter 11 covers parsing, intent resolution, and understanding. You learn more about intents, ontologies, and using tagging guides and middle layers.

Next is a look at misunderstandings—avoiding them and recovering from them:

- Chapter 12 investigates how to maximize robustness. You learn several useful techniques for minimizing errors, including contextual help, recognize-and-reject, one-step correction, examples, tutorials, hidden options, confidence scores, and others.

- Chapter 13 shows you how to recover when miscommunication happens, as well as when to stop trying. Topics include meaningful error messaging, tapered and escalating errors, and various backoff techniques.

The last two chapters in this part dive into topics that are crucial to powerful and natural voice solutions:

- Chapter 14 focuses on context: how to create context-aware dialogs using anaphora, proactive behaviors, proximity, geolocation, and domain knowledge to create smarter interactions.

- Chapter 15 explores personalization and customization. Topics include identification, authentication, and privacy and security concerns. You also learn about system personas and TTS vs. recorded prompts.

At the end of this part, you have a solid understanding of voice systems, how to make them robust, and how to address the issues you're most likely to encounter.

CHAPTER 6

Applying Human "Rules of Dialog" to Reach Conversation Resolution

This is the first chapter of Part 3, where you learn in depth the ins and outs of voice design and development, one key topic at a time. *Don't sweat the details* might be good advice for life in general, but as you've started to see, in voice development it's all about the details. To make a conversational UI seem "smart," it can't only make the voice sound human, add conversational phrases, recognize and understand what the user said, get the context, and know about that user and about the world in general—it has to do all those well to seem at least as smart as your average 3-year-old.

This chapter covers the basic building blocks of conversational VUI dialogs. You start by getting familiar with three conversational dialog patterns and what distinguishes each one. This is important for two reasons. First, these patterns cover most of the voice interactions you'll build, no matter the type of device or topic. Second, by understanding what people expect in each dialog pattern, you can predict responses and build robust voice interactions, even as reusable templates for any platform. You learn how to write prompts for the core dialog patterns that'll keep you out of trouble. Code samples cover turn-taking, initiating vs. responding, single slot vs. multi-slot, question answering (QA), action requests, and task completion requests.

© Ann Thymé-Gobbel, Charles Jankowski 2021
A. Thymé-Gobbel and C. Jankowski, *Mastering Voice Interfaces*, https://doi.org/10.1007/978-1-4842-7005-9_6

Dialog Acts, Games, and Turns—and Grice

At the core of all VUI designs today is the conversational interaction, or dialog. When both of us authors were first at Nuance, a common title for folks specifying the flow and design details was in fact "dialog designer." No matter if you're creating VUIs for mobile apps, in-home assistants, IVRs, games, or cars, to a great extent the same dialog design patterns apply (with predictable variation based on multimodality and context) because you're dealing with the same strengths and limitations of human speech communication: a VUI dialog is a joint activity of audio-based communication between two participants.

This book focuses on what can be described as targeted goal-oriented cooperative dialogs. These dialogs cover most of today's VUI interactions. In these dialogs, it's assumed that Participant A has some intention in mind (yes, that's why we refer to intents) when initiating a dialog with Participant B, to which B is expected to respond. The VUI working assumption is that A and B share an understanding of A's goal and that they will cooperate to fulfill it, if possible. A dialog consists of two or more dialog turns: minimally, A initiates, B responds, and...done. One dialog turn is one participant "holding the floor" by talking or doing something; turn-taking is the behavior of switching between participants taking on the role of initiator vs. responder, or speaker vs. listener. Turn-taking is ruled by all those subconscious rules of language you learned about in Chapter 2. A set of turns and their expected interaction through turn-taking is sometimes referred to as a dialog game; the turns are dialog acts or speech acts with particular characteristics. Examples of high-level dialog acts are Greeting, Yes/No question, WH question,[1] Statement, Acknowledge, Hedge, Thank, and Request.

SUCCESS TIP 6.1 USE DIALOG ACT LABELS IN VUI DESIGN   The dialog act terminology works well for early designs and design patterns. You don't have to stick with a particular theoretical framework if you don't want to; just make use of the parts that help your work. You'll also find that some natural language processing and machine learning work actively makes use of these categories in various ways.

---

[1]WH questions are ones starting with When, What, Which, Who, Why, Where, or How.

Each dialog game has required turns and optional turns, and they can be nested, but at a high level they all follow the same pattern. This is illustrated in Figure 6-1, where asterisks indicate required turns and parentheses indicate optional turns.

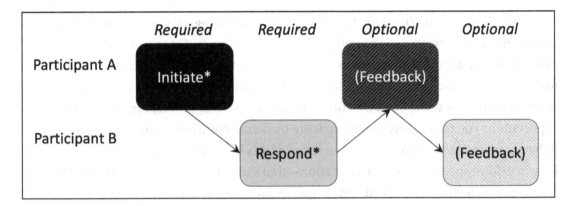

Figure 6-1. *VUI dialog pattern archetype*

The beauty of thinking this way is that you can abstract from people's subconscious conversational patterns to design and implement robust VUI interactions, applying specific patterns to specific contexts.[2] You learn how in this chapter. In many VUI dialogs on today's voice assistants, Participant A is the user (initiator), and Participant B is the VUI (responder). In VUI dialogs for IVRs, it's often the other way around once the call has been initiated. Here are two more definitions that are applicable to the dialog types you'll be most interested in when creating VUIs:

> *A dialogue appears as an alternation of turns, each a sequence of speech acts performed by the same actor...each turn may well be formed by more than one speech act.*[3]

---

[2]If you're interested in learning more about the related research, do an online search on these terms and "discourse structure." Different methodologies use different names and slice the space differently depending on the goal, but they all address the same overall questions of how to categorize and describe spoken dialogs. We're staying agnostic to specific frameworks to focus on the concepts in general.

[3]Airenti, G., Bara, B., and Colombetti, M. (1993). Conversation and Behavior Games in the Pragmatics of Dialogue. Cognitive Science 17, 197–256.

> *Dialog games are cooperative activities of information exchange: the players strive to achieve a common understanding on a true and informative answer to some problem or question on the basis of observation and considered opinion.*[4]

Now you might say, *Hang on. I've been in plenty of dialogs that weren't particularly cooperative and some that were mighty one-sided!* Absolutely. One feature in the procedure prep app steps the user through a set of instructions. You'll learn about how to deal with out-of-context requests later, but there's only so much you can do if your users want to mess with your VUI—the more of that you respond to, the greater the expectations you create. Any dialogs that are by nature confrontational, like political debates, are interesting but outside the scope of this book. We also don't focus on fully free-form speech-to-text like dictation—that's too one-sided to be a cooperative conversation. Social bots and adventure games are also not our focus for space constraints. However, the details we cover apply to those applications as well, once you realize those conversations are sets of shorter distinct dialogs, or dialog acts, that are chained together through additional "rules of engagement."

Turn-taking is done differently across device types and implementations. While common dialog rules say to avoid interrupting the current speaker, as humans we do it often. Telephones allow interruptions since people can talk and listen at the same time. This is full-duplex; and you take advantage of it in over-the-phone VUIs, such as IVRs, by implementing barge-in: allowing users to interrupt the VUI simply by speaking instead of first saying a wake word or pressing a button (half-duplex).

We separate the targeted goal-oriented dialog games into three similar yet distinct usage patterns: question answering, action requests, and task completion requests. Table 6-1 shows examples of each type, what the user might say and how the VUI might respond.

---

[4]L. Carlson (1985). *Dialogue Games: An Approach to Discourse Analysis.* Springer Verlag.

Table 6-1. *Goal-oriented dialogs with general utterance examples, dialog acts, and VUI responses*

	Question answering	Action request	Task completion request
User utterances	When does Na Na's open? Did Tolstoy write *War and Peace*?	Mute the TV! Play "Waterloo" by ABBA.	Send a message to David saying, "I'll be there in ten." Get a table at Na Na's for six people at 7 PM tonight.
Dialog act	WH question, Yes/No question	Command	Command
VUI response	Statement	Action + (statement)	Action + statement

Now look at Table 6-2 for examples of the three dialog types within the procedure prep assistant. The utterances should look familiar: they're archetypes from Chapter 4.

Table 6-2. *Goal-oriented dialogs for the procedure prep helper application intents*

	Question answering	Action request	Task completion request
User utterances	How long will the procedure take? Can I eat rice today?	Call my doctor's office. What should I do today?	Make an appointment. Walk me through my procedure prep. For lunch I had a hamburger, fries, and a diet Coke.
Dialog act	WH question, Yes/No question	Command	Command
VUI response	Statement	Action + (statement)	Action + statement

In-Depth: Reaching the End of a Dialog Through Grice's Cooperative Principle

Language philosopher Paul Grice analyzed many hours of dialog, leading to his conclusion that people make assumptions about how dialog participants behave.[5] We expect truthfulness, relevance, brevity, and clarity, with the goal of efficiently reaching a mutually shared dialog "end." Grice captured this in his Cooperative Principle (*Make your contribution such as is required, at the stage at which it occurs, by the accepted purpose or direction of the talk exchange in which you are engaged*) and a set of four maxims, or rules of conversation that people subconsciously follow:

- **Quality**: Speakers are truthful and don't lie on purpose.

- **Quantity**: Speakers provide as much as info as is needed for understanding.

- **Manner**: Speakers try to be clear and brief, avoiding ambiguity and vagueness.

- **Relation**: Speakers aim for relevance to the current conversation.

There's more to conversations, of course, including how politeness and uncertainty play in and cultural dependency. These don't lessen Grice's insights; it just means the details may need to be modified depending on language and domain. Today's voice designers and developers assume this default conversational behavior, whether they're aware of Grice or not.

Question Answering

You may be familiar with question answering (Q-A) systems from information retrieval. A Q-A (or more acurately QA) dialog is just what it sounds like: the user asks a **question**, and the VUI **answers**. The user expects an informational response, ideally the answer to their question or at least a response explaining why the VUI can't help. There may

---

[5]Grice, H. P. (1975). "Logic and conversation." In Cole, P., and J. L. Morgan (Eds.), Speech Acts (41–58). New York, NY: Academic Press.

be a follow-up from either with a response from the other (more later in this chapter). Minimally one initiates and the other responds—this is one of those dialog turn adjacency pairs you learned about in Chapter 2:

Initiates*	**User**	*<Wakes up VUI, if needed>*
Initiates*	**User**	*When does Na Na's open?*
Responds*	**VUI**	*<Data lookup>*
Responds*	**VUI**	Na Na's *Chinese opens at 7 PM today.*
(Feedback)	**User**	*Thanks!*
(Feedback)	**VUI**	*You're welcome.*

Figure 6-2 illustrates the QA dialog pattern based on this sample dialog—notice how it's a more concrete instantiation of the pattern in Figure 6-1, showing one of the utterance examples from Table 6-1.

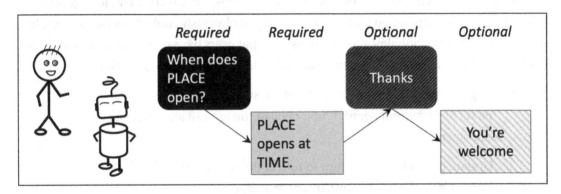

Figure 6-2. *Question answering (QA) dialog pattern with a restaurant example*

Building Out the Question Answering Example

Now it's time to get back to Dialogflow and make this sample dialog a reality.[6] Take a look at two more representative QA sample dialogs, this time for the procedure prep assistant (for brevity, we'll stop including the note to make the VUI listen).

---

[6]Load the files from 6-1.zip if you don't want to create everything from scratch.

User* *How long will the procedure take?*

VUI   *[Lookup]*

VUI* *The procedure normally takes between 45 minutes and an hour.*

~ ~ ~   ~ ~ ~   ~ ~ ~   ~ ~ ~

User* *Can I eat rice today?*

VUI   *[Lookup in context: rice + today]*

VUI* *You can still eat rice today.*

User   *Yay!*

As you can see, they follow the same general pattern from Figure 6-2. There are two basic types of QA interactions: those where the answer is always the same (**context-insensitive**) and those with dependencies or variables (**context-sensitive**). The first one, *How long will the procedure take?*, is the simpler one because the VUI response is constant; it's a general answer that doesn't depend on user context (though it obviously could be personalized). In a helper with FAQ functionality, it's safe to assume that users have many other questions that fit this pattern, so let's start by building a reusable context-insensitive QA dialog:

1. Log into the Dialogflow console. Make sure you're in the Voice First Development agent. If not, click in the left rail and choose that agent.

2. Update the welcome prompt to reflect the name and task. Choose Intents ➤ Default Welcome Intent ➤ Responses.

   Change "Welcome to Voice First Development." to "Welcome to the Procedure Preparation Helper." Click Save.

3. Delete any old intent. Because you've deleted the only "regular" intent, you'll see a notice to that effect, offering to Create the First One.

4. Create the new intent. Click Create the First One; name it qaProcedureLength.

5. Add a sample phrase. Choose Training Phrases ➤ Add Training Phrases; then type "How long will the procedure take?" Click Save. Note that when you click Save, a new empty box will appear in which to enter more phrases. You won't add any more yet.

6. Add a response. In the Responses section of the Intent, click Add Response. In Enter a Text Response Variant, type the response from the sample dialog: "The procedure normally takes between 45 minutes and an hour." Click Save.

7. Set dialog completion. Click the slider next to Set this intent as end of conversation. Click Save. Your Dialogflow should look similar to Figure 6-3.

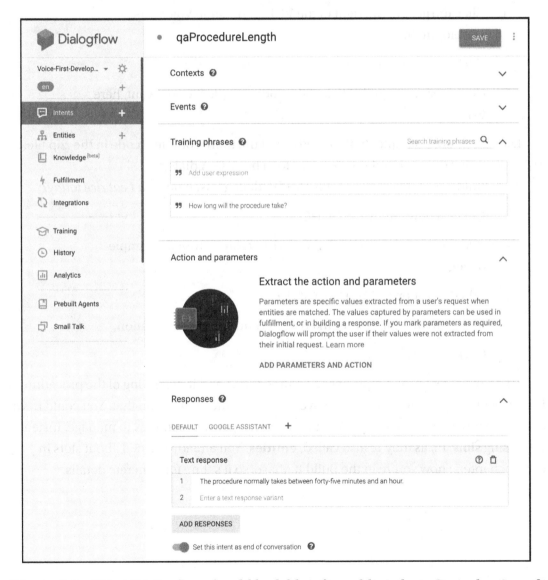

Figure 6-3. *What Dialogflow should look like after adding the qaProcedureLength intent*

8. Now test! As you learned in Chapter 3, you have many options: test with a Google Home device or mobile Google Assistant if you can. To get started, say, *OK, Google. Talk to Voice First Development.* Test early and often (Chapter 16).

We don't show any code listings in this chapter since we are building the interaction exclusively in Dialogflow at this point, rather than writing Python code from scratch. Remember from Chapter 3 that you can pull a configuration into Dialogflow:

1. Click the gear to the right of the VUI agent name Voice First Development.

2. Click Export and Import.

3. Click Restore from ZIP. Select the code sample file you want, here 6-1.zip.

Look at the code sample that's pulled out of the more complete code in the .zip file. This is your first dialog template, a pattern for a basic Q-A dialog.

Next, build a reusable context-sensitive QA dialog based on *Can I eat rice today?*[7]

1. Create a new intent. Call it qaCanEat.

2. Add the sample phrase "Can I eat rice today?" from the sample dialog.

3. Add the response: "You can eat rice today."

4. Make sure the intent is marked as the end of the conversation.

5. Click Save. Test it!

This works great if all people ever consume is rice and if the timing of the procedure is irrelevant. Fortunately, most of us have a more balanced diet than that. You could have a separate intent for each food item, but that would get very complex to manage. Instead, start using **slots**, or, as they're also called, **entities**. You already learned about slots in earlier chapters; now you're in the Build It phase, so it's time for concrete details.

---

[7]Load files from 6-2.zip.

Recall that slots (or entities, which is the term used by Google) are the variables capturing pieces of information in a voice or text request. One way to think of slots is something in your request that comes from a list: if you change the element of the list in your request, it still makes perfect sense. In the utterance *Can I eat rice today?*, rice is one of many candidates to fill a slot—you could replace "rice" with any food, and the sentence would still make sense.

Slots can occur in question answering, action request, or task completion request dialogs. There can be one or several in a dialog turn. Both terms are used by people in the field, so we want you to be aware of both—what term you use depends on where you first learned about them and what framework you use for your VUI work. In the Google framework, entities is the term commonly used at the time of writing.

Technically, "rice" isn't the slot itself, but the slot value assigned to the slot. The slot itself might be called something like `foodDrink`. After you define "rice" as a value of the `foodDrink` entity, you can then add many more possible values to it. Get in the habit of using meaningful slot names and settle on those names in conjunction with others on your team so the same names are used throughout design and implementation.

The great thing about slots is that you can separate the intent of the sentence (*Can I eat this or that?*) from the item asked about (*rice*). Without slots, you'd have to have at least one sample phrase for every single type of food or drink you might be asking about. That's crazy and not what you want. With entities, you can add more and more possible values without changing the sample phrases one bit. The carrier phrases of the intent, the ways in which users word a request while keeping the same meaning (*Can I…*, *Is it OK…*), remain the same in your intent, while the number of slot values can be arbitrarily large.

This is very much like writing a function in code, separating out the one used frequently so that you only need to define it once and can reuse it at will. Let's make "rice" from the sample phrase into a slot or entity:

1. Choose Entities ➤ Create Entity.

2. For Entity Name, type `foodDrink`.

3. Choose Click Here to Edit Entry and then enter "rice." Save. Your Dialogflow should now look similar to Figure 6-4.

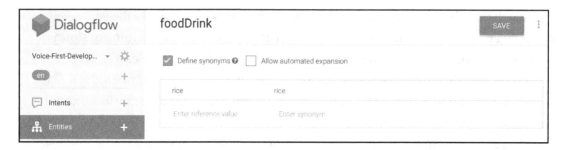

Figure 6-4. *Dialogflow after adding the foodDrink entity with "rice" as it's only value*

You've done the first part, defining the slot foodDrink. Now you need to tell Dialogflow where that fits in the sample phrase:

4. Find the qaCanEat intent.

5. Find the training phrase "Can I eat rice today?" and double-click the word "rice."

6. A menu with many choices appears. Select the one at the top, @foodDrink. Save.

7. The top of your Dialogflow should now look like Figure 6-5. You'll notice the following:

    •   There are both entities and parameters. They're distinct creatures, not the same. See the "In-Depth: Entities, Parameters, and Slots" section.

    •   Below the sample phrase "Can I eat rice today?" in Training Phrases, you see a section that defines which parameters are set if you speak the phrase, as well as the entity that it fills. Here, @foodDrink is the entity you just defined, and the resolved value (the entity value) fills that entity; that and the parameter both get set to "rice." Note that in general we'll refer to entities in Dialogflow with a @ prefix to distinguish them from parameters.

- The Actions and Parameters section was previously empty; now it contains an item for the new foodDrink parameter that was automatically defined when you specified "rice" as filling the @foodDrink entity. For every entity that is filled in all the sample phrases of an intent, there will be an associated parameter in the Actions and Parameters section. We'll get back to the usefulness of parameters momentarily.

8. You should have something like what's in Figure 6-5. Test it!

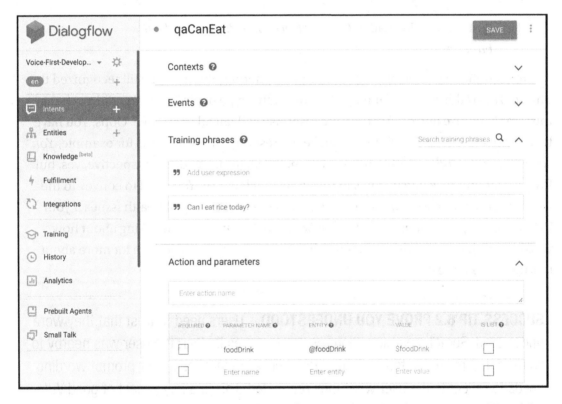

Figure 6-5. *Dialogflow after defining "rice" in the sample phrase as a value of the foodDrink entity*

Wait. It does exactly what it did before; what's the big deal? Hold on. We'll get there.

9. Go back to the foodDrink entity.

10. Edit the rice value. At Click Here to Edit Entry, type "banana." Save. Your Dialogflow should look like Figure 6-6.

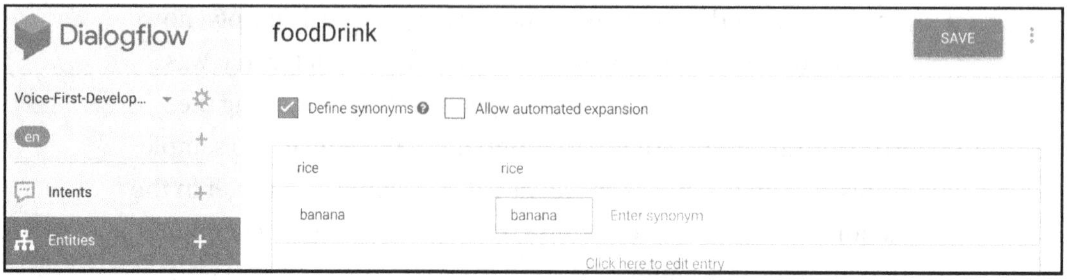

Figure 6-6. *Dialogflow after adding "banana" as another value of the* `foodDrink` *entity*

11. Test the app: instead of *Can I eat rice today?*, say, *Can I eat bananas today?*

You'll notice a couple of things: First, just by adding "banana," it still recognized the phrase! This is the convenient magic of slots in this type of platform. You didn't change the sample phrase one bit. Second, the response still talked about rice. Oops. You have two options for fixing that. One is to make the response more generic, for example, *You can still eat that today.* Problem solved, right? Well, from a coding perspective, yes, but from a user interface perspective, in this case, much worse. You need to convey to the user that you understood what they asked. Imagine the potential health issues if your VUI heard *bangers and mash* instead of *bananas, mashed.* Start thinking about how you'd prove that you're giving patients the right answer—you'll learn a lot more about this throughout the book.

SUCCESS TIP 6.2 PROVE YOU UNDERSTOOD   Users need to trust that they were understood. Sometimes the action response makes it clear: the user was nearby to witness that music muted or lights turned on. At other times, your prompt wording needs to reflect to the user what they requested. This is a key aspect of good VUI design that everyone needs to be on board with—designers, coders, and business owners alike.

The other option is more specific responses. Parameters to the rescue! When you fill a slot @foodDrink with a value "rice," it sets the parameter foodDrink to "rice." Let's use that:

12.   Find the qaCanEat intent and open the Responses section.

13.   In the "You can eat rice today" response, double-click the word "rice."

14.   Type a dollar sign $. A menu appears with a single item: foodDrink. Select it. Save. The Responses section should look like Figure 6-7.

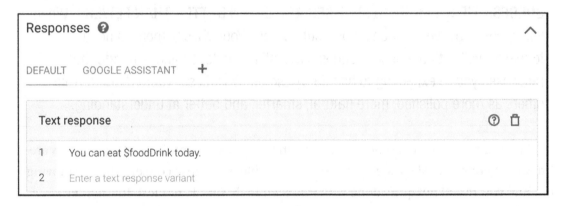

Figure 6-7. *Dialogflow* qaCanEat *responses after replacing "rice" with the* foodDrink *parameter*

15.   Test! Say both *Can I eat rice today?* and *Can I eat bananas today?* Both should work well now. Note that you need to restart the interaction for the second test utterance since you called the qaCanEat intent the end of the conversation. You'll fix that shortly.

What happened with "bananas"? Why did it say *banana*? That's because "banana" is the name you gave the entity value and therefore fills the foodDrink parameter. Let's fix it:

16.   In Entities, find the foodDrink entity.

17.   Click the leftmost "banana" and change it to "bananas."

18.   Now add another synonym "bananas." We didn't need to do this with "rice" since that works correctly in "You can eat rice today." Save. It should look like Figure 6-8.

19.   Test it! It should now work the way you want it.

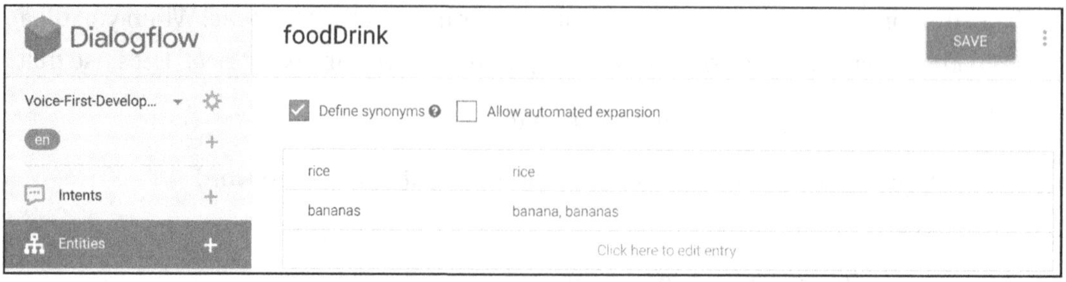

Figure 6-8. foodDrink *entity after changing to "bananas"*

SUCCESS TIP 6.3 MORE RESPONSES ARE OFTEN BETTER THAN FEWER   When you choose how you respond, don't cut corners. Your VUI's responses need to match well with the users' requests to instill confidence and generate the responses you're expecting to handle. These details will set your VUI apart from others as more polished, more natural, smarter, and better at understanding.

We spent quite a bit of time going through this, because entities and parameters are important concepts. Make sure you feel comfortable with these concepts before moving on. And you're still not quite done with this seemingly simple request. In Chapter 7, you'll learn how to deal with relative time, like "today."

With this background to understand the "how," you're probably itching to make changes for your own VUI. We want you to be well versed in the "why" as well, so let's first look at some of the finer design issues.

In-Depth: Entities, Parameters, and Slots

You may be confused about the difference between entities and parameters, especially since they're not always clearly differentiated and sometimes also called slots. Entities are the Dialogflow constructs that let you understand sentences with one of a (potentially) large number of values, such as city, or first name, without having to define all the options as training phrases. Parameters are the variables that entities fill when a user says that particular entity. For example, for a city name, the entity might fill the parameter with "Boston," which you might use in the response or in the fulfillment webhook. Normally, entities and parameters look like the same thing, but you can change that, and sometimes you'd need to. For *I want to fly from Boston to New York*, you use the city entity twice, filled with two different parameters: one with the source city ("Boston") and the other with the destination city ("New York").

The "banana/bananas" issue in the example you just worked through is one you'll run into again. When using entities, you need to make sure that the system can recognize what you say no matter how you say it (*Can I eat a banana today?* or *Can I eat bananas today?*) and that the response is good (the response *You can eat banana today* was not).

On the recognition/understanding side, you haven't (yet) added more training phrases, "Can I eat X?" or "Can I eat a X?", and let's not forget "Can I eat an X?" for foods like "apple." Even with the one phrase we have now, Dialogflow will probably pick it up; this is one of the advantages of the machine learning NLP. But we want to raise the issue so you understand the issue because you can't always count on it being handled for you.

On the VUI response side, you may think, *What's the big deal? It still works; it gives the right answer*. True, the content is correct. Responding with *banana* and responding with *bananas* are both understandable. And the VUI needs to understand both; it's a slip of the tongue by a user. But it's exactly this kind of detail that separates great VUIs from so-so ones. Users notice, even if subconsciously. And even such a small thing affects user trust and their desire to engage with a VUI.

This issue becomes more interesting later when you use large lists or databases of items like foods or medication names. If you do VUI work in other languages, think about how this issue will be different, either more or less complex.

Design Notes on Question Answering

As you'd expect, users often initiate a QA dialog with an utterance phrased like a question, that is, a WH question (*When does Na Na's open today?*) or a Yes/No question using a form of the verb "**BE**" (*Is Na Na's open today?*) or "**DO**" (*Does Na Na's stay open late today?*). But people aren't logical creatures that consistently follow grammatical rules, and yet listeners still—usually—understand. Users can ask questions phrased like statements and signal that they're questions, either through intonation (*Na Na's is open*, rising at the end) or with wording (*Na Na's is open now, right?*). Or maybe it's just a statement because a question is implied by the topic (*Na Na's hours of operation*) or a Yes/No question phrased indirectly (*Do you know if Na Na's is open now?*).

Why is this important? For two reasons: coverage and response wording. First, your coverage needs to handle all reasonable expected versions of questions—you can't rely solely on someone else's prefab models, because context will matter. You learn more about this in Chapters 9 and 14. Second, your VUI's response needs to reflect the style both of the user's question and of the VUI. When people talk to each other, the default answer to a Yes/No question is of course *yes* or *no* with optional additional content. For listeners, both responses in Table 6-3 are acceptable and appropriate; *yes* is actually optional here. The bottom row shows the level of appropriateness of each response, a checkmark indicating good and an X indicating not good.

Table 6-3. *Yes/No responses don't need yes or no*

Who	Dialog	
User	*<Wakes up VUI, if needed>*	
User	*Is Na Na's open at 7?*	
	A	**B**
VUI	*Yes, Na Na's opens at 7 PM today.*	*Na Na's opens at 7 PM today.*
–	√√	√

There are good reasons why you might not want to just answer *Yes* here even though it's appropriate in a conversation. You'll learn about those reasons in Chapter 7. What if the user asked a WH question aimed at the same content? Look at Table 6-4. Here, only options without a *yes* are good since people consider it very odd to respond with *yes* or *no* to a WH question, more so than not including it in a Yes/No question.

Table 6-4. *WH question responses can match Yes/No responses*

Who	Dialog	
User	*When does Na Na's open?*	
	A	**B**
VUI	*Yes, Na Na's opens at 7 PM today.*	*Na Na's opens at 7 PM today.*
–	X	√√

To handle both user question styles as well as ones formed as sentences, you have two options: either you respond to both in a way that's acceptable for both or you handle them separately. If you choose the former, you can treat them as a single intent. For the latter, you need to separate them into two intents, or one intent with different conditions. The latter is more work but allows more targeted and intelligent-sounding responses. Maybe you want that. There's no one-size-fits-all here. It would be appropriate to choose the simpler approach first, until you find a reason to choose the more involved one. Here, it also works for the other phrasings mentioned earlier, as you can see in Table 6-5.

Table 6-5. *Responding without yes or no can allow greater flexibility*

Who	Dialog	
User	Na Na's is open at 7. Na Na's is open at 7, right? Do you know if Na Na's is open at 7?	
	A	**B**
VUI	*Yes, Na Na's opens at 7 PM today.*	*Na Na's opens at 7 PM today.*
–	√√	√

This level of granularity in your responses is an important topic that differentiates well-crafted VUI designs from more rudimentary implementations. Don't skimp: give some thought on implementing this. How much effort are you willing and able to put in? In Chapter 12, you learn how to get your VUI to sound smart based on its level of certainty.

Remember earlier in the sample code, you made sure to say the understood food item name in the response. It might not seem that important—the user gets the answer after all— but it subtly instills confidence in the user to hear a response that fits their question at all levels. When you look at transcriptions of user data from in-production VUIs, you can sometimes find exactly where responses are failing in robustness: users are quite happy to mock your voice app or comment on its responses.

Our examples so far are pretty generic, even bland, in that they don't focus on VUI stylistics. Your VUI's response could be *Na Na's opens at 7 PM today* or *Na Na's is a great choice. They open for dinner at 7 every Wednesday evening, and they're usually not busy midweek* or something else. Both are fine responses, and depending on the VUI system persona, one is more appropriate than the other. You'll learn the how-to of system persona design in Chapter 15.

SUCCESS TIP 6.4 KNOW THE FOUNDATION BEFORE YOU IMPROVISE   Delivering the right VUI system persona is important; it's closely interconnected with prompt wording but can still be discussed separately, and both depend on underlying ASR and NL system performance. Clarity and conciseness of prompting must take priority. No style and delivery can fix unclear or inaccurate prompt content.

Action Requests

What we call action request dialogs differ from QA dialogs in that the user's goal is a direct and fairly immediate action: changing volume, turning something on or off, playing music, and so on. The user makes their request or gives some command, and the VUI responds. Here too, there may be a follow-up from the user, in which case it may be appropriate for the VUI to respond. Figure 6-9 illustrates the action request dialog pattern.

Notice how, again, the pattern is the same basic pattern as in Figure 6-1, but here the response includes an action, in this case playing a song.

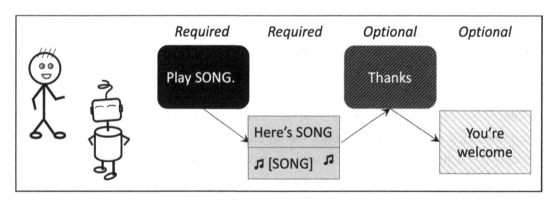

Figure 6-9. *Action request dialog pattern*

The expected VUI response is an action that may or may not be accompanied by a voice response—remember the old saying "actions speak louder than words." The implementation needs to be well coordinated with fulfillment, including handling latency and responding appropriately for what's delivered. Here're some representative action request dialogs:

User   *Play "Waterloo" by ABBA.*

VUI   *Here's "Waterloo" by ABBA. → [Requested SONG plays]*

~ ~ ~

User   *Mute the TV.*

VUI   *[TV mutes]*

~ ~ ~

User   *Call my doctor's office.*

VUI   *OK, calling Doctor Jones, office phone. → [Calling begins]*

Building Action Requests

Let's implement[8] some procedure prep helper action requests. The first example is simple on the surface: *Call my doctor's office.* Create a new intent arCallDoctor, add the training phrase "Call my doctor's office" and a response "OK, calling your doctor," and don't forget to set the conversation to end after that. Don't forget to test! You'll notice in this sample that you're not actually calling anyone yet. Actions allow us to do that, by sending information to the Fulfillment back end, where something could be done. For now, we're just focusing on the dialog.

Similarly, a very simple static implementation of *What I should do today?* is straightforward. Start a new intent arTodaysTasks, with the training phrase and response as listed in the sample dialog. Note that you need to stick the text together in one response; multiple responses are for allowing Dialogflow to randomly select which one to play. After you're done, that intent should look like the one in Figure 6-10. Test!

---

[8]Load files from 6-3.zip and 6-4.zip.

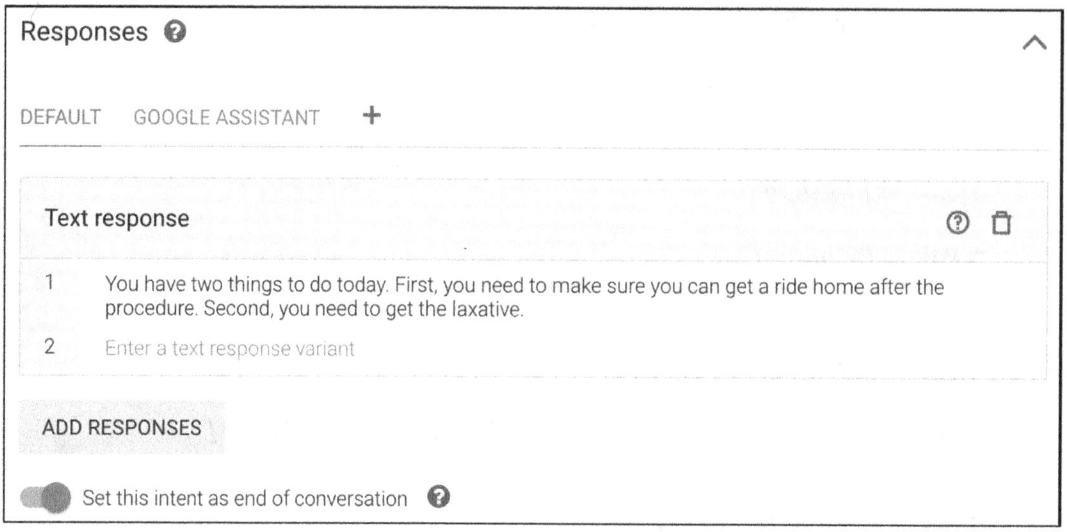

Responses ❓   ⌃

DEFAULT   GOOGLE ASSISTANT   +

Text response   ⑦ 🗑

1   You have two things to do today. First, you need to make sure you can get a ride home after the
     procedure. Second, you need to get the laxative.
2   Enter a text response variant

ADD RESPONSES

◉ Set this intent as end of conversation ❓

Figure 6-10. A first arTodaysTasks intent with one static response

You've realized that for a real application, you'd not hard-wire the tasks like you did here. Later, you'll build more complex logic, taking into account the current time and date and the date of the procedure and figuring out what today's tasks are and allowing for dynamic content responses. You'll do that by treating "today" and "tomorrow" and even "tonight" as slot values.

Design Notes on Action Requests

Action requests are commands, so the default user utterance will be in command form: *Mute the stereo, Play "Waterloo" by ABBA, Turn on the kitchen lights at 6 AM, Stop!,* and so on. But of course, there's also a lot of variation in how users ask for things. Some are more polite than others, so your coverage needs to include *Please play…* and *Play… please.* No need to track level of politeness for different responses—unless your VUI is training kids to be polite! Just make sure various carrier phrases are handled. It might seem obvious, but there are many easy-to-find examples today where this isn't correctly implemented. An action request can often be superficially phrased as a question (e.g., *Could you play…*), even combined with politeness (*Can you please play…*).

Let's look at what determines how your VUI responds to action requests. The only required response is the requested action, so if the request is to mute the stereo, then mute the stereo. If the request is to play a particular song, then play it. But what does the VUI say, if anything? Well, it depends. The short answer for now is to build in flexibility that you can use later. If you think a verbal response is not necessary, implement it anyway in such a way that it's empty but has a reference. Here's why: If the request is to *mute the stereo*, think about what happens. Assuming there's no problem, the stereo mutes. Under default conditions, you don't need the VUI to tell you: it's obvious that it worked, so let the action speak for itself. If you insist on a spoken response, make it short. One word is enough, as long as it's relevant—say *Muted* rather than *OK*, which contributes no information. Don't be wordy: it's annoying and not helpful. Under some conditions, a verbal response is in order. If the user is not so near the device that they can hear that it muted or if the request differs from some default setting, then a verbal response is appropriate (Table 6-6).

Table 6-6. Variation in responses depending on context

Who	Dialog					
User	*Mute the stereo.*					
Action result	*<STEREO MUTES>*					
	A	B	C		D	E
VUI response	*Muted.*	*Stereo is muted.*	*OK, I have muted the music on the stereo.*		*OK.*	--
Stereo is nearby	√X	X	X		X	√√
Stereo not nearby	X	√√	X		X	X

Think about the best VUI response to the request *Close the garage* or *Lock the door*. Whether or not the door or garage is nearby, it's more important to get this right, so be explicit in your response: *The door is locked.*

Task Completion Requests

What we'll refer to as **task completion requests** are action requests where the requested outcome is typically less immediate, indirect, or more complex. It may not be obvious yet why this is treated as a separate dialog type, but it'll become clear. Where action requests don't always need a VUI verbal response, task completion requests do. They often involve multiple steps, often alternating who "has the floor," the user or the VUI. Task completion requests are core to the more complex tasks in enterprise domains, such as financial transactions, reservations, or health-related tasks. It's where VUI interactions need to shine to go beyond simple commands. Figure 6-11 illustrates task completion request dialog patterns. The top example is initialized and driven by the user. The bottom example is a portion of a dialog driven by the VUI.

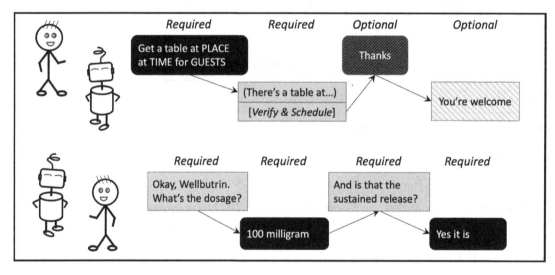

Figure 6-11. *Task completion request dialog patterns*

Look at a few representative examples of task completion, and notice how they differ in how much the user provides in their initial request—we'll discuss the implications of that later in this chapter:

> **User** *I'd like to make a reservation at Na Na's tonight at seven o'clock for six people.*
>
> **VUI** *Na Na's has a table available for six people tonight at 7:30 PM. Would you…*

~ ~ ~   ~ ~ ~   ~ ~ ~

User   *I want to pay the current balance on my credit card.*

VUI   *Scheduling a payment of 510 dollars from your checking account ending in 13…*

~ ~ ~   ~ ~ ~   ~ ~ ~

User   *For lunch, I had a hamburger, fries, and a diet Coke.*

VUI   *Great! Thanks for tracking your lunch in your food diary.*

Building Task Completion Example 1

Let's implement task completion,[9] starting with *Make an appointment.* You'll notice from the sample dialogs that you'll need to collect some follow-on information to complete this task. Recall that that's one of the defining features of a task completion request: you'll need multiple dialog turns from both the VUI and the user to get the job done. Luckily, Dialogflow makes it easy to do exactly that. First, you need to understand **built-in entities** and **required parameters**.

Remember assigning "rice" to @foodDrink and seeing a whole bunch of entities already in the entity menu? These are the built-in system entities that can make your job easier. Dialogflow includes several entities that are commonly used in dialogs. Categories include date and time ("two thirty p m july thirteen," "tomorrow," "noon"), numbers ("one," "ten," "third"), amounts with units ("ten square feet," "two liters"), geographic locations, first and last names, and so on. You'll recognize the system entities by their "sys." prefix.[10]

You already learned about parameters and how they're set when entities are filled. Dialogflow allows you to mark a parameter as required in an intent, which means that it automatically collects the information necessary to set that parameter, before generating a response. Without this feature, you must do that yourself.

---

[9]Load files from 6-5.zip.

[10]https://dialogflow.com/docs/reference/system-entities offers a good breakdown of the available system entities.

How does Dialogflow know to ask for the information? You tell it to make it required! Let's use built-in entities and required parameters to implement making an appointment:

User   *Make an appointment.*

VUI   *OK, you want to make an appointment. For what day and time?*

User   *Thursday, August 5th, at 2 PM.*

VUI   *OK, I've set it up, Thursday, August 5th, at 2 PM.*

1. Create a new intent tcrMakeAppointment and add the training phrase "Make an appointment."

2. Specify the first required parameter. Under Actions and Parameters, click the checkbox under REQUIRED for the first row.

3. Call the parameter name dateTime under PARAMETER NAME.

4. Under ENTITY, choose from the menu @sys.date-time. The VALUE $dateTime will be filled in.

5. Under PROMPTS, click the column; a box appears. Type your information prompt, like "OK, you want to make an appointment. For what day and time?" Save.

6. Create the text response "OK, I've set it up. $dateTime.original." Remember when you used $foodDrink to play back the food item that was spoken? Here you're doing the same with the system entity. The .original specifies how dateTime is spoken. Set the response as the end of conversation. Save. Test!

It should be clear from this detailed walk-through that Dialogflow makes it easy to automatically collect complex information and how system entities make things simpler to develop and save you the pain of doing it by hand. Of course, you want to take advantage of anything pre-built when you can, and this is a great way to build something decent quickly. Soon you'll encounter situations where things are not quite so simple, and you learn why it's not always enough to use built-ins. It's also why we're sneaking in dialog patterns from the start. Don't expect to create complex voice systems with simple drop-in modules—but do start building your own core set of templates.

Building Task Completion Example 2

The example you just worked through involved multiple turns because the user didn't start with a fully specified request. Now let's work through a task that always requires multiple turns: the procedure prep task.[11] This is where contexts apply. Contexts are a key part of every dialog, as you learn in Chapter 14. Until now, all your contexts have been global: an utterance is recognized and handled the same, no matter the context or conditions. But that's not always the case. For procedure prep, the first instance of *next* applies only after the initial step; the second *next* makes sense only after you told the user the second step. In many dialogs, you need to keep track of the **state** of the dialog: which phrases are recognized, how they're interpreted, and what the responses are depend on the state you are in, which is a combination of contexts including what was said earlier in the dialog.

Dialogflow implements this idea of conversational state or "location" in the flow of a conversation with contexts. A Dialogflow context is very much like a dialog state, keeping track of where you are in the conversation. To use this machinery, modify the Contexts section of your intents. You can specify input contexts (basically "this intent is triggered with the training phrases only if one of the dialog's current contexts matches one of the intent's input contexts") and set the dialog's current contexts with an intent's output contexts ("After Intent A, activate contexts X and Y, and make them current"). Here's a concrete example:

User	*Walk me through my procedure prep.*
VUI	*OK, the first step is to prepare the laxative. When you've done that, say "Next."*
User	*Next.*
VUI	*Now drink the laxative completely. After you're done, say "Next."*
User	*Next.*
VUI	*Great job!*

---

[11]Load files from 6-6.zip.

1. Create a new intent `tcrProcedurePrep`, with the training phrase "Walk me through my procedure prep."

2. Add the response, "OK, the first step is to prepare the laxative. When you've done that, say "Next.""

3. **Do not** set this intent as the end of the conversation, as you've done before. The dialog needs to keep going here.

4. Now start the contexts. In the intent's Contexts section, click the down arrow to open.

5. In Add Output Context, type `tcrProcedurePrepStep1` and press return. This means doing step 1 and then waiting. Save. It should look like Figure 6-12. We'll talk later about what the 5 means in the output context.

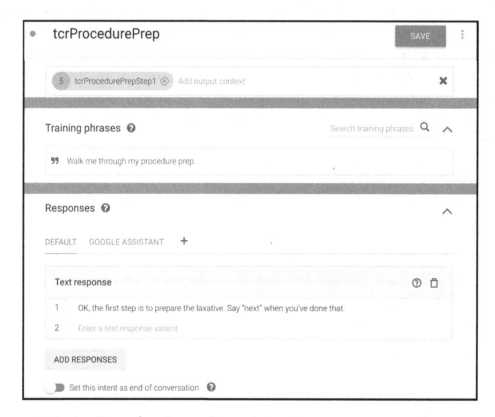

Figure 6-12. `tcrProcedurePrep` *after training phrase, response, and output context*

1. What's the next thing the user can say? It's the first *Next*. Create a new intent tcrProcedurePrepNext1, with the training phrase "Next" and the response "Now drink the laxative completely. After you're done, say 'Next.'"

2. This time, you'll set both input and output contexts. At Add Input Context, start typing "tcr…" and it will auto complete tcrProcedurePrepStep1, since that's the only context you've defined yet. Select that.

3. In the output contexts, it will have auto-added the input context of tcrProcedurePrepStep1. Use the X to delete that, and then type in a new context tcrProcedurePrepStep2, and press return (Figure 6-13). Save.

Figure 6-13. *The tcrProcedurePrepNext1 intent, with both input and output contexts*

4. Do it again. Create a new intent tcrProcedurePrepNext2 with training phrase "Next" and response "Great! You're all done!"

5. Set this intent to be the end of the conversation.

6. In Contexts, add the input context tcrProcedurePrepStep2. As before, delete the auto-added output context with the same name. Save.

7. You've now built a multistep dialog. You know what's next: test!

You now have the beginnings of a procedure prep dialog. Let's look at another task completion dialog: updating the food diary:[12]

1. Start a new intent `tcrFoodDiary` with training phrase "Food diary," response "OK, food diary. What did you have to eat?", and output context (that's new from the last example!) `tcrFoodDiary`. Don't forget: Do not make this intent the end of the conversation! Save.

2. Now add the intent that actually collects foods. Create a new intent `tcrFoodDiaryCollection`, with a training phrase "For lunch I had a hamburger, fries, and a diet Coke" and response "OK, you had a hamburger, fries, and diet Coke for lunch. Thanks!" Make it the end of the conversation, and add the input context `tcrFoodDiary` (don't forget to remove the auto-generated output context). Save.

3. Next, you need to define some slots in your training phrase. Remember you did this earlier in the chapter when you turned "rice" into the slot `foodDrink`. You're going to do that some more.

4. In the training phrase, double-click "lunch." A menu will appear. You haven't defined this slot yet; go to the bottom of the menu and click Create New.

5. You'll be directed to the screen to create a new entity. Call it "meal." Note that it's pre-populated with the sample item "lunch" from our training phrase. Save.

6. Now that you've defined the meal entity, go back to the `tcrFoodDiaryCollection` intent, double-click "lunch" again, and select `@meal` from the menu. Save.

---

[12]Load files from 6-7.zip.

- You were able to go straight into defining the new entity from the training phrase. This is a very handy shortcut. Remember, though, that after defining the new entity, you need to go back to the intent and set the word or phrase (in this case "lunch") to the new entity @meal.

7. Let's do that again for "hamburger." Define a new entity... Wait. There's no need! Remember "Can I eat rice?"; you defined a @foodDrink entity. You can use that! Double-click "hamburger" and pick @foodDrink as the entity. Save.

   - Open the foodDrink entity. Note that "hamburger" has been added without explicit entry. Another great advantage of defining entities. As you build out the application, you can reuse the @foodDrink entity for this new intent. Now go back to the intent.

8. Same for "fries"; define it as a @foodDrink.

9. It's time to call "diet Coke" a foodDrink. You can't just double-click, since it's two words. Click and drag across "diet" and "Coke"; then define it as a @foodDrink. Save.

10. Again, go back to the entity to verify that "diet Coke" has been added.

11. Almost there! The static response has "lunch" in it; replace that with the $meal parameter since the user might have said another meal or none. Save.

12. In the response, click and drag to select the entire phrase "hamburger, fries, and diet Coke" and replace it with $foodDrink. Save and test!

Your intent should now look like Figure 6-14.

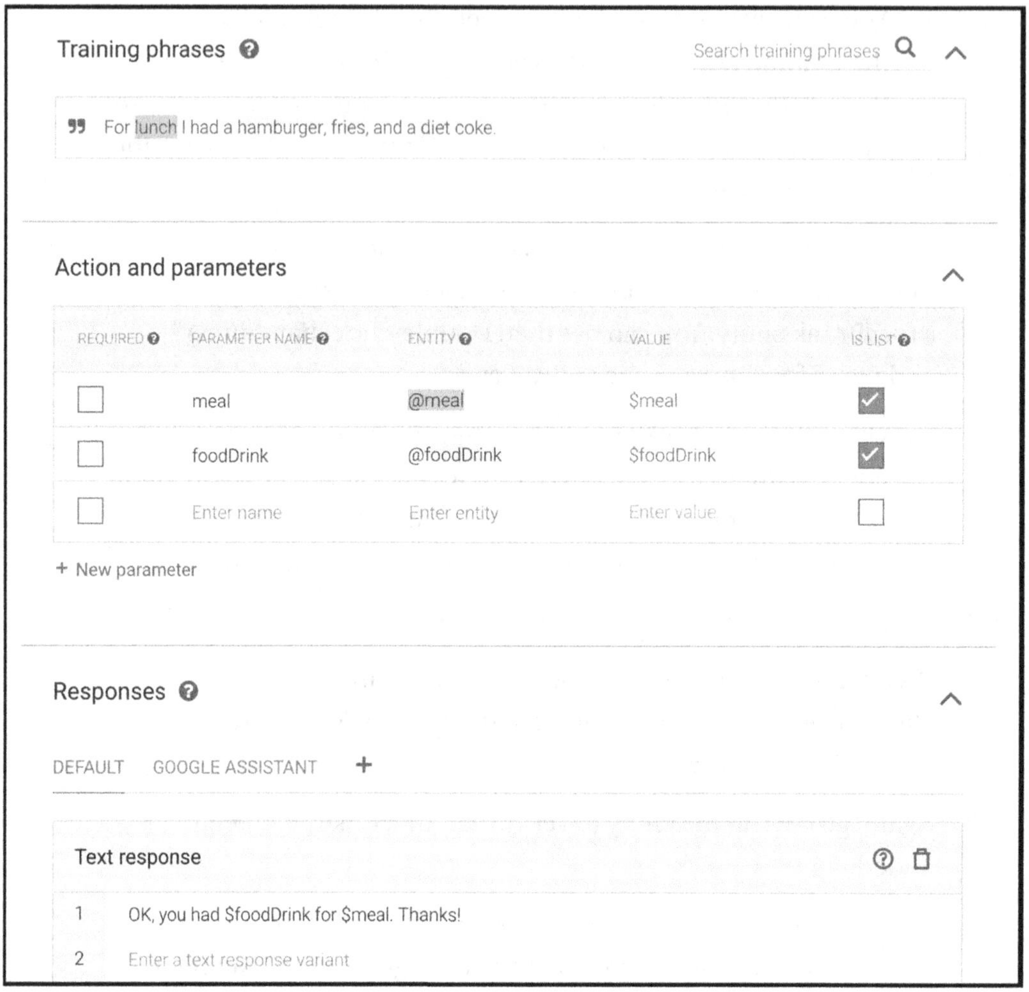

Figure 6-14. `tcrFoodDiaryCollection` *intent*

You probably noticed that Dialogflow and Google Home magically did the right thing when reading back the food items! Remember you defined "hamburger," "fries," and "diet Coke" to all fill the entity `@foodDrink`. When you have multiple items filling an entity, that's known as a list entity, because the value of the entity and parameter is a list. You may not know ahead of time how many items are in a list—you don't always eat three items!

Note that after you made "fries" a `@foodDrink`, in the intent's Actions and Parameters section, `foodDrink` now automatically checks the box in the IS LIST column, indicating that this is indeed a list, even though it only contains one item. `@foodDrink` is not intrinsically a list entity, but it's defined as such in the `tcrFoodDiaryCollection` intent. In the previous `qaCanEat` intent where you used `@foodDrink`, the entity was not defined as a list. Also, note that Dialogflow even added "and" before the last list item. Pretty cool!

Design Notes on Task Completion

If your reaction to the sample dialogs was "Those seem too easy" and "What about making sure it's right?" then good for you! We'll address your concerns soon. For now, notice how much wordier these responses are compared to the action requests. Also look at how they're expressed: all pieces of relevant information are read back to the user because that's the only way they'd get feedback showing they were understood—there's no action, like lights turning off, conveying understanding. Saying nothing, or just *OK*, is both poor options. Information should be read back clearly and follow expectations users have based on their cognitive models of the conversation. Because people can provide the information items in different orders, you need to capture that variation, but you don't need to vary your VUI's responses to reflect it. In fact, it's better to stay consistent. More on that soon. Notice also that users give you hints on meaning that might at first glance not seem clear: user requests for *tonight at 7* or *dinner at 7* clearly mean 7 in the evening, but your VUI can stick with "7 *PM*" to be clear and brief. Here are some additional prompt guidelines:

- Be neither wordy nor overly terse—provide all the content needed, no more, no less.

- Don't be vague just to save a syllable or two—"7 PM" is better than just "7," even if it seems clear from context.

- Chunk information logically according to how people tend to provide it, typically starting with more general topic content—this lessens cognitive load.

- Start responses with a short introductory carrier phrase, even a definite or indefinite article—this can help users not to miss the first bit of content.

Table 6-7 shows you some concrete examples of how to apply these guidelines. Think about why some responses may be better than others.

Table 6-7. *Balancing clarity with conciseness*

Who	Dialog				
User	*Get a table for six at Na Na's tonight at 7.*				
	Make a reservation for dinner at Na Na's for six at seven o'clock.				
	Response A	**Response B**	**Response C**	**Response D**	**Response E**
VUI	*OK. A table's reserved at Na Na's Kitchen tonight at 7 PM for six people.*	*Tonight, for six, at 7, Na Na's Kitchen.*	*OK. This is a popular place!* *I found a lovely table for you. All set for 7!*	*Done.*	*[Silence]*
	√√	X	X X	X X	X X

Fully Specified Requests

The main goal of VUIs and voice-driven devices is to fulfill the intent of the user's request and do it accurately and quickly. In other words, as soon as the VUI has all the information necessary to fulfill a request, it should do so. We call these **fully specified requests**. All examples so far in this chapter were fully specified: no unclarity or ambiguity, one initiating turn by the user followed by the VUI response turn, and voilà. Done.

These are **one-shot** dialogs, or **one-and-done**. One-and-done dialogs are still the most common VUI interactions to date because the technology and implementation makes them the "low-hanging fruit." They're also the base case that needs to be handled for more complex and interesting VUI behaviors. One-and-done dialogs come in two flavors: simpler **single-slot requests** and more complex—and more powerful—**multi-slot requests**.

While the intent is the overall goal of the user's request, slots are the variables relevant for successfully handling that intent. All slots must be filled for the intent to be fully specified and fulfilled. Slots can be filled explicitly by the user or indirectly (implicitly) by the VUI assigning values based on some coded logic. To determine the appropriate number and types of slots, you need to understand what your users will request, what matters to them to feel successful, and what information they are likely to have available.

Single-Slot Requests

Each of the three core dialog patterns in this chapter can be intents with a single required slot. The necessary information is either there or not (Table 6-8).

Table 6-8. *Single slots across dialog patterns*

	Question answer	**Action request**	**Task completion request**
User utterance	*What is* War and Peace *?*	*Play some Rammstein.*	*Pay my credit card.*
Intent and slot	Intent = queryInfo Slot = {thing} Slot value = war_and_ peace	Intent = playMusic Slot = {artist} Slot value = rammstein	Intent = pay Slot = {payee} Slot value = credit_card
VUI response	War and Peace *is a novel written by the Russian author Leo Tolstoy.*	*Here's "Links 2 3 4" by Rammstein.* [SONG plays on default device.]	*Scheduling a payment of 240 dollars and 63 cents to your VISA credit card from your checking account.*

Implementing Single-Slot Requests

Can I eat rice today? is an example of a single-slot request, the slot filled being @ foodDrink.

Design Notes on Single-Slot Requests

There's obviously much more going on behind the scenes here. First, each utterance needs to be interpreted correctly by the VUI. Then, appropriate lookups are necessary to fulfill the requests. For the task completion request, some earlier setup would have happened. The main point is that there's only one required slot, it's filled, and therefore the intent is fully specified. The VUI response to the task completion payment request assumes defaults are set for interpreting payment details.

Multi-slot Requests

Each of the three dialog patterns can also take any number of slots. To the uninitiated, these are the one-and-done requests that are so impressive that they border on magic. Long and complex but fully specified requests like *What is the name of Arnold Schwarzenegger's character in* True Lies*?* or *Make a roundtrip reservation for one person from Los Angeles to San Diego leaving tomorrow at 8 AM and returning on Sunday at 4 PM* are not necessarily more difficult than shorter requests, assuming the user speaks clearly and recognition is good. In fact, the more precise the request, the easier it is to handle. Table 6-9 shows a few more examples, each showing what three or more slots might look like. Notice that the VUI response in this task completion example is the same as the single slot, but here all slots are filled by the user.

Table 6-9. *Multiple slots across dialog patterns*

	Question answer	Action request	Task completion request
User utterance	Who played the character Natasha in the 1956 movie version of War and Peace?	Play "Links" by Rammstein from Spotify in the living room.	Pay 240 dollars and 63 cents on my credit card bill from my checking account.
Intent and slot	Intent = queryActor Slot = {movieTitle: war and peace} Slot = {movieYear: 1956} Slot = {role: natasha}	Intent = playMusic Slot = {artist: rammstein} Slot = {song: links} Slot = {service: spotify} Slot = {endpoint: living room}	Intent = pay Slot = {payee: credit card} Slot = {amount: 240.63} Slot = {fromAcct: checking}
VUI response	Natasha was played by Audrey Hepburn in the 1956 movie *War and Peace.*	Links by Rammstein. Playing in the living room. [SONG plays.]	Scheduling a payment of 240 dollars and 63 cents to your VISA credit card from your checking account.

Implementing Multi-slot Requests

You've already seen examples of multiple slots being filled in our procedure prep helper:

- "For lunch, I had a hamburger, fries, and a diet Coke" fills the slots @meal and @foodDrink (as a list) for the tcrFoodDiaryCollection intent.

- "Thursday, August 5th, at 2 PM" fills the @sys.date-time built-in entity for the tcrMakeAppointment intent.

Both examples are actually interesting in their own right, for different reasons. In the food example, there are several information bits: *lunch* for @meal, *hamburger* for @ foodDrink, *fries* for @foodDrink, and *diet Coke* for @foodDrink. Is that two slots or four? It's actually two, but the @foodDrink is filled as a **list**, as discussed earlier. It's important to make the distinction between filling multiple slots and filling one (or more) slot with multiple slot values. Here you fill one slot (@meal) with one value and another (@ foodDrink) with a list (which, mind you, could include a list of one item, but as you'll see when you start writing fulfillment code, a one-item list is different from a non-list or scalar).

For the appointment time, you can specify one built-in entity, @sys.date-time, but that entity has different components: day of week (*Thursday*), date (*August 5th*), hour of the time (*2*), and *PM*. If you look in the system entities documentation, you see that @sys.date-time will match a date **or** a time **or** a date and a time **or** even more things like an interval (e.g., it matches just *August*, returning an interval starting at midnight August 1 and ending at midnight on August 30). So filling the @sys.date-time slot could include from one to all four of the needed slot components that you need to make an appointment.

Here, you see a new concept of filling a single slot and its associated parameter with a list, or several values. Why do we need the list? Without lists, you need a training phrase where there's only one food and another for two and so on. Those with any programming experience realize this is not a good approach and why list slot filling is added as a feature. In some contexts, users even will specify a list, so you want the dialog and code to be flexible enough to intelligently handle all cases. Another option if you don't use lists is to first ask "What's the first thing you ate?" followed by "And the next?" and so on. Avoid this approach unless truly necessary as a backoff strategy; it's obviously not a pleasant user experience.

Design Notes on Multi-slot Requests

It's technically possible to consider all requests as separate intents, but that quickly becomes impractical because you'd need to implement handling for each intent rather than utilize practical grouping. You can have voice interactions where you define intents without slots—it may even be appropriate if you're sure that you'll only handle a very small static set of requests. But we recommend getting into the habit of breaking intents into slots from the start—it allows for cleaner modular code and easier future expansion. If something lends itself to be handled as a slot, make it one for easy future expansion. For example, if you decided to subtly encourage users to be polite (and we're not saying you should; it's just an example—we comment on this later in this chapter), you could fill a "polite" slot every time users include a *please*—the informational content of your response is not affected, but it allows targeted variation in your responses, making it more natural.

SUCCESS TIP 6.5 NAMING SLOTS AND INTENTS   You probably have conventions for how you name your variables in your favorite programming language. You will and should establish a standard for how you name your voice slots and intents. Use names that are short, meaningful, and unambiguous, and combine them as needed. You and others should be able to look at the name of an intent or slot and have some sense of what interaction, content, and utterances are expected. Examples of actual intent names we've used include GetZip, GetLastName, GetFromAcct, PlayArtistAlbum, ReadStockPrice, and YNConfTrx. Slot names might be month, amount, DOB, zip code, and so on. Smart naming convention helps for discussions and reviews, as well as for scaling through modularity.

Determining Dialog Acts Based on Feature Discovery

We've talked at length about various types of requests and dialogs and showed code for how to implement them. Table 6-10 summarizes the dialog features for each procedure prep core functionality you've designed and implemented so far:

- **Functionality**: In Chapter 4, you first formulated an overall summary of what your VUI would do and then defined the tasks that users likely would expect—the feature functionalities. After that, you started designing details and coding.

- **Request type**: One of three task-oriented request types: question answer, action request, and task completion request.

- **Sample phrase**: An utterance example to initiate or interact with a task.

- **Slots (entities)**: The number of expected and needed slots to fill for the request. For example, *Make an appointment* fills no slots, but the subsequent date collection (via one or more turns) fills several. It's the same for the food diary.

- **Turns**: The number of dialog turns expected or necessary for the user to accomplish a task. In many cases, you don't yet know how many turns there will be; there could be multiple steps including for disambiguation.

Table 6-10. *Features of the procedure prep helper dialogs designed and implemented so far*

Functionality	Request type	Sample phrase	Slots	Turns
General info	Question answer	*How long will the procedure take?*	0	1
Food search	Question answer	*Is coffee still OK? Can I eat rice today?*	1–2	1
To-do info	Question answer	*What should I do today?*	0	1
Contact	Action request	*Call my doctor.* *Call Dr. Brent Jones' cell phone.*	1+	1+
Scheduling	Task completion	*Make an appointment for tomorrow morning.* *Reschedule.*	0–N	2+
Prep task	Task completion	*Walk me through the prep. Next.*	0	2+
Food diary	Task completion	*Food diary.*	0–N	2+

Dialog Completion

Once all your slots are filled and your VUI produces a response, are you done? Well, yes and no. Or maybe. The simple answer is *You're done when the VUI has what it needs to give the user what they asked for.* But, of course, it's a bit trickier than that. Technically, the dialog for some intent or task is complete, but the overall conversation might still continue, just like in a human-to-human conversation. Users might ask follow-on requests, either refining the first request (*Play the version by Metallica*) or asking the same question with a different slot value (multiple stock price requests or ticket prices for different seats). Correctly tracking and using short-term context is what makes a conversation—and therefore a theme throughout this book. It's challenging to do it well, but not impossible and well worth it. Like many challenges in voice, it isn't difficult implementation, but careful tracking of details.

Some platforms implement some type of short-term dialog context. For example, Alexa's optional follow-on mode allows additional requests without the wake word for a constant length of time (4 seconds) after the end of a response. The crux of this is twofold. First, in human dialog, follow-on is semantic and contextual, rather than based only on time. Second, the time during which we expect others to remember the topic of conversation is short, but it's not a constant number of seconds. In conversations, people don't often suddenly jump from topic to topic—something you can make use of to increase interpretation success.

Furthermore, even if the user is getting the information or result they asked for, they might not realize it—or even trust the response—if your response is vague or worded differently from what they expected. You've seen this already: including a *yes* or *no* in response to a WH question. This matters because it affects the user's cognitive load.

MULTIMODAL CORNER

Multimodal interactions follow the rules of dialog too: turn-taking applies, and task completion is a goal. In some cases, spoken requests will be simpler because details and references are handled by pointing or tapping. If a user looks up restaurant information on a screen, a multimodal follow-on might be *Make a reservation here.* Obviously, your architecture needs to coordinate the info stream across modalities. Multimodal interfaces can allow simultaneous modalities in a single request (spoken *here* + tap/point) or allow a choice of modality for each response (spoken *6 PM* vs. type or tap on a reservation time). For more on this topic, read anything by Sharon Oviatt.

Responding to "Goodbye" and "Thanks"

Human conversations often end with some type of spoken closure. Is that necessary for a conversational VUI? Usually not—the assistant doesn't usually need closure, and users simply stop interacting when they feel complete, depending on the task and the platform. But be aware of when users say *Goodbye* or *Thanks*. Some cultures, age groups, and individuals are as polite to your VUI as they are to people, and they appreciate, even expect, politeness in return. So, yes, even if you don't explicitly respond to "conversation enders," you should at least not interpret it as something else!

FROM THE VOICE TRENCHES

We've seen IVRs where users wouldn't hang up the phone until the IVR said *Goodbye* or expected the IVR to end the call after they said *Goodbye*. If you don't expect it and don't handle it, the interaction can quickly spiral into failure, reaching the max error count as users wait for it to end. There's been concern about kids barking commands at voice assistants (we personally don't share that concern[13]). In response, home voice assistants have added features that respond to politeness to encourage politeness among its users. This can backfire. In fact, when interacting with her Google Home Hub, Ann's mom, of a generation where most interactions involve a *please* and *thank you*, became gradually less polite as the VUI commented on her excellent politeness!

---

[13]Just because a machine produces responses that sound like human speech doesn't mean it should be treated as if it's human. If anything, kids should be taught that a human is different from a machine; one has feelings, and the other doesn't.

Implementing the End of a Conversation

In the dialogs you've implemented so far, you've just ended the conversation after the final task is finished, without allowing for a *goodbye* or *thanks*. You can add final intents in support;[14] those intents become the new conversation enders. The need for conversation enders depends on the platform (IVRs more than home assistants that go on standby by default after a few seconds)—we'll add some here, just for practice and illustration. You can even have separate intents for the responses, for example, for *Thank you* vs. *Goodbye*:

1. Create a new intent goodbye with a training phrase "Goodbye," input context end, and response "Goodbye. Talk to you later!" End the conversation.

2. Create another new intent thanks with a training phrase "Thanks," input context end, and response "You're welcome. Goodbye!" End the conversation.

3. Pick a dialog where extra politeness fits, like after making an appointment. In the intent tcrMakeAppointment

    •   Add the output context end.

    •   In Responses, set the end of conversation slider to the off position.

    •   Add something polite to the end of the response: "When you're done, just say goodbye."

4. Save. Test!

You could have done this at the end of any of the dialogs, and in general this behavior would be supported for almost all dialogs. Later implementations of this feature will be a bit subtler and not force users to be polite, but allow the option and "timing out" or ending the conversation if the user says nothing after some time.

---

[14]Load files from 6-8.zip.

What's Next?

You've now been properly introduced to the main dialog patterns needed for the vast majority of VUIs you'll create. They can be combined for different purposes and take particular flavors for specific uses.

When you worked on the food diary code, you might have wondered, *Wow, there're a lot of foods we could ask about. Are we really going to do all that typing inside this Dialogflow GUI?* Fear not. Remember from Chapter 3 that Dialogflow has an API that lets you programmatically edit intents and entities. In fact, you'll learn about that next in Chapter 7.

Summary

- Grice's Cooperative Principle and a basic understanding of discourse structure help you understand the three core patterns of VUI design, which in turn helps you create reusable design patterns and code templates.

- Three core patterns cover the vast majority of VUI conversations: question answering, action requests, and task completion requests. Each has its own set of characteristics that you need to develop toward.

- Understanding the interactions within each pattern helps you create more robust prompts, resulting in better user experiences that instill more trust in your users.

- User utterances can be fully or partially specified. When partial, you either let your VUI fill in the missing information or ask your user to complete the empty slots.

- Built-in NL features take care of use cases and utterances you might have forgotten to handle, but you still need to know how to respond.

- Your functionality discovery feeds into the three core patterns and predictions of the number of slots you need to fill.

- The end of a dialog isn't always the end of the conversation.

## CHAPTER 7

Resolving Incomplete Requests Through Disambiguation

In human conversations, people are basically only as clear as they think they need to be, no more, no less. People assume their listener is following, so they take shortcuts that can lead to incompleteness. Or they're vague, which leads to ambiguity. In human dialog, as you know, this happens all the time. When the speaker isn't clear, the listener asks for clarification or "fills in the blanks" in their head. Sometimes they're correct and sometimes not. The same situation happens in VUI dialogs, which is why ambiguity resolution is one of the most important topics in voice design and development. At other times, the listener doesn't even realize they misunderstood until much later—getting back on track is the topic of Chapter 13. In this chapter, you learn about disambiguation: what it is, why it's important, and how and when to implement different approaches. You also learn about why dialog management is needed to accommodate users' different mental models. Code samples cover disambiguation, multi-turn dialogs, and using webhooks.

Incomplete Requests

Take another look at some of the sample fully specified user utterances in Chapter 6:

- *Get a table at Na Na's tonight at seven o'clock for six people.*

- *Pay 240 dollars and 63 cents on my credit card bill from my checking account.*

© Ann Thymé-Gobbel, Charles Jankowski 2021
A. Thymé-Gobbel and C. Jankowski, *Mastering Voice Interfaces*, https://doi.org/10.1007/978-1-4842-7005-9_7

- *Who played the character Natasha in the 1956 movie version of* War and Peace*?*

- *Play "Links 2 3 4" by Rammstein from Spotify in the living room.*

Are users always this precise when making requests? No, of course not. Both of us authors have seen many examples of robust voice implementations where no more than a small percentage of multi-slot interactions were fully specified in the first turn. When the VUI doesn't have the information necessary to fulfill a user's request, we refer to the intent as being incomplete or underspecified. Underspecification has several causes, including the following:

- The user thought they provided all the necessary information, but didn't.

- The user provided all the information, but was misunderstood by the VUI.

- The user didn't know what information was necessary, so let the VUI take control over the dialog to ask for the missing pieces.

- The user didn't want to overwhelm the VUI, so started with the main request, knowing that follow-up questions would come later.

- The user didn't care about some details, so left it to the VUI to "fill in the blanks."

All of these happen and are completely normal in any conversation—well, as long as it's not two lawyers reading legal contracts to each other, because that's what all conversations would be like if you couldn't make assumptions during speech conversations. For a voice system, it would be awesome if people talked like legal code— this chapter would be irrelevant! But, of course, people don't talk like that.

If an intent expects N slots, users can and will make requests with any combination of slots, in more or less any order. You have to handle every situation, either by asking the user or by filling the slots by some other method.

In the restaurant finder VUI example, let's say you want to handle reservations. Add an intent makeRes, and then look at *Get a table at Na Na's tonight at seven o'clock for six people.* OK, looks like it takes at least four pieces of information to fulfill the request— day, guests, place, and time—that translate to four required slots, or entities. You quickly realize other ways people start a reservation: *Get a table* followed by *...at Na Na's Kitchen, ...at Na Na's tonight at seven o'clock, ... at Na Na's Kitchen for six people,* and *...for six* *people at Na Na's.* Putting aside for now different ways of saying *Get a table*, you realize that people can provide only a portion of what's needed for the reservation and that these pieces can appear in different orders. What to do? You need a way to complete the user's request that's quick and accurate. You have two options: ask the user or "guess" the answer (Figure 7-1).

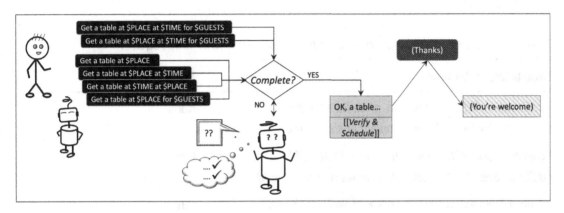

Figure 7-1. *First step to expand the task completion dialog pattern to handle underspecified requests*

Turns out, there's a time and place for both approaches. For a reservation, asking seems wise. A basic but functional disambiguation dialog goes like this:

User	*Can I get a table at Na Na's tomorrow night?*	→ $PLACE, $DAY
VUI	*At what time?*	
User	*Seven o'clock*	→ $TIME
VUI	*For how many people?*	
User	*There will be six of us.*	→ $GUESTS
VUI	*OK, a table at…*	

The user initiates the request by specifying *any slots* in *any order* that fits their mental model, after which the VUI takes over as the initiator to fill the missing slot values needed to fulfill the request. In general, the more familiar they are with the task, the more likely they are to fill more slots at once—this is why it's easier to create successful voice solutions for power users and for tasks with well-defined slot values, like stock trades.

Table 7-1 shows two examples for each slot combination. Only one of 16 cases is fully specified; all others need to be completed somehow by the VUI. Notice that slots can be filled in practically any order, though some orders are more common than others: most people will name the restaurant before any of the other information because place is the most relevant filter to apply first. The "Easter Sunday" request adds complexity: the date changes by year.

Table 7-1. *Representative variation to handle in a four-slot request*

Sample user utterance	Slots unspecified
A reservation, 8 PM, two people, at Na Na's tomorrow. *Get a table for five at Na Na's tonight at six o'clock.*	None
Reserve a spot at Na Na's Chinese tonight at 7 PM. *I'd like a seven o'clock reservation at Na Na's for tonight.*	Guests
I'd like a table for four at six o'clock at Na Na's please. *Make a reservation for Na Na's for four people at six.*	Day
A table for two please, tomorrow at eight in the evening. *Two of us want dinner somewhere tonight at 7:15.*	Place
Dinner tomorrow at Na Na's, three people please. *I'd like a Na Na's reservation for two tonight.*	Time
I'd like to go to Na Na's tomorrow. *Could I get a table on Sunday at Na Na's please?*	Time, guests
Get me a reservation please for Na Na's at 6 PM. *Six o'clock dinner reservation at Na Na's please.*	Day, guests
Table at Na Na's, there will be five of us. *Please make a reservation for five at Na Na's Kitchen.*	Day, time
I want a reservation at six on Friday. *Reservation please for tomorrow for 6 PM.*	Place, guests
Could ya reserve a table please, six people at 5 PM? *Get me a reservation for six at seven.*	Place, day

(*continued*)

Table 7-1. *(continued)*

Sample user utterance	Slots unspecified
Reservation for three adults and a toddler tonight. *Reserve a table Friday of this week for five.*	Place, time
Please request a table at Na Na's. *A Na Na's reservation please.*	Day, time, guests
A reservation at sunset. *Reserve a table at 7:30 or so.*	Place, day, guests
Get a table next Sunday. *I'm looking for a place for dinner on Easter Sunday.*	Place, time, guests
I need a reservation for six. *Where can I get a table for maybe ten people?*	Place, day, time
I need a dinner reservation. Can you do reservations?	Place, day, time, guests

Reaching Completeness Through Dialog Management

Filling unspecified slots becomes a game of combinatorics. This is where **dialog management** is key. When you branch your dialogs and follow up with prompts to fill empty slots, avoid asking for information the user already provided. It sounds stupid and wastes their time, which means they'll be less likely to engage with your VUI. Asking again also adds risk of getting it wrong the second time. Figure 7-2 shows an incomplete request in the procedure prep helper for making an appointment.

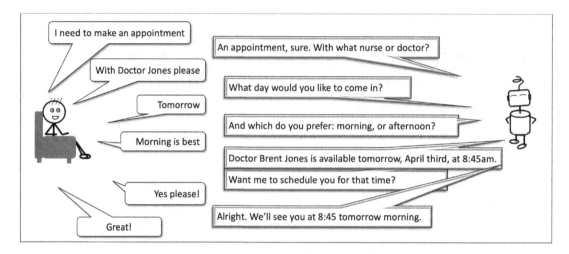

Figure 7-2. *VUI filling an incomplete procedure prep helper request*

Your goal is to balance a solid user experience with robust and maintainable code. Here's one way: find a flow that's familiar and logical to users to fill any missing slots. Turn that into a pattern where each slot-filling dialog can follow the same order of steps no matter what information the user said initially. Look at the third column in Table 7-2: the missing slots in each case are listed in the same logical order of {place → day → time → guests}. This allows you to create a single flow that steps through the necessary prompts and skips unnecessary ones.

Table 7-2. *Simple dialog manager for a four-slot request*

	If {SLOT} needed	Go to prompt	Prompt wording
1	{place}	GetPlace_init	At which restaurant?
2	{day}	GetDay_init	For what day?
3	{time}	GetTime_init	At what time?
4	{guests}	GetGuests_init	How many people?

You have a set of nested Initiate-Respond dialog acts, where the main dialog brackets the sometimes needed slot-filling subdialogs. Table 7-3 steps through an example of putting the dialog manager (DM) to use filling a partially specified utterance. A dialog manager does what you'd guess: manages the dialog. It takes as input a representation of what the user said and decides the VUI's next action based on its interpretation of the utterance within the contexts and conditions it tracks, including domain, dialog history, number of retries, authentication, settings, and so on. The most immediate decision point for the DM is to determine if any required information is missing, that is, if any slots are empty. If so, then DM rules apply to fill those slots, either with additional questions to the user or based on other settings or assumptions.

The success of your voice app depends on your DM. It's the one part of the voice experience you will have most control over. You can have access to the best speech recognition engine, amazing NLP/NLU, and superb TTS, but it's all for nothing if you don't respond appropriately to the result.[1]

Table 7-3. *Detailed sample dialog illustrating the process of filling in missing slot values, reaching resolution through explicit dialog or implicit rules*

Who	Turn	Slot-filling logic needs	Resolution
User	I[1]	New dialog detected.	*Get a table at Na Na's for dinner tomorrow.*
VUI	--	{place nanas}, {day tomorrow}, {time **null**}, {guests **null**}	Assign unambiguous values to slots.
VUI	--	Apply rules to fill empty required slots or clarify ambiguity without dialog.	{day tomorrow} → expand to absolute date and day of week
VUI	I[1]	Fill next empty slot via dialog: Fill {**time**}.	Query: *At what time?*
User	R[2]	{place nanas}, {day 20190816}, {time **9**}, {guests null}	Response: *Nine.*

(continued)

---

[1]Each platform provides you with its own dialog manager tool. Dialogflow is an example. No matter what platform you work with, it's worth looking at what else is available. For example, RavenClaw is a framework for task-oriented spoken dialog systems developed at CMU. www.cs.cmu.edu/~dbohus/ravenclaw-olympus/index-dan.html. Allen et al. provide a good overview of DM challenges here: www.cs.rochester.edu/research/cisd/pubs/2001/allen-et-al-aimag2001.pdf

Table 7-3. (*continued*)

Who	Turn	Slot-filling logic needs	Resolution
VUI	--	Apply rules to fill empty required slots or clarify ambiguity without dialog.	{time 9} → "dinner" means PM → convert to {time 2100}
VUI	I³	Fill next empty slot via dialog: Fill {**guests**}.	Query: *How many people?*
User	R³	{place nanas}, {day 20190816}, {time 9}, {guests **6**}	Response: *There will be six of us.*
VUI	R¹	All slots filled; no ambiguity remains.	*OK, here's what I found...*

SUCCESS TIP 7.1 USE DATA AND LOGIC TO SIMPLIFY USER TASKS   Always try to make a dialog easier for users by using data and logic. When users leave details unspecified because they expect to choose (*a table tomorrow*), look ahead, pinging the reservations database before your next question. If there's only one time available, offer that instead of asking an open *What time?* If something is annoying in a human conversation, avoid letting your VUI do it, even if it's extra work.

Implementing Request Completion

You want to fill slots with values that reflect the underlying semantic interpretation, or meaning, and also simplify any database access and value assignment needs. Looking at Table 7-3, you might already think about how well this would work as a structure similar to this:

```
{"place": "nanas_kitchen",
 "day": {"weekday": "friday",
 "date": "20180608"},
 "time": "2100",
 "guests": "6"}
```

The earlier appointment example was a fully specified request where all needed slot components had been filled. We filled one built-in slot @sys.date-time, but there are multiple possible subpieces, like date, time, and AM/PM. You can imagine many other requests like *tomorrow* where you need the time, *three o'clock* where you need the date, and so on. So you need logic to determine what to fill and how the VUI should ask for it. For that, you need to write code for fulfillment instead of the built-in logic. You'll learn how later in this chapter.

Notes on Implementing Request Completion

Take another look at the utterances in Table 7-1. They're just a few ways to ask for the same thing. There are many possible carrier phrases, the typical sentences that are questions or commands and also include the verb that forms the intent (*I'd like a reservation...*, *Get a table...*, *Make me a...*, etc.). There's also big variation in the order of information: the name of the restaurant could be the first or the last thing said, for example. Think about how that impacts your code. Did you notice some potential confusion around numbers? Good. We'll come back to that in a moment.

We were a bit cagey about how to deal with time in Table 7-3. In this particular example, you could rely on *dinner* in the first utterance and capture "PM" as a separate slot or part of a structured {time} slot. If Na Na's is open for all meals or if the user didn't specify the meal, you might need to ask explicitly if it's *AM or PM*. Maybe you can build on assumptions to speed up the dialog: reservations are only taken for dinner, or Na Na's is only open for dinner. The take-home message is that you need to understand the domain as well as what people are likely to expect. There is pre-built handling for time, but you still need to understand what your users are likely to do and say.

Users often "overanswer" and provide more information than the VUI asked. If the VUI asks *At what time?*, some users will respond with more than the time, for example, *At nine o'clock, for six people.* They're being helpful—great! And they might break your VUI—oh no! Capture the number of guests, rather than ignoring it and immediately asking, *And for how many people?*

Don't demand a response with all remaining fields at once—that gets messy. But accept those utterances if they happen. It's OK to ask for multiple fields at once when those fields are logically connected in the user's mind, like month and year of a credit card expiration date.

Voice development platforms tend to include some handling for things like a date or day of the week. Nobody wants to redo work someone else has already done, so if you can make use of such handling, do so. But any time you rely on built-in modules, you also need to understand what your users will say in that specific context to make sure their utterances are covered. Will they say a date or part of one ("the nineteenth"), an absolute day ("Sunday"), a relative day ("tomorrow"), or a combination of those ("Sunday the nineteenth")?

Because we teach you best practices no matter what modules a platform offers, we mostly avoid built-ins.

Earlier, we decided that a reservation request without an explicit date probably means "today." Making that assumption makes the dialog shorter and quicker. But your choices affect your recovery methods (Chapter 13), confirmation prompting (Chapter 8), and even coverage and performance (Chapters 10 and 12).

Finally, users give you information you might not need or might not think to handle—even information that at first seems irrelevant:

- *I'm looking for a place for dinner on Easter Sunday.* This person hasn't withheld information about where on purpose; they need help finding something for that day.

- *Reserve a table at 7:30 or so.* This person is flexible about the time. Should you track and use that? Absolutely. Will you, and how? Depends on your scope and schedule.

- *Make a reservation for three adults and a toddler tonight.* Is that a table for three or four? It probably matters to the restaurant. What will you do with that information?

- *Can you do reservations?* This probably is both a question and a request. Will you just respond *Yes*, or will you offer to make one?

You can capture this information as additional **optional slots**. The more of these you fulfill or at least respond intelligently to, the more impressed and happier your users will be.

SUCCESS TIP 7.2 DON'T THROW AWAY INFO USERS PROVIDE   If you only worry about filling required slots, you miss an opportunity. Seriously, making use of everything your users say and don't say is one of the best ways to make your VUI sound "smart." Include optional slots in addition to required ones. For example, an optional slot tableType could track requests for "quiet," "by the window," or "close to kitchen" for future use.

Ambiguous Requests

You just filled missing slots, which you'll do a lot in any voice interactions that aren't one-shots. Sometimes during slot-filling, ambiguity happens—you need to resolve that.

If an **intent** is the user's intended meaning, how can you know what the user means? You can't read their mind! Think about how often you're not sure if you completely understand what someone just said or if they understand your point. VUIs have to deal with all that without the benefits you have as a human. Even when we speak the same language and have similar understanding of the world, someone might be vague, mumble, make references to something you don't know, or pronounce a word differently. They express a request as a question (*Can you mute the TV?*) when it's actually a command (*Mute the TV!*). So how can you know the user's intent? The answer is you can never be sure, but you can maximize your chances of success by relying on the "rules of engagement" you learned in Chapter 2 and by providing ways to get back on track when there's misunderstanding. A longtime VUI designer says that 50% of your VUI design effort should be spent on handling non-best path interactions; another VUI designer says that number is optimistic!

Ambiguity as we use it here refers to user vagueness that the VUI needs to resolve in order to proceed and fulfill the user's request. User ambiguity has many causes: vague wording, responses that ended prematurely, homonyms (words that sound the same but have different meaning), names with multiple matches, near-synonyms, VUI misrecognition, and others.

The process of resolving ambiguity is called disambiguation. It's one of the most important aspects of voice interactions and one you need to understand and implement appropriately. Let's use more reservation utterances to illustrate ambiguity:

- *Get me a reservation for six at seven.*

  - **Issue:** No units are specified for the quantities, and both numbers are plausible to mean guests or time.

  - **Solution:** Prepositions are key here: *for six* could be the number of guests or time, but *at seven* would not refer to guests. Apply logic to resolve as $TIME.

- *I'd like a Na Na's reservation for two tonight.*

  - **Issue**: "Two" can refer to time (2 PM, late lunch) or number of guests.

  - **Solution**: A reservation for "tonight" is not likely to mean either 2 AM or 2 PM, so *two* can be assumed to mean guests. Apply logic to resolve as $GUESTS.

- *I need a reservation for six.*

  - **Issue**: *Six* can be time or number of guests; *for* can introduce every piece of info: *reservation for 7 PM for Na Na's for five people for Sunday.*

  - **Solution**: It's too important to get this right. Ask the user to resolve.

- *Get a table next Sunday.*

  - **Issue**: People differ on what *next DAY* means. To some, it's in a week or more; to others, it's the very next one coming up.

  - **Solution**: It's too important to get this right. Ask the user to resolve.

People are sometimes aware of confusion as they speak and sometimes not. Sometimes the rest of the dialog takes care of ambiguity by process of elimination. This is advanced stuff right here. Deep language and cultural knowledge is necessary; details differ between languages and user groups. Just think about what's considered "dinner time" in different cultures. For space considerations, we're focusing on standard dialect US English, but your users won't all be native speakers or speak perfectly grammatically at all times. Far from it.

Your disambiguation needs to acknowledge that the user tried but that you need clarification—if you simply repeat the question, the user will be just as ambiguous the second time. Instead, build on information the user already provided, so they don't have to restate the whole utterance including the added clarification. And track the context. Compare the two examples in Table 7-4. Dialog A keeps the context; Dialog B does not.

People shouldn't need to restate the fully specified *Call Doctor Jones' mobile*, though some will. That's not conversational. Instead, handle all relevant responses within the scope of the disambiguation, and assume that responses are made within the scope of the already specified current context. Context of all types is integral to conversational dialogs, both human and VUI, which is why you hear about it throughout the book, including all of Chapter 14.

Table 7-4. *Disambiguation sample dialog showing the importance of keeping context*

Who	Dialog	
	A	**B**
User	*Call Doctor Jones.*	*Call Doctor Jones.*
VUI	*Brent Jones. Which phone: home or mobile?*	*Brent Jones. Which phone: home or mobile?*
User	*Mobile.*	*Mobile.*
VUI	*Calling Brent Jones, mobile…*	*Mobile is a port city on the coast of Alabama…*
	√	**X**

The general pattern of ambiguity resolution and resolving underspecified requests is illustrated in Figure 7-3. Participant B (the VUI or the human listener) is "stuck" until all required slots are unambiguously filled either by asking Participant A or by applying predefined logic. You may need to fill slots or resolve vague slot values—or both!—more than once in a dialog, as you've seen. The process is the same for both: switching between who's initiating and who's responding. The difference is that in ambiguity resolution, the user has tried to provide the necessary information, whereas in underspecified requests, the user hasn't tried yet. This is important for two reasons. First, some disambiguation techniques work better in one case than in others. You need to understand how to choose the right one for your task and users. Second, to sound smart, your prompts should be slightly different in the two cases. It's subtle and extra work that many voice systems don't bother with. But you want to seem smart, right? Beyond sounding smart, it also helps users succeed.

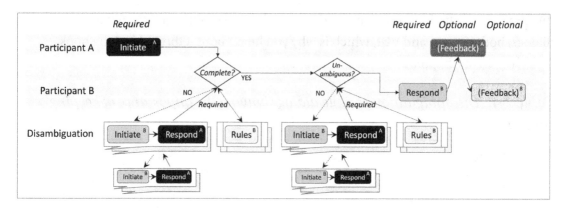

Figure 7-3.   *Core dialog pattern for resolving ambiguity and fully specifying a VUI dialog*

Figure 7-3 is pretty abstract. It covers what's needed in any VUI dialogs you'll build, though the architecture details will be dependent on your environment. Later in this chapter, you'll see how closely it reflects how Dialogflow handles ambiguity. It looks like a call return subroutine—that'll be important later when you learn about keeping context in stateless models.

Applying Figure 7-3 to the sample dialog in Figure 7-1 gives you something like Figure 7-4, with step-by-step slot-filling, what's called a directed dialog.

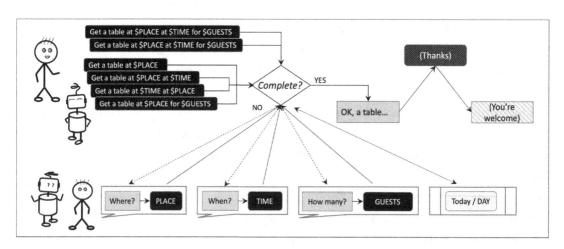

Figure 7-4.   *Disambiguation dialog pattern for multiple slots in a task completion request*

Combining sample dialogs for the other two core dialog types gives you Figure 7-5. These diagrams are simplified by only showing slot-filling. After you learn about disambiguation methods, we strongly recommend returning to these figures. Expand them for a few sample dialogs with multiple slots and ambiguity. It's a surprisingly useful tool for the different roles on a voice team to focus on expected behavior without getting stuck in details.

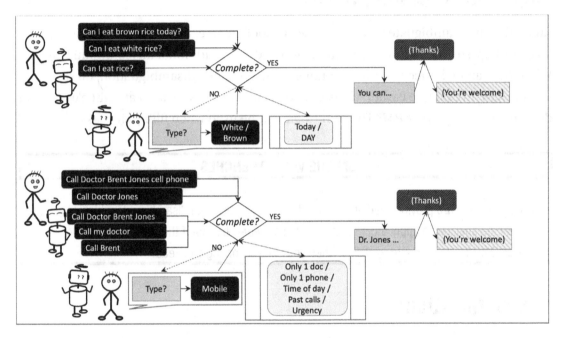

Figure 7-5. *Applying the disambiguation dialog pattern to a question answer interaction and an action request*

MULTIMODAL CORNER

Ambiguity is less of an issue and easier to resolve in a multimodal VUI—pictures really do speak a thousand words sometimes. Combining an initial spoken search with a follow-on screen with the possible choices is a quick and easy way to disambiguate. And if options are vague, images can clarify.

Disambiguation Methods

There are several well-established approaches to disambiguation. As you'll see, your choice depends on the task, the type of content, the likelihood of a particular user choice, and the overall number of choices.

Logic-Based Assumptions

Rule #1: Only disambiguate when you have to. Spoken, or explicit, disambiguation is an extra step, so it slows down the interaction and risks additional miscommunication. When you can make accurate assumptions without explicit disambiguation, do so.

You saw an example earlier: if a user asks for a *dinner* reservation at eight o'clock, you don't need to ask, *AM or PM?* The same logic can be used when filling slots as well.

FROM THE VOICE TRENCHES

An audio hardware provider had an Alexa skill that asked users to disambiguate which connected speaker to apply a command to. That's great—but not if the user has only one device. Never disambiguate explicitly when you can rely on logic instead.

Yes/No Questions

Rule #2: You can't always second-guess your user—you often need to ask them. Yes/No questions are the simplest disambiguation method. Easy for users to process and easy to recognize the response. Use this approach when one option is more likely than any others and the cost of getting it wrong is higher than just assuming.

If a user has one contact named Brent who has two phones in the contact list, use some logic to pick the most likely one and offer that one as the "yes" response in a question. Typical logic includes "most commonly used" and "most recently used":

User	*Call Brent.*	{"name": {"first":"brent", last:"jones"},}
VUI	*Brent Jones, mobile phone?*	"phone ": {"type":"mobile", "number":"4155551212"}}

User   *Yes.*

VUI   *Calling Brent Jones, mobile...*

If most users prefer regular crust when ordering pizza, it's simpler and less error-prone to offer that instead of listing all choices every time:

User   *I wanna order a large pizza.*

VUI   *Regular crust?*

User   *Yes, please.*

VUI   *And what toppings...*

An example of a Yes/No question in the medical domain could involve making sure an emergency doesn't get directed to an answering service. There are reasons why you won't see this exact dialog in real life—think about why—but it's a good illustration of a Yes/No question:

User   *Call my doctor.*

VUI   *Are you calling about a life-threatening emergency?*

User   *No.*

VUI   *OK. Calling Doctor at Maple Clinic...*

Implementing Yes/No Questions

Let's add a disambiguation turn before we call the doctor's office—load the sample code in 6-8.zip to follow along and make updates easily. In Chapter 6, you had some follow-on questions for the tcrProcedurePrep dialog, with a couple of "next" intents. You learned how to implement these using contexts, partly because we wanted to introduce that important concept. Now you'll learn about **follow-up intents**, which are a related concept in Dialogflow. Follow-up intents are intents that only follow some specific intent. Follow-up intents have some pre-built training phrases for common follow-ups, like "yes" or "no." Other pre-builts include navigation commands like "more," "next," and "previous" and universal commands, like "cancel" and "repeat" (Chapter 9). Let's use follow-up intents. After you're done, your intent list should look like Figure 7-6.

Figure 7-6. *Intent list after adding follow-up yes and no intents to* arCallDoctor

1. Change the response of the existing arCallDoctor intent to the new "Are you calling about..." prompt. Turn off the slider marking arCallDoctor as ending the conversation.

2. Click Intents on the left. In the arCallDoctor intent, click Add Follow-Up Intent on the right. A menu opens; choose yes.

3. A new subintent has been created, arCallDoctor-yes. You may need to click the down arrow by the intent name to see it. Click the intent. Notice the "yes" training phrases already populated.

4. Add a response: "Call 911 immediately." Set this intent as the end of the conversation.

5. Do the same for "no." In arCallDoctor, click Add Follow-Up Intent. Choose no, and then choose arCallDoctor—no subintent.

6. Add a response: "OK, calling your doctor." Set intent as end of conversation. Test!

Notes on Implementing Yes/No Questions

You need to be careful about how you handle "no" responses. This may sound weird, but will users know what a "no" means? Is it the opposite of "yes"? Sometimes. If you dictate an email and you hear, *Do you want to send it now?* you might hesitate; yes, you want to send it but not yet, not until you review it. Will "no" save it for later or delete it? Carefully work through how users will be successful in the "no" cases, and clarify prompts as needed.

In a health insurance VUI, more than two-thirds of user interactions were prescription refills. By changing from offering "refills" as one of several options to starting with a simple *Are you calling about a refill?*, overall success rates went up significantly.

A/B Sets

A choice of *A or B* sounds like a choice between two options, but it can be **logically constrained** to various degrees. When users understand that there's the constraint, they know they need to pick one of the two. This works best when the options are **mutually exclusive**. *AM or PM?* is a perfect example. *Hot or cold?* is another.

> **User**   *I'd like to schedule a phone appointment for tomorrow at 7:30.*
>
> **VUI**   *AM or PM?* [Assuming a schedule where this is an option]
>
> **User**   *AM.*
>
> **VUI**   *OK, an appointment for...*

If there's a natural or standard order of options in regular conversation, use that same order in your VUI. So your prompt should ask *AM or PM?* rather than *PM or AM?* If there's no such order, you can do alphabetic, recency, frequency, or just what sounds better!

Implementing A/B Sets

The appointment dialog is a good example of A/B disambiguation (AM vs. PM). You won't know if disambiguation is needed until you parse the result of the built-in @ sys.date-time entity to determine what information you have. Here's another way to implement disambiguation.

When you built tcrMakeAppointment in Chapter 6, you learned about **required parameters**, where a follow-on prompt automatically collects needed information if not filled. You used that to fill the time: in *Make an appointment*, time is a required parameter with an automatic prompt, such as *OK, a new appointment. For what time?* If the user had said, *Make an appointment for three*, that prompt wouldn't play, because you'd already have the information. If you think this looks a lot like Figure 7-3, you're right. Dialogflow has a built-in notion of using required parameters to determine if a request is complete and prompt if it's not. In this example, the time (*three*) is settled.

Let's code AM vs. PM. First, add an entity for disambiguation (Figure 7-7).

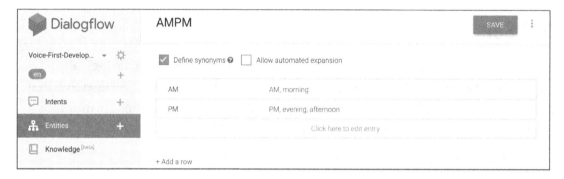

Figure 7-7. *Entity for AM/PM disambiguation*

1. Click Entities on the left bar.

2. Create a new entity called AMPM. Add a reference value "AM" with synonym "morning" and another reference value "PM" with synonyms "evening" and "afternoon."

3. Save (Figure 7-7). Now add the required parameter (Figure 7-8).

Training phrases ❓   Search training phrases 🔍 ⌃

> 99 Add user expression

> 99 Make an appointment for three PM.

> 99 Make an appointment for three

> 99 Make an appointment.

Action and parameters   ⌃

Enter action name

REQUIRED ❓	PARAMETER NAME ❓	ENTITY ❓	VALUE	IS LIST ❓	PROMPTS ❓
☑	dateTime	@sys.date-time	$dateTime	☐	OK, you want t o...
☑	AMPM	@AMPM	$AMPM	☐	AM or PM? [1]

+ New parameter

Figure 7-8. *Adding AM/PM disambiguation as a required parameter to* tcrMakeAppointment

4. Click the intent tcrMakeAppointment.

5. Add a new parameter: name AMPM, entity @AMPM (the one we just created), and value $ampm. Make AMPM a required parameter.

6. Click Define Prompts in the PROMPTS column. Add a prompt "AM or PM?"

7. Test the automatic disambiguation by adding a couple of sample training phrases. First, add "Make an appointment for three."

   Double-click the word "three," right-click, and select @sys.date-time:dateTime. This sets the parameter dateTime that you've already defined to the value "three."

8.   Next, add the training phrase "Make an appointment for three PM." Again, double-click three and choose `@sys.data-time:dateTime`. Then, double-click PM and choose `@AMPM:AMPM`.

9.   Verify that AMPM returns in the response. Add $AMPM to the existing prompt: "OK, I've set it up, `$dateTime.original $AMPM`. When you're done, just say goodbye." Your intent should look like the one in Figure 7-8.

10. Test in the Dialogflow console with all three sample phrases. It should only ask for the information when it needs to. Figure 7-3 in action!

Everything looks good, but you're actually not done yet. Here, you see some of the powers of Dialogflow's system entities to accelerate development. But beware! You'll test this dialog on a device to find additional issues that require you to understand more about what's going on in the system entities.

Are you disambiguating or filling a required parameter? Both! Required parameters are a powerful way of implementing the general disambiguation framework of Figure 7-3. Is all disambiguation like this? *Make an appointment, Make an appointment at three,* and *Make an appointment at 3 PM* are all very likely. But *Call my doctor; it's not life-threatening* is very unlikely.

Notes on Implementing A/B Sets

Because users are familiar with the options, mutually exclusive A/B sets are easy disambiguation prompts to write. Wording that can cause trouble in less constrained sets is fine for *AM or PM?* because the meaning of "morning or evening" implies that there's an "either or" here.

Options may be mutually exclusive to you, but not to your users. It's a common mistake when you're not a naïve user yourself, and it will cause problems. If a user is familiar with some lunch options, they'll know that *soup or salad* is a choice of one or the other. But there's nothing logically mutually exclusive here, not like AM vs. PM. Therefore, some users will say *yes* or *no* or even *both*:

User   *I'd like a lunch special.*

VUI   *Soup or salad?*

User   *Soup/Salad/ No/Yes/Both/What's the soup?/Can I have chips instead?*

The question seems so simple! Predicting what confuses users is important because you need to minimize unexpected responses and handle any variation that disambiguation introduces. When people talk to each other, they often use a Yes/No format when they actually mean "pick one" rather than "say yes or no." Avoid this wording unless you handle all the responses. The options are much clearer to the user if you instead ask a WH question (a question starting with Who, What, Where, etc.), for example, *Our lunch specials come with soup or salad. Which one would you like?*

The details of what causes issues are language-dependent, but the concept is universal in that you need to be very aware of what structures and words are easily confusable, whatever spoken language you're developing for. Keep it simple to help your nonnative users as well.

FROM THE VOICE TRENCHES

In a financial services system, a change from a Yes/No structure to a WH structure alone increased user success significantly. Prompts such as *Are you calling to __, to __, or to __?* were changed to *Which are you calling about? __, __, or __?* In a flight information system that allowed user barge-in, *Is that for today, tomorrow, or yesterday?* resulted in many *yes* and *yes, today* responses as users answered right after hearing only *Is that for today?*

Static Lists

Static lists are small lists, no more than four or five items, always with the same set of options. Longer than that, users won't remember, but longer lists can work if barge-in is available. You use lists when there are a few options that aren't obvious or you want to remind the user of the wording you're looking for.

If a user is familiar with US pizza ordering, they understand that the options for size are mutually exclusive:

> **User** *I wanna order a pizza.*
>
> **VUI** *Sure. What size: small, medium, large, or extralarge?*
>
> **User** *Medium.*
>
> **VUI** *And what toppings...*

Because the user said they want one pizza, the VUI expects one of the four sizes in response. Now try this: say out loud like you would to a person, *I wanna order pizza*, not including *a*. Notice how hard it is to hear if there's an "a" there or not? It's hard for the VUI too! Think about what you'd do differently if you're not sure how many pizzas the user wants to order or if it's a large multi-pizza order. If most people only want one, avoid asking everyone *How many pizzas are you ordering?* But you start by offering a special case, like *If you're getting four or more pizzas, ask for our group order. Otherwise, what size...* You can also imply that there will be a chance to order more than one: *What size for the first one...*

If the user is initiating a task with several options, you might remind them of the options—if they're power users, you might shorten it to *Which meal?*:

User   *Add a meal to my food diary.*

VUI   *Which meal: breakfast, lunch, dinner, or snack?*

User   *Dinner.*

VUI   *OK. What did you have for dinner? ...*

Implementing Static Lists

That last sample dialog is a great example for the food diary functionality. In the tcrFoodDiaryCollection intent (Chapter 6), you added parameters for meal and food type. Now you need to make the meal a required parameter like you did earlier in this chapter for dateTime and AMPM. The new intent will look like Figure 7-9.

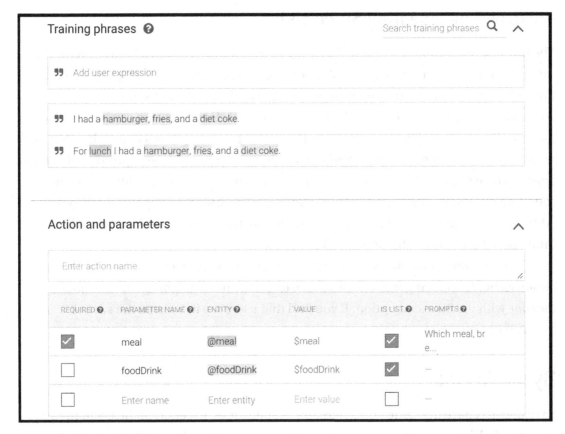

Figure 7-9. tcrFoodDiaryCollection after making "meal" a required parameter for disambiguation

1. Open the tcrFoodDiaryCollection intent.

2. In the Actions and Parameters section, make the meal parameter required.

3. In the new PROMPTS column, click Define Prompts and enter the prompt from the sample dialog: "Which meal: breakfast, lunch, dinner, or snack?"

4. Add a new training phrase without the meal: "I had a hamburger, fries, and a diet Coke." Note how it automatically filled the slots with the right food items. Save.

5. Test with the new phrase. It should ask for meal type.

Notes on Implementing Static Lists

The trickiest thing about designing lists is the carrier phrase wording. Watch out for the same wording issues as for A/B sets. When choices are logically exclusive, you can relax. But even with careful intonation to emphasize the options, hearing a question like *Do you want sprinkles, nuts, or raisins?* can throw users off. Their answers can be names of the three items or *all of them* or *yes* or *no*. Handle all those responses gracefully. Does *yes* mean all of them? Or one of them and the user is waiting for your next question of *Which one?* You'd be surprised how often utterance logs show user confusion for such normal-sounding questions. Minimize the "yes" and "no" responses by using WH questions (*Which one do you want: …?*). Or be ready to handle the variation and be aware that intonation doesn't work the same in all languages.

The common approach for voice is to have users pick from a list by naming the option rather than saying *that one*. It's tricky to get the timing right to correctly match *that one* with the intended option. If you find that users say it, shorten the silence between the options.

Dynamic Lists

Dynamic lists have the same characteristics as static ones, except that the list items are contextual, different for different users or contexts, like time of day, type of account, or number of matching names in a contact list. The order of the items can be alphabetical, by some common standard like time or by most likely choice first. If a user has four contacts named Brent but typically calls Brent Jones, you might have this dialog:

> **User**   *Call Brent.*
>
> **VUI**   *Which Brent: Jones, Adams, Barnes, or Carletti?*
>
> **User**   *Brent Jones.*
>
> **VUI**   *Calling Brent Jones …*

Choosing between filtered search results is a common use case for dynamic lists:

> **User**   *Reservation at Na Na's tonight for four people.*
>
> **VUI**   *Na Na's Kitchen has a four-person table available at 6:30 PM or at 9 PM. Which would you like?*

User   *6:30, please.*

VUI   *OK…*

Implementing Dynamic Lists

With "static" Dialogflow you've used so far, it's tricky to create truly "dynamic" grammars based on context or user-dependent content. This is important because of recognition: dynamic coverage where only valid slot values are accepted allows users to be less precise while still being understood. For that reason, you now start relying more on code rather than on built-in features even though you could handle both list types similarly. More in the following.

Notes on Implementing Dynamic Lists

Be careful with carrier phrase wording, same as for static lists. If the number of items in the list is large, if users are unfamiliar with the choices, or if the number of choices varies from time to time, it can help to be clear about the number of options (*Which of the following five…*; *There are five…*). It's useful to set expectations and prepare the listener for what's coming. When each choice is long, such as a street address, you can offer a couple of items, with a *Which would you like: the first one or the second one?*

Make use of any additional information about the options: offer the most likely choice first in the list. But don't change the list structure so often that users have to pay attention to something they thought they knew.

In a local traffic and directions system, users had to listen to the end of disambiguation prompts because the structure used depended on the number of ambiguous items. A "yes" could mean using an alternate destination (*Would you like to use that instead?*) or hearing alternatives (*Would you like to hear others?*). This makes interactions longer and increases cognitive load—aim for parallel options.

Open Sets

Open sets refer to lists with too many items to list individually because of the cognitive load. Choosing from a list is easier for users, unless the set is large, so for open sets you don't provide an explicit list of options; you just ask the question. If a user wants to make a reservation at a restaurant, you don't start by offering every restaurant in town by name:

> **User**   *Make a reservation.*
>
> **VUI**   *Sure, a reservation. At what restaurant?*
>
> **User**   *Oh... Um... Na Na's.*
>
> **VUI**   *Sure, Na Na's Kitchen. For what day?*

Use this for larger sets of names or amounts and for limited well-known sets like days of the week or months in a year. There's no need to list *What month? January, February, ...*

Implementing Open Sets

We mentioned earlier that you don't want to add long lists by hand in the Dialogflow GUI, but instead use the API. Implementing open set disambiguation isn't very different than a small set, other than that the entity has many more items.

Notes on Implementing Open Sets

The trick with handling open sets is figuring out what to do when users say something you don't handle. An open set is what you face at a restaurant when a server asks, "What would you like to drink?" Just like you might respond "Well, uh, what do you have?", you'll need to be ready to respond to a request for more information. Add synonyms for *What are my choices?* as well as a response. The response can often be the same as for *I don't know*—be sure to handle both. In an open list, giving one or two representative examples can be a great approach. You'll learn about techniques for this and how to incorporate examples in Chapter 12.

Menus

Menus are not different from other lists per se, but the options are often "buckets" of additional options, or starting points for multistep dialogs. They can even be buckets of other buckets! Menus are important for many customer service VUIs because they narrow the scope in a large and potentially overwhelming search space, making them useful when most users are not power users and need some hand-holding.

You might think menus belong only in IVRs, but they have wider use, including offering a few choices to avoid decision paralysis:

User   *I'd like a reservation for five people tonight.*

VUI   *We can seat your party of five at 6:15 or 9:15 tonight. Which do you prefer?*

~ ~ ~   ~ ~ ~

User   *What wine can I serve with dessert?*

VUI   *I can pair wine to anything. What kind of dessert: sweet, savory, or cheese?*

User   *It'll be cheese.*

VUI   *Tasty! What type of cheese: cow, sheep, or goat? Or a mix?*

User   *I'm thinking cow's milk.*

VUI   *And will it be a hard, semisoft, soft, or blue?*

User   *Definitely blue.*

VUI   *OK. Blues can be tricky to pair with. How about this...*

Implementing Menus

For the procedure prep helper, imagine an addition to the functionality that asks what kind of medication you're using. Table 7-5 shows an example of the additional dialog.

Table 7-5. *Procedure prep functionality with new menu for menu disambiguation. Gray rows are new turns[2]*

Who	Dialog
User	*I'm ready for my procedure prep.*
VUI	*OK, let's begin your prep. First, which are you using: Miralax, Dulcolax, or Colase?*
User	*I'm using Miralax.*
VUI	*For Miralax, step 1 is to prepare a dose. Each dose is one cap full. Now, measure one dose, and add it to an 8-ounce glass of water. Stir to dissolve. When you're done, say "Next."*
User	*Next.*
VUI	*Great. Now drink that dose completely. After you're done, say "Next."*
User	*Next.*

You can now build the code additions corresponding to the gray rows in Table 7-5. It will be similar to the calling example—add an additional intent for disambiguation and use contexts to control the flow of the dialog:

1. In intent `tcrProcedurePrep`, change the response to the new next prompt "OK, let's begin…" in Table 7-5.

2. In `tcrProcedurePrep`, change the output context to a new one, `tcrProcedurePrepLaxative`. Save.

3. Create a new entity laxative with items Miralax, Dulcolax, and Colase. Save.

4. Create a new intent `tcrProcedurePrepLaxative` with the training phrase "Miralax." Note how it automatically assigns "Miralax" to the `@laxative` slot!

5. Add the `tcrProcedurePrep` response "For Miralax, the first step…"

6. Add the input context `tcrProcedurePrepLaxative` that we defined earlier and output context `tcrProcedurePrepStep1`. Save. Test!

---

[2]Miralax, Dulcolax, and Colase are registered trademarks of Bayer, Chattem, and Avrio Health, respectively. All are common products—we use the names for realism without making any medical claims whatsoever.

Notes on Implementing Menus

The wording for each menu option needs to convey what's in each "bucket"—users shouldn't need to peck around for the right path. Use names that are short, distinct, and parallel in style. Make it obvious what to say to lessen cognitive load, but avoid being overly repetitious:

- ☹ *To hear instructions, say "Hear instructions." To order forms, say "Order forms."*

- ☺ *You can say "Hear instructions" or "Order forms."*

- ☺ *You can "hear instructions" or "order forms." Which would you like?*

Be very careful using company-specific product names unless users actually know those names. And always include a wide set of synonyms for robust coverage.

If you use menus, also handle all direct requests reaching anything within those buckets. It's too common to see voice enabling of an existing GUI with pull-down menus where only the same step-by-step navigation is implemented for voice. That's terrible. One of the benefits of voice is that users can drop past any steps or buckets right away. Don't force users through a step-by-step flow when they know what they want; they won't like it, they'll hate your VUI, and they'll risk more misrecognition—everyone will be unhappy.

All this doesn't mean menus are bad—quite the opposite. They can guide users who are unfamiliar with the VUI. New users and power users, happily living together. VUIs should never force all users through the same path. Different paths allow different mental models to reach the same goal; your VUI should handle all those models and paths.

IVRs got a bad rap as "trees that kept users away from talking to a person." That's not the technology's fault; instead, underlying causes included poor design or implementation due to failing to understand user needs or behavior, unreasonable schedules, or overzealous business rules.

MULTIMODAL CORNER

Figure 7-10 shows some possibilities you have with a multimodal interface, conceptual versions of a few 22otters app screens. At each screen, an audio prompt plays. You can clarify vague options with pictures (1), and you can offer different input methods depending on the question and expected user responses. Notice how the Yes/No question (2), the small menu (3), and the open question (4) differ in the input controls they offer: each one has a mic for spoken input; Yes/No and small menu also have buttons for the closed set of options, while the open question has a keyboard option and a button linking to an online version of the procedure prep instructions.

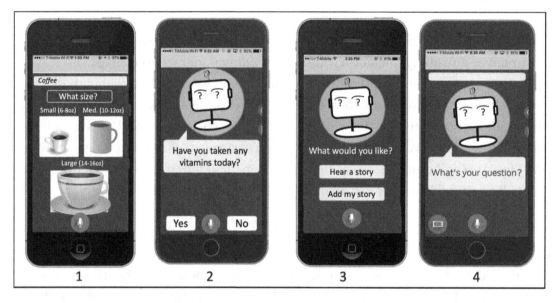

Figure 7-10. *Multimodal disambiguation and choice. (1) clarifying sizes, (2) Yes/ No question, (3) small menu, (4) open set*

FROM THE VOICE TRENCHES

Menus, like lists, can be static or dynamic. One banking system had five possible items that could go in a menu of options. Not all items were relevant to all users at all time, but depended on account type and calendar month. Some options were more applicable than others depending on the same variables, so the bank wanted users to hear options in a personalized order of relevance. This lent itself to a dynamic implementation. Each user would hear menus with anywhere from two to five options in differing order. Managing the dynamic prompts was a huge undertaking. Was it worth the effort? Unclear—we have no comparative data from static menus for this system. But it worked and didn't cause confusion or complaints.

Testing on the Device to Find and Solve Issues

Let's return to see what happens when you test with Google Assistant. Say *Make an appointment for 3 PM.* Oh no, something went wrong! It asked, *AM or PM?* It's important that you understand why this failed, so let's work through it. If you did what we described, you should have gotten the response *AM or PM?* And you'd wonder, *Hey, what gives? I told you PM; it shouldn't have asked!* Let's see what happened.

In Chapter 3, we explained why you need to test not only in the console but also on a device, like a Google Home. Testing on a device also gives you a history of conversations, so you can look at what happened. With the conversation history, you can debug some hard-to-find issues in your dialogs. Dialogflow has a nice capability of showing a conversation history (Figure 7-11).

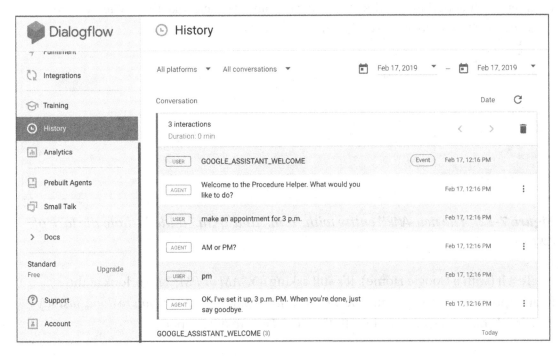

Figure 7-11. *Taking a look at a conversation in History*

Let's use History to debug what's going on with AM and PM:

1. On the left pane in Dialogflow, click History. You see a list of conversations (Figure 7-11).

2. Find and click the last conversation where you tested, "Make an appointment at 3 PM." The conversation history shows the user utterances (USER) and the system responses (AGENT). You see the statement about making the appointment and then the AM/PM response for disambiguation.

Compare the user utterance in History to what we've been writing:

- **Text**: "Make an appointment for 3 PM."

- **Dialogflow History**: "make an appointment for 3 p.m."

They're not the same! There's a capital M vs. a lowercase m. Turns out, that doesn't matter. What else? There's "PM" vs. "p.m."; could that be it? How can you find out? Remember, "PM" is part of the AMPM entity that you defined. What if you add "p.m." as a synonym for the PM entity and the same for AM? Let's do that carefully: there's no space between the first period and the m. You have to add it exactly like that. When you're done, the entity should look like the one in Figure 7-12.

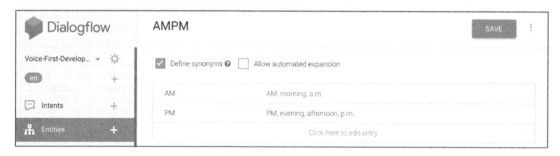

Figure 7-12. *The new AMPM entity with "a.m." and "p.m." added—note the lack of spaces*

Test it (with a Google Home). It's still asking for "*AM or PM?*"! Also, look at the final response from the system: *OK, I've set it up, 3 p.m. PM. When you're done, just say goodbye.* What's up with it saying "PM" twice? Time to dig deeper.

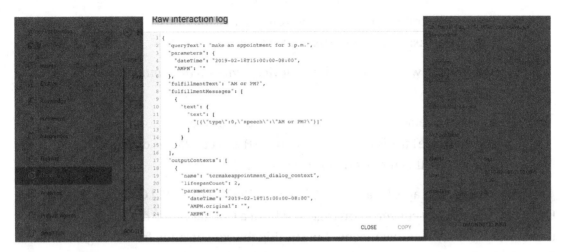

Figure 7-13. *History raw interaction log for "AM or PM?" in the failed conversation*

Find the conversation from the last test step. In the AGENT response "AM or PM?" on the right, click the three dots and select Raw Interaction Log (Figure 7-13). There's a lot of information in here. For now you're interested in the first Parameters section, under queryText. Remember how you defined parameters in the Dialogflow intent (Figure 7-7)? This raw interaction log tells us how Dialogflow actually set those parameters. This level of detail will become increasingly important as you move toward writing more code outside of Dialogflow and using fulfillment:

- dateTime is set to a string "2019-02-18T15:00:00-08:00", which is essentially date, time, and time zone. The time is 15:00, which is 3 PM. Interesting.

- AMPM is empty; it's not filled with anything! Interesting.

Here's what happened. You actually wanted to set dateTime to 3 and AMPM to PM. Instead, Dialogflow set dateTime to (a representation of) 3 PM, which left nothing to fill the AMPM parameter, so AMPM was left empty. Let's fix this first and then look at why it happened and what you need to watch out for:

1. In the tcrMakeAppointment intent, under Actions and Parameters, change the entity of the dateTime parameter from @sys.date-time to @sys.number. Left-click the @sys.date-time in the ENTITY column and choose @sys.number.

2. Look at the training phrases now. You'll notice that the three's now are all using the new @sys.number entity.

3. Test it again with a Google Home device. *Make an appointment for 3 PM*. Finally!

4. Find the interaction log for the new successful conversation. You'll see that dateTime is now set to 3 and AMPM is set to PM, as desired. The fix is in the interaction log (Figure 7-13).

When testing your app, be aware of GOOGLE _ ASSISTANT _ WELCOME. It's the first USER utterance in any conversation triggered from a Google Home device. It's basically the fake USER statement that means "I'm starting the conversation from Google Home." From there, it goes immediately to the Default Welcome Intent, the source of the introductory prompt. You won't see GOOGLE _ ASSISTANT _ WELCOME when testing with the Dialogflow console, but you do if testing with Actions on Google or with an actual Google Home device.

Two Big Lessons

You discovered two important issues while doing a simple disambiguation between morning and evening. We're not picking on Dialogflow or any other tool—this is complex stuff, and these issues happen all over. We go into detail because we want you to understand the pitfall of relying on any platform without verifying the implementation details, in this case for system entities. With more precise control, you can avoid these types of issues—or get tripped up in the same way because you overlooked something. It's easy to do and it happens to us all.

Lesson 1: Know what's in the STT box. The speech-to-text (STT) component of a voice system feeds a string of words into natural language understanding (NLU) (Figure 1-3). So far, we've treated STT as a "black box," not worrying too much about what was going on inside. Most of the time, you don't need to know. But here you discovered that you sometimes need to pay attention. For the PM entity you had synonyms "PM" and "evening," but no "p.m.," which is exactly what the STT returned. And it returned "3" instead of "three." What STT returns isn't under your control on most platforms. So just know what it returns and include the training phrases and entity synonyms that match what STT returns. You wouldn't have discovered either issue if you only tested in the Dialogflow console with text; it only appeared when testing with voice, incorporating STT.

Lesson 2: Know what's in the system entity box. "3 p.m." was not setting the parameters as you expected them to. This issue is a little thornier than the STT issue. System entities can save you a lot of time and effort. But sometimes they produce unexpected behavior that you need to be aware of. Specifically, the @sys.date-time entity can support many different ways of saying the time, including "3" and "3 p.m." Dialogflow can set the dateTime and AMPM parameters based on either the @sys.date-time or AMPM entity (Figure 7-14).

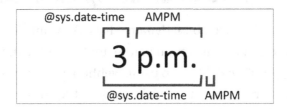

Figure 7-14. *Two different ways "3 p.m." could be parsed by the* @sys.date-time *and AMPM entities*

Which of the two schemes will Dialogflow pick? We can't really say. With more training phrases, it's possible it would pick the top one, the one you wanted, but here it picked the bottom parse, which is to set dateTime to the string representing 3 PM and AMPM to nothing. Because AMPM was set to nothing and it's a required parameter, not only did Dialogflow ask for AM or PM but it included both the PM from the time and the PM from the AM/PM disambiguation in the output response.

How did you fix this problem? By switching the dateTime entity to @sys.number, which only understands "3," not "3 p.m.", the phrase "3 p.m." can only be mapped in one way using @sys.number (Figure 7-15).

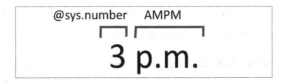

Figure 7-15. *There's only one way that Dialogflow can parse "3 p.m." using* @sys. *number and AMPM*

Now AMPM is set, it won't disambiguate when it doesn't need to, and there's no extra PM in the response.

Why not just use @sys.date-time? It understands "3" and "3 p.m." and returns the right 24-hour time. If someone says *3 p.m.*, then yes, @sys.date-time would have been fine by itself. But if they say only *3* or *3 a.m.*, @sys.date-time actually returns the same thing: a lone *3*. You don't know if the user said *a.m.* or not, so you don't know whether to disambiguate or not.

Webhooks 1: Toward Code Independence

Earlier in this chapter, you learned about dynamic lists. We wanted you to understand the concepts behind a solid VUI interaction before implementing them because this involves moving from "pure" Dialogflow to using webhooks and what most developers would think of as "code." From now on in the book, you'll see more use of webhooks and code outside Dialogflow. At the time of writing this, you can't create some designs inside Dialogflow, and some aspects of your application are more manageable with outside code. But tools and software change, and we want you to be as platform-independent as possible.

First, dynamic lists—review the dialogs in that section now if you need a refresher. The goal of step 1 is to create an intent that calls anyone in a contact list, not only one specific doctor:

1. Create a new intent arCallByName.[3]

2. Add some training phrases: "Call Brent Jones" and "Call Brent." This allows asking both by full name and first name only.

3. In the training phrases, set the entities used and parameters that will be used. Click each "Brent" and set the entity to sys.given-name. Click "Jones" and set the entity to sys.last-name. The Parameters section is filled automatically.

4. Set the response to "OK, calling $first-name $last-name ." Note that you need a space between $last-name and the period, or Dialogflow will think you're accessing a part of $last-name.

---

[3]Sample code files in 7-5.zip. Note that if you use these, you still need to edit the URL for the webhook.

5. Now something new: in the Fulfillment section, select the first slider, Enable webhook call for this intent. This tells Dialogflow to use your web service to process the intent. Save the intent.

You're not done yet. For the sample question *Which Brent:...,* you need an intent to disambiguate the last name:

1. Create a new intent `arCallByNameDisambigLastName`.

2. Add sample phrases "Jones" and "Brent Jones." As with `arCallByName`, set the entities of the training phrases to `sys.given-name` and `sys.last-name`.

3. Add an input context `callbyname`—you'll set it later in the code.

4. Add the same response as for `arCallByName`: "OK, calling $given-name $last-name."

5. Enable webhook fulfillment as you did with `arCallByName`. Save.

Fulfillment and Webhooks

Now that you have your intents, the next step is the webhook code. When you enable Fulfillment for an intent, Dialogflow calls some code (in a web service that you specify) with a ton of information about the intent (which intent was triggered, what the user said, what parameters were filled, what the contexts were) and what Dialogflow will do in response to the intent (response to user, output contexts, and parameters). This information sent to the web service is the **webhook request**.

Simplified, the components interact as shown in Figure 7-16:

- **The Google Home (or similar) device**

- **Actions on Google**: The platform for building applications for Google Home

- **Dialogflow**: The platform for developing conversational dialogs

- **Webhook web service**: The web service for implementing a webhook for fulfillment

- You can also access and write applications for Actions on Google using the Actions on Google SDK, but Dialogflow is the easiest place to start and offers additional integrations for Skype, Twitter, Slack, and others.

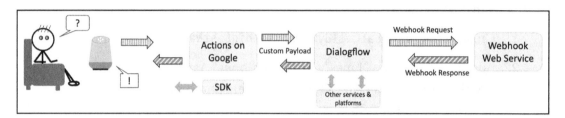

Figure 7-16. *Architecture of Dialogflow in terms of systems*

The code in your web service takes all that information and sends back a webhook response: another bucket of information that potentially modifies Dialogflow's behavior from what it was going to do based only on the intent. The code can change the response text, output contexts, and parameters, and it can trigger an event, which in turn can trigger another intent. The web service sends back the webhook response, and Dialogflow processes it. Your webhook (the web service code) essentially says to Dialogflow, "Do what you were gonna do," "Play the prompt in the intent," and so on. Or it could say, "No, you need to do this differently." You'll see examples of both in dynamic list disambiguation. Both request and response have specific formats, as you'll see shortly.

There's a lot of infrastructure around Google Cloud and related components—this is just a taste of what's involved in fulfillment (Figure 7-17).

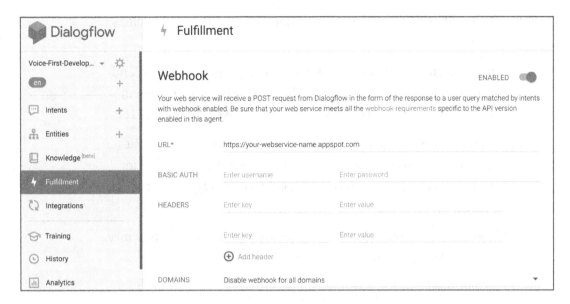

Figure 7-17. *Enabling Fulfillment and specifying the URL of the web service*

1. If you don't have one, get a Google Cloud account. This is different from a Dialogflow account. `https://cloud.google.com/` is a good resource.

2. In the Google Cloud Console, create a project. It generates a project ID for later use.

3. Download the Google Cloud SDK. `https://cloud.google.com/sdk` is a good resource. You'll use this SDK to set, authenticate, and deploy the code.

4. In the Google Cloud Console, enable the App Engine. Then, navigate to Compute ➤ App Engine ➤ Dashboard.

5. Start your App Engine application. Choose Python and standard; they're the defaults.

6. There should already be a service account created for App Engine. In the Name column, find App Engine Default Service Account. Under Actions, select Create Key.

7. Choose JSON format ➤ Create.

8. A file will be downloaded to your machine; the path to this file is the KEYFILE. Keep this safe!

9. In your terminal, create a working directory, navigate into it, and activate the service account with the KEYFILE you just created: `gcloud auth activate-service-account –key-file=KEYFILE`.

10. Set the project to the project you created when you created the Google Cloud account. In the Google Cloud Console (home for your project), this is the project ID: `gcloud config set project PROJECTID`.

11. Download and unzip the 7-5b.zip file into your working directory. You should see the following files:

    a. `app.yaml`

    b. `main.py`

    c. `webhook_request.py`

    d. `webhook_response.py`

    e. `ar_call_by_name.py`

    f. `ar_call_by_name_disambig_last_name.py`

    g. `requirements.txt`.

12. Start your web service: gcloud app deploy.

13. After a while, you see a lot of output similar to Listing 7-1. Find the line for `target URL` and copy that URL.

Listing 7-1. Output of gcloud app deploy (path left out as "..")

```
Services to deploy:

descriptor:        [/Users/.../app.yaml]
source:            [/Users/.../]
target project:    [voice-first-development] target service: [default]
target version:    [20190825t121121]
target url:        [https://voice-first-development.appspot.com]

Do you want to continue (Y/n)? y
```

In Dialogflow, choose Fulfillment. Under Webhook, enable the webhook. Where it says URL, paste the URL you just copied. Save. Your Dialogflow app is now pointing to a web service you've deployed in the Google Cloud App Engine.

Webhook Overview

Before diving into the webhook code, let's do an overview. For now, don't worry about the `app.yaml` and `requirements.txt` files; just focus on the other `.py` files:

1. Pull out the information from the webhook request to make it available later. This happens in the separate file `webhook_request.py`.

2. Now, the actual dialog logic. You'll use this name list—later you'll use a more realistic database:

    Brent Jones

    Brent Adams

    Brent Barnes

    Brent Carletti

    Joe Jones

    Kim Smith

    Mary Poppins

3. If the intent is `arCallByName`

    - If the user specified both first and last names (*Call Brent Jones*), you wouldn't need disambiguation. This is the do what you were going to do case: the webhook doesn't modify what Dialogflow was going to do.

    - If the user specified only a first name (Call Brent), check if you need to disambiguate the last name.

    - Then change the response to ask the Which Brent... question.

    - Add the output context `callbyname`. When you created `arCallByNameDisambigLastName`, you added that as an input context and might have wondered where you set it. Here's the answer.

- Add a parameter `context-given-name` to the `callbyname` context. Adding parameters to contexts is very useful, as you'll see.

- If you don't need to disambiguate (such as there's only one name: *Call Mary*), then find the last name and respond with that. No need to ask. Remember, don't disambiguate unless you need to!

- If the list doesn't have the name (*Call Donald*), play a response that says so.

4. If the intent is `arCallByNameDisambigLastName`

- Get the first name from the previous `arCallByName` intent from the `context-given-name` parameter that was set in the `callbyname` context. The user could have said the full name *Brent Jones* in response to *Which Brent...* instead of just *Jones*. You need to expect both.

- If the last name supplied in the disambiguation is valid, then play the *OK, calling...* response. You're done.

- If the last name isn't in the list, respond appropriately.

5. For any other intent, just return what Dialogflow was going to do anyway; don't modify the behavior.

6. You're not quite done yet. You need to set the right parameters in the webhook response and return the response to Dialogflow. Otherwise, all that logic is useless. The `webhook_response.py` file contains the code to create the response in the right format.

Webhook in Depth

Let's look at the webhook in more detail. `main.py` does three things:

- Loads the webhook request information into the `df_request` object using the code in `webhook_request.py`.

- Directs the logic depending on the Dialogflow intent that was activated. Each intent function takes the `df_request` object and modifies the `df_response` object.

- Returns a formatted version of the webhook response from the `df_response` object.

We'll come back to the details of formatting the webhook request and response. For now, focus on the logic for the two new intents you created in the previous section. First, Listing 7-2 shows the logic for the arCallByName intent.

Listing 7-2. Logic for the arCallByName intent

```
def ar_call_by_name(df_request, df_response):
    """

    Call by name.
    """

    given_name = df_request.parameters.get('given-name')
    last_name = df_request.parameters.get('last-name')

    if (given_name and not given_name == '' and
            last_name and not last_name == ''):

        # If the caller specified both the first name and the
        # last name ("Call Brent Jones"), we don't need disambiguation,
        # just do that. This is the "do what you were going to do case,"
        # where the webhook does not modify what Dialogflow was going to
        # do anyway.

        df_response.output_text = df_request.fulfillment_text
    elif (given_name and not given_name == ''):

        # This section of the code is very specific to the name list
        # that we've set up. Later on we can make it more generic, and
        # hit databases and such.

        # If the caller only specified a first name

        if given_name == 'Brent':

            # If you need to disambiguate last name (e.g., "Call Brent")

            # Change the response to ask the "Which Brent..." question.

            df_response.output_text = \
                'Which Brent: Jones, Adams, Barnes, or Carletti?'
```

```
    # Add the output context callbyname.
    # Remember when you created arCallByNameDisambigLastName,
    # you added that as an input context, and might have
    # wondered where you set it? Here's where that is.

    new_context = {
        'name': ('projects/${PROJECT_ID}/agent/sessions'
                 '/${SESSION_ID}/contexts/callbyname'),
        'lifespanCount': 5,
        'parameters': {}
    }

    # The full context name is long; "callbyname" is only the
    # last part.

    # Add a parameter context-given-name to the callbyname
    # context. You can add parameters to contexts, and you'll
    # see in a bit how useful that is.

    new_context['parameters']['context-given-name'] = given_name

    df_response.output_contexts.append(new_context)

else:

    # If you don't need to disambiguate, there's only one name
    # (e.g., "Call Mary"), find the last name, and respond with
    # that. No need to ask. Remember, don't disambiguate unless
    # you need to!

    if given_name == 'Kim':
        df_response.output_text = 'OK, calling Kim Smith.'
    elif given_name == 'Mary':
        df_response.output_text = 'OK, calling Mary Poppins.'
    else:

        # If you don't have that first name (e.g., "Call Donald"),
        # play a response that says so.

        df_response.output_text = \
            f"Sorry, there is no {given_name} in your list."
```

And second, Listing 7-3 shows the logic for the intent arCallByNameDisambigLastName.

Listing 7-3. Logic for the arCallByNameDisambigLastName

```python
def ar_call_by_name_disambig_last_name(df_request, df_response):
    """

    Get the first name from the previous arCallByName intent, from the
    context-given-name parameter that was set in the callbyname context
    (we told you that would be useful). The caller might have said
    the first name in the response to "Which Brent...", e.g. "Brent
    Jones" instead of just "Jones," but you can't be sure, so you need
    to go get it.
    """

    context_name = ''
    given_name = None
    last_name = df_request.parameters.get('last-name')

    for context in df_request.input_contexts:
        fullname = context.get('name')
        parameters = context.get('parameters')
        if parameters:
            given_name = parameters.get('context-given-name')

        if fullname:
            # fullname is a very long string; we only need the last part
            # of it, after the final /.
            match = re.search('/([^/]*)$', fullname)
            if (match and match.group(1) == 'callbyname') and given_name:
                context_name = parameters.get('context-given-name')

    if (last_name in ['Jones', 'Adams', 'Barnes', 'Carletti']):

        # If the last name supplied in this disambiguation step is valid,
        # then play the "OK, calling..." response, and you're done.
```

```
    df_response.output_text = f"OK, calling {context_name} {last_name}."
else:

    # If the last name is not valid, say so

    df_response.output_text = \
        f"Sorry, {context_name} {last_name} is not in your list."
```

The logic in Listings 7-2 and 7-3 have quite a few branches customized for our particular sample name list. In reality, you'd probably use some sort of database of names. Those familiar with databases and SQL might imagine a query along the lines of `select first_name`, `last_name`, `phone_number_type`, `phone_number` `from directory where` … where the elements of the `where` clause come from the information you have already collected, including any disambiguation. Depending on what comes back, you would decide if any additional disambiguation is needed and what to do next. When you finally get only one record from the database, you'd confirm and potentially make the call.

Time to test! Try various cases to verify that they all work:

- "Call Brent Jones."

- "Call Mary Poppins."

- "Call Mary."

- "Call Brent" and then "Jones."

- "Call Brent" and then "Brent Jones."

- "Call Brent" and then "Smith."

What about the inline editor? And why Python? When you enabled the webhook and supplied the URL for it, you might have noticed the Inline Editor section. It lets you specify code for the webhook without going through all those steps you just went through. So why not just use that? There are a couple of reasons.

First, the inline editor uses Node.js, but our examples are using Python and we're assuming you're writing your code also in Python. This makes the Google App Engine more suited. We use Python because it's the language of choice today for natural language processing, which is closely related to what you're doing here. Also, the Google App Engine, which we're using for deploying the web service, is currently more developed for Python than for Node.js. We prioritize making our Python code samples easy to read for non-experts over optimizing them—we're here to teach you about voice, not Python, after all. ☺

Second, with tools like the inline editor, you run into limitations like code management and scaling to many intents and complex interactions. You can use any existing infrastructure to develop the webhook as long as it follows the rules. As your solutions become industrial-strength, you want those tools and processes, so why not start now?

Contexts, Context Parameters, and Follow-Up Intents

You set contexts for the `tcrProcedurePrep` intent in Chapter 6. There are also **context parameters**: parameters associated with a specific context. They're how intents communicate, to say "This happened in a previous intent, in case you need to know." In the contact calling example, the first name that was spoken during `arCallByName` needed to be kept so the right response could be played. More on contexts in Chapter 14.

You can set output contexts from the Dialogflow GUI, but you need the webhook to set parameters. The parameter names can be anything, but you have to be careful: if you give a context parameter the same name as a parameter from the Parameters section of the intent, some unexpected behavior can happen. When the intent is processed, parameters are taken from all active input contexts and any parameters filled from user utterances, such as slots.

If you implement follow-on questions with contexts or with follow-up intents, how do you know which one to use? Here's a guideline:

- If the next question can occur after more than one intent, use contexts. Otherwise, you have to duplicate the phrases and responses multiple times. Of course, sometimes you want to do some duplication, but don't worry about that now. Think of this as having completed the dialog and moving to the next dialog.

- If the next question only makes sense after the current intent or within its scope and the question is Yes/No or a navigation command like *next*, use follow-up intents. They already have common training phrases, so you don't have to worry about contexts. Think of this as not having completed the current dialog yet.

Sooner or later, you need custom follow-up intent phrases for fuller control of how to converse with the user or for adding synonyms not in the pre-built version. You learn about tuning in depth in Chapter 17. For now, it's a bit of a toss-up between using contexts or follow-up intents, but follow-up intents can be a quicker start.

What's Next

We wrap up the topic of dialog completion for now with an important placeholder. You may have noticed that we didn't discuss where in the flow the back end is contacted. If your user makes a restaurant reservation, when do you figure out what's available, and how does that impact the dialog? If the user asks for *a reservation at Na Na's for 5 PM* but Na Na's doesn't open until 6 PM or has no tables before 8 PM, should you ask about the number of guests only to respond *Sorry, that's not available*? Probably not. You learn more about this and additional uses of webhooks next in Chapter 8.

Summary

- Tools don't protect you from missing or misinterpreting details in user utterances that can have unintended poor consequences.

- Users are only as precise as they think they need to be. That means your VUI often needs to ask for clarification. The more pieces of information are required for the VUI to complete the request, the more dialog turns you'll need.

- Users can give you indirect clues about what they want in how they word their requests. Those clues help you fulfill requests by "filling in the gaps" instead of asking.

- Users listen to how your VUI asks a question. You might think your VUI is precise and clear, but your users might not. Implementing the right disambiguation method for a task increases user success significantly.

- When you use a dialog manager approach, your users can be more flexible and make requests in ways that better match their mental models.

- When debugging, be sure to test on the device your VUI ultimately will run on.

- Find out what's really going on in your application using the tools at hand such as History and raw interaction log.

- Sometimes speech-to-text can be a black box you don't need to worry about; at other times you need to know.

- Be careful using system entities. Sometimes, they provide unexpected results.

CHAPTER 8

Conveying Reassurance with Confidence and Confirmation

Every dialog depends on shared understanding. It's as true for two people talking as when one participant is a computer. When you talk to someone, how do you know if you're being understood or not? By the listener's responses. They either reassure you that you're understood or suggest that some correction is needed. When something's important, you even check that your listener is paying attention by confirming (affirming, saying *yes*) that information with your listener. And when you're the listener, you sometimes want to verify your understanding or show that you're still listening. When you're talking to someone on the phone and can't see each other's faces and body language, verbal reassurance is even more necessary. This chapter focuses on how to create a VUI that's reassuring and confirms information only when necessary using the best method in each context.

Reassurance is an important topic in voice systems for three related reasons:

- VUI accuracy, verifying that recognition and interpretation is correct

- User confidence that the VUI got it right, contributing to user trust in the VUI

- Overall success, helping conversations reach their goal with minimal backtracking

© Ann Thymé-Gobbel, Charles Jankowski 2021
A. Thymé-Gobbel and C. Jankowski, *Mastering Voice Interfaces*, https://doi.org/10.1007/978-1-4842-7005-9_8

Conveying Reassurance and Shared Certainty

In any dialog involving money, health, or privacy, you'd want reassurance of being understood. As a user, if you say *Pay 900 dollars to Holiday Cruises from my VISA card* and hear in response only *Okay*, are you confident that your money is going to the right place? Probably not. You'd want a little more assurance that you were heard correctly so you know who's getting your money. You'd even want a chance to say *no* before a wrong payment is made.

Even simple questions need clear responses. This is a transcript of an actual interaction with one of today's voice assistants:

> **User**   *How much is 14 by 15?*

> **VUI**   *The answer is 29.*

No, it's not! The word "by" implies multiplication, not addition. Reassurance is easily added: the response could be *14 plus 15 is…* vs. *14 times 15 is…* Not much longer, but much clearer. If you ask a friend a question, they'll probably answer differently from a VUI (Figure 8-1, panel 1). This is in part because of how easy it is to ask your friend for clarification and your ability to sense the certainty of their response. The less familiar you are with the person you talk to or the topic, the more reassurance you need. When understanding fails, you need to get back on track, which can slow down the conversation. But we still do much of that fixing and reassuring so easily that it just feels like it's part of natural conversation. Getting back on track, or **recovering** through **repairs**, is a bigger challenge for a VUI, so staying on track in the first place is key. We'll get back to repairs in Chapter 13.

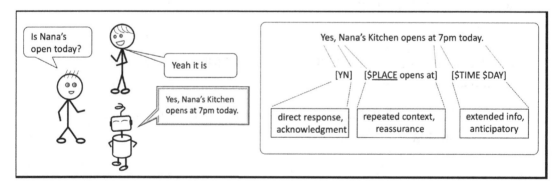

Figure 8-1. *Core components of reassurance: acknowledge, signal understanding, respond, and anticipate*

Take another look at the sample dialogs in Figure 8-1. They form a pattern of sorts (panel 2). A request needs a response. In voice, that might be a *yes* or *no* or *29* or an *okay* that acknowledges task completion. Context is often included: Na Na's *Kitchen opens at...*, *14 plus 15...*, or *900 dollars to...* It's that context that provides reassurance. And if you know that people often follow up with some specific information request, you can make your users' lives easier by anticipating that and including that information, even if it isn't strictly part of the direct response to the initial request. For example, include the actual hours when the question is just *Is it open?* In a VUI, it can save users time and increase success.

In Chapter 2, you learned about the characteristics of voice interfaces and how they differ from visual and tangible interfaces. The biggest difference involves continuity and feedback. GUI interactions are discrete: users tap or click something; it's obvious if there's a result and what it is. VUI interactions are continuous: user requests can be incomplete or ambiguous, as you learned in Chapter 7. Importantly, users don't believe they're unclear. In the other dialog direction, a spoken VUI response needs to be understood by the listener. If users are uncertain about that response, they'll experience higher cognitive load and less trust in the VUI. The higher the stakes, the more important it is to convey reassurance and to be confident in the accuracy of any response.

The trick with reassurance is to strike the right balance between clarity and speed. Your guideline should be "What's the 'cost' of being wrong?" That addresses both the VUI having recognized or interpreted incorrectly and the user misunderstanding or needing reassurance. That cost adds up—misunderstanding low-risk requests often means users won't trust the VUI for higher-risk requests.

SUCCESS TIP 8.1 BREVITY IS "NEVER" MORE IMPORTANT THAN CLARITY

CLARITY   Don't overload users with long audio prompts. At the same time, clarity—within reason—is almost always more important than brevity. Don't remove a few words just to speed up a dialog. Remove "fluff" while keeping the intended meaning, style, and cognitive model. Sometimes it's not even word count that matters. People complain about long prompts when pauses are missing. So make sure you "chunk" your prompts. It helps cognitive load issues.

Take a moment to brainstorm: When are reassurance and certainty important? For money and health tasks, of course. What else? There're lots of factors to consider. Recognition complexity, risk of user embarrassment, user urgency, and user familiarity with the task are just some of them. In a multistep interaction, being confident that the dialog is going in the right direction at the start saves potential backtracking later and so on. The good news is it all comes down to the same thing: balancing cost/risk at any level with speed and simplicity. Think about what this cost is all about. Look at Figure 8-2.

Less costly/risky		More costly/risky
Music; weather; trivia ←----------- **Domain** -----------→		Finance; health; medical
Info lookup; IoT control ←----------- **Task** --------→		Rx refill; reservation; purchase
Short; few steps ←------------- **Interaction duration** ----------→		Long; multiple steps
Little or none ←------------------ **Dialog branching** --------------------→		Considerable
Few ←---------------------------- **Required slots** ----------------------------→		Several
Multimodal support ←---------------- **Modality** --------------------------→		Voice-only
Free; unlimited ←----------- **Lookup/fulfillment charges** -----------→		Not free; limited
Reliable & available ←--------- **Logic to narrow search** ------------------→		None
Narrow; mature; stable ←------ **Recognition difficulty** ---------→		Broad; new; changing
High confidence ←---------------- **System certainty** ------------------→		Low confidence
Few choices or features ←------- **System complexity** ------→		Many choices or features
No difficulties ←----------------- **User performance** ---------→		Retries; no-match; help
None ←------------------------ **Social consequences** -----→		Potential embarrassment
Power users; known info ←-------- **User familiarity** ----→		Novice users; unfamiliar info
Infrequent ←---------------------- **Task frequency** ------------------------→		Frequent
Less urgent ←------------------------ **Urgency** ------------------------→		More urgent

Figure 8-2. *Some of the many factors and dimensions of determining cost of being wrong*

We'll come back to the details at the end of the chapter. At this point, don't fret. Just remember to not ignore these details.

Setting Expectations with Your Implications

Understanding isn't simply on or off, true or false. There's a continuum of certainty and confidence both on the speaking side and hearing side of a dialog, for both user and VUI. In human conversations, our words, intonation, and non-verbal cues convey our confidence in what we say and hear. Person Q might get four different responses to a question:

Person Q	*Do you know where Tegucigalpa is?*
Person A1	(high confidence) *Sure, that's the capital of Honduras.*
Person A2	(mid-confidence) *Hmm, I think maybe Honduras...?*
Person A3	(low confidence) *Teguwhat did you ask?*
Person A4	(high confidence, wrong) *Sure, that's the capital of Mexico.*

When we're certain of our response—both understanding the question and knowing the answer—we use words like "sure," "yes," and "no." When we're less certain, we hedge our responses with intonation and words like "I think," or we double-check our understanding before responding. Below some level of certainty, we don't even try to answer.

Your VUI sets expectations by its responses, just like people do. A VUI should respond *Sure* only when it's sure of the answer and the request itself, never like the preceding Person A4. IVRs and other voice systems have incorporated hedging and multi-tier responses for a long time. Today's voice assistants haven't made use of confidence to the same degree yet. You'll learn more about this powerful topic in this chapter and in Chapter 12.

SUCCESS TIP 8.2 UNDER-PROMISING IS BETTER THAN OVER-PROMISING

We humans are copycats. If a VUI uses certain words in prompts, users expect to be understood when using the same words. If multiple slots are accepted in one task, users will expect multiple slots to be handled elsewhere in the VUI. Be careful and thoughtful in what you imply and promise. Once a VUI doesn't live up to its promises, it doesn't sound so smart, and user confidence starts eroding—and their behavior changes.

Webhooks 2

Even if a platform doesn't provide a built-in that gives you the level of reassurance you want for your VUI, there are ways to implement your own. You used webhooks in Chapter 7 to handle the more complex logic of name dialing. When webhooks are enabled, Dialogflow sends a webhook request to the web service and expects a webhook response in return. You learned how to enable webhooks for the application as a whole and on a per-intent basis. Now let's look at both and use webhooks for reassurance.

JSON

Dialogflow uses a webhook request to initiate a conversation with the web service. JSON is the format for both the request and the response. JSON, or JavaScript Object Notation, is a lightweight data interchange format commonly used for passing information back and forth between software pieces, especially web services. Listing 8-1 shows an example of JSON.

Listing 8-1. Example of JSON

```
# String value, surrounded by double-quotes
{"stringValue":"string",
# Numeric value, no quotes. Can be integer or float.
"numberValue":-1234.567,
# Boolean value, true or false
"booleanValue":true,
# Null value
"nullValue":null,
# Object value. Objects are specified by curly braces {}.
# An object is nested within the overall object.
"objectValue":{"stringValue2":"string2","numberValue2",123},
# Array value. Arrays are specified by square braces [].
# The values in the array can be any of the other values, including arrays.
"arrayValue":["string3",456,false,{"stringValue3","string3"}]}
```

The main concepts are as follows:

- **Objects**, surrounded by curly braces {}. An object contains a set of comma-separated keyword/value pairs. Each pair consists of a keyword (a string, basically a name for the value), a colon, and the value. Keywords are strings, so surrounded by double quotes.

- **Arrays**, surrounded by square braces []. An array contains any number of comma-separated values.

- **Values** can be

  - A string, surrounded by double quotes

  - A number, which can be an integer or float, without quotes, or a Boolean, which can be true or false (no quotes, or it's a string!)

- A null value, which is null (again, no quotes!)

- An object

- An array

The JSON that you pass to or from a service can be any type or value, but it's usually an object or an array of other values. Objects and arrays can be nested.

The Webhook Request

Expanding the final webhook example in Chapter 7, here's a sample webhook request. Listing 8-2 shows what's triggered when the user says, *Call Brent Jones*—it's the JSON in Listing 8-1.

Listing 8-2. A fulfillment request for "Call Brent Jones"

```
{
    # Unique identifier for the request:
    "responseId": "72ed99c2-e05e-42c3-9f201268b11bda58",
    "queryResult": {
        # What the user said:
        "queryText": "Call Brent Jones",
        # What parameters were filled from the user text:
        "parameters": {
            "given-name": "Brent",
            "last-name": "Jones"
        },
        "allRequiredParamsPresent": true,
        # What Dialogflow planned to respond to the user before the
        webhook:
        "fulfillmentText": "OK, calling Brent Jones",
        "fulfillmentMessages": [
        {
            "text": {
                "text": [
                    "OK, calling Brent Jones"
                ]
```

```
            }
        }
    ],
    "intent": {
        "name": "projects/voice-first-development/agent/intents/60bbb90d- \
            b0e7-408d-9efb-a7ab50ffc1b9",
        # The name of the intent triggered:
        "displayName": "arCallByName"
    },
    "intentDetectionConfidence": 1,
    "languageCode": "en"
},
"originalDetectIntentRequest": {
    "payload": {}
},
"session": "projects/voice-first-development/agent/sessions/d02a16a8- \
    5dc6-8dfa-6089-c90740aba732"
}
```

Stepping through this request

- Start with a unique ID for the request.

- The overall value is a JSON object with several key/value pairs. You know that because it starts with a left curly brace {.

- The queryText keyword of the queryResult object shows your VUI's interpretation of what the user said, in this case *Call Brent Jones.*

- In the parameters JSON object within the queryResult object, you see the parameters filled from the queryText. The JSON keywords in this object are exactly the same as the Parameter Name in the Actions and Parameters table for the Dialogflow intent (compare Listing 8-2 with the Dialogflow GUI).

- The fulfillmentText value of queryResult has a string with the Dialogflow response based only on Dialogflow information before the webhook request is made. This comes from the Responses section of Dialogflow.

- The parameters and response are all determined by Dialogflow before making the webhook request. This is important: if the webhook doesn't respond within some time (10 seconds when using Actions on Google, 5 seconds otherwise), Dialogflow continues the dialog as if the webhook were never involved.

- In the intent object of `queryResult`, there's a very long string and a `displayName` string that you'll recognize as the intent name from Dialogflow.

- Dialogflow will show you that a webhook is enabled for an intent. While not all intents need to have webhooks enabled, later you'll enable them for all intents because of the nice features webhooks provide, such as detailed logging.

The Webhook Response

The web service implementing the webhook responds with a JSON webhook response. Listing 8-3 shows the VUI response to the user's *Call Brent Jones*.

Listing 8-3. Webhook response for "Call Brent Jones"

```
{
    "fulfillmentText": "OK, calling Brent Jones"
}
```

It's that simple! All you have is a JSON object with a `fulfillmentText` string showing Dialogflow's spoken response. If the webhook response has set `fulfillmentText`, Dialogflow responds with that. If the web service doesn't set `fulfillmentText`—or spells the keyword wrong!—Dialogflow proceeds as planned with the phrase from the intent Responses section and the `fulfillmentText` field in the webhook request.

For now, the response is very simple, with only `fulfillmentText`. Later, you'll add more components to the response including

- **Contexts**: Intents can set output contexts. You can also do this in the webhook (Chapter 7)—if the user says only *Call Brent*, the VUI disambiguates by asking which Brent. That required setting the output context from the `arCallByName` webhook to allow only the `arCallByNameDisambigLastName` intent.

- **Events**: There are two ways to trigger an intent: from speech or text or by triggering an event from the webhook.

- **Payloads**: For some integration-dependent features, `fulfillmentText` isn't enough. You need to add custom payloads.

Custom Payloads

Dialogflow offers integrations to many other platforms besides Actions on Google. Depending on the platform, you provide custom information about the response that makes sense only to that specific integration. For example:

- If you integrate with a multimodal platform, like Slack, you can display images or indicate a state that only makes sense to Slack.

- For audio output, Actions on Google supports Speech Synthesis Markup Language (SSML), which is useful for non-verbal audio (NVA) and for providing detailed output pronunciation instructions, how to say a name, where to pause, and for how long.

- Ending the conversation. Remember setting the "Set this intent as end of conversation" switch in Dialogflow? It signals ending the conversation after the intent's response. With webhooks, you need to end the conversation via the Actions on Google custom payload.

Implementing the Webhook

Dialogflow doesn't care how the webhook is implemented as long as it accepts and understands the request and provides a response using the correct formats. If the URL specified in the Fulfillment page accepts requests and provides responses, Dialogflow is happy.

There are many ways to implement the webhook for Dialogflow:

- Using Node.js in the built-in inline editor on the Fulfillment page in Dialogflow. We won't use the inline editor for various reasons, including the following:

    - The single page limits the size and complexity of the code you can develop. You'll see that you'll already start breaking up your code into functional pieces, which is critical for good software development.

- You want to apply software development principles, like source code control, to your voice application—that isn't possible with the inline editor.

- Setting up a web server yourself with your software language of choice, such as Node.js, Python, or Java. Because we focus on voice application development rather than web server administration, we'll deploy using another method.

- Using a serverless platform such as Google App Engine or AWS Lambda, letting you focus on the important code, not the mechanics of web servers. Because you're using Dialogflow, you'll use the Google App Engine option.

You may wonder how we got the samples for Listings 8-2 and 8-3. If you test using text input in Dialogflow, you see DIAGNOSTIC INFO at the bottom. Click that. You'll see various details, including the webhook request (Figure 8-3) and response.

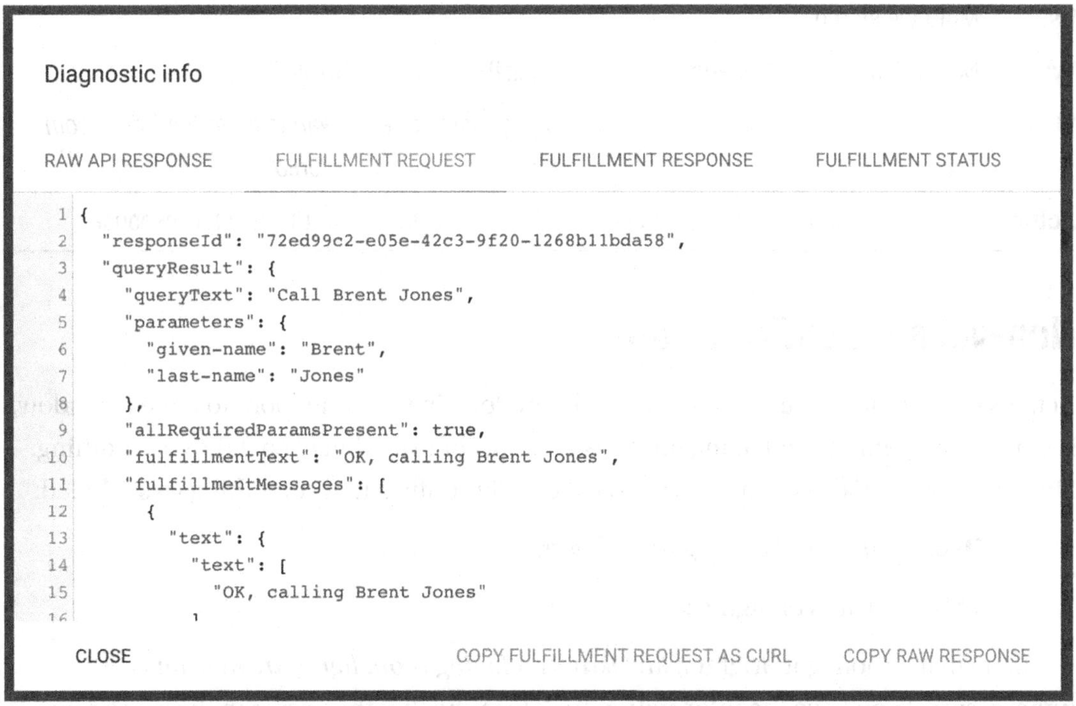

```
Diagnostic info


RAW API RESPONSE        FULFILLMENT REQUEST        FULFILLMENT RESPONSE        FULFILLMENT STATUS

 1  {
 2    "responseId": "72ed99c2-e05e-42c3-9f20-1268b11bda58",
 3    "queryResult": {
 4      "queryText": "Call Brent Jones",
 5      "parameters": {
 6        "given-name": "Brent",
 7        "last-name": "Jones"
 8      },
 9      "allRequiredParamsPresent": true,
10      "fulfillmentText": "OK, calling Brent Jones",
11      "fulfillmentMessages": [
12        {
13          "text": {
14            "text": [
15              "OK, calling Brent Jones"
16            ]
```

CLOSE   COPY FULFILLMENT REQUEST AS CURL   COPY RAW RESPONSE

Figure 8-3. *Diagnostic info from a test phrase, including fulfillment request and response*

With all that as background, let's get back to confirmation methods.

Confirmation Methods

Some type of confirmation is always important; it's just a question of what type is best suited for each context. Just like there are different disambiguation methods, there are different confirmation methods. Which one you choose depends on the cost of being wrong: the more important it is to get it right, the more explicit—or heavy-handed—your confirmation strategy will be. Never be more heavy-handed than necessary based on the cost of being wrong: the more explicit the confirmation, the longer the interaction takes.

Table 8-1 illustrates the main four approaches to confirmation in the same context. In the rest of this chapter, you learn about these four methods, including coding and usage—and why some approaches are better than others in this particular example.

Table 8-1. *Comparison of four main confirmation types in response to the same user request*

Who	Dialog			
User	Mute the stereo.			
Type	Non-verbal	Generic	Implicit	Explicit
VUI	--	*Okay.*	*Living room stereo is muted.*	*Wanna mute the living room stereo?*
Action	<Stereo mutes>	<Stereo mutes>	<Stereo mutes>	<VUI waits for response>

Non-verbal Confirmation

Actions speak louder than words. If you ask someone in the same room to open a window, seeing them opening it or feeling the air is enough confirmation even if they say nothing. Similarly, your VUI doesn't always need to verbally confirm that something was fulfilled:

> **User**   *Turn on the living room lights.*
>
> **VUI**   <Turns on lights.>

If the living room got brighter, an *Okay* or a *Living room lights are now on* is unnecessary if you have the information to determine that the user is in the same room as the light and can see the result. The same is true when the result can be heard, like when asking to mute music that's playing. We'll come back to incorporating this type of context in Chapter 14.

Confirmation can use sounds to indicate success or failure. Non-verbal audio can make interactions quicker and is preferred by some users.

Code for Non-verbal Confirmation

We'll come back to this code later in the chapter to show you how to add non-verbal audio by using the webhook request and response and the custom payload and SSML capabilities of Actions on Google you just learned about.

Notes on Non-verbal Confirmation

Do seen or heard actions ever need verbal confirmation? Oh yes. Think about contexts where spoken audio cues are still useful for reassurance. There are accessibility situations, like reassuring a blind user that a visual request was successful. Some people prefer verbal reassurance, so allow user customization. And if the action takes place away from where the user can verify the result or if their eyes are busy, then reassurance is needed. Knowing the user's location compared to the action result is nontrivial and therefore interesting (Chapter 14).

Verbal confirmations aren't always a great idea. If the content is private, don't assume users want to hear the information repeated back to them. So don't read back an entered PIN or login. If additional verification is needed and no screen is available, there are other approaches. You can ask twice and compare the results without asking for user confirmation. You'll learn about such "behind-the-scenes" techniques in Chapter 16.

Generic Acknowledgment

Generic (or open, or general) acknowledgments, like *okay*, are best combined with a transition to the next thing—*Okay. (And how many?)*—or an implicit confirmation *Alright, a new appointment.* On its own, *okay* doesn't contribute much.

A great way to not sound smart is to give the wrong response while sounding really sure it's right or to ignore details that are obvious to a human. Remember: Users don't know or care why a request failed, only that it did. The good news is that people are willing to cut your VUI some slack the more truthfully it behaves.

More response granularity makes for a more varied and natural user experience. But it also means more to track and more effort on your part. Your responses must fit the user's request in terms of content, syntax, and level of certainty. All three contribute to reassurance. *Okay* and *Alright* are noncommittal for certainty, while *Sure* implies certainty of your answer. Look at these two responses, based on an actual interaction with a voice assistant:

> **User**   *Play "Let It Be"*
>
> > **VUI1**   (acknowledge only)
> > *Sure.* → [Plays "Let It Be Love"]
> >
> > **VUI2**   (acknowledge with implicit confirmation)
> > *Sure. Here's "Let It Be Love."* → [Plays "Let It Be Love"]

Not only does the user hear the wrong song; both VUIs also imply it's the right one. That won't reassure anyone! If your VUI lets users turn lights on or off, make sure it doesn't respond *Okay* when the wrong light turns on or off or if nothing at all happens. There are ways to hedge a response, including phrases like *I think you're asking about…* or *Here's what I found.* In Chapter 12, you learn about the **recognize-and-reject** approach used when a VUI can't fulfill a request. Response granularity plays an important role in that approach.

This topic is more complex than you might expect. Practice finding the right level of commitment in your responses. In Chapter 11, you learn how tagging guides can help with response granularity.

FROM THE VOICE TRENCHES

Both of us authors have worked on voice-first projects with several hundred intent endpoints. Those endpoints can be information readback, multi-turn dialogs, transactions, further disambiguation, or even connections to talk to a person. It's a little extra work, but you'll quickly get the hang of it. Overall, user satisfaction is often higher with carefully worded implicit confirmation prompts because users feel reassured and understood, so it's worth the extra effort.

Implicit Confirmation

Implicit confirmation is very common across VUIs, particularly when interrupting through barge-in is available. It's based on the idea of "silence means agreement." Look at the following dialog comparisons:

User   *Play "Let It Be"*

    VUI1   (implicit and correct)   *Here's "Let It Be," by*
                                            The Beatles. <SONG>

    VUI2   (implicit and incorrect)   *Here's "Let It be Love," by*
                                            Craig Armstrong. <SONG>

    VUI3   (incorrect)   *<SONG>*

~ ~ ~   ~ ~ ~   ~ ~ ~

User   *I wanna make a reservation at Na Na's.*

    VUI1   (implicit and correct)   *Okay, a new reservation for*
                                            Na Na's. What time? ...

    VUI2   (implicit and incorrect)   *Okay, a new reservation for*
                                            Panama. What time? ...

    VUI3   (incorrect)   *What time?*

~ ~ ~   ~ ~ ~   ~ ~ ~

User   *Call Doctor Jones.*

    VUI1   (implicit and correct)
      Doctor Brent Jones, office phone. Calling...

    VUI2   (implicit and incorrect)
      Doctor Linda Jonas, office phone. Calling...

    VUI3   (incorrect)
      Calling...

The idea is to give users enough information to reassure them of shared understanding without unnecessary slowdown—just enough to allow users to stop an incorrect action. For the reservation request, implicit confirmation makes it clear right away if the conversation is about to go off in the wrong direction before multiple dialog turns were wasted. For calling, it avoids potential embarrassment and cost:

User   *I wanna make a reservation at Na Na's.*

VUI2   *Okay, a new reservation for Panama. What ...*

User   *Start over.*

~ ~ ~

User   *Call Doctor Jones.*

VUI2   *Doctor Linda Jonas, office …*

User   *Cancel!*

Code for Implicit Confirmation

The webhook response in Listing 8-3 had only the `fulfillmentText` value. There are two more things left to do for implicit confirmation:

- Add non-verbal audio.

- End the conversation, when appropriate.

Let's first look at the webhook response[1] needed to do these two additions (Listing 8-4).

Listing 8-4. Webhook response after ending the conversation and adding NVA

```
{
    "fulfillmentText": "OK, calling Brent Jones",
    "payload": {      # A
        "google": {       # B
            "expectUserResponse": false,      # C
            "richResponse": {
                "items": [
                    {
                        "simpleResponse": {
                            "textToSpeech": "<speak><audio
src=\"https://actions.google.com/sounds/v1/cartoon/cartoon_metal_thunk.
ogg\" clipBegin=\"1.5s\" clipEnd=\"3s\">DING</audio>OK, calling Brent
Jones</speak>"      # D
                        }
                    }
                ]
            }
        }
    }
}
```

---

[1]The full code listing for the webhook code is in 8-1.zip.

Here are the detailed steps in Listing 8-4:

- Add the Actions on Google custom payload section by adding the `payload` JSON object and under that the `google` JSON object (A).

- Add the `expectUserResponse` value of `false` to the Actions on Google custom payload (B, C). This is how you end the conversation with webhooks.

- Add the `richResponse` information in the format needed (D). Finish it with the `textToSpeech` string value that contains the SSML markup needed for the NVA, as well as the response text. The SSML has the following parts:

  - The `<speak>` tag, which begins every SSML command.

  - The `<audio>` command, which plays audio from URLs. The `<audio>` command has three attributes:

  - `src`, which points to the URL of the audio.

  - `clipBegin`, which tells Actions on Google when to start playing the audio. Note the very specific format `1.5s`; this is specified by the SSML standard.

  - `clipEnd`, which specifies when to stop playing. Same comment about the format, but here it's `3s`.

  - Some text (here it's `DING`), which the VUI speaks if the audio can't be loaded.

- End the audio section with `</audio>`.

- The text of the TTS response you want spoken after the NVA.

- End the SSML section with `</speak>`.

You learn more about SSML in Chapter 15; SSML can keep your device from saying things like *less than speak greater than less than audio* ... Yes, that's a real-world example!

Where do you find audio for your implementation? Technically, you can get audio from any URL, but it must meet the formats for Actions on Google. Avoid a situation where some audio suddenly doesn't play (the URL changed, permissions changed, licensing issues, etc.). For that reason, it's smart to stick with audio that your platform provides by default. To get started, use some stock audio examples that Actions on

Google provides, just as we've done. The Google Developer's site has many good references. You can find documentation on SSML, accepted audio formats for the <audio> tag, and a library of audio for Actions on Google.[2] If you need other audio, hardcode acceptable backoff audio that always plays if code-external audio isn't available, in addition to incorporating alerts that inform you that your backoff played.

To end the conversation and add NVA, you used the webhook as follows:

- You initialized variables for whether you're ending the conversation and playing NVA (both false to start).

- At a conversation ending phrase, you set the end conversation variable to true.

- When you did an implicit confirmation, you set the play NVA variable to true.

- When you created the webhook response JSON, you added the custom payload and Actions on Google section (if needed). If you're ending the conversation, add the expectUserInput=False and add the richResponse and SSML info for any NVA. You can see the result of adding the new custom payload information in Listing 8-5. The variable addPayload always has the same value as endConversation, so you don't need to check that it's added.

Let's look at the details of creating the webhook response in Listing 8-5, from the file webhook_response.py. (A) is the main part for setting the output text; you've only used that part until now. In (B) you add the end-of-conversation information, and in (C) you add NVA, both to conform with the required webhook response format in Listing 8-4. In (D) you set the output contexts—you saw this used for disambiguation in Chapter 7. Finally, in (E) return the JSON of the webhook response.

---

[2]Take a look at https://developers.google.com/actions/reference/ssml and https://developers.google.com/actions/tools/sound-library/

Listing 8-5. Core of the code to generate the webhook response, including ending the conversation and adding NVA

```python
def response_json(self):
    """
    Return the JSON response dictionary.
    """

    # Set the response text.
    self.respdic['fulfillment_text'] = self.output_text.      #A

    # Did you add the Actions on Google payload?
    add_payload = False

    # End the conversation if that's relevant.         #B
    if self.end_conversation:
        self.respdic['payload'] = {}
        self.respdic['payload']['google'] = {}
        self.respdic['payload']['google']['expectUserResponse'] = False
        add_payload = True

    # If doing pre-NVA, add the payload for Actions on Google. #C
    if self.do_pre_nva:
        if not add_payload:
            self.respdic['payload'] = {}
            self.respdic['payload']['google'] = {}
        self.respdic['payload']['google']['richResponse'] = {}
        self.respdic['payload']['google']['richResponse']['items'] = []
        tmpdic = {}
        tmpdic['simpleResponse'] = {}
        tmpdic['simpleResponse']['textToSpeech'] =\
            ("<speak><audio src=\"https://actions.google.com/sounds/v1/"
             "cartoon/cartoon_metal_thunk.ogg\" clipBegin=\"1.5s\" "
             f"clipEnd=\"3s\">DING</audio>{self.output_text}</speak>")
        self.respdic['payload']['google']['richResponse']['items']\
            .append(tmpdic)
```

```
# Set the output contexts if needed.        #D
if len(self.output_contexts) > 0:
    self.respdic['outputContexts'] = self.output_contexts

# Return the webhook response.    #E
return self.respdic
```

Tell the webhook response to end the conversation and play NVA. Previously in your dialog logic files (e.g., in ar_call_by_name.py), you set the text by modifying the df_response object:

```
df_response.output_text = …
```

Now whenever you do that, you also need to end the conversation

```
df_response.end_conversation = True
```

and, if you're confirming the calling of a contact, play the NVA:

```
df_response.do_pre_nva = True
```

When you test your code with NVA, you need to do it from either the Actions on Google simulator or a Google Home device; you cannot test only within Dialogflow as SSML is a custom payload and feature for Actions on Google. The Actions on Google simulator provides some nice debugging features for testing SSML.

JSON AND PYTHON

There's a fairly strong mapping between the various values (strings, numbers, objects, arrays) in JSON and the various programming languages that work with JSON. For Python, the JSON object maps to a Python dictionary, and the JSON array maps to a Python list. Strings are strings, numbers are numbers, and Booleans like true and false in Python map to true and false in JSON. Python has a "json" module that takes a dictionary or list and converts it to JSON (json.dumps( ), used in Listing 7-3). It also has a reader (json.loads( )) that goes from a string representing a JSON value to the corresponding Python object. You used json.loads( ) when reading in the webhook request and parsing out the necessary information. Other programming languages have similar routines.

What If the User Says *No*?

You may have noticed that in the case of implicit confirmation, we're playing the *Okay, doing that...* prompt with some NVA and then ending the conversation. But wait! What if the user says *no*? Handling that is part of the point!

At the time of writing, it's not (yet) possible to customize the dialog within the constraints of Dialogflow. The key missing feature is being able to set the noinput timeout to be very short, like a second. You can't implement implicit confirmation with the usual noinput timeout of several seconds; that long a timeout would be very confusing to the user. Instead, let's look at how to support implicit confirmation at a higher level:

- Play the implicit confirmation prompt and NVA, like you're doing here.

- Set a context that indicates that you just played the implicit confirmation prompt.

- Wait for a response, or lack of a response. Remember, "silence is acceptance" with implicit confirmation. Don't wait too long, maybe a second or so.

- Create an intent for *no* and its variants that's only active during the output context of the VUI's having just played the implicit confirmation prompt. If the user says *no*, then respond with something appropriate like *Okay, canceling...* and end the conversation.

- If the user says nothing, which is the usual case, you go ahead with the action, make the call, or whatever the action is; then end the conversation.

Notes on Implicit Confirmation

Use implicit confirmation often to reassure your users. Imagine a dialog where each step implicitly reassures the user that they're understood:

User   *I wanna make a reservation.*

VUI   *Okay, a new reservation. At what restaurant?*

User   *At Na Na's.*

VUI   *Sure, Na Na's Kitchen. At what time?*

User   *At 7:30.*

VUI   *7:30 this evening. For how many guests?*

User   *Six people.*

VUI   *Let me check... A table is available...*

Notice that the implicit confirmation for time included the day: *this evening*. This is a fine approach if most people make same-day reservations at this restaurant—and if it's clear to users how to change the day. But you might be better off asking an additional question such as *And is that for tonight?* if the user doesn't volunteer the day.

Look at the initial VUI response. It's not just *Okay*. On its own, *okay* only conveys "I heard you, and I think I understood you, so I'm ready to take action." But the user doesn't know if they were understood, just that the VUI heard something. A generic acknowledgment is usually not enough on its own, only as a preamble for more reassurance.

The phrase *a new reservation* reassures understanding of the overall intent: the user wants to make a reservation, not change or cancel one. Think about how a dialog can break down if the first request is misrecognized or if the implicit confirmation phrase is too wide or too narrow. What happens if the phrase is just *a reservation*? Let's look:

User   *I wanna **change** a reservation.*   → Misrecognition

VUI   *Okay, a reservation. At what restaurant?*   → Phrase too broad

User   *At Na Na's.*

VUI   *Sure, Na Na's Kitchen. At what time?*

User   *At 7:30.*

VUI   *7:30 this evening. For how many guests?*

User   *Six people.*

VUI   *Let me check... A table is available...*

User   *I know! I want to change it!*

This time the user wants to change a reservation, but because the confirmation phrase is only *a reservation*, nothing conveys to the user that they're actually making another reservation instead of looking up an existing one until the end of the interaction.

"Implicit" implies many things. You'll find that the term "implicit" is applied to several related but different voice features. To us, "implicit" means conveying reassurance without getting an explicit response: the speaker says something that may or may not be clear, and the listener responds in a way that says, "Here's what I understood." You'll also see "implicit" refer to the assignment of a device as the endpoint that plays some output, either a "sticky" assignment based on some context or a predefined default. This allows the user to not have to disambiguate or specify that endpoint every time. It's an important feature— always look for ways to use context and settings—but it relates more to the logic of resolving ambiguity or setting a command shortcut than to communication reassurance. Unless you work in a framework that uses only one meaning, be careful that everyone on your team uses the word to mean the same thing without having to, well, confirm it!

Explicit Confirmation

In explicit confirmation, the dialog doesn't move forward until there's a verbal go-ahead. In a VUI, you use it when understanding is important before continuing. Because explicit confirmations add length and complexity to a dialog, they're mainly used when the extra step outweighs dealing with getting something wrong. Again, it's a cost balance, not because it's more work to develop the dialog but because the user experience might suffer. In the voice world, explicit confirmation usually refers to the VUI asking the user to confirm something before proceeding, rather than the other way around.

User *Pay 900 dollars to Holiday Cruises from my VISA card.*

VUI *That's 900 dollars to Holiday Cruises from your VISA card ending in 5098. Is that correct?*

~ ~ ~   ~ ~ ~

User *Call Doctor Jones.*

VUI *You want to call Doctor Brent Jones, right?*

User *Yeah, that's right.*

VUI *Calling...*

~ ~ ~   ~ ~ ~

> **User**   *I wanna make a reservation.*
>
> ... [Reservation dialog] ...
>
> **VUI**   *There's a table available at Na Na's Kitchen, for six people at 7:30 PM tomorrow, Saturday.*
>
> *Want me to reserve it?*
>
> **User**   *Yes, please.*

SUCCESS TIP 8.3 STRIKE A BALANCE WITH YOUR CONFIRMATION PROMPTS   Brevity and clarity are your guiding lights. They need to be broad enough to include what the user requested even if they used different words, but also narrow enough to cover the meaning even if the words differ. Avoid *You said...* because the user may have used synonyms with the same meaning. Make it clear when it's time for the user to respond.

Code for Explicit Confirmation

There're a few things we need to do in the application to add explicit confirmation:[3]

- Add a confirmation intent in Dialogflow and an associated entity.

- Modify the webhook code to do the explicit confirmation instead of an implicit one.

- Modify the webhook code to handle the result of the confirmation.

First, let's add the intent and entity we need for confirmation:

- Create a new entity "confirm" with two values "yes" and "no" and some synonyms that make sense in the context of a *Do you want to do this?* question (Figure 8-4). You can reuse this entity in any confirmation intent.

---

[3]The Dialogflow files with the new intent and entity are in 8-2a.zip; the webhook code is in 8-2b. zip.

Figure 8-4. *New* confirm *entity*

Now you need to modify the webhook to use explicit instead of implicit confirmation and to handle the new intent `arConfirmName`.

First, the explicit confirmation change. Previously you had

```
df_response.output_text = df_request.fulfillment_text
df_response.end_conversation = True
df_response.do_pre_nva = True
```

Now change it to the explicit confirmation logic (Listing 8-6), from `ar_call_by_name.py`:

Listing 8-6. Adding the option to provide explicit confirmation

```
if df_response.explicit_confirmation:  # A
    df_response.output_text =\      # B
        f"You want to call {GIVEN_NAME} {LAST_NAME}, right?"
    df_response.output_contexts.append(      # C
        confirmation_context(GIVEN_NAME, LAST_NAME)
        )
else:
    df_response.output_text = df_request.fulfillment_text  # D
    df_response.end_conversation = True
    df_response.do_pre_nva = True
```

`GIVEN_NAME` and `LAST_NAME` come from different places, depending on what part of the dialog you're in. The variable `explicit_confirmation` in the object `df_response` (A) dictates if you confirm or not. If you are, set the output text differently (B) to confirm.

Then add an output context to the response using the new function `confirmation_context` (C) defined in its own file. If you're not confirming, do what you did before (D), including ending the conversation and adding NVA.

Second, add code to support the new intent `arConfirmName`, as shown in Listing 8-7. If the user confirms *yes* (A), play the acknowledging *OK, calling...* and the NVA. If the user disconfirms *no* (B), just say *Sorry* for now and end the conversation. You'll fix that unfriendly placeholder response soon.

You'll notice that from time to time we introduce new helper functions like the `confirmation_context` one used earlier. Typically, they're placed in their own Python files for maximum modularity and readability. These functions create the formatting that Dialogflow demands for the webhook response elements. You don't have to worry about them, but you can certainly look if you're interested. Specifically, the `confirmation_context` function adds the output context `confirmName` and adds the first and last names as parameters to that context—remember, the Dialogflow intent `confirmName` is looking for that input context. We'll discuss in the next section why adding the names is needed.

Listing 8-7. Supporting the new intent `arConfirmName` (in `ar_confirm_name.py`)

```python
def ar_confirm_name(df_request, df_response):
    """

    Result of an explicit name confirmation
    """

    if 'confirm' in df_request.parameters:
        if df_request.parameters['confirm'] == 'yes':      # A
            # The caller has confirmed the name. Play it.
            df_response.output_text = 'OK, calling.'
            df_response.end_conversation = True
            df_response.do_pre_nva = True

        elif df_request.parameters['confirm'] == 'no':     # B
            # Negative confirmation
            df_response.output_text = 'Sorry.'
            df_response.end_conversation = True
```

Dialogflow, App Engine, and Statelessness

Let's look in depth at why you had to add the name to the output context (C in Listing 8-6). As with many frameworks, when using Google App Engine with Dialogflow, the webhook is **stateless** in that it doesn't remember anything from previous requests. Anything you want the webhook code to know from previous requests must be passed in. It's worth repeating **anything you want the webhook code to know from previous requests must be passed in.**

This sounds like a pain, and it would seem useful to have some sort of memory between the requests, but that opens up all kinds of scalability issues. Being stateless, App Engine can deploy the code anywhere it sees fit without having to worry about if it still has access to the history of the conversation. This is one of the features of App Engine and other such frameworks; whether you're making one or one million requests an hour, you don't have to worry about where the code is or if it has access to history. Imagine the nightmare if you had the code running on multiple servers distributed all over the grid; how would you ensure that any history was accessible to requests being executed in all locations? The very next request might be executed a thousand miles away from the current one. With much of the code in the cloud, being stateless has become key.

Okay, so it's not a bug but a feature. But it adds some overhead on your part; if you have some conversation state you need maintained, you need to send it out in the webhook response and then pass it back in to any subsequent webhook requests. How do you do that? With contexts and their parameters. The webhook response adds history information (like the name of the person you're calling) to the output context, and the handler for the intent must grab those parameters from the input context. You'd do this in the handle for `arConfirmName` if you were actually calling someone; it wasn't necessary this time because all you did was respond with *Okay, calling...* and some NVA.

SUCCESS TIP 8.4 USE DATABASES TO DEAL WITH HISTORY   As you learn about interacting with databases, you realize that there's another way. Recall from Listing 8-2 that the webhook request has a unique session ID. You can use this with a database to build your own conversation session store. Now you need to worry about both where the code is executed and potential latency due to accessing a database far away. The key is to understand that stateless is not the same as context-less.

Notes on Explicit Confirmation

The key to robust explicit confirmation is to be clear about what exactly is confirmed. If you changed a dialog from an implicit confirmation *Okay, a reservation* to an explicit *A reservation, right?*, the same unclarity remains. As a user, I don't know if it means all reservation request types or only some. Confirmation prompt wording is key.

If your voice system has many intents or endpoints, the wording takes some serious thought and testing. A good approach is to have several more narrowly worded options (e.g., *a new reservation, an existing reservation*) as well as a more general one (*a reservation*). This allows you the most robust handling by using the broader phrase only for requests that don't fit the narrower phrases and for backoff strategies (more in Chapters 11 and 13).

Be careful about how you phrase your confirmations. Different questions result in different responses—be sure you handle the expected responses:

- *Do you want to call Brent?* → More *Yes (I do)* and *No (I don't)*

- *You want to call Brent. Right?* → More *(That's) Right, Wrong, Not right*

- *You want to call Brent. Is that correct?* → More *Yes, it is, Correct, No, it's not*

We have seen situations where including an explicit phrase like *Please say yes or no* actually improved user success, but don't start with that. It's a last resort in recovery (Chapter 13) because it's unnatural conversation and a sign of other issues. Clearly worded explicit confirmations should make the phrase unnecessary: if your VUI asks *Do you wanna call Brent?*, the natural response is *Yes* or *No*. Done. No explanation needed.

Don't confirm a Yes/No question. If you must confirm, you can just ask a second time and compare the results to decide on your next step. This is not a dialog experience any user should have:

VUI   *A refill of Prozac. Is that right?*

User   *Sure isn't.*

VUI   *Was that a "no"?*

User   *A no ... Yes, no!*

You should expect that some people volunteer additional information beyond *yes*. This is a type of **mixed-initiative** interaction. It's called that because the VUI initiated but the user took over the initiator role, at least temporarily:

> **User**   *Order a refill.*
>
> **VUI**   *You want to refill a prescription, right?*
>
> **User**   *Yeah, for Prozac.*

The format is DIRECT RESPONSE + NEW INFORMATION. If this new information turns out to be a required slot, you want to capture it, so you don't have to ask for it later.

SUCCESS TIP 8.5 YES/NO QUESTIONS—YOUR GATEWAY TO SUCCESS   As a general rule, fewer dialog turns are preferable for several reasons, including speed and less risk of introducing misunderstandings. That said, asking an easy-to-answer Yes/No question early on is a proven way to help novice users be successful in their first conversation even with a complex dialog. There are few better ways to instill confidence in a user than maximizing their chances of early success. It generates goodwill for interactions down the road that potentially are less smooth, and your users will give your VUI more chances after that point than they otherwise would have.

MULTIMODAL CORNER

If you have a screen, implicit and explicit confirmation is easily done using that screen. You saw an example in Chapter 7 of an explicit Yes/No screen. Figure 8-5 shows procedure prep examples of implicit confirmation. The food diary list displays each separate item that was recognized and offers a keyboard for adding food items and "X" buttons for deleting misrecognized items. The open question responses provide enough feedback to assure the user their question was understood—notice the text field at the top showing the recognized utterance, either just abstracted content or verbatim. The spoken prompts often contain a little more detail, but audio and image can stand alone for those who only rely on one or the other.

Figure 8-5. *Multimodal implicit confirmation: listing recognized foods, responding to open questions*

Confirmation Placement: Slots vs. Intents

You've decided what to confirm. But when do you confirm? In the reservation dialog, you have an intent (new reservation) plus four slots (place, guests, time, day). Do you have to use the same confirmation approach for each slot and intent? No, you don't have to confirm every slot using the same method nor every intent in your VUI. Do you confirm them one at a time or everything at once? Well, that depends.

If recognition and interpretation perform well, you can get away with not reassuring on every dialog turn. If the outcome matches a default setting or if some information isn't important to the user, you can also cut down on the reassurance, like in more concise VUI2:

User	*I wanna watch* Chef	→ default output=den TV; default provider=MoviesRUs

VUI1 Chef, *from 2014. Playing now from Movies R Us on the den TV.*

VUI2 *Here's* Chef.

You often end up with some combination. Here are some guidelines:

- **First, confirm that you're on the right track.** Particularly important for multi-turn multi-slot dialogs. You usually want to determine the topic of the request by confirming the intent before continuing.

  - If the user utterance filled both the intent and some slots, such as *I want to make a follow-up appointment with Doctor Jones on Monday*, you'd usually first confirm the general intent (a new appointment) and then confirm the slot information you captured rather than try to do it all in one take. Just don't throw away the slot information the user gave you. That will annoy them.

- **Avoid confirming the same information multiple times.** This is where dialog management shines. If the user backtracks and changes something, don't reconfirm what's still valid from previous confirmation.

- **Confirm anything you can use to narrow down later options.** This simplifies the user's task or fulfills their request faster. For example, if you have verified someone wants a reservation on Saturday and a table is only available for 5 PM, the rest of the dialog will be quick.

- **Confirm logical groups as one.** For example, a card expiration can confirm month and year at once rather than in two steps.

- **Make use of context to cluster multiple slots into one confirmation**. You'll learn about N-best and skip lists in Chapter 16.

- **Never ask users to confirm something you can't give them.** If a restaurant only has one table that can seat a large party, or even no tables at all, don't ask the user to go through the whole dialog before telling them nothing is available. Do your data dips as early as makes sense for the interaction and make several if you need to unless you have a very good reason not to. You want to avoid this:

User   *I wanna make a reservation at Na Na's tomorrow.*

VUI   *Okay, a reservation, for Na Na's Kitchen tomorrow.*

VUI   *What time?*

User   *At 7:30.*

> **VUI**   *And for how many guests?*
>
> **User**   *Six people.*
>
> **VUI**   *[Lookup] Sorry, Na Na's has nothing available tomorrow.*
>
> **User**   *...#$@!!*

Instead, you could do something like this:

> **User**   *I wanna make a reservation at Na Na's tomorrow.*
>
> **VUI**   *Okay, a reservation, for Na Na's Kitchen tomorrow. Let me check...*
>
> **VUI**   *[Lookup] Sorry, Na Na's has nothing available tomorrow.*

If only a few choices are available, make sure you know what those are so you can offer them to the user:

> **VUI**   *... Let me check...*
>
> **VUI**   *[Lookup] Na Na's can seat six people at 5:30 or at 9 PM...*

Disconfirmation: Dealing with "No"

So far, we have mostly ignored what happens if the user disconfirms (denies, rejects, says "no" to) a confirmation. But nobody's perfect, including any VUI:

> **User**   *Call Doctor Jones.*
>
> **VUI**   *You want to call Doctor Brent Jones, right?*
>
> **User**   *No.*
>
> **VUI**   *Who'd you like to call?*
>
> **User**   *Doctor Lena Jones.*
>
> **VUI**   *Doctor Lena Jones. Calling...*

Chapter 13 is all about how to recover from misunderstandings; for now, let's look at only confirmations. You want to

- Minimize the risk of "no."

- Make sure users know how to disconfirm.

- Make it simple for users to make changes and continue without starting over.

You may have noticed that an acknowledgment and implicit confirmation often look identical. We glossed over the difference earlier: an implicit confirmation really implies that the user can respond, either accepting or rejecting the confirmation. That means the user needs to be able to interrupt, either by only saying, for example, *Cancel* (typical in IVRs), by saying a wake word plus *Cancel* (typical for voice assistants), or by some other interaction, like pressing a button to engage the microphone.

Of course, this works only when users understand how to interrupt! Implicit confirmations therefore often include some hint about how to disconfirm—this can be important because the confirmation sounds like a statement, not a question. You can include something like *If that's not what you want, say Cancel/Go back/Start over* depending on what works best for the situation.

What do you do if the user rejects what the VUI offered? If they already filled other slots, you don't want to force them to redo everything. You typically have several choices:

- Ask again. It's the most common situation, especially after an explicit confirmation rejection. If it's clear what slot's the problem or if it's the starting intent, you'll have a retry method.

- Ask the user what slot to change, and then get the new information. That can work if it's clear to the user what to say, but it gets tricky if several slots are wrong.

- Confirm each slot as the user fills it. That interaction can become much too long.

- Guess! Offer another match. You need to be careful with that, as you'll learn in Chapter 13. If there're only two options, it's pretty safe to continue with Option B after A has been rejected without confirming again.

- Throw out everything and start over. This can be the right approach if fixing things step-by-step will take longer.

Code for Disconfirmation

Remember when you added explicit confirmation? If the caller responded *No*, they heard an unceremonious *Sorry*, and the dialog ended. That's a bad experience. Let's fix that now to provide a smoother disconfirmation for the user:

- Add an `arCollectName` intent to collect only a name:

    - Training phrases are the same as for `arCallByName`, but without the "Call..."

    - The response can be the same as in `arCallByName`; it doesn't matter since you're using webhooks.

    - You need to add the `collectName` context in the input and the output.

    - Enable the webhook! Figure 8-6 shows the new intent.

- Make changes to the webhook code:

    - For negative confirmation, add the new response instead of saying "Sorry" and ending the conversation.

    - Add the new `collectName` context to the output contexts.

    - Handle the `arCollectName` intent.

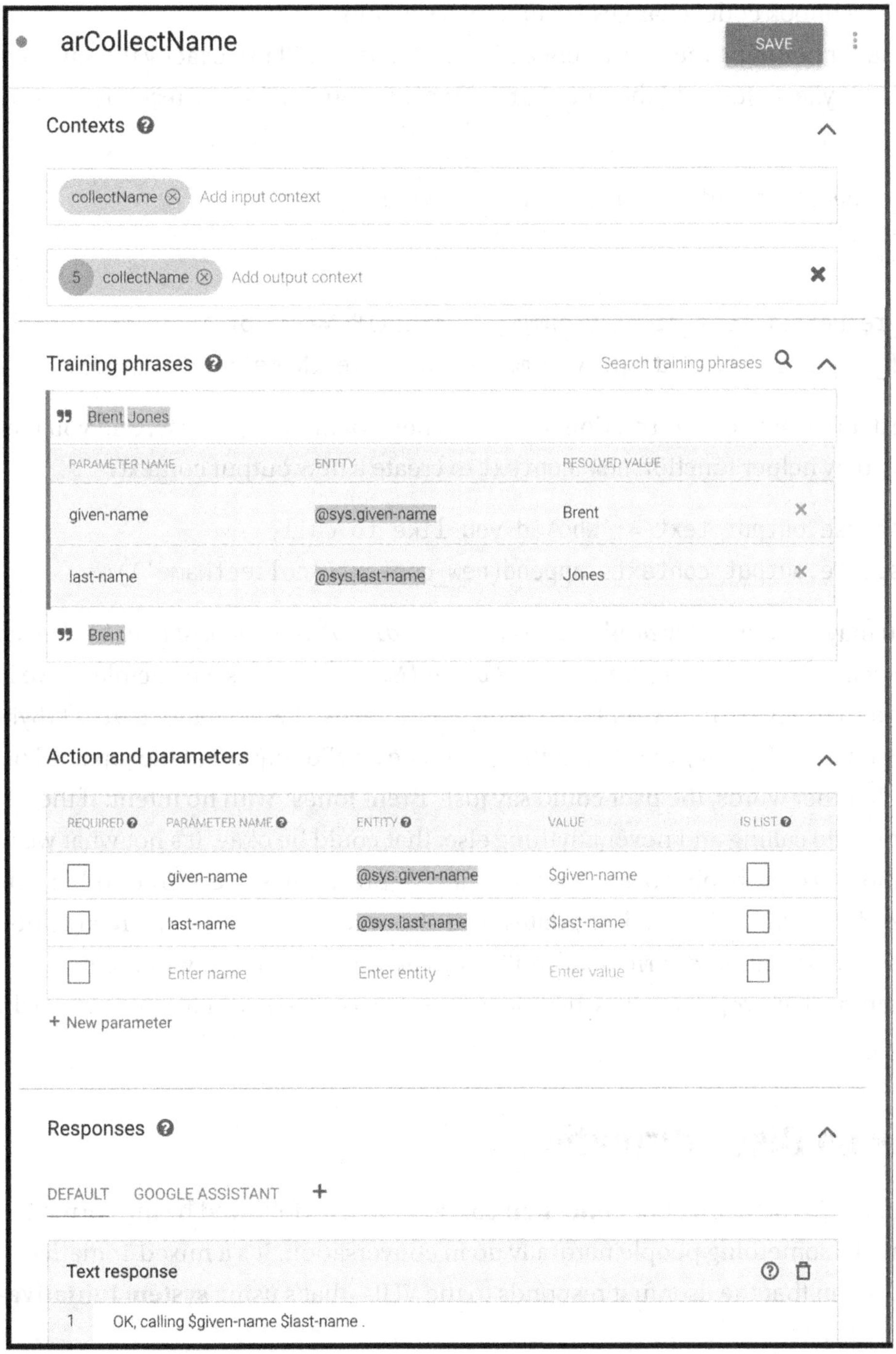

Figure 8-6. *New* `arCollectName` *intent for handling negative confirmation*

The webhook code[4] changes occur in two sections:

First, for handling the new intent arCollectName, you'll use exactly the same code as for arCallByName. Just add the intent arCollectName to that logical test line in main.py. So instead of

```
if df_request.intent_display_name == 'arCallByName':
```

you have

```
if df_request.intent_display_name == 'arCallByName' or \
    df_request.intent_display_name == 'arCollectName':
```

Next, on negative confirmation, you add a new friendlier response, and you use another new helper function new_context to create a new output context:

```
df_response.output_text = 'Who\'d you like to call?
df_response.output_contexts.append(new_context('collectName'))
```

You may wonder: *Why don't we just reuse arCallByName and just tweak it to recognize just the name instead of adding a new arCollectName intent?* It's a principle we've hinted at already: cutting corners won't lead to great interfaces. If we expanded arCallByName to recognize just "Brent Jones," then that would be a valid request at the top level of the dialog. In other words, the user could say just "Brent Jones" with no intent. If the VUI could only do calling and never anything else, that could be okay. It's not what we want here, and you'd probably not want it for a calling app either, since it limits other valid features like making contact list updates. You also want to maximize the recognition in both contexts (another principle you'll learn about in the next few chapters), so constraining it appropriately to what the user is expected to say in the context is what you really want.

Notes on Disconfirmation

In Chapter 12, you learn about **one-step correction**, a *no* followed by the corrected content. It's something people naturally do in conversation. It's a mixed-initiative interaction in that the user first responds to the VUI—that's using **system initiative**—and

---

[4]The Dialogflow files with the new intent are in 8-3a.zip; the webhook code is in 8-3b.zip.

then immediately in the same sentence provides information that the VUI hasn't asked for yet—that's **user initiative**. As you'll see, one-step correction can improve your VUI success rate significantly:

User   *Call Doctor Brenda Jones.*

VUI   *You want to call Doctor Brent Jones, right?*

User   *No, Brenda!*

VUI   *Doctor Brenda Jones. Calling…*

It's important to keep context when reconfirming without starting over. Here, it's clear to us that the user wants to call someone, just not Brent. Users will either restate the full request or a part that—to them—is enough to identify what to change. Your VUI must stay in intent and keep the right context to handle both (Chapter 16).[5]

With other platforms, you have several options for making telephone calls, but the basic pieces are very similar. Several years ago, this was quite an involved process involving telephony hardware and a dedicated connection to a telecommunications provider, like AT&T or others. These days, it can be quite a bit simpler. Twilio and others worry about the hardware and the telecom parts, so all you to do is handle the VUI dialog. You'd also need an application server that would behave much like Dialogflow or the webhooks that we've seen; the communications provider would hit your server with a request, and the server would respond with what it wants to speak to the user.

FROM THE VOICE TRENCHES

Ann's mobile phone has a single contact named "Ronda" and no others with similar names. Even if Ronda's address is set as a favorite destination, the spoken request *How long will it take to get to Ronda's house?* fails for one reason: the text interpretation returns *Rhonda*. The names sound identical, but to a user this is an annoying lack of connecting the dots that can and should be avoided. In another VUI, name search fails when asked to *Call Ann*, either because of mapping to the indefinite article "an" or to the name spelled "Anne" that isn't in the contact list.

---

[5]Can your VUI actually call someone with what you just created? As of now, no. Cloud communications providers like Twilio offer various integration options. At the time of writing this, Google itself has a Dialogflow Phone Gateway beta that allows inbound calls. Expect this to expand over time.

Additional Reassurance Techniques and Pitfalls

Certainty and reassurance impact just about every aspect of a successful VUI. The more accurate the recognition and NL and the more precise the search, the better the results, the simpler the interaction, and the more users will engage and explore. We mentioned earlier that what people like the least in VUIs today by far is not feeling understood and not getting the expected response. Therefore, you want to focus on every aspect of accuracy in your VUI.

SUCCESS TIP 8.6 REASSURANCE IS THE DEVIL IN THE DETAILS   There's a lot of fine detail to conveying reassurance; it's an area of VUI design that differentiates functional from superior. And it's crucial to your VUI success. So be aware that details matter, think about what you're doing, analyze user responses, and be ready to make changes.

System Pronunciation

One of us authors lives in Brisbane, California. California's Brisbane is not pronounced the same as Brisbane, Australia. Hearing that isn't just annoying; it also affects trust in the VUI. The following dialog is an actual transcript from a conversation with a voice assistant:

> **User**   *What's the weather in Brisbane today?*
>
> **VUI**   *In Brisbane today, it will be rainy with a forecasted high of 84...*
>
> **User**   *What's the weather in Brisbane, California?*
>
> **VUI**   *In Brisbane it's 62 and partly cloudy...*

With the same pronunciation and lacking contextual reassurance of an included *Australia* or *California*, only awareness of the likely weather in each place gives the user some idea of which Brisbane they're hearing about. Avoid this situation.

Pronouncing things wrong is one of the quickest ways to get your users to lose trust in your VUI. It's one reason why you might not want to greet your users by name—if you do, offer an easy way for users to fix mispronunciations. Pronunciation may be out of your control if you rely on built-in TTS and databases for convenience, but do what you can. It's equally important to stress the right word in a sentence based on context.

Emphasizing a word signals to the user "Pay attention to this." You learn more about this in Chapter 15.

What about pronunciation of unusual words like medication names or foreign names of places, foods, or artists? Medications are difficult for any user to pronounce. You'll use tricks to expand what's accepted on the recognition side. For confirmation, it can be a challenge if the official pronunciation is far from what the user said. If you can rely on a screen, all the better. What's read back to the user needs to be easy to understand and correct. Users will learn, so if your system pronunciation is off, your recognition will suffer when users copy it.

Earlier in this chapter you used SSML to add NVA. SSML is what Actions on Google uses to control pronunciation, stress, and pausing. Since you now know how to add SSML as a custom payload in the webhook response, "all" you have to know now is how SSML controls all these things, which is a bigger topic we'll cover in later chapters.

SUCCESS TIP 8.7 PRONUNCIATION MATTERS   Learn how to edit TTS output on whatever platform you use. It's worth the trouble. If you record prompts, make sure your voice talent has information about how to pronounce words in context. Users learn from VUI pronunciation, affecting future recognition success.

Backchannels

Backchannels are verbal (lexical or non-lexical) and non-verbal utterances by a listener to reassure the speaker that they're paying attention without taking over the dialog. Backchannels often convey some emotional content (Table 8-2).

Table 8-2. *Backchannels, types, and examples*

Type	Example
Verbal, lexical	*Really?, Right, Yeah, No way!*
Verbal, non-lexical	*Uh-huh, Hmm,* laugh, sigh
Non-verbal	Nodding, facial expressions, gaze

Backchannels are covered by Grice's Cooperative Principle: they efficiently provide feedback to the speaker. The emotional content also affects how the speaker continues.

People use backchannels a lot in conversations. Should your VUI? Probably not a lot. Avoid making it sound too human for one reason: it's not human. The danger of using backchannels in a VUI is to promise too much. Don't behave like you can understand conversation like a human unless you really can. Backchannels are human traits and are imprecise, so they often lead to misunderstandings and dialog repairs (Chapters 12 and 13). Having said that, you can use backchannels carefully in some situations. By signaling *I'm still listening*, backchannels encourage the current speaker to keep talking. For example, think about how you say a credit card number to someone: in groups of four separated by a short pause to give that person time to write it down. You might even wait for so *go on* feedback from the other person. When the listener is a VUI, you need to account for users doing that same pausing. The complication is that users won't know if they should wait for feedback or not. And different people will naturally do it different ways, so you need to allow for both and continue to listen. Backchannels can help here:

User   *4 1 9 8...*

VUI   *Okay.*

User   *9 2 6 5...*

VUI   *Uh-huh.*

Discourse Markers

Discourse markers are "those little words" speakers use to move along or change direction in a conversation—words like *so, and, but, first, although, by the way, on the other hand, actually,* and many others (Table 8-3). These words pack a fair bit of meaning on top of other things said in a conversation. They link ideas across phrases and sentences, add meaning, and decrease cognitive load—without them, communication becomes odd and disconnected.

Table 8-3. *Discourse markers, concepts they convey, and examples*

Concept / Meaning	Example
Add, connect	*And, Also, In addition, Then*
Contrast, qualify	*However, Although, But, On the other hand, Instead*
Compare	*Like, Similarly, Likewise*
Cause and effect	*So, Because, Therefore, As a result*
Illustrate	*For example, Such as, For instance*
Persuade	*Clearly, Obviously, For that reason*
Opinion	*It looks like, I think, Personally*
Emphasize	*Actually, In fact, In particular*
Enumerate, sequence	*First, Second, Next, Before, After*
Conclude	*Finally, In conclusion, To summarize*

People use discourse markers a lot in conversations. Should your VUI? Yes—and you should be careful to use them appropriately because they're not interchangeable across type.

SUCCESS TIP 8.8. DON'T OVERDO DISCOURSE MARKERS   You might remember what websites looked like when people could first easily change fonts and colors. They were a hideous mess because it was easy to make them so. Just because you know that people use discourse markers doesn't mean you should add them everywhere for no reason. More doesn't make your VUI seem smarter or more human, just verbose.

VUI Architecture

Does it matter if you treat *Okay, a new reservation. At what restaurant?* as one, two, or three separate prompts? Yes, it does. How you split things will depend on your overall architecture, number of tasks, and general dialog flow. The key is to treat the acknowledgment as a response wrapping up the previous dialog. It usually makes sense to keep the confirmation separate from the onset of the next dialog because it keeps things modular and flexible.

Think about what happens to a prompt where one dialog act ends and the next begins. Sample dialogs often show the response to one dialog together with the initiation of the next:

User   *I wanna make a reservation.*

VUI   *Sure, a new reservation. At what restaurant?*

That's how it sounds to the listener, like it's all part of one dialog turn. But it's really two separate turns by the same speaker:

User   (initiates)   *I wanna make a reservation.*

VUI   (responds)   *Sure, a new reservation.*

VUI   (initiates)   *At what restaurant?*

It's an implicit confirmation followed by a question to fill the first empty slot. This detail matters: it affects how you think about your design flow and architecture for prompt playback. When you deal with larger VUIs with branching flows and combinatorics, you want to "complete" one dialog before starting the next dialog. You'll see the importance of this when implementing retries (Chapter 13).

Choosing the Right Reassurance Method

With all these factors to consider, how do you choose the right confirmation strategy? As with everything voice, don't freak out. If you feel overwhelmed, just follow these guidelines:

- Explicitly confirm if an incorrect result is costly to the user (financially or time spent in dialog), unless it could affect their privacy (someone else hears it).

- Avoid explicitly confirming every step in the dialog (makes the dialog long).

- You don't have to use the same strategy everywhere. In fact, you probably won't.

Figure 8-7 summarizes the key features of the confirmation strategies you've learned about in this chapter.

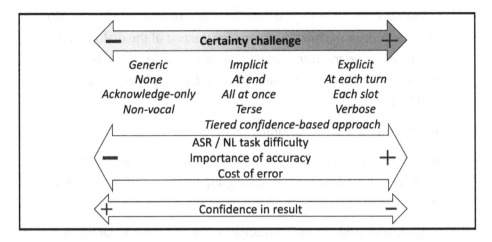

Figure 8-7. *Guideline for choosing a confirmation method*

If you have access to ASR and NL confidence scores, you can use different confirmation methods based on the VUI's confidence in its understanding and response (Chapter 12).

SUCCESS TIP 8.9 CONSISTENCY ACROSS CONFIRMATION METHODS   In a larger VUI with multiple intents and therefore multiple confirmation methods, keep the user experience consistent by keeping voice, persona, wording, and level of formality consistent.

Summary

- Balance the need for reassurance with the cost of misunderstanding.

- A VUI response should reflect the appropriate level of confidence both in the accuracy of the response itself and in having understood the user. Your implementation should allow contextual use of discourse markers and acknowledgment.

- Users who don't trust a VUI's responses are less likely to engage with it in the future.

- Lack of confirmation can severely impact the overall success of a VUI dialog.

- Confirming an intent is fundamentally different from confirming slot values: the former narrows the scope for the rest of the dialog (*You want to make a reservation, right?*); the latter verifies information before a potentially costly mistake (*That's five people tomorrow at 7 PM, right?*).

- Stateless is not the same as context-less.

- Choose the right level of confirmation to increase the overall success of the interaction while balancing keeping the interaction as short as possible.

- By adding code and enabling webhooks, you can have flexibility for how your VUI responds to nuances in user requests. It gives you more independence from tool and platform changes while still providing the advantage of letting the platform handle many details.

## CHAPTER 9

Helping Users Succeed Through Consistency

In Chapter 8, you learned the importance of reassuring both user and VUI that a request is correctly understood. There's an additional piece to user reassurance: feeling in control. If users can navigate a VUI to get what they want, know how to start over, or get help when needed, then they feel comfortable with the whole interaction. The outcome is greater willingness to explore and try new requests and greater success in reaching their goals; it's greater discoverability and findability. When users feel in control of their own fate, they're happier users—even when they don't reach their goal! If you're familiar with usability heuristics, you'll recognize several in this chapter: consistency, standards, familiar metaphor and language, help, feedback, and user control. Consistency is reached by

- Consistent dialog strategies, prompt wording, and voice throughout

- Recognizing what users say if they use the words the VUI uses

- Responding to the same words and phrases throughout a VUI—even across VUIs

- Handling and fulfilling a request identically in the same context throughout a VUI

You can easily find lots of information about usability heuristics online and in books; we'll of course focus on how they apply to voice-first interactions. This chapter is about helping users help themselves.

© Ann Thymé-Gobbel, Charles Jankowski 2021
A. Thymé-Gobbel and C. Jankowski, *Mastering Voice Interfaces*, https://doi.org/10.1007/978-1-4842-7005-9_9

Universals

Universals, or globals, are a small set of commands always available to users, no matter the task or domain or what they're currently doing in the VUI. Universals provide ways for the user to get clarification (repeat, help), redo part or all of a task (start over, go back), or temporarily or permanently end the VUI conversation (pause, stop, cancel, exit, transfer). Universals contribute to familiarity and consistency that makes users more self-sufficient—they're the users' security blanket. Users rely on them for clarification and getting unstuck because they're inherently familiar to the users:

> **VUI**   *Your prescription number is 5 9 2 2 7 6 9.*
>
> **User**   *Can you repeat that please?*
>
> **VUI**   *Sure. Your confirmation number is 5 9 2 2 7 6 9.*
>
> ~~~   ~~~
>
> **User**   *Call Deborah Jones.*
>
> **VUI**   *Dr. Ben Jones. Calling mobile...*
>
> **User**   *No, stop. Cancel!*
>
> **VUI**   *Canceled.*
>
> ~~~   ~~~
>
> **VUI**   *What is the patient's latest MELD score?*
>
> **User**   *Um... What does that mean?*
>
> **VUI**   *The MELD score for liver disease is a number from 6 to 40 based on ...*

As commands, universals should always be available to users, but their content and behavior are contextual. If a user asks to *repeat that*, something should always be repeated, but what exactly gets repeated depends on what happened immediately before the user's request.

Universals are there when users miss what the VUI said and want to hear it again. Or when they need clarification before responding or selecting an option. Or when they get stuck or change their mind in a multistep transaction and want to change something in their request. Or when they need to pause the conversation to find some information the VUI needs. Or when they're done or just don't want to deal with the VUI anymore.

Universals are based on people's common reactions and behaviors even without any previous interaction with a particular VUI. Users should be able to expect the same general behavior from any VUI conversation, no matter the platform or who developed it. Alexa and Google platforms both include some built-in universals, which can make your life both easier and harder. More about that later.

Universals are "universal" not only by their availability; to work well, they need to be based on what real users naturally say across VUIs. Universal commands shouldn't need to be taught; coverage should include the words and phrases people naturally say without being instructed. Ideally they should be short, unambiguous, easy to say, and not sounding like other commands. Map the most commonly used few phrases to each universal. You want those to work well without risking ambiguity that affects other requests. In later chapters, you learn why this is important and how to make mapping to universals more or less likely. Once universals are implemented, the functionality is available everywhere in the VUI.

SUCCESS TIP 9.1 COORDINATE YOUR UNIVERSALS   Make sure the same synonyms are recognized everywhere in the VUI. Also, check that there's no conflict between your added universals and any built-in platform-specified universal's behavior. If your VUI is multimodal, coordinate across all modalities to check that any command words shown on screens and spoken in voice prompts result in the same behavior and are well recognized by the VUI. That does not mean that the full text of prompts should also be on the screen. It means if your voice prompt says *…then say "Next"*, the button to move forward should also say "NEXT" rather than "FORWARD" or "CONTINUE" or "GO ON." All of them should be recognized if users say them, but for least cognitive load, the actual command word or phrase you expect people to say—or the one you want to encourage them to say—should agree across modalities.

Providing Clarification and Additional Information

The first set of universals cover user requests for clarification: the user either wants to hear something again, do something again, or get more information to help them get closer to some goal. Repeat and help are our shorthand names for these intents, but they're not the only phrases the user can say. Both play a big part in recovery strategies, the topic of Chapter 13.

Clarification is always contextual, so your VUI response must take into account what the user just did or said and what else is going on:

User   *Play "As Time Goes By."*

VUI   *[Plays song, to end]*

User   *Repeat that.* → Meaning: I want to hear the same song once more.

VUI   *[Plays song again from the top]*

~~~   ~~~

VUI   *[Plays a song as part of a stream]*

User   [while song is playing] *What song is this?*

VUI   *This is "As Time Goes By" performed by Dooley Wilson.*

User   [a few seconds later] *Repeat that.* → Meaning: I want to hear the info again.

VUI   *This is "As Time ...* → A bit ambiguous if at the end of a song, so you need to decide how to interpret. Low cost to be wrong, so don't ask the user if they meant the info or playing the song— they'll ask again less ambiguously if you got it wrong, and saying the info is less overhead so the best choice here.

~~~   ~~~

VUI   *[Plays a song as part of a stream]*

User   *Volume up by 5.* → While song is playing

VUI   *[Increases volume]*

User   *Repeat that.* → Meaning: I want it louder by another five steps.

Table 9-1 summarizes points to keep in mind. Chapter 14 is all about context, one of the most important topics for creating conversational interfaces. Short-term memory dictates that this should not happen:

VUI   *You have a notification from FedEx: your frozen food has arrived.*

User   *Repeat that.* → Meaning: I want to hear that again because I missed some detail.

VUI   *There's nothing to repeat.*

Table 9-1. *Guidelines for successful repeat and help dialogs*

Universal	User expects VUI to	Default phrases	Complexity
Repeat	Say/do most recent thing again.	*Repeat (that), (Say that) again*	What's "most" recent? How far back to repeat. What to repeat (prompt, content, or action).
Help	Provide info to clarify how to respond (examples, detailed descriptions).	*Help, More info* *Tell me more, What can I do?* *What are my options?*	Keep it concise AND informative. Mic open or closed after? Keep context (help on WHAT). Handling out-of-context requests.

Providing a Do-Over

The second type of universals covers user requests to change something before continuing. This can be a complete redo (start over) or a one-step-at-a-time redo (go back).

> **VUI**   *Next, prescription number 2 1 0 0 5 4 6...*
>
> **User**   *Go back.*
>
> **VUI**   *OK. Here are your five available prescriptions...*
>
> ~~~   ~~~
>
> **VUI**   *Prescription number 2 1 0 0 5 4 6 has been refilled. Here's your confirmation number...*
>
> **User**   *Go back.*
>
> **VUI**   *Your prescription has been filled. To fill another prescription...*
>
> ~~~   ~~~
>
> **User**   *[Has given four food items for the food diary]*
>
> **User**   *Start over.*
>
> **VUI**   *Start over what?*

The key to handling redo requests is tracking context, including content provided by the VUI and input from the user and even the path taken in past dialog turns. You need to handle requests that are spoken in mid-transaction: if the conversation has involved multiple turns, confirm the VUI interpretation and that the user understands that information will be lost.

Users expect start over to "forget" everything. Almost. If the user has gone through some login process, don't forget who they are. But if they haven't finished logging in, then do forget and go back to the start of login. If the user is in the process of refilling a prescription or adding items to their food diary, start over within the task that's in process. That means go to the start of that intent or task. Sometimes it's just a synonym for home/top level/main menu, but when the distinction makes sense, it keeps the intent to start that task again.

The action of go back is mainly relevant in list navigation, content playback, browsing, and some multistep transactions. But people are very similar in how they ask for that action, so it fits well among universals for that reason. If you include *go back* everywhere in your VUI, you need to test it carefully to make sure things work as planned. There will be contexts where you need to tell the user going back isn't possible, like after some financial transaction has taken place. Think about how you might address that condition. Table 9-2 covers the main points.

Table 9-2. *Guidelines for successful StartOver and Back dialogs*

Universal	User expects VUI to	Default phrases	Complexity
StartOver	Stop current dialog, forget all provided info and turns, and keep intent.	*Start over*	Do you keep the intent? Avoid restart by mistake. Forget earlier confirmed info? External changes since start, impacting current options. When can't you start over?
Back	Back up one step, undo only the last info provided, and keep the rest in context.	*Go back*, *Back (up)*, *Previous*	Does "one step" in user's mental model match yours? One step can be several prompts. When can't you go back?

Providing an Exit

The third and final set of universals cover user requests to get out of whatever is happening now. It can be a temporary exit from the task to have time to find something (pause). Or an exit from a task and current dialog but intending to start a new conversation (cancel, home/main menu). Or an exit from the VUI to somewhere else, either to a human or another automated system, including voice mail (transfer). Or a complete exit from the interaction and any further conversation (goodbye).

Note that while *main menu* is mainly used in phone-based call center apps, the concept of a home, top level, or starting point applies to a wide set of voice apps. We use it here as shorthand for any top level. In your VUI prompts, you should use a word or phrase that fits best with your task—but should also handle other common user utterances that fit the concept of *top level* or *home* or *main*, especially if you find that people aren't being understood. That makes your universals even more universals and helpful to users.

In a prescription refill IVR, we allowed users to pause the interaction while finding their prescription number. Every 10–15 seconds while paused, the user would hear a reminder to say "Continue" when ready:

VUI	*If you need some time to find your prescription number, say "One moment."*
User	*Yes, one moment please.*
VUI	*Sure. I'll wait till you're ready. When you're back, just say "Continue"...*
	[10-15s] When you're ready, say "Continue" ...
User	*OK, I'm back. Continue.*
VUI	*Great. What's your prescription number?*

Because this VUI conversation was a phone call, pausing was the only way for the VUI not to forget and the user not to have to call back and start over. Users were successful; the same approach is good anytime the user needs to look for information they don't know by heart. The details are different if your VUI is a mobile app or home assistant skill or action, but keeping context so your user can "hold everything" is no less important.

Similar to the do-over set of universals, think carefully about how to handle exit requests when your VUI is in the middle of unfinished transactions. What if your VUI misunderstood the user? What if they're in the middle of a transaction, like making a reservation? You want to verify that the VUI "heard correctly" before acting. If exiting a conversation can be costly to the user for any reason, use what you learned in Chapter 8 about confirmation strategies.

SUCCESS TIP 9.2 CAREFUL WITH THAT CANCEL   When your VUI interprets what the user said as *Cancel*, don't cancel everything the user did unless you're sure that's what they want. Sometimes you need to explicitly confirm the request. *Cancel* and *stop* are great examples of commands users say more or less automatically but that have different consequences depending on the current context. You should recognize and handle them everywhere, but **how** you handle them will depend on context and flow.

Transfer requests out of the VUI are important in IVRs, but there's no reason that other VUIs can't also involve a transfer from automation to a human-to-human dialog. As voice dialogs become more complex and involve money and health transactions, having some human backup will become increasingly important, especially for voice-only conversations. Include appropriate acknowledgement as a transition to assure users they'll be transferred. Table 9-3 summarizes exit strategies. More on this topic at the end of this chapter.

Table 9-3. *Guidelines for successfully halting or exiting dialogs*

Universal	User expects VUI to	Default phrases	Complexity
Pause	Wait for user input; remember context until "*Continue.*"	*Pause* *Wait* *One moment*	How long can/should you wait? Telling user how to end pause. Keeping context Platform limitations.
Cancel	Stop current dialog turn and forget some or all of what was provided and requested so far.	*Cancel* *Stop*	Avoid cancel by mistake. What to cancel if multi-turn. When is it too late to cancel?
Home	Stop current dialog; forget all provided info and turns, including intent; go to "home base."	*Main menu* *Home* *Go to the top (name of VUI)*	If in mid-transaction, should you forget everything? Avoid forgetting by mistake.
Transfer	Connect with a human (via voice or chat).	*Representative* *Agent* *(Talk to a) person/human*	When to offer it or not. Off hours and time zones affect prompts and availability.
Goodbye	Stop listening and talking; handle any bookkeeping to finalize transactions.	*Goodbye* *Thank you* *I'm done* *Exit*	Avoid ending by mistake. Avoid ambiguity "buy" ~ "bye." Avoid ambiguity "exit" ~ "next."

Coding Universals

To build universals, you first add the intents corresponding to the universals in question. Then, add the code needed to respond appropriately.[1] You'll extend the procedure prep helper VUI, starting with repeat. In English, people naturally use words like *repeat* or *again,* so you'd typically make use of that in a prompt to instruct users how to hear or do something again. Using familiar words lowers cognitive load, and *repeat* is also a word that's easy to recognize.

---

[1]The Dialogflow export for the code is in 9-1a.zip, and the webhook code is in 9-1b.zip.

Repeat requests can be ambiguous: Does the user want to hear what the VUI said or hear a recently played song again? Or do some action again, like turning up the volume more? Sometimes users know it's ambiguous and automatically clarify by saying *Repeat that song* or *Say that again* or similar. Never ignore such information. Be ready for it so you can capture and use it. That's real smarts. But don't waste time by explicitly disambiguating—make a best guess what "repeat" means based on the context. Here're some general guidelines—as with most things voice, they're based on likelihood, not absolutes:

- A song or video is playing or has just ended -> "repeat" = "play the same content again."

- The user made a request in the past few seconds that makes sense to do again -> "repeat" = "do the last thing I asked for again."

- The VUI most recently played a prompt -> "repeat" = "play the same prompt(s) again." If the prompt consists of multiple concatenated voice segments, make sure your logic plays all of them from a sensible starting point. This isn't trivial!

SUCCESS TIP 9.3 ANTICIPATE REPETITION   If your VUI speaks some important and unfamiliar information like a reference number or contact phone number, play that information twice automatically, just like a person would repeat such information without being asked to: *Your prescription order number is 4522890. Again, that's 4522890.*

Before continuing, we'll go into depth on why universals are special and describe two ways to implement them. Universals are very context-dependent; how the VUI responds depends on what the user has been saying and doing. This makes sense: as a user, what you expect from *help* depends entirely on the last thing you heard in the dialog and what you're trying to accomplish. Create this context dependence in two ways:

- Have a separate universal intent for every context, and put the responses in the Dialogflow GUI. You'd have a help intent `help_arCallByName`, another for `help_arCallByNameDisambigLastName`, and so on for all the other universals. As you can imagine, this is a nightmare and is definitely not best practice.

- Have one intent for each universal, and do the context-dependent handling in the webhook. This is much better and what you'll do right now, starting by adding the intents for the universals.

Step 1: Creating Intents

Create a new intent `repeat` with the training phrases listed earlier in this chapter (Figure 9-1). No responses are specified; you'll do those via the webhook. Don't forget to enable Fulfillment, since the universal logic will be coded soon in the webhook.

Figure 9-1. *Repeat intent example within Dialogflow*

Do the same thing for all other universals: `help`, `startOver` and `goBack`, and `pause/continue`, `cancel`, `main_menu`, and `transfer`. `goodbye` is already there; you added that in Chapter 6. But you need to make a slight change to the existing one; we'll get to that now. `main_menu` and goodbye are important for IVRs, less so for home assistants, though some observations can carry over between devices and interaction types. As mentioned in Chapter 6, even when callers are explicitly instructed by an IVR to "simply hang up" when done, a few of them won't hang up without saying *Goodbye* or *Thank you* and hearing some closing response in return. It's one of those little details worth paying attention to, a place where you can gain or lose user trust in your system. A little goes a long way here; don't overdo it. Your goal isn't to call attention to the user saying these phrases, but to handle it gracefully if and when they do.

You didn't specify any responses for these intents because the webhook will take care of that. You also haven't specified any input contexts; these new intents are always available. This is the key feature of universals: they're always active. So you need to remove the end input context for goodbye to make it available at any point in the dialog. You also need to enable Fulfillment for goodbye, as it wasn't enabled when you created it in Chapter 6.

Step 2: Coding the Webhook

Now comes the interesting stuff: adding responses in the webhook, which is needed because you didn't have any responses in the Dialogflow GUI.

You've already learned that universals are context-dependent. So are other aspects of conversational dialogs. The response depends on the current state of the VUI dialog at the time when the user spoke the universal, what they're in the process of doing, what slots are filled, and the most recent VUI action. But many approaches, including the Dialogflow webhook, are fundamentally stateless. This is the core issue of universals: how do you know "where" in the dialog your user is when saying some universal, so you know how to respond for the context? Unless you do something special, you have no history of what's happened previously in the dialog. Let's work on that now.

How do we know "where the user is," so we know how to respond? For now, you can approximate this by keeping track of the most recent intent. For many cases, this approximation is good enough, but not for all, as you'll learn later in this chapter. Since Dialogflow is stateless, you first need to "save" the last intent the dialog processed. This can be done with output contexts. Recall that you have a Python function newContext that creates a new context to send out in the webhook response. In Listing 9-1, you see where to include that, right before the webhook response. We're calling the output context intent_xyz where xyz is the lowercase version of the intent name of the current request. Making it lowercase is important for comparison because Dialogflow applies lowercase automatically when sending context in the next request. You also need to remove spaces from the intent name using the replace method for strings to substitute spaces with underscores. If you don't do that and a raw intent name has spaces, you'll get an error that the application is not responding when you test with Google Home.

Listing 9-1. Adding an output context to note what intent the dialog processed (main.py)

```
# Add an output context with the intent,
# so we can determine the last intent for universals.
```

```
output_intent_name = df_request.intent_display_name.lower().replace(' ','_')
df_response.output_contexts.append(
new_context(f"intent_{output_intent_name}"))
```

Now take a look at the function new_context in Listing 9-2 (from new_context.py); it's a little different from the previous version.

Listing 9-2. Function new_context() to create a new output context to put in the response

```
def new_context(name):
    """

    Return a new output context with a given name.
    """

    context = {
        'name': ("projects/${PROJECT_ID}/agent/sessions/"
                f"${{SESSION_ID}}/contexts/{name}"),
        'lifespanCount': 5,
        'parameters': {
            'timestamp': time.time()
        }
    }

    return context
```

The code adds a parameter timestamp to the intent output context. Python folks will recognize time.time() as a built-in function that returns the current time in seconds. You need this because

- You need a way to find the most recent intent to approximate dialog state.

- By Dialogflow default, contexts have a lifespan of five dialog turns, so there'll be multiple intent_xyz contexts active at once. You need the newest one.

- You could just set the lifespan of the intent output context to 1, so it only lasts one turn, but there are reasons not to, as you'll see soon (hint: "repeat, repeat").

In Listing 9-2, we've added the strings ${PROJECT_ID} and ${SESSION_ID} to the context name. Dialogflow will fill those with the project ID and the session ID. You can find the IDs in the Diagnostic info—Figure 9-2 shows an example for the intent arCallByName. The context name in line 22 is the same as in Listing 9-2, with the variables filled in.

```
Diagnostic info


Raw API response      Fulfillment request      Fulfillment response      Fulfillment status

17              }
18          }
19        ],
20        "outputContexts": [
21          {
22              "name": "projects/voice-first-development/agent/sessions/8776247b-22ff-1cfe-
          8c7a-7b8899970c4a/contexts/callbyname",
23              "lifespanCount": 5,
24              "parameters": {
25                "context-given-name": "Brent"
26              }
27          }
28        ],
29        "intent": {
30            "name": "projects/voice-first-development/agent/intents/60bbb90d-b0e7-408d-9efb-
          a7ab50ffc1b9",
31            "displayName": "arCallByName"
32        },
33        "intentDetectionConfidence": 1,

     CLOSE                          COPY FULFILLMENT REQUEST AS CURL        COPY RAW RESPONSE
```

Figure 9-2. *Diagnostic info showing context name filling for the intent* arCallByName

Listing 9-3 shows you how to get the most recent intent to use for context approximation. We use a regular expression to find everything from the last "/" to the end of the string, checking if this context is an intent_xyz context (A). Get the context timestamp (B) and check if this intent context is more recent (C) and if the most recent intent is not a skippable universal (D) that you'll learn more about shortly. If this is the most recent intent, set intent name (E) and timestamp (F).

Listing 9-3. Getting the most recent intent (set_most_recent_intent.py)

```python
def set_most_recent_intent(df_request, intent_name, context):
    """
    See if this is the most recent intent.
    """
    match2 = re.search('^intent_(.*)$', intent_name)    #A
    if match2:
        if 'parameters' in context:
            if 'timestamp' in context['parameters']:
                context_time = context['parameters']['timestamp']    #B
                if (context_time > df_request.most_recent_intent.get('time') and #C
                        not is_skippable_universal(match2.group(1))):    #D
                    df_request.most_recent_intent["name"] = match2.group(1)    #E
                    df_request.most_recent_intent["time"] = context_time    #F
```

Step 3: Adding Repeat

Now that you (kind of) have dialog state context based on the last intent, you can add logic for the repeat universal. Let's do that for arTodaysTasks. Today's Tasks needs repeat, because it potentially tells you a list of things you need to do today. Listing 9-4 shows the new piece of the main code for the repeat logic (in universal.repeat.py). First, get the more recent intent from the Dialogflow request (A). Check whether arTodaysTasks was the most recent intent (B). If it was, respond with today's tasks again—don't forget to lead with a phrase that signals that it's a repetition (C). Round it off by including a safety out if you haven't implemented full "repeat" handling yet (D).

Listing 9-4. Adding the logic for repeat for arTodaysTasks

```python
def universal_repeat(df_request, df_response):
    """
    repeat universal
    """

    most_recent_intent_name = df_request.most_recent_intent.get("name") #A
    if most_recent_intent_name == 'arTodaysTasks'.lower():  #B
        df_response.output_text = \
            ("Again: You have two things to do today. First, you need "    #C
```

```
        "to make sure you can get a ride home after the procedure. "
        "Second, you need to get the laxative.")
else:
    df_response.output_text = "Sorry, repeat is not enabled here."   #D
```

A few things to notice here. First, you can see why we highlighted the importance of using lowercase intent names for comparison for the most recent intent: Dialogflow automatically assigns lowercase to context names.

Second, you might wonder if there's a way to not have to repeat the `arTodaysTasks` content again, but specifying it only once. You could do that by using an **event**, which is another way to trigger an intent, other than to say something. But you don't necessarily want that, and here's why. You added *Again:* to the front of the main `arTodaysTasks` prompt; you want something like it. It'd be disconcerting for the user to keep hearing the same phrase over and over with no hint that the system has understood that they want to repeat. But you also want variation. You want an approach that allows you to control what discourse markers fit best in each context, which ties single dialog turns into natural conversations.

Third, now that you're relying on the webhook code for output contexts, you need to enable Fulfillment for **all intents**, not just the ones whose responses are generated by the webhook. Recall that this is done in the Dialogflow GUI for each intent. It's OK to enable the webhook even if you're not doing any special processing with it because the default webhook response is to just return what's already in the Dialogflow GUI for a certain intent.

Step 4: Checking Context Robustness

"Now, where were we? Read me back the last line."

"'Read me back the last line,'" read back the corporal who could take shorthand.

"Not my last line, stupid!" the colonel shouted. "Somebody else's."

"'Read me back the last line,'" read back the corporal.

"That's my line again!" shrieked the colonel, turning purple with anger.

"Oh, no, sir," corrected the corporal. "That's my last line. I read it to you just a moment ago. Don't you remember, sir? It was only a moment ago."

—From *Catch-22* by Joseph Heller (Simon & Schuster, 1961)

What if the user wants to repeat the same thing again? Try it: say *What should I do today?* and then *Repeat.* Great, that worked. Now say *Repeat* again. Uh-oh! You got the *Repeat is not implemented* prompt. What happened? Remember that you added logic to get the most recent intent using the timestamp of the intent. When you said *Repeat* the second time, the most recent intent was…repeat! Of course, you don't have a handler for repeating a repeat. What you really want to do is repeat the last non-repeat intent. And if the VUI just provided some important information like today's to-do list, it's not unreasonable that a user wants to hear it two or three times.

So you need to amend your "most recent intent" logic slightly, adding a test to only allow an intent to be the most recent intent if it's not a universal. Listing 9-5 shows the new function for deciding if the last intent was a universal, which you'll find in the `utils.py` file. Recall you used that function in Listing 9-3.

Listing 9-5. The most recent intent can't be a universal

```
def is_skippable_universal(intent_name):
    """

    Is this a skippable universal?
    """

    return intent_name in ['cancel', 'continue', 'goBack', 'goodbye', 'help',
                           'pause', 'repeat', 'startOver', 'transfer']
```

Listing 9-5 uses the actual names of the intents to determine if the intent is a universal or not. There's no special tag in Dialogflow you can set to indicate this special property of the intents, so you have to rely on the intent names.

Now you have the pieces necessary to repeat the correct bits depending on if the user asked for information and wants to hear that again or if they heard a song and want to repeat that. Let's build out the core for the other universals (Listing 9-6). It includes help messaging for `arTodaysTasks` that you saw in Listing 9-4 and a main menu handler (in `universal_main_menu.py`), which is not context-dependent.

Listing 9-6. Core handling code for universals

```
dialog_functions = {   # A
    'arCallByName': ar_call_by_name,
    'arCollectName': ar_call_by_name,
    'arCallByNameDisambigLastName': ar_call_by_name_disambig_last_name,
```

331

```
            'arConfirmName': ar_confirm_name,
            'cancel': universal_cancel,
            'continue': universal_continue,
            'goBack': universal_go_back,
            'goodbye': universal_goodbye,
            'help': universal_help,
            'mainMenu': universal_main_menu,
            'pause': universal_pause,
            'repeat': universal_repeat,
            'startOver': universal_start_over,
            'transfer': universal_transfer}

# Get the handler function based on the intent name.
handler_function = dialog_functions.get(df_request.intent_display_name)  # B

    if handler_function:
        # The core.
        # If handler function is found, call it with request and response.

        # This is how to call a function without knowing ahead of time
        # what function you're calling.

        # The arguments are always the same even if the handler function
        # doesn't use them, so sometimes we'll turn off pylint warnings.

        handler_function.__call__(df_request, df_response)  # C
    else:
        # If the intent is anything else, just return back what Dialogflow
        # was going to do anyway; don't modify the behavior. Use the given
        # response from Dialogflow

        df_response.output_text = df_request.fulfillment_text  # D
```

Let's look in more detail at the core dialog logic in main.py in Listing 9-6. First, define a dictionary that maps intent names from Dialogflow to handler functions (which each have their own .py file) (A). At runtime, you get the handler function from the intent (B) and call that handler function with arguments as both the webhook request and response objects (C). Finally, if you didn't find a handler function because it's not in the dictionary, the response is what Dialogflow was going to say anyway (D).

In (C) you see a way of calling functions in Python that you may not be used to. We use the `__call__()` function of the handler function, always with the same two arguments of the webhook request and response objects. Why? The alternative, now that there are many more intents, is to have a spaghetti of `if/elif/else` statements; this code is much clearer. In the dictionary (A) are the actual function objects themselves (not the names of the handler functions); that's why we can do a `__call__()` on the values in the dictionary.

You saw the handler for repeat in Listing 9-4; many of the new universals' handlers don't do anything other than say "This is not supported," but "repeat" and "main menu" are more complete. Some notes on `mainMenu`:

- You'll notice that the `mainMenu` handler is not context-dependent; it plays a modified intro prompt, modified because the context of returning is not the same as hearing something for the first time. Something like *You're back at the main menu* is an appropriate navigational landmark if your VUI is a complex voice-only interaction with an explicit main menu.

- In any large complex VUI, users' mental models include some type of "home base." In IVRs, it's usually a main menu, which is how it's referred to in prompts. In other VUIs, it might be more appropriate to call it "home" or "start" or something related to the VUI name or persona.

- A safe default VUI response is a simple *OK* followed by a landmark and a reentry prompt for the top level.

- Keep track of what the user did before their main menu request—if the next thing they say is *Go back*, you'll look smart if you can take them back without losing details.

At this point, `output_text` fields are placeholders for the universals not yet enabled. Even if some universal isn't enabled, your response should be more informative and conversational than these prompts.

As you enable other universals, you'll find that more changes are needed. Consider the following request sequence: *What should I do today? [VUI reads today's tasks]* → *Main menu [VUI returns home]* → *Repeat.* What should be repeated? The main menu.

As you've written it in Listing 9-5, you'd repeat arTodaysTasks, because universals were not allowed to be the most recent intent. Main menu is a valid most recent intent, though. Maybe you need to modify the code so that universals can't be the most recent intent, except for mainMenu. The new isSkippableUniversal() function does what isUniversal() does in Listing 9-5, but it doesn't include mainMenu, and that's the function you used when looking for the most recent intent.

You're still not done: help prompts can be repeated—maybe other universals as well. We come back to this later. The key point, which we continue to highlight, is that some complexity is necessary to do what's right for the user; overly simple approaches are relatively easy to design and code but don't usually lead to the best user experience or system performance.

SUCCESS TIP 9.4 USE PLACEHOLDER PROMPT CONTENT DURING DEVELOPMENT   Settle on a temporary prompt wording that's easy to find, like *Placeholder for help on updating the food diary*, and record it in a voice that's noticeably different from the production voice. Use this prompt during development in cases where design is still changing though coding is under way. That makes it easier to find and replace later during development and easier to notice during testing.

Step 5: Ending the Conversation

Until now, you've been ending the conversation after playing an answer like the one in arTodaysTasks. Now that you can repeat, you don't want to do that anymore. Go back to all the intents (except for goodbye!) and remove the slider to end the conversation. This is what "goodbye" is now for.

You've added universals! OK, you've only added repeat, and only to a single intent, but you have the core. You can modify the logic in Listing 9-6 to add other universal handling.

There are several paradigms with which to view dialog design for voice application development. Dialogflow utilizes an "intent-centric" paradigm, where the basic unit is what the user wants to do. This paradigm works fine for most "one-and-done" conversations and is more understandable with little introduction. But most large enterprise voice applications, especially ones with complex transactions, use a "dialog state–centric" paradigm, which is more focused on "where" in the dialog the user is at any point in time. This is a more involved effort, but makes it easier to do many things, like tracking the context dependence that's so important for universals. You learn more about this in later chapters. Dialogflow does not incorporate the dialog state–centric approach, but tries to approximate some of its elements using things like contexts.

SUCCESS TIP 9.5 UNIVERSAL MEANS "ALWAYS" AVAILABLE   As the name suggests, universal means always available. There are valid reasons for limiting availability when there's potential ambiguity, as you learn in this chapter. What happens after the universal is also based on context. But even if you need to limit universal behavior, you should still recognize the common universal phrases so that you can at least tell the user why you can't fulfill their request this time.

Sidebar: Cleaning Up the Code

We want our code to be easy to read, especially for the Python code we discuss here. To help accomplish this, we use the `pylint` tool on our code. It flags both flat-out errors, like undefined references, and stylistic issues, such as

- Not enough or too many spaces or blank lines

- Lines that are too long (we actually modified our `pylint` runs to flag lines longer than 80 characters so that code listings in the text are more readable)

- Too many class instance variables

- Not enough comments

- Too many branches in a function (this is actually why we started using the `__call__()` function in Listing 9-6)

In general, we recommend tools like `pylint` to increase code structure and readability. You can selectively disable `pylint` warnings. In Listing 9-7, we disable the usual warning that a function argument (here `df_request`) is not used. Normally, we'd remove the `df_request` argument, but if you recall from Listing 9-6, we need to call the intent handlers with the same two arguments, so the only solution here is to disable the warning.

Listing 9-7. Disabling specific `pylint` warnings

```
def universal_cancel(
    df_request,      # pylint: disable=unused-argument
    df_response):
    """

    cancel universal
    """

    df_response.output_text = 'Sorry, cancel is not enabled here.'
```

Navigation

Voice navigation commands are tools that help users get around in an audio-only space. Obviously, that's extra important for voice-only VUIs, when there're no screens to see or buttons to push. Consistent navigation commands let users take advantage of the strengths of voice as they jump past multiple levels and pop back up, start over, pause, and so on. Through all that, audio feedback quickly tells them if they're on the right track or not, as you learned about in Chapter 8. Most universals allow the user to navigate through the VUI at their own pace. Navigating the flow is not the same as controlling content playback.

Landmarks

Landmarks are the audio equivalents of product labels or door entry signs. They're short phrases or audio signaling to the user that they're interacting with a specific feature or area of a VUI. Landmarks are a quick way of setting baseline expectations for the upcoming dialog. If your VUI is large with many different functionalities, you can use landmarks to introduce each one, like an IVR main menu or the food diary in our procedure VUI.

By default, landmarks should be brief and clear, like a verbal *Main menu* or *Food diary* or a short chime if non-verbal. How you choose to implement landmarks, if at all, depends on the complexity of the VUI, the interaction platform and modality, and your users' cognitive model of the interaction. Landmarks provide reassurance of being on "the right path." You can notice landmarks doing their job when analyzing real user data from systems with many branching paths: less hesitation and uncertainty in user utterances following the landmark, faster barge-in, and quicker requests to *start over* or *go back*. Overall, the experience is faster and with fewer errors.

SUCCESS TIP 9.6 IMPLEMENT A HANDOFF STRATEGY   Be careful to not end up with multiple adjacent landmarks or acknowledgments. It's a common pitfall in large systems with many paths and with multiple people working on separate modules. It happens if one is part of the "departure" (as a response prompt or call routing confirmation prompt) and the other of "arrival" (at the start of the first intro prompt in the requested subapp function): *Your food diary, sure. OK, food diary …* To avoid this, settle on a convention; most common is to handle them at departure because they're responses.

Non-verbal Audio

In Chapter 8, you learned how to add non-verbal audio to your VUI. Non-verbal audio, or NVA, is sound other than spoken words. As promised, we'll now take a deeper look at how to use NVA for navigation and universals.

Another word for NVA is **earcons**. Good earcons, like graphical icons, decrease users' cognitive load. Instead of a bunch of words, a sound symbolizes a feature or action. That's sound symbolism. The main issue with sound symbolism is that it's not as generally recognized or agreed upon by people as many visual signs are. For earcons to be meaningful, users need to somehow associate them with the intended meaning. The best way to do that is to first of all pick the right sound. Then, play the sound together with the feature or action the first few times users encounter it. Meaning assignment through association is usually better than explicitly telling people what some sound is supposed to mean.

Because short distinct sounds are quicker to process than words in a sentence, NVA landmarks are particularly useful for repeat users who learn to associate a sound with a meaning like success vs. failure.

So how do you pick the right sound? Earcons can be representational—recorded sounds (or synthesized versions) naturally connected with the thing they're supposed to represent. They can be more or less concrete: the sound of a door shutting when a file closes, a toilet flushing (not recommended!) or paper scrunching for emptying trash, running steps for something fast, rising tones and major chords for something that

337

starts or is successful, and falling or minor chords for something ending or unsuccessful. Earcons can also be abstract, with a specific melody or rhythm or instrument being associated with a feature or action. That can be important for branding and can be effective if you're dealing with power users, but it can also be tricky for people to learn.

Common uses of earcons include VUI activity status (listening starts, listening stops, processing, no result found, timing out, successful completion, standby), an alarm or notification, helpful hint or more information, navigation (backward, forward, home/ main menu, subarea of an app), and each item in a list. A brief earcon at the very start of phone-based VUI is very effective to signal automation and setting caller expectations. Audio is also used to mask processing latency. Studies show that when latency is longer than 3–4 seconds, you need to start thinking how to tell the user basically *I'm still here*. The more critical it is for users not to lose contact with the VUI, the shorter the silence should be. That means shorter silence for voice-only VUIs and IVRs, multi-turn conversations, and "important" topics like money and health and longer one for multimodal, one-and-done interactions like requesting music by some artist.

Just like visual sign symbolism, sound symbolism is partly universal, partly culture-specific. Keep that in mind if your user population is diverse. Within a culture, people tend to have similar reactions to a sound. This is important because you can and want to take advantage of it when you create NVA. Table 9-4 shows some common Western culture reactions to sounds; for example, higher-frequency sounds are more often perceived as referring to something smaller, while lower-frequency sounds are associated with something larger.

Table 9-4. *Examples of how specific sounds are typically perceived in the Western culture*

Category	Sound characteristics	Perceived meaning
Frequency	Low // High	Big // Small
Rhythm	Rapid // Slow	Urgency // Waiting, processing
Tone	Rising // Falling	Start, wake, open mic // End, sleep, close mic
Chords	Major // Minor	Success // Failure
Melody	Harmonic // Dissonant	Success // Failure
Duration	Short, distinct // Long, continuous	Call to action // Waiting, idle
Audio	Sound // Silence	Activity, "liveness" // Idle, standby

NVA can be a powerful tool. To avoid major pitfalls, follow a few guidelines:

- **Appropriate symbolism**: Avoid sounds whose natural symbolism implies something opposite. For example, don't use a dissonant falling sound to indicate success or a closing door to indicate the VUI opening the mic to listen for a response.

- **Sound quality**: In general, you want sounds to be pleasant. Even alerts shouldn't be so obnoxious that users cover their ears exactly when you want them to pay attention. Woodwinds are often preferable over brass and and xylophones and marimbas over vibraphones and glockenspiel because of sharper onset of metal compared to wood, though octave choice matters for the same reason. Test with real users in real conditions on intended devices.

- **Volume**: NVA volume should match the VUI as a whole, not be drastically louder or quieter. Depending on the instrumentation of your earcons, there's more to this than pure decibel level. A bit of testing in realistic environments will solve this.

- **Duration**: Earcons in general should be short with a distinct onset and end. Experiment—a good starting point is 50 ms. If an earcon is supposed to mean "VUI is listening" but the audio trails off gradually, it's difficult for users to know when to start speaking—they may even wait so long the microphone stops listening! Latency NVA should be something that can loop easily for flexible duration.

- **Theme**: Define a "family" of sounds that works for your VUI persona and domain. If it's a restaurant app, maybe food-related sounds make sense. If it's a health-related topic, don't use "haunted house" sounds or sounds of ambulances. You don't want to give users a heart attack! If your VUI is associated with an existing strong audio brand, you'd want to incorporate jingles or melodies.

- **Usage**: Be consistent. If your VUI uses an earcon for some functionality, play it every time that context appears. But don't overdo your earcon use. You don't need an earcon for every type of VUI activity status or meaning. That becomes overwhelming and tiresome instead of useful.

SUCCESS TIP 9.7 NVA IS POWERFUL—A LITTLE GOES A LONG WAY   Using the "right" audio for something is a great way to convey meaning quickly. But if users hear a sound in every context or even multiple sounds strung together, NVA loses effectiveness and gets annoying. Use NVA where it makes the most sense. Too many sounds and users tune out.

Code for NVA

In Chapter 8, you used Actions on Google custom payloads and very basic SSML to add NVA to our app. Now you'll add another NVA, this one for the main menu. That means you need to modify the code slightly to specify which NVA to use. Listing 9-8 from webhook_response.py shows how.[2] When you create the webhook response, you initialize the NVA (A). There are four components: whether you play NVA or not, source audio, and the start and end times of the source audio. During runtime, if you haven't specified the NVA source, set it (B) as well as the start (C) and end times (D). Then build SSML with the source (E) and start (F) and end (G) times.

Listing 9-8. Allowing multiple NVA sounds

```
# NVA
self.nva = {"do_pre": False, "src": None, "begin": None, "end": None}  # A

# ...... Code cut for listing focus

# If we are doing pre-NVA, add the payload for Actions on Google.
if self.nva.get("do"):
    # Select our NVA src, begin, and end if it hasn't been specified
    if self.nva.get("src") is None:
        self.nva.update({
            "src": (https://actions.google.com/sounds/v1/    # B
                    "cartoon/cartoon_metal_thunk.ogg"),
            "begin": "1.5s",      # C
            "end": "3s"})      # D
```

---

[2]9-2a.zip (Dialogflow) and 9-2b.zip (webhook) contain files for the rest of this chapter.

```
if not add_payload:
   self.respdic['payload'] = {}
   self.respdic['payload']['google'] = {}
self.respdic['payload']['google']['richResponse'] = {}
self.respdic['payload']['google']['richResponse']['items'] = []
tmpdic = {}
tmpdic['simpleResponse'] = {}

# Put together the SSML
ssml = f"<speak><audio src=\"{self.nva.get('src')}\""          # E
if self.nva.get("begin") is not None:                          # F
   ssml = f"{ssml} clipBegin=\"{self.nva.get('begin')}\""
if self.nva.get("end") is not None:                            # G
   ssml = f"{ssml} clipEnd=\"{self.nva.get('end')}\""
ssml = f"{ssml}>DING</audio>{self.output_text}</speak>"
print(f"'SSML: {ssml}")
tmpdic['simpleResponse']['textToSpeech'] = ssml
self.respdic['payload']['google']['richResponse']['items']\
   .append(tmpdic)
```

Now that the webhook response code is modified, let's use it. Listing 9-9 shows the new universal_main_menu handler (in universal_main_menu.py), where you set the NVA source (A).

Listing 9-9. Setting the non-verbal audio (NVA) source

```
def universal_main_menu(
      df_request,     # pylint: disable=unused-argument
      df_response):
  """

  main menu universal
  """

  df_response.output_text = \
     "You're back at the main menu. What would you like to do?"
  df_response.nva.update({
     "do": True,
     "src": "https://www.soundjay.com/button/beep-01a.wav"})    # A
```

Content Playback Navigation

Control and transport commands are the commands people use when navigating through content playback. We're not going into depth about these. Navigation commands are often connected to device development, so they involve their own specific hardware and software needs, even their own specialized platforms. That gets complex and specialized fast and goes beyond the scope of this book. But the words used for navigation—next, previous, pause, stop/cancel, and continue—are universal in that people use the same words even without instruction. And navigation also applies to lists, which you'll learn about next.

SUCCESS TIP 9.8 NAVIGATION NEEDS QUICK RESPONSE   For navigation to work well, recognition must be fast. This is especially important if your VUI allows voice-only barge-in, the user's ability to interrupt the VUI simply by speaking instead of first saying a wake word or pressing a button. They also need to be easily and accurately recognized without getting confused with other commands. For these reasons, it's not uncommon for a voice system to use a different recognizer for navigation commands, handling recognition on-device instead of in the cloud.

List Navigation

Any kind of browsing, such as list navigation, is challenging to do well in voice. By now, the reasons why shouldn't surprise you. Using lists on a screen is easy: as a user, you look at the list, scroll, and choose something off the list once you're good and ready. With voice, things are different: you need to keep all items in working memory until you make your choice, and if you hear only a few options in each set, you need to know how to move between sets.

Here's an example of a plausible conversation between a user and a VUI. The user is browsing a list of drug names available for refill. You're highly likely to hear users say any of the options listed in the last dialog turn; how will you handle each one?

> **VUI**   *You have six available refills. Here're the first three:*
> *Metformin, Prinivil, and Prednisone.*
>
> *Say the name of the one you want or say "Next set."*

User   *Next.*

VUI   *Here're the last three: Wellbutrin, Oxycodone, and Prednisolone.*

Say the name of the one you want or say "Previous."

User   *Prinivil/The last one on the first list/Previous/Go back/Next/ That one/Repeat that/Read the whole list again/The very first one/Predozone*

You need to allow the user the flexibility to interact with lists using the same range of words and phrases they would use when talking to another person while also keeping things simple and clear and making sure the user is confident that your VUI understood correctly. Expect commands like *next, forward, previous,* and *back,* but don't expect people to differentiate meaning between *next* and *forward* or between *previous* and *back* even if you instruct them to. You can implement the most amazing list structure and it will still fail if you expect your users to remember any special instructions for how to navigate and pick items.

MULTIMODAL CORNER

Multimodal VUIs can make great use of universals by providing a set of universal commands when they're most needed and for choosing from a list. Without screens, VUIs may need to play long prompts explaining how to repeat or start over—that gets annoying to hear over and over. It's common in voice-first multimodal mobile apps to show a few examples of common requests—make these examples into tappable buttons as well. A screen makes universals and hints available visually while the audio conversation continues. Referring to "main menu" in a multimodal VUI may not be what you want. A screen change would speak for itself, or you'd use some icon or non-verbal audio. Your choice of "home" screen will depend on the app tasks. A day-by-day checklist of to-do tasks worked well for the 22otters procedure prep app (conceptual drawing in Figure 9-3).

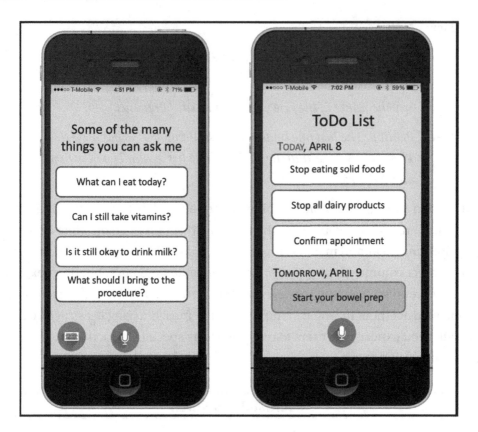

Figure 9-3. Multimodal use of examples and a targeted home screen

Consistency, Variation, and Randomization

We admit it: we're not above mocking voice apps when they respond in ways we think are suboptimal. One example happens in our houses when a voice assistant answers *OK!* in exactly the same way every time, including when connected lights don't turn on and the assistant still happily says *OK!* People don't say things exactly the same way every time. Your VUI sounds robotic without any variation, less interesting, and even less smart. The trick is to add variation without affecting consistency. Consistency is not the same as lack of variation.

Your VUI's responses can vary in several ways, including the words used, how they're pronounced, and when they appear in the flow:

- If your VUI uses acknowledgments, you can randomize words like "OK" and "Alright," but remember that "Sure" isn't exactly the same because of the extra meaning of certainty. Vary within the same set of discourse markers.

- Different pronunciations can be difficult to manage if you rely on TTS to generate output, but it's possible to modify the TTS with available platform tools and markup languages (more in Chapter 15). If you use recorded prompts, adding pronunciation variation is of course easy, just a little extra work.

- Your VUI could add variation by asking for missing slots in a different order at different times. It's variation, but it's not smart variation. Adding variation in ways that impact how users respond makes the VUI inconsistent, adds to users' cognitive load, and creates more work for everyone. Power users get particularly frustrated because now they have to pay attention to something they thought they knew, resulting in more retries. Consistent structure is important particularly for lists, as you learned in Chapter 7. It acts like verbal bullet points that helps users process the information.

For any given context, don't vary structure or flow, the order of items in a constant list, voice and persona, phrases referring to universals, terminology (if you refer to a "food diary," don't sometimes call it "meal diary," but do recognize both), landmarks, or the overall delivery of prompts across the whole VUI. Instead, look for opportunities to randomize the prompt audio output and the "conversational glue" of acknowledgments and carrier phrases in ways that sound natural without affecting meaningful consistency.

Code for Randomization

There are two ways to randomize prompts in Dialogflow:

- **Using the GUI**: In the Responses section of an intent, Dialogflow picks one prompt at random if you defined multiple prompts for the same context. It also won't pick the same prompt twice in a row—so a handy built-in capability to create variation.

- **Using webhooks**: Because you can make outputText anything you want, including a variation of the input fullfillmentText, that can be a great choice. You can use all the power of Python to decide what to play.

The best method is the one best suited for the variation you want. If you're making sweeping changes to the variations of the prompts, the Dialogflow GUI might make sense. For smaller more self-contained tweaks, code could be simpler. We'll show you both methods; the use case you'll implement is randomizing specific prompts. There are several prompts in your procedure prep helper that start with an acknowledgment, either "OK" or "Alright." As you just learned, it's often good practice to randomize those phrases, so you'll cycle between "OK," "Alright," and no acknowledgment in the intent tcrProcedurePrep.

First, in the GUI. Right now, tcrProcedurePrep has a single prompt in Reponses, starting with "OK." Add two prompts, one with "Alright" and one with neither (Figure 9-4).

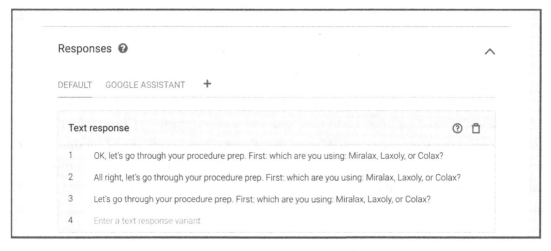

Figure 9-4. tcrProcedurePrep *after randomizing the intro section of the prompt*

Now, the same thing using webhook code. It's fairly simple (Listing 9-10). Use the Python random.choice() function to randomly select between prompt variants. Make sure you "import random" in the code. Each variant is an entry in a Python list.

Listing 9-10. Randomizing prompts in the webhook

```
outputText = random.choice([
    ('OK, let\'s go through your procedure prep. '
     'First: which are you using: Miralax, Laxoly, or Colax?'),
    ('Alright, let\'s go through your procedure prep. '
     'First: which are you using: Miralax, Laxoly, or Colax?'),
    ('Let\'s go through your procedure prep.'
     'First: which are you using: Miralax, Laxoly, or Colax?')])
return outputText
```

For this use case, which method is better?

- In the Dialogflow GUI, you need to find all the prompts that start with "OK" or "Alright" and manually add the variants. That's a bit of a pain.

- In the webhook (Listing 9-8), you'd have to do the same, so you might as well do it in the GUI.

- There's actually an interesting third option that exists only in the webhook:

- Find the GUI prompt (`fulfillmentText`); check if it begins with "OK" or "Alright."

- If it does, randomly pick a version using `random.choice()` as before.

- Replace the existing intro with the random one (can be empty).

Let's see what that looks like (Listing 9-11). You'll search for "OK" or "Alright" at the beginning of a prompt (A), using `random.choice()` to pick a random substitute intro prompt (B).

Listing 9-11. Automatically randomizing prompt introductions

```
# Possibly replace prompt intro with a randomized variant.

if (re.search('^OK,', self.output_text) or
    _re.search('^OK.', self.output_text) or
    _re.search('^All right,', self.output_text) or
    _re.search('^All right.', self.output_text)):

    random_intro = random.choice(['OK','All right',''])
```

```
if random_intro == '':
    self.output_text = re.sub('^OK,','',self.output_text)
    self.output_text = re.sub('^OK.','',self.output_text)
    self.output_text = re.sub('^All right,','',self.output_text)
    self.output_text = re.sub('^All right.','',self.output_text)
else:
    self.output_text = re.sub(
        '^OK,', '%s,' % random_intro,self.output_text)
    self.output_text = re.sub(
        '^OK.', '%s.' % random_intro,self.output_text)
    self.output_text = re.sub(
        '^All right,','%s,' % random_intro,self.output_text)
    self.output_text = re.sub(
        '^All right.','%s.' % random_intro,self.output_text)
```

The code in Listing 9-11 is a little complex, mostly because you had to search for different variants and because the handling is different if the acknowledgment prompt is empty, in which case you need to remove any commas or periods after the intro text. So what's so great about this scheme? Well, you don't need to worry about explicitly adding all prompt variants in the GUI; all that is required is to include an "OK" or "Alright" at the beginning of the GUI prompt to make the potential replacement. This makes it more robust; an acknowledgment doesn't always make sense and should be separated from the content for best handoff.

Working with Built-In Global Intents

Many application development frameworks incorporate some notion of built-in universals, so designers and developers don't need to worry about the complexities that you've seen in this chapter. Great, right? Yes, and as you've seen, there are complexities. Dialog aspects like universals are not given the full attention that they deserve in voice applications because

- They're complex and context-dependent. We've not yet even addressed if or when to give up. After two or three help requests in a state, the user might be less likely to succeed, and another strategy may be needed.

- They're not "best path," but are instead thought of as "edge cases," so it's appealing to just tack them on at the end after the rest of the dialog is done. But usability and long-term engagement can suffer substantially with this approach.

The main takeaways we want designers and developers to get from this section are to know how any built-in functionality is designed and what assumptions you make and whether the platform architecture supports your assumptions. You can't stop thinking about how universals are implemented just because they seem "automatic." Maybe you can treat it as a black box, but it's important to know more if you want to change some behavior. Here are some things you might see in a built-in framework:

- **Spotty implementation and coverage**: Not all universals are implemented, especially some of the hard ones like pause and continue.

- **Inflexible context dependence**: Some built-in universal responses are, well, too universal! Some responses are so generic that the VUI sounds clueless about previous actions and dialog turns. Some commands, like "stop," may have assumptions built in that don't apply to your specific VUI's needs.

- **Superficial dialog flow**: An extension of context dependence: what happens with multiple repeats of the universal?

- **Limited discourse marker prompts**: Sometimes all you can do is circle back and replay the original prompt for some context, but that doesn't necessarily match the user's mental model nor give the right impression of the VUI's level of understanding. If the UI just keeps looping and saying the same thing, that's not helpful to already confused users. Being able to include a *Here's some help*, a *You're back at the main menu*, or a *Again, that number is…* can help get users unstuck.

Thorough testing of your voice app, in its intended environment, is key to finding any discrepancies and uncovering where wrong assumptions are made (Chapter 16). Specifically

- Test all universals, even the ones that may not make sense in certain contexts like cancel, and check what happens.

- Test repeats of each universal (*Repeat. Repeat.*) and one after another (*Main Menu. Repeat.*) to check if the responses make sense.

- Check your discourse marker prompts. Bonus points if you don't always hear the same one.

Consistency and Standards Across VUIs and Frameworks

We hope by now you're getting a sense of the importance of conversational standards, though you'd be hard-pressed to find clear standards across the voice field for several reasons. Some tasks need navigation; others do not. A voice-only IVR has different demands from a mobile multimodal app for how to help users help themselves. Development is understandably focused on implementation on a specific platform. On the design side, there are limits on how to approach a particular conversation because of what the implementation offers. But remember, universals and standards are one path to the consistency users need. Separate the consistency based on human abilities and the nature of voice from the restrictions of a particular platform. You need to understand and work with both. A new user should be able to talk to any new VUI and expect certain consistent behaviors, whether it's Alexa, Google Assistant, Siri, Cortana, Bixby, an IVR, a mobile app, in-car, or anything else. There needs to be consistency between VUIs within a platform, but also across them at a sensible level that feeds user expectations.

Are there industry standards for voice? This whole book is about understanding and applying best practices for voice. In that lies the answer to the question: the real industry standard is maximizing interaction robustness, expecting and correctly interpreting user variation to let users speak naturally. A VUI succeeds only if it allows users to converse in ways that are natural to them in that context. For example, there's a standard spelling alphabet (*A as in alpha*), but that doesn't mean you can expect everyone to use it nor teach them.

There have been various attempts to set VUI standards. Do an online search for current VUI standards—you might find that what's available is minimal and, again, focuses on a particular development platform rather than on actual universal standards across all platforms and integrations. Hey, voice practitioners don't even use unified terminology to refer to basic VUI building blocks, so how can we expect users to know what's universal?

Do people use universals? As usual, the answer is "it depends." Some do; some don't. Some try—you want to handle those attempts. The ones that come most naturally to people without instruction are *repeat* and *stop/cancel*. As a rule, if a VUI mentions a universal in context where users are likely to need it, they'll use it and remember it and use it elsewhere. When explicitly offering an agent transfer in an IVR, you can expect anywhere from a small percentage to 40% of callers to request a transfer. Even with no mention, 5% is not unusual. Requests for transfer or help coincide with specific events, like a bill due date or new features having been added. The more naturally and robustly your VUI talks, the more likely users are to speak to it like to a person. And at the core, universals are simply implementations of what people do naturally in conversation under similar circumstances. By handling common phrases, you anticipate the needs of your users. It's designed discoverability.

What's Next?

If you're interested in sound symbolism, you can find lots of research on the topic by searching for any of the terms you read in the "Non-verbal Audio" section of this chapter. And listen for how sounds are used in apps and other contexts, even when it's not a VUI. How do you react to alerts for end of timer, removing a card from a cashier pay point, signaling payment went through or not, closing the refrigerator, or GPS instructions to turn right or left?

Universals, findability, and discoverability are a big deal in voice-first and voice-only systems because of the human audio processing constraints and the need to clearly and quickly converse with a diverse user population without having to give long instructions. Chapters 10 and 11 go deeper into how to achieve robust VUI understanding. Findability and discoverability play a big part in Chapters 12 and 13 where you learn about conversation robustness and strategies for recovering when understanding fails.

Summary

- Users are more successful when they can rely on consistent VUI behavior. Consistency contributes to discoverability and user trust.

- Universals contribute to consistency when predictably and robustly designed; they're a user's "security blanket" that helps them navigate an unfamiliar voice conversation and encourages them to try new interactions.

- **User requests** for help and system navigation need to be understood without any need for the user to learn and remember a special list of commands. The whole point of universals is to map the words and phrases that come naturally to any user when wanting those behaviors.

- **VUI responses** to universal requests need to be handled as if in a state-based system: responding within the right context based on task, user, and previous dialog turns.

- Avoid unintended "destructive" requests. If you interpret a request to cancel or start over, ask for user confirmation before deleting any content they provided in the conversation.

- The right audio earcons can help users navigate a complex VUI quicker and more easily.

- You can "fool" a stateless system into behaving like a state-based system by using webhooks.

- Your ability to modify how universals behave depends on the platform. Incorporate VUI design best practices as best as you can into whatever development framework and architecture you're using. When best practices are "built in," they'll happen with minimal effort instead of getting dropped under time pressure.

## CHAPTER 10

Creating Robust Coverage for Speech-to-Text Resolution

Today's speech recognition (ASR) engines are amazing and better than ever, but they're still not perfect. If you use dictation on your mobile phone, you see the mistakes that can happen. Correctly turning a spoken utterance into text is challenging—and all meaning interpretation and responses that follow depend on it.

Multi-turn dialogs complicate the situation further: anything that goes wrong early in the recognition process is amplified in each later step with odd results. If sounds aren't recognized, users' words are misinterpreted, meaning the speech-to-text (STT) is wrong. If STT produces incorrect or unexpected words and phrases, NL processing and intent evaluation won't have what they need to succeed.

Anyone with experience in voice design and development knows that successful understanding starts with correctly capturing what the user said. And doing that depends on great ASR and on robust grammars, the patterns and models used in capturing what users say by matching the words in utterances and turning those into representations for intent evaluation.

The next four chapters are a deep dive into maximizing understanding through accuracy and course correction when recognition and understanding fail. This chapter is step 1: STT and grammars. Our goal is to show you that there are things you can do in both design and development that will improve STT even if you don't have direct access to the core recognizer. We'll go into quite a bit of detail, but stay nontechnical enough for everyone to understand the issues and solutions.

© Ann Thymé-Gobbel, Charles Jankowski 2021
A. Thymé-Gobbel and C. Jankowski, *Mastering Voice Interfaces*, https://doi.org/10.1007/978-1-4842-7005-9_10

Recognition Is Speech-to-Text Interpretation

By now, you're familiar with the components of voice systems. It's time now to learn more about the first component, STT. Its input is a user utterance, and its output is a representation—usually text—of that utterance. Figure 2-11 is copied here for reference (Figure 10-1).

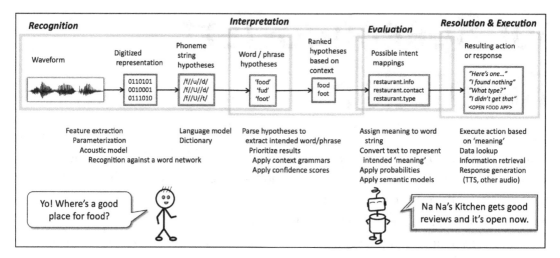

Figure 10-1. *Detailed yet oversimplified diagram of the process of the computer understanding and responding to a spoken utterance*

Speech recognition is hard. Avoiding or at least minimizing "catastrophic failure" is the goal of both recognition and interpretation, and it needs to be your focus as well. We use "interpretation" on purpose: as amazing as ASR is today, it's not perfect; the text result represents the recognizer's "best guess" of what the user said. There's no guarantee that this representation accurately corresponds to what the user said. Interpretation is different from **transcription**: the text typed by trained humans listening to logged user utterances. Transcriptions are very accurate; they're the ground truth used in performance tuning. This distinction is often ignored; it's misleading because it hides the important fact that recognition isn't perfect, and it obscures the need for addressing that understanding on a deeper level. Developing high-performing voice systems needs to involve humans listening to what was said in order to analyze the causes of any performance issues and to transcribe it for tuning. What's important is that the data is kept secure and anonymized and used appropriately, not that someone's listening to improve the VUI experience. Transcription for tuning VUIs is good and necessary.[1]

Inside the STT Box

So far we've mostly treated the speech-to-text (STT) component as a black box, only hinting why you need to know what's coming out of this black box to create your entities and training phrases to match the STT. It's time to look at what's inside this STT box.

Creating Sentences with Smaller Pieces

There's considerable structure to a phrase or sentence. Figure 10-2 shows how to break down the relatively simple phrase *one two three* into smaller fundamental pieces, like Lego bricks.

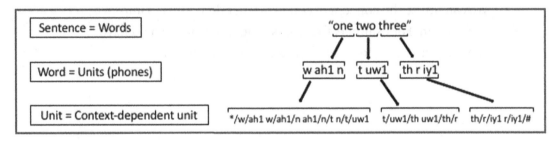

Figure 10-2. *Illustration of how a sentence can be built up from smaller units*

---

[1]www.speechtechmag.com/Articles/Editorial/Features/Curbing-Speech-Data-Overreach-143539.aspx

The sentence *one two three* can be broken down as follows:

- The sentence is a sequence of words.

- Each word is a sequence of units, or linguistic building blocks. The mapping from words to units is the lexicon. The units typically correspond to phones, the smallest distinctive sound in a language. In standard US English, there are approximately 50 phones. This is reflected in the similar number of symbols of ARPAbet or SAMPA, common sets of machine-readable phonetic transcription symbols representing vowels and consonants as well as word stress. For example, the word "two" is represented as "t uw1" where "t" is the consonant and "uw1" is the pronunciation of the vowel sound, including primary stress. These schemes are used widely to represent sounds and words for both STT and TTS. You can see one version of the ARPAbet inventory in Figure 10-3.

- Because of coarticulation, the way in which a sound is produced can vary substantially depending on what the surrounding units are. The context of surrounding phones affects the pronunciation of each unit. We can utilize the concept of context-dependent units to improve recognition. For example, the words "one" and "fun" would have separate /ah/ units, one after /w/ and another after /f/.

Vowels	Example	Consonants	Example	Additional	Description
AA	calm, cot	B	buy	1	primary stress; e.g. "button" [B AH1 EN2]
AE	bat	CH	chew	2	secondary stress
AH	butt	D	do	pau	pause
AO	bought	DH	this	sil	silence
AW	how	DX	butter	h#	utterance intitial and final silence
AX	about	EL	bottle	BCL	B closure
AXH	potato	EM	rhythm	DCL	D closure
AXR	letter	EN	button	GCL	G closure
AY	bite	F	four	PCL	P closure
EH	bet	G	guy	TCL	T closure
ER	bird	HH	hi	KCL	K closure
EY	bait	JH	jazz		
IH	bit	K	kite		
IX	roses	L	lie		
IY	beat	M	my		
OW	boat	N	no		
OY	boy	NG	sing		
UH	book	NX	winner		
UW	boot	P	pin		
UX	dude	Q	uh-oh		
		R	read		
		S	see		
		SH	she		
		T	toe		
		TH	think		
		V	very		
		W	wise		
		WH	why		
		Y	yes		
		Z	zoo		
		ZH	measure		

Figure 10-3. *The ARPAbet inventory of most common symbols with US English examples*

What constitutes a minimal unit differs between languages; so does the inventory of units. In English, the basic unit is a phone. In Chinese languages, for example, the unit is typically syllable-initial and/or syllable-final, which may correspond to a phone, but may not.

Using STT to Build Up Sentences

Figure 10-4 shows the pipeline of speech-to-text components.

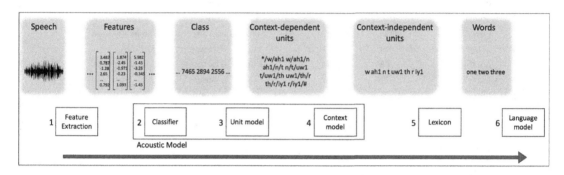

Figure 10-4. *The components forming the STT pipeline*

Many STT components are trained automatically using machine learning techniques, from a large amount of speech and language data. The components are

Feature extraction: Takes the speech waveform and automatically produces features, a set of numbers generated periodically (usually every 10 milliseconds) representing the waveform in a machine-usable format for the next steps.

Classifier: Takes each set of features and outputs one of a number of classes. There are often several thousand classes, generated at the same frequency as the features. Just like with feature extraction, the classifier output doesn't really correspond to anything we think of as a clear category of sounds. Think of them as the next step in finding patterns of distribution, vectors of features, feeding into the next step.

Unit model: Takes the sequence of classes and produces the context-dependent units you saw in the last section. This often involves Hidden Markov Models (HMMs). Basically, there is a mathematical model for what the feature classes look over time for each context-dependent unit. That's a lot of units: with 50 possible phones, training every possibility of left context/center/right context means $50 \times 50 \times 50 = 125{,}000$ possible context-dependent units. The number is actually a bit smaller, because many left/center/right combinations don't occur. But still, that's a lot; you'd not have enough data to train each one. Fortunately, the training process is very smart. It works out how training data can be shared across similar combinations and only trains the full context-dependent unit (called a triphone) if there is enough data; otherwise, it can use only one context (left or right biphone) or even no context at all (monophone) when data is very limited.

Context model: Maps the context-dependent units to context-independent units. The word "one" is specified in the lexicon with the context-independent units "W AH N." For the vowel AH, you might have a full triphone model W/AH/N, left and right biphone models W/AH and AH/N, and even a monophone model AH. The context model combines the possible unit models to get the best model for AH in the word "one," or for any other words in the W/AH/N context ("once," "swung," "wonder").

Lexicon: The lexicon maps words to units. It's basically a big table, generally not trained but hand-generated (or at least hand-checked) by linguists. A common English dictionary, the CMU Pronouncing Dictionary, has over 134,000 words.[2] It's a living document, as words enter and leave the language. The CMU Pronouncing Dictionary specifies the words in "one two three" like this—note that there can be multiple pronunciations for words:

```
ONE HH W AH1 N

ONE W AH1 N

TWO T UW1

THREE TH R IY1
```

Language model (LM): A model of allowed word sequences and the likelihood of each word co-occurring with other words. A good LM is critical to top-performing STT as it basically matches the sound segment hypotheses to the most likely word.

The classifier, unit model, and context model together are commonly referred to as the acoustic model. A good model is trained on thousands of hours and terabytes of data—this is why US English performs better than most other languages still, thanks to the large amounts of training data.

Recognition Engines

It's very unlikely that you'll create your own ASR engine from scratch—and if you're currently on an ASR development team, thanks for reading! People don't create their own recognition engines because of the huge effort involved and the massive amount of speech data required for a high-quality end result. Instead, we recommend you use one

---

[2]There are some great databases available, including the MRC Psycholinguistic Database, with words tagged for pronunciation, frequency, and so on. https://websites.psychology.uwa.edu.au/school/mrcdatabase/uwa_mrc.htm

of several ASR engines created by people with resources for continued improvement. Your effort is better spent on all the other aspects of voice-first design and development.

You need to understand the differences between the available recognizers because there's more to choosing one than raw accuracy rate or budget. You're buying into an ecosystem of both benefits and limitations. Which one is right for you depends on many things including response latency, in-cloud or on-device processing, multilingual availability, tools, parameter access, raw data access, domain, conversation tasks, type of device, and so on. Not long ago, it was next to impossible to do top-quality ASR on-device because of the processing and memory requirements. That's already changing, but the big players who control the best ASR engines are likely to want to keep things in the cloud for several reasons, including controlling access to the voice data that, again, feeds recognizer performance. Here's an overview of some of your recognizer options at the time of writing—it's always a moving target:

- **Cloud-based APIs from major AI companies**: Google, Microsoft, and IBM all have very well-performing US English models and full-featured APIs. Amazon has the same capabilities, but is somewhat less open; for example, you can't currently access only the STT without using the entire Alexa stack. Facebook and Apple are even more closed in that they don't (at time of writing) offer developer APIs at the speech/language level. While US AI companies support many languages, Chinese firms such as iFlytek and Baidu also offer APIs and often perform better on the Asian tone languages. You mostly tailor these for your own voice app by adding sample phrases that language models will be based on.

- **Domain- and channel-specific server-based solutions**: Nuance and others have long been providing high-performing server-based solutions for applications, primarily for call center automation. These are also in the cloud, not on-device, but are typically even more locked down than the previous set, as well as more specialized. Telephony-based models are different in that they're based on 8 kHz–sampled telephone speech, while cloud-based APIs using microphones on mobile devices not going through the telephone network typically use 16 kHz–sampled audio. Because the audio is so different between an 8 kHz telephone and 16 kHz mobile device, you get better performance with separately trained acoustic models for the two cases. The lexicon and the language model are usually the same for the same use case. These often involve a mix of statistical models and rule-based grammars.

- **On-device**: STT can be right on the device. The main application today is the wake word (*Alexa…, OK, Google…*) you see on home devices. After the device wakes up, the rest of the STT happens in the cloud. Another on-device use case is command-and-control for when cloud access isn't available or a quick response is crucial to the use case. Until recently, large vocabulary ASR had to be done on powerful servers accessible only via the Cloud. Today, we see great signs of a future of high-performance on-device recognition models. This is exciting: it creates new use cases for wearable devices as well as for security and privacy applications. As a starting point, take a look at Sensory and PicoVoice.

Grammar Concepts

You'd have noticed by now how much we emphasize writing well-crafted prompts. Clear prompts help users feel confident about how to respond, which makes their responses predictable, which allows your VUI to respond successfully. This happens only when grammar creators and designers coordinate with each other and with app developers.

Coverage

Coverage may be the most important concept in grammars. It refers to the words and phrases that have been included or trained on; in general, better coverage means better VUI performance.

Different people use different words to mean the same thing; they use synonyms. Your grammars need to account for your users' expected synonym variation for all requests you handle and map it to a single slot value, not different ones. For best synonym coverage, you need to know what words users say, including dialect variation and familiarity with the topic. *I'd like a soda* and *One pop for me please* are synonyms; they have the same meaning, so they should result in the same slot value.

SUCCESS TIP 10.1 RECOGNIZING SYNONYMS DOESN'T MEAN ACT ON IT   There are clues about the user in the synonyms they use, such as where they're from. That's cool, but be careful about assigning too much importance to variation you hear. Don't assume someone is from a particular part of the country just because they say *pop* instead of *soda*. For the same reason, if a user is perceived as speaking with a particular regional dialect, don't tailor your VUI's speech on that. Not only might you be wrong but you also don't know how the user feels about where they're from. The risk is too high that they'll be insulted or confused or even change their responses in a way that results in VUI failure.

Different types of grammars handle synonyms differently, as you learn later in this chapter. To understand coverage, it's helpful to differentiate core content from carrier phrase content, or filler. Core content is the word or phrase that fills a slot and captures meaning your VUI needs for acting on. Drug names are core content in *Let's see. I take Lipitor and also Motrin* and *Yeah, this is for more Wellbutrin please* and *Metformin*; everything else is a carrier phrase. Carrier phrases are not unimportant—they carry syntactic meaning and context, so they matter for parsing and correct interpretation.

Core content is the required information the VUI needs to proceed—the piece you'd think of as filling a slot. Carrier phrases are typically optional, but grammars need to account for them since people say them—think of them as the carrier or container for the content. Context matters: there's nothing magic about certain words or information to always make them core content. The same word can be content in one grammar and filler in another. If the VUI asks *Do you want to refill your Wellbutrin prescription?* and the user responds *Yes, the Wellbutrin*, only the *yes* is strictly necessary, making the drug name optional (and filler-like) here—you need to recognize it in both contexts so you can handle it in both. Be careful about carrier phrases when mistakes are costly. Imagine shopping for potentially expensive theater tickets:

VUI   *Wanna buy this Orchestra seat for* Hamilton *now?*

User   *I need to think.*

VUI   [Drops *think*; *to* is interpreted as "two."]

VUI   *You're in luck! Two seats are yours. Enjoy!*

Recognition Space

Coverage affects recognition space. The more similar words are to each other in a grammar, the higher the risk that one will be confused for another. One approach is to make grammars very narrow in what they accept, forcing users to be careful with their pronunciation or word choices. By now it should be clear why this is wishful thinking. Sure, you want some limits, but you also want to allow natural language and normal variation in wording and pronunciation. Our restaurant finder includes "Na Na's Kitchen." That's the official name, but everyone calls it "Na Na's." Because there's no other local restaurant with a similar name—and locals know that—users should be able to say either. Both names should be handled. If there also was a "Nanny's" or a "Na Na's Cafe," you'd need to take into account the potential for confusion.

Now look at medication names: many of them look and sound very similar. Take a look at Figure 10-5. Each gray cloud represents recognition space for a drug name.

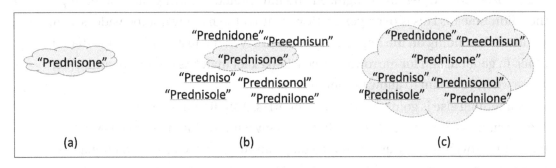

Figure 10-5. *Recognition space for one item (represented by gray cloud): (b) narrow, (c) wide*

In 10-5 (a), the recognition space is narrow: users are recognized well with high confidence each time they say the drug name in the expected "correct" way. But if they stumble saying the name, they'll probably get rejected, again thanks to the narrow recognition space (b). That is frustrating for non-expert users who really try saying these weird names. What if we widen the space a bit and include names as if they're synonyms even though they're technically wrong (c)? Now the coverage is more accepting, allowing more successful STT. Cool. But hold on. What if other similar drug names exist? That's Figure 10-6.

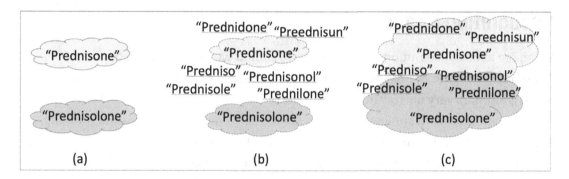

Figure 10-6. *Interacting recognition spaces for two items (represented by gray clouds): (b) narrow, (c) wide*

In 10-6 (a), there's a second drug name (yes, both are real names). With narrow spaces, only proper pronunciations are recognized correctly (b). If you want to handle more variation by adding synonyms, the spaces get so broad they overlap (c)! That means users sometimes are recognized and interpreted as having said something they didn't mean. This is **over-generation**. Neither too narrow nor too wide is a great solution; depending on the importance of accuracy in the task, one is worse than the other. In general, aim for narrower space when exact match is important and wider space when you want to allow fuzzier matches.

Something else is going on here: dictionaries. ASR dictionaries encode pronunciations of words to match what users say with the intended word. Most platforms provide some way for you to add pronunciations to custom dictionaries. In the drug name example, if you somehow know that some people pronounce the name "Prednisone" like *Preednisun* and that there's no conflict with such name, then you can add a phonetic representation to that effect, expanding the recognition space accordingly. Dictionaries can play an important role in STT accuracy: one speech science coworker points out how he added 42 distinct pronunciations to an airline voice system for *Heathrow* based on actual user pronunciations. You'll learn more about this when you learn about tuning in Chapter 17.

Figure 10-7 summarizes the word-level ambiguities that speech-to-text and NL must cope with, including synonyms. Homophones (same sound, different meaning and spelling) can be problems in some grammars or domains: don't encourage users to end a stock purchase interaction with *bye*—it sounds the same as *buy*!

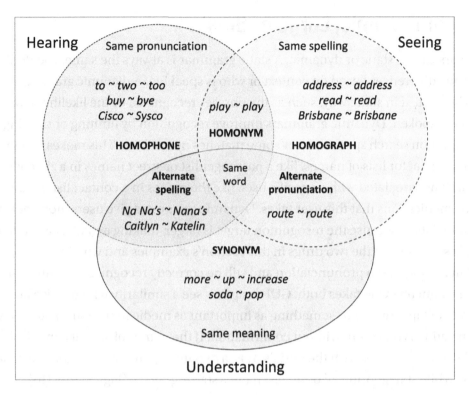

Figure 10-7. *Word-level ambiguity that speech-to-text interpretation needs to handle*

As a rule of thumb, your prompts should avoid homophones and homonyms that are not synonyms, which discourages users from saying words that are easily confused. You'll most likely rely on the core recognizer to handle alternate pronunciations, but here too you influence users by how your VUI pronounces words. If you expect users to say a product name with an unusual pronunciation or multiple pronunciations, make sure you add those pronunciations. Also add any expected synonyms that aren't already handled by the recognizer.

Near-homonyms can be particularly tricky for recognition when your VUI expects a word that sounds similar to (or same as) a word that's statistically more common. For example, a medical voice app that allows users to ask about *stents* will have trouble with an unmodified grammar that includes the word *stints*.

Static or Dynamic, Large or Small

Grammars can be static or dynamic. A static grammar is always the same; you don't expect any differences based on context or who is speaking. A dynamic grammar differs by context in some way, such as the phrases recognized or the likelihood of each item being spoken. Dynamic grammars improve recognition by limiting or skewing the recognition search space to favor some matches over others. This makes dynamic grammars great for lists of names, like a passenger list or street names in a zip code, and for situations associated with a specific user, like the names in a contact list or names of only the medications that this user takes. Dynamic grammars give users more leeway in pronunciation because the recognition target is larger, making a match easier. A user who takes only one of the two drugs in this section's examples and who is ordering a refill can be sloppier in pronunciation and still be correctly recognized (Figure 10-8 (a)) than someone who takes both. GUI designers see a similarity with the size and proximity of tap targets. For something as important as medication, you'd still limit what pronunciations you accept without confirmation. If the names of staff at a medical clinic include only two names with the initials A. P., a dynamic grammar allows some variation of those while still ignoring all other last names starting with P (Figure 10-8 (b)).

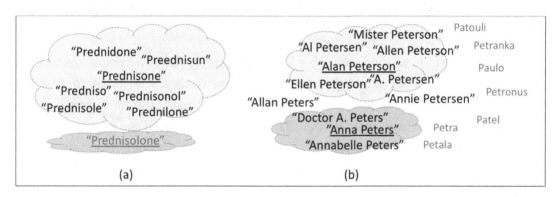

Figure 10-8. *Recognition space for a dynamic grammar. (a) Only Prednisone is valid; (b) Alan Peterson and Anna Peters are both staff at a clinic*

Finding ways to narrow the search space is very important if the set of possible items is large, like the names of all traded stocks or the full National Drug Code (NDC) database of current drugs, each set consisting of tens of thousands of unique items.

SUCCESS TIP 10.2 PROMPTS DIRECTLY INFLUENCE USER RESPONSES   User responses are closely tied to the wording of the prompt. Therefore, all prompt changes must include a grammar review at a minimum and often involve grammar changes. A common rookie mistake is to consider only content coverage and not realize how much prompt changes can influence the filler part of utterances as well.

End-Pointing

Speech-to-text needs a good end-pointer, the algorithm that determines when a user is done talking so it's time to stop listening and start processing. End-pointing is very complex and very important. If it triggers too soon, the user is cut off before reaching the end of their utterance. If it's too slow to end, side speech and other noise may be picked up and mistaken for words. Either way, the result won't accurately represent what the user said, and the conversation fails.

Multiple Hypotheses

During the STT process, and while still listening, the recognizer keeps active multiple hypotheses of what's being said. The reason is that as long as there's speech still coming in, there's information that will change the most likely interpretation of the utterance. Once the user has stopped speaking, the recognizer settles on a top hypothesis. This has many uses that we'll come back to in Chapter 12.

MULTIMODAL CORNER

If your VUI uses push-to-talk (PTT), a button that controls the mic and starts and ends recognition, then end-pointing doesn't have the same impact on detecting start and end of speech, but there are other timing difficulties. It can be tricky for users to get the timing right to coordinate the pushing and the talking. Audio earcons help but they're not enough. In part it depends on your particular users. In the 22otters multimodal procedure prep helper, we used PTT and earcons to signal the start and end of the app listening. We found that users were more successful and their utterances more complete with the earcon hint than without it because of the slight lag caused by the cloud-based recognition. If you dictate to a multimodal VUI with a screen, you probably see how one interpretation is displayed word by word while you still speak. Once the end-pointer decides you're done, you might see the words suddenly changing—sometimes for the better and other times not! You're seeing the final swap of top hypotheses. This can be disconcerting and confusing to some users, so if your VUI has a display, you may or may not want to show the hypotheses in real time. In our own procedure prep helper app, we chose to not display real-time results. We also didn't display the actual word-by-word word string interpretations but a close curated version that removed extra words or stutters while still providing enough information for the user to implicitly verify they were understood (Figure 10-9).

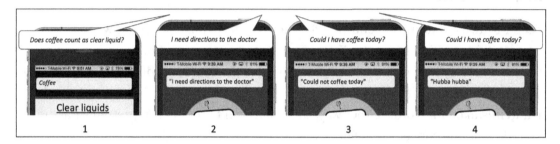

Figure 10-9. *Different text result fields: (1) word-by-word result converted to content only; (2) verbatim, perfect recognition; (3) verbatim, close recognition; (4) verbatim, poor recognition*

Types of Grammars

There are different types of grammars, quite distinct from each other. All have one thing in common: someone had to do something to create them. They don't appear out of thin air. Either you create them yourself, or you get them from somewhere else. If someone else created them, you may be able to modify them. They can be completely handcrafted string matches or statistical matches based on automated training on data corpora. You might have access to pre-populated grammars for some specific domain or topic, like postal address, money amounts, or dates. When such grammars exist, use them— someone else spent a lot of time tuning for robustness, allowing you to focus on your VUI-specific grammars.

In this section, we introduce four types of grammars you're likely to create or come across. You'll learn how coverage and recognition space play into choosing the right type of grammar for each context in a VUI. After this, you'll get concrete experience with how to create grammars.

Rule-Based Grammars

Rule-based grammars are patterns written to match exactly to every expected utterance in some portion of the VUI. They can be static or dynamic. If you can write regular expressions, you can write rule-based grammars. Writing robust rule-based grammars takes a lot of work: coverage is achieved by exactly matching every possible utterance, including both core content and fillers. But if you know what you're doing, you can get a decent grammar in place quickly. They're a good option for structured multi-slot utterances with fairly constrained fillers. Because they're handwritten rather than generated from statistical distribution, they're good for handling low-frequency items. They also allow more visibility into why a specific utterance resulted in a certain outcome by tracking what pattern matched. This is important for medical and financial VUI implementations. One core difficulty with rule-based grammars is balancing coverage with over-generation (Figure 10-5 (c)). The more crowded the recognition space, the higher the risk of matching with the wrong item.

Statistical Models

Statistical language models (SLMs) are not handwritten but generated from training data. Training data consists of a large set of user utterances, collected in the same context as the SLM will be used in a VUI, then transcribed, and fed into appropriate software. Importantly, training data needs to be responses to the same prompt that will be used in the VUI with the SLM. Training an SLM takes a lot of up-front effort. If you can't get the data needed, your models suffer. But once you do have good SLMs in place, they're robust almost by definition. Because statistical distribution is built in, common requests are more easily handled.

And utterances match more easily on near-matches, so SLMs are your friends when users' responses are so varied that it's hard to identify patterns for rules. Sometimes you even see different SLMs depending on context. Some reuse is possible, and the more training data, the more robust the SLM. But if prompts change, user utterances also change, so new training data is needed to keep performance high. Because the SLMs are generated representations based on training data, SLMs are more of a black box than rule-based grammars. This makes it harder to predict exactly what will match with what, especially for uncommon utterances, and harder to show why an utterance matched to a particular intent. That's an issue for medical VUIs where predictability and

369

accountability are your marching orders. You'll see later that combining rule-based and statistical approaches can be the answer. Over-generation is not a concern, assuming it's "real" data and doesn't use the same utterances for different intents.

Hot Words, Wake Words, and Invocations

A hot word grammar looks only for one word or phrase with no synonyms or very limited synonyms. Much like *The Far Side* cartoon of what dogs hear (*blah blah blah Ginger blah blah*), hot word grammars do word spotting, ignoring all other words while keeping the mic open and listening. That makes them great options for navigation commands and continuing a dialog that's been paused, for example, while the user is looking for a prescription number or while finishing a step in a multistep conversation. If done right, the user can be in a noisy room or have side conversations until the magic word is picked up by the recognizer. As you can imagine, this works best when the word or phrase is distinct and easy to say and recognize—but not so easy that it triggers by mistake.

As happens quite a bit in the voice tech space, people differ in the terminology they use and what it refers to. The term "hot word" has become overloaded. Google now uses it to refer to the *Hey, Google* portion. We find it useful to differentiate the use cases, so we tend to use "hot word" to refer to something that's temporarily halted in an in-progress conversation. To us, *Siri, Alexa, Hey, Google*, and similar are better thought of as wake words, a type of hot word associated with "always listening" smart devices to open the microphone for utterance capture in a new dialog. You'd only work on wake words if you're on a team at one of the relevant companies or creating a stand-alone platform or device not built on one of those platforms. The invocation name is the name of your Google skill or Alexa action: it's the name your users need to say to engage with your particular VUI interaction.

Invocation names have to follow specific requirements imposed by each platform— it's best to look at the current rules online for each. Here, we'll focus on the general recognition and UX issues. A wake word is the ultimate hot word: only one word is in grammar, but that word needs to be understood by every user in all kinds of contexts and conditions. And similar words should ideally be ignored. Because branding is often involved, it can be hard to create a good invocation name. An ideal name should be memorable, meaningful, and easy to say and recognize. That's surprisingly difficult. The shorter the word, the easier it is to say but the harder it is to recognize well. You don't deal with wake words or invocation for every voice system. For phone-based IVRs, invocation is the start of making a phone call; for mobile apps, it's opening an app; for purpose-built devices with their own microphone, it might be pressing a manual push-to-talk (PTT) button.

Hot words make in-home assistants possible, but getting the trigger level "just right" for all users is an ongoing challenge. Google now lets you tweak that sensitivity, which is great. And it's important to get it right. When it doesn't work as expected, users either complain that it doesn't understand them or that it's eavesdropping on conversations not intended for the VUI. You want to avoid both.

Working with Grammars

You're most likely to either write your own regular expressions or make use of the tools each platform offers for using or extending SLMs. You can use rule-based grammars for all of the procedure prep VUI. Really. In particular, you'd use them for the content in food diary, contacts, and anything involving names of medications or foods. SLMs would be best for the FAQ, because of the variation you can expect in how people ask general questions. We won't cover the details of from-scratch SLM creation for space considerations.

SUCCESS TIP 10.3 LET EVERYONE TRY BUILDING GRAMMARS   It's worth saying again: the best way to succeed with voice is for everyone on a team to understand what's difficult and why. There's no better way than to try creating robust grammars. It doesn't mean everyone will be an expert at it—far from it—nor that they should write production grammars. But it's instructive to try and it's a lot of fun!

Writing Rule-Based Regular Expressions

So far, you've specified what users are expected to say for each intent by providing training sentences in Dialogflow. That's not writing a grammar per se; it's providing examples that Dialogflow internally converts into some sort of grammar, generally the statistical kind described earlier. Providing examples takes considerably less skill than manually writing grammars, and we have technology these days that is pretty good at creating decent (not perfect) grammars automatically from examples. Another way to specify what users are expected to say is by providing a rule-based grammar.

Regular Expressions Defined

Rule-based grammars are typically based on regular expressions, which programmers might be familiar with. Regular expressions are phrases with wildcard characters that make it very easy to specify multiple possibilities. Instead of having to list them all, regular expressions allow you to say "anything can go here." You can use regular expressions to specify the sequences of words expected in a specific context. You can easily find tutorials and test tools online, so we're only going to walk you through a simple example here. Assume your VUI just asked the user *Would you like to refill that prescription?*; a common response would be *yes*, so a regular expression could be

```
yes
```

Sounds simple, right? Not everyone says just one word. As you've learned, some people add *please* at the end; so you'd better add an optional "please":

```
yes( please)?
```

You might notice that spaces matter, like they do in Python. The ? at the end of a word is a wildcard construct that means the word is optional. Let's assume some users add a *well* at the beginning of sentences, so add an optional "well":[3]

```
(well ?) yes( please)?
```

Of course, users don't always say *yes*. Some say *yeah* or even more unusual phrases. Putting a number of words in parentheses separated by the | (pipe) character means any of the options are valid. So

```
(indubitably |well )?(yes|yeah)( please)?
```

---

[3]Adding handling for common fillers and hesitation is not necessary for all recognizers. Remember: Even though we use Google here, we want to show you in detail how to implement the things we talk about on any platform. You would be more likely to use sub-grammars, which we'll define shortly.

Regular expressions are simple yet powerful and easily available; there are other more complex languages created specifically for the purpose of defining grammars.[4] With regular expressions, you can also extend existing grammars if you find patterns of utterances that don't get correctly recognized. Your grammars need to handle the opposite/negative of an expected utterance, for example, making sure that *not very good* doesn't map to *very good* when a patient is responding to a health check. Think about how you'd test, implement, and handle something like *I take Prednisone but not Prednisolone* or *My husband takes Prednisolone. I only take Prednisone.*

Grammars and Training Phrases

Table 10-1 shows the coverage of your sample grammar—it's a tiny fraction of the ways in which a user might respond in the affirmative to the question *Would you like a refill?*

Table 10-1. *The relationship between grammars and training phrases*

Grammar rule	Phrases		
(indubitably |well)?	yes	well yes	indubitably yes
(yes|yeah)(please)?	yes please	well yes please	indubitably yes please
	yeah	well yeah	indubitably yeah
	yeah please	well yeah please	indubitably yeah please

The point here is that even with something as simple as *yes*, the number of possible phrases is large. Imagine a more complex question with responses that aren't already defined. Having to write out all sample phrases as training phrases becomes unwieldy and error-prone quickly. Some platforms also have limits on the number of sample phrases—limits you hit surprisingly fast. All this is why regular expression–type grammars are so useful. With a very short description, you can specify coverage for hundreds or thousands of possible utterances.

---

[4]For more, take a look at www.w3.org/TR/speech-grammar/ for the W3C Speech Recognition Grammar Specification (SRGS).

Sub-grammars

Just like when you write code with functions for things you do repeatedly, grammars can also be built up from other grammars, or **sub-grammars**. Using the same grammar example, rewrite it to use a sub-grammar for the *yes* portion:

```
(well )? YES ( please)?
YES =: (yes|yeah)
```

The uppercase YES refers to the sub-grammar; it's "defined" using the =: construct. Now you can use YES repeatedly in other grammars, defining it only once.

If you use Google Cloud ASR with your regex's, you'd create a set of sub-grammars, like YES and YEAH, that either specify or ignore all other words around them, using simple AND/OR logic. These are still rule-based, but they leave much of the work to the platform, making these more like hot word grammars, so you don't need to specify entire sentences with every possible way to say *yes* and still interpret *Well, I guess I'd have to say yes to that* as a *yes*. This will work well enough in most situations, but not all, especially if you build your own system for a new domain or a new language. It's good to know you have options.

Dialogflow has sub-grammars too; they're the entities you've worked with. In Chapter 7, you added training phrases for making an appointment. Figure 10-10 reminds you how you did that.

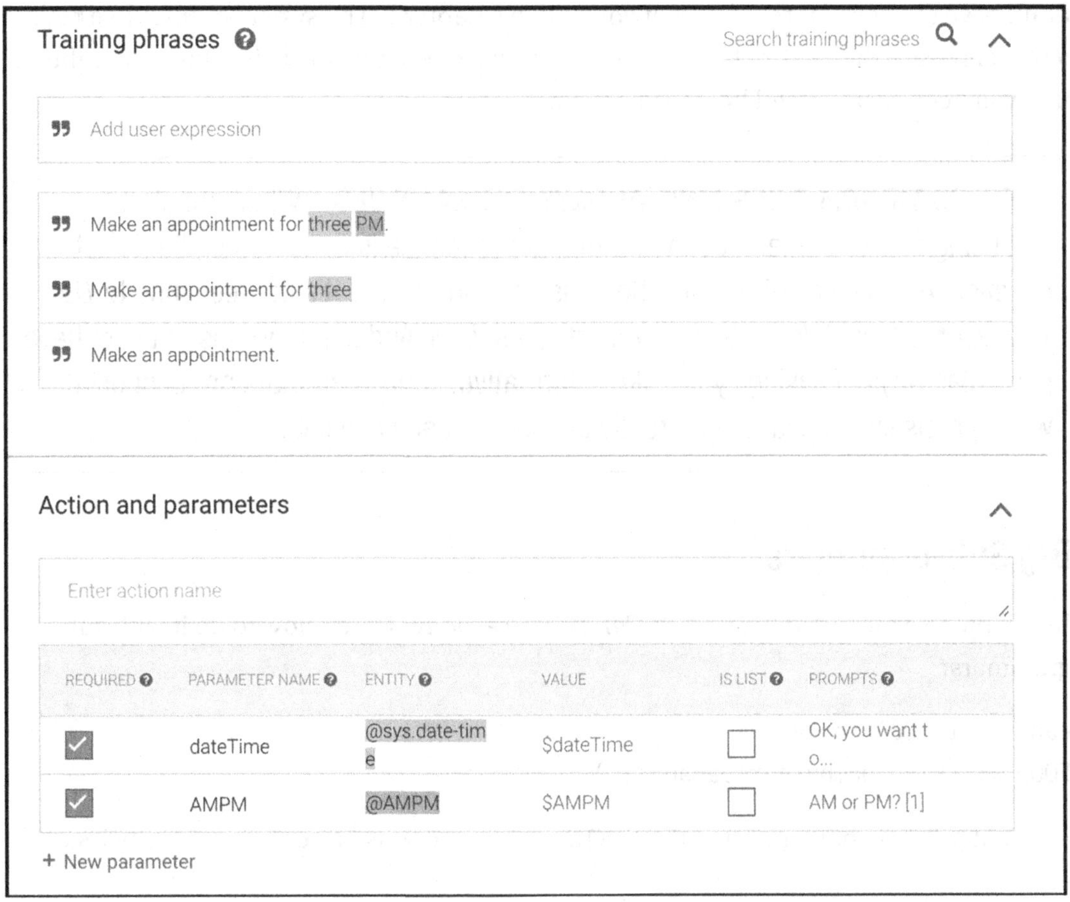

Figure 10-10. *Snippet of intent definition for making an appointment in Dialogflow*

How would you do the same with regular expressions? Like this:

```
make an appointment (at TIME)?
TIME =: NUMBER AMPM?
NUMBER =: (one|two|three|four|five|six|seven|eight|nine|ten|eleven|twelve)
AMPM =: (AM|PM)
AM =: (am|morning)
PM =: (pm|evening|afternoon)
```

Here you make liberal use of sub-grammars. Note that you can surround multiple words and/or sub-grammars with parentheses and make the whole group optional with the question mark. You had to explicitly write out the NUMBER for the time, since here you don't have the @sys.date-time that you had in Chapter 7. The system entities like @sys.date-time save the work of having to write out the grammars explicitly, but remember that you need to be careful how to use them.

SUCCESS TIP 10.4 A YES ISN'T ALWAYS THE SAME YES   When creating and using sub-grammars, be aware that the response is impacted by the exact question. A *yes* takes different synonyms depending on if it's the response to *Do you want…* (*Yes, I do*) or *Is that correct?* (*Yes, it is*). And some groups of users have particular ways of saying "yes," like "affirmative." Sub-grammars are best used when precisely defined and correctly chosen for each use case.

Big Sub-grammars

In Chapter 5, you added the phrase *Can I eat rice today?* Here's how to do it with sub-grammars:

```
can i eat FOOD today
FOOD =: (rice|hamburger|bananas|…)
```

That "…" placeholder part of the FOOD grammar opens up some complexity issues because

- It's huge. It's a grammar of anything you could possibly eat!

- It's not static. If your favorite fast-food restaurant has a new special item, it should be there! So you need to maintain that grammar, not just adding names but also properties of each item to fit it into the ontology resulting in correct answers.

Pronunciations

Assume one of the items missing from the FOOD grammar is "lumpia" (a Filipino egg roll). You add the word to the grammar, but is that enough? Maybe.

Recall there's a lexicon, or dictionary, with pronunciations of each word in the covered language. Words can even have multiple pronunciations; remember the word "one" has two pronunciations in the CMU Pronouncing Dictionary. The pronunciation is the mapping of words to ARPAbet units or similar. With any mature voice platform, you have a basic lexicon that handles most common pronunciations—speech scientists and others will have spent much time creating and refining the lexicon so you don't need to. If a word is not in the lexicon, any speech recognizer has an auto-pronunciation module that comes up with best guesses of pronunciations for words not in the lexicon. The auto-pronunciation methods are good, but not perfect. So ideally, especially for words with nonstandard pronunciations, you want to be able to add additional pronunciations. We've run into this when working with medical drug names. For example, for the medical drug name "Enbrel," a recognizer using a standard dictionary is likely to return umbrella. You can add that to the grammar as a quick hack. But any such hack opens up unintentional over-generalization and potential misrecognition. A better course of action is to add a custom pronunciation that can match correctly with what's spoken. Using ARPAbet, two pronunciations you'd add are [EH1 N B R EH2 L] and [EH1 M B R EH2 L].

How to Succeed with Grammars

Grammar creation is obviously a big topic. In this section, we give you some guidelines on things to look out for.

Bootstrap

How do you know what people will say? The short answer is you don't really—not until you have real user data from a production system. But if that were completely true, you couldn't ever get started! Here are a few data sources you should use for early grammars:

- User studies and background research that show you what words people use today when doing the task, including branding terminology, phrasing, and synonyms.

- A solid understanding of how people speak in general; how they ask questions, make requests, and respond; what variation is more or less common; and so on.

- Grammars that are used for similar tasks in other VUIs.

- Prompt wording and branching in the VUI flow, what people are likely to ask for at each point in the flow, clarification questions they might have, and disambiguation that's likely. If there are multi-slot utterances, make sure to capture all combinations. If users are likely to overspecify the response, make note of that too. In Chapter 12 you learn how to use this for one-step correction.

- Data from real users when you have access to such data. You can collect useful speech data from Wizard of Oz studies—studies that mimic automated recognition while being controlled by a "human behind the curtain"—record free-form user requests, then follow up with a directed grammar, and get data from other modalities, like text chats. You can learn something from every piece of data; just remember where it came from—spoken and written commands are not phrased the same.

Normalize Punctuation and Spellings

If you use your mobile phone for dictation, you see how names often show up with different spellings than the ones you want. You also type differently from how you speak, with different uses of abbreviations, punctuation, capitalization, and so on. The spelling of first and last names is notoriously varied: the name "Katelyn" occurs in well over 100 different spellings! If you use written data for voice grammar creation, you need to normalize all that. Normalization lets the restaurant finder match a text interpretation of <nanas> or <nannas> to [Na Na's].

FROM THE VOICE TRENCHES

A great example illustrating the difference between speech and writing was the voice prompt response when we asked a voice assistant to play music by the Canadian band La Volée d'Castors. The rather unexpected response was a Spotify playlist whose name included *spouting whale upside down face sun face poo* (Figure 10-11). On insights.spotify.com (or https://redef.com/source/541b6febb6f3a22559bee547), you can see that there are more than 35 million user-created Spotify playlists containing emojis in the title. Think about the recognition challenge that presents!

Figure 10-11. *Actual playlist name consisting only of emojis*

Handle Unusual Pronunciations

You've already seen the difficulties with drug name recognition. Pronunciation of brand names and foreign words and names can also be challenging. And what about dialects?

Brand names can be tough if they're invented words. Users don't necessarily know a company's "official" pronunciation. That means your grammars need to capture various pronunciations, not just the official one. This can be an issue if you're building a skill or action and the platform demands a single pronunciation trained into a huge SLM. Foreign names and words need to be recognized when users say them in the language of the VUI. So, if you're building a travel VUI for US English, any locations or points of interest in other languages need to be understood when spoken by a typical US English user. Think about the pronunciation of foreign words in prompts. How does it correlate and interact with recognition? More on that in a later chapter.

What about dialects? This is surprisingly not a problem. Here's why. Dialects could come into play on two levels: using different units to pronounce words and having the units themselves sound different.

To understand the first one, take a look at the entries for tomato in the CMU Pronouncing Dictionary (the ARPAbet symbols were in Figure 10-3):

```
TOMATO      T AH0 M AA1 T OW2
TOMATO      T AH0 M EY1 T OW2
```

How are the two pronunciations different? The EY sound is the vowel in *bait*, which is how most American English speakers pronounce *tomato*. The AA sound is like *balm*, how many British English speakers would say it. So well-developed dictionaries take care of common variation. Chapter 15 provides details for adding pronunciations.

Good STT systems are trained on tens or hundreds of thousands of hours of speech data from actual field conditions, including speakers of different dialects. If a unit or sound is articulated slightly differently for a dialect, it will show up that same way in the training data, and the system will learn it. If it's very different, then maybe it's actually a different unit that should be addressed in the lexicon—like tomato.

Use Domain Knowledge

When you're creating grammars for some domain—like names of medications, foods, or restaurants in some area—you don't want to start from scratch. It's a huge task, and you'll forget to cover something. There are many sources available online; some free, some not. For restaurant names and locations, look at Yelp, Google, and other directories. Restaurants' own websites provide menu details. For names of food items, Wikipedia and other online sites are a good start, and USDA has a searchable database of foods including nutritional information (`fdc.nal.usda.gov`). For medications, you have various options depending on what you're building. Do you need names, dosage and strength, chemical composition, and generic names? Look at fda.gov for the National Drug Code (NDC) directory. After building your data set, you'll still need to modify that data for voice, both for pronunciations and vocabulary variations. You'll learn about creating large data-based grammars in Chapter 11.

Understand the Strengths and Limitations of STT

You've learned that different grammars are appropriate for different tasks or even each step in a task. You also learned the limitations of relying on general machine learning: STT drops information that it's not set up to explicitly capture. Word order and intonation carry information on meaning, emphasis, and emotion, but neither is captured well by most systems; once an utterance has been turned into a representation, this information is lost from later interpretation and logic.

The restaurant finder we've used for examples is for the town of Brisbane, California. That name rhymes with *lane,* which is different from the much larger and better known Brisbane in Australia, which ends much like the name *Ben*. They're both close enough to be recognized, but because both cities are spelled exactly the same, nothing in the text interpretation will capture the difference. The pronunciation difference carries information that's discarded. You'll learn how to address this when we look at parsing and NL understanding.

SUCCESS TIP 10.5 GRAMMAR DOESN'T MEAN GRAMMATICAL   We talk about "grammars" and "syntax" and relying on what you know about the language you create voice system grammars for. At the same time, it's perfectly correct to include ungrammatical phrases in your voice grammars if they match what people actually say. Voice grammars are **descriptive**, not **prescriptive** (for you language nerds out there).

Hands-On: Taking Control over Coverage

We've talked quite a bit about theory; let's put it all together in a simple example: taking an intent for which we're currently providing training phrases in Dialogflow and moving those phrases over to the webhook to illustrate how to specify your own regular expression grammars. Since you just worked with universals, let's use one of those: repeat. The high-level plan is to

- Remove training phrases from the Dialogflow intent (but keep the intent), since you now want the webhook to handle the phrases.

- Have the intent handle an event, which is the second way that an intent in Dialogflow can be triggered. We'll come back to events shortly.

- Make the needed changes to the webhook to support the phrases.

Changes in Dialogflow

Remove Existing Sample Phrases

First, go into the Dialogflow intent for "repeat" and remove all the training phrases. Just click the trash cans and then Save.

Add an Event

Now, back to events. There are two ways to trigger a Dialogflow intent:

- The user says something that matches a sample phrase. This is how you've handled it so far in this book.

- An event is triggered that the intent responds to, such as from the webhook. For this you need to add a `repeat` event in the Events section of the repeat intent.

If the webhook triggers a `repeat` event, that intent is triggered as usual, and the system speaks the designated response. You'll learn how to trigger events next.

Actually, we lied a little when we said events are new. You've been using events, but so far they've been hidden. If you look at the Default Welcome Intent, you'll see an event named Welcome. Every Dialogflow agent is created with that exact event. This is how Actions on Google knows where to start the app. When you say *OK, Google, talk to APP_NAME*, Actions on Google triggers the Welcome event, which triggers the Default Welcome Intent.

Regular Expressions in the Webhook

Here's the overall idea for implementing the grammar in the webhook:

- In the webhook, add logic to handle the Default Fallback Intent.

- In that logic, use regular expressions to check whether the text representation of the spoken utterance matches the phrase(s) you expect.

- If it matches, trigger the `repeat` event from the webhook, which activates the `repeat` intent with its usual response behavior, either what's in the GUI or what's specified in the webhook, as you've been doing.

Why handle the fallback intent? This intent is triggered when the user's utterance doesn't match any of the existing intents (within the constraints of any contexts). If you're using explicit grammars, that has to be done in an intent that's not triggered by the user speech matching sample phrases; this is the Default Fallback Intent. Remember, in the last section, you took the "repeat" phrases out of Dialogflow, so now those phrases will hit the fallback intent. As you might expect, to get more control, you also need to handle more of it.

Handling the Phrase If No Other Intent Does

Listing 10-1 shows the webhook code[5] for handling the Default Fallback Intent. Just like before, you define a function (A) `fallback` in its own file `fallback.py`. As always, the two arguments are the webhook request and response objects (B). Search the `query_text` in the request object (which you haven't used until now) to see if the user has spoken a repeat phrase, using regular expressions (C). If so, we set the event to trigger in the webhook response (D). In `main.py`, as with other intents, we have to add the Default Fallback Intent to the dictionary of handler functions (E).

Listing 10-1. Handling the Default Fallback Intent for repeat

```
def fallback(      # A
    df_request,      # B
    df_response):
  """

  fallback
  """

  if re.search('((say( that)? )?again|repeat( that)?)( please)?',    #C
           df_request.query_text):
    # repeat

    # Trigger the repeat event.
    df_response.event_to_trigger = 'repeat'      # D

# ...... in main.py ......

dialog_functions = {

  # ...... Code cut for listing focus
```

---

[5]Files for this chapter are in 10-1a.zip for Dialogflow and 10-1b.zip for the webhook.

```
'Default Fallback Intent': fallback,      # E

# ...... Code cut for listing focus

'transfer': universal_transfer}
```

You're almost done. Now, add some JSON to the webhook response in webhook_response.py to get Dialogflow to trigger the repeat event, as shown in Listing 10-2. Check if the event is set to trigger above (A). If so, add the needed JSON to the webhook response—here it's the event name—as well as language (B).

Listing 10-2. Using the webhook to tell Dialogflow to trigger an event

```
# Trigger an event if needed.
if self.event_to_trigger is not None:                    # A
    self.respdic['followupEventInput'] = {}
    self.respdic['followupEventInput']['name'] = /
    self.event_to_trigger                                # B
    self.respdic['followupEventInput']['languageCode'] = 'en-US'
```

That's it! Now you've seen how to do this in two ways. This was a very simple example; the logic in Listing 10-1 could be much more complex, accessing data sources and doing processing to settle on a system response and trigger the appropriate event. You can also add parameters to the event when you trigger it, so that Dialogflow uses those parameters in the response.

Why Do It This Way?

These are several reasons for why you'd want to do this:

- One nice thing about this approach is how compact it can be and how easy it can be to support a number of possible phrases. From (C) in Listing 10-1, we can see that a one-line regular expression was equivalent to five sample phrases in Dialogflow. Actually more, since we snuck in the optional "please" at the end.

- As we've touched on, using the webhook opens up many possibilities for using dynamically created grammars from data sources like databases and such, which may not be possible with just Dialogflow or other similar platform tools.

- And, as we've also mentioned, matching on regular expressions can give you very precise control over conversation behaviors. This matters a great deal if you're building some cool new VUI where you don't have ready access to either trained SLMs or a lot of speech data you can train your own models on.

- It can be part of a multi-pass approach. Attempting to first match on an exact narrow expression and then using a broader statistical model for fallback if there's no match is an excellent approach that gives you the best of both worlds. It also increases your chance of correctly matching something that occurs infrequently and may otherwise run into trouble with a purely statistical approach. We'll come back to this in the next chapter.

We'll explore the limitations in the next section. You'll need to weigh pros and cons for your situation. Want another reason? It's really fun. ☺

Programming Sidebar: Debugging the Webhook

As we do more and more with the webhook, Python programmers may wonder: how about debugging, either printing out statements or using the pdb debugger? So far, we've been pushing our webhook code to the Google App Engine, but there is another way, which is useful for debugging purposes:

- Get an account on ngrok, `https://ngrok.com`. Ngrok gives you a URL that redirects to your local machine, so you can run your webhook locally, including any debugging.

- Download the ngrok software.

- In the directory where you have ngrok installed, start it up: `./ngrok http 8080`. This gives you a URL that redirects to your local machine, port 8080.

- Go to the Fulfillment section in Dialogflow and change the webhook URL to the one provided by ngrok (use the https version; ngrok gives you both http and https).

- In the directory containing your webhook code

- If you haven't already, start a Python virtual environment. Make sure the Python version is the same as in the `app.yaml` file that you upload to Google Cloud.

- Install the needed modules into your environment: `pip install -r requirements.txt`.

- Start your webhook: `python main.py`. This starts the webhook listening on your local port 8080. For those of you who wondered about the block of code at the bottom of `main.py`, here's the reason why it's there. This code is executed when the webhook is run locally, while on Google Cloud another process runs the server.

- Test! Now any webhook hit will come to your machine through ngrok, and you can do any debugging and testing that you need to do. Stop the locally running webhook anytime with `Ctrl-C`.

- When you're done debugging, deploy to Google Cloud, and change the Dialogflow fulfillment URL to the one provided when you deploy the app with `gcloud app deploy`.

As we were testing this code, we noticed that sometimes the `query_text` field in the webhook request (part (C) in Listing 10-1) was not filled in. We couldn't find a reliable reason as to when this did or didn't happen.

We bring this up because it underscores something we've discussed about tools and platforms. Remember that these are complex systems; don't be surprised if you see issues that you may have to work with or work around. In industry practice, this is pretty much well known, especially with highly moving targets. Recall our discussion way back in Chapter 3 about whether to use the older Dialogflow Essentials or some of the newer tools; these kinds of issues are why we frequently choose the older but more stable path.

Limitations on Grammar Creation and Use

There are pros and cons of creating your own grammars. Be sure you understand what you're getting into. Having control over recognition and intent resolution to support a user-focused design for specific users and topics is the only way to truly innovate with voice. Creating and maintaining robust grammars of any kind is a skill that takes practice but has great potential rewards. First, decide if you need to create your own. We've discussed reasons why you might want to: new domains, special words or pronunciations, unsupported language, limited training data, and so on. If you choose to create your own, realize that you'll need to continue maintaining them as long as your VUI is "live." That can be a lot of work, but it's far from impossible. If you're a product manager/owner, you need to work this into your plan, and you need a process in place for testing, making sure the grammars don't "go stale." Your reward is the ability to create superior user experiences, thanks to having more control over the whole VUI conversation. If you work with a team without designated speech scientists, figure out who on the team has the interest and abilities to work with grammars. It's not automatically an engineering task—an understanding of language and human speakers is more important.

You learned a little about built-in grammars in Chapter 7, including some of the pitfalls. Remember the complexity even with doing something as simple as disambiguating AM and PM and how using the built-in entity `@sys.date-time` caused issues. Relying on built-ins has its own challenges: you depend on someone else who may or may not share your focus and priorities. Such grammars will also be identical to everyone else's, so your VUI won't stand out.

Even if you have the ability to do your own grammar work, there's still an issue of controlling grammars freely on your platform. Do you even need to? SLMs have been used for voice-first VUIs, including IVRs, since at least the early 2000s. Robust call routing was—and is—possible, thanks to large data collections, which are very time-consuming. SLMs are also behind the rapid spread of voice assistants today. They allow anyone with platform access to create grammars without writing grammars, but instead providing a few training phrases as seeds to the platform's machine learning algorithms that "fill in the blanks." Sort of.

Those blanks might be incomplete or wrong for what you're building. Any phrases you don't provide need to be covered by algorithms, which are powerful but are still—by necessity—more general than your specific needs.

When using platform tools like Dialogflow or tools on the Alexa Developer Console, you don't explicitly write the types of grammars you saw earlier in this chapter. This is partly for convenience: the promise of creating a VUI without becoming a speech expert is tempting, and it's feeding the explosive growth of VUI interactions. It means some limitations are necessary to avoid developers getting themselves into trouble. In part, it's because the NLP technology is such that you actually can generate pretty good results by specifying a limited number of training phrases.

You learned earlier that you can in theory exhaustively specify the training phrases corresponding to all the optional components of a grammar, but you probably wouldn't want to do that because of the number of phrases involved. There are also built-in limitations of the platforms. For example, at the time of writing this, Dialogflow doesn't allow more than 2,000 training phrases for an intent, and practically, things slow down quite a bit when you get to 400 or 500. You can import training phrases from a file, but you still have these limitations.

What's Next

We'll wrap this chapter by reiterating why you should care about recognition, even if you're not a speech scientist. Prompts must be written for clarity: if users feel certain what to say, there's less hesitation or search for how to express something, which means your predictions for what should be "in grammar" are more likely correct, which in turn means users are more likely to be recognized correctly and therefore successful. Prompts must also avoid encouraging users to say words that are phonetically similar but have different meanings (like *buy* vs. *bye*). And if phonetically identical words can't be avoided (like *Sysco* and *Cisco* in a stock trading app), then designers and developers need to know that special confirmation strategies are needed. Anyone responsible for the ultimate performance of a voice system or quoting and planning resource needs to be aware of when to worry about recognition space and methods for addressing it. Stephen Morse and Alexander Beider wrote a very informative article[6] on the complexity of and solutions to phonetic matching of names using Soundex, a common phonetic algorithm for pronunciation-based indexing. The article is detailed while written for a nontechnical audience, so quite accessible for all.

The architecture of platforms where your VUI becomes part of a larger ecosystem of VUIs limits your ability to add your own grammars if there's a top level available for all users and developers. A top-level trained SLM needs to account for every utterance to avoid ambiguity at that level. But if your VUI is a stand-alone conversation on an independent device and you can access the raw recognition results to build grammars (static, dynamic, or SLMs) for only that VUI, your world opens up. You can probably tell how important we think this is. What you learn in this book applies no matter what platform, focus, and resources you have. The more you have free hands to build

---

[6]https://stevemorse.org/phonetics/bmpm2.htm

something less platform-dependent, the greater your potential reward. Being able to write your own grammars opens up new doors to more sophisticated conversational behavior because of how they feed into semantic models and natural language understanding. That's the topic of the next chapter.

Summary

- The highest possible recognition and STT accuracy is crucial for overall VUI success because everything "downstream" depends on it.

- Understanding recognition space means you can sometimes allow users to say "the wrong thing" and sometimes not, balancing robustness and accuracy.

- Relying on built-in grammars and a few training phrases isn't always enough to create a superior voice user experience. When you need to, you can have more control over recognition results with rule-based grammars.

- Platforms can get you started quickly, but they also put constraints on your VUI that may limit its apparent smarts unless you can incorporate more advanced techniques.

CHAPTER 11

Reaching Understanding

Chapter 10 covered the first component of a conversational system: speech-to-text (STT). Now it's time for step 2: natural language processing (NLP) and natural language understanding (NLU). If Chapter 10 focused on recognizing and understanding what a user said, this chapter focuses on what those words mean, as NLU takes the STT representation and interprets the intended meaning behind those words to determine how to respond. Here, you learn what "meaning" means to a voice system, why it's not a solved topic, and how to reach the best result anyway.

If your recognition goes wrong, your meaning interpretation probably will too: you can't "make sense" out of the wrong words—though sometimes you can still get to the right meaning with clever logic, turning a "too" into a "two." Accurate understanding lets you respond sensibly to users and give them what they ask for. It lets you create more complex and sophisticated VUIs that handle ambiguity and pronoun references, and it lets you deal with mistakes intelligently when they occur (Chapter 13). In this chapter, you learn about some of the methods involved in NLP and NLU. NLP assigns structure to a text string, while NLU uses that additional information to more accurately determine and assign a representation of the user's meaning that the VUI can act on or respond to. We'll discuss intents: why they're really "representations of semantic interpretation," what they're good for, and what they're missing. You learn about annotating data and improving conversational resolution through middle layers and multiple parsing passes.

We'll cover important points around the need for voice-appropriate data preparation. It'll be a big part of your effort when building voice apps, and it may seem pretty daunting at times. The good news is that you don't need to get it all right immediately. Recall the application lifecycle from Chapter 1: after you deploy, you assess and quickly iterate and update based on real user speech data. So don't get discouraged! Instead, get comfortable and let us tell you about assigning meaning to what your users said so you can respond the right way—one of our favorite topics in voice. It's where you have an opportunity to let your VUIs shine.

© Ann Thymé-Gobbel, Charles Jankowski 2021
A. Thymé-Gobbel and C. Jankowski, *Mastering Voice Interfaces*, https://doi.org/10.1007/978-1-4842-7005-9_11

From Words to Meaning

The path from user speech to VUI understanding goes like this (Figure 11-1):

1. The user says something.

2. The speech recognizer turns that speech into some representation, often a text string, that (hopefully) captures what the user said.

3. The text, or word string, passes through parsing and matching algorithms resulting in an interpretation that (again, hopefully) represents the meaning behind what the user said.

4. Settling on the right intent that represents the meaning, purpose, and goal of what the user said is the necessary first goal—you can't very well respond appropriately unless you figured out the meaning—figuring out how to respond (step 4) has to wait.

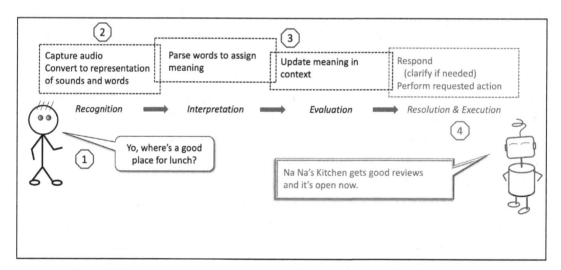

Figure 11-1. *The path from user speech to VUI understanding*

Assigning meaning to a text string involves parsing the word string into its parts of speech, then finding and categorizing lexical items, and ultimately settling on the most likely hypothesis of what the user actually means and wants, all within the domain of what the VUI can handle. That's hard! When learning about what's involved in assigning meaning, it's convenient to differentiate the text processing part from the interpretation part, although not everyone makes that distinction or splits them the same way. The input to understanding is the word string from STT; the output is a representation of the meaning that the voice system can act on within some context and conditions. NLP can be thought of as the glue between pure STT and NLU. NLP relates more to syntax and NLU more to semantics. In our diagrams of the speech-to-understanding processes, we show the steps as overlapping boxes, though one of the challenges dealing with natural language is that the steps can't be completely modularized.

Let's look at an example of meaning (Figure 11-2). In the question *What time does McDonald's close?*, meaning is a combination of the intent (here, an information request or search) and the slots capturing details that refine that intent (here, a required search item name and optional additional refinements of the search).

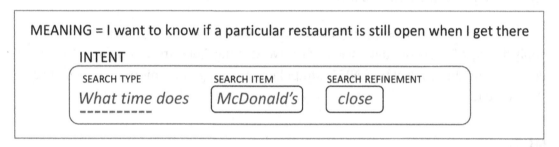

Figure 11-2. *Meaning is encoded as a combination of intent and slots*

This isn't the only way to represent meaning, but for task-based systems, the intent/slot model makes it easy to convert to a structured query like SQL to extract the information from a database and for dialog management (DM) to determine if there's any missing information that needs follow-up. For non-task-based use cases, a more general framework might be needed.

As humans, we interpret what we hear through filters of world knowledge, conversation topic, assumptions of what is known or new information, dialog structure, and so on. We are also amazingly good at understanding even when we hear incomplete sentences, stutters, restarts, mispronunciations, and even the wrong word used in a phrase. What STT passes on to NLU is a best guess based mostly on sound and far from always correct. You can probably think of examples of dictation gone wrong, similar to the examples in Figure 11-3. Knowing that it was raining at the time, what do you think was actually said in the rightmost example? Read it out loud and you'll hear it.

Figure 11-3. *Examples of dictation where the text result is based on sound but represented with the wrong words*

The first step in addressing any incorrect representation coming out of STT is to apply the right "filters" to make sense of the word string. Let's first look at how NLP does that and then look at how NLU extrapolates meaning from this more informative structured text.

NLP

NLP is the process of assigning structure to a text string through various techniques that categorizes the parts involved and their relationship. The purpose of doing this is to clarify and disambiguate the text string so that the correct intention can be assigned. Look at this example of an instruction you might hear:

> Take ***a pill*** out of ***the bottle*** and swallow ***it***.

Most people don't have to think hard to understand that *it* refers to *the pill* here, not *the bottle*. It's easy for us humans, thanks to our world knowledge, but it also involves parts of speech to resolve **pronoun reference** and **anaphora**, using a word like *it* to refer to something defined elsewhere. Some linguists spend their whole careers analyzing references like these; they're that complicated. This means VUIs stumble on them.

NLP can be rule-based or statistically based; you learned about both types of grammars in Chapter 10. Here are some interesting details for the NL processes—you don't need to be an expert in any of these to create good VUIs, but it can be helpful to have a clearer idea of the process:

- **Part-of-speech (POS) tagging**: Labeling the grammatical category (noun, verb, article, etc.) of each word in the string. In English, the basic set of grammatical categories is no more than ten, but there are many possible subcategories that can be relevant depending on the task and domain of your VUI, so 100 or more tags are not uncommon. Tagging is complicated in various ways. Do you tag "what's" as "what" + "'s" or as one? Is "play" a noun or a verb? In language with grammatical gender, should you label all articles as the same category or different ones?

- **Entity extraction**: Also called named-entity recognition, it's the process of finding and labeling concrete examples of some category, like personal names, names of drugs or foods, or amounts. A little like finding all the values of a slot, it might remind you of the keyword recognition you learned about in Chapter 10.

- **Syntactic parsing**: Words in a sentence have a syntactic relationship with each other based on rules and their part of speech. The trick is that parsing rules typically apply to written language. As you know by now, spoken language is a different thing altogether, with incompleteness and all. Yet, parsing is crucial for correct interpretation, so it needs to handle spoken utterances.

- **Coreference and anaphora resolution**: Using pronouns ("it," "them," etc.) while still being clear is characteristic of conversational speech. It obviously speeds up communication. Your conversational VUI needs to correctly handle pronoun references; if your VUI demands fully specified entities only, your users will hate you. Parsing plays a role here.

You'll learn more about these processes in this chapter though we'll only scratch the surface of the many fascinating topics of NLP.

NLU

NLU focuses on turning the processed text string into something that (hopefully!) makes sense within the VUI topic and task such that the VUI can then act on it. In particular, NLU is about matching an utterance with the right meaning or resolving the semantic intention, within the scope of what some conversational system can handle, while also not forcing a match of out-of-scope requests to something in scope. Let's look at a couple of examples of handling meaning:

> *I've got time between 10 and 12. Can you book me time for a trim?*

This request to a salon means *I can be there at 10 AM and need to be done by noon. You know how long a trim takes; make it happen.* It doesn't mean that starting at noon will work for them. If a trim takes 20–30 minutes, that means a start time no later than 11:30. Simple for a human, less so for a machine, but not impossible.

> *Can I... Is **rice** ... Is it still fine?*

In our procedure prep app, is *rice* enough for an accurate response? What if the user specified quantity or type? In some cases, that could make a difference to the response. You should expect questions about *cooked rice, white rice, brown rice, rice pudding, rice cakes, bibimbap, rice and beans*, and so on. And a question of *Is it OK to have a couple of grains of rice?* is likely to really mean *Oops, I had OK food but a little rice was in it. I hope I didn't mess up my prep*, so that needs a different response from *Can I eat a bowl of rice?*

Let's take a quick look at some NLU concepts—again, you won't always have to address these, but it's good to know something about them, especially the more of the NL you create from scratch, rather than relying on what a platform provides:

- **Semantic ambiguity**: The same word can differ in semantics (or meaning) depending on domain (or topic/subject or vertical). You need to assign the right meaning for your VUI. Is "Manhattan" a place or a drink in a bartender VUI? It's both, depending on the context of the request: *Find me a bar in Manhattan* or *What's in a Manhattan?* And *Find me the best Manhattan in Manhattan* isn't a problem if your parsing works!

- **Lexicon and ontologies**: You may need to map alternative words and synonyms to the right entity based on meaning, both in general and specifically for your VUI. For this you need a lexicon (or vocabulary or dictionary). And it needs to work for spoken words and phrases, not written ones. Ontologies capture relationships between words and concepts needed for understanding. For example, it would show all rice dishes being related while also showing which ones are cooked, but probably not anything about the amount of rice—another ontology section would focus on measurements.

- **Sentiment analysis**: Sentiment refers to opinion or attitude; sentiment analysis refers to extracting emotional or subjective information from NL. Sarcasm, humor, and emotional tone are part of human conversation—sometimes the listener gets it and sometimes not. It's very difficult for any VUI. We'll discuss why later in the book.

- **Inference**: Inferring (drawing conclusions by reasoning) and handling new NL phrases is still challenging for machines for several reasons including the limitless variation and vagueness in how people express themselves and the need for deeper world knowledge.

No, you probably won't have to explicitly handle all the pieces of NLP and NLU, but the more you know, the more you can find solutions when you run into issues. NLU isn't real intelligence. But you can get close to sounding smart if you use what's available to map to the right intention and respond appropriately.

In-Depth: What's "Smart," AI, and Understanding?

Although we and others toss around terms like "meaning" and "understanding," that doesn't mean there's human-level intelligence in any of today's VUIs. Real understanding implies being able to generalize to new situations in new contexts. Highly accurate cross-domain NLU (a general AI) is the real Holy Grail of voice, and it's far from solved, and many VUIs limited to a task or domain (relying on narrow, or weak, AI) are much more brittle than most humans in the same situation.

What is intelligence? The Turing test can't tell us; it's a test of a human's perception of a machine. It tests if the machine can imitate human behavior such that the human believes they're having a conversation with another human. "What is intelligence?" is an extremely complex question far beyond the scope of this book. It's also highly relevant to conversational systems. Fortunately, we don't really need to answer the question. What we do need is to avoid user disappointment.

There have already been several "AI Winters"—periods of time of little or no interest and limited funding. The term usually refers to one in the 1970s and one from the late 1980s well into the 1990s. There are several reasons why the AI Winters occurred when they did, but at the core it was disappointment caused by unfulfilled expectations after a period of hype and overoptimistic promises.

Considering how much optimism and hope there has been around "intelligent" voice applications, what does this mean for us all who want to build them? Are we doomed? Of course not. We can avoid a potential Conversational Voice Agent Frost by setting appropriate expectations and fulfilling them with voice solutions that meet or exceed those expectations—ones that make users feel understood. And the good news is that conversational voice agents can already be improved with the tools and methods available today—you're learning exactly how throughout this book. It's not hard; it's just a matter of paying attention to details. It's possible to appear more or less "smart" just based on how fine-grained and robust your VUI logic and responses are.

Parsing

Both of us authors can relate to parsing—one as an engineer and the other as a linguist. Parsing is the process of assigning a syntactic (grammatical) structure to a string of units (words) for further analysis. The purpose of parsing is to determine if the resulting structure is valid within some language, whether natural or computer. In other words, parsing involves matching some string to existing patterns (representations) and assigning a structure based on that match. Parsing a string can help "fix" STT interpretation errors like the ones in Figure 11-3. It can also help capture utterances that otherwise fall outside grammar coverage. Parsing (also called shallow parsing or chunking) assigns a coarse structure that can be used for a general response. More on that later in this chapter. If you rely on Dialogflow or other similar tools, parsing will be handled for you. But understanding something about parsers still helps you analyze and fix issues when they happen and even helps you create your own parser.

Parsing usually involves lemmatization—keeping the core stem of a word, the lemma—and segmentation—separating words into their morphemes (smaller pieces, like prefix "un-" and plural suffix "-s") and classifying based on that process.

One of the hardest things about parsing natural language is dealing with ambiguity (multiple parses) and long-distance dependencies, like pronoun references (what does "it" refer to). Only one parse should remain at the end for meaning to be derived from it. Remember the earlier example, *Take a pill out of the bottle and swallow it*. When there's ambiguity, human listeners will either ask for clarification or apply a best guess based on world knowledge, context, and so on. A computer needs ways to deal with this.

The other difficulty with parsing is that we're dealing with spoken language. Natural conversational speech is filled with stutters, jumbled word order, hesitations, restarts, pauses, coughs, and so on. Results are often incomplete or ungrammatical from a technical point of view. This is why you use the different grammar approaches you've learned about: looking for patterns, matching on key phrases, fuzzy matching based on probability, and so on.

SUCCESS TIP 11.1 WORDS ARE THE SOURCE OF MISUNDERSTANDING[1]   Text is a convenient representation of spoken utterances. But remember written and spoken languages differ from each other. Parsing conversational speech has to handle restarts, disfluencies, pauses in midsentence, and even ungrammatical sentences.

Figure 11-4 shows a parsing example using the Stanford Parser, a commonly used NLP parser that you can try yourself at `http://nlp.stanford.edu:8080/parser/index.jsp`.[2] The example is the same one: *Take a pill out of the bottle and swallow it*.

---

[1]Quote from *The Little Prince*, by Antoine de Saint-Exupéry.

[2]Some additional resources for the Stanford Parser: Tutorial, `https://github.com/stanfordnlp/stanfordnlp#online-colab-notebooks`; Stanford CoreNLP, `https://stanfordnlp.github.io/CoreNLP/StanfordNLP`; Python package (to be renamed Stanza), `https://stanfordnlp.github.io/stanfordnlp/`

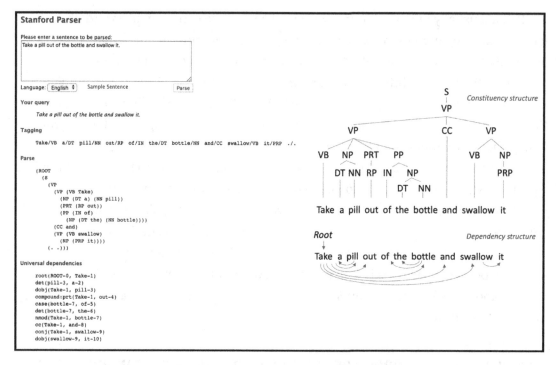

Figure 11-4. *Example of the Stanford Parser and its associated parse trees*

Look at some of the different components of the NLP parser:

- **Tagging**: Determining the part of speech for each word, such as NN for noun or VB for verb.

- **Parse**: Dividing the sentence into parts of speech using a hierarchical tree. This is not just one tag per word: it's the relative structure of an entire sentence. You see notations like NN for nouns and NP for noun phrases, VB and VBP for verbs and verb phrases, and so on.[3]

---

[3]You can find the complete list of possible tags here: www.ling.upenn.edu/courses/Fall_2003/ling001/penn_treebank_pos.html

- **Universal dependencies**: Creating a tree with the most salient words closer to the root and less "relevant" ones at the leaves of the tree. This is getting one step closer to the meaning of the sentence. In this example, the verb *take* is the root of the tree; the verb often is. The direct object (dobj) is the thing that's taken, so you see the dobj relationship between *take* and *pill*. And so on. Compare the relationship strength between words in the constituency structure tree and the dependency tree.

Using these kinds of parses, you can specify rules to derive an intent (perhaps from the root of the dependency parse plus any modifiers) and slots (children of the root node).

The bag-of-words model is a popular approach in some NLP applications. As the name implies, it's like cutting up sentences into separate words and putting them in a bag, disregarding syntactic structure and word order, but keeping information about how many instances of each word there is. Because articles like "the" and "a" or prepositions like "to" are by far the most common words, they're often normalized in some way. This technique is useful for categorizing documents or establishing the domain topic, but it should be obvious why this doesn't provide enough information for understanding in an English conversation: word order matters in English—note that this is not true for all languages. So do those little words like articles, pronouns, and "to" vs. "from." Without that information, you lose meaning that matters. For example, how do you think your users would react if your VUI can't handle the difference between *Transfer 500 dollars from my checking to Joe's savings* and *Transfer 500 dollars from Joe's checking to my savings*? We recently asked a voice assistant *Tell me about requirements for European travel to USA* and were told about US travel requirements to Europe. Don't expect to use a bag-of-words approach for a language that uses word order to encode meaning unless you have additional ways of capturing these important differences in meaning.

Machine Learning and NLU

We've covered very little about deep learning (DL) and how it has made possible great strides in STT, NLP, and NLU. This important topic is too big to cover here, but let's take a quick look.

DL uses distributed representations; it takes as input a vector of numerical features (or sequence of them) and outputs one of a number of classes, where a class represents something like an intent in your VUI. You need numerical features for DL, but you have words. How do you bridge this gap?

A **word embedding** is a conversion from a word to a vector in an n-dimensional space. Based on the idea that "You shall know a word by the company it keeps,"[4] words that occur in the same context should be semantically synonymous and have similar feature vectors. Words with very different neighbors would have very different feature vectors. Very simplistically, restaurant names appear in similar sentence positions, so a new name is easily understood to be a restaurant:

What time does	*McDonald's*	*close?*
What time does	*Na Na's*	*close?*
What time does	*McDonald's*	*open?*
Is	*Na Na's*	*open?*
What time does	_____	*open?*

These word embeddings are trained on corpora of millions (or billions!) of words. You can get pre-trained word embeddings, train your own, or take a pre-trained one and refine it with your particular corpus of data, but you need a lot of data—clearly a limiting factor of DL.

Most modern systems, including Dialogflow, make heavy use of DL to learn and generalize because it improves performance over shallower machine learning techniques and requires less custom work. Double win! DL techniques tend to be more robust to slight changes in phrasing, so users don't need to say something exactly like it's trained; the system learns what words are important and acts accordingly. This is why you don't need lots of training samples for Dialogflow intents to work reasonably well. Later in this chapter, you'll see that there's still a place for more handcrafted NLP.

---

[4] J. R. Firth, 1957.

Ontologies, Knowledge Bases, and Content Databases

In Chapter 10, you learned about creating and using grammars. We didn't tell you about how to find the data to populate large content grammars, like names of foods or medications. If our procedure prep VUI handles *Can I have Kentucky Fried?*, it's because it was taught to handle *Kentucky Fried* as `<food fried_chicken>`, in part thanks to ontologies.

Ontologies are knowledge bases. They show how a set of words and concepts are related within some domain. Ontologies are large hierarchies connecting synonyms and antonyms, showing what features each entry has and what's a subset of something else. Sometimes you're able to use ontologies that others have created—the Google Knowledge Graph is one such example. Various large corpora of spoken language exist that can be useful, like the British National Corpus,[5] but you may need to build your own domain-specific ontology. Think about what you'd need for the procedure prep food questions. How do food names need to be classified for your VUI to respond appropriately? Which classifications are relevant and which are not? Where do you get that info from? And what changes are needed for voice?

Creating such a knowledge base can be an overwhelming undertaking—again, don't worry! We'll show you how to tackle this, step by step. It's well worth the effort, as you'll see. You might be able to start from something that's already available, like the National Drug Code (NDC) directory, a database with names of all US medications and their classifications. But it doesn't provide pronunciations or alternative ways people say those names. You also can't go online to grab an ontology that covers all foods in your food diary or food FAQ. You can find names of dishes and foods in recipes or menus and even nutritional information. But where do you find a comprehensive knowledge base of foods and how people say them, including their color and fiber content if that's an issue for your VUI procedure? Take something as simple as cottage cheese. There's *organic cottage cheese*, *low-fat cottage cheese*, and *small curd cottage cheese*. Is it *low fat* or *lowfat* or *low-fat*?

---

[5]`www.natcorp.ox.ac.uk/corpus/index.xml`

Or *2%*? There's *non-fat* and *clabbered*—even combinations: *fat free small curd.* Is *ricotta* the same as *quark* for this purpose? How do you pronounce *chhena*? And there's *cottage strawberry cheese* or *mix-in cottage cheese.* Oh, dear. The food diary wants to capture everything; the food FAQ wants to give the right answer based on all those details.

Now think about drug names. Most medical drugs come in both brand name versions and generic versions, and many drugs have different dosage versions, different forms, and even different versions with additives. Brand and generic names are drastically different, and most patients don't know what's called what or pay attention to dosage. Go to the NDC online database search[6] and look up your favorite headache or cold medication to see just how many variants there are. And it gets worse. The most common pain medications have different generic names in different parts of the world: in the United States, the accepted generic name of para-acetylaminophenol is acetaminophen, but in Europe it's paracetamol. Try searching for Paracetamol in the NDC—it's not there, but there's over a thousand entries for Acetaminophen. But wait. There's more! Acetaminophen is different from Ibuprofen, and both are different from Aspirin. Some people incorrectly call everything aspirin (Figure 11-5)!

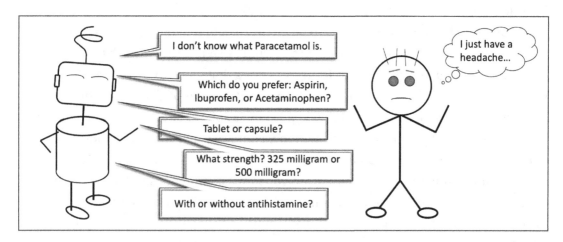

Figure 11-5. *Provide users options that make sense to them for their context*

_____

[6]www.accessdata.fda.gov/scripts/cder/ndc/index.cfm

What does it all mean for the VUI? It comes down to context and user expectations. Should your VUI understand both paracetamol and acetaminophen? Probably, your users may have grown up in different countries. The two will likely have different responses—and definitely not the same as aspirin. If you use the NDC database (or similar), you use only some database fields, but you need to add others for what voice needs: pronunciations—for the VUI and for common user variation—disambiguation needs, and slot values. From there, you can map to next steps. If the user is a patient with a refill request, VUI responses will be different from those for a medical practitioner looking up options for dosage or an NDC product label. And if a generic version is substituted for a brand name, be careful about how to make that clear to the user. Compare these three VUI response dialogs:

User   *I want a refill on my Deltasone.*

~ ~ ~   *Missing explanation*

VUI1   *OK, your Prednisone refill will be shipped tomorrow.*

User   *Wait. What? That's not what I asked for!*

~ ~ ~   *Missing explanation*

VUI2   *You want a refill of Prednisone, right?*

User   *I have no idea what you're talking about...*

~ ~ ~   *Includes clarification*

VUI3   *OK, your refill will be shipped tomorrow.*

You'll receive Prednisone, which is the generic of Deltasone.

User   *Great.*

SUCCESS TIP 11.2 BOOTSTRAPPING YOUR TAGGING   If you need a tagged or annotated data set, always check if something exists already so you don't have to start from scratch. Tagging of any type is a huge effort, it takes a long time, and it needs to be accurate. If you don't find anything that's exactly what you need, you can often find a starting point, such as a list of medication names, foods, restaurants, first or last names, city names, and so on. If other implementations exist in other modalities, such as product name databases or websites, start with those and modify them based on your voice app task. Some businesses specializing in creating data for voice tech use are starting to appear.

As mentioned in the chapter intro, it might sound like a lot of work to get all this right. Ontologies and databases tagged exactly for your needs may be hard to come by because much of it is fairly task-dependent. Therefore, it's likely that you (or your team) will do at least some of the work. Keeping your tagged data up to date can be a challenge. Tagging guides (and test scripts based on those) will help with this task—you'll learn about those next. Remember that you don't need to get it all right immediately because you'll be iterating and improving based on data, adding phrases and terms to the ontology in the process. This is where backoff strategies will help: something that provides an "out" for your users if you haven't yet implemented the coverage and variation of a final product. It can be talking to a live person or pointing to online material or an email, or some backoff menus with general, less targeted, answers. Your users will encounter this backoff strategy less over time as you expand and tune the voice system, but there's seldom any reason to remove backoffs. There will always be some reason why a user isn't understood—maybe simply because something like a new prescription is introduced and you haven't yet added this name.

Intents

You don't need to include every possible training phrase for every intent before rollout, but you do need to be ready to quickly iterate and update training phrases that reflect real user utterances and capture the intended meaning. The less accurate your first set is, the worse your VUI performs with real users, as you'll see in Chapter 17 (tuning).

Intent Tagging and Tagging Guides

You define your set of intents no matter what platform you're using. You'll have some idea of what you expect people to say to your VUI and categorize those in generalized intents that you can respond to. At the very least, you'll have filled in a few sample expressions that the platform's NLU can build on. But you want to do a great job so you've collected utterance data that you want to respond to intelligently. What do you do with this data? Well, you tag it with detailed intent labels that you define and then you capture what you did in a tagging guide so you don't forget what you did and so others can help.

Start with a set of annotated and transcribed utterances—both ones you expect people to say and ones you have been able to collect in early testing. In some platforms, this data is easily available, including with the Google SDK; in others, it's more challenging. You can use the Dialogflow training function that captures OOG utterances. You can even set up a separate data collection, recording and transcribing what your testers say.

This is a good place to mention the use of crowdsourcing platforms like Amazon's Mechanical Turk for collecting text data for early system bootstrapping. It works best for getting data for simple everyday tasks, like representative common responses to *What did you eat for breakfast?* or *What time do you typically set your alarm for on weekdays?* It's inexpensive and fast; we have used this approach ourselves many times.

Once you have some data, start your tagging by putting all text results into a column in a spreadsheet, one utterance per cell ("Utterance" column in Figure 11-6). In other columns, start categorizing utterances by similarity in meaning and explicitly mentioned content detail. As you process more utterances, you resort and see patterns evolve that you can use to formalize your groups. You start adding tags ("Tag" column in Figure 11-6).

Let's assume you have some users who really want a drink to calm their nerves before their procedure. You have a bunch of utterances asking about what's OK to drink during procedure prep. The answer is that it depends not only on how soon the procedure is or that it's alcohol but also on the color and cloudiness of the drink. Some people ask very specific questions and others more general ones. Look at the excerpt of a tagged set in Figure 11-6. Notice the variation in filler phrases, level of detail, content, generic vs. specific (one or more Xs in a column), and so on. And they're not all complete sentences. A likely first tagging scheme excerpt is overlaid.

Start slicing, adding, and modifying categories as you go. Whatever your tagging scheme and level of detail, the key is consistency. Here are some guidelines for how to tag:

- You're categorizing the users' utterances for meaning, so different content matters, but fillers and overall wording don't if the overall meaning stays the same. *Can I still drink milk?* and *Can I still drink coffee?* will be given different tags, but *Can I still drink milk?* and *Is it still OK to have milk?* get the same tags. Sidenote: *drink* has a different meaning in *Can I drink milk?* and *Can I have a drink?*—careful with that word spotting.

- The more similar two utterances are in meaning, the more similar their tags are; tags incorporate dependency similarity.

- If two utterances always result in different responses in the same context, they should have different tags; it means the meaning of those utterances are different. Ideally, your tagging scheme lets you look at a label and have a good idea what utterances belong there.

Utterance	clarity	color	type	time	Tag
what can I drink					canidrink.general
any types of wine or other alcoholic beverages that i am not allowed to drink			x		canidrink.alcohol.wine
can i consume any alcohol					canidrink.alcohol
can I have a drink					canidrink.alcohol
does alcohol count as clear liquid	x				canidrink.alcohol
is it okay to drink alcohol while i do my cleanout if it's clear	x				canidrink.alcohol
may can i still drink any alcohol					canidrink.alcohol
may i drink alcohol					canidrink.alcohol
okay do I have to avoid alcohol while i take my medications					canidrink.alcohol
is it all right to drink clear alcohol	x				canidrink.alcohol_clear
i can have green alcohol since I can have green jello		x			canidrink.alcohol_color
bee- beers okay if so which ones can I drink			x		canidrink.alcohol.beer
can i have a beer					.beer
can i can i drink beer still					cohol.beer
could drink a beer					.beer
is beer clear enough					.beer
light beer					.beer
is it alright if i drink beer					.beer
may i drink beer					.beer
should i abstain from drinking bee					.beer
is dark alcohol okay or no					_dark
can i drink vodka					.vodka
what alcohol would be okay vodk					.vodka.beer
when could i have a single malt sc					.whiskey
I seriously want some whiskey					.whiskey
can i have a glass of wine with dinner or would that affect my medication			x		canidrink.alcohol.wine
so i usually have glass of wine as part of my dinner should i skip it tonight			x	x	canidrink.time.alcohol.wine
may i have wine			x		canidrink.alcohol.wine
since i can't eat grapes can i drink wine			x		canidrink.alcohol.wine
would it be all right if i have a small glass of wine with my supper			x	x	canidrink.time.alcohol.wine

Draft naming scheme

Tag	Description
canidrink	Base intent; any question about **consuming any beverage**
canidrink.alcohol	Question about **consuming alcohol**
canidrink.alcohol_color	Question about **consuming alcohol of some color**
canidrink.alcohol_clear	Question about **consuming clear alcohol**
canidrink.alcohol_dark	Question about **consuming dark alcohol**
canidrink.alcohol.*	Question about **consuming named alcohol**
canidrink.alcohol.wine	Question about **consuming wine**
canidrink.alcohol.wine_red	Question about **consuming red wine**
canidrink.time.alcohol	Question about **consuming alcohol** at a specific time
canidrink.time.alcohol.*	Question about **consuming named alcohol** at a specific time

Figure 11-6. *User utterances, sorted by intent tags, and initial tag set*

Take a moment to really study the utterances and mapping in Figure 11-6. Think about where you might have to expand your original training utterances because of surprising ways of wording a question. Also think about what you'd need to know about the content. If there are limits on some colors of food and drink before a medical procedure (that's common), you need to know that wine and beer come in different colors and shades and that chartreuse is green or yellow. This is a tiny set of all questions to the VUI about what's allowed to drink—an even tinier set of all questions. Not a single duplicate. It gets complex fast!

Once you've settled on a tagging scheme, capture it in a tagging guide. Your tagging guide should include each tag, a description of the intent for that tag, an example utterance or two, keywords, and any additional helpful notes for using that tag. Figure 11-7 shows what a segment of a tagging guide might look like for this data.

Intent (Semantic tag)	App tag	Description	Keywords	Archetype example	VUI response in context
canidrink.general	FAQ.drink.general	Question about consuming beverages during prep; general questions not covered by other tags	drink	What can I drink	FAQ-drink for {TIME now}
canidrink.alcohol	FAQ.drink.alcohol	Question about consuming alcohol during prep. Type or color of alcohol is not specified.	alcohol booze a drink	Can I drink any alcohol	FAQ-drink for {TIME now} {DRINK alcohol}
canidrink.alcohol_ color	FAQ.drink.alcohol_color	Question about consuming alcohol during prep. Color of alcohol is specified.	alcohol + COLOR drink + COLOR	Can I drink green alcohol	FAQ-drink for {TIME now} {DRINK alcohol} {COLOR any}
canidrink.alcohol_ clear	FAQ.drink.alcohol_color	Question about consuming alcohol during prep. Clear alcohol is specified.	clear (alcohol)	Can I drink clear booze	FAQ-drink for {TIME now} {DRINK alcohol} {COLOR any}
canidrink.alcohol_ dark	FAQ.drink.alcohol_color	Question about consuming alcohol during prep. Darkness of alcohol is specified.	dark (alcohol) dark color (alcohol)	Is dark alcohol okay	FAQ-drink for {TIME now} {DRINK alcohol} {COLOR any}
canidrink.alcohol.*	FAQ.drink.alcohol.*	Question about consuming alcohol during prep. Type or color of alcohol is specified.	NAME/TYPE OF ALCOHOL	Can I have beer	FAQ-drink for {TIME now} {DRINK alcohol} {ALCOHOL *}
canidrink.alcohol. wine	FAQ.drink.alcohol.wine	Specific question about consuming wine during prep. Type or color of wine is not specified.	(QUANTITY) wine	Is it okay to drink wine	FAQ-drink for {TIME now} {DRINK alcohol} {ALCOHOL wine}
canidrink.alcohol. wine_ sparkling	FAQ.drink.alcohol.wine	Specific question about consuming wine during prep. Type or color of wine is specified.	champagne sparkling wine cava	Can I have sparkling wine	FAQ-drink for {TIME now} {DRINK alcohol} {ALCOHOL wine}
canidrink.time.alcohol	FAQ.drink.time.alcohol	Question about consuming alcohol at a specified time. Type or color of alcohol is not specified.	alcohol + TIME and/or DAY booze + TIME and/or DAY a drink + TIME and/or DAY	Can I drink alcohol after 10 pm	FAQ-drink for {TIME *} {DRINK alcohol} {ALCOHOL wine}
canidrink.time. alcohol.*	FAQ.drink.time.alcohol.*	Question about consuming alcohol at a specified time. Type or color of alcohol is specified.	NAME/TYPE OF ALCOHOL TIME and/or DAY	Is beer okay the day of my procedure	FAQ-drink for {TIME *} {DRINK alcohol} {ALCOHOL *}
canidrink.time.alcohol .white_wine	FAQ.drink.time.alcohol. wine	Specific example of canidrink.time.alcohol.*	ALCOHOL + TIME and/or DAY	Is white wine ok after 10pm	FAQ-drink for {TIME *} {DRINK alcohol} {ALCOHOL wine}

Figure 11-7. *Excerpt of a tagging guide covering for representative utterances in Figure 11-6*

How do you know how granular to make your intents? As usual, the answer is *It depends*! Some guidelines: The more granular your semantic tags are, the more flexibility you have to respond in ways that sound smart. It's also more work. In this set, you could have just one intent, `canidrink`, which maps to a single general response about what's OK to drink leading up to the procedure. But that's not as helpful as it could be: a conversational VUI that recognizes what's said should respond to it as well. Note that we decided to respond to exact times, like *10 PM*—we simplified by planning to cover that more generally in the response.

Tagged data is useful at every step of your voice project, during design and development and for testing and tuning (Chapters 16 and 17).

SUCCESS TIP 11.3 TAG, YOU'RE IT!   It might be tempting to offload tagging to a group who's a step removed from the data they're tagging. If you choose that route or if your organization demands it, be sure to create a detailed tagging guide and stay in contact to address questions when new utterances come up. Taggers have the best of intentions but may be unfamiliar with the domain, product, or task that makes it harder for them to know what's important. In addition, treat your tagging guide as part of your IP: it's part of your "secret sauce" if your intent models are based on many hours of your work that's often involved in creating them. Don't underestimate their value.

Middle Layers: Semantic Tags vs. System Endpoints

When we worked on creating NL solutions for call center routing at Nuance, a distinction was made between **semantic tags** and **application tags**. Semantic tags label user intent, staying as close as possible to what most likely was the user's intended meaning of the utterance based on transcriptions and context. Application (or app) tags label the VUI behavior, the system's response to each interpreted request. This distinction forces you to separate what the user wants from what you can give them. Semantic tags represent the user's meaning based on transcriptions and context, while app tags encode the fulfillment. Semantic tags tend to be more fine-grained than app tags, so you end up with many-to-one or one-to-one mappings from semantic to app, but never one-to-many—in fact, that would result in ambiguity. So `canidrink.alcohol_clear` and `canidrink.alcohol_color` are two semantic tags that map to the app tag `FAQ.drink.alcohol_color`, and the response includes information relevant to both. Think of app tags as a way to map the user's raw requests to slots and intents that the VUI can deal with without having to deal with variation that doesn't matter in a particular case. It's a way to control variation from getting out of control: interpreting what the user said without losing meaning by ignoring "irrelevant" variation. If an app tag covers a set of utterances that needs disambiguation for the VUI to respond appropriately, then the semantic-to-app mapping will highlight what disambiguation options are expected.

Figure 11-7 showed how the two interact. A "VUI response" column formalizes the expected destination in the flow, or type of VUI response expected in the dialog. This column could also link to other VUI modules and destinations by any naming convention you have in place already. For large systems, this mapping is extremely useful when testing that transitions sound smooth in context.

This distinction between semantic and app tags is useful not just for IVRs but for any conversational systems with a broad set of topics or requests with different outcomes. We've used this approach for different types of voice systems and devices. Here's why it's handy:

- Users don't know your story. They're not asking for a specific VUI behavior or call center group; they're asking for some content or information and will ask similarly for other similar VUIs even if the VUIs respond differently.

- The app tags serve as a middle layer that can be more quickly and easily remapped with semantic tags than having to redo the per-utterance tagging, reminiscent of dependency injection.

- All the effort spent on semantic tagging of a large data set can be reused for similar domains and tasks or for other clients by updating the mapping between tags rather than redo the per-utterance tagging.

- When something changes in your system, like the addition of a feature or a handoff to a human, it's quick to modify the app tag destination and change the response.

- You can combine semantic tags into fewer tags if you notice few people make a distinction you made. Or split them when you notice a pattern you can develop for.

There are many reasons for creating a tagging guide for utterance tagging:

- Design
    - Provides a concrete basis for design decisions
    - Helps fine-tune response wording to match user utterances within each tag
    - Clarifies what slots and values are needed to cover requests
- Grammar development
    - Helps with verifying grammar robustness and coverage
    - Provides a structure when using tagged data for SLM training
- Testing and tuning
    - As a companion to the dialog spec, a basis for creating test cases
    - Helps verify that design and implementation handles all cases
- Productivity and team communication
    - Provides a guide for others to use and refer to
- Insights
    - By categorizing utterances, provides an understanding of variation in speech
    - Helps in tracking changes over time and analyzing utterance distribution
    - Provides data for determining future feature expansion

If your VUI gives snarky responses—and we're not suggesting it should—like *Yes* to *Can you turn up the volume?*, then you'd use different tags for that and for *Turn up the volume*; if you simply try to help the user, you'd label them the same because the user meant the same with both.

Putting It All Together

We've covered a lot of information about how to understand the words and meaning of a user's utterance to map it to a response. Let's look at how to put all the pieces together to maximize your chance that this response is the best one.

Matching Wide or Narrow

Think of intent matching as a set of funnels or sieves going from finer to coarser: if the user is specific, give an equally narrow response; if they're general or vague, respond with something more general. It's better to respond with something reasonable than to not respond at all or to respond with the wrong level of detail. Here are four sample dialogs:

1. **User**   *Can I eat brown rice today?* → Specific, in ontology

   VUI   *Brown rice is off the menu till after your procedure.*

~ ~ ~

2. **User**   *Can I eat rice today?* → general, in ontology

   VUI   *You can still have white rice, but brown rice is off the menu...*

~ ~ ~

3. **User**   *Can I eat sticky galangal rice today?* → specific, not in ontology

   VUI   *I haven't heard of that, but most rice dishes are off the menu till after your procedure.*

~ ~ ~

4. **User**   *Can I eat galangal today?* → general, not in ontology

   VUI   *I'm not sure what that is. In general, today you can still eat some solid food. Do not eat high-fiber food till after your procedure.*

   1. In the ontology, *brown rice* is detailed enough for a detailed targeted response.

   2. The response to the more general *rice* explains the relevant difference between the specific types.

3. Assuming that *sticky galangal rice* isn't in the ontology, the response is more general, acknowledging that it's outside the VUI's knowledge but still providing a cautious response based on what it did understand (*rice*).

4. If the item isn't understood, you still know it's a food question here (*eat*) and can give an answer rather than reject it outright. Or ask the user for more information. For example, *I'm not sure what that is. Does it have high fiber, grains, or red sauce?*

Multiple Grammars, Multiple Passes

Earlier in this chapter, you learned that parsing lets you capture utterances that would have fallen outside your domain grammar coverage. Multiple passes can give you the most robust intent resolution. We've been successful combining a first pass of exact matching on carefully ordered regular expressions with a second pass of parsing or SLMs. The benefit is that regular expressions are powerful mechanisms for catching complex patterns succinctly—when they match, they're predictable and a match (or lack thereof) is easy to explain. SLMs are more powerful for broad utterance variability, but less predictable. And, since they're statistical, SLMs might needlessly punish rarely occurring requests, making it harder for users to be understood in those cases. This approach is particularly useful for VUIs that deal with costly domains where you need to be able to show why something was or was not recognized, like in the medical domain. You can even implement different paths through the dialog depending on which grammar was engaged. Because of the precise match possible with a regular expression grammar, a match can be less in need of confirmation or disambiguation than when the match is only with an SLM that captures the general gist (Figure 11-8).

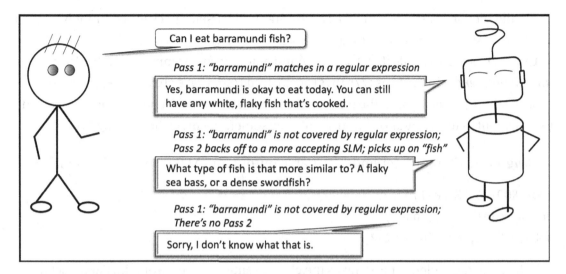

Figure 11-8. *Multiple passes can lead to better overall coverage and responses with different dialog paths*

This approach is also useful for disambiguation contexts. Let's say you have an open-ended prompt with a broad and large set of possible destinations or endpoints, like a shopping app. If there's ambiguity, the app might follow-up with *Which do you want: X, Y, or Z?* One way to implement this is to create a dynamic grammar that only allows X, Y, and Z. A more efficient method could be to use the full grammar, but postprocess the results, allowing only X, Y, or Z. This postprocessing can be done by using the STT in N-best mode. An N-best list returns a ranked list of possible matches; starting with the top ranked result, you traverse the list until a result is considered valid that's then returned. You'll learn more about N-best in Chapter 12.

You can also use this approach with a third-party STT engine like Google or others. Even if you can't access or control the main grammar that's used, you can still postprocess the results to return the result that makes sense within the current context.

The Stanford Parser Revisited

Let's use one of our intents to see how to apply rule-based NLP techniques. Take another look at the `tcrMakeAppointment` intent, the intent encoding user requests for making an appointment with their care provider. You added these sample phrases for the intent:

- "Make an appointment."
- "Make an appointment for three."
- "Make an appointment for three PM."

In the section "Parsing," you first saw the Stanford Parser, a package commonly used for parsing sentences into their various syntactic structural components. Go to `http://nlp.stanford.edu:8080/parser/` and enter the first sample utterance *Make an appointment* or here `https://nlp.stanford.edu/software/lex-parser.html` to download the parser. Look at the parse in the section Universal Dependencies, Enhanced (an augmented representation). You should see something much like Listing 11-1.

Listing 11-1. Stanford dependency parse output for "Make an appointment"

```
root(ROOT-0, Make-1)
det(appointment-3, an-2)
dobj(Make-1, appointment-3)
```

Here, the dependency parse takes the classic sentence parse from the Parse section and uses a large set of rules to create a different kind of parse tree that tries to put the more important meaning-bearing words at the root of the tree, with modifiers and filler words further down toward the leaves.

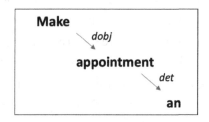

Figure 11-9. *Stanford dependency parse tree for "Make an appointment"*

Figure 11-9 shows the dependency parse tree for *Make an appointment*: a graphical representation of what you saw in Listing 11-1. Each element in Listing 11-1 has the following components:

- The type of relationship between the parent in the tree and the child, for example, ROOT, dobj, and det. More about these relationships in a moment.

- A parent node, such as ROOT-0 or Make-1. The numbers represent the word in the sentence in order of appearance. They're necessary to make sure the nodes are unique in case there are multiple of the same word in the sentence.

- A child node.

Here, *Make* is the root node of the tree. In a dependency parse, the main verb in the sentence is usually at the root of the tree. Next down the tree is "appointment" that has a **dobj**, or direct object, relationship with the root node "Make." Finally, there's "an" that has a **det**, or determiner, relationship to "appointment." Again, the most "meaningful" words are at the root of the tree, and the less meaningful words are lower, or more leaf-like. This means that to determine the meaning of the sentence, you'd focus on the root of the dependency parse tree.

Next, enter the longest of the three sentences *Make an appointment for three PM* and look at the parse result (Listing 11-2 and Figure 11-10).

Listing 11-2a. Stanford dependency parse output for "Make an appointment for three PM"

```
root(ROOT-0, Make-1)
det(appointment-3, an-2)
dobj(Make-1, appointment-3)
case(PM-6, for-4)
nummod(PM-6, three-5)
nmod(appointment-3, PM-6)
```

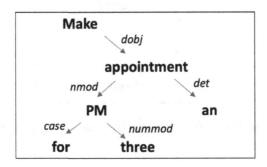

Figure 11-10. *Stanford dependency parse tree for "Make an appointment for three PM"*

As you can see, the root part of the tree is the same, but the addition of *for three PM* results in additional elements branching off the main part. This is what you want: sentences with the same meaning should have the same structure near the root to reflect this similarity.

What if your user wants to schedule an appointment but words it differently (Figure 11-11)? As you've seen, you can get away with not handling that explicitly on many platforms, thanks to statistical models basing understanding on the sample utterances you provide. But that's not always the case. If your user says something like *Arrange a meeting*, it's not handled by the sentences used to train `tcrMakeAppointment`.

Listing 11-2b. Stanford dependency parse output for "Arrange a meeting for three PM"

```
root(ROOT-0, Arrange-1)
det(meeting-3, a-2)
dobj(Arrange-1, meeting-3)
case(PM-6, for-4)
nummod(PM-6, three-5)
nmod(meeting-3, PM-6)
```

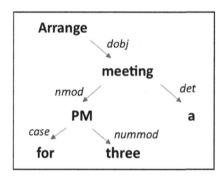

Figure 11-11. *Stanford dependency parse tree for "Arrange a meeting for three PM"*

Determining Intent

So parse trees are fun, but how do they help with determining intent? Take a look at a tree again:

- There's a root node: "Arrange."

- There's a dobj node as a child of the root node: "meeting."

That sounds like the meaning of the intent! Imagine having additional rules for determining slot values, like the time of the appointment—these rules would be based on child nodes of the "meeting" node. Time for some code for these rules.

Introducing spaCy

For the code, we're using a different intent, `arTodaysTasks` (for questions about what needs to be done today). `tcrMakeAppointment` was good for illustrating the usefulness of dependency parses, especially when there's qualifying information to add. But in this example, we don't want to focus on the complexity of filling slots like time and AM/PM, so instead we start with an intent that doesn't need slots.

Because we're changing things up, we're also using another dependency parser: the open source spaCy.[7] We're using spaCy because

- We wanted to stress that there are multiple packages out there for NLU; many provide very similar representations and are equally good options.

- Many industrial applications lately use spaCy.

- The code for using spaCy is a little simpler than for the Stanford Parser.

- The non-web-based Stanford Parser is written in Java, so it doesn't fit well into our Python framework.

- The web-based Stanford Parser relies on a web service that is usually up, but we've seen it not be.

- spaCy has some performance advantages that we'll discuss.

Let's dive in!

---

[7]`https://spacy.io/`

Loading spaCy

The first thing is to load spaCy into your system. This involves adding some lines to your `requirements.txt` file, as shown in Listing 11-3.

Listing 11-3. Changes to requirements.txt to load spaCy

```
setuptools
wheel
spacy>=2.0.0,<3.0.0
https://github.com/explosion/spacy-models/releases/download/en_core_web_sm-
2.3.1/en_core_web_sm-2.3.1.tar.gz#en_core_web_sm
```

We don't recommend that you type these in; just copy the `requirements.txt` file from the code example. That complicated last line (which is long, so it spans two lines in the text) loads the models that spaCy uses to do NLU. There are a number of models available in several languages.[8]

After changing `requirements.txt`, you need to load the software, which will depend on your deployment method:

- When you deploy with gcloud app deploy on Google Cloud, the new needed software and models get installed automatically.

- If you're running the webhook locally with ngrok (as you saw in Chapter 10), you'll need to install it manually via pip install -r requirements.txt.

Calling spaCy

The next step is to call spaCy, providing a dependency parse for a given piece of text. Listing 11-4 shows this new code, in a new file `spacy_parser.py`. First, load the models (A), making sure to use the same models that were loaded in the requirements.txt file. Then, run spaCy on the input text (B). Next, initialize the empty list of dependency parse nodes (C), and loop through the nodes in the spaCy output (D), adding to the list of dependency parse nodes (K). Each parse tree node is represented by a dictionary with

---

[8]https://spacy.io/models

420

- The text (E)

- The lemma (F), or stem of the word ("run" is the lemma of "run," "ran," "runs," "running," etc.)

- The index of the token (G) in the entire sentence (0 for the first word, 1 for the second, etc.)

- The relation to the parent node (H), which is "ROOT" for the root node

- The index of the parent node (I)

- The part-of-speech tag for the node (J)

Finally, return the list of dependency parse nodes (L).

Listing 11-4. Calling spaCy to provide a dependency parse

```
def dependency_parse(text):
    """

    Get the spaCy dependency parse.
    Each node has:
    text
    dependency relation to parent (ROOT) if root
    parent node
    part of speech
    """

    # Load the spaCy models
    nlp = spacy.load('en_core_web_sm')          # A

    # Run spaCy
    doc = nlp(text)                             # B

    # Initialize and collect the dependency parse
    parse = []                                  # C

    for token in doc:                           # D
        node = {"text": token.text,             # E
                "lemma": token.lemma_,          # F
                "index": token.i,               # G
```

```
            "relation": token.dep_,                    # H
            "parent_index": token.head.text,           # I
            "pos": token.head.pos_}                     # J
        parse.append(node)                              # K

    return parse                                        # L
```

Using spaCy's Dependency Parse

Now that you can get the dependency parse from spaCy, let's use it! First, let's take a look at the dependency parse for the "What should I do today?" phrase from the arTodaysTasks intent. Similar to what you did with the Stanford Parser, you can get the spaCy parse on the Web at https://explosion.ai/demos/displacy. Figure 11-12 shows what the parse looks like.

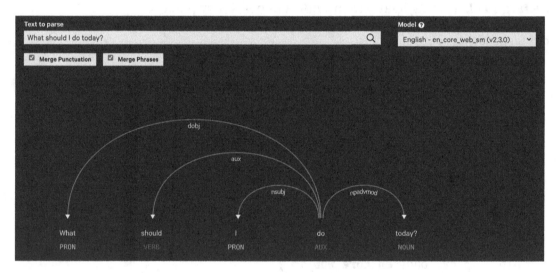

Figure 11-12. *spaCy's dependency parse for "What should I do today?"*

It looks a little different from the tree-looking structures you saw earlier. This is how dependency parses are frequently visualized (the Stanford Parser used a similar visualization in Figure 11-4). We have our root "do" and then all the other words ("tokens" in NLP parlance) hanging off "do," notably "What" with the dobj relationship to the root.

From this, we can imagine a sensible set of criteria for the `arTodaysTasks` intent to be as follows:

- The lemma of the root is "do."

- There is a dobj off the root that has a lemma "what."

You may ask why both these rules are based on the lemmas rather than the raw text. Typically for determining meaning, the prime interest is the stem of the word of interest, not, for instance, whether it was capitalized or lowercase, singular or plural, present tense or past tense, which are all different for the raw text. It's much easier to write a single rule looking for the lemma "do" than to use the various possible raw texts: does, did, doing, done, and all the capitalized forms. The lemma is basically capturing the core meaning.

Now that you have some sensible rules, let's see the code (Listing 11-5, in `fallback.py`). The first part (A) may be familiar from Chapter 10; here you try using regular expressions on the sentence text to look for the repeat intent. If that doesn't succeed (B), you get the dependency parse from spaCy (C) and then start looking for features that you can use for rules. The first feature is the root node. Loop through the dependency parse nodes (D); when you find the one with relation ROOT, set the index (E) and lemma (F) of the root node. Next, look for a token that has the relation of dobj to its parent (G) and the root node as its parent (H), setting the feature when you find it (I). Finally, you can implement the rules (J) using the features. When you find it, trigger the intent (K), exactly like in Chapter 10. If the dependency parse didn't find anything, return what Dialogflow was going to say anyway (L).

A nice "feature" of breaking this task into subtasks of determining features and then applying rules based on them is that with a small number of features, you can implement rules for many kinds of intents that are of interest.

Here you're only looking for one intent, but you can imagine a lot of intents of the form "do this ACTION to that THING" that can be coded with the root node verb corresponding to the ACTION and the direct object (dobj) off the root node corresponding to the THING.

The Stanford Parser has a tool called `semgrex`: basically regular expressions for dependency parse trees. It's designed to do exactly the kinds of things we're doing here: search for patterns in the trees. The very new 3.0 version of spaCy includes the same sort of semgrex-like functionality for finding patterns in dependency parses—exactly what you're doing here, but you just do it manually.

Listing 11-5. Using spaCy dependency parse to look for arTodaysTasks

```
if re.search('((say( that)? )?again|repeat( that)?)( please)?',      #A
            df_request.query_text):

    # repeat

    # Trigger the confirmYes event.
    df_response.event_to_trigger = 'repeat'
else:      #B
    # No hit with regular expressions; try dependency parse

    parse = dependency_parse(df_request.query_text)     #C

    # Collect features from the dependency parse tree

    # Get the root node in the dependency parse tree
    root_verb_index = None
    root_verb_lemma = None
    for node in parse:      #D
        if node.get('relation') == 'ROOT':
            root_verb_index = node.get('index')     #E
            root_verb_lemma = node.get('lemma')     #F

    # Get a dobj off the root node
    dobj_lemma = None
    for node in parse:
        if (node.get('relation') == 'dobj' and      #G
                node.get('parent_index') == root_verb_index):     #H
            dobj_lemma = node.get('lemma')     #I

    if root_verb_lemma == 'do' and dobj_lemma == 'what':      #J
        # "What should I do today?."

        # Trigger arTodaysTasks
        df_response.event_to_trigger = 'arTodaysTasks'      #K
    else:
        # No dependency parse match; do what Dialogflow would have

        df_response.output_text = df_request.fulfillment_text     #L
```

Dialogflow Changes

Almost there! You do need a couple of Dialogflow changes, just like in Chapter 10:

- Remove the sample phrases from the arTodaysTasks intent, so you hit the Default Fallback Intent when the user says those phrases.

- Add the event arTodaysTasks to the intent.

CHOOSING AN NLU ENGINE

You've seen two NLU engines in this chapter, the Stanford Parser and spaCy. They're only two of many, which is great: you can find one that best fits your needs—make sure to add this step to your discovery (Chapter 4). Two performance criteria many people use for NLU engines are accuracy of parses and throughput (number of words/sentences the engine can process per second). Choi, Tetreault, and Stent (2015)[9] compare ten different NLU engines based on a set of metrics including these two criteria and show one of the reasons why spaCy is so popular in real-world industrial applications: it has mid-to-high accuracy of 89.6% and the highest throughput (14000 tokens/second). Also, spaCy is accessible from Python, which continues to be the language of choice for NLP and machine learning in general.

In-Depth: Understanding, Parsing, and Knowledge in Practice

This chapter has introduced some pretty advanced topics because we want you to have some understanding of what you can do today without a massive effort to improve understanding while also realizing why it's tricky and not solved. This is the most exciting and challenging area of language technology today and will be for years to come. It involves deeper understanding and representation of cognition—we'll wrap up this chapter with some additional comments, and we encourage you to search online for the latest developments and solutions.

---

[9]Choi, Jinho, Tetreault, Joel, and Stent, Amanda (2015). It Depends: Dependency Parser Comparison Using A Web-based Evaluation Tool. 1. 387–396. 10.3115/v1/P15-1038 (www.aclweb.org/anthology/P15-1038.pdf).

Revisiting Intents

In this and the previous chapter, you've seen two distinctly different ways to use NLP to determine users' intended meaning:

- Using regular expressions from the raw text (Chapter 10)

- Using higher-level natural language constructs to write more general rules (this chapter)

There are other knowledge-based methods as well. spaCy has a Rule-Based Matcher that allows you to write rules based on the text, lemma, part of speech, and other attributes. It has a lot of similarities to what we did in this chapter, without the hierarchical tree-based structure to the tokens. You can interactively try out the Rule-Based Matcher at `https://explosion.ai/demos/matcher`.

So far in this book, we've talked a lot about intents, or what the user wants to do. The intent is an incredibly useful structure for simplifying the development of voice applications; first, you determine the intent from speech and text, and then based on the intent, you decide what to do next in the dialog. This is simplified in Figure 11-13.

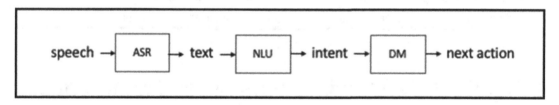

Figure 11-13. *Current dialog system pipeline using intents*

There's been a movement lately in the voice development community to do away with intents and that intents are an artificial creation that actually hinders our evolution to more fully conversational systems. See, for instance, `https://blog.rasa.com/its-about-time-we-get-rid-of-intents/` where the following example illustrates some of the complexities:

User   *I'm looking for a restaurant.*

System   *How about Chinese food?*

User   *I had that yesterday.*

System   *How about Italian food?*

You can see why this natural (for a human) dialog can be tricky to handle. Within the context of intents, or the way you'd do this in Dialogflow, "I had that yesterday" would be a sample training phrase for a `confirmNo` intent. But you probably would never use that phrase for such a generic intent; it only makes sense as a synonym for "no" in that very particular context. It only implies "no" in this context, so it's domain-specific. That makes it no less valid as a response, so it needs to be handled correctly, but not as part of a general "Yes/No" intent. It's valid, or salient, within the intent "`restaurant.recommendation`." You can of course (and you did in the last two chapters) expand your grammar by adding custom meaning determination in the webhook that's very specific to the current domain (and intent) and then trigger the negative confirmation. All that custom work significantly increases complexity, which is why people search for alternatives, but its importance is the reason for much of the discussion in the last two chapters. The argument is to bypass the notion of intents and determine or train the next dialog step directly from training phrases and not have the intent "in the middle." Figure 11-14 shows this schematically, where intents can be bypassed, but don't have to be.

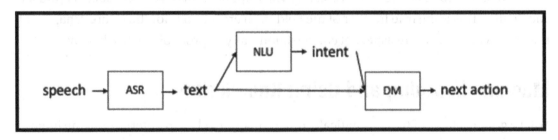

Figure 11-14. *Optional bypass of the intent, to determine next action directly from text*

From the standpoint of enabling fully conversational systems, there is a point to this in that the concept of an intent limits what you can do in most platforms today. However, it's still a useful concept, especially if you think of "intent" as a way to capture for "semantic interpretation" or "result of interpreting the core meaning of what the user said in the context of the current dialog," which is how we think of it. W3C, an organization that focuses on standards and guidelines, puts it this way: "What is needed is a computer processable representation of the information, the Semantic Result, more than a natural language transcript. The process of producing a Semantic Result representing the meaning of a natural language utterance is called Semantic

Interpretation."[10] The key here is to not throw out the baby with the bathwater, but keep what's meaningful and useful while improving the tools and representations used to make it easier to create ever-better and complex conversational voice interactions. The need for robust dialogs that allow users flexibility while also recognizing underlying meaning has long been acknowledged by speech folks, in fact. If you're interested in diving in deeper, check out a dense but informative paper by Lemon and Gruenstein.[11]

Of course, the question is: how do you directly determine the next dialog action from text—another interpretation of what was actually said—without the intermediate representation of contextual meaning? This is a very complex problem and where the need for deeper semantic models comes in, models that can be incorporated in the frameworks or tools that enable the development of such systems. Conversations are not just superficial statistical predictions. Nor are they stateless or dependent only on what one thing was said 5 seconds ago. It's not just being able to build a proof-of-concept or a prototype. It's a question of understanding how people talk and think and building something that they will use because they feel understood in their specific context, including domain and speech acts, as mentioned by Lemon and Gruenstein. And it's a question of how to scale the process, so that voice application developers such as yourself can do this. This is the true frontier of the field, with great hopes for the future. Chapter 14 is all about context, a core aspect of conversations, as you probably realize by now.

Machine Learning and Using Knowledge

You've gotten a taste of two dramatically different approaches to determining the intent of an utterance:

- **Statistical approaches**: Machine learning (ML) that automatically learns intents from training phrases, as we showed earlier, and that Dialogflow relies on.

- **Rule-based approaches**: More knowledge-driven human-in-the-loop methods, like the example we just went through using the Stanford Parser.

---

[10]www.w3.org/TR/semantic-interpretation/

[11]Multithreaded Context for Robust Conversational Interfaces: Context-Sensitive Speech Recognition and Interpretation of Corrective Fragments. O. Lemon and A. Gruenstein. ACM Transactions on Computer-Human Interaction, Vol. 11, No. 3, September 2004, pages 241–267.

The tension between these two approaches is real, and it's been a hallmark of the speech/natural language community for a long time. Fred Jelinek, a big name in early ASR and NLP research, famously said that their system performance went up every time a linguist left the project.[12] Well, there's no need to be that rude to linguists (read "Part-of-speech tagging from 97% to 100%: Is it time for some linguistics?" by Chris Manning[13]). There's room for both approaches, even a need for both, as we've suggested in this chapter. Rule-based approaches require a lot of careful work by people who understand the domain of the VUI as well as how people talk. This makes rules precise and predictable, but rules won't capture every possible wording. Statistical approaches, on the other hand, are powerful, as long as they're trained on relevant data. SLMs need to be trained on a lot of data to be robust enough for people to want to use such a voice system. By nature, the most common interpretations are favored at the cost of less common requests.

With the advances of deep learning in the past few years, it's become possible to reach high performance on previously out-of-reach tasks like broad conversational NLU using automatic machine learning techniques. Dialogflow in particular takes advantage of this; 15 years ago, it wouldn't have been possible to get passable intent accuracy when specifying only a few sample training phrases. Today, you can, at least to a point. But as you reach into domains and tasks that don't rely on mature data models or that demand predictable high accuracy, you'll want to incorporate some rules. If nothing else, rules will allow you to go into production faster so that you can collect data that will feed your statistical models.

A big benefit of current ML approaches is that they open up voice development to more practitioners. Like you! You can live happily with ML and never worry about rules. But understand that there are cases where rule-based approaches provide a better answer, especially with little data, which is why we encourage you to learn about them. You become more independent and able to create robust VUIs in new domains, but you will need to move toward something like the raw Google Cloud Speech-to-Text API. Rules force you to think carefully about language, and that's good—voice systems are all about understanding language, after all.

---

[12]https://sciencenonfiction.org/2014/12/18/why-computer-scientists-and-linguists-dont-always-see-eye-to-eye/

[13]https://nlp.stanford.edu/pubs/CICLing2011-manning-tagging.pdf

The Not-So-Distant Future?

Taking machine learning to its current extreme, OpenAI's latest language model GPT-3[14] has 175 billion parameters and is trained with 5 data sets of almost 500 billion words captured from web crawling and book text, though OpenAI used "only" 300 billion words for training.[15] Training the model required three million-billion-billion flops (floating-point operations), or 3000 years on a single new Apple M chip.

GPT-3 is designed for what's known as few-shot learning: basically, you give a few examples of the correct response for different phrases, and the model does the rest. This should sound familiar. Dialogflow does something similar with training phrases, but isn't as generic as GPT-3. In theory, GPT-3 is also designed to not only provide intent but also the NL response, so it incorporates the NLU, DM, and NLG functionalities of our generic voice system.

So is the future of voice apps a "one-stop shop" API for all your understanding and dialog needs? Maybe, but…don't wait for that before you build your next conversation system, especially not one that gives medical advice to its users. If your knowledge representations are based on website training data unrelated to your domain and the NLU is a black box in terms of the responses your users get, you can't just turn it on and hope for the best—OpenAI would be first to warn you.[16] You also still need to handle some contextual domain-specific knowledge. Even with 175 billion parameters, a generically trained language model won't know what time your local McDonald's closes this Wednesday. What you're learning in this book will still be useful!

What's Next?

Chapter 10 and this chapter have brought you further into the core of speech science. You can't have a successful conversational VUI without robust recognition and understanding. Good VUI design can compensate for some shortcomings, but not all. The more you understand how STT and NLU work on the platform you choose for your VUI, the more successful you'll be. In Chapter 16, you'll learn about how to refine STT and NLU based on the user data you collect. If you're interested in NLP and NLU, we

---

[14]https://openai.com/blog/openai-api/

[15]https://arxiv.org/pdf/2005.14165.pdf

[16]www.nabla.com/blog/gpt-3/

strongly encourage you to look at what's available, including open source options. It's exciting and constantly changing. There's no doubt that the future of voice lies in deeper understanding, NLU that incorporates semantics, discourse structure and real-world knowledge, as well as some representation of rules.

No matter how solid your STT and NLU are, there will be misunderstandings. Chapter 12 covers how to minimize them in the first place; Chapter 13 shows how to get back on track when they happen.

Summary

- NLP is the syntactic and structural pipe through which STT output passes to become useful for NLU.

- Tagging utterance data has many uses that will help your VUI be robust and successful.

- Using multiple passes with different grammar types and parsing can increase VUI performance by capturing ever-broader user requests while also handling rarely spoken utterances.

- There's still a place today for doing intent determination using classic NLP techniques like parsing and knowledge-based rules, as well as using machine learning techniques such as those incorporated into Dialogflow.

CHAPTER 12

Applying Accuracy Strategies to Avoid Misunderstanding

With the background you gained about recognition and intents in Chapters 10 and 11, this chapter is the first of two on specific techniques you can apply to make VUI conversations more successful for users. These strategies focus on increasing the chances that the VUI recognizes and interprets correctly and that it can recover when misunderstandings happen.

This is actually one of our favorite topics. No, it's not because we love misunderstandings—we're not that crazy. It's because misunderstandings will always happen, no matter the state of the technology or the user's expertise. Figuring out how to minimize those misunderstandings is like a puzzle for a good cause; the rewarding goal is happy successful users and a successful VUI. Our experience with enterprise solutions may be behind our interest. In a 2019 episode of the podcast *This Week in Tech*, the host and guests commented on their dislike of working on enterprise solutions while also noting how happy they were that someone wants to do it. Enterprise-level development involves a lot of work with demands of high accuracy and often less "fun" designs. But if you learn the techniques that address enterprise performance needs, you can apply them to build superior conversational VUIs for any domain on any platform. The same general concepts apply across all VUIs.

We introduce a lot of accuracy strategies in this chapter. We don't expect you to learn everything about them after reading this chapter, so don't get overwhelmed. Instead, just appreciate that there are many approaches for a reason, you don't need to implement all of them at once, and if you find that your voice system is having trouble, there's probably a particular method you can apply to address the issue. We summarize all the methods at the end of the chapter.

© Ann Thymé-Gobbel, Charles Jankowski 2021
A. Thymé-Gobbel and C. Jankowski, *Mastering Voice Interfaces*, https://doi.org/10.1007/978-1-4842-7005-9_12

Accuracy Robustness Concepts

First, some definitions (Figure 12-1). Out-of-coverage (OOC) and its superset out-of-grammar (OOG) are both relevant concepts: both can result in misrecognition and misunderstanding, but the solution is different. You have direct impact on coverage by expanding the words in a grammar; noise and fragments may be outside your abilities to do much about, but you learn more about them in Chapter 17 (tuning).

Table 12-1. *Common speech accuracy concepts*

If an utterance is...	The utterance is...
In-grammar (IG)	Included in relevant grammars; matches what's expected.
Out-of-grammar (OOG)	Not in-grammar, including noise, fragments, and side speech.
Out-of-coverage (OOC)	A phrase that's valid in the language but not covered in-grammar.
If the outcome is...	**The utterance is...**
Correct accept (CA)	In-grammar and handled successfully.
Correct reject (CR)	Out-of-grammar and rejected successfully.
False accept in-grammar (FA-in)	In-grammar but recognized as another in-grammar utterance.
False reject (FR)	In-grammar but not recognized as anything in-grammar.
False accept out-of-grammar (FA-out)	Out-of-grammar but recognized as an in-grammar utterance.

Figure 12-1 illustrates the concepts in Table 12-1 using two actual drug names, Prednisone and Prednisolone and a few possible user pronunciations of them. The two darker clouds represent grammar coverage: the darkest cloud represents the grammar for Prednisolone, and the lighter gray represents Prednisone. The two white clouds represent what's recognized and mapped to something in each grammar. Some utterances are similar enough that the recognizer matches them even when not strictly covered by the grammar; others are miscategorized or even thrown out by the recognizer because of how they're pronounced.

In this example, one of the Prednisolone utterances is incorrectly matched to the grammar for Prednisone (making it a falsely accepted in-grammar item, or FA-in), and another is not matched to anything (it's falsely rejected, or FR). Prednilone is not a real drug name and is correctly not mapped to anything in-grammar (correct reject, or CR). Prednidone also isn't a real name, but was mistakenly mapped to the Prednisone grammar (a false accept of something out-of-grammar, or FA-out). When you learn about tuning in Chapter 17, you build further on these concepts.

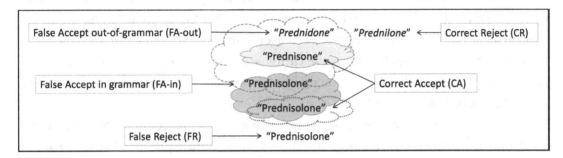

Figure 12-1. *Accuracy concepts illustrated with medication names*

Accuracy Robustness Strategies

Maximizing the proportion of correct outcomes while minimizing false ones is of course the goal. In this chapter, you learn about some of the strategies involved.

SUCCESS TIP 12.1 FINDING ROBUSTNESS CLUES   The best place to get ideas for how to improve robustness is to look at the wording and interpretation of OOG utterances and what utterances came before and after the current one in the dialog flow.

Examples

People are surprisingly good at generalizing from examples—assuming they're good examples! Good examples are better and shorter than instructions. Work done at Nuance[1] suggests that well-chosen examples can help users succeed when formulating their requests at an open prompt for a statistical language model (SLM). Use natural phrases and make clear that they're examples, not a menu of two options.

---

[1]Say it Like You Mean it: Priming for Structure in Caller Responses to a Spoken Dialog System. Sheeder, T. and Balogh, J. *International Journal of Speech Technology* (2003) 6: 103.

The best examples show the depth and breadth of what can be requested. Make examples relevant to each user and include common requests; something about the to-do list is a good example in the procedure prep VUI. Another example asking about a specific food item shows how detailed a request can be: *For example, say "What's on my to-do list today?" or say "Can I still eat whole wheat bread?..."* If you're building a VUI for a bank and have metadata on the users' account types, you can even use those names to make the examples more relevant to each user than generic names: *You can say "Transfer 200 dollars from checking to education savings" or "When's my next credit card payment due?..."* It's more work for you up front, but a better user experience with more successful users down the road.

Fun fact: Over the years, we've seen a surprising number of examples of people not separating instructions from commands. That's why we phrase prompts like this: *For example, say "Order a refill"* instead of *Say, for example, "Order a refill."* Or *Enter or say your PIN* instead of *Say or enter your PIN.* Otherwise, some people say things like *Or enter your PIN.*

Implementing Examples

Be sure to test any examples you tell your users to say, as well as any other phrases you explicitly mention in your VUI prompts. Pay special attention to risks of examples clashing with other phrases users are likely to say. If people can't be understood when saying exactly what you told them to say, they won't be happy. This is where combining regular expression rule-based grammars with statistical models comes in handy: use rules for your example phrases and pass the utterance through that grammar before handing off to the SLM. You learned about doing regular expressions from the webhook in Chapter 11. If your recognition accuracy is handled via training phrases, like with Dialogflow, make sure the exact phrase mentioned in a prompt has been added as a training phrase, as well as any close variants. You'll learn more about this when you dive into tuning (Chapter 17).

Providing Help

In Chapter 9, we introduced universals, including "help" and "more info." It turns out that asking for help is a universal concept people use even when they don't strictly know it exists in the VUI. People probably won't say the word *help* unless they're told that's an option. What they **will** do is ask questions and voice their confusion. Therefore, you add synonym coverage to your help intent in response to *What are my options?* or *What does that mean?* or *I don't know* or *How do I find my prescription number?* or whatever else users might say in the context if they feel stuck. It's a good idea to start help prompts with a landmark (*Here's some help* or *Here's how to…*). At each step of your VUI conversation, think about what's likely to confuse users and what information can help. That's your contextual help prompt. Good help gives users the information they need to phrase requests to reflect their intended meaning while being understood by the VUI.

A general request for *Help* or *Tell me more* is always assumed to be contextual: your VUI response should be based on what the user just did or asked for and what they're in the process of doing. We have also worked on systems that allow noncontextual help. Here, users don't just say *Help* and let the system figure out the context. Instead they can specify what they need help with, like "*Help me* add a contact" or "*Tell me more about* clear liquids." This allows users to ask for help on specific topics when they need it—though they're not a free-for-all. The available topics are still related to what users struggle with in a particular context and won't be available in the middle of a conversation unless they're relevant. So, for example, "*Tell me more about* clear liquids" won't be available in the middle of scheduling an appointment. This is starting to feel like a conversation with some smarts:

> **VUI**   *Do you have someone who can drive you home after the procedure?*
>
> **User**   *Why do I need a ride?*
>
> **VUI**   *After the procedure you'll be drowsy. It won't be safe to drive yourself.*
>
> *So will someone drive you home after the procedure?*
>
> **User**   *Ah yes, I have.*

FROM THE VOICE TRENCHES

In one financial voice-only bill pay system, the ability to ask for *help on TOPIC* allowed users the freedom to help themselves. They could ask a more precise question, such as *Help me change a payee address*, instead of hearing a more generic and broader bill pay explanation that might not have helped them. With this approach, users gained confidence in the system, and support staff got fewer questions. Win-win!

SUCCESS TIP 12.2 LISTEN POST-HELP   After your VUI provides some help, leave the mic open to allow the user to respond without extra steps. Because help prompts tend to be a bit verbose, end by directly telling the user you're expecting them to respond, either with a repetition of the original prompt or with a differently worded one.

Notes on Designing for Help

Sure, here's some help is a great response if the user explicitly asked for help and you're sure recognition was correct. Avoid starting a help response with an acknowledgment like *OK* or *Sure* unless you're tracking the details of how users worded their question. It's better to treat acknowledgments and landmarks as separate prompt segments that you can choose to include or not, depending on context such as the exact wording of the user request. That way, the same help prompt preamble can be used no matter what the user said, and the core prompt can be used whether or not the user explicitly asked for assistance. To see the issue, try responding *Sure, here's some help...* to the four help requests earlier in this section. Do any of them sound odd as a response? They should, as you see in Figure 12-2, together with some better lead-in alternatives.

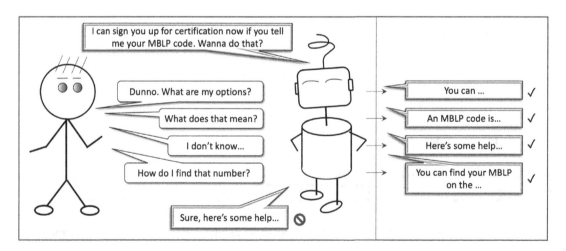

Figure 12-2. *Help messages can't start with the same preamble in all contexts without sounding odd*

Just-in-Time Information

Just-in-time (or JIT) information is a way of providing help. The difference is that the user didn't ask for help or voice confusion; it's a helpful hint made available when the conversation context makes it relevant. JIT information is useful right after a user has completed some request or task, but they had some difficulty with it or did it in more steps than necessary:

> **User** *I'd like to make a reservation for Na Na's.*
>
> **VUI** *A reservation at Na Na's. When?*
>
> **User** *Tomorrow night.*
>
> **VUI** *What time?*
>
> **User** *7:30.*
>
> **VUI** *And for how many people?*
>
> **User** *Six.*
>
> **VUI** *Alright. I've made a reservation for...< details >*
>
> **VUI** *By the way, here's a quicker way to make reservations.*
>
> *Just say "Make a reservation for Na Na's for six people tomorrow at 7:30 PM."*

The key to JIT is that by showing how to do it faster right after the user experienced the dialog step by step makes the information more relevant and therefore more useful. If you offer JIT information, track and limit how often you offer it—some users know they can do it in one sentence but prefer stepping through complex requests. Let them.

Notes on Designing for JIT

Information is helpful when it's relevant to the user, both for content and when it's provided. A mistake in some IVRs is to immediately direct callers to a company website. Don't do that: this person just called; if they wanted a website, they would've gone online instead. It wastes the caller's time and starts the call with irrelevant information that makes people tune out. We've seen several examples of how removing irrelevant information and unnecessarily long wording led to fewer agent transfer requests.

SUCCESS TIP 12.3 JUST-IN-TIME IS NOT ALL THE TIME   Be sparing about your JIT info. Think carefully about when it makes sense and how often to provide it. Track when a JIT was offered to each user to avoid repeating it next time or often. Also, seriously limit using it for anything that feels like upsell, like offering a more premium service.

Hidden Options and "None of Those"

Hidden options don't mean you hide how to ask for something. It means there are options that the VUI understands and handles but that aren't explicitly mentioned to users in prompts. Grammars are identical with or without hidden options; only the prompts are different. Because audio as a modality is limited, you need to be concise, so there're commands and options that you don't want to repeat in every prompt. Universal commands are often hidden options. Sometimes there may be reasons to not mention an option that tempts users to choose it for the wrong reasons or even have a hidden "access" for some group of users.

Another common use case is to provide a way out during any login or authentication process and to help with questions like the ones in Figure 12-2. The key is to cover the expected ways users naturally ask, making handling broad and robust—the purpose is easy discovery and highly successful recognition and resolution:

~ ~ *VUI with hidden commands* ~ ~

VUI   *What's your membership number?*

User   *Umm, I don't have one.*

VUI   *Alright, new member registration.*

~ ~ *VUI with explicit commands* ~ ~

VUI   *Please tell me your membership number or say "I don't have one" or say "I forgot."*

User   *Umm, I don't have one.*

VUI   *Alright, new member registration.*

~ ~ VUI without hidden commands ~ ~

VUI   *What's your membership number?*

User   *Umm, I don't have one.*

VUI   *Sorry, tell me you membership number.*

User   *I said I don't have one!*

Always include handling for these types of responses if your VUI involves user login, though you may be restricted on how to do so by your development platform. Watch out: avoid hidden options that are easily misrecognized as something that's in-grammar or explicitly mentioned in a prompt. That gets confusing to users.

SUCCESS TIP 12.4 HIDING IN PLAIN SIGHT   Hidden options are powerful conversational tools when correctly balanced. On the one hand, the wording that's recognized has to be something that comes naturally for the user in the context, without explicit instructions. On the other hand, users must believe that the VUI can understand utterances beyond ones that have been explicitly mentioned in prompts. The best hidden options are therefore requests like *I don't know, I forgot, Repeat that, What are my choices?*, and *None of those.* In other words, what you might say to a person when you're stuck.

Phrases like *None of those* or *I don't want any of those* and similar are common responses to menus or lists of options that don't cover what the user wants to do. These responses come naturally—people don't need to be instructed to say them. It's therefore a special hidden option use case. Depending on context, map this to a prompt that gives more information that explains how to proceed if a user feels stuck, such as more explanatory versions of options or even additional options.

Recognize-and-Reject

Recognize-and-reject is one of the most useful techniques for giving an intelligent response to something your VUI can't help with. You include the word or phrase in grammar so that you can recognize it and respond in a helpful informative way, even if you can't actually fulfill what the user asked for. It's the catch-and-release of VUI design. Recognize-and-reject is more useful and less frustrating to you and your users than ignoring a request because it's out-of-coverage (OOC). This is why it's important to differentiate fulfillment from intent resolution. While **intent resolution** means "figure out what the user meant," fulfillment means "give the user what they asked for." If someone tells you "Give me a ride to the airport at 4 AM tomorrow," you can understand what they want without actually doing it. Use this technique for out-of-range requests and requests that fit your VUI's domain but that you haven't yet fully developed. By capturing these requests, you also learn what users want to do so that you can decide on where to put your efforts next. It also makes overall performance more accurate because you control the outcome of something that's otherwise OOC. When an utterance is OOC, there's no guarantee it's not FA-out, mapped incorrectly to something that is IG. If, however, the utterance is IG, it's more likely that it will match what's IG:

> ~ ~ *Without recognize-and-reject (and too wordy)* ~ ~
>
> **User**   *I want to order food for delivery.*
>
> **VUI**   *Sorry, I didn't understand.*
>
> **User**   *I said, order delivery.*
>
> **VUI**   *Sorry, I still didn't get that.*
>
> **User**   *Oh for... You stupid...*

> ~ ~ *With recognize-and-reject* ~ ~
>
> **User**   *I want to order food for delivery.*
>
> **VUI**   *Sorry, I can't help with food ordering yet.*

One-Step Correction

When people talk to each other and some information is misheard by one person, the other person often uses one-step correction, a conversational shortcut that combines a rejection with the corrected content. Your VUI can and should as well:

> **VUI**   *And what's your date of birth?*
>
> **User**   *March 9, 1989.*
>
> **VUI**   *That's March 9th, 1981. Right?*   → YEAR is misrecognized.
>
> **User**   ***No, 1989***   → One-step correction
>
> **VUI**   *March 9th, 1989. Is that correct?*
>
> **User**   *Yes, correct.*

Without one-step correction, the dialog has to be longer and clunkier for everyone: first *no*, then reprompt, and finally the corrected content. Instead, with a little more effort, you allow users to provide natural conversational feedback. When implementing it, keep in mind that some people jump straight to the corrected content without first saying *no* or *that's wrong* or similar. As humans we understand that it's a rejection and correction even without the *no*—will your VUI?

One-step correction comes naturally to people when they're very familiar with the content of what's being corrected. In a healthcare IVR, we added one-step correction for date of birth after analysis of the out-of-coverage utterances. This alone increased in-grammar handling by about 10%.

Implementing One-Step Correction

Let's look at the steps involved in implementing one-step correction for the date of birth example using Dialogflow:[2]

1. Create an intent `arEnterDOB` with a few training phrases that mean "provide date of birth." Set an output context `DOB`, and add a prompt asking for a date of birth, such as "Please tell me your date of birth." Don't forget to enable the webhook.

2. Create the follow-on intent `DOB` that captures the date of birth (Figure 12-3).

3. Add an input context `DOB` to match the output context from `arEnterDOB`.

4. Add an output context `confirmDOB` for the follow-on intents confirming date of birth:

- Be careful here: when you enter a training phrase containing a date, Dialogflow automatically picks `@sys.date` as the system entity. You need to delete that and change it to what's shown in Figure 12-3: break up each phrase and define slots for month, day, and year. `@sys.date` will recognize a date without issues, but when the date is read back for confirmation, it'll sound something like *That's 1987-03-03,*

---

[2]One-step correction code files are in 12-1a.zip (Dialogflow) and 12-1b.zip (webhook).

right?, which isn't a great user experience. It increases cognitive load unless the user said it using that same format. This happens because `@sys.date` puts the output in a specific format. Once again, use system entities with care.

5. The parameter `$day` you add should be a `@sys.number` instead of `@sys.ordinal` so that both *March third, 1987* and *March three, 1987* are understood. Users will say both.

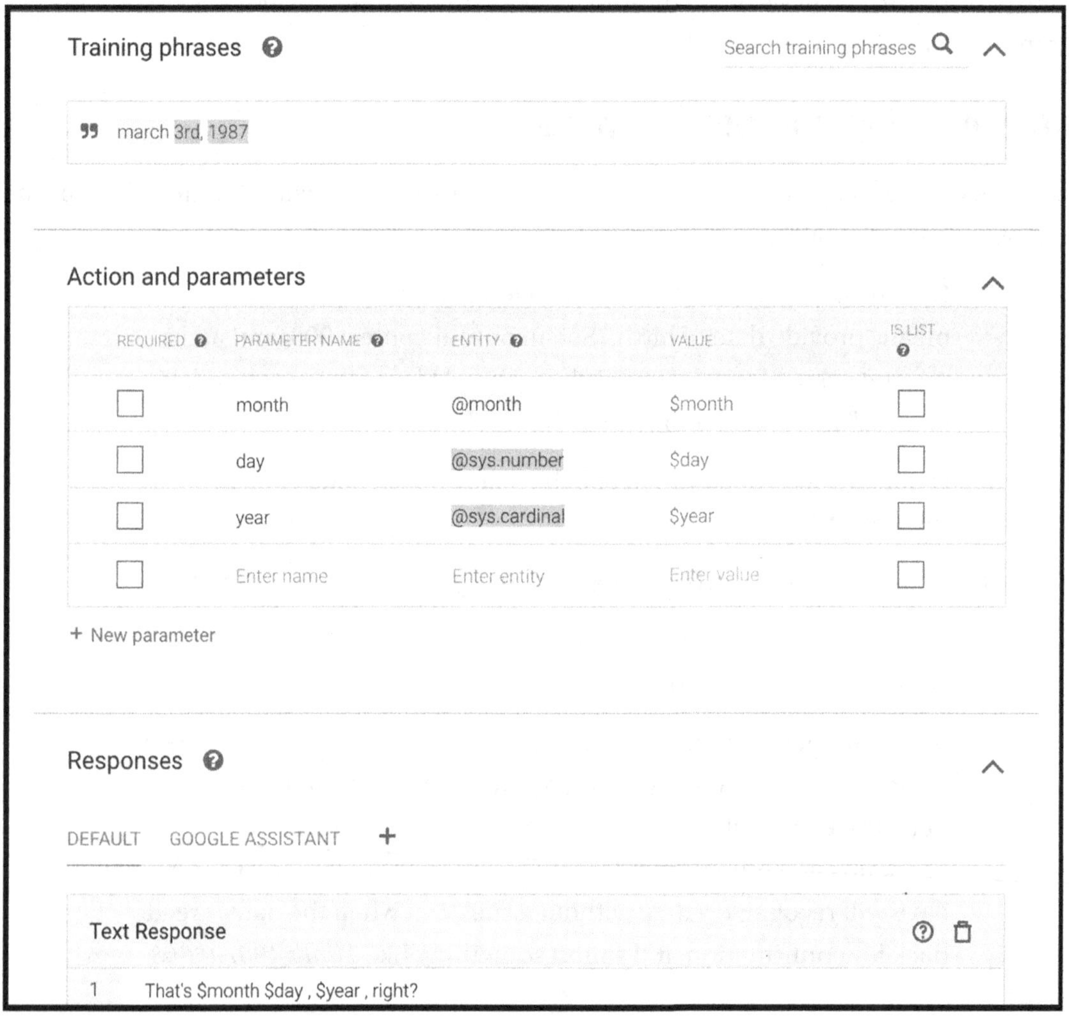

Figure 12-3. *New DOB intent*

6. Add a custom entity @month.

7. Next, provide handling for the happy path case of when the date of birth is correct (Figure 12-4). Create an intent confirmDOByes. Don't forget to have confirmDOB as the input context.

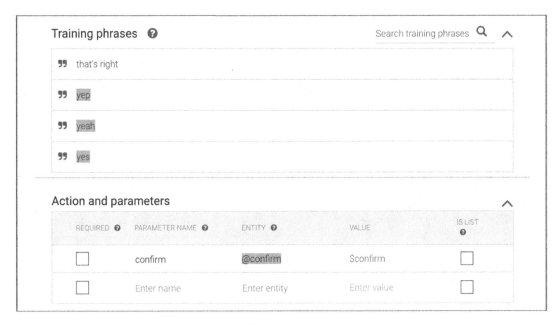

Figure 12-4. *New intent* confirmDOByes

8. Now add handling for the correction case. Create a new intent confirmDOBcorrect (Figure 12-5). Don't forget to add the same input context confirmDOB as you did for confirmDOByes. For now, only add one training phrase with a full date correction. Remember to change the parameters and entities like you did in the DOB intent.

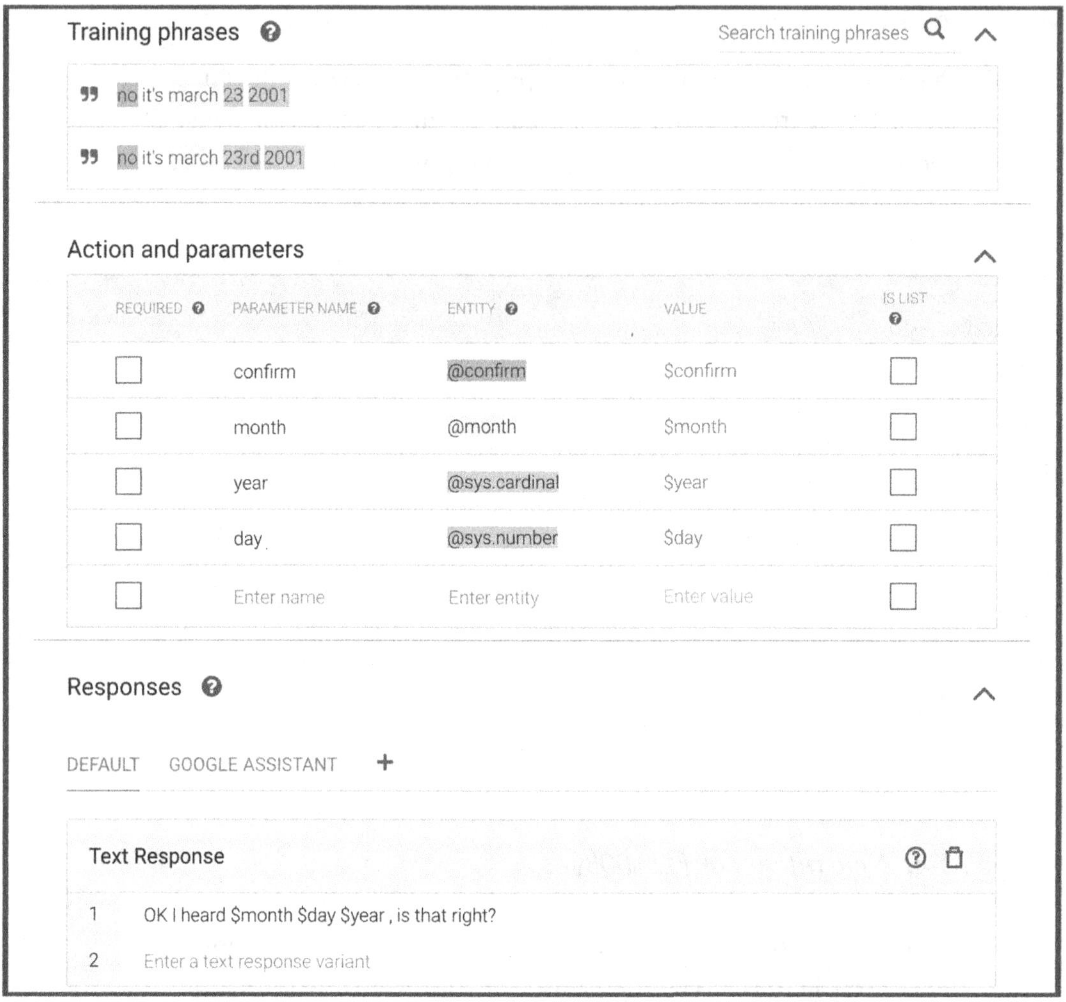

Training phrases ❓   Search training phrases 🔍 ⌃

> 99   no it's march 23 2001

> 99   no it's march 23rd 2001

Action and parameters   ⌃

REQUIRED ❓	PARAMETER NAME ❓	ENTITY ❓	VALUE	IS LIST ❓
☐	confirm	@confirm	$confirm	☐
☐	month	@month	$month	☐
☐	year	@sys.cardinal	$year	☐
☐	day	@sys.number	$day	☐
☐	Enter name	Enter entity	Enter value	☐

Responses ❓   ⌃

DEFAULT   GOOGLE ASSISTANT   ✚

Text Response	❓ 🗑
1 OK I heard $month $day $year , is that right?	
2 Enter a text response variant	

Figure 12-5. *Initial* `confirmDOBcorrect` *intent, allowing only full date correction*

9. Test it. First, say *date of birth*, give a date of birth, and then say *yes*. That should work. Now, try one-step correction with a complete date. Say *No, it's [another full date including month, day, year].* You should hear a confirmation prompt. Say *yes*. So far, so good!

It turns out that users will not only one-step correct with a complete date (*No, it's March third, 1987*) but also correct only the part that was wrong, like *No, it's March, No, it's the third, No, it's 1988,* and *No, it's March third*. Let's handle that.

10. For `confirmDOBcorrect`, add a training phrase "No, it's March," using the custom entity @month.

11. Test it again. Correct with only "No, it's March." We have a problem! The intent `confirmDOBcorrect` was recognized, but there was no response. Note that the response has all the parameters $month, $day, and $year, and in this case, only $month was filled because that's all the user said. The day and year were from the last DOB intent, but they're not active now. What do we do?

You need to go to the webhook, which you haven't done yet for one-step correction. You need the webhook to save the date parameters from the DOB collection and use them later if the user corrects only one or two pieces of the date. There are actually things you need to do for two different intents; we'll take them one by one.

First, for the DOB intent, you need to save the date parameters month, day, and year into the output context confirmDOB. Remember that you can set parameters associated with contexts from the webhook. This way they'll be available during later intents as long as the context is still active; recall the default lifespan of five dialog steps for contexts, which should be fine. Listing 12-1 shows this piece of webhook code, from a new module dob.py, as we've done with all the other intents. Start an empty context to add to later, using the function new_context() that you created earlier (A). Add month if it's in the query input parameters, and call the parameter currentmonth to not confuse with month (B). Add day and year, if there are any (C, D). Append the new context to the list of contexts to set (E). Use the response text from the Dialogflow GUI (F). Though not shown in Listing 12-1, as always, in main.py, you add the function dob() to the dialog_ functions handler dictionary.

Listing 12-1. Saving date of birth parameters for future use

```
def dob(df_request, df_response):
    """

    Date of birth
    """

    # Set the confirmDOB context with date parameters.

    context = new_context('confirmdob')    #A
```

```
# Add month, day, year parameters to the output context
# so we have them for later.

if 'month' in df_request.parameters:    #B
  context['parameters']['currentmonth'] = df_request.parameters['month']

if 'day' in df_request.parameters:
  context['parameters']['currentday'] = df_request.parameters['day']   #C

if 'year' in df_request.parameters:
  context['parameters']['currentyear'] = df_request.
parameters['year']   #D

# Append the new context
df_response.output_contexts.append(context)   #E

# Use the response in Dialogflow
df_response.output_text = df_request.fulfillment_text   #F
```

The second step is to use the parameters you saved in the intent
confirmDOBcorrect. First, extract the date parameters from the context confirmdob.
These are the parameters that you saved in Listing 12-1. Now, get the date parameters
from the correction phrase, if there is one, or from the saved parameters. For example,
if someone says *No, October*, then the month would come from that one-step
correction, and the day and year would come from the saved parameters. Listing 12-
2 shows this starting with a separate function to pull out the month, day, and year for
the confirmation. First, you initialize date parameters (A). Loop through the input
contexts (B). When you find the confirmdob context, get the parameters (C). Get the
month, looking first in query parameters (D) and then in saved context parameters (E).
Then, get the day. There are two cases to handle for parameter query, either day (F) or
dayoryear and < 32 (G). Finally, get the year. Again, there are two cases where you need
to query parameters: either year (H) or dayoryear and >32 (I). Provide the confirmation
text using the collected date parameters (J).

Listing 12-2. Webhook code for intent `confirmDOBcorrect` for confirming corrected date (`confirm_dob_correct.py`)

```python
def confirmation_month(df_request, params):
    """

    Month to confirm
    Get from parameters, then context.
    """

    month = None   # A

    if (('month' in df_request.parameters) and
            (df_request.parameters['month'] != '')):  # D
        month = df_request.parameters['month']
    elif (params is not None) and ('currentmonth' in params):  # E
        month = params['currentmonth']

    return month


def confirmation_day(df_request, params):
    """

    Day to confirm
    dayoryear hits this if < 50, e.g., "25" for the date.
    """

    day = None     # A

    if 'day' in df_request.parameters and \
            df_request.parameters['day'] != '':
        day = df_request.parameters['day']     # F
    elif (('dayoryear' in df_request.parameters) and
            (df_request.parameters['dayoryear'] != '') and
            (df_request.parameters['dayoryear'] < 50)):
        day = df_request.parameters['dayoryear']   # G
    elif params is not None and 'currentday' in params:
        day = params['currentday']

    return day
```

```python
def confirmation_year(df_request, params):
    """

    Year to confirm
    dayoryear hits this if > 50, e.g, "1985".
    """

    year =      # A

    if 'year' in df_request.parameters and \
            df_request.parameters['year'] != '':
        year = df_request.parameters['year']      # H
    elif (('dayoryear' in df_request.parameters) and
          (df_request.parameters['dayoryear'] != '') and
          (df_request.parameters['dayoryear'] >= 50)):
        year = df_request.parameters['dayoryear']      # I
    elif params is not None and 'currentyear' in params:
        year = params['currentyear']

    return year


def confirm_dob_correct(df_request, df_response):
    """

    One-step correction for DOB.
    """

    # Get the parameters from the confirmdob context.
    for idx, name in enumerate(df_request.input_contexts['names']):  # B
        if name == 'confirmdob':
            context = df_request.input_contexts['contexts'][idx]
            dob_context_params = context.get('parameters')      # C

    # Get date params to confirm.
    # If they are not in the request parameters, get them from the context.
    confirm_month = confirmation_month(df_request, dob_context_params)
    confirm_day = confirmation_day(df_request, dob_context_params)
    confirm_year = confirmation_year(df_request, dob_context_params)
```

```
# Confirmation text using extracted parameters
df_response.output_text = (
    f"I heard {confirm_month} {int(confirm_day)} "
    f"{int(confirm_year)}, is that right?")    # J
```

During our testing, we ran into an effect that resulted in a small change to webhook_request.py. Some of the parameters came from Dialogflow as a list rather than a singleton, so we added a piece of code (Listing 12-3) to avoid errors later by making them all singletons. We point this out as a reminder: when working with "black box" tools or platforms, you won't necessarily know when data appears in unexpected formats, so remember to test in different environments.

Listing 12-3. Making sure parameters are singletons

```
self.parameters = query_result.get("parameters")
# Go through the parameters, and turn any list into a singleton
for param in self.parameters:
    if isinstance(self.parameters[param], list):
        self.parameters[param] = self.parameters[param][0]
```

What happens if someone says *No, it's 8* or *No, it's 1998*? These are both valid cases for correcting only the day or only the year. But both are numbers, so how do you know what to correct? The parameter dayoryear in the intent confirmDOBcorrect is what you can use together with the webhook to figure out which one it is. Fortunately, days must be less than 32, and years in most VUIs will be greater than 1900 (ignoring for now the case of *"I heard March 5, 2019. Is that correct?" "No, 18."*). You have to slightly modify the intent confirmDOBcorrect as shown in Figure 12-6 and use the webhook code to disambiguate.

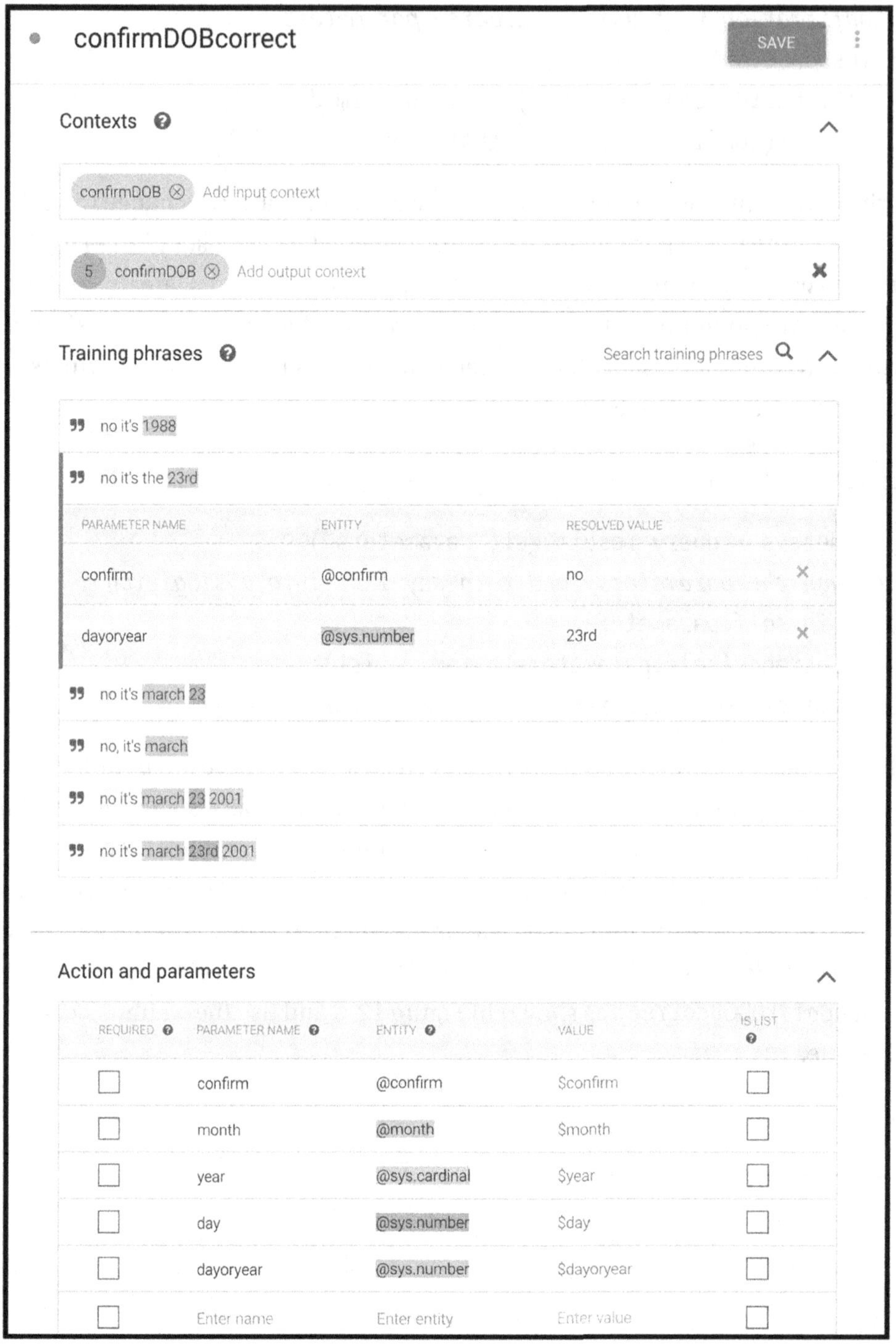

Figure 12-6. New piece of confirmDOBcorrect *intent handling* dayoryear *parameter*

Notes on One-Step Correction

You can use this code as a baseline and make changes needed for your VUI's use cases. All the examples here started with a *no*, but some people only correct the content: *Was that June 12, 1985? July.* For human listeners, that's clear enough without the *no*.

In the final example, the two numbers are easy to tell apart because their ranges don't overlap. That won't always be the case: what if people use numbers for both days and months or if you're asking for something like quantity and dosage of medications? Think about situations where they'll overlap and how you'd need to modify design and code. Also think about how you can constrain the valid ranges; any such information is crucial for highest-accuracy performance. The good news is that people tend to be aware of what's ambiguous when they use one-step correction, so they'll include enough context. If the year *2009* is misrecognized as *2005*, most people would repeat the whole year, not just the final digit.

Tutorials

Targeted tutorials can be useful for some tasks and user groups. Tutorials can be more or less complex. Sometimes just a simple recorded sample interaction between a "user" and the VUI is all that's needed to illustrate how something is done. Just hearing what's basically a recorded sample dialog with prompts and common requests or responses can improve user success and happiness. When the conversation involves a task or device that's brand-new or one that's complex or risky for any reason, an interactive demo is worth considering. It gives users a chance to "learn by doing" in a sandbox without any risk. We have implemented both types and seen their benefits. Some simple guidelines to keep in mind:

- Keep it short.

- Use a clearly distinct voice for the user part. If your VUI voice has a low deep voice, your tutorial user should have a higher voice, for example.

- Offer the tutorial; never force users to listen to it. And don't keep offering it every time the user engages with the VUI. Offer it when the user is new or if you track error behaviors and notice that they're having trouble getting what they want. A simple *Wanna hear about what I can do?* (or whatever fits the context) is good because the user only needs to say yes or no.

- Remember to update tutorials any time your features or grammar coverage changes. As with examples, a tutorial must reflect what actually works in the VUI.

MULTIMODAL CORNER

If your VUI is multimodal, you want to make use of the screen to convey recognition, offer disambiguation, and so on. Tutorials and helpful hints are particularly great when you have a screen. If something involves steps that the user isn't familiar with, step-by-step multimodal tutorials are a great approach (Figure 12-7).

Figure 12-7. *Multimodal tutorials are a great tool*

Spelling

The hardest recognition tasks are some that seem the most basic: single digits and letters of the alphabet. This shouldn't surprise you: you've been on the phone with someone spelling a name using a phonetic alphabet like *A as in apple* or *alpha*. Air traffic controllers and pilots say *niner* instead of *nine* to decrease risk of misunderstanding and confusion with *five*. Many letters in the US English alphabet's **e-set** (B C D E G P T V Z) are very hard to tell apart when listening without seeing the speaker's lips. F and S are also problematic.

If you're creating a voice solution for military or aviation use, you can expect users to know and use the official phonetic alphabet. But it's pretty unlikely that you'll only design military VUIs for the rest of your career. So what do you do? A partial solution is to find out what the most common words are that people use and include them in your grammars. Another is to use any available logic to cross-reference with plausible answers, our next topic.

Narrowing the Recognition Space

One way to increase accuracy is to gradually narrow the search space for your VUI to make the recognition task easier. This can be done through disambiguation and confirmations and also by focusing the grammar structure. You already know that you don't want to limit users to only say a few keywords you're imposing on them. You want to allow natural variation—but sometimes they say things like *Can I have a glass of red wine with my wife after dinner?*, and that might throw your VUI for a loop because you only expected *Can I have red wine?*

Most data sets have some structure or limitations. For example, a bank's account numbers might be numeric, 8–14 digits long, and the third digit from the end is always a 1 or 2. Phone numbers are a certain length depending on country or area code. Credit cards use checksum digits. US address grammars are linked to zip codes so that every street name isn't in-grammar at all times, which helps recognition a lot. A large but sparse data set could be checked against. You should incorporate anything that's reliable and narrows the recognition space to improve accuracy.

Now back to how to handle spelling. If someone is spelling their name to an airline app to confirm a reservation, it's very likely the flight has a passenger list to check against. If someone is reading an alphanumeric prescription or confirmation number, it's highly likely this number is available to check against and that only some combinations are valid. If your VUI recognizes *5 D 4 4 9* but there's only a valid *5 T 4 4 9*, it's likely the *T* was misrecognized. One solution is to attempt a fuzzy match; the VUI captures the approximate matches as a separate result that can be verified by the user:

VUI   *Please spell the passenger's last name.*

User   *J O N E S.*   → Recognized as J O M E S

VUI   *[Finds no Jomes, but finds Jones]*

VUI   *That's J O N as in Nancy E S. Is that right?*

User   *That's correct.*

~~~   ~~~   ~~~

VUI   *What's your prescription number?*

User   *5 T 4 4 9.*   → Recognized as "5 D 4 4 9"

VUI   *[Finds no "5 D 4 4 9" but finds "5 T 4 4 9"]*

VUI   *To verify, please tell me that number again.*

User   *5 T 4 4 9.*   → Recognized as 5 T 4 4 9

In low-security circumstances, you can "auto-correct" it or correct-and-verify. Other times an option is to log the discrepancy and ask again. You'll learn another interesting solution in this chapter. Recognition space can be narrowed by having grammars or understanding customized for a particular context. You saw an example in Chapter 7 for disambiguation based on custom phone lists and knowing what names were in the list.

Advanced Techniques

To work with voice technology is to embrace uncertainty. In the world of conversational voice design and development for IVRs, a few techniques have long been useful to get a grip on uncertainty, but haven't (yet) been implemented commonly in other voice interfaces. Because these techniques are so powerful, we want you to learn about them: confidence scores for multi-tier recognition behavior and N-best and skip lists for picking the right recognition result.

Multi-tier Behavior and Confidence Scores

Most of us have a pretty good sense of whether or not we heard something correctly or how well we expressed ourselves. There may be background noise, or maybe the speaker talked quietly or slurred their words, or the topic was unfamiliar. We base our assumptions and responses on our level of certainty: we forge ahead, or we first verify that we understood, or we ask for a clarification or even a do-over.

This is the concept behind using **tiered recognition confidence scores** in VUI design. Multiple tiers, usually two or three, are defined with different VUI responses based on the VUI confidence that the user utterance was correctly understood. Every recognition result has an associated score based on how closely the result matches its hypothesis. A multi-tier design lets you verify utterances with lower recognition scores to avoid later problems while moving more quickly through the conversation and avoiding extra steps when they're unnecessary—like what people do. Here's a typical multi-tier design:

VUI   *What's your prescription number?*

User   *5 T 4 4 9.*

~ ~ High confidence score ~ ~

   VUI   *Thanks. You have two refills remaining for Prednisone...*

~ ~ Medium confidence score ~ ~

   VUI   *Just to confirm, that's 5 T 4 4 9. Right?*

~ ~ Low confidence score ~ ~

   VUI   *Sorry. What's that number?*

At high confidence scores, the VUI assumes its recognition result is correct and doesn't confirm it with the user—though including an implicit confirmation is still important. At a medium score, explicit confirmation verifies that the result is correct before moving on. Below some score, just ask again because the chance of being wrong is too high.

You use confidence to tailor confirmation strategies (Chapter 8) based on the likelihood that your VUI understood the user and certainty about the accuracy of the response. If confidence is high, you do less confirmation, mostly implicit, and use words like *Sure*. At medium confidence, you explicitly confirm and hedge responses with phrases like *I think you want...* And at low confidence, you reject and retry.

```
                      FROM THE VOICE TRENCHES
```

We've both experienced our home smart devices triggering when we didn't address them, even when several feet away. You've probably had similar experiences. A conversation including the phrase *This is not acceptable* somehow resulted in the device asking *Should I play Blake?* If multi-tier confidences were broadly incorporated and set correctly, fewer such misfires would take place.

Implementing Multi-tier Confirmation

Not all platforms make confidence scores available to developers. When creating a VUI, both designers and developers need to share the same understanding about the availability. Here's where Google is a perfect choice for our book: at the time of writing this, confidence scores are available via the Google Cloud Speech API, but not directly or consistently via Dialogflow. This is great because it allows us to address both situations.

Multi-tier confirmation can be implemented in several ways. Using recognition confidence scores from the recognizer is the best approach when those scores are available. A simple approach that works in some contexts is a string match: an exact word-for-word match with a known item in a multi-word phrase would result in "high confidence," while a not exact match gives a lower confidence and different behavior. This works best for long search phrases, like names of movies or descriptions of meals.

Since Dialogflow doesn't currently make confidence scores available, your ability to implement such a strategy is limited. If or when it does—or if you're working within a platform that does—the implementation goes something like this:

1. Create an intent to collect the number. Name it `arCollectNumber`.

2. Create an intent to read back the information. Name it `arReadInformation`. Make sure this intent responds to the event `readinformation`.

3. Create a confirmation intent `arConfirmNumber` for medium confidence. Make sure this intent responds to the event `confirminformation`.

4. Add the `reject` event to the existing Default Fallback Intent.

5. Add logic in the webhook to process the intent `arCollectNumber`:

   a. Save the number as parameters in an output context like you did with date of birth collection earlier in this chapter.

   b. If the confidence from the webhook request is high, trigger the event `readinformation`.

   c. If the confidence is medium, trigger the event `confirminformation`.

   d. If the confidence is low, trigger the `reject` event.

The webhook code for the intent `arReadInformation` takes the number from the context, as it was set when responding to `arCollectNumber`. The result is something like Listing 12-4.

Listing 12-4. Output of Google Cloud Speech-to-Text API

```
{
    "results": [
        {
            "alternatives": [
                {
                    "transcript": "1 2 3 4 5 6 7 8 9 0",
                    "confidence": 0.88398576
                },
                {
                    "transcript": "one two three four five six seven eight
                        nine zero",
                    "confidence": 0.9059588
                },
                {
                    "transcript": "one two three four five six seven eight
                        nine 0",
                    "confidence": 0.86726743
                },
                {
                    "transcript": "1 2 3 4 5 6 7 8 9 zero",
                    "confidence": 0.87917966
                },
```

```
            {
                    "transcript": "1 2 3 4 5 6 7 8 9 0 0",
                    "confidence": 0.8787717
            }
        ]
    }
]
}
```

Notes on Multi-tier Confidence-Based Design

Where you set the boundaries between tiers is not set in stone. It depends on how important it is to be correct before moving on and on the overall platform scores. Think of confidence scores as percentages where 100% represents absolute certainty. Good general starting points are often around 85% and 50–65%. Trial and error, and tuning once you have real data, will help you pick those boundaries. The right levels maximize correct accept (CA) results in the high confidence bucket and correct reject (CR) results in the low bucket. Results that would have been false accepts or rejects (FA or FR) are the ones you want in the medium bucket so that your VUI doesn't base decisions on incorrect information and also doesn't make the conversation longer than necessary.

You probably realize that all VUI interactions in fact use tiers. It's just that the default is two tiers: accept or reject. You're unlikely to use multi-tier designs everywhere for all interactions—imagine the horror of confirming a Yes/No: *You said "no," right?* You can also have additional tiers and other confidence-based behavior, like "hedging" your response when confidence is lower:

>   **User**   *I'm looking for a fusion Scandinavian-Japanese restaurant.*
>
>   ~ ~ ~ High confidence score ~ ~ ~
>
>   **VUI**   *Sure. SamurHej is the perfect place for you…*
>
>   ~ ~ ~ Medium confidence score ~ ~ ~
>
>   **VUI**   *You might like SamurHej…* ← Hedging implied by
>   carrier phrase

Regarding confidence scores in Actions on Google, you'll sometimes find results in a field called speechRecognitionConfidence in the queryResult section of your webhook request. However, the current Dialogflow documentation says, "This field is not guaranteed to be accurate or set. In particular this field isn't set

460

for `StreamingDetectIntent` since the streaming endpoint has separate confidence estimates per portion of the audio in `StreamingRecognitionResult`." For that reason, you currently can't rely on having access to confidence scores in Dialogflow. If you need them consistently for your implementation, you'd have to use another STT provider such as the raw Google Cloud Speech-to-Text API.[3] This API provides confidence scores as well as the N-best list, which you learn about next.

All platforms have some limitations—what you're able to implement depends on your particular development situation. Enterprise-level IVR platforms typically allow access to confidence scores, but many "plug-and-play" platforms trade this level of information for ease of use for non-experts, and that's fine. Choose the right setup for your goal and resources, and make sure everyone involved understands the limitations to settle on the right solution.

N-Best and Skip Lists

Remember how recognition works: multiple hypotheses are formed and tracked by the recognizer until end of speech is reached, and then the hypothesis with the highest score moves on to the next step of interpretation. This arrangement produces a single top-scoring hypothesis; it's a system with "*N-best* = 1." If you're lucky, you work with a platform that makes available more than just the top score. You can use N-best > 1 (where N is maybe 5 or 10) to create some pretty clever conversations when combined with other lookups to see if the result is valid in the context. This was the technique we hinted at earlier in this chapter when discussing recognition space and how to remove invalid options without asking the user. For a system with alphanumeric UK postal codes, a coworker used N-best=100!

N-best is usually combined with a skip list within a dialog: if the N(1) hypothesis is rejected for some reason, it's put on the skip list. The N(2) hypothesis is evaluated, checked against the existing skip list, and so on. It's a common technique for challenging recognition tasks, such as long alphanumeric strings. It's particularly useful when the same incorrect hypothesis is returned multiple times:

~ ~ ~ Without N-best and skip lists ~ ~ ~

VUI   *What's your prescription number?*

User   *5 T 4 4 9.*

---

[3]`https://cloud.google.com/speech-to-text/`

VUI   *That's 5 T 4 4 1. Right?*   ← Misrecognized number

User   *No. It's 5 T 4 4 9.*

VUI   *OK, 5 T 4 4 1. Right?*   ← Misrecognized again

User   *No!!*

Instead, here's what N-best and skip lists can do for you:

~ ~ ~ With N-best and skip lists ~ ~ ~

VUI   *What's your prescription number?*

User   *5 T 4 4 9.*

VUI   *That's 5 T 4 4 1. Right?*   ← Misrecognized number

User   *No. It's 5 T 4 4 9*   ← "5T441" is put on skip list.

VUI   *OK, 5 T 4 4 9. Right?*   ← Misrecognized again; check skip
list; go to N=2.

User   *That's correct, yes.*

Implementing Skip Lists

As with multi-tier confirmation, Dialogflow (with Actions on Google) does not give you the N-best list. If it did, you'd do something like this:

1. Create an intent `arCollectNumber`.

2. In the webhook for `arCollectNumber`, save the recognized number in a context parameter, like you did for date of birth.

3. Create an intent `arConfirmNumber` that handles number confirmation; again, you can do one-step correction as you did for date of birth.

4. If the user corrects, step down the N-best list from item #1 until you reach the first item that hasn't already been attempted. Use this item for your confirmation; if the user rejects it, add this item to the skip list, ask again, and pass by anything on the skip list until confirmation is successful or a max attempts counter is

reached. This way you will not confirm with a wrong answer more than once.

Again, as with confirmation, it depends on your voice platform whether you have access to the N-best list or not. You currently don't with Actions on Google, but you do if you use the standalone Google Cloud Speech-to-Text API as shown in Listing 12-3. You also do on many enterprise-level IVR platforms.

Notes on N-Best and Skip List Design

N-best is obviously a powerful approach that can be used in various ways. But be careful: think about how skipping to another option comes across to the user. When we cover error handling in Chapter 13, you learn about some pitfalls to avoid. Make sure to reset skip lists appropriately: they're temporary tracking devices that should end when the dialog ends.

Probabilities

Another technique is to assign probabilities to individual words and phrases based on expected frequencies. Probabilities can affect the chance that an utterance is recognized and interpreted correctly. SLMs assign probabilities on their own by virtue of being statistical creatures. But there are reasons to influence this probability, and training on a certain data set isn't always the answer. Maybe you know there's a seasonal or event-related spike of a specific phrase, but you don't have the training data yet. Maybe you use regular expressions rather than statistical models and need to weigh some recognition results more heavily. Maybe your universals are being misrecognized as other entities. All are valid reasons—and all should be based on real user data even when the events are rare. For that reason, you'll learn more about probabilities when you learn about tuning (Chapter 17).

As with confidence scores, platforms differ in what they provide. Some more explicit grammar constructs and enterprise IVR platforms allow this functionality, either on a per-slot or whole-utterance basis. At this time, Google Cloud Speech API makes some probabilities available to developers, but Dialogflow doesn't provide a method for weighing the likelihood of specific utterances at the time of writing this. In some sense, it's included automatically based on the bias introduced by the training phrases that weigh certain options or variants more than others.

Timeout and Latency

If you have the ability to change the timeout settings for when to close the microphone and stop listening, you can avoid this situation:

> **VUI**   *What's your card number?*
>
> **User**   *4143 ... 9743 ...*   ← User reads numbers off card and pauses
>   too long.
>
> **VUI**   *Sorry, card numbers are 16 digits long.*
>
> **User**   *Well, I wasn't bloody done yet...*

Some situations need a longer timeout than others. Even if you don't have access to that parameter, you can recognize that only half the number was recognized and give a better response or offer another method of entry. Don't make the user feel like they're at fault.

Many of today's voice platforms don't provide developers with the ability to customize at this level. The default is to set a longer-than-always-needed timeout to avoid the cut-off behavior you just saw in the sample dialog. Some enterprise-level platforms do allow changing timeout duration, so it might become available in the future. One downside of a default long timeout is that users have to wait when their responses are very short, like *yes* or *no*.

Enterprise-level IVRs that support VoiceXML (a cross-platform W3C standard format for specifying voice interactions) actually have two timeouts: an `incompletetimeout` that is used in tracking whether what has been said so far makes sense in the current context and a `completetimeout` that kicks in when the user has said something that makes sense. `Completetimeout` is always shorter, so that the system doesn't wait as long after the user has said something that is a reasonable response for the context. With these different timeouts, you can avoid situations like cutting off a 16-digit credit card number; the `incompletetimeout` is in effect early in the utterance, allowing the user time to finish, and the shorter `completetimeout` applies after the system has detected 16 digits. You can have your cake and eat it too!

What's Next

We hope this chapter illustrates why you can't simply rely on tools if you want to implement something beyond the basics, showing that some may have what you need while others don't, and change is constant. Make sure your choice of platform makes available the parameters your design expects.

It's natural for us all to think *Hey, I speak this language, so I'm an expert!* Because we use language all the time, we automatically "clean up" what we hear. We can ignore stutters, silences, mispronunciations, side comments, missing words, and bungled grammar. We're not even aware of how much we compensate to keep a conversation going. If this surprises you, do this experiment: record a natural conversation, and then carefully transcribe every detail of what's said, including length of silence, interruptions, partial words, and so on. First, you'll notice how choppy conversations are. Then you'll start to wonder how computers ever manage to understand anything we say!

There are many interesting books on conversational and discourse analysis. Here are two places to start: *How We Talk: The Inner Workings of Conversation* by N. J. Enfield is a very accessible quick introduction to the core topics—no need for any background. *Conversation Analysis*, by Rebecca Clift, is a Cambridge textbook in linguistics, so it has a more academic focus, but is still very accessible for anyone interested in the topic.

Summary

- To succeed with interpretation, you need to start from correct recognition.

- You can't control what users say to your VUI, but you can nudge them and help them succeed by providing the right information at the right time. Work with them, not against them—assume people actually want to talk to your VUI and will appreciate assistance that's relevant and unobtrusive.

- Different platforms make available different recognition and interpretation information. Therefore, it's important that you (and your whole team) understand what's feasible to design and implement in your situation.

- For conversations that are closer to human abilities, use advanced techniques that enable more fine-grained responses. Examples include multi-tier confidence scores and N-best and skip lists. If you can't access the data needed for those, you can still create better conversational dialogs with simpler techniques, including examples, contextual and user-specified help, hidden options, and one-step correction. Table 12-2 summarizes the strategies we've covered.

Table 12-2. *Summary of strategies*

Strategy	Key implementation points
Examples	In open prompts, give two to show depth and breadth.
Help	Contextual response to universal command.
Just-in-time info	Short hints and shortcuts for next time, given right after a successful request completion.
Hidden options	Info responses to natural user utterances ("I don't know") that are not explicitly offered in prompt.
None of those	In menus, contextual response for when user doesn't pick any offered option.
Recognize-and-reject	When answer and task is not (yet) implemented, a response that's more informative than a nomatch-and-reject.
One-step correction	In explicit confirmation, recognize user's correction without a "no" step.
Tutorials and demos	For novice users or complex tasks, pre-recorded sample dialog of VUI and distinctly voiced "user"; can be interactive.
Spelling alphabets	For names, allow users to use military spelling or common words; users should not need to choose one over the other.
Narrowed recognition space and skip lists	Numbers: Match recognized string to checksum; skip till match is found. Dynamic/context grammar: Look for match in smaller set (itinerary, contact list). Ask twice "to verify..."; match two recognition results.

(continued)

Table 12-2. (*continued*)

Strategy	Key implementation points
Multi-tier recognition and confidence scores	Confirm only lower-confidence results to speed up interaction.
N-best and skip lists	Add disconfirmed results to list to avoid asking user to confirm the same wrong result twice.
Probabilities	Improve recognition match when a less common word too often is misrecognized for a more common one.
User-controlled pause	For access, orders, or payment, allow users time to find needed info without conversation resetting.
Timeout duration	For long number strings, allow for longer silence where users naturally pause briefly to group digits.

## CHAPTER 13

Choosing Strategies to Recover from Miscommunication

Recognition is never perfect, not even with today's amazing ASR. Nor is it so accurate that you can just ignore any utterances that fall off the happy path because of misrecognition or incorrect intent mapping. You've already learned about many of the reasons why recognition fails: not covering the words spoken by users or the way users pronounce words that are covered, interfering similar words, noisy background, and side speech are just a few reasons. Or suddenly someone changes a feature or adds a branded product name, and bam! People don't get recognized and get frustrated. This chapter is all about getting back on track by designing and implementing the best recovery and backoff method for a particular context.

Recovery from What?

You tried so hard to maximize recognition performance with robust grammars, good prompts, and a design that fits the users' mental models. And yet, things went off track! Why? And how do you even know? Even with the best of intentions, failure to communicate will happen.

When communication fails, you need to get the conversation back on track. This is referred to as error handling or error recovery. Some people don't like the word "error," but it's commonly used—it's easy to say and people know what you mean. It doesn't mean that the user is in error; it means that the VUI needs to fix some situation. Always let the VUI take any blame, never the user. Blame, bad; information, good. Even when some mistakes are technically caused by the user—like saying a partial prescription

© Ann Thymé-Gobbel, Charles Jankowski 2021
A. Thymé-Gobbel and C. Jankowski, *Mastering Voice Interfaces*, https://doi.org/10.1007/978-1-4842-7005-9_13

number or not pronouncing something how it's "supposed" to be said—it serves no purpose telling the user they did something wrong. Besides, it should be clear by now that voice is not binary: you can't guarantee that the VUI wasn't at fault. The point is not to blame anyone but to get back to shared understanding again quickly.

The exception is the rule—your key to VUI success is not only a great experience on the happy path but what happens when there are exceptions. The difference between great and poor recognition is only in how many people go down error paths; the difference between great and poor design and implementation is how quickly and painlessly those people get back on the happy path.

Poor performance affects trust, which affects future use. A study on users' voice system likes and dislikes (Chapter 1, Figure 1-1) illustrates this perfectly. The top two responses to "Describe the traits of your ideal voice assistant" and "What do you like least about voice assistants?" were **getting the right result** and **being understood**. "Right result" responses mentioned correct fulfillment (correct content, information, or action) and responses matching the request in level of detail, relevance, and certainty. "Being understood" included recognition of words used, correct interpretation of the intended meaning, and minimal need of retries.

FROM THE VOICE TRENCHES

A financial voice app wrapped up with *Do you want another stock quote?* to which a *No* answer resulted in *No is not a recognized name.* An attempt of *Exit* resulted in a quote for Exxon. The tester didn't try *bye* for fear they'd "buy" something!

Recognition, Intent, or Fulfillment Errors

There are clear and important differences between different errors:

- Recognition errors (not hearing the right words)

- Intent mapping errors (not understanding what the words meant)

- Fulfillment errors (not being able to do what was requested)

A recognition failure can be a **no match**: what was said doesn't match anything in your grammar coverage. If it's a **no speech**, the user said nothing when the VUI expected speech, or the ASR didn't pick up anything that sounded like speech. If input can be multimodal input—like button pushes, typing, or touch-tones (DTMF)—the outcome can even be a **no input**.

You need to understand users' mental models for mapping a request to the right intent, to minimize errors in the first place, and to provide the most helpful recovery strategy. In-home assistants like Alexa and Google convey omnipresence: the same voice by the same name comes out of different devices throughout the house. But if you set a timer in the kitchen, then go to the living room, and ask how much time is left, you'll get told there's no timer set. That breaks most people's mental model. If your VUI controls volume on another device, users' mental models will differ on the scale (10 or 100 steps? Half-steps? Start at 0 or 1?) and how much louder it gets for *Turn it up a little*.

You want to avoid responding with the wrong fulfillment as well as inappropriate responses like *Sure, here's "House of the Rising Sun"* when the user asks to hear the song "Risingson."

With only slight wording changes, you can let the user know something about why the VUI had difficulty, similar to what you might do when talking to a person. The clearer the VUI is about why it can't do what's asked of it, the more trustworthy and smart it appears, and the easier it is for the user to address the issue and try again:

> **User**   *Play the song "Risingson" from my music library.*

~ ~ ~ Recognition fails ~ ~ ~

> **VUI**   *Sorry, I didn't get that.*

> **VUI**   *Sorry, what song did you want to hear?*

~ ~ ~Intent mapping fails ~ ~ ~

> **VUI**   *Sorry, I don't know that song.*

~ ~ ~ Fulfillment fails ~ ~ ~

> **VUI**   *Sorry, I can't find "Risingson" in your music library.*

> **VUI**   *Sorry, I can't search for music in your local library.*

SUCCESS TIP 13.1 COVERAGE ≠ HANDLING ≠ FULFILLMENT   Recognizing what the user says is not the same as responding to it. Handling a request is different from fulfilling it. Even if you can't fulfill it, it's better to understand an utterance and respond in some way than to just ignore (reject) it, for several reasons. It's an opportunity to track requests for future expansion. Users are also much happier if you respond intelligently than if you ignore them or don't understand them, even if you can't give them what they want. It's more intelligent and it's more human. For example, if the user says, *Call my doctor*, your response options include

> *I didn't get that.* → Intent not assigned or not recognized
>
> *I can't help with calls.* → Intent + acknowledgment
>
> *I can't place the call, but the number is…*   → Intent + handling
>
> *Calling Doctor Anderson's office…*   → Intent + fulfillment

---

Recovery Strategies

Your guiding light is to make the VUI recovery response as clear as possible in context so that a reprompt is as successful as possible. You can learn a lot about recovery strategies by listening to how people try to get conversations back on track after misunderstandings.

FROM THE VOICE TRENCHES

We watched a friend try to ask for a specific song from one of his home VUI assistants. After an attempt resulted in a seeded music station instead of the exact song, he did what most clever VUI users would do: he rephrased his request. He assumed that he hadn't been specific enough, so he tried again, now specifying the type of each slot value: *Play the song "Risingson" by the artist Massive Attack from the album Mezzanine.* Another fellow voice designer exclaimed, "He's not supposed to say that!" much to our amusement. Whatever users say that's reasonable has to be handled by the VUI. What a user specifies is your clue as to what matters to them. Don't ignore it. (He still didn't get his song.)

Meaningful Contextual Prompts

Dave   *Open the pod bay doors, please, HAL. [...]*

Do you read me, HAL?

HAL   *Affirmative, Dave. I read you.*

Dave   *Open the pod bay doors, HAL.*

HAL   *I'm sorry, Dave. I'm afraid I can't do that.*

Dave   *What's the problem?*

HAL   *I think you know what the problem is just as well as I do.*

—*2001: A Space Odyssey* (1968); Stanley Kubrick, Arthur C. Clarke[1]

The famous dialog on spacecraft Discovery in *2001* between Dr. Dave Bowman and the HAL 9000 computer is the 1968 version of an intelligent assistant gone wrong. Good error handling should be clear and concise, informative when possible, and appropriately worded for the intended user base. Don't point fingers: your user may have said something incorrectly, but so what? You may have recognized or interpreted it incorrectly. All you want is to get back on track: quickly let the user know that you couldn't answer a question or fulfill a request. HAL is doing that, but is too smarmy and long-winded. If you're confident that your interpretation is accurate, follow up with a brief explanation of why you can't answer and/or a relevant suggestion for the user. HAL clearly fails on that. If you're not confident, reprompt. And start working on a process for collecting data for tuning (Chapter 17). A noncorrupt helpful HAL could have responded this way:

Dave   *HAL, open the pod bay doors, please.*

HAL   *Sorry. The pod bay is offline, but the emergency airlock is available.*

It's a good idea to use different recovery strategies within your VUI depending on context. The default recovery strategy for many VUIs is an optional error alert preamble followed by a context-sensitive message and reprompt. For example: *Sorry. What time do you want to come in?* or *I still didn't get that. If you need time to find your number, say "Pause."*

---

[1]Easily found online, for example, `https://youtu.be/ARJ8cAGm6JE`

Because your goal is clarity, reprompts are often more verbose than initial prompts. They don't have to be: the simplest reprompt is a short preamble and a repeat of the initial prompt. Sometimes that's perfect, especially in contexts where you don't expect a lot of issues. Sometimes, all you need is an audio earcon (Chapter 9).

You can avoid some unnecessary problems by following a few simple guidelines when writing your recovery prompts. Keep in mind that you're writing for voice, so keep it concise! Take a look at Table 13-1.

Table 13-1. *Guidelines for how to word recovery prompts for voice*

	Avoid	Instead
Keep prompts concise	*My apologies, I didn't understand what you said.*	*Sorry.*
Recognition is never certain	*The number you said...is incorrect.*	*The number I heard... doesn't match.*
Request spoken input	*Provide.../Enter...*	*Say.../Tell me...*
Mic triggered on no speech	*I'm sorry. I don't know the answer to that.*	*(Nothing)*
Respond to spoken input	*You said...*	*I heard...*
Respond to input when modality isn't tracked	*You said...*	*That's ...*

A big reason to never blame the user is that you can't be sure that the user actually did say something incorrect, like a six-digit number instead of an eight-digit number—the recognizer might not have picked up the missing digits.

SUCCESS TIP 13.2 DON'T BE TOO SORRY   If your error prompts start with an apology preamble, don't overdo it. Avoid starting every reprompt with a long *I'm sorry. I didn't understand that* or similar. It wastes the user's time and feels heavy-handed. But you do need to acknowledge to the user that you know you're asking again. A simple *Sorry* is often enough, and even that isn't needed every time.

Escalating Prompts

Escalating prompts are a common approach to error recovery in IVRs—the concept applies well to most contexts and types of VUIs. The idea behind escalating prompts is to balance concise prompts for a quicker dialog with more detailed prompts when necessary. A common approach is a short Retry-1 that escalates to a detailed and explicit Retry-2:

VUI   *You have one refill remaining. Want me to order that refill now?*

User   *Ummm...*

VUI   *Should I place the order?*

User   *Hang on. When will it get here?*

VUI   *I didn't catch that. If you'd like me to order a refill for Prednisone, say "Yes." If not, say "No."*

~ ~ ~

VUI   *You can add, update, or remove a meal. Which would you like?*

User   *This is for yesterday's lunch.*

VUI   *Sorry. Say "Add," "Update," or "Remove."*

User   *What do you mean update?*

VUI   *To add a new meal from scratch, say "Add." To change what's in a meal you already added, say "Update." And if you want to start over or delete a meal, say "Remove."*

Either type of retry can be preceded by an optional short apology fitting what's known about the reason for the retry, for example, *Sorry* or *I didn't catch that*—but, again, go easy on those.

Notice that the escalated prompts sound more like a "heavy-handed" directed dialog? That's done on purpose for added clarity. It doesn't mean that you now only accept the options mentioned in the prompt—coverage should be the same for initial tries and retries. It means that you understand the user's mental model well enough to have a good idea what the most likely issues are based on what they were trying to do when failure happened.

FROM THE VOICE TRENCHES

Data analysis of error prompts from multiple voice systems suggests that including explicit directions like *Please say "yes" or "no"* in fact does decrease out-of-coverage (OOC) rates significantly, sometimes by more than half. Clarity should always be your goal, and sometimes it's OK to be extra clear. You just need to find the right balance: extra clarity is needed where there's confusion, like in retries, not everywhere. Then it sounds stilted and becomes annoying.

Code for Escalating Prompts

Let's look at how to implement escalating prompts. Recall that when no intent is recognized, the response comes from the Default Fallback Intent, which has very generic responses like *I didn't get that*. You're going to add a second-level fallback prompt that has more specific information to help the user. There'll be no work in the Dialogflow GUI for this; it's all done with the webhook:[2]

1. To implement escalating prompts, you need to create a custom handler for the context where the Default Fallback Intent is the same as both the current and previous intents. Your handler also needs to track and check the last non-fallback intent the dialog saw, because that determines the content of the escalating prompt. Luckily, you already have some machinery in place to do that, as you'll see in a moment. You need two modifications to the webhook:

   a. Find the last intent that was not a fallback intent. This drives the content of the escalating prompt.

   b. Implement a handler to provide a second-level escalating prompt for the context.

   Listing 13-1 shows the first change, built on the existing code from implementing universals in Chapter 9. To keep track of the most recent non-fallback intent, you need

---

[2]In 13-1.zip.

to add the following: In webhook_request.py, extend the existing code to initialize name and time of all the most recent intents (A) and the most recent non-fallback intent (B). Then add two more tests for last intents: all intents including universals (C) and non-fallback intents (E). Update the name and time of the most recent of all intents (D) and non-fallback intent (F).

Listing 13-1. Keeping track of the most recent non-fallback intent

```
# ....... In webhook_request.py

# The most recent intent.

# name/time are for excluding universals.

# name_all/time_all are for all intents, including universals.

# name_non_fallback/time_non_fallback are excluding fallback.

# Need that for notion of dialog state for universals.

self.most_recent_intent = {"name": None,

                           "time": 0,

                           "name_all": None,   # A

                           "time_all": 0,

                           "name_non_fallback": None,   # B

                           "time_non_fallback": 0}

# ....... In set_most_recent_intent.py
def set_most_recent_intent(df_request, intent_name, context):
    """

    Set the most recent intent.
    """

    match2 = re.search(r'^intent_\d+_(.*)$', intent_name)
    if match2:
      if 'parameters' in context:
        if 'timestamp' in context['parameters']:
          context_time = context['parameters']['timestamp']
```

```
# Set the last intent, including universals and fallback
if context_time > df_request.most_recent_intent['time_all']:  # C
  df_request.most_recent_intent["name_all"] = match2.group(1)  # D
  df_request.most_recent_intent["time_all"] = context_time

# Set the last non-skippable intent: no universals or fallback
if (context_time > df_request.most_recent_intent['time'] and
    not is_skippable_universal(match2.group(1))):
df_request.most_recent_intent["name"] = match2.group(1)
df_request.most_recent_intent["time"] = context_time

# Set the last non-fallback intent, for escalating prompts.
if (context_time >
  df_request.most_recent_intent['time_non_fallback'] and
    not match2.group(1) == 'default_fallback_intent'):  # E
  df_request.most_recent_intent["name_non_fallback"] = \  # F
    match2.group(1)
  df_request.most_recent_intent["time_non_fallback"] = \
    context_time
```

Now the second change: adding the actual escalating prompts. You can implement this all in the block of code that tests whether the current intent is the Default Fallback Intent (Listing 13-2). You first saw this block of code in Chapter 11 when learning about regular expressions and the spaCy parser. Now you want to add a new condition (B) that checks whether the last intent is the same as the Default Fallback Intent. If they're the same, then it's a candidate for escalation. This test is the reason behind adding the feature to track all intents, including universals and fallbacks.

As you learned, escalating prompts work best when they're both content- and context-specific. That means you need to implement each second-level prompt separately for each context. Remember the main intent handler code in main.py? You'll do the same again here: define a dictionary of handlers (A), get the handler (C), and then apply it (D). If you don't find a handler, do what you were going to do (E). In Listing 13-2, we only show the logic and detailed nomatch prompt for when the last non-fallback intent was arEnterDOB. Using this, you can easily add and expand to other intents and situations.

Listing 13-2. Adding second-level nomatch handling

```
else:
  # No dependency parse match

  # Look for a handler for nomatch 2 prompts
  nomatch2_dialog_functions = {  # A
    'arenterdob': ar_enter_dob_escalating_nomatch}

  # Get the handler function based on the intent name.
  handler_function = None

  last_intent = df_request.most_recent_intent["name_all"]
  if last_intent == 'default_fallback_intent':  # B
    # 2nd and above nomatch
    intent = df_request.most_recent_intent["name_non_fallback"]
    if intent:
      handler_function = nomatch2_dialog_functions.get(intent).  # C

  if handler_function:
    handler_function.__call__(df_request, df_response)  # D
  else:
    # No escalating handler; do what would have been done
    df_response.output_text = df_request.fulfillment_text  # E
```

Now, add the handler in a new file ar_enter_dob.py (Listing 13-3).

Listing 13-3. Escalating nomatch prompt handler for arEnterDOB.

```
def ar_enter_dob_escalating_nomatch(df_request,
                                    df_response):
    """

    Escalating nomatch prompt for arEnterDOB
    """

    df_response.output_text = ('Sorry, I still didn\'t understand. '
                               'Please give your date of birth as month, '
                               'day, and year. For example, say, '
                               'March third, 2001.')
```

Test it: say *date of birth* and then two nonsense phrases in a row. As a response to the first nonsense phrase, you should hear one of the standard default fallback phrases, like *Sorry, I didn't get that*. The response to the second nomatch should be the escalated prompt you just added.

Tapered Prompts

Tapering refers to the gradual shortening of wording within a longer prompt. This is used when offering a list of options, especially when referring to other modalities, like tapping or entering a numeric option. Again, the purpose is to balance clarity with conciseness. Tapering can be used in initial prompts or retry prompts.

For example, *To get a refill, press 1. For order status, press 2. Address change, press 3. Adding dependents, 4. Policy information, 5.* The instructions get gradually shorter with each option as the pattern is established. Tapering is used less in voice-only contexts because it saves very little in conciseness while potentially adding confusion.

Rapid Reprompt

When you say "What was that?" or "Huh?" because you didn't hear or understand the speaker, that's **rapid reprompt**. The idea behind rapid reprompting is that the prompt is very short and natural, so the hope is for a natural and more carefully spoken repeat of a request or response. There are potential problems with rapid reprompting. The user will probably repeat the same thing again, just louder—it's typically what people do as a response in conversation. That means if the utterance was OOC the first time, it still is the second time. If they didn't actually say anything but the VUI triggered, that's also an odd experience. Rapid reprompting doesn't make clear if an utterance wasn't understood or not loud enough to be heard (Figure 13-1).

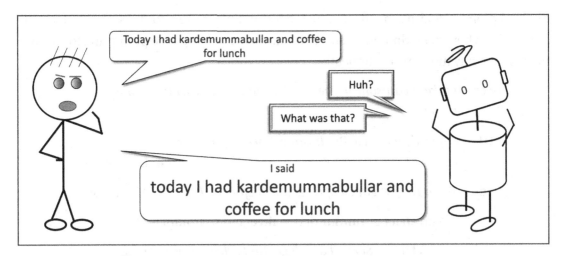

Figure 13-1. *Rapid reprompting often results in the same utterance repeated, but louder*

Some rapid reprompts are more likely to succeed than others. If your implementation is able to differentiate between not hearing (a no-speech timeout) and not understanding (a recognition reject), then yes you can have different responses for different conditions resulting in awesome natural conversations. Avoid stand-alone general reprompts like *Pardon?* or *Sorry?* or *Could you repeat that?* Especially don't use that last one—you don't want someone to repeat what's OOC! Generic ones may be easy and quick to implement, but you have more success with contextual reprompts: *What's that prescription number again?* or *An appointment for when?* or *Who did you want to call?* Conciseness, great; clarity, obligatory. It signals a shared mental model to the user.

Backoff Strategies

If your VUI isn't understanding the user, especially when asking an open-ended question, back off to a more directed dialog. It's OK. There's nothing inherently bad about a more directed dialog. It's still natural and conversational; it's just clearer what response is expected. People use the same strategy, so why shouldn't your VUI? The immediate goal is to get that conversation back on track. Importantly, backing off to directed prompts doesn't mean you remove the ability for users to still speak as naturally as they did when you didn't understand them. You just change the prompting to clarify; the abilities stay the same underneath:

> **User**   *I take Prednisone in the morning and... no, evening... one tablet.*
>
> **VUI**   *Sorry, do you take Prednisone morning, day, or evening?*   ← Directed
>
> **User**   *Yeah, 10 milligrams of it, usually before bed*   ← Multi-slot
>
> > ~ ~ ~ With **strict grammar** tied to **directed** reprompt ~ ~ ~
> >
> > > ~ ~ ~ **VUI1**   *Sorry, I didn't get that. Please say morning, day, or evening.*
> >
> > ~ ~ ~ With **open grammar** handling **multi-slot** responses ~ ~ ~
> >
> > > ~ ~ ~ **VUI2**   *I added Prednisone, 10 milligrams, evening, to your meds list.*

An important backoff strategy for a question-answer VUI is to respond with a broader and less specific answer to a user's question. You saw this in Chapter 11: the VUI doesn't recognize the dish in *Can I eat sticky galangal rice today?* but knows about *rice*. So instead of rejecting the question, the answer is *I haven't heard of that, but most rice dishes are off the menu till after your procedure*, a much better experience.

There are many other backoff approaches:

- **Do nothing**: Close the mic, stop listening, and go idle. This is common when a wake word has triggered by mistake.

- **Ignore the "error-ness" in the reprompt**: Act like it wasn't an error by not calling it out. No apologies or explicit requests to try again. Instead, follow up with additional details as examples or explicit options. This incremental prompt is particularly useful in free-form open questions when the user doesn't know how to respond:

> **User**   *Can I eat chicken still?*
>
> **VUI**   *What type of chicken?*
>
> **User**   *Umm, stupid ones with two legs?*

> **VUI** *Examples are fried chicken or chicken cacciatore or even a chicken sandwich. Describe the type of chicken you're wondering about.*

- **Automatically provide the next N-best item**: If the user disconfirms N(1) and you put it on a skip list, can't you just ask if N(2) is the right one? If there only are two options, then it can work. But if there're more possibilities, be careful. The conversation can become disconcerting, sounding like the VUI is guessing. In the next example, the recognition fails on "for one," resulting in N-best results of "9" and then "1":

User	*A table for one.*	← Misrecognized number
VUI	*Nine guests. Right?*	← N(1) = "9"
User	*No!*	← Put "9" on skip list
VUI	*Sorry, that's one guest, right?*	← N(2) = "1"
User	*Yes (phew).*	

- You can use skip lists for intents to not give the same answer again. If a user asks the same question again right after asking it the first time, but phrasing it differently, chances are you didn't answer their question the first time.

- **Tiered retry methods based on confidence scores**: If you have access to recognition confidence scores, you can create sophisticated conversations by using different error handling methods for different levels of confidence. For example, in a multistep financial interaction, you can confirm only results with lower confidence until the final overall confirmation. Also track which entities were confirmed earlier in the dialog. You can then combine scores and known confirmations to focus later error handling on the entities that you're less sure about.

In Chapter 12, you learned conceptually how to use confidence and/or N-best lists to create smart dialogs to reduce errors—Dialogflow doesn't reliably give access to confidence scores or N-best lists, though the Google Cloud Speech-to-Text API does.

MULTIMODAL CORNER

If your VUI is multimodal, **offer another modality** for retries. This is a common approach in IVRs, where touch-tone entry is encouraged when voice is unsuccessful. Point out the option of typing when there's a keyboard or tapping when there are buttons. Don't remove the option to speak; let your user decide what works best for their situation. You can use the same approach across all retries while staying with voice in all initial prompts, or you can offer to switch over completely to another modality if the user has wider difficulties. In the drug name dialog, in addition to *Please say morning, day, or evening*, you'd have three buttons on the screen, labeled "Morning," "Day," and "Evening." Having both reinforces the options in either modality; any content words need to match across modalities. If the full text of a spoken prompt appears on the screen, it needs to match word by word—a mismatch even in non-content words increases cognitive load. We found the strongest cross-modal reinforcement when content words appeared on screen alone or in highly modified (compared to voice prompts) short phrases.

When to Stop Trying

Your ability to control the number of retries and the wording or method of those retries is platform- and device-dependent. You'll need to choose the right number of retries depending on context and task. Your VUI should try harder for anything that's costly, such as health or money tasks, privacy or security, or when the rest of the conversation builds on getting this piece of information correct. Most home voice assistants either don't try again or try only once if some piece of information is necessary for the conversation to continue and some request to be fulfilled. When a response is necessary to proceed, many IVRs attempt two retries for a maximum number of three total (1 initial + 2 retries); after that, the caller is transferred to customer support, or some other behavior takes place to move toward task completion.

Three attempts is a lot. IVRs tend to "try harder" exactly because the dialogs often are multi-turn, filling slots toward transaction completion. It's appropriate to attempt some retries in that situation, because just stopping the conversation and forgetting everything the caller said is rude and aggravating. On the other hand, never force callers to keep trying. At times, businesses try to keep callers in the IVR by setting a very high number of retries before transferring the caller to a person. That serves no purpose other than annoying the caller, resulting in bad PR for that business and IVRs in general.

FROM THE VOICE TRENCHES

A Nuance comparison of error handling success rates across many voice IVRs in different domains suggests that one retry of a particular prompt or dialog state was beneficial, but a second retry on average gave less than 5% incremental success rate. At the same time, half of the users faced with a second retry failed, either because they were still not understood or because they simply gave up. Other data analyses elsewhere have come to similar conclusions. It's an important tradeoff to understand: always ask yourself if a task makes it necessary to ask users multiple times or if you can move the conversation forward by making a "best guess" assumption or by using one of the other techniques in this chapter.

Max Error Counts

Some VUIs make use of error counts for a whole dialog interaction, often in addition to error counts for each particular dialog state. When the max error scope is the whole conversation, it means the interaction can move forward, even when a user (for whatever reason) needs multiple attempts for each slot or step.

Once the max error count is reached, the VUI behavior changes under the assumption that the user is having trouble overall for some particular reason, like background noise or a strong accent. Typical behavior changes include switching to a more directed dialog, offering additional help or transfer, or encouraging use of another input method (if that's an option), like keypad entry for numbers. Be aware that changing something about the interaction can confuse and annoy users. Some financial voice systems automatically switch from voice to touch-tone input after the max error count is reached. That helps some users, but it's definitely not great for everyone—some VUIs even ask the user, *We seem to have trouble understanding each other. If you want to switch to touch-tones, press 1...* If you switch input modality, clearly alert the user about what's happening, and continue allowing previous methods.

Remember to reset error counters after the conversation is done. And by "done" we mean a combination of a short time and reaching successful endpoints in a dialog.

Code for Keeping Track of Max Errors

You implement max error counters via the webhook. There are several things you need to do:

- Slightly modify the format of the output contexts that track intents. Right now the name of the context is intent_INTENT, where INTENT represents the name of the intent. This has worked fine so far, but what happens if you have more than one intent with the same name? It just overwrites the previous one. That clearly won't work if you want to count and track the number of errors. You need to add a timestamp to the intent name to guarantee that you get a context per intent.

- Count the number of errors in a time window. Here, you'll use 30 seconds, but that may or may not be a good length for all situations. It's something you'd reevaluate when you have real user data for tuning your system performance (Chapters 16 and 17).

- Add a different behavior for the condition of maximum number of errors allowed in the time window. To illustrate how to implement it, we use max = 3, but a lower number is usually appropriate.

Listings 13-4 and 13-5 show the changes needed to include the timestamp in the output contexts.[3] The first step is to modify the new_context function (Listing 13-4). Get the current time at the beginning of the function now since it will be used later (A). If the name is for an intent context, add the integer (seconds) part of the timestamp (B). If it's an intent context, make the lifespan longer so that it can be tracked (C). Use the current time that was set at the beginning of the function (D).

Listing 13-4. Modifying the new_context function to add timestamp to the context name

```
def new_context(name):
    """

    Return a new output context with a given name.
    """
```

---

[3]Code for this section is in 13-2.zip.

```
time_now = time.time()  # A
lifespan_count = 5

# If it's an intent context, add the timestamp.
if name.startswith('intent'):
    name = re.sub('^intent_', 'intent_%s_' % int(time_now), name)  # B
    lifespan_count = 50  # C

# The full context name is long; "callbyname" is only the last part.
context = {
    'name': ("projects/${PROJECT_ID}/agent/sessions/"
             f"${{SESSION_ID}}/contexts/{name}"),
    'lifespanCount': lifespan_count,
    # Add the time to find the most recent context
    'parameters': {
        'timestamp': time_now  # D
    }
}
return context
```

In Listing 13-5 (in set_most_recent_intent.py), you see the modified code that checks for intent contexts now that you have timestamps in the context names. Add \d+ to the regular expression to find the new intent context format (A).

Listing 13-5. Accounting for the timestamp when searching contexts for past intents

```
def set_most_recent_intent(df_request, intent_name, context):
    """
    Set the most recent intent.
    """
    match2 = re.search(r'^intent_\d+_(.*)$', intent_name)     #A
    if match2:
```

Now that the intents are tracked properly, you need to count the number of error intents in the time window. Listing 13-6 (from webhook_request.py) shows how: Initialize the number of errors seen (A). Specify the length of the error window in seconds (B) and the maximum number of errors in the time window (C). Get the current time to find the number of errors relative to now (D). Check if the intent is within the time window and an error for the default intent (E). Increment the number of errors (F).

Listing 13-6. Counting the number of errors in a time window

```python
# Error information

# numErrors: How many errors have we seen in the past time period

# errorWindow: Error time window in seconds

# maxErrors: The maximum number of errors in the window before we

# change strategies

self.error_information = {"numErrors": 0,  # A

                          "errorWindow": 30,  # B

                          "maxErrors": 3}  # C

# Get the current time

self.current_time = time.time()  # D

#...... Code listing cut for focus
    context_time = context['parameters']['timestamp']      # E

#...... Code listing cut for focus
    if (df_request.current_time - context_time <  #F
            df_request.error_information['errorWindow'] and
            match2.group(1) == 'default_fallback_intent'):
        df_request.error_information["numErrors"] = \  # G
            df_request.error_information['numErrors'] + 1
```

Finally, in `fallback.py`, add whatever behavior you want for the user who experiences a max error count in their conversation. Listing 13-7 shows how this might look: Test if the max number of errors is reached; use -1 since current intent is an error (A). Include a placeholder for the fallback behavior so you can move on even if that's not designed or implemented yet (B).

Listing 13-7. Handling max errors

```
def fallback(
    df_request,
    df_response):
"""

fallback
"""

if (df_request.error_information.get('numErrors') >= \
    df_request.error_information.get('maxErrors') - 1:  # A
    # If already too many errors, try another method
    df_response.output_text = 'OK let\'s try this another way.' # B
```

Listing 13-7 includes the logic for checking whether or not the max number of errors has been reached and a placeholder for the custom handling you want to happen in the max error case. We don't specify the handling here, but depending on context and strategy, you might take the user down a different dialog path, such as a directed step-by-step dialog, or give some other detailed assistance. Importantly, this added test needs to be the first one done in the code block.

Transfers

There are many reasons for transferring the conversation to another modality, another app, or even a person. Having human backup isn't just something for IVRs. Any voice system on any device could allow handoff to a person for assistance, either as a routing endpoint or for assistance under some circumstances. Here are some guidelines for incorporating transfers:

- Include prompt wording that assures users they will in fact be transferred. If the wait is long, tell them how long.

- If your VUI has human backup only during some times of day, don't offer to transfer during off-hours only to then say nobody's available. You need different versions of prompts where you offer transfers. This works best if you know your user's approximate geographical location; if not, make sure to include time zones in prompts.

- Transfer requests are more likely in some dialogs than others. They're most likely in menus and at the start of multistep transactions—less likely for simple Yes/No questions or A/B "this or that" options. Costlier tasks are more likely to see more transfers.

- Transfer requests are more likely when prompts are unclear to users, so review transfer rates at each prompt, if you can. Expert users are less likely to request a transfer than novice users unless they know they need to speak to someone to get their task handled.

- Agent requests typically decline over time and often spike at specific times depending on task: before tax time, after bills are mailed out, or before a scheduled procedure.

- If users have some type of relationship with a human or expect one, like medical staff, be clear about how to get in touch. A multimodal voice app could include a direct call button. On a home voice assistant, you may or may not be able to do a direct call. If not, provide a phone number or something else that works for the situation.

When talking about transfers, the elephant in the room is that some stakeholders think the best way to save money is keeping users away from human help. The truth is some people prefer automation; others prefer talking to a human. Some want different interactions depending on context and topic. What people **do** want is the ability to choose. If you find yourself arguing for making transfers explicitly available, here's some information to use:

- In a financial VUI, agent transfer was explained up front as an always available option. Because of this easy out, users were more willing to give things a try and were overall quite successful staying in automation. The same was true in an airline VUI. Overall transfer rates were not higher than VUIs where the transfer option was hidden from users; only 5–6% chose immediate transfer rather than trying automation.

- The Harvard Business Review (HBR) confirms this behavior in several controlled studies. Their results show that users are happier just by having the option to contact a human and, importantly, having that option doesn't mean people use it. The HBR concludes that "Merely offering access to talk to a person can be enough to restore customer confidence, improve trust in the firm, and strengthen long-term relationships" (`https://hbr.org/2019/04/why-anxious-customers-prefer-human-customer-service`).

SUCCESS TIP 13.3 NEVER HIDE YOUR HUMANS   If you work with or for a company that has live representatives, don't hinder your end users from talking to them. Really, just don't. People have many valid reasons to want to talk to a person. You'll only annoy them if you try keeping them in automation. Automation of any conversation should be in addition to rather than taking the place of. It also breaks trust and Grice's principles of truthfulness and providing necessary information in dialogs (Chapter 6).

Choosing a Recovery Strategy

Your ability to use a particular strategy depends on the platform you're using. The more you rely on built-in modules, the less choice you have for prompt wording and retry method. You'll also be limited in terms of the specific error conditions that are tracked. You may or may not be able to tell the difference between a no-speech and nomatch or between different backend errors. This impacts your ability to give the user targeted information to help them understand what went wrong.

You'll use different strategies in a single VUI, choosing the best method for each situation based on context, device, modality, dialog flow details, and so on. Here are some guidelines:

- Make error prompting clear and focused; anticipate the types of issues a user might have and target those in contextual prompt wording.

- If your prompt addresses the type of issue (recognition, intent mapping, or fulfillment), make sure you respond with the appropriate prompt for the situation.

- If your prompt wording encourages a directed dialog or alternative input modality, you still need to accept the same open-ended input your initial prompts did.

- If your initial question is open-ended, include concrete options in your retry prompts, as examples, as a list of options, or as more directed dialog backoff.

- If you have access to error condition details, such as reasons for a backend failure, use them for contextual error prompting rather than using a single generic error prompt.

- If available, use N-best and skip lists for large or confusable grammars (Chapter 12) to avoid retrying with a result the user already said wasn't a match.

- Allow one-step correction (Chapter 13) when users are asked for explicit confirmation; without it, error counts can escalate quickly exactly when users speak very naturally.

- Keep the number of forced retries as low as possible:

  - If an accurate response isn't necessary to continue, don't keep asking. Use other information to make a best guess, or just stop.

  - If an accurate answer is needed to continue, it's better to change methods than keep trying the same way, but don't remove any option from handling.

What's Next

You learn more about how to handle failed fulfillment when you dive into customization and working with data in Chapter 15. The only way to minimize failure and maximize overall conversation success is to collect relevant data and analyze issues based on an understanding of both the technology and the users. Chapters 16 and 17 cover this in detail—it's important enough for two chapters.

Testing VUIs by straying off the happy path teaches you better VUI design and development by noticing what goes wrong and how the result sounds. Be curious about what works and doesn't, and figure out why. Notice what happens when you yourself get misunderstood: how do you react, why do you think it happened, and how did you change your behavior to get back on track? Translate that into what could have been done better and test your assumptions on others. You're on your way to becoming a well-rounded voice practitioner!

As you can imagine, your overall design and implementation can get quite complex if you want to make use of different error handling methods for different intents and contexts. Next in Chapter 14, you'll see how different error conditions combine with a variety of contexts. You'll understand why careful design and development efforts are necessary to track and handle the many resulting combinations.

Summary

- Although recognition performance today is excellent, there's still no guarantee that people are recognized correctly. That means your design and implementation always has to account for misrecognition and nomatches to assist the user in getting back on track if and when errors happen. The difference between a great and a so-so VUI is in how many people go down error paths and how easily they get back on track.

- Never blame your users—they're seldom the cause for things going wrong.

- Not everyone thinks the same way and not everyone's environment is the same. Backoff strategies need to help users across mental models and contexts to succeed.

- Know when to stop trying—try more times if the rest of your dialog depends on getting it right.

- Choose the appropriate recovery type for the task, domain, users, and platform—your recovery methods are constrained by what's available on the platform you're using.

## CHAPTER 14

Using Context and Data to Create Smarter Conversations

Context refers to all the knowledge, perception, language, and environment that affect the exact interpretation of an utterance and conversation. To understand context, think of a simple request you'd make of someone—maybe *Open the window upstairs* or *Turn down the volume* or *What time do we need to leave?* What assumptions do you make when saying this? How does your wording change depending on who you're talking to, their current location as well as your own, how well they know you and the topic, who else is nearby, what they're doing, and what else is happening around you? How might the response differ depending on the assumptions you make?

Context is important enough for its own chapter. We'll cover designing for short- and long-term contexts, how to use proactive data and domain knowledge for better user experiences, and how to work with dynamic data. In most of our discussion, we use "context" when referring to the general concept in human communication of interpreting meaning based on circumstances and details of a situation. When we show you how to implement context as strings in Dialogflow, it'll be clear—from context! — that we're referring to the platform-specific details.

Why There's No Conversation Without Context

Look at Figure 14-1. By asking to *Turn up the game*, the speaker assumes a lot of shared context. One listener is near enough to see and hear what the speaker sees and hears; the other is in another room. All responses here are the results of the listener's interpretations and the speaker's assumptions about shared knowledge (what sport,

A. Thymé-Gobbel and C. Jankowski, *Mastering Voice Interfaces*, https://doi.org/10.1007/978-1-4842-7005-9_14

what teams, where, turn it up how much), information accuracy (when is it on, what channel), proximity of the listener (what else is the listener doing, are they able to fulfill the request, do they even know they're being addressed), earlier conversations (has the request been made more than once), ambiguity, ability and desire to help, and so on. In addition, there's misrecognition and misinterpretation. If any assumptions are incorrect, the listener response shows it, and the speaker responds based on the new context. Easy enough for a person, but far from trivial for a voice system.

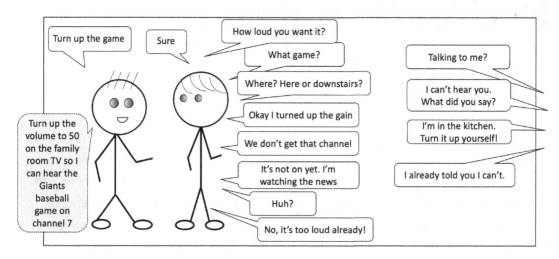

Figure 14-1. *Many context qualities and dimensions interact, resulting in assumptions made by speakers and listeners*

Context is king in VUI conversations as well as in human dialogs. With each dialog turn, shared understanding is created and refined based on knowing (or not knowing) the user's immediate environment and location, past experiences, likes and dislikes, time and day, and what is or isn't possible in the world. People don't usually communicate in fully specified single utterances—the kind of utterance shown in the gray bubble in Figure 14-1—or in impressive "one-and-done" fully specified VUI requests: *Find a movie I can watch for free online tonight and that stars Will Smith and is no more than 5 years old.* You need to handle both the well-specified and the vague or incomplete requests; in some contexts users are very precise in what they ask for, like power users who place a bet or make a stock option order. But most natural conversations are a back-and-forth with each person questioning, explaining, clarifying, narrowing down, and verifying understanding—not to mention hesitations, incomplete phrases, and topic jumps. Each step builds on previous turns, refining and changing the overall context, directly affecting the next response and dialog turn. If your VUI "forgets"

496

the context of a request as soon as the microphone stops listening, it can't handle conversational interactions. VUIs need contextual awareness to respond sensibly; people expect to be able to refine a search built on information from preceding dialog turns, to be asked for clarification only when necessary, and not to have to waste time when the relevant context has already been established.

Conversational context is complex; it covers many dimensions—basically anything that affects what someone says and how they say it and what assumptions they make. Some contexts, like time of day, are easy to quantify and apply to the dialog. Other contexts, like user's frame of mind, are less so. Take a look at the context examples in Table 14-1.

Table 14-1. *Examples of common types of context*

Context type	Example
Domain and topic	Medical, food, entertainment
Task	Info lookup, play music, make reservation, call someone, order something, get instructions
User identity	Identified, unidentified; number of known users; child/adult
Time	Absolute: 2 AM, "January 4th," "2021"; every Sunday, weekdays
Clock and calendar	Relative: *tomorrow, before my appointment, last time*. User availability,
Time zone	calendar events
Location	Geolocation: Brisbane, London, Canada
Environment	Environment: indoors, at home, in the kitchen, proximity to VUI
Device	One device, multiple connected devices, has screen, wearable, stationary, physical dedicated or built-in
Conversation history	Pronoun reference *(When do **they** open?), the first one, go back, repeat that*. Recognition certainty Time since last user utterance
Past interactions	Past appointment history
Customizations	Language, volume, user expertise level, music preferences
Device activity	Device idle/off/playing other audio; urgency of response
User frame of mind and activity	Distracted, hands busy, eyes busy, driving, upset, nervous
Security and regulation	Legal, business, limited data access

This can seem like an overwhelming mountain to climb. We get it. Remember: We're pointing out many areas where today's voice implementations can be improved, and context is one of those areas. That doesn't mean you need to design, implement, and test every context that possibly applies to your VUI before you launch a product. We just want to make you aware of how important context is and what incorporating context lets you do. What you'll do is to figure out what contexts are important for your particular VUI task and users and then start with the one or two that are most important. For example, for the procedure prep helper, the most important context is relative time, so that users can ask *Can I eat __ **today?*** If your VUI lets users play music from speakers in different rooms, the most relevant contexts are the current activity on the speaker (on/off/idle/playing) and speaker location (*Play __ **in the kitchen*** or *Play __ **here***).

FROM THE VOICE TRENCHES

Ann added voice-controlled lights under her kitchen bar counter. When she asked one of her home voice assistants to *Turn on bar counter*, the VUI's response was to bark like a dog! After a moment of annoyance, she eagerly recorded the interaction for posterity as a great example of how things should not work. The issue here is tripping over phonetic similarity (*bark* vs. *bar counter*) while prioritizing contexts incorrectly (the architecture favored a never-before-used skill that barks over the user's name for their local device) when matching utterance to intent.

Your VUI's responses should be the product of all relevant implemented contexts—and you usually need to evaluate them in combination! For example, if your VUI asks for a calendar date, user responses differ depending on task: people often say credit card expirations like they're written on the card (*1 0 2 4* or *ten twenty-four*), but others convert it to *October (twenty) twenty-four*. But if the VUI collects work history, you can expect responses for start or end dates to include the names of the months, not digits.

When several responses are possible, contexts need to be layered and prioritized appropriately, taking relevance into consideration. In this example, the user-named device bar counter should take priority over something that barks and has never been engaged by the user. And, no, limiting what the users can call their lights is never the right solution, assuming it's a pronounceable word.

SUCCESS TIP 14.1 TAILOR RESPONSES FOR EVERY CONTEXT   This is a core VUI best practice. If a VUI responds well to different contexts across conversations and understands the contextual assumptions in what the user says, people will think of those conversations as interesting, smart, and successful. Your design and implementation should focus on incorporating that variation. Sure, more tailored responses are more effort. But you don't have to include a lot before your initial product launch. Even adding a single context, when it's the right one, makes your VUI seem smarter and your users will notice. Start simple and iterate.

This complexity is reflected in any well-defined detailed VUI dialog design spec. In fact, it's a core reason why many specs we've worked on are in table or spreadsheet format. It's the most efficient and easy-to-read format when many dimensions are at play, and it reflects the dialog manager aspect of complex designs. You'll understand why after reading this chapter.

Figure 14-2 gives you some idea of how complex context can get—and why you pick one or two to start. The drawing is from an informal discussion about contexts affecting users' conversations with connected devices (lights, speakers, screens, thermostats, locks, etc.) in a house. We stopped when we ran out of room on the paper!

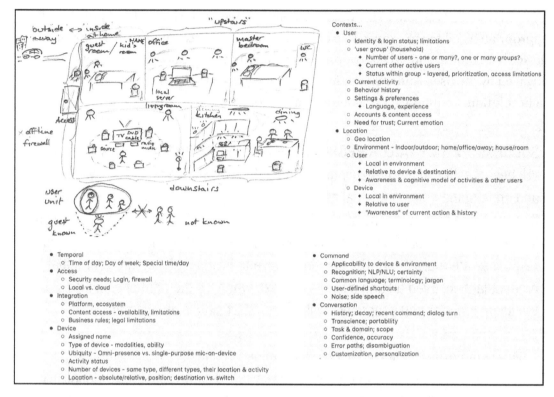

Figure 14-2. *Illustration of context complexity affecting user behavior with various devices in a house*

Hands-On: Context Complexity Thought Experiment

To get a sense of how contexts interact to provide a good user experience, anyone involved in voice technology should try this exercise: create voice timers for a home.

Assume your home has multiple rooms with multiple VUI assistant devices that are in the same ecosystem and potentially connected. You live with other people, maybe roommates, maybe family. How would you design a timer voice app for maximal flexibility and convenience for all in your household? Think about use cases, contexts, and implications. Here's a start:

Interaction flow: Should there be a limit on the number of timers? If so, how many? Do users want to hear a list of all current timers? If so, how do you present the list in a brief and meaningful way? When and how do you need to disambiguate? When and how do you offer retries and provide help? What type of retry is appropriate? How will users know that the time was set correctly? How can users change, add on to, or cancel a timer? What type of help is helpful at different parts of the dialog? Is a tutorial useful? Or examples? What should happen to timers if the power goes out?

User location: Does behavior depend on where/what room a user is in when they set a timer? What should happen if users move between rooms (assuming VUI access in each room), maybe starting a timer in one room and querying or ending it in another? Can users—and should they be able to—interact with timers from a mobile device or car if you leave your house?

Coverage: What utterances are recognized? How do you deal with partially specified or misrecognized requests? What makes some requests unambiguous?

User access: Do you know or care who set it? How does your decision affect the dialog? Can anyone cancel a timer they didn't set? Do users expect secure access and privacy?

Device: Does current device activity impact your design? What's the prioritization hierarchy when multiple contexts are in conflict? And under what circumstances does that hierarchy shift? If the device is actively playing some content or answering a user question or even sounding another timer or alarm, what happens? Pause, lower ("duck") the content volume, wait till previous action is done, interrupt?

Integration: Any design decisions need to be changed due to integration limitations? How long will the end alert play if nobody stops it? Limits on number of timers or durations? Can you allow users to name their timers? If so, any limitations on those names? Why or why not? Will you use TTS or record the user for those names? What if multiple timers have the same name or duration? Are timers linked to power or settings of other devices? If so, how do these devices communicate with each other? Can you track timers across connected devices in different locations? What behaviors do you need to track to implement the flow?

Temporal: Does time of day or day of week need special handling?

User personalization: Can timers play user-specified tunes on completion?

Access: Any legal or geolocation limitations? Ecosystem limitations?

You get the idea. These are the types of questions you should address when building any VUI. Most of all, practice your empathy skills: really think about different use cases, understanding that different people have different needs. Ask some people what they'd want. Write sample dialogs and create flow diagrams. If you try building some of it, great, but even if you don't, this is a useful exercise that brings home how quickly things get complex.

FROM THE VOICE TRENCHES

Ann's house has several lights that are controlled via home virtual assistants. She has not enabled any shopping-by-voice feature. Beside setting a timer, turning the lights on or off is the only thing done when speaking to the assistants in the kitchen. One evening, she made a typical request to *turn off the under-cabinet light*. Imagine her surprise when instead, this assistant put some hideous kitchen cabinet door handles in her shopping cart. There are multiple issues with this outcome, as well as multiple ignored contexts: First, shopping is a financial transaction; therefore, it needs user confirmation. Here, it should not happen at all since the functionality was not enabled. The utterance audio quality was poor (Ann had turned away from the device and was heading out the door). Any utterance with such poor quality should either be rejected or be matched to something that has been requested many times before. It certainly should not be interpreted as something that's never been requested, especially something as high risk as a purchase of something never viewed.

The multiple contexts affect conversations at every level, from recognition to interpretation to fulfillment. Before exploring how to make use of contexts to create smarter-sounding conversations, let's first understand the underlying pieces needed for implementing context: data access and persistence tracking.

Data Access

To make use of context, you need timely access to relevant and accurate data. You've seen examples where data is used to set the right context for an intelligent dialog: getting business hours and availability for making a reservation, accessing a contact list to call someone, requesting to hear a particular song from a specific music provider, changing volume where music is playing, ordering remaining refills, asking about eating some food relative to the time of a procedure, narrowing down a search for a restaurant, and so on.

You need the ability to read data from several sources, capture data, and track the changes that result from information collected in the conversation and even make updates to more permanent user settings and accounts. You also need to decide when to stop tracking each piece of information, how long to keep that information available for later dialogs, and what to do if different pieces of information affect each other.

VUI conversations are influenced by data from two sources: the user (through an utterance or response) and the VUI (based on lookup, confidence, and availability). As soon as user data is captured and interpreted, your integration turns it into information that can be accessed for some period of time until it's no longer relevant for the current or future conversations, at which point you can let it go. Different information differs in context permanence and relevance:

- **Static**: Unchanging information. It's not that it never changes; it just doesn't change during the conversation. Examples are currently assigned device names (*bar counter light*) or a restaurant address.

- **Dynamic**: Information that's filled or changes as a result of further information collected during the conversation. Examples are the time in a restaurant reservation, amount for a bill payment, and remaining refills for a prescription.

- **Relative**: Information that changes relative to contexts outside of the dialog, such as current time and day, device status, the song currently playing, or changes in user conditions and environment. An example is diet recommendations that change as the user gets closer to their procedure date.

- **Fleeting**: What's "remembered" from one dialog turn to the next in an active conversation. This is maybe the trickiest aspect as it's related to how people think and converse. The intent of the user's previous utterance and the VUI response they got are relevant if the user asks for a repetition, but only for a few seconds. The number of retries in a conversation, what slots are filled and with what values, and even in what order they were filled all can influence the dialog flow, but only for a short time until the goal of the conversation has been reached. The data is either temporarily kept within your VUI, or it's owned and updated more permanently through some external service.

External Accounts and Services

General context (like time of day) and conversational context (like user behavior and recognition results) are tricky enough to handle correctly, but at least they're local and accessible. Sometimes you need to set context that relies on access to data from external accounts or services, like entertainment content providers, drug name databases, store hours, and hotel room availability. That's a whole other level of complex—not just because of technical issues, but because of business rules and legal access limitations.

Imagine you're on a flight and ask for a *Diet Pepsi* but the airline has an agreement with Coca-Cola, so you're handed a Coke Zero instead. Or vice versa—we're not playing favorites. If you're a fan of sugar-free cola drinks, you know they taste different. If you like one but not the other, you won't be happy. You'd have liked to know in advance to set your expectations or choose another beverage. The same is true for voice solution fulfillment.

Let's assume that your VUI allows music search. A user requests to *Play "Hallelujah" by Leonard Cohen*. Try this yourself with any smart speaker you have nearby. After recognizing what was said, the VUI must make some choices:

1. What is this thing I'm being asked to play?

    a. Is it a song? An album? Maybe a whole musical? Is there a definitive version? Is Cohen the performer or the one who wrote it or both?

2. Where can I get it?

    a. What music services has the user linked to? Maybe it's available on a local server? Is one source the default—what if it's not there?

3. If I find several matches, how do I pick one?

    a. Which one should I play? The highest-quality one? The most recent? A studio or live version? Are cover versions OK? What's the definition of "closest match" anyway? Is it more important to play the song or the artist?

    b. Are there business rules to prioritize one match over another? What about regulation for content access based on geographical location? Does the user have a limit on the number of songs they can play from one of the providers?

4. Picked one! I'm ready to play it...but where?

   a. How many devices are there? Is there a default device? Is it on?
      Is it already playing something now? What's near the user?

These aren't just hypothetical brainteasers or technical questions with a single right answer. In fact, technology is seldom the limitation in these situations. Business goals, data ownership, platform cross-functionality, and laws all create contexts you need to handle; and they potentially limit your ability to fulfill users' requests exactly how they had hoped. The point of context here is to give the user what they asked for without having to specify every detail. To keep things simple, settle on defaults for all search criteria. Make the music provider with the largest catalog the music source default. Make the active audio player the default; if everything is idle and the device the user is talking to can play music, then play it there. For picking specific content, apply default rules there too so users don't always have to specify *Play **the song** __ by **the artist** __*. Your defaults also interpret the media type of any names in the request: choose a song over an album or playlist. If you have a history of songs the user played in the past, return the same version. Otherwise, play the most frequently requested version over others. When you break it down like that, it becomes quite manageable and gives you a rule set that you can expand later with more detailed defaults: the original artist over a cover version, a studio over live version, and so on. Your defaults allow users to hear their music without having to be long-winded. And remember these are defaults: if the user specifies media type (*the album, live*) or source (*my local server*) or destination (*in my office*), you use that instead to fulfill the search. External data from a system perspective.

In Chapter 1, you learned about the general architecture of a voice system (Figure 14-3). Recall the dialog management (DM) component and the three data sources it connects to: the application database with information useful for answering queries, the conversation database that tracks what's happening in the VUI, and the user database relevant to personalized behaviors. All three are involved in the context that determines how your VUI responds.

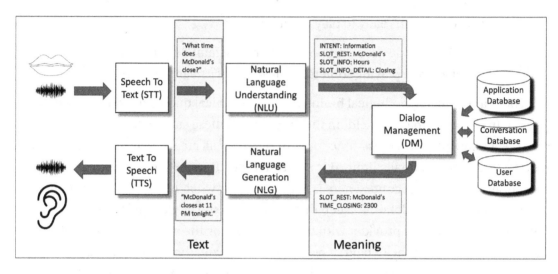

Figure 14-3. *Generic voice-first system*

Interacting with the application and user databases can be one of the most challenging parts of deployment efforts because of your lack of control over the details. It's a big topic that we don't fully have room for here, but we'll cover a few points about the three.

First, some high-level comments. When we talk about "databases" (Figure 14-3 and elsewhere), we're not necessarily meaning formal databases that developers are familiar with like MySQL or Elasticsearch or the offerings from the cloud providers. It may be a "conceptual" database in that we're storing information about a conversation or about the user, not necessarily a "database" per se. Or you may get information from a custom API that's developed specifically for that purpose (common with the application database). You'll see quite a few examples of this in the current and upcoming chapters. The point is we're using "database" in Figure 14-3 in a generic sense as you'll see in the following when we step through a few examples of how you've already been storing conversation information.

First, the conversation database is often the most manageable because you typically have the most control over that by defining and building the VUI interaction. In the context of Dialogflow, there are some limited "conversation database" capabilities already; recall, for example, the notion of required parameters and how the application will ask for them if the user hasn't yet specified them. This is the beginnings of a "poor man's conversation database" for cross-conversation history. A more complete conversation database would store a user's detailed conversation history, such as which restaurants had been asked for in previous conversations. You could then not only avoid making the same suggestions again but also improve future suggestions and have smarter references, like "the last place." For that, you'd need an actual database; it'll be a little beyond Dialogflow's simple context passing. Aside from cross-conversation context, within-conversation context is something you handle yourself; you'll see more examples of that shortly.

Second, the application database contains information needed to answer queries, such as business hours, product availability, reservations status, and so on. Some of the biggest challenges are as follows:

- The information you need probably already exists in a data store somewhere, so you think *Great, less work for me!* Yes, but there are many such databases, systems, and protocols, for saving, accessing, listing, and deleting this information; it's a project in itself to connect your VUI with these sources. Unless the data is already aimed at voice applications, it doesn't cover pronunciations and other formatting you need.

- All the information you need is probably not in one place. Store hours are in a different place than reservations, for example. In some projects, someone in the organization provides a single Application Programming Interface (API) for accessing any needed information, doing the legwork of integrating with these various sources of data. But not always!

- This data is frequently "held" by another organization than the one building the voice system. You may think *Well, it's all the same company, right?*, as we have, only to find out that organizational politics arise. If the data comes from an external source, it's just that much more complicated.

And third, for the user database, you have these challenges:

- **Account access:** How do you identify and authenticate the user? For a Google app or action or an Alexa skill, you can use existing Google or Amazon accounts; otherwise, you might need a whole new independent and separate infrastructure that you have to manage with this data store. In many respects, this is a VUI question and a storage question.

- **Significant privacy concerns**: Users are very sensitive about being monitored and having their personal information in some organization's system—rightfully so, given the data breaches they hear about on a regular basis.

- **Location-dependent regulations**: The organization may have specific privacy policies, and there may be international regulations, like Europe's GDPR, which impact your VUI.

- **Domain-dependent regulations**: There are significant regulations around keeping data secure with severe penalties for violations. In the US healthcare domain, HIPAA regulations constrain how personal health information (PHI) is stored and accessed.

The good news is that you've been slowly adding more and more context to your VUI as you've worked your way through this book. Here are some examples:

- You've been adding multiple responses to intents. Dialogflow randomly picks one except it won't pick the last one that was picked. This is a form of context: knowing what the last response was and not choosing that one.

- In Chapter 6, you implemented an appointment dialog using the Dialogflow feature of required parameters, which automatically asked for missing information. This is context: knowing what information the user has provided and what's still needed.

- Also in Chapter 6, you implemented a procedure prep dialog that walked the user through a number of steps to complete a task. The context here is knowing where the user is in the dialog flow, responding with the appropriate next step.

- Chapter 7 dealt with incomplete requests and disambiguation. Here, context consisted of tracking information: what's required, what's missing, and what's been specified.

- Chapter 9 was all about universals, which as we mentioned are inherently context-dependent; the response depends on the most recent intent. You built out that tracking and added more context to handle the cases of multiple universals in a row.

- In Chapter 12, you implemented one-step correction to allow *No, it's 1984*. The context there was date of birth collection.

- In Chapter 13, you implemented escalating prompts and max errors, both of which require context knowledge of how many errors the user has experienced.

So, you see, you've already been using quite a bit of context, even when it wasn't formally stored in databases.

Persistence Tracking

FROM THE VOICE TRENCHES

A recent interaction in Ann's home illustrates incorrect persistence:

Ann	*What are my notifications?*
IVA	*You have one notification… <information about delivery>*
Ann	*Repeat that.*
IVA	*You have no new notifications.*
Ann	*{Response not fit to print}*

Persistence is what ties dialog turns together into a conversation instead of isolated phrases. It's the stickiness of information within and across conversations. Well-implemented persistence allows more human-like mixed-initiative dialogs. It allows users to build and refine a request in the current dialog as well as into later conversations. In human cognition, short-term memory and working memory are behind the active temporary context associated with the listening, refining understanding, and question-response parts of the current conversation. Long-term memory is the tracking and storing of names, preferences, or account numbers—information that's remembered and can be brought into the conversation without having to be explicitly mentioned. It's short-term and working memory that's the source of most of VUI complexity.

The simplistic approach to listening is to leave the mic open for a set number of seconds. The simplistic approach to persistence within a dialog is to listen and retain information until all necessary slots are filled or the user stops responding or says

Thank you. At that point, you update any backend data and clear slot values and intents, because you consider the conversation to be done. That's a start, but it's not enough for a natural conversation.

Persistence is tricky because it's not about waiting for some constant number of seconds. It's not only about how long you listen but also how context affects what you remember for how long. People don't remember every conversation word for word forever; neither should your VUI. Nor should it forget everything the moment it stops listening. It's a bit squishier than that, alas.

A better approach to short-term and working memory is to use a memory decay together with the details of the user's most recent requests or responses, any retries, the VUI response, the fulfillment result, user location, and so on—just like people do. If I ask you to *Repeat that* 2 seconds after you give me some information, I expect you to tell me the same information again. But if I came back 30 seconds later and said *Repeat that*, I'd expect a *Repeat what?* because the conversation would've reached a natural conclusion and you'd probably have mentally moved on to think about other things. If I'd asked to *Play "Hallelujah" by Leonard Cohen* and 2 minutes after the song ended I said, *Play that song again*, I'd expect you to remember if no other similar conversation or behavior took place during that time and only if no other songs played since. Any intervening event would've changed the context. And if I'd been in the kitchen and had originally asked to play it in the living room, I'd probably expect the same location again unless I said *Play that song again in the kitchen* because as a lazy human I'd expect persistence of information and would only need to specify things that had changed. Persistence influences the scope of interpretation.

As you saw in Figure 14-2, context has many dimensions involving time, place, communication type and history, people present or absent, and so on. More general contexts, like current geographical location and date, have longer persistence and won't change from one conversation to the next, unless a fair bit of time has passed—or if we're all in some science fiction story with instant-travel wormholes. More specific contexts, like slot content in a request, will change more quickly, so should have a shorter memory decay time.

Context-Aware and Context-Dependent Dialogs

Your VUI conversations will shine if and only if you incorporate context. It seems subtle—and it is—but responding differently to the nuances of intertwined contexts brings your VUI that much closer to appearing natural and intelligent. With context, your VUI's responses can be more precise and informative. Let's take a deeper look at some of the cool things you can do with context, why you'd want to, and how they affect the conversational flow. With different context correctly incorporated, you can build the following conversation:

User	*Can you tell me when the Giants are playing next?*
VUI	*Sure. The San Francisco Giants are playing the Dodgers tomorrow at 7 PM.*
User	*And where's that game?*
VUI	*That game will be at Dodger Stadium.*
User	*Are the Giants playing at home this week?*
VUI	*No, their next home game is against the Reds on Monday, September 9th.*

This conversation uses all kinds of context: anaphora (*that, their*), date and time, domain knowledge, and geolocation ("Giants" are also an American football team, but it's currently only baseball season and both of us authors are in San Francisco). Let's learn more about how to make use of context.

People don't jump randomly from topic to topic in most conversations, especially ones aimed at VUIs. In fact, much about how people respond in the next dialog turn is fairly predictable when the dialog isn't yet complete—if the conversation seems to go in a different direction, it's usually caused by a need for clarification or disambiguation. This is important because ASR and NLP rely on it and make use of it in the dialog manager. Using predictability, a VUI can favor more likely interpretations of utterances. You learned about context grammars in Chapters 10 and 11, and you'll learn even more in Chapter 17.

Discourse Markers and Acknowledgments

In Chapter 8, you learned about discourse markers and what each type implies. Remember discourse markers are contextual conversational glue. Each one depends on several contexts, including the type, certainty, content, and outcome of the previous dialog turn and what the speaker is about to say. You can create very natural dialogs if you incorporate appropriate discourse markers based on the context of what slots have been filled:

User   *I wanna add my dinner to my food diary.*

VUI   *Sure thing! What did you have for dinner?*

User   *I had a salad with oil and vinegar, a roll with butter, and broiled salmon.*

VUI   *Got it. Anything else, like dessert?*

User   *Yeah, a cup of strawberries.*

VUI   *Alright. And to drink?*

User   *Just water.*

VUI   *OK. Here's what I got...< order summary >*

With a bit of extra work, tracking context across dialog turns gives you the tools to create natural-sounding dialogs. A bit of randomization is good—just be careful to randomize among markers and acknowledgments with the same meaning and "value." For example, remember that *sure* implies a greater level of certainty than *OK* does, so only use it when you're certain you understood the request.

SUCCESS TIP 14.2 NATURAL IS, UNTIL IT'S NOT   Yes, anaphora and discourse markers are integral parts of human language. But it's easy to take it too far and make something sound unnatural by overemphasizing it. Clarity always takes priority in your VUI dialog choices. Remember people misunderstand each other and micro-correct their conversations all the time—it's a lot harder for VUIs to do that.

Code for Context-Aware Dialogs

A good example of context awareness is responding differently if the user makes the same request twice in a row. There's a good reason to this beyond simple randomization: when the VUI hears the same request twice in a very short time window, that's often a sign it didn't understand the user the first time. We'll use the name dialer again.[1] You'll notice how similar the code in this section is to the skip list implementation in Chapter 12. That's on purpose to make it easy for you; the focus is just a little different this time. The implicit confirmation tells the user if they were correctly understood. You obviously want to avoid giving the same wrong answer a second time, and you want to acknowledge it with a different discourse marker as well:

User   *Call Brent Jones.*

VUI   *Calling Brenda Jones.*

User   *Stop! Call Brent Jones.*

~~~ *VUI-1: Same incorrect response again* ~~~

~~~ **VUI**   *Calling Brenda Jones.* ☹

~~~ *VUI-2: Explains and does not call* ~~~

~~~ **VUI**   *I can't find anyone with that name.* 👆

When you get the name dialing intent, check to see whether you've had the same intent with the same name within a very short time period (try 30 seconds for now; real-life applications would likely use a shorter window). If you did, let's play a different implicit confirmation prompt. From a coding standpoint, you'll make three changes:

1. Save first and last names in the intent context.

2. Look for a recent name intent and store the name.

3. Use the recent names to give alternate behavior.

Let's walk through those steps in detail:

Step 1: First, in the name dialing intent, save the first and last names in the intent context that you created in Chapter 13 (that will come in handy again!). Remember that that intent context has a timestamp in the name, so you'll know if it was recent. The code listing for this is in Listing 14-1.

In the new `context.py,` add a new `params` argument to `new_context()` with a default of None (A). If the new `params` argument is not None, add the parameters to the new context (B). In `webhook_response.py`, initialize parameters for the intent context to an empty dictionary (C). In `main.py`, pass in the intent parameters (D). If it's a name dialing intent, set the first name if you have it (E) and the last name if you have it (F).

---

[1]Code in 14-1.zip

The reason why we're using given_name2 and last_name2 as parameter names in the contexts is because Dialogflow fills in given_name and last_name from the slots of the last utterance—the naming is to make sure there's no confusion.

Listing 14-1. Adding parameters to the intent context

```python
# In new_context.py:
# add a parameter params; add params to the context

def new_context(name, params=None):    #A

# ...... Code cut for listing focus ......

    # Add params if you have them
    if params is not None:
        for key in params:
            context['parameters'][key] = params[key]    #B

    return context

######
# In webhook_response.py: Initialize the params

class WebhookResponse():

# ...... Code cut for listing focus ......

    def __init__(self):

        # Parameters in the intent context
        self.intent_params = {}    #C

######
# In main.py: add the params to the new context

def main():

# ...... Code cut for listing focus ......

output_intent_name = df_request.intent_display_name.lower().
replace(' ','_')
```

```
df_response.output_contexts.append(
    new_context(f"intent_{output_intent_name}",
                params=df_response.intent_params))   #D

######
# In ar_call_by_name.py:
# set the intent params based on the input parameters

def ar_call_by_name(df_request, df_response):

# ...... Code cut for listing focus ......

    given_name = df_request.parameters.get('given-name')
    last_name = df_request.parameters.get('last-name')

    # Set first name and last name in intent context as parameters

    if given_name and not given_name == '':
        df_response.intent_params['given-name2'] = given_name   #E

    if last_name and not last_name == '':
        df_response.intent_params['last-name2'] = last_name   #F
```

Step 2: When stepping through contexts for a request, find a recent name dialing context and retrieve the first and last names. Listing 14-2 shows how to search for a recent name intent: Initialize the variables in webhook_request.py. Set the repeat window to 15 seconds. This is how far back you look for an identical intent (A). Set the time of the most recent name intent (B). Set the first and last names in the most recent intent (C). Check if it's an arCallByName intent within the repeat window (D). In set_most_recent_intent.py, set the recent last name (E) and the recent first name (F).

Listing 14-2. Looking for a recent name intent and storing that name

```
# Repeat window repeatWindow = 30            # A

# Recent first and last names and time of most recent arCallByName
mostRecentNameTime = 0   # B
recentGivenName = None   # C
recentLastName = None
```

```python
# Parameters in the intent context that we always create
intentParams = {}

# Get the current time
currentTime = time.time()

# Parameters that were supplied, either from the
# user speech/text or from contexts.
parameters = []

# An event to trigger
eventToTrigger = None

# Initialize output contexts
outputContexts = []

if 'queryResult' in requestJSON:
    queryResult = requestJSON['queryResult']
    queryText = queryResult.get('queryText') or ''
    parameters = queryResult.get('parameters') or []
    if 'intent' in queryResult:
        intentDisplayName = queryResult['intent']['displayName']
    fulfillmentText = queryResult.get('fulfillmentText') or ''
    inputContexts = queryResult.get('outputContexts') or []

    for dic in inputContexts:
        fullname = dic.get('name') or ''
        m = re.search('/([^/]*)$', fullname)
        if m:
            # See if this is the most recent intent.
            m2 = re.search('^intent_\\d+_(.*)$', m.group(1))
            if m2:
                if 'parameters' in dic:
                    contextTime = dic['parameters'].get('timestamp') or 0
                    if contextTime > mostRecentIntentTime:
                        if not isSkippableUniversal(m2.group(1)):
                            mostRecentIntentName = m2.group(1)
                            mostRecentIntentTime = contextTime
```

```
        if contextTime > mostRecentNonFallbackIntentTime:
            if m2.group(1) != 'default_fallback_intent':
                mostRecentNonFallbackIntentName = m2.group(1)
                mostRecentNonFallbackIntentTime = contextTime
        if currentTime - contextTime < errorWindow and \
                m2.group(1) == 'default_fallback_intent':
            numErrors += 1
        if currentTime - contextTime < repeatWindow and \
                m2.group(1) == 'arcallbyname':  # D
            if contextTime > mostRecentNameTime:
                mostRecentNameTime = contextTime
                recentLastName = \
                    dic['parameters'].get('recent-last-name') #E
                recentGivenName = \
                    dic['parameters'].get('recent-given-name') # F
```

Step 3: If the current intent is a name dialing intent and we have a recent first and last name and they both match, play a different prompt. Listing 14-3 (ar_call_by_name.py) shows using the recent names to give alternative behavior: Check if you have recent first and last names and if they're the same as the current ones (A). Context-sensitive alternative response (B).

Listing 14-3. Context-aware alternative behavior if the name is repeated within 30 seconds

```
givenName = parameters.get('given-name') or ''
lastName = parameters.get('last-name') or ''

if givenName:
    intentParams['recent-given-name'] = givenName
if lastName:
    intentParams['recent-last-name'] = lastName
if givenName and lastName:
    # If the caller specified both the first name and the
    # last name ("Call Brent Jones"), we don't need disambiguation,
    # just do that. This is the "do what you were going to do case,"
    # where the webhook does not modify what Dialogflow was going
    # to do anyway.
```

```
if givenName == recentGivenName and lastName == recentLastName:  # A
    outputText = (
        'I\'m having trouble with that name. '
        'Maybe it\'s not in your contact list?'  # B
    )
```

Try it! Say *Call Brent Jones* twice within 30 seconds, and you'll see the new context-sensitive response.

Anaphora Resolution

Here's a common anaphora example:

> *Keith needs a ride to the airport. Can you drive **him**?*

> *Sure. When does **he** need to be **there**?*

Pronouns like *him* and *he* and adverbs like *there* are examples of pronouns and anaphors, words used to refer to something already established in the conversation, in this case a person and a place. We all use anaphora all the time because it makes conversations shorter. Without using or understanding anaphoric references, our conversations would take longer and sound like legal proceedings. You can't have natural dialogs without anaphora.

An anaphor must agree syntactically with its reference. In English, that usually includes gender (male/ female), number (singular/plural), and case (subject/object). In the example, "Keith" is one person and male; therefore, "he" and "him" were used. There's no risk of confusion here because only one person was discussed. The problem is that it can be difficult to figure out what the anaphor refers back to:

> *Joe offered to let Bob take the car. Unfortunately **he** couldn't find the keys.*

Based on syntax, it's unclear if Joe or Bob couldn't find the keys. People rely on semantics and context to resolve anaphora when it's vague: knowledge about the world and the specific topic and what's established earlier in the dialog as well as immediately after. When we get the reference wrong, we clarify or self-correct in our heads after we hear additional clarifying information, or we misunderstand, resulting in a confusing conversation. Anaphora resolution is very challenging and a big topic in NLP, far outside the scope of this book. If natural conversation is your goal, your VUI needs to both understand anaphora reference and use it appropriately in prompts. Resolution ambiguity is a great source of amusement for listeners who notice a resolution conflict. A classic example is from the King James Bible: *And he spake to his sons, saying, Saddle me the ass. And they saddled him.*

MULTIMODAL CORNER

Put that there is a perfect example of multimodal anaphora, where voice and gesture together result in a short, efficient, yet precise interaction. It's also the name of an early important system[2] demonstrating multimodal communication.

It's useful to combine an initial voice search with a tap or point-and-click to choose between a small set of results: a spoken restaurant search (*What's available at Na Na's for six people for dinner on Friday?*) followed by seeing the results of available times for a table, thinking about the options, and picking one by tapping on it. It's basically the best of both worlds, taking advantage of the strengths of each modality, speeding up the dialog, and minimizing cognitive load. Note that modalities can build on each other, or overlap, but anaphora implies some context awareness. If your VUI is multimodal, is the user able to look at what's on the screen and ask, "What's this a picture of?" If not, it's not using context appropriately.

Because anaphora resolution is so difficult, your main goal should be to minimize confusion in your prompts and confirm anything that needs to be clear for later dialog turns. When a response is vague, don't rely only on anaphora. Compare these two responses:

User   *What time is it in Hong Kong?*

VUI1   *It's 4:02 PM **there**.*

VUI2   *It's 4:02 PM **in Hong Kong**.*

Even though a person might use *there* in their response, it's safer for the VUI to be more explicit to avoid uncertainty on the user's part. It's not worth cutting a few words for conciseness, though you can get away with it if your VUI is multimodal and a screen or other action provides some implicit evidence of understanding.

---

[2]Bolt, R.A., 1980. "Put-That-There": Voice and Gesture at the Graphics Interface. ACM SIGGRAPH Computer Graphics, 14(3), 262–270.

Watch out for anaphora mismatch, using the wrong anaphor for the situation. Anaphora mismatch is why you need to be careful even with what you think is a generic error response, like *I don't know that.* Look at the following dialogs:

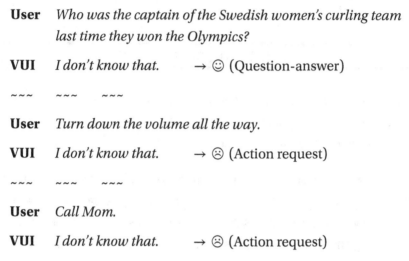

User   *Who was the captain of the Swedish women's curling team last time they won the Olympics?*

VUI   *I don't know that.*   → ☺ (Question-answer)

~~~   ~~~   ~~~

User   *Turn down the volume all the way.*

VUI   *I don't know that.*   → ☹ (Action request)

~~~   ~~~   ~~~

User   *Call Mom.*

VUI   *I don't know that.*   → ☹ (Action request)

I don't know that is a fine response to a question, but a poor response to an action request, where *I don't know how to do that* works much better. A general *I can't help with that* can fit all three examples. Avoid this common pitfall with randomized responses by grouping all responses of the same meaning, function, and confidence level; then randomize from within that group. It's a subtle but important point for sounding intelligent; you learn more about it in this chapter.

SUCCESS TIP 14.3 CAREFUL WITH THOSE REFERENCES   You're sometimes safer using names and nouns a bit too much than risk using anaphora in ways that are odd, vague, or incorrect. And that's just in English. If you're building VUIs in languages with grammatical gender, you can't just use an equivalent of "it" and "that" without knowing what word it's referring to, so your design becomes that more complex.

Follow-Up Dialogs and Linked Requests

As you just learned, persistence is closely tied to scope: how long something stays active and applicable in a conversation. Follow-up dialogs are the perfect anaphora use case because anaphora links meaning back to preceding dialog turns. Anaphora and follow-up requests typically have short lifespans; references are "active" until some other item or topic interferes or till the topic hasn't been discussed for a few seconds. But this time window is not constant; it decays quickly as it fades out of our working memory, unless it's fed by continued references in the conversation. This is important and overlooked in many implementations.

A constant N-second delay for closing the mic and clearing active content is easy to implement but can actually be more confusing to users than not having any mic closure delay at all. Users shouldn't need to look at a light to see if the device is still listening, and a follow-up question that semantically and structurally builds on the previous interaction can easily have a longer timeout for users than you'd want the mic to stay open. In the current climate of concerns caused by ideas that *they're always listening to our conversations*, leaving the mic open means there are more situations of a VUI responding to something not intended for its "ears," feeding negatively into trust issues and affecting future use of voice technology.

The answer lies in understanding when people respond and when they don't. Precise wording, relevance to the topic and previous dialog turn, conversational structure, source and direction of the utterance, and the loudness and prosody all feed into a human listener's interpretation of the next spoken thing they hear. A VUI worthy of being called "intelligent" should correctly choose when and how to respond.

You want to avoid the response for the follow-on to *What are my notifications?* you saw in the Voice Trenches example in the section "Persistence Tracking". You also can't hardcode a general follow-on question to a particular response: *What about in CITY_NAME?* isn't a synonym for *What's the weather in CITY_NAME?* unless it directly follows a question about the weather somewhere else (also an actual voice assistant example).

This is where tracking the most recent activity comes in handy. Because people mostly follow up with dialogs that are somehow related to the preceding conversation, you can limit or favor interpretations to those that build on the previous conversation and create natural conversational dialogs with discourse markers and anaphora. By tracking the most recent request and result, you can create dialogs like these:

User *Turn up the volume in the kitchen.*

VUI <Volume up>

User *A bit more.*

VUI <Volume up>

~~~   ~~~   ~~~

VUI   *The light's on in the garage. Should I turn it off?*

User   *Yes. And on the patio as well.*

VUI   *OK. Both are now off.*

SUCCESS TIP 14.4 LOOK FOR FOLLOW-ON CLUES   When subsequent requests include anaphora, phrases like *What about…* or *How about…*, or similar intents with different slot values, build on the most recent requests and results to favor interpretations that are logical follow-ons.

Code for Follow-Up Dialogs

Earlier you created an intent supporting phrases like *Can I eat rice today?* A follow-on might be *How about tomorrow?* or *What about on Wednesday?* For this, you first need a new Dialogflow intent qaHowAboutOtherDay as a possible follow-up to the qaCanEat intent you already have, not forgetting to add an output context to qaCanEat and the same input context in qaHowAboutOtherDay, because *How about tomorrow?* only makes sense as a follow-up to qaCanEat. Also, don't forget to enable the webhook in the new intent, as you now do with all intents.

Next, you need to save the food queried in qaCanEat for use in future intents, much like you did with first and last names. Listings 14-4 and 14-5 (qa_can_eat.py) show this in two segments.[3] First, in Listing 14-4, you're adding a function can_eat() for determining if it's OK to eat something or not. It isn't a lot of code because you're building on work that you've done before. For now, some fake business logic for deciding if it's OK to eat something (A). It may be good or bad news, depending on your opinion about brussels sprouts (B)! The time argument will come in handy later for follow-on questions.

---

[3]The Dialogflow code is in 14-2a.zip and in 14-2b.zip for the webhook.

Listing 14-4. Creating can_eat() function

```
def can_eat(
            food,
            time=None)

    if food == 'brussels sprouts':    #A
        return False                  #B

    return True
```

Listing 14-5 shows how to handle the intent (A). In a production system, this type of business logic often gets quite complex. Here, you save the food or drink in the intent context (B) and call the fake business logic (C). Based on the outcome, the user is told either that they can eat it (D) or that they cannot (E).

As always, when you need to support a new intent, add the new handler qa_can_eat to the dialog_function dictionary in main.py. Otherwise, the webhook won't find your new handler and will simply do what was in Dialogflow.

Listing 14-5. Supporting the qaCanEat intent and saving into context

```
elif intentDisplayName == ''qaCanEat'':  # A
    # Save food in intent context

    foodDrink = parameters.get(''foodDrink')
    # foodDrink slot not shown as required in intent definition
    # unlikely that intent can fire without slot, but be careful!
    if not foodDrink:
        outputText = 'Sorry, try that again?'
    else:
        intentParams['foodDrink'] = foodDrink  # B
    # TBD consult database for logic
    if canEat(foodDrink):  # C
        outputText = f'You can eat {foodDrink} today.'
    else:
        outputText = f'Sorry, you cannot eat {foodDrink} today!'
```

Now, as you've done before, you need to search the previous most recent intent contexts for interesting information like food. Earlier you relied on a fixed time (30 seconds for errors or 15 seconds for repeat requests). Now you'll be a bit more general and introduce the notion of "Are you still in the same conversation?" In the current example, assume the answer is yes. Instead of a new variable for each new special context, keep all the information in a conversationContextParams dictionary (Listing 14-6). Now that we're getting more into saving context, we'll use this variable as a general store for any context-based information that needs to be saved between dialog turns in a conversation. We're getting closer to the notion of a generic data store for context, even if we're not storing it in a formal database.

As before, you'll do this in two steps. First, add a function to check if the conversation is still the same one (Listing 14-6). It only depends on a timestamp now, but the dependency could be something else, such as allergies or interaction with other medications.

Listing 14-6. Adding params to the general conversation context

```
def sameConversation(timestamp):
    return True
```

Next, in set_most_recent_intent.py, use this function to decide if you should save the parameters into the context (Listing 14-7). Again, you check if you're still in the same conversation based on your parameters, here time (A). If so, add the intent parameters to the conversation context (B).

Listing 14-7. Storing parameters into the conversation context if needed

```
for dic in inputContexts:
    fullname = dic.get('name') or ''
    m = re.search('/([^/]*)$', fullname)
    if m:
        # See if this is the most recent intent.
        m2 = re.search('^intent_\\d+_(.*)$', m.group(1))
        if m2:
            if 'parameters' in dic:
# ...... Code cut for listing focus ......
                if sameConversation(contextTime):        # A
                    for param in dic['parameters']:
                        conversationContextParams[param] =\
                            dic['parameters'][param]   # B
```

Almost there. You need to handle the new qaHowAboutOtherDay request. This should be relatively easy since the food has now been stored in the conversation context. And finally, in Listing 14-8 (qa_how_about_other_day.py), add handling for qaHowAboutOtherDay, using the time given in the user statement. Check if foodDrink is in the conversation context (A). Add a new "you can eat this" clause, including date (B), and a new "you cannot eat this" clause, including date (C). If there's no foodDrink in the context, you need an appropriate response—we've added a placeholder for you.

Listing 14-8. Handling "How about tomorrow?"

```python
def qa_how_about_other_day(df_request, df_response):

    params = df_request.conversation_context_params
    food_drink = params.get('foodDrink')
    date = params.get('date')
    date_original = params.get('date.original')

    if food_drink and not food_drink == '':      #A
        if can_eat(food_drink ,time=date):      #B
            df_response.output_text = \
                f"You can eat {food_drink} {date_original}."    #C
        else:
            df_response.output_text = \
                f"Sorry, you cannot eat {food_drink} {date_original}!"
    else:
        df_response.output_text = "I don\'t recall you asking about a food."
```

You'll notice that we're using two date parameters, date and date.original, used for different purposes. If users say *How about tomorrow?*, Dialogflow fills the date value with a formatted date, for example, "2021-02-14T12:00:00-08:00", because of the built-in @sys.date parameter. That kind of formatted date is what you want for backend functions that implement business logic, like can_eat(). On the other hand, date. original will get filled in with exactly what the user said, *tomorrow*, which is what you want to use for the response in this use case.

Note that as you've gone through the examples both in the previous chapter and this one, you've saved a great deal of context in the dialog history so you can access it later, be it name or food or any other interesting information from the conversation.

This is precisely what implementing context-sensitive dialogs is all about! It's a bit of extra work from the development perspective, but what it adds to dialog naturalness makes it worthwhile.

Proactive Behaviors

Most VUI behavior is **reactive**, a direct result of responding to a request. **Proactive behavior** includes offering or completing steps in a dialog rather than waiting for the user to ask for it. It includes using scheduled events for time-sensitive reminders and actions, such as telling a user it's time to take their medication or to leave for an appointment—just like a helpful human assistant would. It's how your VUI can seem smart while also making conversations easier and more relevant for your users:

VUI	*Your credit card balance of $46.23 is due in 5 days. Wanna pay that now?*
User	*Yes, please.*
~~	~~~
VUI	*The light's still on outside. Want me to turn it off?*
User	*Make it so!*

Proactive behaviors are based on scheduled events, past user behavior, settings, reminders, expected follow-up requests, and so on. The context can be user-dependent (*Time to start your prep!*) or user-independent (*Tax Day is 2 weeks away*). It can be based on static information, like user settings and favorites (*Tickets for Massive Attack at The Arena on November 5th just went on sale. Want me to find tickets?*), or relative to an event (*Brent's on his way, so I turned on the oven. It'll be up to temperature at 425 in about 10 minutes*).

Be sure any proactive behaviors are helpful and appreciated by the user:

- Think about time of day and other activities. Many of us have experienced devices that speak or light up in the middle of the night, complaining about a lost connection or updating its firmware. Ask yourself if the message is even needed.

- Consider wording of personal notifications. Instead of loudly announcing *It's time for your colonoscopy*, potentially embarrassing your user (yeah, we almost did that once), use a text box pop-up for a mobile app or a vague *You have a task reminder* type of prompt. Prescription refill and other medical service IVRs need to be vague about medication details and appointments.

- Offer settings for type, timing, and frequency of proactive behaviors, and do it very clearly during initial setup. Some want those spoken notifications; others don't. Also make sure users can change those settings later.

Implementing proactive behaviors provides personalization without the user having to take any steps themselves. Good IVRs have long made use of proactive behaviors, reminding callers of upcoming due dates and offering different options or examples depending on context, usually time or date. Just-in-time information is proactivity based on context. A procedure prep helper has many proactive behaviors, both user-dependent and time-sensitive for context. As you'd expect, the multimodal procedure prep helper we built at 22otters used a combination of contexts for its proactive notifications, including procedure type, date of procedure, medication details, and current time and day, to name a few. Figure 14-4 illustrates the concepts of a couple of the proactive alerts: notification of a diet change and an alert about starting the prep. Most screens in the app had voice-overs; voice and graphics were coordinated to strengthen the message while also reaching more users and contexts by providing interaction alternatives, each modality standing on its own. Voice is a better fit for some notifications than others— we've already mentioned the risk of embarrassing users by loudly announcing their upcoming procedure, but during the preparation phase, an audio notification is helpful.

Figure 14-4. *Proactive alerts in a multimodal system (22otters procedure prep helper)*

We don't have space here to do this topic justice, but we'd encourage you to think about if and how to incorporate proactive behavior in your own VUI. And we'll return to it in the next chapter because it goes hand in hand with personalization.

Code for Proactive Behaviors

It's straightforward to add proactive behaviors now that you've been tracking time! Listing 14-9 shows a new section in the webhook[4] with a dummy function (in utils.py) that checks for upcoming events and adds a notification of such events to the existing prompt (in main.py). The check happens after the intent test; it could apply to any intent.

---

[4]Webhook code is in 14-3.zip.

528

Listing 14-9. Adding proactive notification of upcoming events

```
def upcoming_events(timestamp):
    """

    pylint: disable=unused-argument
    Returns proactive list of upcoming events
    """

    return []
def main():

# ...... Code cut for listing focus ......

    # Add an optional proactive prompt as a reminder of an upcoming event.

    for message in upcoming_events(df_request.current_time):
        df_response.output_text = f"{df_response.output_text} {message}"
```

Topic, Domain, and World Knowledge

Context influences recognition and interpretation for people, so it needs to do so for machines as well. Context determines how to interpret **homonyms**, words that sound the same but have different meaning, to avoid the following actual voice assistant dialog. A classic example of confusion caused by a lack of conversational context is the old Abbott and Costello comedy routine *Who's on First?* where players on a made-up baseball team have nicknames like *Who, What,* and *I don't know.* You can easily find a recording of it online. Look at what can go wrong with "here":

User	*What time is it in Hong Kong?*
VUI	*It's 7 AM.*
User	*What about here?*
VUI	*"Do you hear what I hear?" is a song ...* → ☹ "Hear" instead of "here"

Fortunately, knowing something about context usually makes conversations less ambiguous, not more. It also helps us, as listeners, to understand words that were maybe muffled or unclear—the same's true for VUIs.

Figure 14-5 illustrates the interaction between domain-based interpretation and recognition/interpretation.

Figure 14-5. *Topic of conversation context influences ASR and NL interpretation of an utterance*

Your VUI needs to match the domain knowledge of its users for each task. Even if you know that a peanut technically isn't a nut but a legume, you won't be happy if you're asking for a list of nut butters for sale and don't get any peanut butter info, and when you ask the VUI it informs you that's not made from nuts. Nobody likes a smartass VUI.

If you talk to someone who shares your deep level of knowledge about a topic, you have a different conversation than you would if that person knew nothing. You can make use of that in a VUI as well. We've seen amazing voice solutions over the years that wouldn't be thought of as "natural" in that they're not like a chat over coffee; instead, they're successful because they incorporate knowledge of how people speak in a particular situation, like making a bet on horse racing, ordering freight pickup, or buying and selling stock options. Expert vs. novice domain knowledge is a context you should pay attention to.

If common words are said differently depending on the domain, make sure your VUI understands as well as speaks them as expected in prompts. Think about how you'd say a number like *1120* if it referred to time, money, street address, or TV channel. The suboptimal situation in Figure 14-6 is built on actual VUI interactions.

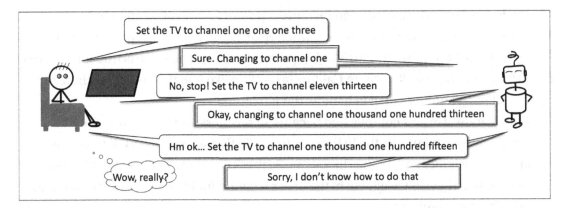

Figure 14-6. *Domain influences how common words are spoken; prompts must reflect expectations and ASR and NL must interpret correctly*

FROM THE VOICE TRENCHES

From a voice assistant user: "I asked [IVA name] *What's the weather?* and it told me the weather in Santa Rosa. I've never inputted my location into any [company] website field, so it just told me the current temperature from where my ISP node originates. The app geolocates to tell me the current temperature in my actual location via the weather API built into the app's front page. Why doesn't it push that to its own devices?"

Geolocation-Based Behavior

Weather, traffic, movie times, restaurant search results—they're all dependent on the user's location. If you can make use of location to make life easier for the user, do so. But at the same time, don't always assume they want to know about something close to where they are right now. Make the most likely assumption based on the task while allowing the user to specify other locations and find ways to tell users how to change it or set their own default.

Again, think about how people talk. If they're in the same location, the assumption is "here" for questions about time and weather. So, if you ask a home assistant *What's the weather?* or *What time is it?*, no explicit location should be expected. If a location name is ambiguous with another location but near enough to be considered local to the user, then the local one should be preferred.

Geolocation should also be used for correct pronunciation of location names: *Versailles* is pronounced very differently when referring to the French palace (ending like *sigh*) or the borough near Pittsburgh (ending like *sails*). The same is true for *Brisbane* in Australia (ending like *Ben*) vs. in California (ending like *bane*). This isn't technically difficult; it's just another detail to handle. But it matters.

Geolocation also gets complicated because of business and legal rules related to content access. In Europe, the VUI needs to explicitly ask users if it's OK to base a response on their location; in the United States, that's currently not needed. If someone asks for content that isn't available in the user's location for business reasons, you need to handle that gracefully.

FROM THE VOICE TRENCHES

Ann was listening to music on a voice-enabled speaker and asked to *skip* to the next song. The music continued while the voice integration tried launching "SkipIt TiVo," an app that was irrelevant to both the current media stream and the device and had never been launched by anyone in the household.

Proximity and Relevance

Proximity applies to many levels of conversational dialog design. Proximity usually refers to physical closeness: where the user, the VUI, and the interaction target object (if any) are located with respect to each other. When people are nearby, we share physical context, like knowing if a light is on or not. We expect the same shared context from smart automation—otherwise, it's not very smart. If I set my alarm in one room and ask the same assistant in another room how much time is left, I expect it to know.

Relevance is related to proximity. Something that's relevant is close in importance or awareness, so it's mental proximity even if not physically close. That includes ownership, accounts, family, household, and so on. *My workout playlist* has a level of proximity to me that *Bob's workout playlist* or *a workout playlist* doesn't. If I just asked for my playlist in the office, then my office speaker has closer proximity to me in time and relevance than all my other speakers.

How you track proximity affects how you interpret potentially ambiguous requests and how you respond. Anaphora is based on proximity because it refers to something that's been established "nearby" in the conversation. If only one device is playing something, a question of what's playing or a request to turn it up is most relevant to that one device.

You need to decide when to assume something and when to ask. It's a balance: only ask if you really need to from the user's perspective. User-created content and personal settings should always take priority over defaults; an interpretation that applies to the current device or environment takes priority over something that doesn't. In Chapter 16, you'll learn about asking for immediate user feedback after a response to determine if the VUI got it right.

FROM THE VOICE TRENCHES

Ann asked, *How long does it take to fly from San Francisco to Newark?* A flight with that same itinerary was on her associated calendar, resulting in the voice assistant overinterpreting her question as being about that flight and not answering the actual question: *There's one flight on your schedule. Alaska flight 266 from San Francisco to Newark departs on July 21st at 9:40 AM.* This would have been a fine answer if it also included, for example, *The scheduled flight time is 6 hours and 30 minutes.* An answer was available for the return direction: *Nonstop flights from Newark to San Francisco are about 5 hours and 55 minutes long.* But flight times are not the same in both directions. And once the return flight was added to the calendar, the return flight time was no longer available!

Number and Type of Devices

Understand how people expect devices to interact. Should different devices "know" about each other? If they can, then the answer is likely "yes." If multiple devices are connected in your house, how do they interact? If you set a timer in the kitchen and go to another room for some purpose while waiting, you want to not only hear the timer end notification in that room but also be able to ask how much time is left.

If your home has two devices, A and B, and music is playing on A while nothing is playing on B, should you have to specify where to turn down the volume or disambiguate? Probably not. But if the two devices are playing different content at the same time, then yes—unless one device has a screen and the other doesn't and you're playing video content on one and ask to *turn up the brightness*.

Device input modality is yet another context. If the user speaks their request, they're likely to expect a verbal response as opposed to a silent list on the screen. But, as you've seen, this isn't always true. For example, device control like turning a light on or turning up the volume provides its own response through its action. Similarly, if the input is typed text or a button tap, your starting default assumption should not be to respond with voice. However, this won't always hold true; task and user preferences take priority.

Time and Day

Track current time, day, and dates if your VUI does anything where those contexts are relevant. You've already seen examples of these contexts in this chapter. These contexts have broad use, alone and in combination with others. You might want prompts using relative time references like *tonight* or *in 4 hours*, proactive conversations, and different responses depending on time of day, day of week, or even month. If your VUI has any human handoff, like to a nurse or customer representative, make sure your behavior takes time zones and business hours into consideration. Don't offer a transfer if nobody is available!

We've seen in the last couple of chapters how you've been keeping more and more track of time, either the current time or the timestamp of recent intents. With the infrastructure you've built already in the webhook, it's relatively straightforward to add time-sensitive logic, like you did earlier with proactive notifications.

User Identity, Preferences, and Account Types

Do you know who's talking? Do you need to know in order to respond? Can you expect multiple people using one account, in one location? Chapter 15 dives deeper into authentication and privacy. For now, just remember that user preferences, identity, authentication status, and account type are all contexts that affect responses and therefore need to be tracked. It's particularly relevant the more personal the topic, such as our procedure prep app. If your VUI does music search, a user with three linked premium music provider accounts expects a different interaction than a user with one free limited provider. If you know something about who's speaking in a multi-user household, you want to respond differently to a request for *Play my playlist* depending on who's talking. VUI responses spoken to a young child should sometimes be different from those spoken to an adult. A medical professional probably expects different responses from the ones you give a layperson. You learn more about customization and personalization in Chapter 15.

User Utterance Wording

Throughout this book, you learn about how subtle differences in prompt wording can have surprisingly big effects on how users react and respond. Look at the following sample dialogs; the user asks for the same information but words the request differently:

User   *Tell me how likely it is we'll have rain today.*

VUI   *It's very likely you'll get some rain today.*

~~   ~~

User   *Will it rain today?*

VUI   *Yes, it will probably rain today.*

~~   ~~

User   *What's the forecasted percent chance of rain here today?*

VUI   *Currently, the expected chance of rain here today is 80%.*

Could your VUI respond to all three with the same response? Sure. Try reading the three user utterances with this one response: *Today's chance of rain is high. Right now, it's 80%.* It works, right? But it drops some of the reflection of what the user asked. In particular, it's not responding to the Yes/No question with a *Yes.* This works in English but might not in other languages and sounds just very slightly like you ignored what the user said.

System Conditions

In addition to contexts, intents, and slots, there's one more important context dimension that ties in with Chapters 12 and 13. The missing dimension is error handling, including the number of retries, system error outcomes, and recognition confidence level. Let's call these conditions. Think of context as variation based on user characteristics and conditions as voice system characteristics. What you call them isn't important, of course, but accounting for them is. You may have several conditions for every context combination, each resulting in different prompts and next steps: high confidence, mid-confidence, retry, what other slots have been filled, and so on. Another system condition you need to take into account is the ultimate outcome or fulfillment, which you learn about next.

Tracking Context in Modular and Multi-turn Dialogs

You'll have noticed how various contexts interact with each other and how quickly the combinations increase. It's a core reason behind the need for dialog management and for a detailed VUI design specification beyond only sample dialogs. When you have, say, ten intents, six slots, and five contexts, you need a way to convey what you expect to happen in each case as well as track that each response is appropriate. And that's not even a big system.

The result of all these combinations is many use cases, each one needing to be handled appropriately for what's recognized and the intent it's assigned, the level of confidence in the result, assumptions about new vs. established information, user preferences and location, previous conversations, how the request was worded, and so on.

Natural dialogs are not self-contained modules where all entry and exit paths are predefined; neither are they a completely free-form grab bag of "anything goes" from turn to turn. Sure, there are dialog rules; they're just mostly like predictable suggestions rather than laws. Dialogs are chains of associated modules where some are more likely than others and sudden switches to new modules can happen.

When you're designing and building a larger system, you need a way to track the possible steps a user can take through a dialog, given all contexts and conditions, so that you interpret step-by-step requests correctly and respond appropriately. As you've seen, anaphora and discourse markers depend on a combination of contexts. If you're working on the whole thing yourself, it's hard enough to get it right. If you're dividing up the work with others, it gets even more challenging. You need a plan. The answer lies in combining several concepts you've learned so far:

- Track all relevant contexts and available conditions:

  - Intent labels that encode the meaning of the current utterance based on everything said up to now, including the established conversation topic or domain

  - Tags that encode speech acts, confidence, number of retries, and so on

- Associate context tags with patterns of wording and behavior and tailor them to fit the intent.

- Handle acknowledgments before handing off to the next dialog turn:

  - An acknowledgment should be as targeted as possible without being more targeted than its context.

- Refer to both high-level flows and detailed specifications, and use a dialog manager strategy to track that it all works for the conversation, from start to end:

  - Because dialogs build on what happened earlier, the next dialog turn in a conversation is more likely related to the previous one than not. Build on this predictability: first, try matching to the most detailed context fit with the most on-target response; if the context doesn't fit, move on to broader and more general responses.

The beauty of this approach is that it ties together UX/UI design best practices with something that's implementable. The basic concept is general enough that you can modify it for any platform and for any level of context complexity you choose to handle, including starting with few and broad contexts and expanding in later phrases.

Your detailed spec—and therefore your implementation and test use cases—needs to cover all combinations. That means for each intent you specify behavior (prompt, flow, multimodal action) for all conditions (happy path, retry 1-N) for each fulfillment outcome (found, not found) for each relevant context, including number of days before the procedure in the case of our prep app. In addition, you might have a different behavior for different users in one "family" and multi-tier behaviors.

Scaling can get out of control, but the answer isn't to ignore it or to make fewer coarser contexts but to find ways to modularize and reuse patterns. Combine intent names with a set of speech act labels you settle on that cover the variation you handle across intents. For example, you might use _cm for "close match," _vm for "vague match," and _nm for no match. Look at the following simple example of responses you can imagine for procedure prep questions. Here, the label faq.food-5_cm tells us it's a response to a question about a specific food (*Can I eat rice today?*) five days before the procedure that was recognized as a close match; a database lookup determined the food is still OK to eat:

faq.food-5_cm	*Yes, you can still eat $FOOD today.*
faq.food-5_vm	*$FOOD is OK today if... <clarification>.*
faq.food-5_nm	*I'm not sure. What other food is it similar to?*

~~~   ~~~

faq.drink-5_cm	*Yes, you can still drink $DRINK today.*
faq.drink-5_vm	*$DRINK is probably OK today.*
faq.drink-5_nm	*I'm not sure. What's it similar to?*

~~~   ~~~

faq.med-5_cm	*Yes, you can still take $MED today.*
faq.med-5_vm	*Ask your doctor if $MED is OK today.*
faq.med-5_nm	*I'm not sure. If it has another name, ask me about that.*

These few prompts handle a lot of requests between them. You could collapse the _cm responses by saying *have* instead of *eat/drink/take*, but we wouldn't: some variation is nice, and by using the more specific verbs, you indirectly teach users to say them as well, which in turn allows you to give a more targeted _nm response for food/drink/meds even when the specific item was a nomatch—a great backoff strategy.

The more direct control you have over the data, the more you can address interpretation and fulfillment issues. But keeping data current is a lot of work and might not even be possible. If your VUI has a diet diary that relies on restaurant menus, you need to rely on outside data. If your VUI plays music, you need to first understand the name of the artist and item they asked for—it's hard already! It involves searching music catalogs with foreign names and even symbols. Once you think you have that, you need to know what services users have access to so you can search those. Then how do you know if you found a good match, and how do you respond if you don't find one?

As content providers split and platforms become more protective of their data, they also become less eager to play nice with each other. Users end up holding the short end of the stick. And they'll blame you and your VUI. You need to deal with these limitations to make the experience as good as you can.

Fulfillment

Your VUI needs to respond appropriately based on fulfillment, the final outcome when a request is expected to result in an action, like turning off the lights or making a reservation, or content delivery, like playing a specific movie or song. Your recognition and intent interpretation might be perfect, but if the correct data isn't there to fulfill an action or answer a question, the conversation has failed. There are important differences between recognition errors, intent mapping errors, and fulfillment errors. Your VUI responses should reflect those differences to avoid misunderstandings and annoyance from the user. Most users don't care why they didn't get what they think they asked for; they just know they didn't. They also don't care what part you have no control over. They're talking to your VUI, asking something perfectly reasonable, but ending up with an unexpected outcome.

If you can't guarantee data or content access because it's out of your hands, you need to reflect it in your responses. The key is to track all available contexts, including fulfillment certainty, and use that information to respond as accurately and informative as possible. This way you can avoid the situation in Figure 14-7. These are actual responses by current voice assistants to *Play the song "Risingson" by Massive Attack*, a perfectly unambiguous request that a human DJ would easily handle by finding that song performed by the named artist. The issue isn't only that the fulfillment is incorrect, but that the accompanying voice responses don't admit there's a problem.

Figure 14-7. *Suboptimal music request fulfillment accompanied by response prompts that don't match the result. All observed in recent smart speakers*

This mismatch between expected result and actual result matters because it feeds users' lack of trust in voice solutions and decreases their desire to use voice in the future. As a user, if I ask for "the song," don't give me a playlist—unless you tell me you don't have the song. If you start playing the whole album where the song is the noninitial track, you're just weird. Don't give me a different title—unless you indicate you're unsure somehow of your response. Don't give me some other artist version—unless you don't have the one I asked for. And don't ever ramble off some list of unrelated options or sound more certain than you should be—just say you can't do it. You can get far with short phrases, like *I couldn't find that version, but I found this...* or *This might answer your question...*

Even the most experienced voice developer can get tunnel vision and forget that NL interpretation and fulfillment are not the same. We once had a brief disagreement over whether or not sample phrases in a spec were "invalid" because they couldn't be fulfilled. Fortunately, the disagreement was short-lived after we discussed the difference between *asking* for something that's logically valid and *receiving* it. The content of that conversation was similar to what's in Table 14-2. Imagine a VUI that handles requests for audio and video content from various sources. All five requests in this table are well-formed English requests that are straightforward to parse and assign meaning to, but not all can be fulfilled for different reasons:

- Request 5 is not in scope for this VUI because it's not a media content request; therefore, fulfillment isn't possible for business reasons without changes to the VUI.

- Requests 1 and 2 are both potentially possible: a request for a named movie from a movie content source is clearly in scope of this app. But at the time of writing, the movie isn't on Netflix. Therefore, fulfillment failure isn't a logic issue (the movie exists) but a current availability issue. In the future, Request 2 may well succeed.

- Requests 3 and 4 are both in-scope music requests. But Request 4 is not possible to fulfill because it was never recorded by The Beatles.

Table 14-2. *Different media type content requests with corresponding fulfillment behavior*

Request (media content VUI)	Parse	In scope	Possible fulfillment	Actual match fulfillment
1. Play Green Book *from Amazon Prime.*	Good	Yes	Yes	Success
2. Play Green Book *from Netflix.*	Good	Yes	Yes	Failed
3. Play "Risingson" by Massive Attack.	Good	Yes	Yes	Success
4. Play "Risingson" by The Beatles.	Good	Yes	No	Failed
5. Play my voice messages.	Good	No	No*	Failed

Why is this important? Because you want to respond differently to different outcomes and reflect the different reasons for those outcomes. Table 14-3 shows you how responses can reflect the outcomes. You'll have options for how to deal with fulfillment failure. If possible, help the user get what they want; take a closer look at the "failed" responses in 2 and 4.

Table 14-3. *Responses reflect the media type and fulfillment outcome of each request*

Request	Possible response
1. Play Green Book *from Amazon Prime.*	Green Book. *Casting now to your den TV.*
2. Play Green Book *from Netflix.*	a. Green Book *is not currently available on Netflix.*
	b. Green Book *isn't on Netflix, but you can rent it from Prime for 5.99. Want to stream it from Prime?*
3. Play "Risingson" by Massive Attack.	*Here's "Risingson" by Massive Attack.*
4. Play "Risingson" by The Beatles.	*I can't find "Risingson" by The Beatles, but here it is by Massive Attack.*
5. Play my voice messages.	*I can only play music and video content.*

This level of detail is what makes users think "smart." It's "just" more work, but it's worth it. As content consumers, we hope for easy access to any song or movie at any time. The technology is there, and sometimes we can certainly go into an app or go online and pick exactly what we want. But content is getting more and more fractured between providers who limit our access to some movies at some time or limit streaming to some ecosystems and devices. If it's a live event, we also rely on accurate up-to-date schedules. If your VUI is not in full control of every step to fulfillment, you'd better have the ability to hedge your responses to match.

SUCCESS TIP 14.5 KNOWLEDGE FIRST, RESPONSE LATER   When you don't control content fulfillment or don't have access to all metadata, it's crucial to know what's available to you. One of the worst things you can do in a VUI is say one thing and do another. If your VUI returns content or information from external sources, always determine fulfillment outcome first and then respond with a prompt that reflects the result. It may be an extra step of code with potential latency, but never respond before you know if you can actually give the user what they asked for. Users accept imperfect fulfillment as long as they feel understood, feel like you tried, and understand why they can't have what they wanted.

What's Next?

You might be getting concerned: how does implementation not get out of hand if every combination of contexts and path conditions needs custom follow-on behavior? For contextual responses, as with other topics we've covered so far, implementing voice is always a balancing act. You can include very targeted behaviors, resulting in potentially smarter-sounding dialogs. The price is more testing, especially of intent boundary cases, to verify that responses are clear and sensible in all contexts. With more coarse-grained responses, you can get to successful production faster.

Our recommended approach is to start small, with fewer intents and a more coarse-grained set of responses for the first phase. Remember you need to handle all reasonable requests in voice—you can't just ignore requests you don't fulfill. But you can start with some general responses, collect data, and look at how users word requests and what they're trying to do. Then, in your next phase, split intents and responses so you can more directly respond to questions and requests. You'll still use your phase 1 broader intents for default behavior of requests you haven't accounted for. Having said that, we also strongly believe that implementing context well will set apart successful voice systems from now on. Here's a simple and insightful exercise anyone can do and learn a lot from:

4. Have a conversation with a few VUIs you have access to. Listen carefully to the responses you get, especially when your utterances aren't on the obvious happy path:

    a. Phrase the same requests as statements, Yes/No questions, and WH questions. Try partly and fully specified requests, even out-of-scope ones.

    b. Change your contexts in any of the ways you learned about in this chapter.

5. Did responses differ based on contexts? If so, how did responses reflect your contexts? Were they spot-on? Did they make no assumptions or the wrong ones? What in the response brought you to that conclusion?

6. What changes would you make? Write sample dialogs that reflect your contexts to sound intelligent. Think about what you'd need to track and implement to make these dialogs happen.

Summary

- Context is multidimensional and affects everything in a conversation. The more you incorporate context, the smarter and more interesting your VUI conversations can be.

- Minimize poor dialog transitions and maximize modularity by incorporating a dialog manager strategy that encodes and prioritizes design patterns, contexts, and conditions.

- User retention depends heavily on their trust in the VUI. There's a fine line between helpful and proactive on one side and annoying and intrusive on the other.

CHAPTER 15

Creating Secure Personalized Experiences

This chapter builds on what you learned about context in Chapter 14 as you now explore creating individualized voice interfaces that users will trust. Even while writing this chapter, there were weekly reports of data breaches at big corporations exposing access to health records, financial information, and passwords. In the voice industry, reports that workers listen[1] to your private conversations and that smart speaker apps are vulnerable to phishing contribute to growing concerns around intrusion on privacy. And let's not even get into any international political or legal topics.

Headlines feed on everyone's fears. After all, fear sells! The concerns are not based on lies per se—home voice assistants **do** trigger the mic by mistake when they shouldn't, and there's no excuse for security breaches. The only way to improve VUIs is to collect user data, analyze it, and iterate to improve performance. What's missing is an understanding about what's worth worrying about and how to address it appropriately.

In this chapter, you investigate these topics from multiple angles: how to handle user data securely while also creating trustworthy voice solutions that meet the individual needs of each user. We discuss balancing defaults with letting users customize their experiences, and you'll learn about incorporating user data to create tailored personalized experiences while avoiding creeping out the user by "knowing too much." This leads to the related second topic in this chapter: system persona. Your VUI needs to convey trust, which it does by what it understands and how and when it responds, as well as how much it knows and doesn't know about its users.

---

[1] Two of many examples: https://9to5mac.com/2019/10/21/smart-speakers-can-eavesdrop/ and www.theverge.com/2019/7/11/20690020/google-assistant-home-human-contractors-listening-recordings-vrt-nws

© Ann Thymé-Gobbel, Charles Jankowski 2021
A. Thymé-Gobbel and C. Jankowski, *Mastering Voice Interfaces*, https://doi.org/10.1007/978-1-4842-7005-9_15

The Importance of Knowing Who's Talking

Sometimes your VUI needs to know who's talking to it and other times not. If you, as a user, ask a VUI, *What time is sunset tomorrow in Paris, France?*, you'd expect the same answer whether that VUI is registered to you in your house or you're asking a VUI at a friend's house. But if you ask, *What's my checking account balance?*, you want to hear about your own account, and your friend sure doesn't want you to hear about theirs! If two users in the same household ask to *Play my playlist*, can your VUI interpret *my* based on who's talking?

And in the procedure prep app, *Can I still take Aspirin?* obviously has to provide the right answer for the right user, but *Is tea considered a clear liquid?* is a question with the same answer no matter who asks it.

Knowing who's talking has two purposes: individualized targeted behavior and authorized secure data access. Individualization, or personalization, doesn't have to mean explicit identification at the start of every conversation, but it could. It does imply recognizing that you've talked to this person before and remember something about them. That can be achieved by the user saying who they are, by them using a device that's assumed to be personal, or through voice biometrics, determining user identity based on some type of voice pattern. Authorized access is what you need for tasks that involve private or secure data, like medical history or financial transactions. That too can involve biometrics of various types, or it can involve information tokens, like account numbers and PINs. Personalization and secure access both result in greater user trust and enjoyment, so let's look at each in detail.

Individualized Targeted Behaviors

A restaurant might offer a kids' menu, a choice of sides, or vegetarian options, knowing that not everyone has the exact same needs. And an experienced server at that restaurant interacts differently with different guests depending on their needs, explicitly stated by the guest or perceived by the server: providing the kids' menu to a family, explaining choices to first-time visitors, or offering to bring "the usual" to frequent visitors. The outcome and goal is the same: get guests' food orders accurately and pleasantly and deliver what they requested.

To make a VUI interaction relevant to each user in each context, don't force everyone through the same interaction. No, not even when it's less implementation work. Instead, spend a little extra effort tailoring the experiences. Make something that's useful and usable by more people based on user behavior and preference data. People find proactive suggestions genuinely useful when those are based on analysis of their behavior and needs. Suggestions must be relevant, quick, and infrequent. Look at these experience comments.

TWO VOICE ASSISTANT USERS DISCUSSING SETTING ALARMS

User 1: *Why is [IVA] offering to play me a relaxing song to help me sleep when I set my alarm?? She said something like "It sounds like you're heading to bed. Would you like me to play you a relaxing song to help you sleep blah blah." It's 9 PM! I'm just setting an alarm! And it's like a loong prompt to force you to listen. Would probably play some sh*t like Kenny G. That would so not relax me. LOL.*

User 2: *She asked me if I wanted to set an alarm for the whole week. Why? It's Wednesday! Plus I've NEVER set an alarm with her before! Why assume I want this?!*

A better solution for User 1 would've been not to assume she was going to sleep now (unless data showed that 9 PM was her typical bedtime). A very succinct "more info" offer would have been better for both users. So do find opportunities to be proactive, but do tread carefully. It's great when it's done right, but just because you added a new feature doesn't mean your users want to hear all about it.

Concepts in Personalization and Customization

Time for some definitions and terminology:

- **Proactive vs. reactive**: You've learned quite a bit about proactive behaviors in earlier chapters. Proactive means taking initiative based on some information or event. Reactive is just responding. Where proactive is active, reactive is passive.

- **Personalization vs. customization**: You'll see these terms used almost interchangeably, but they are crucially different as to who decides on a particular change from a default. Personalization is what product owners and implementers do based on their analysis of user data; customization is what the users themselves individually do to modify their experience. Customization is achieved by users through personal settings and preferences (which of course had to be made available by the implementers).

- **Upsell and cross-sell**: Upsell refers to offers from a business to a user to upgrade an account or add features. Upsell is different from personalized proactive behaviors based on an analysis of user data in its focus on primarily benefiting the business—at least that's how it's perceived by the users. It typically involves users paying or signing up for something. Cross-sell refers to related or complementary products, for example, offering additional home assistant devices at a special price. So offering a large pizza for a small price increase over a medium is upsell; offering a cheap six-pack of soda with a pizza purchase is cross-sell.

Figure 15-1 shows examples of how the different approaches can interact. The top three VUI results are triggered by some combination of past user behavior, time of day, user preferences, and business decisions. Only the last VUI result is in response to a voiced user request.

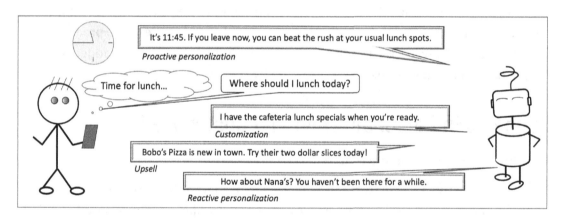

Figure 15-1. *Personalization, customization, and upsell can be both proactive and reactive*

In a GUI, proactive information might be a screen pop-up box that the user can easily dismiss. But remember voice is fleeting and narrow, demands attention, and doesn't allow multitasking. It doesn't take much for some proactive information or just-in-time tip to be annoying. If a user asks a question one time about some sports team, don't assume they want proactive notifications from now on about that team's scores. Instead, track behavior over time, and then ask the user if they'd like to add that notification. At the same time, if a user is doing the same thing several times in similar contexts, like driving to the same location every weekday morning, stop asking every day if they're driving to work—especially if they always respond *yes*. In addition to being annoying and prolonging the conversation, asking irrelevant questions or providing information at unexpected times in the dialog also increases cognitive load—users need to process additional input and respond. This, in turn, increases the risk of errors, timeouts, and missing relevant information, which affects overall success.

There's a fine line between helpful and pushy. Upsell and cross-sell are especially tricky. As a business, you want to sell more, and that's fine. But you won't sell more if users can't succeed and get frustrated due to overwhelm or annoyance. If and when you do this, make it relevant and brief, and track if the user says *no* so that you don't make the same offer again too soon.

SUCCESS TIP 15.1 DON'T BE CREEPY   There's a fine balance between offering to do something for a user and seeming like you're spying on them. People are increasingly sensitive to privacy and data security. It's best to err on the side of caution and not get carried away by your ability to do something. When you test with real users, don't test only the functionality; also test how and when something is offered. Allow users to opt in/out of such behavior. One person's "proactive" is another's "annoying." In Chapter 17, you see examples of how logged user utterances can tell you exactly how much "help" is too much.

A time will come when your business decisions conflict with what you suspect is the best user experience. We've seen this many times. Good news: It's possible to meet business goals **and** have a great UX. The solution always involves everyone on the team working together to maximize ROI by offering the best user experience. This involves understanding the goals of both users and business, as well as understanding contexts and technology challenges, to offer customization and proactive behavior that helps everyone succeed.

SUCCESS TIP 15.2 DON'T THINK YOU KNOW BETTER THAN YOUR USERS   Never ignore a user's explicit request. You don't know their reasons. If a user asks for something you can provide, do so. If you can't, explain why. If you give them a substitute, show them that you know it's a substitute, or they'll not feel heard or understood. Once they feel ignored or lied to, you can't win back their goodwill and trust.

In Chapter 7, you learned that users who are more familiar with a task are more likely than novices to fill all or most slots of a multi-slot request. They're also less likely overall to hesitate or use filler phrases, like *Yeah, I'd like to...* People can be very successful talking to VUIs about complex topics assuming they know the task well. A stock option trading request such as *ACME pizza, October seventeen twenty twenty, sixty two, call at two dollars and eighty cents* doesn't seem very natural to most of us, but it can be handled very well by a VUI. It's not what you'd think of as particularly conversational, but it **is** a spoken interaction using language that's natural for users with trading experience. Catering to what's "natural" to the user is your key to success. A stock trading VUI has to handle the syntax of these all-in-one requests as well as less structured phrases that inexperienced users are likely to say. You'd also need to work with people who have the correct level of official stock trading certification, just like you'd need to work with trained medical staff if building health VUIs.

Novice vs. expert mode is an important concept for design and implementation. Simplistically, novice users need more explanatory prompts, maybe with examples at each step. Expert users tend to just need reminders of what's expected by the VUI at some step. Novice vs. expert is therefore often a distinction of verbose vs. concise, but could also involve speed of readback. The decision of which interaction mode to engage can be left for each user to make explicitly, but more commonly it's assigned automatically. You could do that based on knowing the user's level of expertise via a stored association with an authentication token. You can also do it based on frequency of interaction or number of errors during the last N interactions.

Having two versions of prompts available opens up a lot of flexibility for you and your users. You can use them for personalizing the experience based on what you know about your users, as well as for offering users customization. You'll learn how in the next section on implementation.

No one product is everything to everyone without options and settings. We strongly believe that offering users customization leads to user happiness. It's as true for voice as for other modalities. Consider these quotes from Mary Meeker's 2019 Internet trends report:[2]

Developing a better user experience produces by far the most viral effect & impact when investing in growth. Engagement drives conversion from free consumption to paid subscription.

—Barry McCarthy, CFO, Spotify

The most important thing is to make sure the existing customer [is] happy rather than chasing after new prospects.

—Eric Yuan, Founder / CEO, Zoom

Get to know people... 100% of what we sell is based on recommendations. ... stylists [are] successful [through] listening, empathy & delivering what the client wants & doing that without judgment.

—Katrina Lake, Founder/CEO, Stitch Fix

SUCCESS TIP 15.3 VOICE BUSINESS SUCCESS = GIVING USERS WHAT THEY WANT   Common arguments against customization are it's too confusing to users, nobody uses it, and it's too much effort for too little gain. As always, think it through to offer choices that matter most. Determine the most likely defaults and allow users to change from those to fit their needs in contexts most relevant to them.

Implementing Individualized Experiences

Assuming you have the user's approval, think about what you could provide in your restaurant finder if you had access to the user's current location, typical daily schedule, past behaviors, and preferences. You can do a lot!

Personalization can be based on just about any context and can affect all aspects of a VUI conversation, including content, language, voice quality, verbosity, prompt wording, speed of prompt readback, and so on. The restaurant finder and the procedure prep helper both offer many opportunities for proactive and reactive personalization and customization. In IVRs, different numbers can be given to different caller populations,

---

[2]www.bondcap.com/report/itr19/#view/1

providing tailored dialogs that are targeted at offering the most common choices to those callers and getting them through quickly. A prescription refill IVR was able to personalize the experience for patients vs. pharmacists based on which phone number was called. This is done using DNIS, or Dialed Number Identification Service. The first few dialog turns, including the menu of options and login formats, can be tailored for the needs of each group while many submodules are identical. With two entry points, you can personalize the experience while still avoiding double work.

At the same time—and this is important—think about how to present proactive suggestions so they're useful and not intrusive. Just because you know something about the user doesn't mean you need to mention it! Take a look at Figure 15-2. The voice bot isn't saying anything untrue, but there are safer ways to share the same information— unless, of course, you meant to create a nagging VUI persona. ☺ It's safer to use geographical location and other personalized information in a way that's similar to what a passenger or casual friend would know: *Looks like you're in Oakland…* or *Based on your location/diet goals…* or *Here're your reminders for today: "Mom's birthday"…*

Figure 15-2. *Proactive and personalized behavior doesn't have to explicitly mention personal information*

The procedure prep VUI is built on the ability to provide a personalized experience for each user, so careful implementation and wording choices become even more important. The content and timing of specific responses is not something users should be able to modify because the VUI addresses a medical procedure controlled by their doctor. But you can imagine personalized diet restrictions based on users' specific food likes and dislikes.

FROM THE VOICE TRENCHES

In a multimodal mobile health app, users were horrified when greeted with a cheerful voice reminding them of their next task in a very personal medical procedure. All fine when in private, but loudly proclaiming an upcoming procedure in public is not something most users appreciate.

Code for Personalized Experiences

In Chapter 14, you added context-sensitive code to check if the user asked for the same name twice within the same conversation, so a short time period. If they did, you handled it as an error, and the application responded differently. When you first implemented disambiguation in the name dialer back in Chapter 7, if the user said *Call Brent*, there was a disambiguation of *Which Brent...?* Now, let's add a personalized context-sensitive experience continuing with the name dialer. Let's designate one "Brent" as their "default Brent." The point of a default is to allow the user to say only the first name and not need to disambiguate or say the last name every time. The choice can be something you offer (*I see that you often call Brent Jones. Would you like to add this contact to your favorites for quicker calling?* or similar) or something you assign automatically based on frequency. If you do it without confirming with the user, you also need logic to reset that default if the user starts saying *Cancel* to your *Calling Brent Jones*—notice that the prompt still says the whole name as implicit confirmation.

First, you need a way to store the user context information. Listing 15-1 shows this. For simplicity's sake, you'll use the intent contexts you've been using in the last few chapters and keep building on that user context, passing the current context into the webhook request and storing the new context in the intent context. In `webhook_request.py`, initialize the user context to an empty dictionary (A). Add a function to update the user context (B) and another to update the name history (C) using the previously defined function (D). In `set_most_recent_intent.py`, update the user context from the intent, if defined (E). Add the requested first and last names to the user context. Note that this is pre-confirmation (F). Update the user context with the name history once the name is finalized (G). Listing 15-1 shows some places where this is done in `ar_call_by_name.py`, `ar_confirm_name.py`, and `ar_call_by_name_last_name_disambig.py`. There are additional places in those files; wherever there's a name but no confirmation yet, it's added to the user context (F). When the confirmation is completed (or immediately, if not confirming), update the name history (G).

Listing 15-1. Storing user context information

```python
# webhook_request.py

    def __init__(self):
# ...... Code cut for listing focus ......
        self.user_context = {}   # A
    def update_user_context(self, request_time, key, val):    # B
        """
        Update the user context with a key/val pair at a time.
        """

        if request_time not in self.user_context:
            self.user_context[request_time] = {}

        self.user_context[request_time][key] = val

    def update_name_history(self, request_time, first, last):  # C
        """
        Update the user context with a name request.
        Calls update_user_context with a first and last name.
        """

        self.update_user_context(request_time, 'givenName', first)  #D
        self.update_user_context(request_time, 'lastName', last)

# set_most_recent_intent.py

def set_most_recent_intent(df_request, intent_name, context):
    match2 = re.search(r'^intent_\d+_(.*)$', intent_name)
    if match2:
        if 'parameters' in context:
            if 'timestamp' in context['parameters']:
                context_time = context['parameters']['timestamp']

                # Also set the user context
                if context_time > df_request.most_recent_intent['time']:
                    df_request.most_recent_intent["time"] = context_time
```

```python
        # Set the user context if needed
        user_context = context['parameters'].get('userContext')
        if user_context:
            df_request.user_context = user_context  # E

def ar_call_by_name(df_request, df_response):

    # ...... Code cut for listing focus ......

    # If the caller specified both the first name and the
    # last name ("Call Brent Jones"), we don't need disambiguation,
    # just do that. This is the "do what you were going to do case,"
    # where the webhook does not modify what Dialogflow was going to
    # do anyway.

    if (given_name == df_request.repeat_information['recent_given_name'] and
            last_name == df_request.repeat_information['recent_last_name']):
        # Context-sensitive case where the same name was said in
        # a very short time window
        df_response.output_text = \
            ('I\'m sorry we seem to having trouble; '
             'maybe that name is not in your dialer?')
    elif df_response.explicit_confirmation:
        df_response.output_text = \
            f"You want to call {given_name} {last_name}, right?"
        df_request.update_user_context(    # F
            df_request.current_time,
            'requestedGivenName',
            given_name)
        df_request.update_user_context(    # F
            df_request.current_time,
            'requestedLastName',
            last_name)
        df_response.output_contexts.append(
            confirmation_context(given_name,
                                 last_name))
```

```python
    else:
        df_response.output_text = df_request.fulfillment_text
        df_request.update_name_history(    # G
            df_request.current_time,
            given_name,
            last_name)
        df_response.end_conversation = True
        df_response.nva["do"] = True

# ar_confirm_name.py

def ar_confirm_name(df_request, df_response):

    # ...... Code cut for listing focus ......

    df_response.output_text = \
        f"OK, calling {recent_given} {recent_last}"
    df_request.update_name_history(     # G
        df_request.current_time,
        recent_given,
        recent_last)
    df_response.end_conversation = True
    df_response.nva["do"] = True

# ar_call_by_name_disambig_last_name.py

def ar_call_by_name_disambig_last_name(df_request, df_response):

# ...... Code cut for listing focus ......

    if (last_name in ['Jones', 'Adams', 'Barnes', 'Carletti']):

        # If the last name supplied in this disambiguation step is valid,
        # then play the "OK, calling..." response, and you're done.

        if df_response.explicit_confirmation:
            df_response.output_text = \
                (f"You want to call {context_name} {last_name}, right?")
            df_request.update_user_context(    # F
                df_request.current_time,
```

```
            'requestedGivenName',
            context_name)
        df_request.update_user_context(    # F
            df_request.current_time,
            'requestedLastName',
            last_name)
        df_response.output_contexts.append(
            confirmation_context(context_name,
                                 last_name))
    else:
        df_response.output_text = f"OK, calling {context_name} {last_name}."
        df_request.update_name_history(    # G
            df_request.current_time,
            context_name,
            last_name)
        df_response.end_conversation = True
        df_response.nva["do"] = True
```

In Listing 15-1, we only show one place where you update the user context with the name history: the user said both the first and last names. There are several other places to update, and these are all in the full code sample. Any time you know for sure what name to call, you'd update the history. If you're doing explicit confirmation, you need to wait until the name is confirmed before you update the history.

You just used intent contexts to store user context and history. This was done partly for simplicity. You wouldn't really want the history of a user's interaction with the application to be passed back and forth like we're doing here. In a real application, you'd use some sort of data store like a SQL database, NoSQL tables, or a Redis data structure. We didn't want to make this book about setting up and connecting to databases (which is a big topic in itself), so we kept it simple. If you stay in the Google world, continuing with Dialogflow and the App Engine, you have many choices like Bigtable for NoSQL and Cloud SQL. It's particularly easy to have interfaces to these options from App Engine (the webhook) since it's all Google Cloud. In reality, your choices will depend on availability and constraints in your particular environment.

Now that you have a context and you're setting it, you can use it! If the user says only *Call Brent*, check the context to see if all the "Brents" have the same last name, and there are at least three requests in the history. If so, assume that last name, but use explicit confirmation to make sure. Listing 15-2 (from `ar_call_by_name.py`) shows this with a combination of very generic code for using the context you've stored and a very specific example of the name dialer with the first name "Brent." Initialize a name dictionary to keep track of the last names for the requested first name (A), then the number of the most frequent last name (B), and the most frequent last name (C). Loop through all the timestamps in the user context (D). Initialize, or increment by 1, last name counter (E). If the number of last names is larger than the current max (F), reset the max last name count (G) and the most frequent last name (H). If we only have one last name in the dictionary and we have at least three requests (I), assume that last name and use explicit confirmation (J). If the personalization criterion isn't met (all last names in the history the same and the number >= 3), ask which last name, same as before (K).

Listing 15-2. Using the context to choose the last name

```python
def ar_call_by_name(df_request, df_response):
# ...... Code cut for listing focus ......

    # If the caller only specified a first name

    if given_name == 'Brent':

        # If you need to disambiguate last name (e.g., "Call Brent")

        # Personalization: look through the userContext. If all the
        # Brents are the same name and there are at least 3, assume
        # that one. The logic could be much more complex and look at
        # timestamps and have different rules, etc..., but this is a
        # simple example.

        name_dic = {}      # A
        max_num = 0        # B
        max_name = None    # C
        user_context = df_request.user_context
        for timestamp in user_context:      # D
            context_given_name = user_context[timestamp].get('givenName')
            context_last_name = user_context[timestamp].get('lastName')
```

```
    if (context_given_name and
        context_given_name == given_name and
        context_last_name and
        df_request.current_time - float(timestamp) < 60):    #L
        name_dic_last_name = name_dic.get(context_last_name)
        if name_dic_last_name:              # E
            name_dic[context_last_name] = \
                name_dic[context_last_name] + 1
        else:
            name_dic[context_last_name] = 1

        if name_dic[context_last_name] > max_num:    # F
            max_num = name_dic[context_last_name]    # G
            max_name = context_last_name         # H

if len(name_dic) == 1 and max_num >= 3:     # I
    # Personalization: Use the last name used previously.
    # It has to be the only one and used three or more times.
    # Assume explicit confirmation.

    df_response.output_text = \
        f"You want to call {given_name} {max_name}, right?"  # J
    df_response.output_contexts.append(
        confirmation_context(given_name, max_name))
else:
    # Change the response to ask the "Which Brent..." question.
    df_response.output_text = \     # K
        'Which Brent: Jones, Adams, Barnes, or Carletti?'
```

You may wonder why we added the timestamp in (L). It only adds names to name_dic and thus is considered for personalization, if they happened in the last minute. This is for testing, so you can try different scenarios. If you *Call Brent Jones* three times in a minute, *Call Brent* will assume Jones. If you wait a minute, that history leaves the window, everything gets reset, and you can try again. In a production system, you wouldn't have this timeout. You'd also track usage details for a much longer time, in most cases. You'd also use more complex rules for personalization.

During testing, you can't say *Call Brent Jones* multiple times in a row without hitting the behavior you added in Chapter 14 that assumes that multiple repetitions mean there's an issue of some sort. You can get around this if, after the first *Call Brent Jones*, you use the "default Brent" method and say *Call Brent.*

Note that you're implementing a very simple rule for personalization; if all last names are the same, then assume that name. There could be more complex rules that take into account time, looking at behavior over the past number of days or weeks, or using a lower threshold. You could also have multiple rules for different situations.

In-Depth: Context or History?

You might wonder if we're really storing context or just the history of interesting things that the user has done. The answer is the second, and we have a reason for that. Another alternative would be to store, for example, the contents of the name dictionary in the context, making the application logic simpler.

We chose to go more down the "history" route since we know from experience that the logic you might use to decide and user- or context-dependent behavior can change over time or as a function of many factors that you didn't anticipate when you first built the system. Our philosophy is to defer such decisions as late as possible and make the data we're storing as flexible as possible. It's easy to change the logic in the application, but harder (and it takes much longer) to have to recover from bad decisions when storing the information in the data store.

There are some implementation issues to consider. Storing each history item as it happens can incur quite a bit of latency if, for example, you had to hit a RESTful web service for every history update and that service was far from the webhook—another advantage of deploying such backend systems close to the webhook. Tens of milliseconds of added latency, piled up turn after turn, can easily get very annoying to your user. So you might need to consider options for keeping data local until the end of the conversation, when the back end can be updated. Again, for space considerations, we won't go into the details of these kinds of options here.

Authorized Secure Access

Few voice topics are more important than privacy and security. As you learn more, you'll hear terms like **verification** and **authentication**; you'll realize that not everyone in the field uses these terms the same way. That would be too simple. Instead of getting stuck on terminology, let's first understand the steps involved and then look at some common voice-first options for implementing access restrictions. Figure 15-3 is a happy path overview of the process as questions behind what the VUI needs at each step.

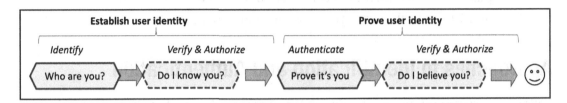

Figure 15-3. *Steps of identification and authentication*

Because these terms are overloaded and often applied slightly differently, you'll hear people refer to the steps as login and password, parallel to non-voice access steps. Whatever terminology you use, just make sure everyone you work with has the same shared understanding. Let's take a closer look at each step:

1. **Identity claim**: *Who are you?* The user makes a claim directly or indirectly about who they are. In some cases, it involves the identity of someone else the user is representing, like a close relative, medical doctor, or financial advisor. Successful verification establishes a claimed identity but doesn't prove that the user is that person. It's the first gate to personalization: it can be all you need for some tasks, like setting music preferences based on who's talking. If you ask for *my workout playlist,* it's not that the list is private; it's just different from your spouse's or roommate's.

2. **Validate identity claim**: *Do I know you?* In this step, the system determines the validity of the identity claim by verifying the claim against some data. The system can base its interpretation of *my* on its certainty that the voice is yours.

3. **Prove user identity**: *Can you prove it's you?* Request some nonoverlapping piece of information or check device access only the "right" person is likely to know or have. If others are messing with your favorite playlist, you might decide to add a password for access.

4. **Validate authentication claim**: *Do I believe it's you?* The final step is parallel to step 2: determine the validity against some stored data for the claimed identity to authorize full access and prove that the claimed identity is true beyond reasonable doubt. Your playlist is safe, thanks to your obscure choice of password!

Approaches to Identification and Authentication

Let's look at some common methods used at each step. You might wonder if security is lacking because methods are repeated—that's because you can often choose different methods at different steps. Just make sure that the whole combination is secure. And remember to allow users to provide secure information silently if they're in a nonprivate setting, like entering numbers on a keypad:

- **Identity claim**: "Who are you?"

  - **Knowledge**: In many IVRs and other voice systems that need to establish identity, this is typically based on something you know, like a unique ID token, such as an account number or (in the United States) a social security number (SSN). Be sensitive to cultural differences around what information is OK to ask for.

  - **Biometrics**: When you talk on the phone with someone you know, they recognize your voice. When used in a voice app, that's voice biometrics: knowing someone's identity based on their voice characteristics. It does need pre-enrollment and works very well when tuned or when the user population is small, in which case it can be used to establish identity without further proof to use that person's settings. This is used today in many home assistants.

  - **Physical control**: Identity based on access to a physical device, something you have or hold. A user's mobile phone is usually assumed to be tied to one person, so it can often be used for verifying identity. When face-to-face, showing an ID card or passport makes an identity claim.

- **Validate identity claim**: "Do I know you?"

  - **Knowledge**: Examples include verifying an account number against a database. This step sometimes uses a checksum digit for a credit card number or N-best for account numbers.

  - **Biometrics**: Voice biometrics compares an utterance against existing voiceprints to determine if the quality of match is high enough to pass some threshold. If you expect users to represent someone else, the biometrics solution needs additional paths, either multiple voiceprints or a knowledge-based backoff. See the "Voice biometrics" sidebar.

  - **Physical control**: The device is recognized from previous use.

- **Prove user identity**: "Can you prove it's you?"

  - **Knowledge**: For voice-only VUIs, this typically involves a PIN or password that the user has set up. Similar to website security questions, another approach is for the VUI to ask for easy-to-remember information that the user previously set up, such as a childhood phone number or grandparent's birthday.

  - **Physical control**: A key fob that generates a time-limited numeric code that can be spoken by the user.

- **Validate authentication claim**: "Do I believe it's you?"

  - Similar to validating identity claim, verify against some data store, but here the matching criteria should be stricter. No N-best, for example.

IVRs have long needed to combine various secure access methods to make calls both secure and efficient: anyone can call a phone number, so how do you share the right information only with the right person while also giving them options for access that work best for them? Secure access will become increasingly relevant and important for non-IVR VUIs as they expand to tasks and domains on new platforms and devices.

VOICE BIOMETRICS

Both of us authors have done work with voice biometrics, the method of verifying who you say you are by your voice.

Here you distinguish between verification ("is this who they claim to be?") and identification ("who is this?"). Verification can work with any population size since you are only comparing against the "voiceprint" for the claimed speaker; identification can work for small populations such as maybe ten or fewer. Voice biometrics has made strides in recent years and can be very useful in the right context.

You can imagine scenarios where identification is handy, such as an app that members of a family share, each member with their own preferences and their own ability to perform certain operations, like purchases. You also need to keep in mind questions of user trust. Is it appropriate for your task to use biometrics?

Depending on the task, your VUI may stop anywhere along the way, from before step 1 to after step 4. The real complexity is in how to deal with retries and no matches. Can you give users some access even if they fail to prove they're who they claim to be? Usually, yes. Figure 15-4 summarizes the ideas you just learned about. This is your "glass half full" situation: with each step, you can give users a little more access without any security or privacy risks to them or to you. Users who don't want to identify themselves or who fail to can have access to the "No gate" information: locations, hours, and other general information. Gate 1 access in a financial VUI might be passive info, like recent transactions, while Gate 2 access includes active money movement, like money transfers. Think of Gate 1 as read-only and Gate 2 as read-write access.

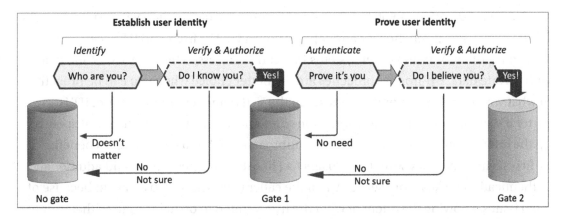

Figure 15-4. *Using identification and authentication methods to grant gated data access*

How do you give the right access to the right user while at the same time making that process both easy and secure? Access approaches fall into one of the following:

- **Open access**: The VUI deals only with general information so doesn't need to know who each user is. It may still use location information and other nonidentifying context. Everything is "No gate."

- **First-time-only sign-on**: Any needed identification and authorization is done only once, when first initializing a device or installing an application, often together with any usage disclaimers. This is a common approach for many skills, actions, and mobile voice apps. No gate, or only one gate.

- **Up-front access**: All-in-one immediate login. Complete all necessary identification and authorization at the start of the interaction, no matter what the user wants to do or know. Access to everything is controlled in one "location," like the front door of a building. Only one gate.

- **Just-in-time (JIT) access**: Delay login until needed. Authenticate only when necessary for the task. This is like the front door being unlocked but some individual rooms being locked. One or two gates.

All are valid options—you "just" need to figure out what method will result in success for the most users given the task and topic of your VUI. Up-front and JIT access are both very common in IVRs and other systems that can be accessed by many users and deal with private data. Up-front approaches are the better choice when you can be proactive in what you offer the user or if most tasks in the VUI demand authentication. JIT is better if a significant portion of interactions don't need full authentication as it speeds up the interaction for those tasks. The JIT approach also has a psychological benefit: by first saying what they want to do, users feel like they progress faster, and additional authentication makes more sense. And if the caller is transferred to an agent because of login issues, knowing the intent of what the user wanted to do helps routing that user to the right agent.

Design and implementation do get more complex for JIT solutions because of the extra work needed to track if identification is needed or even the type of access used. In your design flow and spec, include simple flags and conditional logic to show what's needed when and what should happen in both success and failure conditions.

FROM THE VOICE TRENCHES

In a review of financial voice IVR nonbiometric login methods, we saw a fairly even split between up-front and JIT designs. Identification commonly used account number, social security number (SSN), credit or bank card number, or member or merchant ID. For authentication, a numeric PIN of some length was the most common. Other approaches included the last four digits of SSN, date of birth, ZIP (postal) code, credit card CVV or expiration date, or some other word or phrase chosen by the user. One institution at the time incorporated a liveness test by asking for a specific digit or piece of information from a database of user transactions or account detail. The choices depend on the level of security deemed necessary. IVRs make use of a process (ANI, or automatic number identification) that identifies the incoming phone number and line type—this information can be used for looking up stored account association. It's different from caller ID—blocking doesn't affect it—and it can be used as one of several factors in identification.

Implementing Secure Gated Access

Multi-tier recognition and N-best and skip lists are often used in login approaches. In combination, they allow for "fixing" misrecognition without making the experience less secure or painful for the user. Imagine the following login dialog:

VUI   *Tell me your member number.*

User   *One three five three six one nine.* → High reco score

VUI   *And what's your PIN?* ← Pulls member login info

User   *Two nine three two.* → High reco and matches ID

VUI   *Thanks. Your test results are available...* ← Full access granted

Here, everything works great on the first try, recognition is perfect, and a comparison on the back end validates the two numbers as associated. Now, what if the member number recognition was only in the midrange? Because this member number is on a card and not "secret," it's fine to read it back—a PIN is knowledge you'd not want to read back, but you can ask again if it doesn't match what's in the user's account database:

VUI   *Tell me your member number.*

User   *One three five three six one nine.*   → Mid-reco score

VUI   *That's 1 3 5 3 6 1 9. Correct?*

User   *Yes, it is.*   → Confirmed

VUI   *And what's your PIN?*   ← Pulls member login info

User   *Two nine three two.*   → Heard 2132; match failed

VUI   *Sorry, tell me that PIN again.*   ← Retry without saying "no match"

User   *Two nine three two.*   → Higher recognition score this time

VUI   *Thanks. Your test results...*   ← Full access granted

There are various ways to combine these methods—try writing your own sample dialogs for something that has one or more levels of access security. As you do so, think about potential security holes and how you'd address those. How does the dialog change depending on if the login ID or the password or both have high or mid-recognition scores? When is it OK to explicitly confirm, and when is it not? And remember other methods you've learned about, like one-step correction. Here's one more example, this time showing gated access after authentication failed:

VUI	*Sorry, tell me that PIN again.*	→ Retry
User	*Two nine three two.*	→ Still no match; max tries
VUI	*And finally, what's your phone number?*	← Additional token
User	*650 123 4567.*	→ Match; lower security
VUI	*Thanks. I can tell you about…*	← Partial access granted

Watch out for users who remember their numeric passwords as words. This happens especially when people are used to entering passwords on a phone keypad (Figure 15-5). It's not a problem if you're only handling key presses, but there's a big difference in

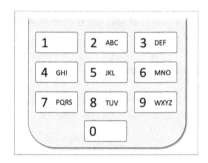

Figure 15-5. *Mobile keyboard showing how digits and letters correspond*

implementation effort and success between handling a spoken *2 7 2 9 9* and *crazy*!

There are some interesting techniques that can be used to maximize accuracy and usability during identification (ID) and authentication. One technique is to use the two-factor authentication mentioned earlier, asking for a second piece of information that is "something you know," like ZIP (postal) code or other information kept on file for the user.

Two-factor techniques can also be combined with the speech recognition N-best lists you learned about in Chapter 10. Alphanumeric strings are notoriously challenging for speech recognition: the "e-set" of letters [b, d, e, p, etc.] are difficult to differentiate in speech—one reason for the use of spelling alphabets. Compare this with differentiating "1" (one) from "l" (lowercase L) in writing, and you immediately see why vision and auditory perception differ in what's easy and difficult. One way to improve accuracy is by using the N-best lists on both the ID token (such as phone number or account number) and the second factor, and keep going down the two N-best lists until you get a matching combination in the database of ID token and second factor. Using this technique, we've achieved over 97% end-to-end identification success, whereas the success on each of the two individual elements would have been much lower.

SUCCESS TIP 15.4 SUCCESS COMES FROM GIVING USERS ALTERNATIVES   You've seen that different synonyms and different paths through a dialog result in more people succeeding. The same is true in any type of login. When possible, provide different methods for users to complete their tasks and stagger access methods so that less private or secure data can be accessed with less authentication. More access options always increase success. Out-of-coverage utterances provide invaluable data on why users fail on login—use that data to decide on what other methods to add.

Notes on Implementing Access

Sometimes the user requesting access to private or secure information isn't the "information owner" but a trusted "stand-in" such as in a medical application where the user is the identified person's caretaker, but a close family member. Some such systems offer two separate identification paths with prompts worded differently to use either "you" or "he/she" depending on whether the user is the patient or the caretaker. Again, extra work, but worth it for a better overall experience.

At times, users may not know a particular piece of information or be willing to use it; US social security numbers (SSNs) belong in this category. In fact, SSN is better used as a backoff strategy, allowing users an alternative optional path if they can't remember an account number. In some countries, a national ID number may be considered more, or less, acceptable to use. Other countries might use passport, tax ID, or driver's license numbers. Voice biometrics might not work well for a user. Find a way to offer alternate methods at similar security levels. The extra effort pays off in the long run through happier and more successful users. And include the ability to *start over* for those who want to do so. You need to understand what your users have trouble with and what's easy for them. Every population is different. In general, expect people to have more trouble remembering their account numbers and PINs than their personal info like SSN, date of birth, and phone numbers.

In many IVRs, an *I don't know* response during identification or authorization acts like a hidden command that takes the user down an alternate dialog path. If your data points to a significant portion of people having trouble remembering one type of login token, you can explicitly offer a way out: *Enter or say your account number, or say "I don't know it."* To encourage people to try, don't mention that option until the retry. In addition, help prompts should explain something about the login and how to transfer to an agent: *You can find the account number on page one of our monthly statements* or *Your plan number is the ten-digit number on your medical provider card.*

You also need to decide how many attempts you'll allow and how the VUI should respond once that maximum is reached. Most IVRs allow only a couple of attempts after which an agent transfer takes place or access is locked, temporarily or permanently. If access is locked, make sure you give clear instructions for how to regain it. As you can imagine, this is a decision that typically involves many people in different roles. Start that discussion early.

Sometimes it's appropriate to allow limited access to a small set of known users, even unidentified guest users. This is what you'd want for most Internet of Things (IoT) tasks in a household, like turning lights on and off: kids and guests should be able to control lights and volume after all!

MULTIMODAL CORNER

If access is multimodal, track the modality used during each part of the login. If someone speaks an account number, you can assume it's OK to read it back for confirmation. Don't assume the same if it's entered on a keypad. Speaking of keypad, some users will think of PINs as words on a phone keypad rather than digits. How will you handle that? If your VUI runs on a device using biometric-capable devices, you can make use of that to avoid the need to ask for logins and passwords. For low-security needs, assume that an app running on a smartphone is secure enough to not need login every time.

Privacy and Security Concerns

More and more customer-company interactions happen on mobile devices. These devices are "always" with us, they're customized and (mostly) personal, and they access data in the cloud and incorporate several modalities, though the smaller the device, the harder it is to type. Look online for statistics on day-to-day financial transactions, and you'll learn that the proportion of digital payments increases year to year in all groups of people. For these reasons, expect the immediate growth of voice to involve mobile devices. That means a broader set of voice dialogs across domains and tasks, much more than we've seen so far. It also means a greater need for privacy and security aimed particularly at spoken data.

FROM THE VOICE TRENCHES

At 22otters, one of our products let cancer survivors share experiences as a community by recording tips and observations. This presented many challenges. One solution for privacy was an option to share stories that were rerecorded using a company-provided voice.

Data storage privacy and security isn't a concern only for voice solutions. But voice brings up additional issues that aren't relevant with other modalities exactly because it's an audio signal and spoken language is a communication tool meant to be heard. There's dialog privacy:

- If your VUI demands a spoken login, that's a potential security hole; allow other login methods for the user when in public settings, including multifactor biometrics and keying in passcodes or other sensitive information.

- If your VUI greets the user by saying something private or potentially embarrassing, make the wording more generic, and allow the user to set the interaction to silent mode where responses are on-screen or even offered to be accessed by other means, like through email or a web link (see Figure 15-6 for a multimodal solution).

Imagine the potential issues if your VUI "overshares" by providing personal information when responding to general questions, like the flight duration dialog in Chapter 14. You might argue, "But it knew your voice!" Sure, but it also read out loud personal information I didn't ask for because it had auto-populated my calendar. What if that trip was a surprise for someone in the same household who now happened to hear it? It's easy to think of use cases where this can both upset your users and create bad PR for your VUI (Figure 15-6).

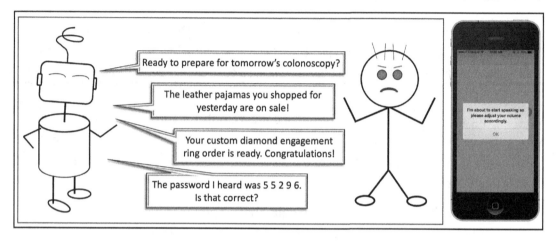

Figure 15-6. *Avoid potential embarrassment and security issues in your VUI dialogs*

As mentioned in the chapter intro, many recent reports focus on issues around workers listening to user data, even private messages being sent by mistake by voice assistants. At its core, the issue isn't—or shouldn't be—with the technology, but valid concerns around data handling and safety nets in the design and implementation. In Chapter 16, you learn why collecting voice data is necessary for improving VUI performance, which ultimately benefits all users.

FROM THE VOICE TRENCHES

Ann was in the kitchen with her husband discussing finding a good recipe based on cupboard contents. No search engine was mentioned. Yet one of the voice assistants in the dining room pipes up: *I think you want to find your phone. Is that right?* After responding *No!* and hearing the follow-up *OK, I wasn't sure*, she forgot all about sourdough and picked up her phone to look for details for what just happened. The VUI had picked out something it interpreted as *find the's good*. Having never set up any phone-finding feature and not seeing an interpretation that was at all relevant and having not addressed the device in the first place, her response to the device's follow-up *OK, I wasn't sure* is not fit for print.

There's another trust aspect around listening: responding to utterances not intended for the VUI. Wake words trigger by mistake, just like you sometimes think someone's talking to you when they're not. Home voice assistants can determine that some are false triggers and stop listening—but not always, which can affect trust and people's willingness to use voice in their homes. Be careful not to respond to something that should have been rejected.

IVRs have a benefit when it comes to user trust: users call a phone number to initiate the conversation. That phone number is on official statements and cards from the company, so there's baked-in trust that the VUI has the company's blessing and is secure. The same isn't automatically true if the communication is through a skill or action or other voice app. Justified or not, we've heard even experienced voice practitioners say they'd not trust financial interactions on home voice assistants without a fair bit of solid login.

SUCCESS TIP 15.5 THERE'S ALWAYS ANOTHER WAY   If your VUI has a screen, use it. Make it an option for users to tap or type and read instead of speaking and listening when they want to. Even voice-only solutions have options. IVRs can always offer touch-tone options for authentication. Phones have volume control and non-speaker options. Sometimes all that's needed is a heads-up that audio is coming and to not move ahead until the user confirms or to offer sending something by email or to an app.

One thing's clear: people love convenience. They also want to learn how to get more out of any product, if it benefits them. Most users don't mind that their data is used to personalize their experience or used anonymously to improve performance and get new features. One study[3] found that 91% of participants preferred brands that provide personalized offers or recommendations and 83% were willing to share their purchase

---

[3]2018 Accenture survey of 8,000 consumers in Canada, France, Germany, Italy, Spain, Sweden, the United Kingdom, and the United States.

history and similar behavior data in exchange for a personalized experience. What's rightfully upsetting users is how some companies and organizations handle their data: not keeping it safe, profiting from selling it, and using it for upsell and advertising. Of course, you want to monetize your product, but pushing paid versions and selling user data isn't the road to loyal customers. What are you offering in return? A customizable experience, a promise not to share personal data, and a well-designed and implemented solution that consistently and accurately solves a problem will win you loyalty and word-of-mouth recommendations and returning users.

SUCCESS TIP 15.6 "YOU CATCH MORE FLIES WITH HONEY THAN VINEGAR"   In other words, being nice gets you further than being mean. A VUI that pushes a business agenda too hard is mean. If an IVR caller asks for an agent, transfer them as quickly as possible. If your VUI is honestly helpful and offers something useful, it's more likely to succeed in the long run. First give users what they ask for and then make your upsell. If they say *no*, they won't suddenly say *yes* after the eleventh time of hearing the same offer.

Protecting user data access is an arms race in all interfaces and modalities. For voice, the only viable answer likely involves a multifactor combination of knowledge and liveness biometrics. Despite pure voice biometrics already raising concerns,[4] it's powerful if used in two-factor authentication. For space reasons, we won't cover the details of how to implement and tune voice biometrics. Just remember that recognizing someone's voice to provide a personalized experience is different from being certain they are who they claim to be for secure data access.

System Persona

Do your users think you created a stern teacher who borders on rude but knows everything or a lying dingbat who doesn't listen but is really cute? Hopefully neither, but just about every choice you make in your design and implementation will affect how users perceive and interact with your VUI's **system persona**. Here we focus on the

---

[4]www.washingtonpost.com/technology/2019/09/04/an-artificial-intelligence-first-voice-mimicking-software-reportedly-used-major-theft/. The first of its kind reported and not likely easily replicated.

persona conveyed by the voice system, not the personas used in UX and UI design to represent a category of user.

Back in Chapter 2, you learned that all of us humans form an image of the person we talk to. It's as if we can't help doing it. And because VUIs "talk" and "listen" like humans do, we anthropomorphize them: we attribute human traits and behaviors to nonhumans. That means your users will form an image of your VUI based on the persona they perceive and that image will affect what they say and how they say it.

Creating a successful VUI is built on this assumption that users are fairly predictable and that when their expectations are met, the conversation is easy and comfortable. When a conversation follows expectations, both dialog participants know what to say and expect to hear certain responses at certain times. That means recognition and NL performance will be higher. So, if your VUI persona meets users' expectations, the outcome is greater overall success and a positive experience.

The point of a system persona is not to create a caricature version of a human— well, unless that's appropriate for your VUI, which is not your most likely situation. The system persona is the overall identity or character of a VUI. It's the style and personality it conveys through its voice range, vocabulary, pronunciation, dialect, expressiveness, grammar, behavior, helpfulness, proactiveness, intelligence, what it knows about its users and what it does with that information, and so on. Bad news: There's no guarantee your users perceive your persona the way you hoped for or that they even like it. Good news: You **can** influence that perception a lot (Figure 15-7).

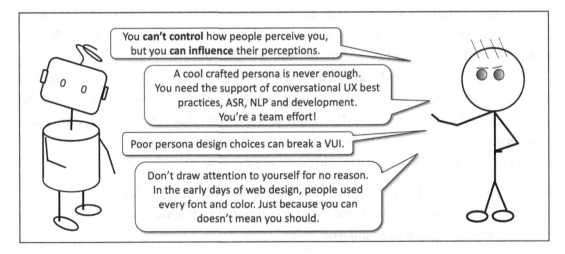

Figure 15-7. Comments from actual VUI users rephrased as persona design guidelines

---

FROM THE VOICE TRENCHES

We once created a wine pairing app. The user said what food they were having; the system responded with a recommended wine pairing. That was the most fun requirements gathering ever! As part of the design process, we needed to define the right system persona; somebody friendly and casual, yet deeply knowledgeable, professional, and helpful. Turns out Ann has a good friend who owns a winery. Basing the persona definition on her friend made the persona spring to life.

Defining and Implementing a System Persona

Defining an appropriate persona for a VUI is not without controversy and difficult choices. At the core is the fact that people simply don't all like the same one. Ask anyone around you what they think of Siri, Alexa, and the Google Assistant, and you'll get a different answer from everyone. We both have our most and least favorites, but we're not gonna tell you what they are. Even choosing a name must be done with care. It needs to be short and memorable, easy to say without a lot of variation for better recognition, yet distinct enough to not be easily misrecognized. If the name implies a gender or age or other characteristics, then the voice you choose needs to match. If it's an Alexa skill or Google action, you obviously don't need to make those choices. But think about the interesting difference in choice made by Apple and Amazon vs. Google: an explicitly chosen personal name vs. the company name. From a practical point of view, that's why you have to say *Hey, Google* or *OK, Google* instead of just a name, or the mic would trigger easily when someone in the room says, "I'll Google it," whereas someone talking about Siri or Alexa need **not** say the name. Ann refers to Alexa as "Pringles" because of the similarity in shape of an Echo and a Pringles can—she's even put an empty Pringles can around one of her Echo devices. But using a company name is also less personal, less anthropomorphic. Does it matter? We're not gonna answer that either. We just want you to think about the implications of choices and understand what matters to your users.

There are many reasons for explicitly defining a persona:

- It serves as a focus for designers and anyone working on prompt content, which helps them create a consistent experience through conversational flow and wording.

- It captures the VUI's cognitive model and branding, which helps product owners and experience designers evaluate the overall implementation.

- It provides information to craft the audio experience, which helps voice talents and voice coaches, or anyone choosing a synthesized TTS voice and creating non-verbal audio, understand how to convey that experience.

- It provides information about wording, which helps speech scientists handle recognition and intent coverage.

The persona definition and style guide often includes descriptive attributes and sample utterances, as shown in the excerpt in Figure 15-8.

Persona Attributes
- Female, mid-late 30s. No strong regional accent. Core attributes:
  - <u>Natural</u>: Human-like, smooth, clear and understandable. Intonation and inflections must connect with the user to be believable and desirable.
  - <u>Responsive</u>: Behaves in a consistent manner; engaging and reassuring to instill confidence. Demonstrates knowledge, flexibility and proactivity.
  - <u>In touch</u>: Her style is current and relevant; classic yet up-to-date. Perceived as knowledgeable and intuitive; a step ahead of the customer.

Vocabulary
- Speaks in short, casual and complete sentences, frequently using contractions. First person singular preferred over plural for self-reference.
  - YES: "Later I'll need your member number..."
  - NO: "Later we will need your member number..."

Figure 15-8. *Excerpt from a typical persona description in a style guide*

Who is the user talking to? Is the VUI ultimately representing the user or someone else, like a company? Imagine wanting a recommendation for something. Think about what you'd expect and how much you'd trust a response from your friend with similar or different tastes vs. an independent reviewer vs. a company salesperson. Users might like their home VUI assistant to know their preferences like an ever-present all-knowing human assistant—without the human part. But if that assistant starts insisting on actions that are more in line with someone else's agenda or profit motive, you'll lose the trust of your users real fast. There're ways to offer something to the user or help them discover something new that might interest them. Make it clear this is based on user preferences and past behaviors; don't push too hard or often. It's a slippery slope, so be very careful and think about who you're ultimately representing.

Get in the habit of creating and using a persona definition and style guide. Define your system persona carefully:

- Stay true to any user expectations for the task, domain, and brand.

  - If your VUI is associated with a brand, you need to incorporate that brand.

  - If users naturally associate your VUI with a metaphor or mental model matching real-world interactions, like ordering food for takeout or describing illness to a doctor, then your system persona needs to fit that mental model. If not, users will be less successful because of increased cognitive load.

  - Who is the VUI representing? If the VUI is a personal assistant, users expect more customization. If it's a company representative, less customization of the persona is fine, as is upsell and cross-sell. A VUI representing a store or utility will speak and behave differently than one who represents a medical doctor, a teacher giving an exam, an entertainer, or a legal representative.

- Never let stylistics of the persona take priority over functionality.

  - Avoid expressions that might confuse some users, such as slang, regional metaphors, or specialized terminology.

  - A persona for a medical or financial VUI should instill trust; avoid using child or cartoon voices.

Be careful of allowing your VUI to make human-like commentary. Something as simple as giving color to commute traffic info can backfire. If your VUI comments that traffic *looks good* or is *lighter than usual*, be sure it's not Saturday morning, and keep in mind that your "good" may not be my "good" if there's any slowdown. Same for weather: some people like rain, and others like sun. If your persona makes this type of qualitative comments, will they contribute to the overall persona or annoy users? There's no one answer, but the more noticeable its traits are, the more divided your users will be. If you want users to love your persona, allow them to set some parameters, like the voice, and build on known user preferences. If you want to annoy your users, let your persona make lots of comments and get things wrong! In Chapter 16, you'll learn about the tricky topic of testing personas.

SUCCESS TIP 15.7 "CONVERSATIONAL" DOESN'T MEAN "CHATTY" When voice systems are described as "conversational," it means they're expected to understand natural speech as well as not breaking the "rules" of dialog. VUI responses are also expected to sound natural. But remember it's a machine, not a person. Some people love a persona who acts like a sentient being and makes subjective comments about the weather; others just like the modality of voice and want nothing but accurate responses. Think about how you can create a persona that appeals to all your user populations. Pro-tip: You can't. Just like there's no person who's liked by everyone. The stronger and more branded the persona, the more likely your users are to be polarized. Some will love it; others won't. So be natural, and aim for something that's generally appealing to most users without irritating a lot of them.

How Persona Affects Dialogs

The system persona affects every aspect of the conversation and affects how users address and respond to the VUI. If you're creating a skill or action, you define a persona for it, but your users address Alexa or Google to access it. Users will only experience your persona if they first open the skill or action; if they give a one-shot all-in-one command, they'll interact with Alexa or Google.

People are very good at copying and mimicking behaviors—this is exactly why examples are a great tool. It also means that users mimic the persona's style, rate of speech, and choice of vocabulary. Make sure all words and grammatical structures your persona uses are in grammar. If users categorize your VUI as having a female-sounding voice, some of them will include words like "ma'am"; if categorized as male, some will say "sir" instead. Neither should throw off your NL processing, and you need to handle both if users can choose the voice. Remember: Just like a person with certain outward characteristics, your persona must understand not only the words it's using but also all other topic-relevant utterances in the language.

If your VUI converses in other languages, things get more complex. In some languages, the gender and age of the person you talk to affect the grammatical form of what you say. In many languages, you can hardly talk about anything without applying the correct grammatical gender to what you're saying. That means different strategies are necessary for different languages as they deal with unknown gender differently.

This is why you can't simply translate prompts from one language to another but sometimes even have to reorganize your code. We talk about internationalization (building something that can be modified easily for different languages and countries) and localization (making those language- and country-specific changes) rather than simply translation (changing sentences in one language to another while retaining the original meaning) to show that there's more to it. Your persona needs to be consistent with any linguistic and cultural expectations. For example, US and UK English differ not only in pronunciation and some word choices but in some basic syntactic behavior: when talking about sports and musical artists, a Brit tends to use the plural, where a US speaker uses singular (Figure 15-9). How will your VUI persona account for this, both in prompt wording and in understanding?

Figure 15-9. *A VUI system persona has to reflect every aspect of the language and style it's incorporating*

SUCCESS TIP 15.8 CONSISTENCY IS IMPORTANT, EVEN FOR A PERSONA   Pay attention to every detail of persona design, especially if you yourself are not a perfect match for your persona definition. Even if you're a fluent speaker of the language of a country but don't live in that country, get a current resident to check for up-to-date expressions.

Choosing an appropriate and consistent persona feeds trust. Ask yourself how you can build user trust in VUI responses, not just in wording but in fulfillment accuracy and system "honesty" when there may be options for what answer to give. What's the source of that answer? Do you tell your users what the source is? If so, how; if not, why not? How much control do you have over the source material? Who checks if the information is correct, and who can make updates? If users address Alexa or Google or another platform assistant rather than your own, who's to blame if the information is incorrect or misleading or if the experience just isn't very good? Who will your users blame?

Remember the barking bar counter in Chapter 14? It's not only a very funny example; it also points to the deeper implications of architectural decisions that affect current and future usage of and trust in voice assistants. If more skills or actions respond automatically to assist users with more complex tasks, they must be trustworthy. As a user, I need to know I can trust what I hear. If I want to buy a plane ticket, do I ask for a skill or action from a particular airline, or does an aggregate skill or action offer to help me? If so, who created that skill or action, and why is it prioritized? In the eyes of users, an assistant persona is one that represents the user's interests first and foremost; the persona of a company or product does not.[5] What happens when the two blend? Thanks to over-promising "AI" smarts, VUIs are already on shaky ground in terms of trust with many users. Together as educated practitioners, we can make voice a success story for everyone, as long as we're mindful of trust.

System Voice Audio

The actual voice audio output—the sound of the voice—needs to fit the system persona as well as the wording. They're intertwined. That includes the delivery and quality of the voice, the perceived demographics, and pronunciation. Think about store clerks who are instructed to address you by name to convey care and personalization. How impressive is that when they struggle to pronounce your name? Not very. In fact the attempted personal touch backfires as being fake. If your VUI addresses users by name, the pronunciation needs to be correct. Provide a way for the user to correct the pronunciation, for example, by typing alternatives in an app, as well as choosing not to be addressed by name. Similarly, don't take shortcuts with place names. As mentioned earlier, the restaurant finder handles requests for Brisbane, California. This isn't pronounced the same as the Australian city. Versailles is pronounced differently when referring to the palace in France or the borough in Pennsylvania. It may save time in development, but mispronouncing words is another way to erode trust—it can even cause confusion and unclarity. With a little extra effort, your VUI will sound smarter.

---

[5]Thyme-Gobbel, "A Matter of Choice: Personalization vs. Personality in Interactive Voice Assistants," 2018 San Francisco AI Assistant Summit.

Another example you may have heard from your home voice assistants: the title of an album recorded *live* pronounced like "to *live*" rather than as in "*alive*." Again, context comes into play: use it to guide pronunciation.

We're finally looking at steps 4 and 5 of the voice-first architecture you saw in Chapter 1: natural language generation (NLG) followed by TTS output (Figure 15-10).

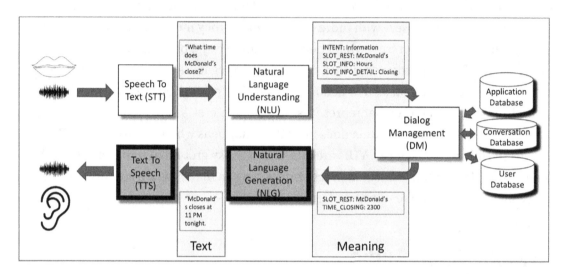

Figure 15-10. *System voice audio output is the result of voice architecture steps 4 and 5*

You can track spoken pronunciations in the user context just like you kept track of last names earlier. In the food diary, you might have lots of examples of alternative pronunciations of words. Figure 15-11 shows a possibility with the Italian pasta "gnocchi."

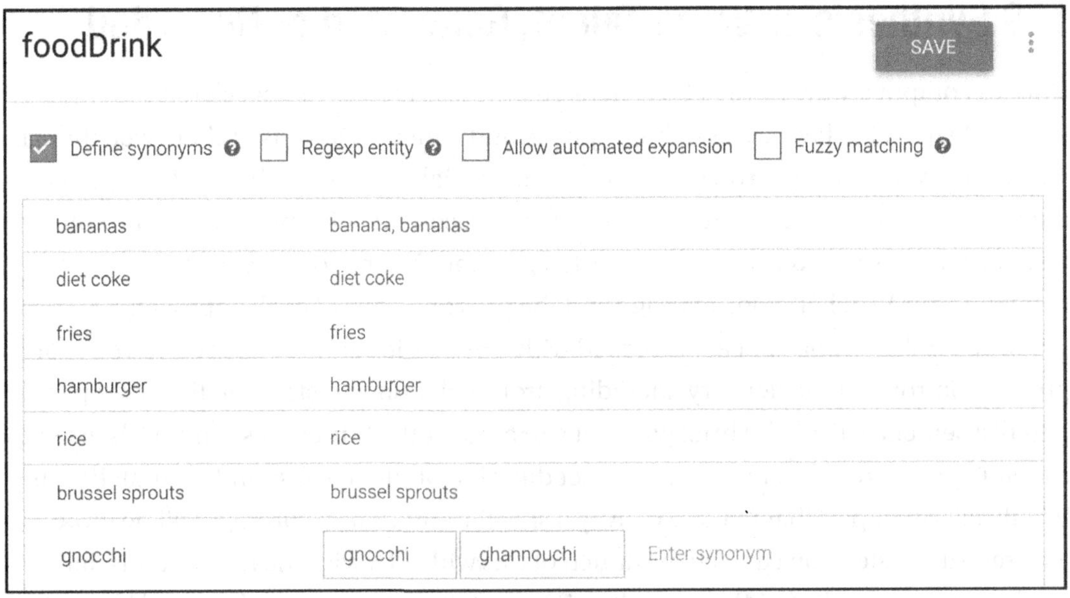

foodDrink		SAVE	⋮
☑ Define synonyms ❷ ☐ Regexp entity ❷ ☐ Allow automated expansion ☐ Fuzzy matching ❷			
bananas	banana, bananas		
diet coke	diet coke		
fries	fries		
hamburger	hamburger		
rice	rice		
brussel sprouts	brussel sprouts		
gnocchi	gnocchi	ghannouchi	Enter synonym

Figure 15-11. *Alternative pronunciations for entities, here "gnocchi"*

You can imagine tracking which version was spoken in the user context:

```
"userContext": {
        "1576461424.7895339": {
                "requestedGivenName": "Brent",
                "requestedLastName": "Jones",
                "pronunciations": {
                        "gnocchi":"ghannouchi"
                }
        }
}
```

The question of course is what to do with that information. Be careful about assuming that, for instance, the VUI should speak a "certain way" to particular users.[6]

---

[6]Dialects differ both in pronunciation and word choices. www.nytimes.com/interactive/2014/upshot/dialect-quiz-map.html illustrates some examples of US dialectal variation and is quite entertaining, but a word of caution: usage is not nearly as clearly regionally defined as the quiz suggests. It does show synonyms that your VUI needs to handle if it covers the relevant topics.

TTS Synthesis or Voice Talent, Generated or Recorded

Does the output always have to be generated synthesized text-to-speech (or TTS for short)? Well, no. Today, access to high-quality and varied TTS is easier than ever, though TTS quality varies widely. You can choose from available voices within each ecosystem, often at no extra cost. Yet, there're reasons to use recorded voice prompts. Some voice systems make use of both TTS and recorded prompts. Your choice depends on the details of your VUI. Let's look at usage and the pros and cons of each approach.

In general, prompts that are recorded with a professional voice talent give you more precise control over the delivery, including pronunciation and stress on the appropriate part of a sentence. Even the brief pause at a comma or the "air quotes" emphasis given to a menu option involves more than a preset duration of silence to sound natural. If your VUI deals with topics that need to convey a specific emotion, recordings will be more accurate and faster. You can achieve much of this with TTS with the help of tools and markup languages like SSML, but it often involves more fine-tuning than you'd expect and can still fall short. Google, Alexa, and other platforms today provide simple ways of doing some TTS pronunciation edits, but it's still a fair bit of work and won't always result in the pronunciation you hoped for. Sometimes the only option is to change the prompt wording, which can lead to other issues, like users now responding with different words. Another potential downside of TTS is the risk of increased cognitive load, even confusion, when, for example, a TTS prompt that's a question doesn't have the prosody that questions are expected to have.

The drawback with recorded voice prompts is the amount of work needed to create and administer them. If your VUI involves broad variation, like account numbers or names of people, places, foods, or medications, you can't really record all of them. Each one involves many thousands of names, and most voice talents record no more than around 200 utterances per hour. And each name or number must sound good in different contexts, which means multiple versions.

The great benefit of TTS is that whatever prompt text you've written instantly generates audio output. No need to schedule voice talent recording sessions or involve audio engineers for postprocessing. No need to handle large libraries of prompt segments. But, as always, there's no free lunch. You need to spend more time testing the final result. With recorded voice, much of the initial unit testing has been handled during recording and postprocessing sessions.

Sometimes it makes sense to pre-record and store TTS prompts rather than generate them from the cloud each time. This can be true if you expect issues with processing or connectivity or if certain prompts are particularly important to "get right" for the experience.

There are reasons to use both TTS and recorded voice in the same VUI:

- If the VUI uses multiple voices or languages, the overhead of multiple voice talents may be too much, so lesser-used languages might be TTS candidates.

- Using TTS during design and development is a convenient placeholder before having recorded voice prompts.

- Finally, some VUIs use TTS created from the voice talent, allowing a mix of recording and TTS. That's the best of both worlds and allows you to limit pre-recording to the most frequently heard prompts or ones where delivery style is critical, such as pronunciation or emotional tone.

When you did non-verbal audio (NVA) in Chapter 8, you used Speech Synthesis Markup Language (SSML) to play an audio file. Another thing you can do with fully implemented SSML, but not yet with Actions on Google/Dialogflow, is customize the pronunciation of a word. If you could, you could imagine an app mirroring the pronunciation of the user in subtle or maybe not-so-subtle ways to make the app seem more natural and responsive.

Finding and Working with Voice Talents

Finding the right voice talent takes effort. Various companies can help you find an ideal voice talent. Such a search typically involves listening to and rating as many as 20 voices on various attributes to match persona definition. Any talent you evaluate has to fit the branding needs in the style guide, but there are additional needs:

- Natural ability to understand the intended meaning and context of a prompt to convert it into a read with appropriate emotional tone and emphasis

- Ability to take direction and needing only minimal retakes

- Voice quality that's easy to hear and needs minimal postprocessing

585

- Consistency in delivery across sessions, even when additional takes happen months apart

- Availability when needed—if your brand calls for a celebrity spokesperson, availability can be a challenge

- Cost, per utterance or for a set amount of time

AN EXPERIENCED AUDIO ENGINEER ON THE TOPIC OF CHOOSING A VOICE TALENT

There's a lot of focus on "conversational" today, resulting in UX designers and media creators seeking out things that are fresh and different. The problem with that is that "new" and "different" have always been the focus of the creative: audio, video, animated, visual, and so on. While constantly attempting to change and update is a reasonable pursuit, never ignore core performance needs that are paramount for great sound. When working with a voice talent, you'll always need to achieve clarity, consistency, trustworthiness, and empathy. The "art" of producing a voice talent for any voice platform is to align the business and technical requirements of each project with a producer's instinct. Only then can you decide which voice is best.

SUCCESS TIP 15.9 GIVE EVERYONE A VOICE ABOUT THE VOICE   When you evaluate voice talents or TTS voices, find a way to include real (or potential) users in the decision process. Product owners and end users don't typically have the same goals or context of use. You take a risk if you don't get end user feedback on the voice and persona.

One or Several Voices

Multiple VUI voices can coexist in some situations. Let's look at a couple of them. Some users will have more than one app or assistant covering similar domains and even speaking out of the same device. Alexa, Google Assistant, and other voice assistants all have different and recognizable voices and personas. They also have different strengths and weaknesses because of their origins and priorities. Sometimes the argument is made that users will get confused if multiple assistants talk through the same device.

All experienced voice designers and developers as well as end users we've discussed this with agree that it's a nonissue. Here's why: as humans, we don't get confused talking to different people. We expect different people to handle different requests and know different information. Those who have multiple assistants usually have clear preferences for when to talk to each. What does get complicated is that assistants on different platforms probably don't have the same content access or shared visibility into all contexts. If you asked VUI1 to start a movie, can you ask VUI2 to fast forward or tell you who directed it? If a group of people is watching the movie, everyone shares the same context, no matter who turned on the movie. Therefore, these limitations are ultimately business constraints rather than user limitations. Today's home assistants offer users a voice choice. In a multi-person household, it can be useful to offer each person a choice such that the VUI responds to each user with their chosen persona.

Using multiple voices within a single solution is an idea that's been around at least since the voice portals of the early 2000s. You'd have one voice for the latest news, another for sports, yet another for arts and culture, and so on. Depending on your branding needs, it may be worth looking into, but be aware that it's a lot of extra work. Using different voices can be great for subtle alerts. In the procedure prep VUI, you could use one voice for answering questions and another voice for alerts, like when it's time for one of the key prep steps. Other uses of multiple voices include one voice that only gives hints for how to interact with the VUI and different voices in short audio how-to demos.

You can also use SSML to change the voice quality. Google and Alexa both offer several voices for some languages; you can even change the voice on the fly, using the voice property of the speech tag. What you can do is use SSML to alter the speaking rate, volume, and/or pitch of the current voice.

In Chapter 8 you used SSML by sending a custom payload in the webhook response. You can use the same approach to make the voice louder for emphasis (Listing 15-3).

Listing 15-3. Making the TTS voice louder for emphasis

```
{
    "fulfillmentText": "It's time for your procedure
    prep!",        "payload": {
        "google": {
            "expectUserResponse": false,
            "richResponse": {
                "items": [
                    {
                        "simpleResponse": {
```

```
                            "textToSpeech":
                            "<speak><prosody volume="loud"> \
                            It's time for your procedure prep! \
                            </ prosody></speak>"
                            }
                        }
                    ]
                }
            }
        }
}
```

You can experiment with different SSML parameters to see what they sound like in the Actions on Google console (Figure 15-12).

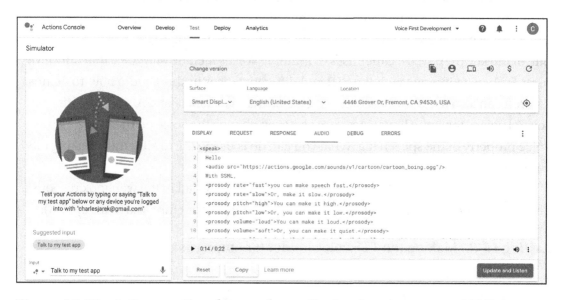

Figure 15-12. *Actions on Google console, audio simulator, to try out SSML changes to the voice*

Prompt Management

VUIs of all sizes and complexities benefit from having a prompt labeling convention. Systematic labels and tags are particularly important if you're managing recorded prompts, but they're handy in all phases of design and development, for your own use and for communicating with others. Use them if your VUI has customization or different modes, like the expert vs. novice modes discussed earlier in this chapter. Prompt labels are a must-have if your VUI is multilingual. As you saw in Chapter 14, detailed dialog specs are often large spreadsheets of prompts and conditions; being able to sort prompt wording based on conditions and context is a big help when reviewing persona stylistics.

Different platforms have different prompt naming requirements, and that's fine. The convention you choose should balance clarity with conciseness and should encode intent, context, and condition. Incorporating the dialog turn concepts "initiate" and "respond" can be useful to quickly find or refer to all prompts in a particular conversational context. When working with others, this lets you quickly refer to *all init prompts* or say *Look at PlayTitleDis_I* instead of *Look at the prompt the VUI speaks on the first try when it needs the user to disambiguate the requested title to play the right thing.*

Avoid hardcoding prompt content in a way that complicates later prompt content changes. Using labels as links instead allows easier systematic modification and reuse.

Emotion and Style

Vector, the fist-sized robot by Anki, understands voice commands but communicates mainly through non-verbal audio, movement, and two "eyes" on a low-res display. Yet it portrays emotion and personality very well. When it does speak, Vector's voice is robotic, and that's OK because it fits its persona and it's intelligible, more so than some real human voices!

Vector's loyal followers respond well to its persona and conveyed emotions. You'll want your users to respond positively to your VUI's emotions as well, and you'll want to respond appropriately to your users' emotions. But recognizing and responding to emotions is not any easier for a computer than for a person:

- How emotions are encoded and displayed in speech is very speaker-dependent. Several emotions often co-occur in a single utterance. And recognizing an emotion isn't the same as knowing what's behind it. To interpret emotion correctly in speech, you need a lot of familiarity with a specific person. That means a lot of validated training data for a computer.

- People respond differently to the same utterance. They interpret emotional content differently, and they differ in what they consider an appropriate response. Even if you recognize an emotion correctly, how do you respond? Should you? What if you're wrong?

Just because you think you recognize an emotion doesn't mean you should respond. When we worked on IVRs, occasionally someone would suggest recognizing swear words and responding, either by an immediate transfer to an agent or by commenting on there being no need for such language. Neither option is recommended. If you get it right, you're enabling and teaching users to swear for faster transfer. If you get it wrong, users who get scolded will certainly be angry now even if they weren't before. Best is to not respond, just like a human listener who is pleasant and professional no matter what. And don't risk sounding fake: your VUI is a machine; it has no feelings. If you're certain some reaction is appropriate and your chance of being wrong is slim, then of course emotion is valid: it's part of human conversation.

FROM THE VOICE TRENCHES

At 22otters, we performed a set of studies on how users interpret the same utterance in different contexts and in TTS vs. recorded speech. We found that the specific words in a prompt conveyed emotion more reliably than a change in intonation and delivery—at least to a point. Users ascribed the right emotional tone based on context unless the delivery was so strong that it came across as fake.

SUCCESS TIP 15.10 GO EASY ON REACTING TO EMOTIONS   Because it's easy to get it wrong, be careful about responding to a user's negative emotions or any perceived emotions. Identify the worst outcome and gauge your response based on that. Getting it wrong is much worse than not responding. Focus on "safe" contexts where stakes are low, like being congratulatory at the end of a task, and use multi-tier recognition, if available.

FROM THE VOICE TRENCHES

An IVR user commented, "I can't use those. I'm blind." That confused everyone until we realized that the comment referred to touch-tone IVRs. We were focused on speech systems that relied on no visual cues. Voice is obviously a great interface for anyone unable to read or look at a screen for any reason. But this user's comment makes an important point: no single modality, including voice, always works for all people or even for any one person at all times.

Voice for Specific User Groups

Every voice app must be created with a particular target population in mind. Even "general population" is a specific target. Subject matter experts, kids, non-native speakers, account holders, color-blind lactose-intolerant dairy farmers...whoever it is, you can't be effective unless you know who you're talking to and understand as much as possible about their context and needs.

Accessibility and design for any specific user group are topics deserving a whole book. Here are just a few things to keep in mind:

- Allow users to control the rate of speech and volume. With voice biometrics, you could automatically associate individual user settings in a multi-person household.

- Are children your intended target users? There are privacy and security concerns you need to meet. Prompt wording must be simplified, age-appropriate, and encouraging. Recognition of children's voices is notoriously harder than of adults, so recognition models and overall design need to account for differences in performance.

- Are children potential users but not the main target? Parental controls of some sort may be needed. Some users will want you to bleep swear words; others will not.

- Are users under physical and/or mental stress, including illness? Slow down. Simplify language, offer more information follow-up, and allow for longer speech timeout and the ability to pause while finding information. As a rule, medical content for patients is written for someone with a seventh grade reading level. Your VUI should be too.

- Are you offering medical or financial advice or asking about the user's health? You must read up on all applicable laws including HIPAA if your users are in the United States and any similar rules if they're in other countries. HIPAA consultants are available if needed. Your servers may even need to be physically located in one of a limited set of countries. If you yourself is not a member of the target audience, it becomes extra important that you involve representative users from Day 1 to avoid pitfalls.

MULTIMODAL CORNER

One of the strengths of multimodality is the flexibility it provides, accommodating more users by allowing them to choose both input and output modalities. Some will always use one modality; for others, it's context-dependent (hands busy, eyes busy, quiet or loud environment). For some, it's not a choice, but a permanent reason; for others, it's temporary (lost their voice, hand in a cast). As much as possible, let users choose whether to use push-to-talk, haptics, or speech to trigger the VUI microphone. Tie VUI action states to other devices and sounds, like an incoming message blinking lamps in a room. Also, don't assume a particular level of tech savvy or interaction preference based on age alone. Sure, vision and hearing get worse with age, so take that into consideration if your user population is on the older side. But contrast makes reading easier and words pronounced intelligibly lower cognitive load for users of all ages (Figure 15-13). It's just good design.

Figure 15-13. *An 80-year-old user with poor eyesight appreciates being able to talk to a procedure prep VUI app*

SUCCESS TIP 15.11 ACCESSIBILITY IS BEST PRACTICE A VUI must function well for all its intended users. That means people in all contexts and with all abilities. Don't think of accessibility as something only for people with special needs. A robust VUI is always accessible to all people. VUI design best practices are also accessibility best practices: low cognitive load, short and clear instructions that can be interrupted or repeated, different paths through a dialog, personalization to speed up the interaction, and robust recognition, NLP, and error handling.

What's Next?

The main topics of the last two chapters are at the core of what will decide the future of voice system success: context (to create complex, accurate, and useful VUIs) and trust (so people will want to use those systems). Check out the work done by the Open Voice Network,[7] a nonprofit industry association focusing on closing the potential trust gap by addressing privacy, security, and equal access through communal development of standards.

This chapter wraps up part 3 of the book. You've learned a lot about how to design and develop toward enterprise-level robustness. You now have the tools to create VUI experiences that will delight any user population no matter the level of complexity of their tasks and requests. In part 4 you learn how to verify that your VUI in fact works as well as you hope it does. Part 4 covers the various types of testing and tuning needed for any voice-first system and discusses how to avoid common pitfalls before, during, and after deployment.

Summary

- Access to private data needs to be gated appropriately for the task and context.

- System persona touches every part of a VUI, from wording and flow to recognition and user happiness.

---

[7]https://openvoicenetwork.org/

- You can't control how users will react to a particular system persona or voice, but you can affect and steer their reactions.

- There are pros and cons of using TTS or recorded speech for VUI prompts related to effort involved and precise control.

- Focus your efforts on gaining your users' trust in your voice app. Trust means staying within the expected persona for the context, displaying just the right amount of knowledge about your users to be helpful but not pushy or creepy, and show that you understand users' requests by providing an accurate response or a reason why you can't. And don't respond when not spoken to.

- Prompt labels are a useful shorthand throughout every phase of VUI development—as long as the naming convention is clear and agreed on by all on the team.

- Accessibility is best practice.

PART IV

The Launch Phase: Verifying and Tuning

No voice-first solution is ever perfect out the gate. While some people deploy their system and spend minimal additional effort working on it, we don't recommend this approach if your goal is to create the best voice system possible. Voice systems are in no way set-and-forget.

This final part covers the third phase of voice system success: testing, analyzing, and fixing issues and doing it quickly and appropriately before and after production launch. You learn techniques for collecting and analyzing data and for mapping your findings to the appropriate solutions.

How do you know if your users like your voice solution? Chapter 16 covers various user testing methods tailored for voice, the coding needed to support them, and what you can learn from such testing. You learn the do's and don'ts of QA testing a voice system and testing recognition and usability.

Chapter 17 teaches you how to improve, or tune, your voice solution. You learn what real user data tell you about the performance of your VUI, what to log and track, how to measure accuracy, and, most importantly, how to interpret your data so you know what to fix. The chapter covers many facets of performance tuning, including coverage, recognition, dialog, and intent tuning.

Congratulations! You've worked hard and learned a lot. Now you're ready to turn any good voice system into a polished great one.

## CHAPTER 16

Testing and Measuring Voice System Performance

So you've built your voice system and applied everything you've learned. Now you're ready for the rest of the world to flock to your implementation. How do you bring it to the world without it breaking in some horrid way? Will you know if people are successful interacting with your VUI or like talking to it? If you followed all the "rules," why do you even need to worry about any of this?

This chapter explores how to test voice systems and measure their performance in terms of both system accuracy and usability and how to identify valid user data. The information and metrics you capture feed directly into your ability to improve system performance (Chapter 17).

Testing Voice System Performance

All software needs testing; voice systems are no different. In fact, voice systems usually need even more testing because the inputs are so varied. And because of that, how you perform testing of a voice system, and across voice development platforms, differs from what you might be used to if you've tested non-voice interfaces.

© Ann Thymé-Gobbel, Charles Jankowski 2021
A. Thymé-Gobbel and C. Jankowski, *Mastering Voice Interfaces*, https://doi.org/10.1007/978-1-4842-7005-9_16

Recognition Testing

A recognition test, or reco test, is a limited and controlled sanity check to see if common expected user utterances are correctly understood. You don't need highly representative users for a reco test, just a small set of people who are reasonably similar to your expected real users. If your VUI is geared to a general population, your testers should represent gender and age variation, as well as some dialects. If your VUI is intended for a specific user group, like speakers who are very young or in a noisy environment, be sure your testers reflect that.

Why is this important? Back in Chapter 2, you learned that everyone's voice and vocal tract is different. All recognizers don't perform the same either. A reco test is not a test of synonym coverage, but a test that the recognizer performs as expected under typical circumstances. For that reason, reco testers typically read from a script that someone on the VUI team has created. The script covers a few representative high-frequency dialogs and utterances that can be taken from sample dialogs and includes any special instructions, such as if a string of numbers should be read as single digits or natural numbers.

Recognition testing should be obligatory if you have access to underlying recognition parameters, such as is the case in some enterprise solutions and IVRs. But even for smaller home assistant VUIs, a reco test can provide peace of mind that users will succeed in the most common situations.

Recognition testing is usually fairly quick to execute. Prepare the script and line up testers in advance, and leave time for analysis, reporting of results, and modifications. Make sure all necessary speech data capture mechanisms have been tested beforehand. A reco test is basically the last bit of testing before any larger rollout happens. It doesn't need to be automated, nor should it be.

Is recognition testing a test of the recognition engine? Well, yes and no. Unless you work in an organization that builds its own ASR engine, you won't have any ability to change the core recognition performance. All recognizers perform differently at the very core. All you can do is choose the best one available for your task and resource needs. What you can do, though, is train the recognizer on your data and look for gaps in grammar coverage. Sometimes you can even modify deeper parameter settings that affect recognition. You learn more about your ability to affect performance in Chapter 17. During pre-deployment reco testing, you only look for major issues that don't need large amounts of user data.

If your VUI is multilingual or in a language that you/your team doesn't speak fluently, you need current native speakers to test. You can't just create sentences in TTS based on machine translation—you need not only realistic pronunciation and intonation but someone who knows real people from a particular country, region, and sociolinguistic context of the user. The same holds true for any VUI design as well, of course.

Dialog Traversal: Functional End-to-End Testing

The purpose of a dialog traversal test is to verify that the VUI's functionality matches what's in the design specification. Think of it as a type of user acceptance testing. Like recognition testing, traversal testing is done with voice commands after the code is stable, but it differs from reco testing in a couple of ways:

- The goal is to test every path under every context and condition in the design specification.

- The tester needs to be a person who's very familiar with the design; if the system is large, multiple testers may divide the work between themselves.

Testing all contexts and conditions means every path and slot combination, every number of retries, every authentication use case (if part of the system), success and failure of any fulfillment, and so on. It should also cover testing of any data access or transfer behaviors at different times of day, days of week, and geographical locations. The point is to follow each possible path in every context that might affect the outcome. The detailed design spec comes in handy here: all use cases are already laid out, including a sample utterance to speak for each.

SUCCESS TIP 16.1 GETTING REALISTIC TEST ACCOUNTS   If you test a production system that runs on someone else's servers, it's best to start arranging for test accounts early. For large enterprise clients where other departments may be involved, it can take a bit of time. In many systems, users have different experiences depending on various contexts. User-specific contexts include new vs. existing account, first login, type of account (savings vs. mortgage), account content (amount of savings, number of stock trades, free vs. paid), and role (patient vs. pharmacist). Other contexts include geographical access restrictions and the reason for talking to the system (different people may route differently through the system and have different experiences depending on their account type). Arrange to have multiple accounts that cover what real users encounter, and make sure those accounts mirror the behavior of real accounts, including any latency or database access hurdles. If it's a health or medical system, it will likely involve setting up test health data in the back end.

Even though traversal testing is not a test of synonym coverage, the combinatorics of all this leads to testing taking quite some time, even for small systems using a single archetype utterance for each use case. If all is done "by hand," traversal testing for a larger enterprise-level VUI can take weeks. Fortunately, there are ways you can speed it up:

- Before any spoken traversal testing, run automated or semiautomated tests to quickly and methodically identify potential gaps in handling, for example:

    - End-to-end tests to identify missing paths through a dialog or missing slot combinations in the code. VUI designers can review and analyze the flagged results and provide feedback to developers about what needs to be updated and what can be ignored.

    - Traversal tests using the text of each sample utterance to verify that the correct intent is returned, slots are correctly filled, and the expected prompts are played in each context and condition. This takes recognition out of the equation and quickly flags mistakes in utterance-to-intent mapping. Identifying incorrect responses can be as simple as automatically comparing the prompt wording in the VUI spec to the wording generated by the system. Watch out for randomized and dynamic prompts if you compare prompt wording.

- Traversal tests using TTS or pre-recorded sample utterances to verify intent, slots, and prompt. Pre-recorded test utterances allow for quick and controlled retesting after each update. They also speed up manual testing by allowing testers to focus on listening to aspects of the dialog that aren't easily automated, such as the delivery and emphasis of responses. Before you use TTS or pre-recorded utterances for testing, verify that each is correctly recognized.

At some point, you need live human testers for dialog traversal testing. You want to listen for misplaced emphasis in prompts that can cause confusion, for odd handoffs between prompts, for pauses that are too long or too short, for quality or volume changes from one prompt to the next, for TTS test prompts that have been left behind, and so on.

SUCCESS TIP 16.2 CHOOSE YOUR TESTERS CAREFULLY   A lot of software testing is outsourced to third-party QA companies. That's fine for a lot of testing, but can be a problem for voice systems if testers speak with strong accents that don't match that of the users or test in environments that don't match what's expected for your VUI. It can still work fine, as long as the QA team is trained, including knowing to retest before reporting any recognition issues. Reco testing can also be a great way to involve stakeholders, giving them first-hand early access to the implemented system while keeping them constrained.

Wake Word and Speech Detection Testing

If your VUI depends on a specially trained wake word (such as *Alexa* or *Hey, Google*) or another mechanism to trigger active recognition of speech, you need to verify that it works well in expected usage contexts. If your voice system uses barge-in, that needs to be tested as well. Recall from Chapter 6 that barge-in is a crucial feature in IVRs that lets users interrupt the VUI simply by speaking instead of by first saying a wake word or pressing a button. This type of testing should be very controlled, thorough, and methodical. Few people do this level of work themselves; more likely, you'd rely on a specialized company or team to develop and test this functionality. Even if you don't do this yourself, be aware of it. Testing should cover not only how often recognition is triggered when it's expected to be but also how often it's triggered by mistake. The latter is much more difficult to test but just as important.

Other Types of System Integration Testing

Some other familiar types of testing are also important for voice system performance. We'll discuss them briefly here; you'll learn more about how they come into play when you learn about tuning (Chapter 17). In each case, testing needs to cover different contexts from the perspective of a conversational user: check that the VUI responds in an informative and timely manner, including appropriately worded prompts or alternative paths as designed. And, to be clear, testing should of course be done iteratively throughout your development effort—we're just collecting much of it in this chapter for practical reasons:

- **Utterance data capture**: Utterances, interpretation results, and tags need to be logged as expected at all times of day and in all authentication contexts. Of course, you must keep in mind the privacy and security issues around capturing and storing speech data that we discussed in Chapter 15. We'll come back to this important topic later in this chapter and the next.

- **Backend data access**: Check that any internal and external databases are accessible. Remove these databases during testing to verify that the appropriate expected error response is returned when they're not available.

- **Latency and response time testing**: Minimizing delays and handling them when they occur for VUIs. Users will be confused by unexpected silences. Test for delays in response time to determine if latency comes from ASR or NL processing, from database lookups, or elsewhere. Longer-than-expected latencies need to be addressed by designed workarounds. That can be done with latency-masking non-verbal audio (Chapter 9) or by additional prompting, such as *Let me look that up for you.*

- **Load, stress, and soak testing**: Check response content and timeliness when the system is underload. Include applicable backup and recovery tests.

SUCCESS TIP 16.3 TESTING IS NOT OPTIONAL   If you're asked for an itemized bid for some voice work, be sure to write your quote and Statement of Work in such a way that the appropriate testing is part of each phase or portion of work and cannot be separated out and potentially pulled out to make the proposal cheaper. We've seen this attempted for usability testing (UT) in particular.

Testing Usability and Task Completion

During dialog traversal testing, it's common to notice something that might be an issue for the deployed voice system, even if it matches the design. Sometimes this happens because the various systems and databases now connected to the VUI don't behave exactly as expected. For example, there might be more latency than expected, resulting in longer-than-expected silences in prompts, or some media or informational content turns out to be different from what you expected. Again, involve designers, developers, and product owners to determine how serious such findings are and how to address them.

Basic system performance is easily measured and quantifiable as long as the metrics are available for capture. But measuring and quantifying user success in an accurate and meaningful way is a lot harder. Usability testing studies are a bit like a set of guided yet unscripted spot-check dialog traversal and recognition tests. It's functional testing without clear "right answers"—even if your VUI does what you planned for it to do, it has to be functional not just in abilities but also for the intended users.

Voice Usability Testing Concepts

In Chapter 5, you learned about user research methods, including how to find out what people want from a VUI before you even have anything designed or built, let alone real users. Now it's time to look at what data you can collect from representative and real users who talk to your VUI pre- and post-deployment. You're not interested in just any data, but the data that tells you if your voice system is successfully giving your users what they want. In this chapter, you'll learn about some underlying concepts to understand why both quantitative and qualitative testing are necessary and what you learn from different testing methods. You'll learn what you can reliably measure.

In a financial services system, we tested two different menu structures; one consisted of a single longer list, and the other split the list into two sets. Both allowed barge-in. The general assumption was that two shorter lists would be the strong winner and that older users would be overwhelmed by the single long list. Turns out some preferred one and some two—and it was just a personal preference, not simply tied to user age or tech savvy. In fact, the oldest participant, well past retirement age, was delighted to not sit through several levels and happily barged in with her requests. Lesson: Be careful about making assumptions based on stereotypes about what some group of users wants.

Study Methodology: Task Scenarios and Surveys

There are many types of studies that can provide valuable data and insight during the late pre-deployment and post-deployment phases. Two of the most useful and common are studies involving task scenarios and surveys. During a task scenario test, a moderator presents several scenarios to the participant and observes the interaction as the participant tries to complete each task. After each task, the moderator asks follow-up questions about the experience. Surveys, or questionnaires, often consist of a set of statements rated on a Likert scale. A Likert scale is a five- or seven-point scale intended to measure to what degree someone agrees or disagrees with a statement like *The VUI helped me get my task done quickly*. The scale is given as phrases rather than number values: for examples, "strongly agree" and "disagree somewhat." They can also include ranked choices to measure preferences. The absolute Likert values are a nice summary for reports and presentations, but be careful not to overemphasize the number when you run tests with a typical small-size (fewer than 12 is common) participant group. Instead, pay more attention to free-form responses or group differences.

Task scenario performance tests focus on system usability and task completion success while also uncovering qualitative user satisfaction information. Surveys are quantitative and focus mainly on user satisfaction. You'll learn more about both later in this chapter. Task scenario studies include Wizard of Oz studies and functional system studies; surveys are discussed as well. When testing usability, analyze the results, make changes in the design and implementation, and iterate the qualitative studies as well as collect quantitative data for analysis.

Study Environment: In-Lab or Remote

You have a choice: bring participants into a lab or leave them in their "native environment." Pros and cons of bringing users into a lab setting aren't just relevant for voice. You can find many studies online that compare benefits of in-lab usability testing vs. remote testing.[1] If remote, the moderator (the person running the study) can come to the participant's location or remain in a separate location—here we're focusing mainly on the latter type of remote. At Nuance, much of our usability testing (UT) was done remotely. This works very well for voice-first and voice-only VUIs like phone-based IVRs; just set up a phone bridge and record the conversation.

A moderator who's familiar with the design and technology can determine where participants have issues with the VUI without watching them. It's actually one of the benefits of the moderator being remote: participants often provide more detail when describing their experiences because it feels more necessary to explain what happened exactly because the moderator isn't there to observe. Sometimes they're even more honest! If you're testing multimodal devices, you do of course need to see what the participant does. You can more easily and reliably set up cameras to capture users' reactions and interactions in a lab.

We've found that users tend to stumble on the same core recognition and interpretation issues in both environments; those types of findings can be equally valid across environments. But taking the user away from their regular environment can remove the context that results in dialog flow and implementation issues. If users need to find some information or refer to something physical, you need to minimally recreate that part of the task. Ideally, do some testing in the lab and some in the user's environment. Table 16-1 summarizes the differences we just covered between in-lab and remote voice UT.

---

[1]Here's a starting point: www.usability.gov/how-to-and-tools/methods/remote-testing.html

Table 16-1. *Comparison of in-lab and remote studies*

	In-lab	Remote
Environment	Controlled, but a step removed from participant's natural environment	"Native" participant environment, but limited interaction
Participant base	Harder to find broad set	Easier to find (no travel needed)
Cost	Can be higher (to compensate for travel)	Can be lower
Time needed for study	Longer (more overhead)	Shorter
Participant feedback	Less wordy, less critical, more personal	More explanatory, more honest, less personal

The more personal a VUI conversation is, the more important it is that participants feel comfortable and safe talking to the VUI. When a use case depends on something in the intended user's environment, it's very important that you collect data that reflects that environment. This can be challenging when the environment is private, potentially embarrassing, or even legally questionable. We've collected user voice data for in-car texting-while-driving, for colonoscopy prep, for financial transactions, for medical urine sample collection, and other VUI conversations that are quite a bit more personal than asking to hear some song or setting a timer. Think about what choices we had to make in terms of in-lab vs. remote testing for those VUIs to still gather valid data… Here are some answers:

For in-car testing, much of it is done in a lab (you saw a picture of the lab setup in Chapter 1). We've also been alpha testers for live in-car tests for safer tasks, like navigation. Those could be safely done while actually on the road since the user never risked taking their eyes off the road. Cameras and in-car observers captured the interactions, including responses, hesitations, and timing. For colonoscopy prep, we enlisted friends and family who had had one or were scheduled to do one. We did interviews to find out what was difficult about the process, and we did in-lab studies where we asked participants to remember their own prep and what they would have liked to know and then asked them to get that information from the app. For those with a scheduled procedure, we used detailed in-app logging to capture all speech-related data; we included a survey as the final to-do task in the app and followed up with phone interviews. For the urine sample collection, no, of course we couldn't record what people said or did in a hospital bathroom. Instead, we studied detailed pictures of those bathrooms and then mocked up similar arrangements locally to determine where the microphone and speaker should be and how that would affect the experience.

Study Administration: Moderated or Unmoderated

Many types of studies can be either moderated or unmoderated; either a human administers the study in real time, or participants answer questions and perform tasks in their own time. Results are collected through behavior tracking or reporting tools or even by participants self-reporting. During our time at Nuance, most usability studies were moderated, whether remote (over the phone) or in-lab. Since then, we've relied more on unmoderated studies.

One benefit of moderated studies is that the moderator can follow up to get clarification on observed behaviors or participant comments. More than once we've seen participants get confused and give a rating at the "wrong" end of a ten-point scale; an unmoderated study can't fix that. On the other hand, unmoderated studies "run themselves," so they can reach lots of participants quickly and cheaply. If time and budget allow, do both. Table 16-2 summarizes typical differences between moderated and unmoderated studies.

Table 16-2. *Comparison of moderated and unmoderated studies*

	Moderated	Unmoderated
Cost	Higher	Lower
Broad participant base	Harder to find	Easier to find
Time needed for study	Longer	Shorter
Participant follow-up	Immediate	None

Results: Quantitative or Qualitative

In their excellent book,[2] Travis and Hodgson explain why you need both data types: "Quantitative data tell us *what* people are doing. Qualitative data tell us *why* people are doing it." In other words, quantitative studies deal with calculations: how many users say X or what percentage of people succeeded. Qualitative studies focus on observations: why did particular users say X instead of Y or how do various contexts affect what users say next. In general, surveys are quantitative, and task scenarios are qualitative, but both types often include some elements of both. More on this topic when you learn about metrics later in this chapter.

Any test that involves looking at logs of user behavior should be quantitative. Depending on how logs were created, they can be qualitative as well, as you'll see in the survey discussion.

For quantitative studies, you obviously need statistical significance for any conclusions and claims. When you set up your qualitative studies, someone will ask you how many participants you need.[3] We've found that task scenario studies need no more than 10–12 participants; the biggest issues are usually found by the time half that many are done. That's good, because it means you can find the big issues in a day or two. Your efforts are usually better spent by running several iterative smaller studies testing different design versions.

SUCCESS TIP 16.4 NEVER SHORT-CHANGE QUALITATIVE STUDIES   Both quantitative and qualitative studies are valid and important—and both can be meaningless if conducted poorly. Quantitative studies are not more believable or important just because they have results from more people. Qualitative studies provide insights into why the numbers are what they are, so do as much qualitative testing as quantitative.

---

[2]Travis, D., and Hodgson, P. (2019). *Think Like a UX Researcher*. CRC Press.
[3]The same arguments apply for voice usability as for other modalities. You can find lots of articles on this topic online, for example, www.nngroup.com/articles/how-many-test-users/

A/B testing is a common UX testing method that provides quantitative data on typically qualitative tasks. In A/B testing, users are automatically and randomly assigned to one of two different versions of some experience. For voice systems, this often means two differently worded prompts, the presence or absence of a confirmation step, and so on. The test is done to prove a hypothesis, like "More users succeed with Task A if there's an explicit confirmation following their initial request." Because these tests need real users and need to be statistically significant, the trick with VUI A/B testing is that you need access to the production system. Depending on your organization and the domain and task, it may either be very difficult to get the go-ahead to run an A/B study or be part of testing for other modalities, like website testing. If you can, use it!

Wizard of Oz Studies

Wizard of Oz (WOZ) testing is the most brilliant VUI testing method you might never have heard of, so we're dedicating a whole section to it. The name comes from the concept of "the man behind the curtain" in *The Wizard of Oz* stories: what appears to be a machine is actually the responses generated by a person simulating the machine— the Wizard.[4] We introduced WOZ in Chapter 5 as one of the early data collection and user testing techniques that's particularly appropriate early in the product design and development process, before you have a functional robust VUI. We go into more detail in this chapter because you now have the necessary understanding of voice design for running a successful WOZ. Also, you can do a WOZ at any time during product development to test a new feature, and the techniques you use in a WOZ are similar to the ones used for functional system tests. In a WOZ, whether in-lab or remote, the moderator asks a participant to perform a task using a VUI; the participant interacts with the VUI, while the moderator observes and then asks follow-up questions—just like in any other usability study (Figure 16-1). The difference is that the VUI system isn't functional—it's a person (usually the designer) listening to the participant's commands and feeding back voice responses to fit the task, as if it were a functional VUI. The moderator doesn't tell the participant that the system is "fake" unless the participant asks, which seldom happens. Don't lie if they do ask!

---

[4]The method has been used since the 1960s, but the term was coined by J. F. Kelley ("An iterative design methodology for user-friendly natural language office information applications." ACM Transactions on Office Information Systems, March 1984, 2:1, pp. 26–41).

Figure 16-1. *The key to a successful WOZ is giving the participant a realistic experience*

The Wizard uses a GUI to generate spoken responses to the participant's spoken requests. That interface needs to be organized so that the Wizard can find the right response quickly—if the response is wrong or takes too long, the experience won't feel realistic to the participant making the results less valuable. Some enterprise voice development platforms, like Nuance and others, provide tools needed for running a WOZ or for automatically generating the test environment directly from the detailed design documentation. If you don't have access to those, don't worry. You can create your own by hand using easily available editing tools. You usually only test a small segment of a VUI design in each WOZ, so handcrafting the Wizard's interface is very doable. Figure 16-2 shows the start of what two WOZs might look like when created in Microsoft PowerPoint: a restaurant reservation system and a timer setting app. The flow provides an easy reference for the Wizard to quickly find the right response for the context; the black labels in the restaurant screen, like "reservation," refer to the participant's initial request. In this context, VUI responses and subsequent dialog paths depend on how many slots the participant filled in that first utterance. The Wizard clicks the audio icon in the chosen dialog path to play a preloaded prompt, and there are some "easy out" prompts in the right corner that can be played when the Wizard needs a little extra time to choose a response or if the request can't be handled with what had been included in the GUI setup. For realism, the audio should appear to come from the device that's claimed to be tested, so through a phone if it's an IVR and from a home assistant device when that's what's tested, even if it's just through a hidden external speaker.

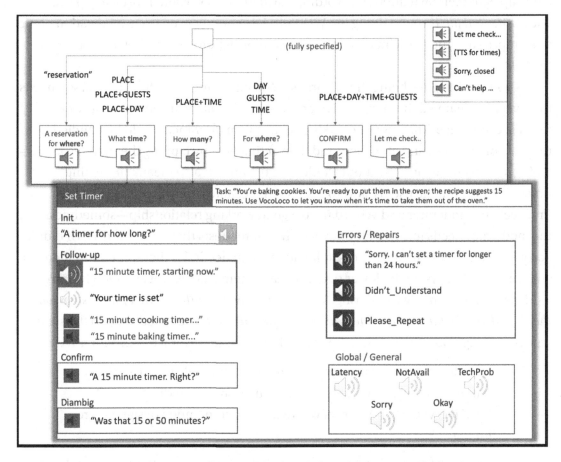

Figure 16-2. *Initial screens of two simple Wizard of Oz tests using PowerPoint*

When done right, WOZ results are highly valid and insightful because of the realistic conversation participants experience. A typical WOZ study includes four to six tasks that are relevant to the participant, and the moderator must present each task in a way that makes the task clear without spoon-feeding the utterance wording to the participant. For example, when testing a prescription refill task, you want the participant to think about how they would do the task, so they use their own words. So, as moderator, you first set the stage by asking something like *Have you ever gotten medication prescribed by your doctor that you picked up at a pharmacy?* Soon you move on to the task description. You might say something like *Let's assume that this morning you took your prescribed medication. You're taking it every day, and you just realized there are only a few days left in the bottle. Go ahead and use the VUI to get more before you run out.* You don't want to give the instruction *Use the VUI to order a refill* because you want the participant to come up with their own utterance wording—with this, they would most likely parrot back *Order a refill.* If you're doing the WOZ in a lab, you can even use a medication bottle as a prop, asking the participant to refer to any information on the label if asked for by the VUI.

As you can imagine, being the Wizard is challenging and stressful. That person needs to be very familiar with both the design and voice technology in general to provide a realistic experience. That means quickly deciding if an utterance would be handled by the real voice system and, if so, how and then acting on it by tapping the right response— typing in a response for TTS output would take too long. It also means simulating timeout behavior if the user is slow to respond or hesitates mid-utterance. Practice! Practice! The moderator and Wizard need a good working relationship—sometimes the moderator needs to cover for unexpected user requests that the Wizard's GUI didn't account for. A common moderator explanation when needed is that sometimes there's a glitch and the test system is slower than the real system will be. Not completely untrue!

Now you're probably wondering, *Why would anyone bother with a fake system when they could use the functional system with recognition?* Glad you asked! You do the same types of testing also with functional systems, but there are several reasons for a WOZ:

- No voice system has perfect performance, especially before tuning. A functional system is likely to fail at times and unpredictably. A WOZ lets you test how users will react to your intended design before tuning.

- You can't force a particular response behavior on a functional system—unless you have special limited versions, but that's a lot of work. If you want to test user response to a particular type of error handling, you'd need a separate version of the system or make other code changes. A WOZ gives you total control of responses without any coding effort.

- You want to test the design of some feature before spending time and money implementing it or even choose between several approaches. A WOZ is a quick way to test those features in conversational context at any point during product development.

- Some backend data, system error conditions, or any of the contexts in Chapter 14 aren't available. A WOZ lets you simulate the whole conversation experience to see how your users will react.

We've only scratched the surface of what's involved. You can find more details online and in books. Here are a few more points to keep in mind:

- At the start of a session, ask participants to approve recording their session.

- After the last task scenario, wrap up with an overall satisfaction survey. Ask about likes and dislikes.

- WOZ tests are qualitative because they usually only involve as many participants as can be handled in a day or two of one-hour sessions, so maybe a dozen. But you'll have collected task success numbers and satisfaction numbers on a numeric scale. You'll want to report those numbers. That's fine, as long as you remember and make clear that those numbers are not statistically significant because of the limited number of participants.

- During the session, the moderator is the boss. Requests and input from observers are welcome if they can be considered in a way that doesn't affect the overall session, but the moderator has final say. Make this clear to all.

When planning and executing a usability study with participants, it's easy to forget a step or not start early enough. If that happens, the sad outcome is a less useful study or even completely cutting out the test. The project schedule needs to allow time for multiple tasks, some happening in parallel, most with dependencies on other tasks having been completed. Key steps, very simplified:

1. Settle on what system features to test. The designer or designers lead this, but you want to involve business owners to get buy-in and approval.

2. Start process of recruiting and scheduling participants. It's never too early. Don't forget to include recruiting fees and participant payments in the budget.

3. In parallel with #2, start creating the WOZ based on the relevant portions of the design. Test that it works well end to end. Give the Wizard lots of practice with available "participants," like coworkers.

4. Run the test.

5. Analyze the results. Create the agreed-upon report. Share results. Update designs.

Developing the WOZ

To conduct a WOZ, you need some software for the Wizard to do their job. From a development perspective, the main concern is building the functionality of the dialog, but instead of using the ASR and NLU from the system, the Wizard is the system and provides the answers. From a Dialogflow perspective, you can imagine a couple of components to such a system:

- **A Wizard graphical interface, often web-based**: This UI has buttons or links for each of the expected Dialogflow intents and an open-ended option for when unplanned requests are made. The web page can be generated automatically from your app's current Dialogflow intents in a couple of ways:

  - **By exporting the app into a .zip file (like the ones in this book) and processing the contents—you did that for your Dialogflow app back in Chapter 3**: The .zip file includes agent.json and package.json, directory entities (an ENTITY.json and ENTITY_entries_LANG.json file for each entity ENTITY), and directory intents (an INTENT.json and INTENT_usersays_LANG.json file for each intent INTENT). These files could be used with, for example, a Python script to create the Wizard web interface. We don't include specific examples of such a script here; the detailed implementation depends heavily on how the WOZ interface is provided to the Wizard.

- **By using various Dialogflow APIs[5] to pull out the intents**: It makes sense to deploy this Wizard UI on Google App Engine, since that's where the webhook is deployed.

- **A way to intercept the normal application behavior and use the Wizard UI input instead**: One strategy is to have some code in the webhook for "WOZ mode." In this mode, the webhook would wait for a response from the Wizard UI and use that to provide the response to Dialogflow instead of responding directly to a user utterance. This can get tricky: you'd need to be careful not to exceed the time limit of how long Dialogflow waits for a webhook response before it went ahead with the non-webhook answer.

SUCCESS TIP 16.5 THINKING OUT LOUD? THINK AGAIN   Having participants think out loud while they perform some task is a common usability testing method for getting insight into people's thought process. Obviously, that's difficult if you're investigating voice commands, especially if testing an "always-listening" system, like an over-the-phone IVR.

The Wizard of Oz is the workhorse of VUI design. Find a setup that works best in your environment and learn how to use it to collect valuable data. And again, practice: a successful WOZ takes experience.

Tracking and Measuring Performance

Before you try improving your VUI, you need to know how it performs right now. Those measures need to be accurate, informative, consistent, and quick to generate. Tracking, logging, and measuring performance isn't just for making changes—even if you're unable to make changes, you want to know what's happening when your users talk to your VUI. And if you built a voice system for someone else, they may have made your payment performance-related. You can see the importance of choosing the right things to track and measure.

---

[5]https://cloud.google.com/dialogflow/docs/reference/rest/v2-overview

Performance metrics availability differs greatly across voice platforms. If you can log it, do, as long as it doesn't violate privacy or security, of course. Importantly, you don't want to limit your logging to what was recognized. In some ways, there's more information in what was misrecognized and what people asked for that you don't yet handle. Do what you can to capture that information. You also want to capture the timing of when the user said something and when they didn't, how long it took them to respond (if they hesitated, that's a sign of cognitive load, and you want to figure out why), or if they barged in with a response. And if you sample periodically, capture variation across user types, times of day, days of week, and so on. In Chapter 17, you'll understand the importance of logging anything you can so you can accurately pinpoint how to improve system performance.

SUCCESS TIP 16.6 IT'S NEVER TOO EARLY TO PLAN FOR LOGGING   Although we discuss logging late in the book, we want to emphasize that you should implement logging and performance metrics at the very start of any project, rather than retrofit it once development is mostly done. Stakeholders, designers, and developers all need to be included in those discussions, ideally even before any client engagement contract is signed. What's logged needs to help users as well as make any promised goals attainable.

To understand how your VUI performs now and over time, you first need a baseline to compare against. Performance metrics fall into three categories: recognition performance, transaction completion, and user satisfaction. There's a fourth category you'll care about: business metrics. Let's take a look.

Recognition Performance Metrics

Voice system performance reporting always involves recognition performance metrics, including grammar coverage, accuracy, and sometimes latency. These metrics help in understanding VUI errors in different types of dialogs, and intent and slot accuracy is dependent on recognition performance. You learned about these in Chapter 12 (repeated in Table 16-3 for easy reference). Performance metrics should cover as many of these measures as you can collect in your framework.

Table 16-3. *Recognition performance coverage and accuracy concepts*

If an utterance is...	That utterance is...
In-grammar (**IG**)	Covered by relevant grammars; matches what's expected.
Out-of-coverage/Out-of-vocabulary (**OOC/OOV**)[6]	Any utterance that's not covered in this part of the dialog.
Out-of-grammar (**OOG**)	OOC plus noise, fragments, stutters, coughs, or side speech.
If the outcome is...	**The utterance is...**
Correct accept (**CA**)	Covered by current grammar and successfully matched as expected.
Correct reject (**CR**)	Not covered by current grammar and therefore rejected as expected.
False accept in-grammar (**FA-in**)	Covered by current grammar but incorrectly recognized as and matched to something else that's IG.
False reject (**FR**)	Covered by current grammar but not recognized or matched to it.
False accept out-of-grammar (**FA-out**)	Not covered by current grammar but recognized as and matched to something else that's IG.

There's one more important concept you need to understand: in-domain vs. out-of-domain. A phrase that's in-domain (ID) is one that belongs in a grammar, whether or not it's currently included. The phrase belongs because in its context of overall VUI topic and current dialog turn, it has the same meaning as the other phrases in that grammar. Here're some examples to illustrate the point that the same utterance can be in-domain or out-of-domain:

---

[6]Depending on who you ask and where they started their voice work, "OOG" and "OOC" are used as shown here, or exactly opposite. Some include an analytical component about whether or not an utterance is in domain and therefore a potential future addition. We prefer to keep these measures objective for automated reporting while tracking both spoken words and other sounds that could affect performance. There's a third name that may be clearer when you want to refer to actual user utterances: out-of-vocabulary (OOV). Stick with the convention used with your platform and make sure everyone on your team shares the same understanding.

VUI   *Who's your favorite artist?*   (Expect artist name)

User1   *Yes.*   ← In-domain (band name)

User2   *9 9 9.*   ← In-domain (band name)

~~~   ~~~   ~~~

VUI   *That order number is 995. Right?*   (Expect Yes/No)

User1   *Yes.*   ← In-domain

User2   *9 9 9.*   ← In-domain (one-step correction)

~~~   ~~~   ~~~

VUI   *A reservation for tonight. Right?*   (Expect Yes/No)

User1   *Yes.*   ← In-domain

User2   *9 9 9.*   ← Out-of-domain

~~~   ~~~   ~~~

VUI   *What's your favorite holiday?*   (Expect holiday name)

User1   *Yes.*   ← Out-of-domain

User2   *9 9 9.*   ← Out-of-domain

You can see how important domain context is. This is one reason why it's difficult to use "off the shelf" grammars as-is. They're a great starting point, but seldom enough and certainly need testing. While in-grammar and out-of-grammar are clear and binary concepts—a phrase is either included or not—determining if a phrase is in-domain gets fuzzier because it involves judgment calls, especially as you approach the edges between intents. And assume the domain is English to avoid any potential counterargument that this is an attempted *no* by a very insistent German (*nein nein nein*).

Look again at the four sample dialogs. You'll realize something else that's important: slot-level performance. You want to track recognition performance for general intents, such as for all utterances responding to the order number confirmation. To understand what specific responses are failing, you also want to capture and report performance on individual slots and values. For example, you want to see order number confirmation slot values for Yes, No, and individual numbers of one-step correction. If you have the ability, capture this information. This level of detail is crucial for tuning your system (Chapter 17).

A fundamental question is how to get the data for this type of analysis. You've already seen that Dialogflow has some built-in mechanisms for stepping through the history of the application and improving performance, including

- The History link that shows conversation history

- The Training link that flags issues and allows corrections such as adding training phrases

Both provide good data, and we've seen a variety of GUI-based tools over the years that do similar things. The main issue here is scale. These tools are fine for analyzing a few conversations, but if you have a deployed app and want to go through thousands of conversations to figure out what phrases need to be added for coverage or you try to understand behavior in a particular intent, these tools are limited. Figure 16-3 shows a sample of a spreadsheet with the type of statistics that provide better insight. In Chapter 17 you learn how to find and work with this kind of data. For a real application, you'll have thousands of rows of this kind of data.

Transcription	Recognized text	Correct intent	Interpreted intent	Filled parameters	VUI response	Grammar result	Recognition result
Call Brent Jones	call brent jones	arCallByName	arCallByName	{"given-name":"Brent", "last-name":"Jones"}	Brent Jones. Calling.	IG, ID	CA-in
yes	yes	arConfirmName	arConfirmName	{confirm":"yes"}	Okay. Calling Brent Jones.	IG, ID	CA-in
Call Brent Jones	call brent jones	arCallByName	arCallByName	{"given-name":"Brent", "last-name":"Jones"}	You wanna call Brent Jones, right?	IG, ID	CA-in
Call Brent	call brent	arCallByName	arCallByName	{"given-name":"Brent"}	Which Brent: Jones, Adams, or Barnes?	IG, ID	CA-in
Jones	jones	arCallByNameDisambigLastName	arCallByNameDisambigLastName	{"last-name":"Jones"}	Okay. Calling Brent Jones.	IG, ID	CA-in
Call Brent Jones	call brent jonas	arCallByName	arCallByName	{"given-name":"Brent", "last-name":"Jonas"}	You wanna call Brent Jonas, right?	OOV, ID	FA-out
Telephone Brent Jones	telephone brent jones	arCallByName	Default Fallback Intent	{}	Sorry?	OOV, ID	CR-out
Pepperoni pizza	pepperoni pizza	Default Fallback Intent	Default Fallback Intent	{}	Sorry?	OOV, OOD	CR-out

Figure 16-3. *Recognition/interpretation statistics sample*

Task Completion Metrics

Where recognition metrics provide a more static picture of performance, task completion metrics look at the whole conversation from a different perspective than pure recognition performance. Tracking what paths users take through multi-turn dialogs is crucial information. So is anything that indicates if users succeeded or where and how they failed.

Ideally you want to capture the spoken utterance audio, the text interpretation of what was said, the intent and slots filled, what happened before and after each request, the time between those steps, any retries, time of day, who said it (based on biometrics or authentication status), the status of any associated devices, how the VUI responded, and the ultimate fulfillment outcome. Include tags in your code so that you can collect data automatically. And remember that those logs need to be anonymized, have personally identifiable information (PII) removed, and be securely stored and accessed.

Log tags should capture the user's progress through the conversation. You want to encode what happens at each step so you can capture that information for later analysis; assigning what's success vs. failure should be left for that later analysis, and it may even change as your system changes in the future. As with the recognition performance metrics, we show you how to configure your app to collect data at a high level next. Then in Chapter 17 you learn more about the details.

For task completion, you need to mark two events:

- The task is starting.

- The task is completed.

For example, a user triggering the intent `tcrProcedurePrep` by saying *Walk me through my procedure prep* marks start of task. End of task is marked if the VUI plays the response *Great! You're all done!* from the intent `tcrProcedurePrepNext2`.

So far, you haven't defined many scenarios in the procedure helper app that involve complex tasks; they're mostly "one-and-done" requests. But even those requests that are sometimes simple, like *Call Brent Jones*, can get complex when there's disambiguation, confirmation, error handling, and so on.

The percentage of start of task that's also end of task is your task completion percentage (TCR). If a transaction starts and then another transaction starts before task 1 reaches completion or if the logs end before completion, then you assume that the transaction did not complete, unless the task has another task within it.

At a high level, there are two strategies for measuring TCR data:

- Put tags in the application, and then measure TCR straight from the logs.[7]

---

[7]Some analytics can be gotten out of the main voice assistant platforms, and there are several commercially available tools (ever changing, of course), including from Adobe, `www.adobe.com/analytics/voice-analytics.html`

- Don't do anything in the application, but have slightly more complex analysis scripts that infer the beginning and end of tasks from other log elements.

We usually gravitate toward the second method when possible. One reason is that things change. We've been through many instances in practice where we spend a lot of time (and money) defining tasks in the app only to realize afterward *Shoot! We missed something!* At that point you have two choices: (1) throw out loads of very useful data, fix the tags, and start over again with the data collection or (2) do post-analysis on the collected data, defining new task starts and ends based on the log data you have. Well, that's the same as the second method, so you might as well start there! Another reason to stay away from hardcoded tags has to do with testing: everything should be tested carefully before data collections start, but it's notoriously difficult to get all the cases right, including disambiguation, confirmation, nomatch and recognition errors, and so on. That's another reason to favor post-analysis on the raw logs. In Chapter 17, you learn more about both approaches.

SUCCESS TIP 16.7 KEEP YOUR SCRIPTS CURRENT   If you use scripts for automated data collection, keep them up to date to match any grammar changes, feature additions, splits or consolidation of intents, and updates made to prompts and flows.

Audio and TTS Testing

All audio earcons and prompts need to be tested. Some testing can be automated, including making sure something plays when it's supposed to and that the volume is within expected range. At some point, though, you need to listen. You're dealing with sound, after all!

If you use temporary TTS prompts during development, preferably it's a voice that sounds distinct enough from the final voice to help you find any overlooked remaining TTS now. If prompts are recorded by a human voice talent, make sure the recording quality hasn't changed between sessions. Check for odd clicks or pauses. With TTS, test comprehension. Get a representative group of listeners to evaluate comprehension of a set of utterances in a survey. It's possible to measure TTS quality and comprehension objectively. You can even measure how well a certain emotion or urgency is conveyed, for example, by asking two groups of participants to listen to the same system responses recorded with TTS (group 1) and recorded by an expressive natural voice (group 2). We've used this approach successfully ourselves. Figure 16-4 shows the result from listeners evaluating the emotion conveyed by two versions (high-quality TTS and recorded human voice) of two identically worded VUI prompts. The TTS and human voice versions convey very similar emotions.[8]

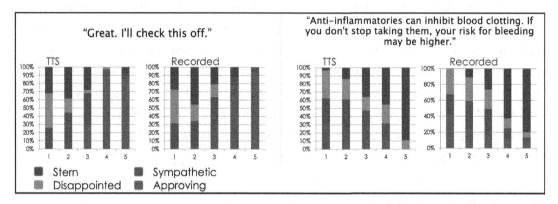

Figure 16-4. *Two prompts, presented as TTS and human voice, evaluated for their conveyed emotion*

SUCCESS TIP 16.8 LISTEN TO ALL PROMPTS IN CONTEXT, EVEN TTS   Even though today's TTS is amazing, it's not perfect. Be sure to test for comprehension as well as thoroughly listen to a large set of generated utterances in context. Does it sound natural? Is there confusing intonation? Sometimes the answer is as simple as changing the punctuation: If you don't like how *I can't find that, but I found this…* sounds, try changing it slightly to *I can't find that. But I found this…*

---

[8]Thyme-Gobbel (2018). A Matter of Choice: Personalization vs. Personality in Interactive Voice Assistants. AI Assistant Summit, San Francisco, CA.

User Satisfaction Metrics

User satisfaction is a combination of direct feedback from users and analysis of what can be inferred from retries and success in giving users what they asked for. User satisfaction correlates closely with transaction completion success—this is no surprise, as people who aren't successful getting what they asked for aren't going to be as happy as those who do. If you have access to OOG data, you can easily see the level of frustration in user utterances. If your VUI makes use of any automated satisfaction metrics, like user thumbs-up/thumbs-down feedback, capture that in your automated reporting. User satisfaction studies are usually handled separately because they're not derived from automatically tracked system metrics. An analysis report might look like the excerpt in Figure 16-5.

Transcription	Recognized text	Correct intent	Interpreted intent	Filled parameters	VUI response	Grammar result	Recognition result
Call Brent Jones	call brent jones	arCallByName	arCallByName	{"given-name":"Brent", "last-name":"Jones"}	Brent Jones. Calling.	IG, ID	CA-in
yes	yes	arConfirmName	arConfirmName	{confirm":"yes"}	Okay. Calling Brent Jones.	IG, ID	CA-in
Call Brent Jones	call brent jones	arCallByName	arCallByName	{"given-name":"Brent", "last-name":"Jones"}	You wanna call Brent Jones, right?	IG, ID	CA-in
Call Brent	call brent	arCallByName	arCallByName	{"given-name":"Brent"}	Which Brent: Jones, Adams, or Barnes?	IG, ID	CA-in
Jones	jones	arCallByNameDisambi gLastName	arCallByNameDisambi gLastName	{"last-name":"Jones"}	Okay. Calling Brent Jones.	IG, ID	CA-in
Call Brent Jones	call brent jonas	arCallByName	arCallByName	{"given-name":"Brent", "last-name":"Jonas"}	You wanna call Brent Jonas, right?	OOV, ID	FA-out
Telephone Brent Jones	telephone brent jones	arCallByName	Default Fallback Intent		Sorry?	OOV, ID	CR-out
Pepperoni pizza	pepperoni pizza	Default Fallback Intent	Default Fallback Intent		Sorry?	OOV, OOD	CR-out

Figure 16-5. Get immediate feedback from users; verify that feedback is on accuracy, not content

More data is pretty much always better, as long as the data is valid. And a word of warning: Just as you shouldn't read too much into single data points, don't assume something is analyzed correctly just because it's based on a large data set. Even numeric measures need to be analyzed with an understanding of human and computer speech processing.

Commonly measured user satisfaction metrics include

- Overall duration of the conversation

- Errors (number and types) and retries

- Overall task completion and type of failure

FROM THE VOICE TRENCHES

In an IVR, the wording of two different welcome prompts was tested. One greeted the caller with the system persona name, and the other also included a brief phrase clearly identifying the voice to be an automated agent. When automation was clearly stated, agent transfer requests increased (about 5%), but fully automated calls also increased. This means that transparency and choice led to accurate expectations and tailored experiences for users, which resulted in overall increased containment, outcome success, and user satisfaction.

As you can imagine, it's very difficult to accurately measure user preferences and satisfaction. That includes testing system persona preferences. You should always try to do so, of course. Just be careful to draw valid conclusions. It's a fascinating topic—search online for "valid experimental design" and similar—knowing more about it will serve you well, not just in evaluating your own and other people's VUI-related claims but also in general critical thinking. We have done various studies over the years trying to measure user preferences of voices and wording. Here are some of what we've learned:

- The biggest pitfall is turning qualitative observations into quantitative measurements and claims. It's fine to report numbers, but unless you know there's significance in a controlled study, focus on capturing qualitative observations.

- You can find many claims online about user preferences of male vs. female VUI voices or human recorded speech vs. TTS. By all means read those, but be aware that preferences depend on many factors and parameters. Preferences are often based on something else or a combination of factors, like recognition accuracy or feature availability.

- When people say they prefer one gender over another for the VUI voice (see persona discussion, Chapter 15), it might simply mean they prefer that particular voice or how some test phrase was spoken.

- When people say they don't like TTS, it may mean they don't like that TTS or its use in this particular VUI.

- The same wording is often perceived as conveying the same level of concern or urgency whether it's TTS or human speech. Content weighs heavier on interpretation in isolated responses, but there may be preference differences with use over time.

- A more robotic voice can be fine, even preferred, in some contexts. Watch out for the uncanny valley, the unsettling reaction people have to something with some strong human characteristics but not others.

- To measure users' satisfaction with voice or persona accurately, you need to measure satisfaction with real users in actual use over time, not just by playing an utterance in isolation during a study. You'll need your testers to interact with several versions of a VUI that differ only in the voice used.

- Ultimately a voice preference is very individual. The best solution is to give users a couple of choices in a voice system that works well and implements best design practices, like clear and concise prompt wording.

The most common and useful methods for measuring voice system user satisfaction involve task scenarios and surveys. Let's take a quick look at what you can learn from both.

Functional System Task Scenario Studies

Task scenario studies using functional ASR and NL basically use the same test methodology as for WOZ studies, except that recognition and intent mapping are functional rather than controlled by a human. Because of that, the experience is realistic; the studies are evaluative in nature and can be used to collect user success and satisfaction metrics data. You get task completion data, dialog path taken, and satisfaction data from follow-up surveys after tasks are done. Importantly, you observe user interactions first-hand rather than rely on users' self-reporting. At the end, you can also include broader questions on branding and preferences, like *Does it match your image of company X?* and *What would you change?*

Administered and Crowdsourced Surveys

As you just saw, some survey element is always part of moderated task scenario studies. Larger voice surveys are usually remote and often unmoderated. Surveys involve self-reporting by the participants, which means you get a filtered version of people's experiences including their perceptions of what works and doesn't.

That's fine, as long as you're aware of it. Surveys don't need to be quantitatively significant to be useful. They can provide useful qualitative data as well: collect performance results on simple tasks with A/B tests, or collect information on preferences, usage, and ideas through multiple choice or short answer questions.

You can conduct surveys using services like Amazon Mechanical Turk, Google Surveys, Figure Eight, and similar human-in-the-loop organizations. They can be inexpensive and quick. For a relatively small payment, each participant provides feedback, responses, or behavior data on some task or topic. Questions and tasks can be targeted to address exactly the topic you're interested in. You can specify the number of participants you need and their demographics. You can get a lot of potentially valuable information from a very broad population.

There are drawbacks as well. You can't follow up with clarification questions. The further you get from asking participants about concrete experiences, the higher the risk they're not accurate or engaged when responding. Questions must be carefully worded to generate valid answers, and it's difficult to find very specific participant groups, such as older users or people with specific health issues.

Crowdsourced surveys can be a great source of performance data if your VUI is intended for a general population and you ask the right questions—creating surveys involves skill and experience. We've had good results using them over the years. The key is to stay as clear and concrete as possible. You can play audio on most survey platforms, but you'll be limited on connecting directly to a functional device or app.

There are testing companies out there that provide those more in-depth services. Yet other companies carry out large-scale survey interviews. That can be a very useful source of user metrics assuming the questions are clear and accurately reflect the voice modality. You or someone experienced in how voice systems work should review all survey questions.

User engagement and data validity is one of the biggest issues with crowdsourcing. Because payments are small, participants rush through each task. You can counter that by asking the same question in several ways to verify responses. For example, ask a free-form question and later a rank-order and/or a multiple-choice question. Also, pay your participants more than minimum and collect data from enough participants that you can toss out any questionable results. In one large crowdsourced survey, we had to remove more than 15% of the responses. By reviewing the data logs, we determined that some were duplicates by a single participant, while others were nonsense responses.

In-App Automated Surveys

Another way to collect user metrics is automated in-app surveys. In your deployed VUI, you include a short survey or feedback question at strategic points in the conversation. In IVRs, it can be a short satisfaction survey at the end of a complex task. In a multimodal mobile app, you can include a thumbs-up/thumbs-down feedback question after information responses. We've built and used both successfully to collect user performance data. If you're able to incorporate in-app surveys, they're inexpensive and flexible once the infrastructure is in place, and they provide you with direct access to user satisfaction and success data.

In-app surveys are a great source for relevant and valid metrics for several reasons. First, feedback is requested immediately after the experience. People forget audio details quickly. It's the nature of the modality—voice is fleeting. Feedback tends to be more accurate, detailed, and relevant than for separate surveys administered after the fact.

Another benefit of in-app surveys is that they're spoken. That keeps the participant in the same modality that helps them when thinking about how well the spoken conversation worked for them. If users also speak their responses to open-ended questions, there's an added benefit of answers in the users' own words.

Participants are guaranteed to be real users because the survey is placed in the app that's being asked about. In crowdsourced surveys, there's often no guarantee that participants are actual users of the app asked about, although they may be representative.

Any in-app survey questions need to be clear and precise so that responses are valid and useful. They also need to be short and appear only sporadically to not annoy users.

SUCCESS TIP 16.9 SURVEY CREATION TAKES SKILL; SO DOES VOICE   Creating valid surveys and analyzing the results are important skills. It's all too easy to ask questions in a way that negates the results. The how-to of survey creation is outside the scope of this book. Understanding voice data is another crucial skill— by reading this book, you already know a lot more than many people who collect and analyze data. If you rely on someone else's data, verify that they have a solid grasp of both survey techniques and voice topics.

Business Metrics

If you're building or improving a product, you need to have a clear understanding of the business goals for the VUI, and you need to know when you first start planning (Chapter 4) to make sure not only that your design addresses those goals but also that you can measure them. In some cases, the goal is increased customer satisfaction, either relative to past company/product performance or against some established standard. This is often measured with surveys. Common business goals include cost saving and increased automation by off-loading simpler and non-troubleshooting tasks from human representatives to voice apps. In cases where companies have large call centers with specialized agents, decreased misrouting is key. In other cases, it's decreased hold-time/time-to-service or increased sign-ups or successful login or reaching the end state of a specific feature successfully. There is also call abandonment, retries, frequency of use, interaction volume, or even an increased rate of success for procedure preparation. Whatever it is, make sure you have access to the necessary measurements. You'll find that business metrics are often combined as well, rather than just depending on a single measure. As you can see, you need reliable logging of user behavior both at each dialog step and cumulatively.

What's Next?

You learned how to test your voice system and make it as robust and ready for primetime as possible. You also learned how to collect different types of system performance and user data.[9] That's the data you need for improving your voice system performance. That means you're ready for the fascinating topic of our final chapter: tuning.

Summary

- More data is always better, as long as it's valid. Don't rely on just one test or one type of test. Instead, perform different types of tests to see if your results agree. They might each uncover different issues as well as the same ones from a different and insightful perspective.

- UI, UX, developers, analysts, and product owners all benefit from understanding qualitative and quantitative data.

- Measure performance even if you can't change anything in your voice system; otherwise, you don't know anything about its success.

- Your ability to accurately measure and report system performance directly affects your ability to tune your system.

---

[9]Here's an easy-to-read article about data that can be collected and what you can learn from it: `https://research.atspotify.com/giving-voice-to-silent-data-designing-with-personal-music-listening-history/`

## CHAPTER 17

Tuning and Deploying Voice Systems

Tuning voice system performance is an iterative and ongoing process of analyzing data from real users and improving their experience based on any issues you identify. It starts during one or several pilot tests after you have worked through integration and functional testing. Limited tuning will be part of your testing during end-to-end and acceptance testing. Full-on tuning is only relevant once you have real user data from a fully tested and integrated system. You'll understand why as you read through this chapter. It covers definitions of tuning concepts and gives you hands-on practice. You also learn about how to tune when data access is limited and how to avoid pitfalls before and after deployment.

Tuning: What Is It and Why Do You Do It?

Tuning refers to the process of collecting and analyzing data from a live in-production voice system utilized by actual end users, proposing solutions, and implementing them. If you like solving puzzles, you'll love tuning. Let's start with some definitions and reasons why you need to tune every voice system to some degree.

The core reason for tuning is that user happiness and success is directly related to system performance. Because human speech varies greatly in pronunciation and word choice and because that variability can only be predicted so far in advance, performance always improves once you have access to real user data and can tweak coverage and parameters for your real users in their real-world contexts. Even after thorough in-house testing of a voice system built by an experienced team, there will always be utterances

A. Thymé-Gobbel and C. Jankowski, *Mastering Voice Interfaces*, https://doi.org/10.1007/978-1-4842-7005-9_17

that are not covered by grammars, not understood, or misinterpreted. Even if you're lucky enough to have access to a relevant annotated training set, it won't cover all utterances or contexts. Every system is different, and every set of users is different; you don't see the full story till you have real user data, data from actual end users talking to the deployed VUI for their own needs in their own environment.

All this probably feels scary: *What do you mean it might not work perfectly?!* We get it—just remember it doesn't have to be perfect. It's to be expected, and it's OK. Really. There is no such thing as a perfect voice system that understands everything, not even after tuning. Just like no person always hears and understands perfectly. That makes some people nervous, especially when coming from more graphical interfaces, where a click or link either works or it doesn't. And if you're a product/project manager interacting with clients who are new to voice, it's a good idea to explain this early on and remind them before tuning begins. All you can do is follow best practices and everything you've learned, do as much testing as possible, and make the interaction and the grammars as robust as possible before launch. It's enough.

Tuning improves handling of what users say by expanding the utterance coverage, either by adding phrases in rule-based grammars or by adding training phrases to statistical models. If recognition doesn't perform as expected, tuning can involve modifying parameter settings or training on more data. It can involve applying or tweaking some of the techniques you learned about in Chapter 12, including skip lists, N-best, and confidence thresholds. It can involve broadening recognition to include alternate pronunciations of some words. You might need to tune your utterance-to-meaning associations. That can involve modifying the phrase-to-intent mapping or splitting one intent into several more detailed intents, each of which needs new prompts, behaviors, and grammars. As you'll learn in this chapter, tuning goes far beyond tweaking grammars. Tuning is seldom code-focused per se, but expect that code needs to change to support necessary prompt and flow changes. This is why it's so important to build tuning into any project schedule, including testing and redeploying production code.

You'll come across signs of user confusion and evidence that your users weren't as successful as you'd hoped. This shows up indirectly as people asking what seems to be the same question twice in a row. If you have access to recorded utterances or logs of out-of-grammar utterances, you may find requests and wording you hadn't accounted for. Some of those issues are addressed through dialog changes or changes in the wording or emphasis of a prompt; others are coverage and intent mapping issues.

All this boils down to one thing: only real users interacting with your VUI for their own needs after it goes live can provide the data showing you if you made the right design and development choices.

Why Recognition Accuracy Isn't Enough

High ASR accuracy is a prerequisite for VUI success. It's the foundation on which you build robust intents and smarter dialogs. But it's not enough. Here's a list of why:

- Recognizing users' words correctly is only the first step.

  - As you learned in Chapter 16, if you rely on the platform's automatic text interpretation of user utterances, you only see what the platform "heard." Transcriptions are still the gold standard, the ground truth. Transcriptions are done by trained professionals and include accurate details describing where pauses occur and how long they are, unusual pronunciations, stutters, restarts, screams of frustration, background noise, side speech, and even clear emotional states of the speaker—all the things that affect what's recognized. Without it, you'll base your interpretations on limited data, and you might try to "fix" something in a suboptimal way, even making the problem worse. You're concerned that your users are drinking too much because you see *liquor* in your diet diary logs. So you add warning prompts here and there...until you find out some people just really like *licorice* and were misrecognized.

- Interpreting users' utterances correctly is the second step.

  - Recognizing the words correctly is only one part of the task; extracting the correct meaning is next, and it's harder. Sadly, for us, people don't often speak in the kinds of complete and grammatically correct sentences that are much easier to interpret. How do you interpret incomplete sentences that are just a few words? And what do you do if your shopping VUI hears users say "BY"? Does it mean *bye* or *buy*? Users won't be happy if you get that wrong.

- Finding and handing difficulties in users' utterances leads to greater success.

    - As mentioned in Chapter 16, if your platform only gives you the automatic results of utterances that are interpreted as something, you won't know anything about those utterances that fall outside of this set. You'd be delighted to see in your diet diary logs that the number of users who ate *broccoli* doubled this month... until you get the transcriptions and notice they all had *broccoli tempura* which was cut off because you hadn't included handling for *tempura*. Your early data collection showed that people want to know about insurance coverage, but now nobody is asking about it. Without out-of-coverage data, you don't know that it's because they don't say *insurance*, just *Is this covered?*

- Ultimately, you need to know if real users are successful.

    - Anyone who's done UX work and usability testing knows that no matter how much research was done to inform design, nothing takes the place of data from real users interacting with the UI in their real-world context and environment. That's true for voice as well. Research feeds into hypotheses that turn into designs. Controlled experiments using prototypes get you one step closer to the data that matters; user data from pilots and full product releases always provides utterances and behaviors you hadn't planned for. There's nothing built into a recognizer or general data set that predicts all the variation of real speech data.

Analyzing Causes of Poor System Performance

You've set up your environment to track and measure a whole set of metrics, you have your baseline numbers, and now you're getting your first set of interaction logs as well as data from user studies and surveys. How do you know what the metrics really mean, and if some results are bad, what do you do about it? Your voice system performance is affected by many factors, which means you need to analyze performance by looking at it from multiple directions. In other words, you apply several tuning methods:

- **Core ASR engine performance**: Unless you're creating an ASR engine from scratch, there's little you can do besides choosing the best one available to you. In some development environments, you might be able to change some recognition parameter values.

- **Quality of the incoming speech signal**: This can be caused by poor microphones, background noise, or side speech in the user's environment. You can't fix a poor signal after the fact, but sometimes there may be indirect solutions like additional instructions in prompts or multimodal backoff strategies.

- **Users' speech**: By now, you've figured out that ASR is far from perfect. If you're building a US English system, you're better off than with most other languages. Not because there's anything magic about English, but because those language models have been trained on vastly more data. In addition, some people's speech simply isn't easy to recognize for what seems like no reason. Indirect solutions may again be your best choice. Other options involve expanding pronunciation dictionaries or training speaker-dependent models, if you have that ability.

- **Grammar coverage**: If people use words you didn't account for but are reasonable for the task, add them now. If words already in-grammar are misunderstood for other words, more in-depth fixes may be needed.

- **Understanding and intent mapping**: If people ask for things you didn't include, you'll see what they're asking for. You can decide how to handle those requests now and when to expand future functionality.

- **Prompt wording and delivery**: If users find words and questions to be confusing or unexpected, their responses will be less definite. Any hesitation or uncertainty in responding leads to greater out-of-grammar and false accept/reject rates, and long-winded verbose prompts can make users miss key information.

- **Dialog path flexibility and clarity**: If users ask for things that map to universals (such as help, repeat, go back) or if you see many retries or incomplete ends to conversations, chances are something in the design needs to be revisited. You may have missed something about the user's context or mental model of the task that causes confusion and now needs additional options or dialog paths.

In the rest of this chapter, you learn how to interpret collected data to find and address issues. You won't always be able to fix issues in the most ideal way due to platform constraints on what's exposed and available to developers. The good news is that what's available changes constantly. The main voice development platforms all employ experienced people who understand both the reasons and consequences of limiting third-party access—data security and user privacy is a big factor. They're working on striking the right balance. Therefore, what you learn in this chapter helps you understand the underlying causes of various tuning issues and shows you what you can do with the access you have right now and ability you have rather than limit the discussion to what's available today on any single platform.

Tuning Types and Approaches

Broadly speaking, tuning is either system performance focused or user success and satisfaction focused. You shouldn't be surprised by now that those overlap—users won't be successful or happy with a system that performs poorly—but it's still a convenient division to make. System performance can be tracked, measured, and improved through automated or unsupervised procedures and controlled offline experiments, as well as by more manual and targeted methods.

Table 17-1 summarizes concepts you've already learned—all relevant to tuning. In general, you want to maximize/increase some (+), while you minimize/decrease others (-).

Table 17-1. *Tuning concepts with examples assuming a single digit grammar*

IG	In-grammar	+	Covered by relevant grammars; matches what's expected.	"0"–"9" → [0]–[9]
OOC	Out-of-coverage	-	Any utterance that's not covered in this part of the dialog.	"twenty"
OOG	Out-of-grammar	-	OOC plus noise, fragments, or side speech.	"twen- twenty"
CA	Correct accept	+	Covered by current grammar and matched as expected.	"nine" → [9]
CR	Correct reject	+	Not covered by current grammar and therefore rejected as expected.	"fine" → [no match]
FA-in	False accept in-grammar	-	Covered by current grammar but matching with something else that's IG.	"five" → [9]
FR	False reject	-	Covered by current grammar but not recognized or matched.	"five" → [no match]
FA-out	False accept out-of-grammar	-	Not covered by current grammar but matched to something else that's IG.	"fine" → [9]

Where you put your focus depends on what your VUI does. For less costly tasks, like responding to general questions or playing a song, you'll aim for increasing CA with less worry about FA-in or FA-out. For tasks where being wrong is a bigger issue, like a payment amount or drug name, you focus a lot on minimizing FA. A change in FA-in or OOG is easily quantifiable. A change in how many users reach a certain point in a conversation or make a specific request is also quantifiable, but how to improve their happiness about it is often not as straightforward.

We can also differentiate between various types of grammar tuning. You've seen a couple of ways to specify grammars ("grammar" is a convenient umbrella term for all approaches): the standard Dialogflow method of adding training phrases and treating NLU as a black box vs. the rule/regular expression–based NLU that can be very useful when you have large numbers of specialized terms, such as in a medical application. When tuning such a specialized application, it's critical to know where the rules are not working, so you know how to fix them. Rules are traceable and explainable beyond most statistical approaches.

SUCCESS TIP 17.1 POOR PERFORMANCE IS NEVER YOUR USERS' FAULT   It's not your "fault" either, but you have to be the adult here. Whatever you do, don't blame users for not succeeding. Your VUI needs to take the high road. You created this thing with the best of intentions: you think your prompts are clear, and you try to tell people how to respond. None of that matters if users don't succeed—it's your baby, and while it's not a human one, you need to teach it to communicate with the existing rules of human language and expectations of your user population.

Log-Based vs. Transcription-Based Tuning

Tuning involves analyzing collected conversation data, identifying issues, proposing solutions, running offline experiments, making changes to the production system, and finally remeasuring and iterating. Much of your tuning can and will be log-based tuning. Performance and transaction logs provide a reasonably accurate picture of system performance very quickly. All major platforms have some type of logging available, and you can add your own as well—what's built-in is often very general, by necessity. You can obviously use more details for more meaningful logging if you have access to specific databases within your system architecture The automatically generated logs provide you with a close approximation of the recognition rates in Chapter 16, user responses, confirmations, and number of retries. With transaction logging, you'll also have a great understanding of the user's full dialog path. With this information, you can find problem areas and even form some analysis of what might be the issue.

Everyone who tunes does some log-based tuning. But to do all tuning activities most accurately and find the best solution to address issues, you need reliable **utterance transcriptions**. Remember from Chapter 10 that transcriptions are text typed out by trained humans who listen to logged user utterances. The text representation you get from a recognizer is an interpretation of the top hypothesis of what the system heard; therefore, it's never guaranteed to be completely accurate. If you really want to know what the user said, you can't rely on the recognizer's text hypothesis. Transcriptions need to be detailed, consistent, and accurate because they're the "answer" that you'll analyze and compare results against. Trained transcribers will not only transcribe the words in the utterance, but they'll also annotate word fragments and the type of noise heard. This level of detail gives you important clues to what went wrong when there were issues. For this reason, we recommend against using untrained crowdsourced helpers for transcriptions. Instead look at companies offering specialized transcription. For smaller sets and simpler systems, you or someone detail-oriented on your team can transcribe.

Not everyone can do transcription-based tuning, simply because the platform doesn't give access to any utterance audio recordings. That includes most home assistant implementations. Most transcription-based tuning is done for large enterprise systems with great focus on keeping recordings secure. Some is done when the VUI is part of proprietary hardware. You can even find some way to record test users to get utterances for transcription. Data from rigging up a mic and recording device is far better than no data: you can learn a lot from the words, pronunciations, and hesitations you collect even in such a simple way.

Lack of access to real user utterance recordings and transcriptions limits your ability to get to the bottom of some issues. But don't despair: there are simple ways to improve system performance, even without that data. Once you understand how people talk and understand speech (like you do now), you know what to look for, and you can do some quick log analysis to identify potential issues. Organize your results in chronological order, keeping the timestamp of each utterance. Then

- Find examples of two adjacent instances of the same or similar request. Unless they're navigation commands, like *next,* it's a sign of someone trying again because their first attempt failed.

- Find requests to *stop, cancel,* and *repeat.* Then investigate what happened immediately before those requests.

- Find adjacent requests with a very short time between them or ones that interrupt your VUI's prompts. This can mean that the user interrupted as soon as they realized the response was not what they wanted.

- Find any nonsensical utterances, like the funny auto-correct results you might see when typing. Read the result out loud and see if it sounds similar to something that's in-grammar. For example, a friend's name is *Nils,* but various voice assistants turn his name into *Niks.*

- Look for a high proportion of *no* responses to confirmations; lots of *I don't know*, *go back*, and *help*; and no utterance where you expect one. These are all red flags that something isn't working well.

Collect and group all similar examples. You already have what you need to identify many common issues and start tuning. We still use these methods, even when we have additional data. Another source of tuning data you might have access to is the data from the "thumbs-up/thumbs-down" user feedback we mentioned in Chapter 16—investigate anything a user gives thumbs-down to so you can determine its cause.

Coverage Tuning

Coverage refers to whether a phrase is in a grammar or not. When coverage is good, a broad set of expected in-domain utterances are in-grammar (IG). It's one of the most important aspects of performance: a recognizer can be excellent at understanding what a user says, but if those words haven't been associated with the right concept, the user won't be understood.

The goal of coverage tuning, or grammar tuning, is a high IG rate and a low OOG rate. You start coverage tuning by determining what core words and phrases, synonyms, and carrier phrases (or filler phrases, such as *I like to…* or *Could you…*) users will say and what they mean when they say them. This is done by analyzing utterance logs and by applying your knowledge of what people are likely to say in that specific context. You then improve coverage by adding missing phrases to either rule-based grammars or to training sets mapping to the appropriate intent. Adding words and phrases is the most basic and common type of tuning—if you only do one type of tuning, this will be it.

Tuning coverage in a Yes/No grammar is easier than in a food name grammar because utterances are more predictable and less varied. However, even Yes/No grammars need tuning. You've already learned about one-step correction: if you have high OOG rates in a Yes/No confirmation, look for content corrections. Make sure you have the appropriate carrier phrases based on the wording of the VUI's prompt. For example:

VUI   *Do you know your prescription number?*

User   *Yes, **I do.***

~ ~ ~   ~ ~ ~

VUI   ***Did you get** a prescription number?*

User   *Yes, **I did.***

~ ~ ~   ~ ~ ~

VUI   *Is that the right prescription number?*

User   *Yes, it is.*

If your voice platform gives you access to OOG utterance logs or audio files, fantastic. You can learn much more than simply what words to add, including data for intent tuning and dialog tuning. As long as users talk to your Google action from "inside" it (after first invoking it), you do have some access to OOG utterance text results that you can use for tuning in Dialogflow. But because of the overall architecture of Actions on Google, and similarly Amazon Alexa, you don't have any insight into any OOG utterances your users spoke "outside" your actions (when invocation and request were part of the same utterance). This is an important difference between these assistant platforms and fully contained custom systems or systems built on some enterprise-level platforms. The difference affects what OOG data you can base your coverage tuning on.

Some systems have dynamic grammars: grammars that change depending on the context, like a flight itinerary or a phone contact list. To tune those, you need an additional level of logging, including what current grammar is used for a particular request, which may be different from the last or next requests. With some types of grammars, coverage over-generation can also be an issue that needs to be addressed during tuning.

FROM THE VOICE TRENCHES

A former colleague recently told us how he was tasked to update a grammar used to recognize a common governmental alphanumeric sequence used in a variety of applications. He reported to us that it was "shockingly deficient" in several ways. It had not been updated in 15 years, so it wasn't aligned with new sequence formats and other changes made during that time. It also allowed the use of *A for alpha* only at some positions in the string and not others. Poorly maintained grammars like this contribute to a negative experience for your users when what should be a valid utterance of theirs is rejected by an ill-fitting grammar. It's an important reminder that maintenance and tuning resources can be needed long past rollout.

Ambiguity Tuning

When you add coverage to a grammar, you might not realize that you've mapped the same item to multiple meanings. This is easier to do the bigger your grammars are, like names of all prescription drugs or financial stocks. If testing doesn't catch it, the result is a no-way-out situation for the user who has only audio to go by rather than visual text:

> **User**   *Call Ann Jones.*

> ~ ~ ~ VUI finds two entries with a slight spelling difference ~ ~ ~

> > **VUI**   *Which one? Ann Jones or Anne Joanez?*

> > **User**   *... Ann Jones!*

> > **VUI**   *Which one? Ann Jones or Anne Joanez?*

> > **User**   **@#!!*

Make sure that there's an unambiguous phrase for all items and no ambiguous dead ends. It's an obligatory and crucial step for financial voice systems handling large mutual fund grammars. Of course, it's more straightforward to do thorough ambiguity tuning if you have complete control over or access to the data, such as a drug name database. But you can tune for this even when you don't have access to the user's contact list. First, you need to define entry matching rules based on pronunciation rather than spelling. This is where Soundex comes in handy, the algorithm we mentioned at the end of Chapter 10. In addition, add a skip list. That keeps the VUI from asking about the same name again and again. For names that sound the same, as in this example, you need to also add a disambiguation mechanism using any other information that's available and helpful to the user, for example, *in area code 650* or *in Menlo Park*.

Recognition Accuracy Tuning

Recognition accuracy tuning is closely associated with coverage tuning. It refers to how well the system correctly recognizes the utterances with in-grammar phrases while rejecting the ones that are out-of-grammar. Remember that a recognizer looks for the closest best match. That match is an **attractor**. If there's no attractor close enough, there may not be a match. More coverage means a more crowded attractor space.

The goal of accuracy tuning is to accurately recognize as many phrases as possible and correctly categorize them as in-grammar or out-of-grammar. In other words, you want high rates of correctly accepting IG utterances and rejecting OOG utterances, paired with low rates of mistakenly accepting OOG utterances and rejecting IG utterances. In addition, you want low rates of matching IG utterances to something else that's in-grammar—these are often the hardest and most important to address. You can see some illustrative examples of these recognition errors in Table 17-2 together with common solutions.

Table 17-2. *Illustrative examples of recognition errors*

Type of error	User said	Outcome
FA-in	*A reservation for five*	Recognized as "a reservation for **nine**"
FA-out	*I called my daughter…*	Recognized as "Call my **doctor**"
FR-in	*Refill for Prednisone*	Rejected

These examples illustrate why false accepts are worse than false rejects: it's better to make users try again than to interpret their request wrongly. The examples also illustrate why you need transcriptions. Error calculations can only be made if you have a "right answer" to compare recognition results to, and the detailed transcriptions point to what went wrong so you can address it.

You might see reports about how people's voice systems have now improved to handle 80% of requests. That's actually terrible—imagine talking to someone who misunderstands every fifth word. Accuracy needs to be as high as possible because ultimately there's no successful conversation when words are misunderstood.

Recognition errors also accumulate over multiple turns as users need to try again and go down unexpected paths. Most speech scientists would continue tuning until the CA-in percentage was at least in the low nineties and FA/FR rates were in the single digits.

SUCCESS TIP 17.2 YOU CAN'T PROVE EVERYTHING WITH STATISTICS   High IG rates are never the whole story. If someone tells you their voice system performs great with a 98% CA-in rate on 1,000 utterances, you should immediately ask about the OOG rates. If a VUI only accepts a small set of phrases, performance on those is likely to be stellar. But if that's paired with just as many rejected utterances, the overall performance from the user's perspective is most likely terrible.

As grammars get larger and more complex, the risk of error increases, and recognition rates naturally decrease somewhat. If you have a grammar with only two words, all your error rates are likely quite small! Before looking at accuracy in depth, let's take a look at four specific types of accuracy tuning that you may or may not have access to—if you do, they'd apply to the examples in Table 17-2.

Acoustic Confusability Tuning

There's no guarantee that an OOG utterance is rejected or an IG utterance is accepted. Grammar coverage should be as broad as possibly to help with this without causing you trouble. *What trouble could more coverage possibly cause?*, you ask. One potential issue occurs when a grammar has multiple similar-sounding words or phrases. This can lead to conflicts where one item acts as an attractor for other similar words, resulting in incorrect mapping (either FA-in or FA-out). The attractor is typically a word that's more frequent than the other words. For example, in a general voice system, *umbrella* is more common than *Enbrel*; therefore, people speaking the drug name will be misrecognized as saying the rain device. Take special care that example phrases used in prompts are not easily confusable. If they are, change one or more of the phrases to minimize false attractors.

Dictionary Tuning

In the voice world, a dictionary defines all the ways a user is expected to pronounce each word in a grammar or voice system. Most platforms allow you to add pronunciations for new or existing words. If you notice that a particular word has high FA-in or FR-in rates, adding or modifying a pronunciation for that word can be the solution. Sometimes an FA-in can even involve changing another word's pronunciation. Dictionary tuning is closely related to acoustic confusability. Both are often relevant when your VUI needs to understand a brand or product name. They're also important when the VUI's domain affects how words are pronounced, like the *Enbrel-umbrella* example you just saw.

Confidence Threshold

You learned about multi-tier recognition in Chapters 12 and 13. If your system uses multi-tier recognition and you see a high proportion of either yes or no responses, it's a sign to change the thresholds. Your goal should be to minimize both: too many yes's mean unnecessary confirmations; too many no's mean incorrect results are returned and recognition accuracy needs further investigation.

Timeout and Probability Parameters

Some voice development platforms give you access to lower-level parameter settings. You learned in Chapter 12 that a longer timeout is appropriate in some contexts, like for 16-digit credit card numbers spoken as four groups of four digits. If you see incomplete cut-off phrases that seem to happen because of user distraction, short timeouts are a likely culprit. Applying probabilities that act as weights on a recognition hypothesis, you can affect the strength of an attractor and ultimate result. That's very handy when there's domain-specific confusability and you want the less common word to be recognized more often than the common word. Again, this is applicable to the *Enbrel-umbrella* example. It's also great for weakening universals and hidden commands while still making them available.

At the time of writing this, Actions on Google and Dialogflow don't let you control many of these low-level parameters, but they may be coming soon as more developers build more complex VUIs, and Google Cloud API does provide some. Some enterprise and other cloud ASR platforms allow specifying custom phrases or language models for a particular domain. This is one way of altering probabilities. For example, Microsoft is expanding features for their cloud ASR engine allowing you to create a custom acoustic model with 10 hours of speech and a custom language model with a million words of text.[1]

---

[1]Xuedong Huang, Technical Fellow and Chief Speech Scientist, Microsoft, Conversational Interaction Conference, February 10, 2020.

In-Depth: Building Accuracy from Sample Phrases

Let's work through a simple example. Recall the `tcrMakeAppointment` intent (Chapter 11) that covers requests meaning *I want to make a new appointment*. Table 17-3 shows how some phrases for that intent can be categorized for grammar coverage and domain. As you learned in the previous chapter, in-grammar (IG) and out-of-grammar (OOG) are clear concepts: a phrase is either included in a grammar or not. If you're dealing with rule-based grammars, something that's in a grammar is very likely to be recognized correctly, but it doesn't always happen, because of all the other factors you're learning about in this chapter. If your grammar coverage is based on training phrases, as is the default case with Dialogflow, it's a little less clear what utterances will be in-grammar. Anything included as a training phrase is highly likely to be correctly accepted as in-grammar, but how similar must other utterances be to be captured based on your training phrases? Determining if a phrase is in-domain (ID)—a sensible utterance for the task but one that isn't covered in-grammar—gets fuzzier still because it involves judgment calls, especially as you approach the edges between similar intents. A perfect recognition/interpretation system would give you 100% correct accept (CA) on all in-domain phrases and 100% correct reject (CR) and 0% false accept (FA) on all out-of-domain (OOD) phrases, or phrases whose meaning differs from others in the intent in a way that's significant in the context of the VUI. Let's step through the six examples in Table 17-3.

Table 17-3. *Categorizing sample phrases by grammar coverage and domain inclusion*

Phrase	Grammar (in/out)	Domain (in/out)	Outcome
Make an appointment.	IG	ID	CA
Make an appointment for three.	IG	ID	CA
Make an appointment for three PM.	IG	ID	CA
Can I make an appointment?	OOG	ID	CA
I'd like to make an appointment.	OOG	ID	CA
I need to cancel my appointment.	OOG	OOD	FA

The first three examples are clearly in-domain (ID). They're also in-grammar (IG); you added them in Chapter 11. Here's where human expert–created regular expression rule-based grammars and defined parsing rules differ from machine learning–based "fuzzy logic" ones algorithmically created from training phrases. The former are easy to test to determine what's in-grammar and what's not. The latter depend on someone else's algorithms and models built from your sample training phrases. With machine learning–based fuzzy logic (like in Dialogflow), you'd like it to **generalize**, that is, to understand phrases you didn't enter as training phrases, but that are similar to the ones you did enter and make sense for the intent.

Now look at the next two, *Can I make an appointment?* and *I'd like to make an appointment.* In most contexts, these are sensible synonym phrases to include in the same intent, so they're also in-domain, but they're currently out-of-grammar because you haven't added them as training phrases (or in a regular expression grammar, if you're using those). If the intent instead was "Direct questions about a tool's feature set," then *Can I make an appointment?* would be in-domain, and all the others in this example would be out-of-domain. As you can see, intents need to be specified carefully for the specific needs and situation of what the VUI covers. Context matters, as always.

Even though Dialogflow had not been trained on these phrases, it returned the correct intent: in-domain, correctly accepted. Great! Again, generalization means you don't need to enter every possible phrase—Dialogflow figures out a lot of it for you. In contrast, a rule-based grammar will not generalize by itself.

Now let's look at the last example: *I need to cancel my appointment.* This phrase clearly is not an acceptable synonym phrase in an intent for making an appointment. But Dialogflow returned the intent tcrMakeAppointment, so it's an out-of-domain, false accept (FA).

What happened? You can't be completely sure since Dialogflow's inner workings are a black box to you, but you can guess. In this case, the system seems to key hard on *appointment.* If you try other variants with *appointment* including *change appointment, move my appointment,* and so on, it'll still return the intent tcrMakeAppointment. These are all OOG and out-of-domain false accepts. During tuning, you look at any OOG utterances and determine what to do with them. If they're in-domain, add these phrases to your training set (or rules); if they're out-of-domain, pat yourself on the back that you got it right. But guess what? In this case, it was a bit of dumb luck that it worked out correctly from the user's point of view—we'll fix it in a more robust way in a moment.

Here's the problem: as you've learned throughout this book, there's never any guarantee that utterance X will map to the desired intent, even when that utterance is spelled out in a rule-based grammar or training set.

There's even less guarantee if it's not part of a grammar or training set. In this case, a false accept (FA) was generalized as you'd want it to be. Next, time it might map to another intent. You definitely don't want that in a health-related VUI. With tuning, you increase your chances that utterances are handled correctly. Generalization can be a great thing and allows nonspecialists to go far in building conversational apps. Just be aware of the pitfalls, and do extensive testing on what users really say (like canceling or modifying an appointment). You need to test not only with in-domain examples but also with out-of-domain ones to make sure both behave as expected.

Now, let's fix this issue. If some intent attracts a lot of out-of-domain utterances, you need to create another intent that can be trained on these utterances. This is due to how recognition works: it basically tries to match everything it hears with something. So if users ask to change or cancel an appointment, you need intents to support those. What you'd do here is simply add a new intent tcrCancelAppointment, map all *cancel* utterances (and others you think users will say) to this intent, and then retrain. Adding the intent doesn't mean you need to implement cancelation in your VUI. Instead, just the intent can just respond with something like *If you need to cancel or change your appointment, please call your doctor's office.* Now, you'll likely get an in-domain correct accept for tcrCancelAppointment instead of a false accept for tcrMakeAppointment—a much better user experience.

This is a very useful approach that should be used liberally. It makes your VUI smarter and broader with very little extra effort. Even if users ask for things you don't support, you can add an intent for those requests and train it with the phrases. Now you can respond with a helpful *I can't do that, but here's what you can do instead* type of prompt instead of just saying *Sorry* or, worse, risking giving a wrong answer. Never rely on rejection (out-of-domain correct rejects) to do the right thing; create new intents for any relevant phrases. If available, confidence thresholds are also useful for this.

What does the explicit knowledge method do with *I need to cancel my appointment*? This is the Stanford Parser you encountered in Chapter 11. It correctly rejects this utterance. Remember that one of the rules was that the root node of the dependency tree had to be *make* or synonyms of it. In this case, the root node would be *cancel*. The explicit parser method paid more attention to the main verb of the sentence (*make* vs. *cancel*) and less attention to the object (*appointment*) compared to Dialogflow. Actually, our parsing rules required both that the verb be *make* and there be a direct object, specifically *appointment*, which in this case would do the right thing.

You see this tradeoff again and again: ease of use and simplicity vs. effort and performance and system transparency. Only you can decide where on the tradeoff scale you want to be; you just need to make an informed decision and understand the pros and cons involved. We encourage you to try out the phrases in Table 16-1 yourself in Dialogflow (or whatever platform you're using). Experiment by adding phrases that are similar but map to different intents. What happens if lots of similar ones map one way and one single one maps another? In your VUI context, what if it's important that some phrase is always recognized correctly but that phrase is similar to others with another meaning? Compare behavior when you vary carrier phrases vs. core content. Really get a sense of what affects accuracy in your world—it's your key to voice system success.

Finding and Using Recognition Accuracy Data

In Chapter 16, you learned that the current built-in Dialogflow tools are somewhat limited in giving you access to the data you want for accuracy tuning. It's time we showed you how to get around that and find some real data. You do, in fact, have some options.

Google Cloud has an operations suite, formerly called Stackdriver, that you can use to get large volumes of application data. You've been using Google Cloud while you've been using Dialogflow, and when you started using the webhook in Chapter 7, you used Google Cloud even more, specifically the App Engine. The operations suite is another of the many Google Cloud pieces; this one provides a unified framework for logging application data to a centralized place so it can be processed later. Other cloud services, such as AWS and Microsoft Azure, offer similar functionality—good to know if you're working on other platforms—but since we're mostly in Google world in this book, we'll focus on the operations suite. To use it, go to the settings for the client in Dialogflow by clicking the gear next to the client name in the left panel. You'll see the option Log interactions to Google Cloud. Click that to turn on logging. Figure 17-1 shows this.

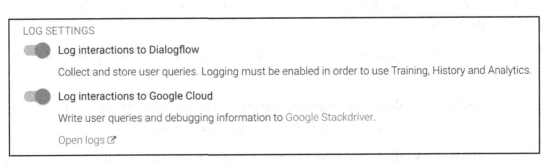

Figure 17-1. *The client settings page where Google Cloud operations suite (formerly Stackdriver) logging is turned on or off*

Once you've turned on logging and made a few interactions, here's how to see the logs:

- Go to the Google Cloud Console (console.cloud.google.com). Make sure you've selected the project you've been using for the Dialogflow work and the webhook.

- In the upper-left menu, choose Operations ➤ Logging ➤ Legacy Logs Viewer. You may not see any logs yet; after you change the time limit drop-down menu to No Limit, you should see something like in Figure 17-2.

- Verify that the leftmost drop-down menu says Global and the menu to the right of it says All Logs.

Figure 17-2. *Operations suite log sample*

Next, click any of the rows; it expands to show the detailed log information. We strongly encourage you to poke around a bit in these logs to see the large amount of data that is produced just from one interaction with Google Home/Dialogflow.

Figure 17-2 shows the four kinds of logs you might see for an utterance, in chronological order:

- **Dialogflow request:** The initial request to Dialogflow, including the text that was recognized.

- **Dialogflow fulfillment request:** The request made to the webhook, if the webhook was enabled for the client and the intent.

- **Dialogflow fulfillment response:** The response from the webhook. If the webhook wasn't available, you still get this entry, but it will indicate there was an error, for example, an HTTP 500 error (server unavailable).

- **Dialogflow response:** The final response from Dialogflow including the response that was spoken back to the user.

Prepare to pull logs from the operations suite using Python.

- Install the `google-cloud-logging` Python SDK. How you do this exactly depends on the operating system that you use.[2] In our Python example, we added `google-cloud-logging` to our `requirements.txt` file. To update, you'd need to rerun `pip install -r requirements.txt`.

- Create a service account in your Google Cloud project. Don't forget to add the role Project Owner:

  - For example, you might click the upper-left menu in the Google Cloud Console and select IAM & Admin ➤ Service Accounts ➤ Create Service Account.

- Create a .json key and store it somewhere locally. This process is also described on the same Google web page.

- Set the path to the service account .json key, also described on the web page. In our case, we ran `export GOOGLE_APPLICATION_CREDENTIALS=<json key filename from last step>`.

You're now ready to pull large numbers of logs. Included in this chapter's webhook code is a Python script `get_logs.py`. This script steps through the four types of logs stored in Google Cloud; when it sees a piece of information needed for tuning, it pulls it out. After detecting a new interaction (a new Dialogflow request, based on the first log), it prints out the information from the last interaction on a single line. In a terminal, run

```
python get_logs.py > logs.txt
```

The next step depends on you having spreadsheet software (like Microsoft Excel, OpenOffice, or Numbers on Mac). It's optional, but as we'll discuss later, we find that using some type of spreadsheet software with powerful filtering capabilities can make tuning and annotation much easier. We'll demonstrate it using Excel—details will vary across spreadsheet software, but you can obviously use others:

---

[2]https://cloud.google.com/logging/docs/reference/libraries#client-libraries-install-python

1. In a new Excel workbook, click the Data menu bar at the top of the workbook.

2. You should see an option called Select it.

3. Select the location of the log.txt file from the last section.

4. Select Delimited, and make sure you select Tab as the delimiter.

5. Finish the import. The spreadsheet should look like Figure 17-3. Save it!

TIMESTAMP	RECOGNIZED TEXT	RECOGNIZED INTENT	FILLED PARAMETERS	APPLICATION RESPONSE
2020-11-08T08:04:27	call brent jones	arCallByName	{"given-name": "Brent", "last-name": "Jones"}	OK, calling Brent Jones.
2020-12-08T02:14:38	call brent jones	arCallByName	{"given-name": "Brent", "last-name": "Jones"}	You want to call Brent Jones, right?
2020-12-08T02:14:42	yes	arConfirmName	{"confirm": "yes"}	OK, calling.
2020-12-08T16:10:28		Default Welcome Intent	{}	Welcome to the Procedure Helper. What question do you have for me?
2020-12-08T16:10:28	can i eat rice today	qaCanEat	{"foodDrink": "rice"}	You can still eat white rice today, but avoid brown rice until after your procedure.
2020-12-08T16:22:09	can i eat kale today	qaCanEat	{"foodDrink": ""}	You can still eat kale today.
2020-12-08T16:22:55	how about tomorrow	qaHowAboutOtherDay	{"date": "2020-12-09T12:00:00"}	Sorry, after today, you cannot eat kale until after your procedure.
2020-12-08T16:23:37	can i eat brussels sprouts today	qaCanEat	{"foodDrink": "brussels sprouts"}	You can still eat brussels sprouts today.
2020-12-08T16:24:18	can I have a latte	qaCanDrink	{"foodDrink": "caffe latte"}	You can still drink coffee with milk today.
2020-12-08T17:05:54	is corn okay	qaCanEat	{"foodDrink": "corn"}	You can still eat cooked corn today, but you cannot have popcorn until after your procedure.

Figure 17-3. *Microsoft Excel spreadsheet with the contents from log.txt ready for tuning*

This spreadsheet looks a lot like the one you saw in Chapter 16, indicating what kind of data you need for tuning. We added the column anyway to highlight that you'd want it when it's available—and you'd have it in some platforms.

This brings up an important point: this whole section has assumed that you're using Dialogflow and Google Cloud. Of course, there are other options, including using a standalone STT API like Google or Microsoft or IBM. In those cases, you'd need to handle the logging yourself. You could potentially still use the operations suite to log transactions, but you'd need to modify the get_logs.py script.

You might wonder why log.txt has tab-separated fields instead of comma-separated ones, like many text files designed to be imported into applications like Excel. Quite simply, if there's ever a comma in your actual data field, you can't use .csv; it will confuse everything. Both the parameters and the application response might have commas, so you need to use tabs.

Task Completion Tuning

Task completion analysis provides information that complements recognition performance. How many users reach a successful endpoint in a conversation, filling all necessary slots and getting an appropriate response? You have a good idea of what is a successful endpoint: confirmation prompt at the end of a reservation, a light turning on after a request, a countdown starting after setting a timer, and so on. Task completion analysis looks at VUI behavior at a higher level or from a more holistic perspective. Think of recognition analysis as more of a static snapshot, whereas task completion and dialog tuning is more like videos: recognition tuning focuses on improving performance for utterances in a specific grammar but hides the fact that conversations are not isolated utterances without context; task and dialog tuning puts performance into the context of the whole dialog, or at least of what happens in the steps right before and after. That means tracking behavior per user is important.

Task completion tuning involves identifying where multi-turn dialogs end without users getting what they wanted. Does it happen in a specific part of the dialog? Why do some users stop before they reach the end? It can be recognition issues or some design problem, but it can also be external factors: maybe refill formats changed, maybe database access is down, and so on. Or you don't define success the same as your users.

FROM THE VOICE TRENCHES

In one bank VUI, a significant number of users did not complete the bill payment request they started, causing a massive tuning effort, before we realized users were choosing that path to find the bill due date and amount—they had no intention of paying right then but still ended the conversation perfectly happy, having heard the information they were after.

Task completion includes fulfillment accuracy. It's not enough to base task completion on reaching a state you've designated as "success" or filling all empty slots. If the user asked for a song by one artist but heard a different version, that's not success as far as the user is concerned. If they wanted a reservation for 7 PM but there were no tables, they didn't succeed. Even if you can't give them what they wanted, you need to analyze how often it happens and how to best respond. A different prompt might be enough; offering a substitute is another. Fulfillment tuning can be tricky and relies on transcription access.

Task completion is also about how users reach ultimate success. A VUI where 95% of users reach a successful goal in 15 seconds, or in three steps with no retries, is obviously better than one with the same 95% success rate over 30 seconds, or six steps and several retries. Improvements are often a combination of recognition and dialog improvements. In a multi-slot multi-turn dialog, there may be specific steps where people have trouble. The more accurately you can analyze the issue, the more likely you can make improvements.

Code for Task Completion Analysis

In Chapter 16, you learned that there are two ways to do task completion analysis: adding tags after the fact—our preferred method—or baking them into the application. Let's look at a piece of the code that helps with adding task tags. Here's a portion of the get_logs.py code showing how to add task tags keyed off the recognized intent. This is in Listing 17-1. Find the Dialogflow fulfillment log entry (A). Perform a regular expression search. It's a multiline entry, which is why you use the re.M and re.S flags (B). Set the JSON for the request from the log (C). Pull out the intent display name (D). Procedure prep start (E). Procedure prep end (F). Print out the log.txt line (G).

Listing 17-1. Adding task tags to get_logs.py

```
def main():

    # Dialogflow fulfillment request (multi-line)    (A)

    pattern = re.compile(
        'Dialogflow fulfillment request : (.*)$', re.M | re.S)    # B

    match = pattern.match(entry.payload)
    if match:
        df_webhook_request = json.loads(match.group(1))    # C

        # Recognized intent
        try:
            recognized_intent = \
                df_webhook_request['queryResult']['intent']['displayName']    #D

            # Add any task tags here
```

```
    if recognized_intent == 'tcrProcedurePrep':    # E
        task = {}
        task['name'] = 'ProcedurePrep'
        task['tag'] = 'start'
        task_tags.append(task)

    if recognized_intent == 'tcrProcedurePrepNext2':    # F
        task = {}
        task['name'] = 'ProcedurePrep'
        task['tag'] = 'end'
        task_tags.append(task)

except KeyError:
    pass

# Filled parameters
try:
    filled_parameters = \
        json.dumps(df_webhook_request['queryResult']['parameters'])
    except KeyError:
    pass

# ...... Code cut for focus

if havelog:
    print((f"{date_time}\t{session}\t\t{recognized_text}\t\t"    # G
            f"{recognized_intent}\t{filled_parameters}\t"
            f"{application_response}\t{json.dumps(task_tags)}"))
```

When you run this modified get_logs.py and import the log.txt into Excel, you should see something like in Figure 17-4 (some columns are hidden to better show the task tags). You can see how you could count the number of task starts and ends; the ratio is the task completion percentage.

RECOGNIZED TEXT	RECOGNIZED INTENT	FILLED PARAMETERS	APPLICATION RESPONSE	TASK
walk me through my procedure prep	tcrProcedurePrep	{}	It's time for your procedure prep. What are you taking today: Miralax, Laxoly, or Colax?	[{"name": "ProcedurePrep", "tag": start"}]
miralax	tcrProcedurePrepLaxative	{"laxative":"miralax"}	Okay, Miralax. Let's prepare your first dose. Measure one cap-full and pour it into a glass..	[]
next	tcrProcedurePrepNext1	{}	Now drink the full glass. When your glass is empty, say "next."	[]
next	tcrProcedurePrepNext2	{}	Great job! You're all done!	[{"name": "ProcedurePrep", "tag": end"}]

Figure 17-4. *Count the number of task starts and ends to calculate the task completion percentage*

Dialog Tuning

Dialog tuning is a common term for the more "hands-on" analysis work focused on improving the overall conversation. Dialog tuning is not easily automated; it often uncovers issues that don't show up in automated quantitative logs or clarifies the right remedy for issues that do. The analysis pays special attention to issues that evolve over multiple turns. Typical discoveries during analysis are prompt wording and delivery issues that cause user confusion and out-of-grammar utterances.

As the name suggests, the remedies focus on analysis and change of the full dialog flow and detailed design. Dialog tuning typically results in prompt wording changes and changes in the pronunciation and delivery of prompts; an emphasis put on the wrong word can easily cause confusion that leads to OOG utterances.

Other prime candidates for dialog tuning are timing issues caused by pauses that are either too long or too short or in unexpected places and anything that unravels across a multi-turn dialog and affects the conversational flow or the users' mental models.

Dialog tuning relies on access to what users actually said (transcriptions) and how they said it (audio files). You can see right away why dialog tuning does best when there's access to transcriptions and voice recordings of IG and OOG utterances from real users. So what do you do if you don't have access to that data? If you have nothing but automated performance logs and some task completion logs, you can still get a sense of what doesn't work and what might be the cause. Focus on looking for performance hotspots. You know the wording of each prompt and you can hear it as well—knowing that there's an issue, can you figure out what it is? You can also look at some text interpretation logs—can you think of similar-sounding words that may behave like attractors? If some error prompts play often, can you figure out what's going wrong? Do users confirm more than expected? Do they fail during authentication? Do you have data from survey studies or usability testing that points to some potential problem?

If logs hint at poor performance in some part of the system, an in-depth investigation is the right next step. This might be triggered by high OOG or FA/FR rates, specific complaints of confusion or poor performance, and high rates of failed transaction completion. Choose or capture a small set of conversations, typically no more than 100. Scrub the conversations of any PII before doing any further listening or analysis. If the audio files don't already include the prompt audio, you may need to recreate the conversations by concatenating prompts and responses. Listen to the full interaction for start-to-end context and transcribe them. In the IVR world, this is called whole-call analysis. Some IVR platforms let you listen to callers' full journey through the system even if you can't record for offline analysis. If none of those are possible, run a controlled in-lab study with naive users who can be recorded. Listen and read transcriptions. What generalizations can you make? Are some users not recognized while others are? You'd find out if confidence thresholds need to be changed or added, if prompts don't make sense in some paths through the dialog, if users hesitate or ask for repetitions, if users have several retries in certain contexts, if they hear information they don't expect, if there are too many confirmations, and so on. This is where you apply everything you've learned about voice design and technology in part 3 of this book: look for opportunities to improve consistency, decrease cognitive load by shortening lengthy prompts, remove unnecessary repetition, add reassurance through implicit readback, provide clarity with examples or explanatory detail, look for confusing or missing options, and so on.

Before you put your design updates in place, you can test memorability or comprehension of new prompts with crowdsourced surveys (Chapter 16). Check the intonation of your prompts: incorrect intonation placement will confuse some and should be fixed. Other signs of confusion can be easily found in the OOG logs: hesitation, side comments, backtracking, repeats, vague responses, voiced annoyances, and so on. OOG data is gold for tuning! Table 17-4 shows some examples of OOG data we've run into and what issue each one suggests.

Table 17-4. *Examples of problems found in OOG utterance logs*

OOG user utterance	What it might tell you
I already gave you that number.	First attempt not recognized; user may have provided it in earlier dialog turn –> opportunity to add multi-slot handling.
Blah blah blah (mocking tone)…	Verbose prompt –> opportunity to shorten.
NO! I don't want that.	Misrecognition or misinterpretation more than once.
Hang on. It's here somewhere…	User didn't expect to be asked for requested info and didn't have it handy –> opportunity for pause handling.
Uhhh, what's that?	Unfamiliar terminology in prompt; user doesn't know how to respond –> opportunity to change prompt or add info.
None of those.	Prompted options don't cover what user wanted, or wording doesn't imply the expected option –> opportunity to add "none" as hidden option and revisit menu options.
Both.	Prompt offers two not mutually exclusive options –> opportunity to add handling.
Why did she start talking?	VUI triggered unexpectedly and user noticed.
Checked that yesterday and the numbers were not the same.	VUI triggered unexpectedly and user didn't notice.

For each OOG utterance in the table, you'd first establish how common the issue is, looking across users and across dialog turns. Then you'd look at the details: What's the context of the issue? Do some options in a prompt sound too similar and cause recognition confusion? Do some words cause user confusion? Missing coverage? Look for the easiest likely solution to try first—sometimes it's the right answer.

But what did your users really say? We've discussed already that with Dialogflow, you don't have access to the audio, so you don't know what the user really said. Luckily, Google STT is very good; if a user says something like *I already gave you that number* or *None of those*, that will probably show up in the RECOGNIZED TEXT column of the log, and it may also show up in RECOGNIZED INTENT as Default Fallback Intent. So, while it won't be the whole story, you can do a lot of useful dialog tuning with the log spreadsheet you've extracted. And you learned ways already to look for indirect signs of issues.

Intent Tuning

We'll call out intent tuning here as a separate tuning focus. It involves maximizing the number of user requests that map to the best fit intent. If there are several possible intents that could match, tuning usually aims for the most specific one that still fits all contexts; more general intents require extra dialog turns, disambiguation, or menus. Intent tuning involves a mix of improvements to accuracy, coverage, task completion, and dialog tuning. Parsing rule changes are possible; updates to your detailed spec and prompt wording are the most likely outcome. Real data from real users is critical for productive tuning. Core happy path utterances are easy; you probably don't need to change those unless you split or combine intents. Instead, focus on the utterances on the "boundaries" between intents, the ones that are vague. If users asked a similar question again, canceled, or backtracked, you can be pretty sure you got the intent wrong. Be careful about introducing ambiguity—if it's hard to separate intents, add tiered recognition to confirm before continuing the dialog. Look for context that can clarify the intent mapping. If the user is asking to *play the first Harry Potter* on an audio-only device, it's more likely they mean the audiobook than the film, so add a context check and map it to mean PlayAudiobook rather than PlayFilm followed by an error message that the device can't handle video content.

SUCCESS TIP 17.3 TUNING ISN'T ONLY ABOUT FINDING AND FIXING ERRORS   If something doesn't work, of course you need to address the issue. But tuning is also about noticing and addressing what could improve the experience overall. Look for ways to help users get what they want faster as well as more accurately.

How to Prioritize Your Tuning Efforts

Now that you've got lots of data in your spreadsheet, how will you make sense of it and work your way through it?

One option is to go line by line through the spreadsheet, filling in the columns that need filling in and noting any needed fixes. We don't recommend this strategy if you have more than 100 lines or so. Once you have several hundreds or thousands of lines—and you want that much data—it's not a practical approach.

Instead, you prioritize, filter, and resort. Click the Data menu bar at the top of the workbook and then click Filter. At the top of each column, you see an arrow; click that arrow. You can select from a list of values; you can type in values and filter that way; you can filter the timestamp to get only certain logs. Start with the most common errors and intents and with intents you know are roadblocks for other intents; then work your way down the list. Here are some concrete strategies:

- Filter on the RECOGNIZED INTENT being Default Fallback Intent. These are your rejected phrases, which may well be OOG.

- You're not done filtering yet. Go for the RECOGNIZED TEXTs that are frequently occurring. If you have an application problem, probably multiple users are going to have the same problem. That's when you can figure out what's wrong, what phrases might need to be added to the intents, and so on.

- When annotating OOG/OOC, filter by RECOGNIZED TEXT, with the most likely first; that way you can just cut and paste after you've entered the first piece of data.

For any decent-size application, you won't fix everything. That's more than OK—it's expected. Start by fixing what happens most often and has the highest cost to users. And don't stop—keep analyzing and fixing. Spreadsheets also help when a user or client tells you *A few days ago I said something like this...and I got a weird response. Why? Can you fix it?*

One more comment about the process. When you pulled the data, we had you immediately import it into Excel. It's because that's what we do. As you apply the tuning strategies in this chapter to your data, you'll quickly notice how a spreadsheet saves you time, thanks to filtering. Can you use other solutions? You certainly can, especially if you have access to some specialized tuning tools. But even when we do, we still use Excel for some of the work.

Mapping Observations to the Right Remedy

Analyzing the data to understand the cause and severity of each issue is hard enough; figuring out the best way to fix the issue and implementing the changes isn't easy either. Each issue often has one of several likely causes and even more possible solutions.

FROM THE VOICE TRENCHES

Watch out for misunderstanding quantitative results. A colleague was presented with A/B test data on how long users listened to a song after they had requested it. In VUI-A, users were not told metadata, such as the title; in VUI-B, they were. Quantitative data showed significantly longer listening in VUI-A; the interpretation by those not familiar with user behavior was that not hearing introductory metadata led to greater user happiness. To verify this interpretation, our colleague performed a qualitative dialog path analysis, looking at the intents of users' follow-on requests, as well as the responses. This data provided a different picture: when told nothing about the content, users often asked about what they were hearing, which of course resulted in longer overall content "engagement" time, especially when the content didn't match user expectations. Making the situation even worse, some follow-on questions were not understood, leading to even longer conversations as users tried rephrasing their questions. Based on understanding the data in context, the correct conclusion therefore is that VUI-B provides the better experience. Introductory metadata provided implicit confirmation so that users quickly knew if the fulfillment matched their request. The lesson is to understand the complete picture and use all available data for any analysis:

User   *Play "Let It Be"*   → VUI misinterprets as another song: "Let It Be Love."

~ ~ ~ Response without metadata ~ ~ ~

    VUI-A   *OK.*   → Plays "Let It Be Love"
                   → Listening needed to determine accuracy

~ ~ ~ Response with metadata ~ ~ ~

    VUI-B   *OK. Here's "Let It Be Love."*   → Plays "Let It Be Love"
                                     → No listening needed

To understand the cause, you need to understand the dos and don'ts of voice design and implementation, as well as the specific details of your VUI, including any resource limitations. The good news is that tuning builds on everything you've learned in this book. It's not rocket science, but it does take some thought and practice.

In this section you get a chance to practice applying what you've learned. Tables 17-5 and 17-6 lay out some simple examples and observations that you're likely to find in a performance analysis. The observations in Table 17-5 include snapshot performance data from a single portion of a voice system or the system as a whole; data in Table 17-6 depends on tracking individual users through a dialog turn or taking multiple turns into consideration. For each observation, we list some likely causes and remedies: it's seldom the case that there's only one cause of an issue. Study the whole table, or cover the second and third columns to settle on your own analysis and solution. Have fun!

Table 17-5. *Tuning based on snapshot performance data mapped to likely causes and remedies*

Observation (set 1)	Analysis and plausible causes	Plausible remedies
High proportion of incomplete responses and shorter than expected: *My phone number is 415...* (expects ten digits).	End-of-speech (EOS) timeout too short. Users providing info that's usually spoken in chunks.	Extend EOS timeout. Keep mic open till matching string is detected. Allow button/screen entry with final #.
High proportion of *yes* responses to confirmation.	Confidence threshold is set too high. Unnecessary steps make the dialog longer, which can annoy users.	Change confidence threshold. Remove confirmations not needed for "cost." Change to implicit confirmation.
High proportion of *no* responses to confirmation.	Confidence threshold is set too low. Recognition is failing for some reason.	Change confidence threshold. Add N-best and skip lists. Look for trends in recognition accuracy and coverage.
High proportion of utterances without recognition/text result in logs (system listening but not finding any words).	No-speech timeouts have many possible causes, including hardware and parameter settings, user hesitation due to confusing prompt wording or missing options, users looking for requested info. User quiet speech, muffled or unintelligible.	Test mic sensitivity. If isolated to some contexts, investigate prompts and modify. Check signal-to-noise ratio and user voice volume.

(continued)

Table 17-5. (*continued*)

Observation (set 1)	Analysis and plausible causes	Plausible remedies
High proportion of OOG strings expected to be digits: *What's your PIN? –> Nola*	Some people turn numbers into words using keypad correspondences (easier to remember)..	Expand grammar. Add clarification in prompt.
High proportion of misrecognized brand names: *IKEA* = [ay-KIY-ax] or [iy-KEH-ah]	Names with unusual pronunciation need to be understood, and users need to know how to say them. If borrowed foreign words, both original and modified versions need handling.	Check and add dictionary pronunciations, including close variants. Double-check TTS pronunciation.
High in-domain OOG (synonyms) for Yes/No confirmation: *Yes, ma'am. Mostly right. Sure, it does.*	Grammar coverage is too narrow. There's more to Yes/No grammars than those two words.. Responses often include different fillers depending on syntactic context and persona.	Check and add synonym coverage. Add one-step correction. Expand grammars to coordinate with prompt wording and persona. Choose Yes/No grammar that reflects context.
High proportion of out-of-domain OOG in a confirmation.	Wrong mental model; confirmation of unexpected or unknown information. Confusing prompt wording or delivery.	Check and update grammars. Add one-step correction. Check and modify prompt delivery.
High proportion of OOG side commentary directed at VUI.	User annoyance with something in system behavior: recognition, wording, delivery, intent mapping, fulfillment.	Check coverage and recognition in the dialog state/turn. If not fixed, then look at bigger context (Table 17-3).

Table 17-6. *Tuning based on multi-turn data mapped to likely causes and remedies*

Observation (set 2)	Analysis and plausible causes	Plausible remedies
User makes multiple consecutive requests, same meaning but worded slightly differently.	Misrecognition or coverage. Utterance-to-intent mapping is wrong.	Update synonym coverage. Look at the utterance in previous and next turns. Update/retrain intent models.
User makes multiple consecutive requests, same content worded the same: *Tell me about stents. → There's no info on stints. → I need info about a stent. → Sorry, nothing on "stint."*	Misrecognition or coverage. Strong attractor exists.	Check and add synonym coverage. Add dictionary pronunciations. Change parameter settings. Add N-best and skip lists.
User disconfirms the same result twice in a row: *4 1 5. → 4 1 9, correct? → No, 4 1 5. → 4 1 9, is that right?*	Misrecognition or coverage. Strong attractor exists.	Add N-best and skip lists. Change parameter settings.
User said something in-grammar but the response seems to answer a different question: *Tune to channel 1 1 3. → Tunes to channel 1* *A refill order… cancelation. → OK, ordering refills.*	System stopped listening too soon (user hesitation). Utterance-to-intent mapping is wrong.	Listen to the whole utterance: Was user cut off? Why? Increase EOS. Update/retrain intent models.
A high proportion of requests are followed by a specific next request: Two-thirds of inquiries about remaining refills are followed by a refill request. If one or more refills remain, 84% of next turns are refill requests.	Opportunity to make the interaction quicker and easier for the user.	Redesign: Add Request 2 as an explicit option after 1, or go directly into 2 while saying how to exit.

(continued)

Table 17-6. (*continued*)

Observation (set 2)	Analysis and plausible causes	Plausible remedies
High proportion of *go back* requests.	Missing option in prompt. Misleading unclear prompt in previous turn. Utterance mapped to wrong intent.	Look for unclear or missing options in prompt; rephrase. Look at utterance in previous and next turns; update/retrain intent models.
High proportion of OOG out-of-domain yet related responses.	User is responding to the previous prompt. Wording isn't meaningful to users.	Look for unclear or missing options in prompt; rephrase. Check utterance in previous turn. If an issue is found, update intent models for the previous turn.
OOG commentary responses and high proportion of *yes* to confirmations followed by incomplete tasks: *You asked when is the Giants first home game?* → *Yes!* → *I don't know about that.* → *Then why did you ask me?*	Unnecessary confirmation. Response structure doesn't match request. Mislabeled intents.	Redesign. Apply design principles. Additional testing of similar requests.

Reporting On and Using Tuning Results

Some platforms offer built-in reporting; others do not. Whatever your situation, set up your reports for your baseline and use the same reports going forward. Your reports should include a brief executive summary highlighting key performance findings, detailed results with accompanying analysis and improvement suggestions, and any numbers related to how business goals are met, such as automation and drop-out rates. Dialogflow (at the time of writing this) offers some out-of-the-box reporting:

- From the History link, you can see the history of conversations; within those conversations, you can see which interactions returned an intent and which ones didn't (first discussed in Chapter 7).

- From the Analytics link, you can

  - Find the details of intents, including how many sessions and how many exits from the conversation from that intent.

  - Look at the flow of sessions, such as users' next steps after the various intents, including exiting the conversation.

This is a terrific start toward seeing how the application is doing. Other features you might find, especially in enterprise-level reporting and analysis tools, include

- Breakdown of key metrics over time, such as task completions for critical tasks, providing a sense of longitudinal application performance.

- Filtering by user type. A VUI often works better for some populations than others—you find yourself having to balance between focusing exclusively on a narrow core population and offering something to everyone.

Typical quantitative metrics that are included in tuning reports are recognition accuracy rates, task completion rates, intent or routing accuracy, and authentication success if applicable. Always include a highlight discussion of improvements made and quantitative comparison with any previous tuning rounds. IVR tuning reports usually also include overall call automation, time spent in call, and transfer rates. If available, you'd also include numbers for new users and existing user retention.

We've covered different tuning types in this chapter; we strongly encourage you to never tune in isolation. Everything you can measure and observe should be analyzed, prioritized, and addressed in the context of all collected data and with an understanding of both the design and development efforts involved. A good approach is to flag any areas of concern coming out of performance logs and look for related data in qualitative usability tests and focused utterance analyses and vice versa. When quantitative log analysis shows how widespread an issue is, qualitative in-depth analysis of utterances and dialog turn behaviors provides information about the nature of the issue that helps you apply the right solution. Invite your whole team to contribute to testing and tuning—the results affect everyone:

- Collect concerns and beliefs and wishes from representatives of all teams.

- Set expectations and explain why things are done in certain ways.

- Set up recording facilities and live observation, if appropriate and possible.

- Establish a working pipeline.

  - Arrange for data collection, privacy measures, and transcription services.

  - Data from different sources need to inform all tuning efforts.

- Determine how best to share findings: make it easy and informative.

SUCCESS TIP 17.4 BEWARE OF QUALITATIVE IN QUANTITATIVE CLOTHING   Most small studies, including usability testing studies, usually provide some quantitative results. Partly that's because it's relevant to say something about how often something happens. Partly it's because people like quantifying everything. It somehow seems to make results more real and certain. And most people like certainty. However, be careful to not turn results from a dozen subjects into percentages that are used to argue for or against something. Better to downplay the numbers in this case. For example, "Five of twelve commented on the length of confirmation prompts" followed by the relevant verbatim comments.

How to Maximize Deployment Success

You know by now that your work isn't done once you've deployed. We'll take it as a given that you applied everything you've learned to implement a superior design and that you tested thoroughly. But there's always room for improvement! Step 1 is to plan for it. Step 2 is to react to issues with the right amount of urgency and the right solution. Let's look at how to succeed with both.

Know When to Tune

Because so many things can go wrong, with issues feeding other issues, you want to perform multiple rounds of tuning. The higher the stakes, the more frequent and/or thorough your tuning rounds should be. Enterprise voice systems typically start small, with beta and pilot releases and ever-increasing user populations.

Then, one or two in-depth tuning rounds should be carried out as quickly as possible in early deployment, followed by "snapshot" tuning rounds and regularly scheduled tuning rounds once per quarter or less often. It often depends on the overall engagement, difficulty or novelty of the task, and whether later phases add new features:

- A phased rollout is always a good idea. Analyze and tune, at least minimally, after each round of data collection, including pilots, alphas, and betas.

- Tune when your system first deploys to the outside world. This is the most critical time for tuning. You have real user data and the eyes—and the ears!—of the world on your VUI. Focus on quick updates, especially anything critical to user happiness that you missed pre-deployment. Don't wait: if recognition tuning is quicker than other types of tuning—it usually is—do a first round of that and implement the changes, rather than wait for a more complete tuning round.

- Measure performance and plan for possible tuning after any new event, such as a feature change or redesign in any part of the system. Focused spot-check tuning rounds are great, especially for areas where your experience tells you might have issues.

- Issues often trickle to and from other parts of a system. Don't limit later tuning rounds to only those recently modified areas of the system. Also don't limit tuning to focus only on your success criteria— those might directly determine payments and future contracts, but other findings can tell you how to build even more successful VUIs in the future.

- Tune after a new user population is added or after any system-external changes you're aware of.

- If A/B testing is an option, it's never too early to lay the groundwork for running those.

- Agree on regular tuning intervals. Make sure everyone who needs to be part of a tuning effort knows when one is scheduled. That can include time to collect and process data, scrubbing data for privacy, getting transcriptions, doing the analysis and tuning work, and retesting before putting the changes into production.

- Monitor qualitative changes in behavior, including any increase in complaints directly to you or second-hand in online forums and product reviews. Perform your own informed analysis of the reported issues, knowing that naive users will tell you their experiences of what's wrong but might not assign the right cause. These complaints are still valid; don't ignore them and don't brush off users by directing them to some generic FAQ.

- Create automated performance tests that provide ongoing monitoring and alert you of sudden changes in any performance numbers. Focus on any high-traffic areas and parts of the system that other dialogs depend on, like identification and authentication.

- You may have experienced this with your home voice assistants: suddenly they don't understand you as well.

Something you've said successfully many times before doesn't work now. This can actually happen after a core recognizer or language model update is put in place. The new version has been tuned on new voice data, which means it will eventually work better for a broader set of users, but also behave differently at first for those in earlier user groups. The smaller set is now less favored at the cost of the whole. The hope is that with time everyone benefits, and that's usually the case.

Understand Tuning Complexities to Avoid Pitfalls

Tuning requires training and experience to do well under the best of circumstances. Many factors come into play to make it even harder to do well. Here are some:

- Sometimes chosen success metrics can't be accessed or measured accurately, or you don't have access to changing what you'd need to improve performance.

- Something changes in a connected external system; you don't know anything has changed until you notice that performance is getting worse.

If you rely on any system-external databases, set up automated unsupervised tests that will alert you to changes. If you're working on a system in a larger organization, find ways from Day 1 to stay in contact. Some changes that involve minimal GUI work can deeply impact VUI performance. For example, a new seasonal product name needs to be pronounced, recognized, and fulfilled correctly, and it mustn't be easily confusable with other product names or commands. A minor layout change on billing statements can affect the conversational flow of step-by-step instructions or result in user confusion, as shown by no-speech timeouts or *help* requests.

- You're limited in how often or quickly you can make updates.

- In some enterprise product environments, even a simple change like modifying a single prompt may take weeks because it needs to fit into overall test phases and scheduled updates.

- Post-rollout usage is low, so data trickles in slowly and gradually, precisely at the time when tuning is most urgent.

- Collect data and tune anyway as soon as you can, but be careful to not overfit to data that's not representative.

- You're unable to do any offline tuning to test your tuning changes before putting them into production.

- You don't have access to the part of the system or the utterances with performance issues:

  - You'll be limited in data access unless you are doing much of the process yourself or have enterprise tool access. If you don't have access to "raw" utterance data, including actual audio files, you don't know what really happened. What did the user actually say? Is the wording not covered by your grammars? Did they cough or pronounce something unexpectedly? Was there noise or someone else talking at the same time? If you can't get that information from a broad set of real users, you might be able to at least collect data from a small group of users. Is there a group of people who have signed up to be early testers and who you can collect data from? Investigate what's possible in your particular environment.

- You're asked to provide a list of "everything a user can say":

  - It's an understandable request by a product owner or those who need to write up PR copy or usage instructions, but it's not a reasonable request. A complete list of what's "in coverage" for even the smallest interaction will be thousands and probably millions of utterances. In addition, unless you're dealing with rule-based grammars, you won't even be able to supply such a list. And even if a phrase is in-grammar, there's no guarantee that it will be recognized and interpreted as planned anytime it's spoken. Instead, provide that explanation together with a set of archetype utterances and expected outcomes for every intent.

- Someone (over-)reacts to high-profile outliers:

  - This has happened on quite a few projects we've been involved in. The Senior VP of Something complains about not being recognized. In one case, a customer stakeholder complained that his mother wasn't recognized when calling the voice system while having her hair dried at the salon! You need to refrain from tuning to a few outlier observations. Remember that a voice system basically looks for a statistical best fit. Even when it can be tweaked to favor one person or a specific environment, that will come at a cost to the whole user population. Instead, educate everyone from Day 1, don't over-promise, and use anecdotal examples as fodder for further studies. If it's a pattern that can be addressed and will be of overall benefit, then include it.

- Analysis and tuning tasks are handled by a specialized team whose members are separate from the product/project design and development team:

  - We've seen well-meaning trained analysts miss issues or propose suboptimal solutions because they're brought in for a week instead of being part of the team all along. They can't see the big picture or the details that the long-term team is familiar with. In contrast, our most successful tuning projects involved design and speech science working together throughout the process, as well as subject matter experts (SMEs). SMEs include medical staff for health apps and experienced call center agents for various domains. Not only do they know technical terminology and official pronunciations but more importantly they know what "regular people" have trouble pronouncing or describing, so they can catch references others would miss. Be sure to update your tagging guides (Chapter 11) with relevant tuning findings.

- User voice data security:

  - Encrypted disks and secure servers are a given. It's also common to either scrub some information from regular logs or to separate logs such that identifying information can't be associated with authentication tokens during tuning. Despite recently reported security concerns, it is possible to keep collected voice data safe; it's been done for decades. Do your part—what you learn from that data is well worth the extra effort, and everyone ultimately benefits.

FROM THE VOICE TRENCHES

Between the two of us, we've worked on well over 100 voice engagements and products ranging from the very simple to complex behemoths that process tens of thousands of calls per day for very large clients.

We're usually able to explain to our client that we want one or sometimes two pilot phases of the app before rolling it out to full production. Sometimes we'd get pushback, and ultimately we were able to argue for some phased rollout. But there were those cases where, either because of client demands ("Haven't you done this before? Don't you know exactly what's going to happen?") or absolutely immovable time constraints, a whole system had to go from 0% to 100% live on Day 1 with no updates possible for weeks. If your goals are great UX, client benefits, and your own sanity, we don't recommend this. There's always something new; we can safely say that there's never been a situation where, after assessment, there was no need for any app updates. What we usually do in such situations is to have in place a mechanism for very quick assessment/updates, so that even though we're at 100% rollout, we turn around changes quickly, sometimes within days. The client has to be ready for this too.

And here's another lesson: yes, we've done this before, and no, we still didn't know exactly what was going to happen—even with solid requirements and customers with past voice project experience. Each voice implementation is different—users are different and expectations are different. A good thing to keep in mind.

What's Next?

After working through this chapter, you know a lot more about the causes of performance issues and how to fix them than most people building VUIs. Really. And even if you can't fix everything, this knowledge will help you find workarounds and contribute to sessions where others are proposing solutions.

This is the last chapter of our book! We packed in a lot of information—thanks for staying with us! Next step is to go out there and build great VUIs, ones that you yourself would want to talk to.

We'll end with some words of wisdom from people who have been in the voice industry for a while, who have used voice technology, or who have worked in supporting roles during VUI development. Here're a few responses to *What advice can you give someone that will help them succeed with building a voice interaction?*

- "I hear the dev team's concern. What does the UX team say? If they say 'Do it this way. Here's why,' then we will, unless there's a reason why we technically can't do it within the scope of product development."

- "Voice has become the hottest ticket in town. Which means every Tom, Dick, and Harry pop up offering their opinions and services. Find out what concrete voice work someone has done themselves before you take their word for anything. If they promise to make everything easy for you, they've not done the work themselves."

- "Under-promise and over-deliver. MVP (minimum viable product) and the 80/20 Rule (the Pareto Principle) don't apply in the way you might be used to. You can't tell people not to ask for something that's reasonable given what your VUI does. The way to limit a rollout is to have a wide net that catches most requests at the source. Say 'Sorry, I can't help you with that yet'; then build out details gradually."

- "Spoken language is special; you can't treat it like any other data set. To succeed with voice, you need to listen, understand, and communicate."

- "Voice is not something you just dabble with if you expect others to use it. Decide if you want to (and can) be a voice innovator or a follower. Successfully doing all of your own voice design and development is a serious commitment—you need to get all of it right. There's no harm in being a follower, especially if your specialty lies in another field, like hardware or domain content. Focus on what you're good at and follow experts' recommendations."

- "If I'm not understood, I'm not gonna use it. I wish I could tell all voice developers to test, test, test before rolling it out."

- "Speech and NL understanding is so cool. When it works, it's like magic. When people experience that, they want to use it more and do more complex stuff with it. Let's help them get there! ☺ We'll all benefit from it."

Summary

- The best way to overall success with voice is to not over-promise. Focus on tuning to create robust systems that perform well; if users are successful, they're more willing to keep using the VUI and try new things.

- The results from quantitative and qualitative tuning and analysis provide most insight when done collaboratively. Capture issues and improvement ideas. Analyze both user behavior and user commentary. They don't always agree but both provide insights.

- Know what you can and can't tune. What's available differs across platforms and is constantly changing.

- Establish a baseline of metrics you can measure and that are meaningful to what's considered success in your voice system. If you have success metrics, be sure they can be measured.

- Test your tuning changes offline.

- It's often difficult to find the exact cause and apply the appropriate solution without looking across all categories of metrics and considering the complete picture of a conversation.

Index

A

Accents, 11, 98
Accuracy
  probabilities, 463
  robustness
    examples, 435, 436
    grammar, 434
    hidden options/none of those,
      440, 441
    JIT, 439
    medication names, 435
    one-step correction, 442, 443,
      446–448, 450, 451, 453
    providing help, 436–438
    recognition space, 455, 456
    recognize/reject, 441
    speech accuracy, 434
    spelling, 455
    tutorials, 453, 454
  timeout/latency, 464
Acoustic confusability tuning, 644
Acoustic model, 56, 359
Action request dialogs
  building, 195
  design notes, 196, 197
  pattern, 194
Actions on Google, 72, 75, 77, 78, 81, 249,
    257, 258, 273, 274
Agile process, 30
Amazon Alexa, 3, 14, 71, 82, 641

Ambiguity, resolution, 219, 229, 231
Ambiguity tuning, 642
Application database, 23, 495, 497, 506
Application Programming
    Interface (API), 507
Application tags, 410
Architecture of voice systems, 16
ARPAbet, 356
  US English, 357

B

Backchannels, 309, 310
Backend data access, 602
Baidu, 360
Bootstrapping grammars, 377, 378
Built-in entities, 200
Built-in global intents
  assumptions, 349
  complexity, 348
  context dependence, 349
  edge cases, 349
  framework dependency, 349
Built-in reporting, 665
Business Associate
    Addendum (BAA), 127
Business requirements
  access/availability, 124–126
  branding/terminology, 123
  device, 117, 120
  legal/business constraints, 127–129

A. Thymé-Gobbel and C. Jankowski, *Mastering Voice Interfaces*, https://doi.org/10.1007/978-1-4842-7005-9

V

Printed in the United States
by Baker & Taylor Publisher Services